AMIDST THE DEBRIS

T0322396

JULIANO FIORI, FERNANDO ESPADA,
ANDREA RIGON, BERTRAND TAITHE
and RAFIA ZAKARIA
(*Editors*)

Amidst the Debris

*Humanitarianism and the
End of Liberal Order*

HURST & COMPANY, LONDON

First published in the United Kingdom in 2021 by
C. Hurst & Co. (Publishers) Ltd.,
83 Torbay Road, London, NW6 7DT
Copyright © Juliano Fiori, Fernando Espada, Andrea Rigon,
Bertrand Taithe, Rafia Zakaria and the Contributors, 2021
All rights reserved.

The right of Juliano Fiori, Fernando Espada, Andrea Rigon, Bertrand Taithe,
Rafia Zakaria and the Contributors to be identified as the authors of this
publication is asserted by them in accordance with the Copyright, Designs
and Patents Act, 1988.

Distributed in the United States, Canada and Latin America by
Oxford University Press, 198 Madison Avenue, New York, NY 10016,
United States of America.

A Cataloguing-in-Publication data record for this book
is available from the British Library.

ISBN: 9781787383968

This book is printed using paper from registered sustainable
and managed sources.

www.hurstpublishers.com

Printed and bound in Great Britain by Bell & Bain Ltd, Glasgow

CONTENTS

Acknowledgements   vii

List of Contributors   xi

1. Introduction: Humanitarianism and Liberal Ordering
   Juliano Fiori, Fernando Espada, Andrea Rigon, Bertrand Taithe,
   and Rafia Zakaria   1

PART ONE
THE POLITICS OF HUMANITARIAN PRACTICE

2. Humanitarianism and History: A Century of Save the
   Children   *Emily Baughan*   21

3. The Rise of the Humanitarian Corporation: Save the
   Children and the Ordering of Emergency Response
                                                             Gareth Owen   35

4. A Pestilential World: Promises of Protection
                                                             Nimmi Gowrinathan   55

5. The Modernity and Liberal Value of Humanitarian Things
                                                             Bertrand Taithe   67

6. The Conscience of the Island? The NGO Moment in
   Australian Offshore Detention   *Eleanor Davey*   83

7. Rights-Bearing Migrants and the Rightfulness of their
   Rescue: The Emergence of a 'New Model of Humanitarian
   Engagement' at Europe's Borders   *Klaus Neumann*   107

PART TWO
THE PRACTICE OF HUMANITARIAN POLITICS

8. The Legitimation Crisis of the Liberal Order: Political
    Minimalism, Humanitarianism, and the Government of
    Inequality   *Simon Reid-Henry*   127
9. Notes on Our Melancholy Present   *Juliano Fiori*   155
10. Warfare on Welfare in the Age of Emergency
                                         Mark Duffield   185
11. The White Moderates: Europe and the Return of the State
    in Mali   *Fernando Espada*   207
12. Deplorable Liberalism: Whiteness, Trump, and the
    Anti-Humanitarian Social Contract   *Stephanie Reist*   225
13. Requiem for a Most Violent Humanitarian Order
                                         José Luís Fiori   247
14. Orders and Disorders of Refugee Humanitarianism in the
    Arab Middle East   *Tamirace Fakhoury*   259

PART THREE
HUMANITARIANISM AFTER LIBERALISM?

15. Violence in a Post-Liberal World   *Brad Evans*   281
16. Where Humanity Ends: Dubai and the Performance of
    Modernity   *Rafia Zakaria*   303
17. Billionaire Philanthropy, Women's Empowerment, and
    the Currency of Modernity   *Serene J. Khader*   313
18. Humanitarianism and Liberal International Order:
    A Necessary Relationship?   *Jacinta O'Hagan*   333
19. Towards an Anti-Racist Humanitarianism in the
    Post-Liberal World   *Patricia Daley*   351
20. What's there to Mourn? What's there to Celebrate?
    Decolonial Retrievals of Humanitarianism
                                         Olivia U. Rutazibwa   369

Notes   377
Index   463

ACKNOWLEDGEMENTS

At the best of times, an edited collection with twenty chapters is a considerable collective endeavour and requires sustained commitment from individual contributors. And this, it would be fair to say, has not been the best of times! The project behind this book was born almost three years before the coronavirus pandemic had infected our sense of shared life and undermined whatever assumptions we may have held about planning. It only survived thanks to the patience, generosity, and resolve of the authors and translators, who, amid a host of unexpected practical demands—home-schooling children, adapting university courses, warding off mental exhaustion—produced the chapters herein. And it is to them that we must first express our gratitude. We are also grateful for fruitful exchanges with Rony Brauman, Elena Fiddian-Qasmiyeh, Paulo Eduardo Arantes, Lilie Chouliaraki, and Andrew Thompson, which have left an impression on these pages.

Changing circumstances forced a number of authors to withdraw along the way. But if changes to the cohort of contributors inevitably affected the scope of this book, we, as editors, take responsibility for any shortcomings with respect to the diversity of perspectives and themes covered.

Two events on the political economy of humanitarian aid contributed to the early development of this project. The first was a workshop, held by Save the Children, in 2018—part of a series of seminars on data and conflict, coordinated by Jonathan Fisher and funded by the Economic and Social Research Council. The second, in the same year, was a panel at the International Humanitarian Studies Association conference, in The Hague. Jessica Field, Patricia Tambourgi, and Marc DuBois participated in this latter discussion with thoughtful presentations.

In December 2019, once the concept for the book was more defined, and chapters were already in development, we held a workshop with many of the authors. It was hosted by The Bartlett Development Planning Unit at University College London, and funded by the Arts and Humanities Research Council, together with Praxis, an initiative at the University of Leeds, which promotes the role of the arts and humanities in addressing global challenges. We thank Gary Grubb, Ian Stanton, and Poppy Cullen, of the AHRC, and Stuart Taberner, Lauren Wray, and Deena Dajani, of Praxis, for their enthusiastic support. The workshop also benefitted from the participation of Andrea Warnecke, Mirella Cooper, Anna Wyatt, Chantal Meza, Gabriella Waaijman, and Mariangela Palladino.

This book is a product of a partnership between the editors and their respective institutions which reaches back almost a decade. Save the Children's Humanitarian Affairs Team was established in 2012 and has since been dedicated to promoting critical reflection on humanitarianism. Its primary object of analysis has been the relationship between humanitarianism and politics. Not so concerned with how humanitarians might adhere to 'good practice', it has questioned what it is that informs humanitarians' conception of 'the good'. Rather than asking how humanitarians can protect themselves from the dirty world of politics, it has explored the agency exercised by humanitarians in processes of political and social change. It has only been able to carry out this work because of the encouragement, support, and protection provided by Gareth Owen, Save the Children's Humanitarian Director, who has championed the idea that critical debate is the cornerstone of ethical practice.

It was this desire to explore and engage critically with broad questions about humanitarianism and politics, about the role of humanitarianism in historical processes, that brought the Humanitarian Affairs Team into contact with the Humanitarian and Conflict Response Institute at the University of Manchester—an academic centre which was already at the forefront of efforts to build bridges

ACKNOWLEDGEMENTS

between humanitarian practice and scholarship. And, soon afterwards, a partnership was formalised with The Bartlett Development Planning Unit, which had six decades of experience in such bridge-building. These institutional relationships provided a basis for the discovery of intellectual affinities and, indeed, for friendship.

Finally, we are grateful to those at Hurst who have helped to get this book to publication. In particular, we thank Michael Dwyer for his early guidance, Daisy Leitch for her work on production, and Lara Weisweiller-Wu, our publishing editor, for her critical support and patience.

While the coronavirus pandemic affected the production of this book and reduced the amount of contact between contributors, it didn't prevent the development of new relationships. For this we are very grateful. And we are sure that these relationships will continue to bear fruit, beyond the pandemic, into brighter times.

LIST OF CONTRIBUTORS

Emily Baughan is Lecturer in 19th/20th Century British History at The University of Sheffield.

Patricia Daley is a pan-Africanist feminist and Professor of the Human Geography of Africa at the University of Oxford.

Eleanor Davey writes about the histories of aid and activism. She is an honorary fellow at Australian Catholic University.

Mark Duffield is Emeritus Professor at the Global Insecurities Centre, University of Bristol.

Fernando Espada is Head of Humanitarian Affairs at Save the Children UK.

Brad Evans is Professor of Political Violence and Aesthetics at the University of Bath.

Tamirace Fakhoury is Associate Professor of Political Science and Global Refugee and Migration Studies at the University of Aalborg, Copenhagen.

José Luís Fiori is Professor of International Political Economy at the Federal University of Rio de Janeiro.

Juliano Fiori is Head of Studies (Humanitarian Affairs) at Save the Children UK.

Nimmi Gowrinathan is an activist, scholar, and founder of the Politics of Sexual Violence Initiative at the City College of New York.

LIST OF CONTRIBUTORS

Serene J. Khader is Professor and Jay Newman Chair in the Philosophy of Culture at Brooklyn College, City University of New York, and the CUNY Graduate Center.

Klaus Neumann is a historian and works for the Hamburg Foundation for the Advancement of Research and Culture.

Jacinta O'Hagan is Associate Professor in International Relations in the School of Political Science and International Studies, University of Queensland.

Gareth Owen OBE is Humanitarian Director at Save the Children UK.

Stephanie Reist is a writer and post-doctoral researcher at the Federal Rural University of Rio de Janeiro.

Simon Reid-Henry is Reader in Geography and Director of the Institute for the Humanities and Social Sciences at Queen Mary University of London.

Andrea Rigon is Associate Professor at The Bartlett Development Planning Unit, University College London.

Olivia U. Rutazibwa is Associate Professor in Human Rights and Politics at the London School of Economics and Political Science and Senior Research Fellow at the Johannesburg Institute for Advanced Study.

Bertrand Taithe is Professor of Cultural History at The University of Manchester and Director of the Humanitarian and Conflict Response Institute.

Rafia Zakaria is an author and political philosopher.

Translation

Ana Naomi de Sousa is an independent documentary filmmaker, writer-journalist, and translator.

INTRODUCTION

HUMANITARIANISM AND LIBERAL ORDERING

Juliano Fiori, Fernando Espada, Andrea Rigon, Bertrand Taithe,
and *Rafia Zakaria*

Unveiling government spending plans for the coming year, on 25 November 2020, British Chancellor of the Exchequer Rishi Sunak spoke of 'tough choices'. With the UK under lockdown, as the second wave of the COVID-19 pandemic surged, the government was facing an 'economic emergency': the largest public deficit since the Second World War. And so it was unjustifiable, he asserted, to maintain government expenditure on foreign aid. Barely one percent of proposed borrowing, the £4 billion saved by cutting the aid budget from 0.7 percent to 0.5 percent of national income would make almost no difference to the government's balance sheet. Yet the measure was of symbolic significance. Not least because it jarred against the promise of a three-year increase in defence spending. Five months after the government folded the Department for International Development into the Foreign and Commonwealth Office, the cut to aid was indicative of a suspension, if not an unravelling, of a political consensus that had held for more than two decades. Commitment to overseas aid had sat squarely in the common ground occupied by the progressive neoliberals of left and right in government since the 1990s. It had reflected a shared assumption of the compatibility between altruistic ethics and self-interested politics—and a shared understanding of aid's strategic role in projecting Britain's soft power, ordering international affairs, and promoting capitalist development.

A few weeks before the publication of Sunak's spending review, Joe Biden was elected president of the United States. Presuming to speak for everyone, American novelist Francine Prose reproduced the *expression du jour*: 'We can breathe again.'[1] 'You know, the *I can't breathe*?' questioned Van Jones, CEO of the REFORM Alliance, during a poignant response to the election result, on CNN. 'That wasn't just George Floyd'—the black man whose murder by Minneapolis police had sparked international protests in June. 'That was a lot of people that felt that they couldn't breathe.'[2] 'I can't breathe' had been adopted as a protest slogan by the Black Lives Matter movement in 2014. But asphyxiation is a grim motif in America's long history of white oppression of black people: hundreds of thousands of slaves died in the Middle Passage from drowning or lack of oxygen below deck; hanging was the most common fate for black victims of white lynch mobs, slave patrols, and the Ku Klux Klan, although many were killed by chokehold—a metonym for racist police violence today. With his talk of 'very fine people on both sides', his Muslim ban, and his characterisation of Mexicans as, 'in many cases, criminals, drug dealers, racists', Donald Trump pressed the boot of the American state further down on the necks of blacks and ethnic minorities; his departure from the White House seemed likely to offer them a reprieve. But in the moment of Biden's victory, the historical experience of black asphyxiation, evoked by the June protests, was somehow conflated with anxieties about disruption of the normal order of things, about dissolution of the ideal of orderly progress. White liberals now renewed their hope of restoration of the normal order of things. But, if this order was less permissive of race-baiting and supremacist pageantry, if it was more humanitarian, if it offered a greater chance of avoiding climate catastrophe, it was also sustained by a racist division of labour, a racist system of legal justice, and a racist enterprise of civilisational expansion. With the death of George Floyd still at the forefront of political debate, the suggestion by white liberals that *everyone* could breathe again obscured continuities—discussed by Stephanie Reist in this volume—between Trumpism and the racial liberalism that predominated before his election in 2016. Despite centuries of whites using asphyxiation as a technique of domination, it was Joe Biden, an elderly white man, whose 1994 crime bill demonised a generation of black boys, who was now imagined as guarantor of (in the words of Achille Mbembe) 'the universal right to breathe'.[3]

In his acceptance speech, Biden expressed determination to 'restore the soul of America'.[4] The white nationalist tattoos, Kek flags, and male tribalist furs on display as Trump supporters stormed Washington's Capitol on 6 January 2021, offered a reminder of the dark side of the American soul, with which, one way or another, Biden will have to contend. But liberals outside the United States will hope that his project of restoration succeeds, with repercussions elsewhere, breaking the wave of popular authoritarianism that has washed across the West and beyond, over the last decade. The referendum vote in favour of Brexit, in June 2016, was decisive. In Europe and North America, new nationalist movements of the far right had been feeding off the discontent of the disenfranchised and the patriotic posturing of political elites, for a number of years. They had even achieved electoral success on Europe's fringes. But the Brexit vote marks the moment when what Christophe Guilluy characterises as the 'emergence of the periphery'—a moral rebellion by those priced out of bourgeois society, stoked by these nationalist movements and decadent sectors of capital—produced the first major shock to the very heart of neoliberalism's transnational regime.[5] As the British government has shifted rightwards since, authoritarian manoeuvres have been downplayed amid the posh-boy pleasantries of Tory chumocrats. Trump's gaudy narcissism would of course be out of place in Westminster; Boris Johnson's demagoguery is garnished with historical allusion and Ancient Greek verse. But there should be no doubt about the elective affinities of the two men. If Johnson is a protean politician, not much chewing is required before ingesting Marine Le

Pen's assertion that he serves as an inspiration for the Rassemblement National, in France; few eyebrows are raised when he is included in the parade of the so-called 'nationalist international'.

Brexit exposed a cleavage in Britain's political establishment, which has widened whenever the government threatens to topple liberal totems of the post-Cold War period. The decision to cut the aid budget provoked an angry reaction from the liberal wing of the Conservative Party, as well as from MPs across the Labour Party. A Foreign Office minister resigned. Former prime ministers David Cameron and Tony Blair warned against the measure, as if in defence of their condominium. Aid agencies inevitably protested too. Danny Sriskandarajah, CEO of Oxfam GB, argued that the cut risked 'significantly undermining one of the UK's genuine claims to global leadership'.[6] For Kevin Watkins, CEO of Save the Children UK, it had 'broken Britain's reputation for leadership on the world stage'.[7]

Since at least the early nineteenth century, British claims to global leadership have rested partly on overseas humanitarian endeavours— not necessarily aid, as understood today, but the sentimental humanist activism with which it is most readily associated. The promotion of relief and reconstruction became one of Britain's principal contributions to international ordering after the First World War, as it grudgingly adapted to imperial decline. As noted by Emily Baughan in this volume, Save the Children, established in 1919, developed close ties with the British state in its early years. And, despite its founding socialistic vision of civic diplomacy, it increasingly aligned itself with British foreign policy. In the decades following the Second World War, the organisation often performed the role of—in Baughan's words—'stretcher-bearer for the casualties' of decolonisation and proxy warfare. But, after the fall of the Berlin Wall, the relationship between aid agencies and the state became altogether more instrumental, not only in Britain, but across the West. In the moment of liberal democracy's apotheosis, aid agencies were conscripted to assist in the periphery's cultural conversion to Western capitalism and in the consolidation of a moral universe subject to American arbitration. During the 1990s, many of them cheered on and collaborated with Western military campaigns launched in the name of human rights and civilian protection—'humanitarian interventions', remembered by many contributors to this volume, most notably José Luís Fiori. Trading on a moralisation of politics in the West, many of the larger aid agencies grew rapidly. A steady increase in private and government funding accelerated the professionalisation of the aid industry. And so, as aid was more systematically integrated into Western strategies of liberal capitalist expansion, aid agencies became more dependent on governments and corporations. In his chapter in this volume, Gareth Owen, one of the longest-serving emergency operations directors in the aid sector, reflects on his experience of this entanglement. Concerned about the impact that the cut to British government aid could have on people affected by conflict and disaster, he nonetheless suggests that it could 'force humanitarian agencies to delink from state power and adapt their financial models for the better'.

Owen's chapter can be situated in a tradition of *auto-critique* by aid workers who question the sustainability, as well as the political implications, of expansionary financial models for multinational charities, even as they recognise the benefits of growth. But it differs from those analyses that would announce a crisis of humanitarianism on account of its pollution by politics, its betrayal by immoral leadership, or its intransigence in the face of modernising imperatives (innovation, professionalisation, technocratic efficiency, etc.). If these elements appear in his account, Owen sees the main challenges for humanitarianism today as intrinsic to its interdependencies with neoliberal political economy, and, more generally, with liberal order. In doing so, he gets to the nub of the first question that has animated the production of this volume—a question addressed directly in Jacinta O'Hagan's chapter: How should we understand the relationship between Western humanitarianism, in its contemporary form, and liberal order?

Liberal Order

The merits of liberal order have never been so intensely debated as in recent years, during which its defenders—G. John Ikenberry, Joseph Nye, Francis Fukuyama, and Richard Haass, among the most prominent—have deemed it to be under threat.[8] Indeed, perhaps the clearest illustration of what the proponents of liberal order have imagined it to be is provided by their description of a *status quo ante* that requires moral defence. Yet such a description tends to rely on selective histories. Nye, for example, overlooks the normalisation of civil conflict on the periphery when he writes of the 'demonstrable success' of liberal order in 'helping secure and stabilise the world over the past seven decades'.[9] It thus revives another debate: Has anything like liberal order ever really existed? In one of the most notable recent exchanges on this question, in *Foreign Affairs*—arguably the most notable mouthpiece for American liberal internationalism—political scientist Graham Allison seeks to demonstrate that liberal order is a myth by exposing the main claims of its defenders as 'more wrong than right'.[10] Elsewhere, historian and imperial nostalgist Niall Ferguson affirms that 'liberal international order... is neither liberal, nor international, nor very orderly'.[11] Michael Barnett, author of the most widely read *longue durée* history of humanitarianism, writes: 'Some might consider the 1990s as a high-water mark of the liberal international order, but my view is that the international order got closer to having a liberal quality but never quite passed the threshold.'[12] If such assertions are to bear scrutiny, they must be accompanied by a delimited conception of liberalism. The 'boundary-work' that enthuses liberal political theorists is not of primary concern in this volume. Moreover, it is by no means clear that bounding liberal ideas and practice gets us any closer to resolving the debate, since there remain intractable questions about the nature and origins of order.

This volume, then, takes the concept of liberal order at face value—as an object of the imagination of self-defined liberals, as well as some of their critics. But also as a dynamic normative construction in which the rhetorical deployment of ideas commonly associated with liberalism, by the powerful, plays a central role in the exercise of authority, the creation of institutions, the hierarchical organisation of potential rivals, and the suppression of threats. Until they undermine the strategic value of liberal discourse, actions that seem to contradict it can be understood as constitutive of this construction. This approach poses a challenge to the conception of order as a steady and peaceful state, which suspends the rupture that will eventually return disorder. It also differs from the conception of order as an organised group of institutions, adopted by John Mearsheimer, among other scholars of international relations.[13] And it focuses attention instead on processes of 'ordering'—in the inter-state system, but also within the nation-state, suggesting a certain fluidity between the two. As such, this volume is not exclusively concerned with 'liberal international order'. Fernando Espada's chapter, in particular, considers how ordering at home affects ordering abroad. Through discussion of the relationship of humanitarian politics and practice to processes of liberal ordering, the chapters in this volume contribute to an understanding of liberal order as a product of power relations and contestation, not necessarily of moral progress or rational evolution. While they are informed by different politics, they all maintain a critical distance from liberal order—indeed, from liberal ideology— without resorting to facile denunciation. Neither invective nor *apologia*, this volume critically interrogates conventional assumptions about our current conjuncture and the historical developments that produced it.

Attention to processes of ordering can contribute to an understanding of historical continuities. But to account for the historical specificities of liberal order, it is also necessary to recognise change. The contributors to this volume do not propose bold revisions of periodisation. Rather, they adhere to four established views on the genesis of liberal order, situating it in the aftermath of either the First World War, the Second World War, the crisis of the 1970s, or the Cold War. The combined effect is a sense that, notwithstanding the undulations and contingencies of History—the push and pull of the struggle for power and profit—liberal ordering became an increasingly prominent feature of world politics as the United States consolidated its global hegemony. Liberal order appears as inextricably tied to the American century, similarly bearing legacies of the age of empire it succeeded, in which liberal humanitarianism nonetheless also played a role in ordering—as noted by Bertrand Taithe in this volume.

It also appears as tied to global governance, under the tutelage of American power—to the establishment of international institutions, not least those of what, since the 1980s, aid workers have referred to as the 'humanitarian system'. Anyone who attends a UN coordination meeting for an emergency response will recognise the importance attributed to the idea of order in the humanitarian system. The hierarchy of interventions is well defined; sessions are structured predictably; discussions, often limited to information-sharing, appear scripted, with disagreement more performative than substantive. Since war and disaster are chaotic—as the innumerable reports published every year by aid agencies testify—the sensible observer would presumably welcome orderly responses to the human suffering they cause. The significant energy invested in developing and reforming humanitarian institutions since the turn of the 1990s, within and beyond the UN, has produced more systematic and coordinated relief operations. But an emphasis on ordering emergency response has also cultivated a bureaucratic denial of politics, leaving humanitarian governance particularly beholden to the neoliberal *zeitgeist*.

In the main, the chapters that follow also suggest an association between liberal order and the rise of neoliberalism. This association is brought out by the conceptual history of 'liberal international order'. Perhaps the earliest use of the term, with more or less the general meaning it is commonly given today, was in 1959, in an essay by German economist Wilhelm Röpke, a leading figure in what Quinn Slobodian has called neoliberalism's 'Geneva School'.[14] As Nils Gilman has pointed out, it came into more common usage in the 1970s, as Western powers sought to define an attractive alternative to the New International Economic Order proposed by the Group of 77. It then became bound up with the neoliberal policies promoted by international economic institutions, which undermined the sovereign claims of non-aligned states.[15]

By the 1980s, neoliberalism had become not only a dominant technology of capital accumulation, but also the ideology of a newly emboldened Western bourgeoisie. The tensions within contemporary liberalism's broad church render its conflation with neoliberalism unsatisfactory. Liberals such as Joseph Stiglitz and Amartya Sen have been among neoliberalism's most prominent critics, pointing to its distortion, if not betrayal, of classical liberal tenets. But for decades, such intellectuals had the ear of neoliberal policymakers, who presented them as markers of the acceptable limits of radicalism. If they diverged on macroeconomics, the 'open society' they advocated could be complementary to the neoliberal logic of social fragmentation; and elements of their critique could be incorporated to broaden its appeal. Across the West, liberal and social democratic parties not only accepted but accelerated the dismantling of the social state. They seemed to conclude that, even if it produced a degree of social friction, neoliberal capitalism fostered an aspirational consumer culture that was beneficial to the progressive pursuit of moral equality and inclusion; its expansion at home and abroad would remove traditional obstacles to the propagation of cultural liberalism, representative democracy, and human rights. In turn, a minimalist conception of human rights would not only fail to challenge neoliberal political economy, but it would become the lynchpin of a moral economy that provided neoliberalism with social legitimacy.[16] From this perspective, financialisation, the explosion of fictitious capital, and the development of transnational labour markets—defining characteristics of neoliberal globalisation—became counterparts to the moral universalism and institutionalism most often associated with liberal ordering.

The End

In a 2017 *Foreign Affairs* article, Jeff Colgan and Robert Keohane warn that, unless globalisation is made to serve the interests of middle and working classes, 'liberal order will wither away'.[17] Such warnings are typical of liberal political commentary over the last decade, not only that of international relations scholars and political scientists. The rise of popular authoritarianism has provoked the production of a considerable body of angsty writings on liberal decline. Often recognising flaws in the normal order of things ('the system is rigged', admit Colgan and Keohane), they nonetheless promote its restoration and improvement. Many imagine liberalism itself to be under threat and in need of renewal. 'Liberalism made the modern world, but the modern world is turning against it', affirmed *The Economist*, on the occasion of the magazine's 175th anniversary, in 2018.[18] But it is not only liberals who consider liberalism to be waning. Conservative critics of liberalism, such as Patrick Deneen, have been quick to announce its downfall.[19]

Whether coloured by glee or by gloom, the starker declarations of liberal decline are expressive of a resurgence of 'endism'. Often associated with the turn of the 1990s, and with Fukuyama in particular, this mode of thought has roots in religious eschatology, which pass through modern philosophies of history. The idea of historical closure found more regular expression in politics, theory, and pop culture in the decades before Fukuyama published his works on the 'end of history'.[20] It was supported by a sense that utopianism had been exhausted. In his chapter in this volume, Juliano Fiori argues that, if, as Samuel Moyn proposes, human rights emerged as the last utopia, it is because they 'reflected an idealism defined by the negation of other utopias'.[21] It is this last utopia, Fiori suggests, that has dissipated in recent years. Notwithstanding pastiches of premodern messianisms produced by fundamentalist religion, presentism is a defining feature of contemporary politics. And yet, social imaginaries are flooded with images of the apocalypse—of incurable disease, of catastrophic climate change. If not a systemic inevitability, human extinction is widely understood to be a distinct possibility. Nonetheless, pronouncement of the end of something or other is a temptation to which political analysts (and their publishing houses) are too readily drawn, not least because it makes for a bold and marketable product.

Curiosity about the end of things has been one of the motivations for putting this volume together. And so here is the second question with which it is principally concerned: Is this really the end of liberal order? The volume does not provide a singular response. Rather, it is intended as an interrogation of liberal declinism. As such, our subtitle, *Humanitarianism and the End of Liberal Order*, should be taken as provocation, not affirmation. Some chapters accept the proposition of liberal decline, speculating as to what a post-liberal world might hold. Rafia Zakaria, for example, considers the possibility that the United Arab Emirates, often referred to as a 'new humanitarian donor', offers a dystopian image of a possible post-liberal future. Others question whether, as Pankaj Mishra has argued, 'liberalism is not so much in crisis as are its self-styled campaigners'—and, if so, what relation this bears to material, as well as normative, changes.[22] Common to the chapters is recognition of a shock to the normal order of things. Historicising this shock, many of the chapters explore possible causes. Mark Duffield emphasises the war on welfare; Fernando Espada, rising inequality and the decline of the Western middle class; Juliano Fiori, the logic of diminishing social expectations. José Luís Fiori discusses the imperial overreach of the United States. Brad Evans, meanwhile, argues that '[a] clue lies amid the ruins of liberalism itself: its narcissistic impulses, which produced ill-fated wars of conversion, and which ontologised insecurity, paving the way for the liberation of prejudice and the normalisation of besieged mentalities only *they* were meant to experience'.

Fukuyama's thesis on the 'end of history' found fewer adherents than its fame would imply. But his enthusiasm about the possibilities of a unipolar moment was widely shared by liberals. Indeed, the recent anxiety of liberal commentators has exposed a particularly affective relationship with what cultural theorist Jeremy Gilbert has called 'the long 1990s'—stretching from the end of the Cold War until at least the financial crisis of 2008.[23] The likes of Bill Emmott, Thomas Friedman, George Packer, Anne Applebaum, and Edward Luce found their place in the sun in this period, as did Fukuyama himself; and their writings on popular authoritarianism bear its intellectual hallmarks—not least an assumption of the uniquely progressive character of Western capitalism. Emmott, editor-in-chief of *The Economist* during much of the long 1990s, claims that the 'idea of the West... the world's most successful political idea, by far', is also 'under threat and under attack'.[24] But he makes it clear that the values this idea promotes belong to liberalism—a term he refrains from using only because it does not quite command 'either the heart or the brain'. Applebaum warns of a possible 'collapse of an idea of the West, or of what is sometimes called the "the Western liberal order"'.[25] The spread of Chinese state capitalism, in particular, surely does pose a challenge to the 'idea of the West'. But the conflation of liberalism and the West in such narratives of decline suggests that it is not only ideology at stake in the project of liberal renewal, but also chauvinism, pride, and self-identity.

Humanitarianism

Humanitarian morality has been constitutive of Western self-identities since the nineteenth century. Advancement of a certain conception of humanity was considered by European social reformers to be a marker, as well as an obligation, of civilisation. Many liberals and socialists who opposed the 'new imperialism' on humanitarian grounds considered the maintenance, even the expansion, of colonial empire to be a humanitarian duty.[26] Patricia Daley's chapter in this volume roots the contemporary racialisation of humanitarian subjects in European colonialism and the civilising mission. Olivia Rutazibwa, meanwhile, reflects on the Eurocentrism of humanitarian studies— and its practical consequences. Today, NGO executives can be heard echoing calls to 'decolonise aid'. But this comes after more than a century of anti-colonial challenges to liberal humanitarianism. As Emily Baughan notes in *Saving the Children*, James Ford, an African American journalist, was dragged off stage at Save the Children's Conference on the African Child in 1931, after protesting against the organisers' association with the exploitation of African colonies.[27] During the Cold War, Third World intellectuals like Walter Rodney and Samir Amin pointed to the function of aid in the underdevelopment of postcolonial states. And, since the 1980s, critical scholars, not least in the anglophone academy, have sought to provincialise the humanitarianism professed by Western aid agencies. Drawing on this critical tradition, Nimmi Gowrinathan's chapter proposes that the Western particularities of liberal humanitarianism are thrown into stark relief when its anti-political premise runs up against the realities of those living through war on the periphery.

In the latter part of the twentieth century, the United States and its Western allies increasingly mobilised moral universalism as an instrument of order and strategy. At the core of Western universalism lies an abstract humanity, rationally deduced. And, in recent decades, this conception of humanity has been most effectively disseminated through the vocabularies of human rights and humanitarianism. Samuel Moyn has argued that the political breakthrough of human rights came in the second half of the 1970s, once they were incorporated into the official discourse of the United States government, under President Jimmy Carter.[28] Into the 1980s, many Western relief workers adopted the language of human rights.[29] The moral radicals at the helm of the French branch of Médecins Sans Frontières believed that their humanitarianism compelled a commitment to human rights. In turn, they promoted an ideal of human rights that accorded with a humanitarian morality of *urgence*. Assuming an anti-communist stance, the leaders of MSF-France explicitly aligned themselves with the West in the final years of the Cold War. And yet, they imagined themselves defending and exemplifying a universal humanity.

In 1965, humanity had been established as the first principle of the Red Cross, 'from which all other principles flow'.[30] In the early 1990s, a code of conduct signed by the Red Cross movement and NGOs affirmed that '[t]he humanitarian imperative comes first'.[31] This recourse to Kantian deontology was aimed at safeguarding humanitarian action from political contestation and manipulation. It also contributed to a tightening of the meaning of humanitarianism. Even as aid workers imagined themselves exercising a growing influence over the transformation of the periphery—through 'stabilisation', democracy promotion, and 'capacity building'—the humanitarian epithet came to be applied almost exclusively to the cross-border provision of aid *in extremis*. In this period, initiatives to professionalise the aid sector through the development of common standards of practice and evaluation were guided by the neomanagerial imperatives of effectiveness, efficiency, and accountability. In 2016, a study involving editors of this volume concluded that the 'humanitarian effectiveness agenda' had created 'an echo chamber in which the ideas of the [aid] sector's dominant actors bounce off each other, validated without modification or critical interrogation'.[32] Turning inwards, away from the sphere of political contestation, aid agencies were able to consolidate a definition of humanitarianism as an exclusively moral, life-saving enterprise—even as it was being politically instrumentalised by Western states. Indeed, the frequent insistence by aid agencies that humanitarianism was beyond politics made it a more useful technology of government.

If today humanitarianism is normally understood as a limited field of emergency response, it has nonetheless incorporated a large number of practices not previously deemed essential to the protection of life: education, 'livelihoods' training, cash transfers. Meanwhile, discussion of aid in general tends to evoke an emergency imaginary. From the Russian famine of the early 1920s to the Second World

War, the Biafran War of the late 1960s to the Ethiopian famine of the mid-1980s, acute crises of mass human suffering produced the twentieth century's largest and most mediatised public fundraising campaigns. As many historians have argued in recent years, the abandonment of revolution in the 1960s and 1970s, and its substitution with activism, increased popular enthusiasm for emergency relief; and it turned aid agencies into sites of a hybrid radicalism, which combined moral idealism with professional aspirations. Much of this historiography underplays the role of humanitarian imagination in the adjustment of social expectations after the exhaustion of modernity's grand utopian projects. Concluding his thesis on the last utopia, Moyn suggests that 'today, human rights and humanitarianism are fused enterprises, with the former incorporating the latter and the latter justified in terms of the former'.[33] Humanitarianism's subsumption within human rights in this way would tend to reaffirm the narrow bounds of its contemporary conceptualisation. If this does not necessarily deny the political forms that concern for human suffering has taken in recent decades, it obscures the function of a minimalist humanitarian reason in not only redefining human rights, but also reshaping the public sphere.

A great deal has been written about the politicisation of humanitarianism in the post-Cold War era—not least by disgruntled aid workers. This volume also offers reflections on how this process relates to the humanitarianisation of politics and society. Collectively, the chapters are suggestive of a broader conception of humanitarianism, as a politics of human life.[34] A minority of them focus directly on relief practices. In so far as they reflect on the merging of relief, development, and security, they reveal a reduction of policy concerns to questions of survival. They also reveal synergies between humanitarianisation and the spread of neoliberal reason, with its technocratic and post-political emphasis on targeting. Serene Khader's chapter demonstrates how billionaire philanthropy has contributed to a depoliticisation of 'women's' empowerment' through targeting, reducing it to a form of survivalism.

The structuring role of humanitarianism's politics of life is captured in Simon Reid-Henry's contribution to this volume, which explores the ethos of 'political minimalism'. More than a 'redemptive façade' for political minimalism, Reid-Henry argues, humanitarianism has been the 'limit point—and perhaps even the last redoubt—of liberalism's willingness to conceive of a better version of itself: to embrace the challenge of thinking through utopia'. Juliano Fiori's chapter also identifies the establishment of this limit point, following the capitalist crisis of the 1970s. Relief from necessity, Fiori suggests, became a maximum expectation of Western societies, as the neoliberal counter-revolution destroyed the social state and the collective sense of society. Construction in the present of a 'society of the humanitarian minimum' has depended on something like a biopolitical pact—Western populations accept the suspension of their political agency in exchange for the promise of life through consumerist inclusion.

The humanitarianisation of Western societies has both responded and contributed to their development of conditions generally associated with the periphery. In his chapter, Mark Duffield plaintively describes how the precarity and informality he witnessed in semi-rural Sudan in the 1970s now characterises his hometown of Dudley, in the British Midlands. Meanwhile, Maiurno, the Sudanese village in which he lived, has developed the trappings of Western consumer society. In recent decades, Western NGOs have taken on a more active role in the reduction of domestic food poverty, filling gaps left by the retreating state. Applying its expertise in the provision of relief, Save the Children has given increased attention to contingency planning for emergency responses in the UK, resuming a role it exercised during the interwar years. Amid large-scale disasters across the West—wildfires, floods, earthquakes, hurricanes—Red Cross societies have come to look more like surrogates for government than auxiliaries. Meanwhile, as Bertrand Taithe explains in his chapter, the COVID-19 pandemic has stretched public health services, drawing aid agency medical teams into the front line of domestic responses, while revitalising the role of pharmaceutical conglomerates in emergency relief.

The normalisation of non-state relief operations in the West destabilises humanitarian self-identities that are based not only on recognition of disposable resources and institutional know-how, but also on historical assumptions of civilisational superiority. 'Humanitarian space'—a space of acute mass suffering, demanding external inter-vention—is conventionally imagined as opening up beyond the West, in those territories described by Stephanie Reist as constituting 'humanitarian place'. When widespread death and destitution expose Western government responses to domestic crisis as negligent, incompetent, or simply insufficient, humanitarian geographies are called into question. Reist's chapter reflects on perhaps the twenty-first century's starkest example: Hurricane Katrina.

For those engaged in the 'perpetual utterance of self-applause', Alexis de Tocqueville wrote, in reference to a majority of Jackson-era Americans, certain truths can be learnt 'only from strangers or from experience'.[35] In recent years, a particular experience of contact with 'strangers', even more than domestic disasters, has revealed to the West hypocrisies of its humanitarian morality. Growth in the number of forced migrants claiming asylum in Europe and North America has been a defining object of recent ideological dispute, invoked by right-wing nationalists as a threat to their cultural identity, and by progres-sives as providing an opportunity to confirm the West as plural and tolerant. But many public figures raising ethical objections to Britain's aid cuts have been silent about the violent, xenophobic harassment faced by forced migrants who survive odysseys to reach British shores. Tory MPs and peers lamenting the possible impact of cuts on global poverty reduction defended their government's suspension of support for Mediterranean search and rescue, in 2014, on the grounds that it was a 'pull factor' for migrants. The provision of emergency aid along what Mark Duffield calls Europe's 'security frontier', has been com-plementary to the attempts of European states to contain refugees as close as possible to their countries of origin. Tamirace Fakhoury's chapter considers the geopolitics of aid to refugees in the Arab Middle East, and its relevance to containment strategies.

The surge in forced migration has reproduced classic humanitarian dilemmas. Aid agency decision-making regarding relief and protec-tion for recent waves of forced migrants has been mediated by con-cerns about financial and political consequences. Eleanor Davey's chapter focuses on the role of the Salvation Army and Save the Children in detention centres off the Australian coast. With its fraught history of border control, and its enduring colonial treatment of

INTRODUCTION

Indigenous peoples, Australia offers a disquieting case study of anti-immigrant policy in the twenty-first century and its relationship to liberal ordering. For Save the Children, in particular, the controversial decision to work in detention centres was partly motivated by a desire to curry favour with the Australian government, while supporting children in a situation it disapproved of in principle. In Europe, meanwhile, the organisation's decision to operate a search and rescue vessel in the Mediterranean has generally been understood as a challenge to the policies of European governments and of Frontex, the European Union's border agency. Of the major aid agencies, Médecins Sans Frontières has been the most active in Mediterranean search and rescue. But the transformation of the Mediterranean into both a cultural battleground and a vast ossuary has also given rise to new movements. Through their operations and civic mobilisation, the likes of SOS MEDITERRANEE, Open Arms, and Sea-Watch have directly challenged anti-immigrant sentiment and fatal border policies, breaking from the anti-politics of liberal humanitarianism. Klaus Neumann's chapter considers the proposition that they represent a 'new model of humanitarian engagement'.

Born of both humanitarian concern and opposition to nationalistic politics, such movements are themselves involved in a struggle to define European identity—even to define an idea of Europe. Advertising the novelty of their approach, they also defend liberal ideals challenged by the new right. Very few who resist today's rightwards shift will reject every aspect of the normal order of things, not least because this order has coopted and incorporated political ideas emerging from the radical projects it previously suppressed. And if, in the current conjuncture, the new right appears as the most revolutionary political force, it too seeks to conserve fundamental aspects of bourgeois society. Despite claims of liberal decline, this moment could be characterised as one of intensified struggle to redefine liberalism itself. That humanitarian arguments should feature prominently in this struggle, deployed by those concerned with restoration, is no surprise. Humanitarianism has been the bedrock of the West's late capitalist sociodicy. It has developed broad appeal as an expression of secular religiosity; and its mobilisation of faith could make it a viable force of liberal renewal.

This will depend on the condition of its social and political bases. To what extent, then, do challenges to liberal order pose a threat to humanitarianism? This is the third and final question framing the contributions to this volume—one that, all too hastily, could be taken as expressive of a preoccupation with 'saving' humanitarianism. Despite the critiques they offer, the chapters in this volume—diverse in content and register—recognise value in the impulse to attend to the suffering of others and in a politics that respects human life. Questioning the institutional forms and the political tendencies historically associated with liberal humanitarianism is necessary to thinking through how a politics of life can be part of building a more just and equal world. This is an endeavour to which we hope to contribute.

January 2021

PART ONE

THE POLITICS OF HUMANITARIAN PRACTICE

2

HUMANITARIANISM AND HISTORY

A CENTURY OF SAVE THE CHILDREN

Emily Baughan[1]

In January 1919, a group of British feminists breached the Allied powers' ongoing blockade of recently defeated Germany by sending packages of rubber teats for baby bottles to German women. When the teats arrived, the bottles remained empty due to milk shortages in war-ravaged Berlin, but this did not matter to their senders. The purpose of the gift was as a government-defying gesture of solidarity on the part of the Women's International League for Peace and Freedom, an anti-war campaigning body.[2] Three months later, in April 1919, these women founded a new organisation, aimed at fusing political protest with humanitarian provision: the Save the Children Fund. Their leader, Dorothy Buxton, believed that publicising the plight of children in the aftermath of the First World War would draw the British public into a broader protest against the inequalities of the emerging world order. Buxton saw humanitarian action as a gateway to radical politics. It was only political change, rather than humanitarian aid, that could end suffering in Europe and create peace.[3]

In its designs for a peaceful, mutually prosperous world order, Save the Children was perhaps slightly ahead of the curve, but it did not remain so for long. What had been radicalism in the immediate wake of the war was, by the middle of the 1920s, a hegemonic vision of liberal internationalism. Advocating for international friendship and the importance of children's health (at home and overseas) for mutual economic prosperity, Save the Children ceased to be pushing at the boundaries of public opinion, but sat comfortably within the status quo. It is an organisation through which we can read the dominant strain of British liberal internationalist thought across the twentieth century. Doing so, we see how this strain of liberal internationalism has been dependent on, but has limited the ambition of, humanitarianism throughout the last hundred years.

In this chapter, I will show how points of convergence between humanitarianism and liberal internationalism resulted ultimately in the constraint of both humanitarian practice and humanitarian ideals. First, I'll show how ideological convergence enabled close relationships between aid organisations and state, which have ultimately served to constrain humanitarian independence. Second, I'll argue that an increasingly individualising liberal definition of rights has, ultimately, influenced both humanitarian work and—more fundamentally—the humanitarian imagination. Third, this chapter will highlight the ongoing legacies of imperialism in the international aid movement: it was, after all, Western imperialism that undergirded the liberal internationalist project.

To do this, I offer a history of the present. That is, a history that seeks not—as it usually should—to denaturalise the present, but instead to explain it. I reflect on the history of Save the Children as it illuminates present concerns, and I take as my starting a conference organised by Save the Children on the occasion of the organisation's centenary, in April 2019, in which the past served multiple functions: simultaneously, the restatement, rejection, and reaffirmation of different aspects of the organisation's present identity. This conference took place in Holborn, London, just down the road from Save the Children's first shabby one-room office, where Dorothy Buxton had furiously scrawled appeals for 'former enemy children'. One hundred years later, Save the Children has become a global organisation, comprising 29 national member organisations that work in 120 countries. Save the Children's UK branch has an annual income of over £300 million. It now employs over a thousand staff, its base a corporate office space in the City of London. Over its first century, Save the Children has moved from being a fringe protest movement to one of the world's largest and most influential humanitarian organisations.

The last ten years have seen a proliferation of histories of aid, and humanitarian organisations are beginning to participate in the production of more serious and honest accounts of their own past.[4] Save the Children's centenary conference was an attempt, driven from within the organisation, to grapple with the complicated history of aid to better understand its troubled present and contested future. The organising committee of the centenary conference held the organisation's first fifty years up to the light, making archival documents and photographs accessible to a practitioner audience. The conference also gathered testimony from those who had seen and shaped Save the Children's more recent half-century, from the end of the 1960s to the present day. In a series of witness panels, the conference drew upon the living institutional memory of Save the Children staff and their collaborators in other humanitarian organisations, in government, and on the ground in disaster-affected communities.

Archival documents recall Save the Children's early work in Europe, ravaged by two world wars, and its expansion into the British empire at the very moment that formal colonialism was being powerfully challenged by nationalist movements. Witness panels reflected on: the era of emergency response in the aftermath of decolonisation, moving from Biafra in 1967–70 to Bangladesh from 1971; the rapid growth of Save the Children as it responded to the Ethiopian famine and civil war in Sudan in the 1980s; a dawning awareness of the limits of humanitarian relief during genocides in Bosnia and Rwanda in the 1990s; and the embroilment of humanitarian organisations in official foreign policy, from the Iraq War in 2003 to the present day.

The conference took place after five difficult years for Save the Children UK. The close relationship between the charity's leaders and the British government, the advocacy of then-CEO Justin Forsyth for military intervention in Syria in 2013, and the organisation presenting an award to former UK Prime Minister Tony Blair the year after, had angered a younger generation of staff.[5] Revelations about sexual harassment during the course of the 2016 'me too' movement had led to senior resignations, including Forsyth's, and funding for the organisation from the British government (accounting for about one third of annual income) had been paused.[6] In this context, there was an appetite for greater transparency and open critique: an opportunity for frank conversations about the future and a demythologised version of the past. After two days of reflection, optimism seemed in short supply.[7] During the final panel of the conference, former Director of Emergencies Relief, Lewis Sida, said of the recent history of Save the Children:

> This is a time of development failure and protracted crises: most places we are working in today, we were working in fifteen years ago… we're often providing substitute service provision in long-term, broken places. I'm not particularly optimistic about these places: they will continue to be the badlands, and they're where we as humanitarians will continue to find ourselves.[8]

The aid sector seemed to have hit an impasse. Save the Children's founders had believed that by saving children, they would save the world. They had imagined that children's education and nutrition held the key to international peace and prosperity. Fifty years later, abandoning this utopia, a new leadership had believed they could save children from a disordered world by specialising in rapid crisis response. Neither approach seemed to have worked as imagined.

Politics, Aid, and the State

Though the situation that Sida described seemed far removed from the utopian vision of Save the Children's founders, it would not have surprised Dorothy Buxton. Buxton had never imagined that humanitarianism, on its own, would be enough to bring about a better world. Rather, humanitarianism was a gateway to forms of political action that would. Buxton had founded Save the Children to inspire socialist opposition to the inequalities of the liberal international order that had emerged from the First World War. It was Buxton's sister,

Eglantyne Jebb, who promoted a narrow humanitarianism as a pathway to a better world. Less politically radical than her sister, Jebb took over the organisation of Save the Children in the latter part of 1919, enabling the Fund's appeal to a wider section of the (largely anti-socialist) British public. Under Jebb's leadership, the Save the Children Fund sought to nourish and educate children, believing that healthy children's minds and bodies would be the basis of peace and mutual prosperity. Unlike Buxton, Jebb did not believe that humanitarians needed to critique or to change the existing political order. Rather, they should lead by example, inspiring states both to advance child welfare programmes and international collaboration.

Jebb believed that the humanitarian ends of Save the Children were above politics, and that they could be attained through existing liberal internationalism. In the interwar era, Save the Children imagined colonial capitalism as a means for Europe to enhance its prosperity and share its 'civilisation' with the wider world. In between the two world wars, Save the Children tasked itself with humanising British imperial rule and with bestowing the benefits of its expertise in foreign relations on a wider, international community via the League of Nations Child Welfare Committee. After the Second World War, the organisation sought to modernise British imperialism through the deployment of internationally garnered humanitarian expertise. In the 1950s and 1960s, its humanitarianism became a form of conservatism, as it sought to protect a liberal and imperial order that was rapidly slipping away.

What happens to a movement when the ideals that it was marshalled to protect begin to disappear? As the British empire disintegrated, Save the Children's leadership ceased to imagine a prosperous future for the world. Their beliefs about the function of humanitarianism started to shift: it would no longer be a midwife to a better world order, but would rather become a stretcher-bearer for the casualties of ongoing global disorder. In the three decades following the Fund's intervention in Biafra, the Director General position was occupied by retired colonial servicemen and army and air force generals. With expertise in rapid mobilisation, off-road transportation, and mass feeding, Save the Children was equipped for rapid responses to the successive crises its leaders imagined would follow in the wake of decolonisation. Embracing disaster response, rather than development, Save the Children diverged from the other major aid organisations that had emerged in late imperial Britain, such as Oxfam and Christian Aid. Where these organisations focused on local 'grassroots' solutions to hunger and poverty, Save the Children used its operational capacity and military experience to respond to complex emergencies. It no longer sought to save children in order to save the world, but to save children from a world that was already broken.

For Save the Children, ongoing survival was not just about playing to its operational strengths, however, but also cultivating its partnership with the British government. It was Save the Children that, in 1921, established a model for a century of state-funded humanitarian aid, acting as a contractor in the delivery of official British aid during the Russian famine. In its first fifty years, the Fund became a ready collaborator with the British military in war, and a partner in the growing development and education work of the Colonial Office. This partnership conferred status and resources on Save the Children, even if it occasionally came at the cost of constraining its action when aid stood in opposition to the British government's economic or diplomatic objectives. For Save the Children's early leadership, these instances were matters of pragmatism rather than a fundamental threat to principles: imagining British power as the basis of a peaceful and prosperous world order, humanitarians and the British state sought the same ends.

But this cooperation had a cost. Over the course of the last century, Save the Children had entrenched the modern British state's self-fashioning as a humanitarian actor. British imperialism had been cast as inherently humanitarian and, with the collusion of humanitarian agencies, its postcolonial foreign policy would be presented this way too. It was this image that would enable the so-called 'humanitarian wars' of the 1990s and the invasion of Iraq in 2003. In these wars, aid agencies followed on the heels of Western armies, funded by Western states, to heal the casualties their invasions had created.[9] A dawning discomfort with state collaboration, described by Save the Children staff at the centenary conference, came at a moment when aid organisations were more dependent on state funding than ever before. In the years since the Iraq invasion, the global humanitarian sector has quadrupled in size, becoming a US$29 billion-per-year industry. Around half of this figure relates to the funding given by (primarily Western) states to so-called 'non-governmental' aid agencies (both directly and via supranational bodies such as the United Nations and the European Union).[10] It is in this period too that humanitarian organisations have increasingly become, as Lewis Sida described at the centenary conference, service providers in 'failed' states in the global South.[11] What the world is left with, then, is aid organisations acting as intermediaries for Western states financing the functions of Southern, often postcolonial, states, almost half a century after the era of decolonisation.[12]

Scholars have been writing about the neocolonial character of international aid since the 1960s. They have shown how aid organisations became vehicles for state power, as well as Western cultural hegemony.[13] By tracing the longer history of the modern international aid movement, we can see that state-led and popular humanitarianism were forged in tandem, shared the same ideological ends, and were performed by the same actors. If crises are endemic, if development is stagnant, then this is a consequence of the same imperial and capitalist principles that animated the humanitarian movement in the first place. Speaking at the Save the Children centenary conference, Sida located hope within the humanitarian ethic itself: 'What Save the Children has been good at is keeping the flame of hope alive: believing that a better world is possible and that it is worth fighting for.'[14] Once the utopian vision of Save the Children's founders failed to materialise, humanitarianism—and its bearing of hope in a broken world—became an end in itself.

Liberalism and Children's Rights

In 1924, Eglantyne Jebb—by then de facto leader of the international Save the Children movement—climbed a mountain just across the French border from Geneva. Hours later, she descended, Moses-like, with the text of the Declaration of the Rights of the Child in her hands. (It seems likely that she ascended with the text too, as archival records reveal it had, in fact, been drafted over a number of years by a specially appointed Child Rights committee.) This is a powerful myth, and during the centenary year, Save the Children's introduction of the Declaration of the Rights of the Child in 1924 was repeatedly commemorated as one of the organisation's primary contributions to the modern humanitarian movement. Since Jebb walked down from a mountaintop, the meaning of children's rights has changed, their contours shifting along with popular understandings of liberalism. When the Declaration of the Rights of the Child was first authored in the early 1920s, it drew upon a late Victorian liberal collectivist tradition. Children were valued not as individuals but because of the contributions they would make to wider society. These contributions were imagined in biopolitical terms: healthy children would become the workers of the future. Child rights, though described as universal, were imagined only to apply to healthy children. The first Declaration of the Rights of the Child did not assume that every child would be equal, nor have the same value. Save the Children drew upon eugenics and colonial racial 'science' to determine the relative value of children. The League of Nations Child Welfare Committee, tasked with implementing the Declaration, imagined that nation-states or colonial powers would be the foremost protectors of children's rights. The Declaration of the Rights of the Child provided no ideological or practical challenge to the major threats to children's rights in this era: colonialism and fascism.

After the Second World War, although the United Nations adopted the League of Nations Child Rights declaration, Save the Children itself moved away from a rights-based discourse, ceding this ground to UNICEF.[15] Save the Children did not rediscover child rights as a framing device for its work until decades later. The early 1990s saw a shift in Save the Children's leadership (towards career voluntary sector workers and away from former military) at the same time as disillusionment grew within the organisation about the long-term impact of disaster relief.[16] In 1989, the United Nations reworked and relaunched the Declaration of the Rights of the Child and, from the 1990s, Save the Children once again styled itself as a 'child rights organisation'. In the 1990s, child rights provided a point for Save the Children, an organisation focused primarily on emergency aid, to re-enter into long-term development work.[17] This re-entry took place, not coincidentally, at the moment when 'development' was shifting away from a focus on economic justice and community-based programmes towards the rights of women and children—and in doing so becoming ostensibly less 'political'.

The contemporary UN Convention on the Rights of the Child—the version of child rights that Save the Children now strives to realise—is an expression of late twentieth-century liberal individualism. It enshrines children's rights to the 'development of [their] personality', 'freedom of expression', and 'individual life in society'.[18] Whereas at the start of the twentieth century, children's rights were vested in their position vis-à-vis the community, today children's rights are understood to exist independently from the society they inhabit. At the same time, the 1989 Declaration locates the child within the family, as the 'natural environment for… growth and well-being'. This shift began in the aftermath of the Second World War, as psychoanalysis posited the stability of the nuclear family as central to the emotional health of children and, in turn, the future of (capitalist) democracy. Save the Children began its first family reunification programme in the aftermath of the Biafran War in 1970. The largest such programme since the Second World War, it marked a belated change in direction for the Fund, which had been reluctant to end its practice of separating children from their families for education and relief. The Biafran War marked the moment, too, when the Fund parted with its iconic bambino logo: an icon of a Christ-like orphan, taken from the walls of a sixteenth-century orphanage in Florence. It replaced this with the bold, modern 'Charlie' logo. In doing so, it removed the icon of an orphan that had been central to its work and its public image for the first half-century.

In the mid-1990s, following the mass refugee crisis and family separations generated by the Rwandan genocide, family reunification became a central aspect of Save the Children's work. In major disasters of the twenty-first century, such as the 2010 Haitian earthquake, Save the Children positioned itself as an expert organisation, advocating for the preservation of families and the prevention of international adoption. This work located Save the Children's concern for the right of children to family life alongside its traditional strength in disaster relief.[19] More recently, Save the Children UK has lobbied against family separation through legal channels. In 2018, Save the Children sponsored a major legal inquiry into the protection of children in conflict, that, like Save the Children's 1938 report on the protection of children in war, advocated the removal of children from conflict zones.[20] In 1938, Save the Children had argued that children should be placed in designated zones and cared for by professionals. In 2018, recognising the difficulty of recreating familial environments and the trauma of separation, Save the Children lobbied for adult civilians in conflict zones to be afforded enhanced protection alongside the children they cared for.

Upholding the right of children to family life, Save the Children also advocates safe passage and settlement rights to be granted to the parents of children who have sought asylum abroad, and for children whose parents have found new national homes. In contrast to its successes in family reunification in the global South, Save the Children has had little success in altering restrictive immigration policies in either Britain or the United States.[21] Nonetheless, attempts to do so are revealing about the changing position of children in the humanitarian imagination. In the 1920s iteration of children's rights, the young claimed their entitlements in relation to their adult selves. In the contemporary iteration of children's rights, it is adults who make claims on sympathy, asylum, and protection through their relationship to children. In neither guise has the language of child rights brought us any closer to a world in which people are valued on their own terms, in the present, as people.[22]

Humanitarian Internationalism in Britain Today

In the last decade, the landscape of international aid in Britain has shifted further. The thirteen-year rule of Britain's last Labour government, in power until 2010, was characterised by an 'ethical foreign policy' that echoed many of the tenets of earlier liberal internationalism. It included the rapid expansion of state aid and the use of military force in the name of humanitarian concern.[23] Now, as I write this chapter, Britain's current Conservative government has just abolished the Department for International Development. The consensus around international aid, the only budget to have been ring-fenced by successive Conservative-led austerity administrations after 2010, seems to have vanished. Under a government that was elected on a platform of nationalism, border control, and xenophobia, Britain has withdrawn from the European Union. At Save the Children's centenary conference, which took place just after the first missed deadline for Britain's withdrawal from the European Union, delegates wondered if they were witnessing the end of Britain's internationalist century, which had begun in 1920 with entry into the League of Nations. Today, 101 years after the League of Nations Health Organization was founded as a collective endeavour to stem the tide of epidemic disease, the fight against COVID-19 is being waged largely on a nation-by-nation basis.

While humanitarian organisations now lament the end of an era of liberal internationalist consensus, their ideals have done little to challenge the rise of right-wing nationalism.[24] British humanitarianism has always been a highly constrained form of internationalism. It is one that promotes a form of compassion at a distance; it breaks down entirely when those who are designated to be in need of aid approach Britain's borders. By externalising need, humanitarianism has failed to offer a successful challenge to a century of British reluctance, or refusal, to welcome refugees. Humanitarianism is also a deeply hierarchical form of internationalism. It places Western states as leaders of—rather than collaborators with—nations overseas. Over the past 100 years, it has been a tool for successive British governments to affirm Britain's 'global leadership' in the face of its diminishing economic and geopolitical significance. This nostalgia for 'global leadership'—a euphemism for imperialism—remains a fundamental aspect of right-wing nationalism in Britain.

Humanitarianism has often provided a means of reimagining the imperial past. Save the Children was engaged in this rewriting of imperial history from its earliest days. In 1931, the organisation hosted a landmark 'Conference on the African Child' in Geneva, which drew together missionaries, doctors, colonial administrators, and international experts. The conference celebrated the centenary of the abolition of slavery in the British empire and the 100 years of imperial benevolence that had followed in its wake. While sentimentalising some aspects of the imperial past, Save the Children has also worked to distance itself from histories of colonial violence—such as its involvement in imprisoning children during the Kenyan Emergency—expunging these from its archives.[25] The 2019 centenary conference represented a growing desire to grapple with Save the Children's imperial origins, but was itself constrained by the contingencies of both the colonial past and present-day international relationships. Delegates shifted uncomfortably in their seats when I spoke about Save the Children's 1931 'African Child' conference, which had just seven African delegates. The audience assembled in 2019 did not look so different. We, the organisers, had failed to locate staff members from the global South who had worked in the successive crises addressed in the conference's witness panels. Many of the conference delegates travelling from Africa or the Middle East had had their visas delayed or denied by the British Foreign Office.[26] The conference, like the contemporary aid movement, reproduced colonial knowledge and power structures.

Can humanitarianism be uncoupled from the imperialism that birthed it? A new movement to decolonise international aid seeks ways to incorporate local traditions of care into humanitarian emergency responses, to vest decision-making in affected communities, and to divest aid financed by Western donors of imposed Western cultural norms.[27] For many humanitarians committed to this decolonisation process, history also has an important role to play in recovering alternative origin stories and visions for the contemporary humanitarian movement. In 2019, Save the Children launched its first ever training course on the history of international aid. While the online course charted the well-known origin story of humanitarianism in the British empire and the international Red Cross movement, it also explored 'southern humanitarianisms'. There is vital historical work to be done to gain a better understanding of how humanitarian agencies spoke to, or co-opted, other traditions of care. There is also important work to be done around understanding how humanitarianism was interpreted, interrupted, challenged, or adapted by local staff and recipients; work that is made challenging by our existing archives, and will remain so for as long as we fail to gather testimony from the vast, but forgotten, Southern staff of the international aid movement.

Yet there is also a danger that, when we search for the global origins of a Western vision of universalism, we are naturalising it. Rather than seeking multiple origin stories for the particular vision of humanitarianism that has spawned a US$29 billion global aid industry, dominated by organisations like Save the Children, historians need to understand both Western and Southern cultures of mutual aid, philanthropy, and solidarity on their own terms. 'Humanitarianism' may not be the best framework for doing so.[28]

Accepting the specificity of humanitarianism as an ethic for international action that grew out of nineteenth- and twentieth-century Western liberalism might also help us move away from overblown claims about its significance. While the interventions of aid agencies were undoubtedly important, even lifesaving, for many recipients of aid, how far have these interventions actually transformed the governance, economies, and environments of postcolonial states? Humanitarianism offers us an important lens through which to examine the establishment of liberal internationalist hegemony in the West, but it may be altogether less useful to our understanding of how this hegemony was experienced, or rejected, in the global South. Humanitarian archives have replicated the power hierarchies of humanitarian aid, and even where there is access to the voices of aid's recipients, historians do not meet them on their own terms, speaking to their own concerns. Perhaps it is time to stop accessing vast sections of the past through the inherently hierarchical humanitarian interactions, just as it is time to stop Western publics accessing vast sections of the present world through the humanitarian imagination. Other stories need to be told.

3

THE RISE OF THE HUMANITARIAN CORPORATION

SAVE THE CHILDREN AND THE ORDERING
OF EMERGENCY RESPONSE

Gareth Owen

This is a personal account of nearly twenty years of lived experience in Save the Children UK (SCUK), the British member of the world's largest independent international children's development and humanitarian agency. It is my own interpretation of SCUK's relationship with, and efforts to influence, the political economy of twenty-first-century humanitarianism. The story starts just over 100 years ago with the founding of the Save the Children Fund by sisters Dorothy Buxton and Eglantyne Jebb, during a period of burgeoning international socialism in the aftermath of the First World War. Having engaged in conventional philanthropy prior to the war, Eglantyne was of a more conservative disposition than Dorothy, whose humanitarian ideals were more explicitly political. Dorothy, in particular, felt humanitarian aid could contribute to a new civic diplomacy and peace.[1] Today, the organisation they founded comprises an association of thirty members worldwide, working together through a wholly owned subsidiary, Save the Children International (SCI). Save the Children's vision is a world in which every child attains the right to survival, protection, development, and participation; its mission is to inspire breakthroughs in the way the world treats children, and to achieve immediate and lasting change in their lives. Collectively, Save the Children is present in over 100 countries and has an annual turnover of over US$2 billion. SCUK remains one of its largest individual members, with an average annual income over the five-year period 2015–19 of over £300 million.[2]

A central theme of this story is humanitarian realism. Acknowledging situations as they are and being prepared to navigate accordingly has usually been the SCUK way, adapting humanitarian intentions to achieve maximum possible impact. I believe such pragmatism is one of the great strengths of the organisation. SCUK has always deliberately placed itself in close proximity to those with wealth, power, and status in order to promote the cause of disadvantaged children. This organisational choice is the story's second central theme. It might be a legitimate strategy to follow. But I contend that, in taking this approach, SCUK has often also been used as a tool by the custodians of liberal order. And I question whether the strategy of proximity has been a means to an end or whether, at times, it has become an end in itself.

The third theme of the story concerns leadership. The way an organisation carries out its mission depends very much on who is leading it at any one time. Here one can question whether the course taken by a particular leader reflects 'humanitarian realism'. Adapting to different leadership approaches as well as changes in the external environment is part and parcel of working in any organisation. As a member of SCUK's emergency programme staff from 2002 until 2007, and Humanitarian Director since then, I have been directly involved in the major events and leadership decisions described herein. I experienced SCUK's loss of 'humanitarian innocence'; and I participated in the deliberately expansive corporatisation that rescued it from financial jeopardy. Later, like many staff, I also questioned the 're-politicisation' of the organisation's humanitarian agenda. It is these events, and the institutional arrangements and governing interests that underpinned them, that are the subject of my critical reflections. As a humanitarian leader at SCUK, the search for meaning in all this is deeply personal. This can therefore never be an entirely objective or comprehensive account, nor is that the intention. Rather it is an attempt to offer an insider's view on events that seem exemplary of a particular historical moment.

My maternal grandfather, John Francis Danby, was a scholar of William Shakespeare and a staunch socialist from Geordie mining stock. During the Second World War, he befriended Jewish refugees and became involved in military intelligence. Danby's best-known writing is a study of Shakespeare's *King Lear*, in which the tragic protagonist finds his core values undermined by cruel experience and arrogance. *Lear* was an exploration of humanity's search for meaning. Danby viewed the play, in part, as a Hobbesian study of human nature. He wrote:

> Behind the shift and drift of the meanings of the word Nature there is the shift and drift of humanity in a setting at once historical and spiritual. Behind the word there is Shakespeare certainly. But behind Shakespeare there is the mining engineer breaking into the bowels of the earth; the Seeker out of the mysteries of brass, and glass, and salt, and the supplier of the Elizabethan navies; the doctor, taking apart the human body to anatomise the mechanism of muscle and bone; the capitalist aware of money as the sinews of war and soon to recognise in it the circulating lifeblood of the body politic.[3]

This passage is meaningful to me as a humanitarian practitioner. It reminds me that we are shaped by a world of constant ethical, political, and economic struggles from which none are spared; where there may be no good choices, but where good decisions made by good leaders really matter.

Humanitarians share a foundational belief in common humanity and respect for human dignity. We have crafted fixed principles and exclusive goals around what we tend to imagine as a timeless ethos, creating structural frames by which we live, work, and think. But in doing so, we have perhaps too often forgotten one of Shakespeare's great lessons on human nature. Danby described it thus: '[I]n the moral sphere one must act in accordance with one's ideas. But in the course of that action, the ideas themselves will undergo development and are subject to change.'⁴ As we move through the world around us, its political and economic forces act upon our neatly constructed humanitarian foundations, bending and bowing them such that at times they may be rendered barely recognisable.

Like many charities, SCUK operates a two-tier governance system. The first tier is an Executive Leadership Team led by a Chief Executive Officer, which oversees the day-to-day running of the organisation. The executive directors tend to be seasoned professionals with substantial careers in the charity sector. They are governed by a supervisory board of non-executive trustees, who are chosen less for subject matter expertise in aid and more for their skill sets in important business areas, such as financial and risk management. Led by a Chairperson, trustees are responsible for maintaining strategic oversight: ensuring SCUK carries out its stated purpose, complies with charity law, manages its resources responsibly and accountably, and upholds its public reputation. The working relationship and backgrounds of the Chair of Trustees and the Chief Executive Officer have a significant influence on the charity's organisational culture and strategic direction of travel.

In a large and long-established charitable institution like SCUK, interpretations of mandate and meaningful action in protection of human dignity vary widely. There are the competing methodologies of developmentalism and humanitarianism; there are differing views on resource allocation and the relative priority of programmes and advocacy; and, of course, there are divergent politics. Members of staff can then experience moral distress and a loss of trust when they perceive their organisation to be straying from the principles they signed up to. Trustees and executives, meanwhile, face a collective challenge to take seriously any fundamental compromise of their organisation's identity. But times change and boundaries blur, trustees and leaders come and go, key staff move on. All the while, an organisation's 'nature' must adapt to the *zeitgeist*, the demands of political economy, and evolving interpretations of 'doing the right thing'. Core values matter enormously, but so does the manner in which they are put into practice. How a humanitarian organisation managerially functions in pursuit of its ends is as important as the humanistic ends themselves.

THE RISE OF THE HUMANITARIAN CORPORATION

SCUK and the 'New Humanitarian' Era

By the turn of the twenty-first century, a substantial 'drift and shift' in the nature of humanitarianism had taken place, as described by Juliano Fiori et al.: 'the [new] humanitarianism, which took shape in the 1990s, focussed more on the consequences of aid, and involved a shift from needs-based to rights-based approaches. Significantly influenced by donor governments, it has often been associated with the promotion of military means to address humanitarian problems.'[5] Mike Aaronson became SCUK's Director General during this 'new humanitarian' period. He had joined Save the Children as a young philosophy student in 1969, immediately participating in the emergency response to the Biafran War. He had then embarked on a career in the Diplomatic Service, before returning to the organisation in 1988. He took on leadership of SCUK in 1994, as genocide was being perpetrated in Rwanda. Shortly afterwards, SCUK entered Kigali from Uganda. The Rwandan Patriotic Front had taken the capital and SCUK had built up an important operation within Rwanda. SCUK chose not to become involved in the horrendous situation in the camps in the Democratic Republic of Congo, focusing instead on the repatriation and resettlement of children.

There was much furore within the aid sector about the humanitarian response to the Rwandan genocide. A large number of underqualified organisations had flooded into the country and almost certainly did more harm than good. Published in March 1996, the Joint Evaluation for Emergency Assistance to Rwanda (JEEAR) delivered a damning verdict on the inadequacies of humanitarian professionalism and coordination.[6] It had profound consequences, landing at a time when

> the deontological basis of humanitarian action was […] being supplanted by a consequentialist ethics prompted by greater expectations, a ballooning sphere of activity, and broadening alliances, but also by the enthusiasm of donor governments for the introduction of results-based management (RBM) in the humanitarian sector. The inadequacy of humanitarian action in response to conflict, genocide and mass displacement in Africa's Great Lakes region would only confirm this realignment.[7]

The JEEAR was followed by a 'torrent of new initiatives aimed at improving performance and accountability'[8] that included the Sphere Project, a massive inter-agency effort to establish common technical standards for humanitarian relief; the Active Learning Network for Accountability and Performance in Humanitarian Action, a membership community of practice; and, later, the Humanitarian Accountability Project.

In 1997, SCUK introduced a new five-year 'Global Programme Strategy' that sought to 'secure the benefits of a more rigorous, child-focussed approach to SCUK's own work' and to 'strengthen and promote a more developmental approach to emergency work', the area of work for which it had been best known in the public domain.[9] Although SCUK had contributed to the proliferation of neoliberal management techniques in the aid sector, through its promotion of professionalising reforms, the new strategy offered a critique of contemporary economic reason:

> The 1990s have seen the dominance of a model of economic and social development across the world which perceives and promotes market forces as the answer to poverty alleviation and social problems at a country, regional and global level. The role of the state is seen as increasingly marginal and government programmes have come under intense pressure to cut expenditure.[10]

The strategy was primarily intended to increase coherence between SCUK's domestic and foreign programmes. It also sought a closer relationship between activities that might have a direct impact on children (service delivery) and those that might have an indirect impact (policy influencing). An upshot of this was a reduction in operations unconnected to developmental advocacy, with negative consequences for the organisation's income in an increasingly competitive charity market. The central importance of emergency programmes to organisational income and profile was then thrown into sharp relief by the Kosovo War in 1999. SCUK was working inside Kosovo before the conflict erupted and therefore had the beginnings of a programme among refugees in Macedonia and Albania. However, its emergency capacity had always been lodged within the Africa team, and, despite internal opposition, that clearly needed to change. So, as the short-lived era of Western 'humanitarian interventions' came to an end in the Balkans, SCUK slowly began to rebuild a central operational capability for responding to emergencies.

SCUK and the Point of No Return

The new millennium opened a new humanitarian chapter for SCUK. An 'Emergency Strategy' speculated that increased competition in the aid sector would lead to 'less analytical, short-term' programmes, 'based on the needs of the organisation rather than the rights of those affected'.[11] If the strategy promoted a revival of the organisation's emergency response culture, it also reproduced the human rights discourse that had inspired humanitarian reforms in the 1990s. By early 2003, SCUK also had in place a new Board Chairman, Nick MacAndrew. With a long career in financial asset management and investment banking at Schroders, his appointment marked a more financially driven approach to trusteeship. This was a moment of accelerated commercialisation of the aid sector; the neomanagerial totems of efficiency, productivity, and effectiveness were becoming synonymous with success. MacAndrew's primary focus, then, was SCUK's balance sheet. He was not expected to be an expert in child rights or humanitarianism, which were considered matters for specialist staff. The introduction of new fundraising techniques would lead to significant staff changes.

Meanwhile, SCUK, like other UK aid agencies, was entering a new phase of its engagement with government. On 24 September 2002, the British government released its Iraq Dossier.[12] Parliament was recalled as *The Sun* newspaper headline screamed, 'Brits 45 Mins from Doom'.[13] By January 2003, it was clear to all that the UK would soon be following the US into war. SCUK had issued a public statement urging that war be avoided, 'casting serious doubt on the wisdom of such an endeavour', and reminding the British government that it was the 'moral duty of the members of the Security Council to invest all their efforts towards a peaceful resolution'.[14]

Mass protests against the war were staged in February 2003, and anti-war sentiment ran very high among SCUK staff. For many, if the US government and its allies intended to invade and occupy another sovereign nation, then it was equally their responsibility to deal with the consequences. It was not the business of humanitarian NGOs to take any part in the planning and conduct of regime change. But SCUK had been present in the Kurdish north of Iraq since the early 1990s and was long-supported by the British government to run development programmes. SCUK chose to stay, and continued to receive British government funding from the Department for International Development (DfID). We had a long-established programme there and took the pragmatic view that it was where we could make our greatest contribution, especially as it was clear we would not be able to operate in accordance with our principles from Baghdad.

Save the Children US (SCUS) was coming under state pressure from the US government, which saw NGOs as 'natural partners' in the management of the aftermath of war.[15] Addressing NGOs shortly after the invasion of Afghanistan, in 2001, Secretary of State Colin Powell had said, 'just as surely as our diplomats and military, American NGOs are out there serving and sacrificing on the front lines of freedom [...] I am serious about making sure we have the best relationship with the NGOs who are such a force multiplier for us, such an important part of our combat team.'[16] But in the eyes of many aid workers and spectators, not least in the Islamic world, it was in Iraq that the humanitarian community passed the point of no return in its relationship to state power. The humanitarian tenets of independence and neutrality, so often knowingly compromised through the pragmatism of circumstance in other conflict settings, had been relinquished before bombs were dropped on Iraq.

We watched 'shock and awe' play out on our television screens on 19 March 2003, as the US unsuccessfully attempted to eliminate Saddam Hussein and his sons with its opening strike.[17] On 25 March, Mike Aaronson issued a statement to calm the continuing disquiet among staff:

> I have great sympathy with those who would like us to take a position of outright opposition to military action against Iraq [...] However, as a humanitarian agency we have to tread a fine line between speaking out boldly and effectively on issues affecting children... and adopting a broader political position that takes us outside our man-

date... I realise that this can be very frustrating, particularly when we all have such strong personal views on the situation, but ever since Save the Children was founded this is the route we have taken in order to maximise our effectiveness as an advocate for children's rights.[18]

As British and American troops were deploying for combat, Save the Children pragmatically lowered its public profile. By the beginning of April 2003, a large build-up of humanitarian agencies was underway in both Kuwait and Jordan. The main body of coalition forces was now driving into the heart of Iraq and meeting little resistance. Most of the Iraqi army was quickly defeated and Baghdad was occupied on the 9 April. Kirkuk fell the following day, and Tikrit, Saddam's hometown, five days later. The Iraqi president and senior government officials went into hiding and, on 1 May, George W. Bush triumphantly declared from the deck of the USS *Abraham Lincoln* that major combat operations were over.

Far from being hailed as 'great liberators', the invading military was quickly met with a brutal insurgency. Aid workers frequently faced open hostility and worried that they were viewed by sections of the local population as partners in the regime change and subsequent occupation.[19] Numerous tragedies befell the humanitarian community, the most infamous being the devastating bomb attack on the Canal Hotel in Baghdad, on 19 August 2003, which killed more than twenty people, including the United Nations' Special Representative in Iraq, Sérgio Vieira de Mello. As Hugo Slim put it, the vulnerability of humanitarian agencies was now 'a matter of their blood-essence as westerners and intervenors'.[20] For SCUK, principled support for anti-war public opinion had now given way to a complex humanitarian field operation with little prospect of lasting success.

Playing a structural role in the opening of markets in occupied Iraq, INGOs became widely acknowledged as 'missionaries of western neoliberalism'.[21] Humanitarian aid budgets rapidly expanded in subsequent years, and increasingly ambitious British aid agencies generally celebrated the outsourcing of government services at home and abroad. A growing anxiety among SCUK humanitarian staff over the perceived subordination of ethical principles was soon to be compounded by the vigorous pursuit of corporate growth.

SCUK and the Rise of Humanitarian Corporatism

According to management expert Michael Pirson, the enhancement of humanity's well-being and dignity is dependent on achieving an acceptable balance between the economistic drives to acquire and defend life-sustaining resources and the humanistic drives to bond with each other and comprehend our own existence.[22] For SCUK, the 'drive to acquire' has been a pursuit of financial resources and access to power, but secured for humanist purpose: to defend the rights of children, to bond globally in international solidarity, to comprehend the changing circumstance and needs of the world's most marginalised and deprived, and to argue for more equitable distribution of wealth and social justice. Humanist and economistic outlooks are often taken to be at odds, but for a humanitarian organisation it is not a binary choice of one over the other. Rather, it is a complex balancing act. The drive to acquire and defend is inherently human and key to survival. In institutional terms, it requires adept political manoeuvring, for the right reasons: to gather the means to act in furtherance of the cause. But in an extreme form, if left unchecked the will to acquisition can have unintended consequences. As aid budgets expanded, SCUK entered a decade of imbalance in which competitive, economistic drives became dominant.

The 'tipping point' came with the Indian Ocean tsunami of 2004, which, in financial terms, remains the largest emergency response in Save the Children's history.[23] This response had a profound effect on the organisation by reaffirming the power of 'getting the big emergencies right'—a mantra that recognises the fact that high-profile emergencies often attract substantial numbers of new supporters who, through effective, targeted marketing, can become longer-term donors of vital unrestricted funds, the lifeblood of all charities. As such, a big emergency response was considered an extremely profitable commercial proposition. And there had been none bigger than the tsunami response.

Leading a major emergency response from the outset is a classically utilitarian endeavour. The proposition of doing the greatest good for the greatest number of people had appealed to Eglantyne Jebb, and has been part of Save the Children's humanitarian ethos.[24] Responding is an exercise in large and rapid planning with very unreliable information. It is a shifting numbers game. Human lives are often reduced to an amorphous mass of tragic victimhood in an effort to solve problems in bulk. In the case of the tsunami, compared to previous disasters, the number of persons affected was significant, but not enormous. The biggest challenge for agencies like Save the Children was to simultaneously scale up its response in multiple countries spread across two continents.

News media tends to focus on the loss of life, but human fatality is not an indicative measure of the severity of an emergency situation. A more accurate account of such disasters is provided by the number of survivors in urgent need of assistance, the damage to national infrastructure, personal assets, and property, and the long-term effects on basic services, livelihoods, and a country's economy. The humanitarian response therefore necessitates an unemotional and economistic planning exercise. But the scale of response depends on the appeal to public sentiment and the monetisation of compassion for distant strangers; it depends on the development, through the press, of a 'credible sense… [of] victimhood'.[25]

Big agencies will pump prime responses with cash from their reserves while they initiate fundraising efforts. But this involves a judgement call, and most managers of aid are instinctively cautious, fearing going too far into the red. In the case of the tsunami, the UK Disasters Emergency Committee (DEC), a long-standing umbrella group comprising all the major British humanitarian charities, launched an appeal early on, and the emotional response from the public was spectacular. A total of £392 million was eventually raised. What prompted such a public outpouring of generosity has often been debated: the time of year—Christmas, a traditional period of giving; the shocking character of an apparently natural event; the fact that so many people knew the beaches of Thailand where so many holiday-makers were killed, including families of the famous like Sir Richard Attenborough; the many compelling survivor stories from multiple countries. Both the impact of the disaster and the response were more international than any aid worker of my generation had experienced. But the enormous publicity generated by disasters like the tsunami can distort the manner in which the response is administered. Like many aid workers, I knew the huge response to the tsunami was disproportionate to the needs of people affected, but it proved impossible to resist the clamour and the funding.

In early 2005, the Tsunami Evaluation Coalition (TEC) was formed to jointly assess the humanitarian response. It was facilitated by the London-based Active Learning Network for Accountability and Performance and coordinated by NGO, UN, Red Cross, and donor government representatives. Despite acknowledging the success of the fundraising appeal, it was critical of the way a 'flood of international agencies' controlled resources and marginalised people affected by the tsunami.[26] The TEC concluded that international humanitarian agencies were driven by institutional imperatives, 'such as the urgency to spend money visibly' and the 'perceived need for quick, tangible, agency-specific results'. The tsunami response was a demonstration of an aid phenomenon that would become increasingly prevalent through corporate responses to competition: humanitarian agencies projected their 'moral authority' through narratives of success, seeking in turn to expand their income and influence.[27]

The long-term effect on SCUK of the Indian Ocean tsunami, and the two other high-profile emergency responses of 2005—to famine in Niger and an earthquake in Kashmir—was profound. In 2006, SCUK adopted an 'Emergency Strategic Implementation Plan' that corporately embedded two key concepts.[28] Firstly, the notion of 'getting the big emergencies right' to enable reach; and secondly, the competitive language of 'becoming a top 3 NGO' in terms of scale and brand recognition.[29] New commercial thinking had entered the humanist DNA, championed by a new director—now with the corporate title of CEO—with a background in international business marketing. Jasmine Whitbread's appointment would prove to be a good choice for the restoration of SCUK's finances. Whitbread introduced new corporate values to the organisation, focusing on the development of a much more ambitious and inspiring culture—and this meant more attention to the spectacular potential of humanitarian response. Her intervention was pivotal in accelerating the revitalisation of the humanitarian cause, leading to substantial investments that quickly transformed our ability to respond to emergencies at scale. The impact was significant: SCUK rapidly expanded in size.

Amid the global economic downturn in 2008, SCUK's leadership decided that operating on a much larger scale was the best way for the organisation to weather the storm. It was a view shared by a new Board Chairman, Sir Alan Parker, founder of global PR firm Brunswick Group. Together, Parker and Whitbread were a potent force. They believed Save the Children globally had been growing slower than other NGOs—an untenable market trend. Together with other branches of Save the Children, they developed a working hypothesis that anticipated the movement substantially growing its annual turnover to secure a leading top-tier position. The expansive strategy would prove to be highly successful in terms of increased financial turnover, programmatic reach, and global brand awareness. Save the Children was by no means alone in following this approach. Big NGOs had long held the view that increasing income would increase impact.[30] Others also grew in this period, though few as much as Save the Children.

SCUK also had a political trump card to play. Parker's friendship with Conservative Party leader David Cameron helped foster good relations with Tories, who were tipped for a return to power. For Cameron, prioritising international aid was a way of rebranding the Conservative Party, and over the coming years he would invest considerable time and political capital on his attempt to write into law the UK's commitment to spending 0.7 percent of gross national income on overseas aid.[31] The Conservative Party opted to launch its green paper on international development from the SCUK office in central London, while Whitbread wrote a comment piece in *The Times* in support of Cameron's ring-fencing of aid spending.[32] SCUK also appointed Cameron's wife, Samantha, as one of its ambassadors. In seeking future influence, SCUK was also implicitly throwing its weight behind Cameron. It was a political realignment, enabled by the proximity on policy between the outgoing Labour government and the presumed government-in-waiting. Moreover, it was the beginning of a re-politicisation of SCUK's humanitarian ambitions, which would be accelerated by a dramatic shift in the international governance of Save the Children.

In 2010, Save the Children International (SCI) was created to deliver programmes on behalf of all thirty national Save the Children members. Whitbread left SCUK to become its first CEO, and the economistic culture of growth and ambition spread across Save the Children globally. In late 2010, Justin Forsyth, a former Whitehall spin doctor, was appointed CEO of SCUK, and he quickly set about coupling financial growth with an aggressive pursuit of political influence. If Parker and Whitbread had propelled the organisation through a process of corporate 'modernisation', Parker and Forsyth were a formidable influencing force, with an ability to reach the ear of political and wealthy elites. Furthermore, in their eyes, no humanitarian idea was too audacious or too risky or too controversial. It was a time of great strategic opportunity for SCUK's emergency responders and one that we sought to harness to the full.

For Save the Children's humanitarian endeavour, the decade of expansive corporatisation, commercialisation, and government contracting that followed the tsunami was a period of extremes and contradictions. The emphasis on ambition and achievement created major opportunities to innovate and expand, such that SCUK competed and collaborated in equal measure: maximising its relative share of DEC funds on the one hand, while on the other jointly authoring and hosting three innovative civil society initiatives aimed at improving humanitarian practice and knowledge sharing globally.[33] However, SCUK's leadership ethos and cultural identity were becoming less distinguishable from those found elsewhere in professional society, whether the civil service or the C-suite of major corporations, from where most of its top executives were now being drawn. SCUK was neither a government department nor a large business. It was an independent humanitarian NGO with 100 years of unique cultural heritage to protect. For staff like myself, there was a marked philosophical boundary between wanting to ensure access to wealth and power in order to have influence and becoming subordinate to party political agendas when fostering such ties. It was now less clear which side of the line those at the helm of SCUK sat. Indeed, the line itself was now blurred.

SCUK and the Re-politicisation of Humanitarian Ambition

David Cameron's international development strategy of 'One World Conservatism' not only reaffirmed the Conservative Party's commitment to the 0.7 percent target; it also retained DfID, by now a widely respected aid institution, as an autonomous department. The role of Britain as a 'development superpower' was viewed as serving national interests by bringing prestige, strengthening security, and tackling the causes of mass immigration.[34] However, after 2010, as the Conservative government implemented its austerity programme of cuts and privatisations, public scepticism about international aid spending increased.[35] In the run up to the 2015 UK general election, SCUK would find itself under the direct influence of these political dynamics. We would be asked to throw our weight behind the Cameron government once more. Only this time it would be on the humanitarian frontline.

In early 2013, Sir Alan Parker was approached by Sir Michael Jay, Chair of Trustees at Medical Emergency Relief International (Merlin), about a possible merger. In fact, it was a huge opportunity for SCUK to acquire a strategic frontline health capability and reputation. By the end of 2013, the takeover had been formalised. SCUK aspired to emulate the medical capability of Médecins Sans Frontières (MSF), the world's premier medical humanitarian agency. And the acquisition of Merlin would be of almost immediate consequence to the political strategy of SCUK leadership.

In February 2014, cases of Ebola haemorrhagic fever were registered in Guinea. With a case fatality rate of up to 90 percent, Ebola is among the world's deadliest diseases. An outbreak in such parts of West Africa was highly unusual. Save the Children immediately began a programme of response focused on prevention through community mobilisation, public health messaging, and basic support to health centres. As the weeks wore on, new cases appeared in neighbouring Liberia and, by early June, cases were also recorded in Sierra Leone. By July, international media attention on the region was increasing. Though global concern was still quite low, it was rapidly moving up the global security agenda. With the Ebola crisis spiralling, in August, *The Guardian* newspaper ran a scathing attack by MSF on the international community's failure to offer adequate help.[36] While MSF's complaints were not necessarily reflective of the perspectives of other NGOs, their criticism had an effect. Governments around the world, which had been slow to react to initial warnings, now sought to speed up the response to a deadly disease outbreak that health experts were warning could become a global disaster. The motive of rich countries in the global North was not primarily humanitarian: they sought to ensure that Ebola would be contained in Africa.

The World Health Organization (WHO) approached the UK government, asking for its assistance to strengthen isolation measures and provide treatment beds throughout Sierra Leone. It also requested the establishment of a large treatment unit in the rural village of Kerry Town, to treat the general population and offer specialist intensive care for national and international health workers who contracted Ebola. National health workers were at particular risk and many had already died, while international staff would have to be repatriated for treatment if the highest level of care was not available in-country. Ensuring that sufficient numbers of health workers were willing to continue to treat isolated patients was essential if the outbreak was to be brought under control.

As the former colonial power, the UK had historical interest in Sierra Leone—and a historical debt. Furthermore, as 2015 was going to be an election year in Britain, Cameron's Conservative-led coalition government needed to be seen to act decisively in the face of a global risk to justify its continued defence of UK aid. The British government agreed to WHO's request and turned to DfID and the Ministry of Defence (MoD) for action. DfID also needed to find a humanitarian agency willing to step up and help run the large treatment facility at Kerry Town, alongside the British military. For this, they turned to SCUK. There was a strong sense among SCUK leadership that, if the organisation could respond well to such a request, the British government would recognise it as a serious emergency health actor—and this would boost the nascent Emergency Health Unit, intended as the Merlin legacy. The British government expected SCUK to take such a lead role in the fight against Ebola after the financial support it had already given to the Merlin merger the previous year. With multiple British government ministries and agencies involved in the effort, the Kerry Town centre quickly became the flagship initiative of the UK's response to Ebola, and, as such, an emblem of the overall effectiveness of the UK aid budget.[37] For an operation that had to overcome enormous challenges and manage serious risks, the expectations were sky high. For SCUK senior leaders, the treatment facility at Kerry Town, though only one element of the Save the Children regional Ebola response, would determine a much wider relationship with DfID for the future.

In September 2014, Foreign Secretary Philip Hammond invited Justin Forsyth to Whitehall to present Save the Children's part in the plan for Kerry Town. Public pressure in Sierra Leone and the UK ramped up the expectation that the centre would reach full capacity in the shortest possible time, not least given the significant cost and high profile of the project. British government ministers kept a very close eye on the scale-up of the centre. On 3 December, Chancellor of the Exchequer George Osborne issued his Autumn Statement, stating that 'even as we speak, they are tackling the horrific Ebola virus in West Africa—a fight that reminds us all of the value of Britain's commitment to 0.7 percent in development aid'. On Christmas Day, the Kerry Town Ebola Treatment Centre reached its full operating capacity. By mid-February 2015, Justin Forsyth was able to report to colleagues that Secretary of State for International Development Justine Greening had spoken to the cabinet about the Ebola response, expressing the gratitude of the British government to Save the Children for stepping up when asked.

The 2015 general election was held on Thursday, 7 May. Polls and commentators had predicted a second hung parliament similar to the 2010 election, but the Conservative Party won an outright majority. Meanwhile, 9 May marked a significant day in Liberia, as President Ellen Johnson Sirleaf and WHO officially declared Liberia free of Ebola. Sierra Leone had just a few cases now, while the situation was also starting to look better in Guinea, where two vaccination trials were underway. There had been no health worker infections in recent weeks. Vital prevention measures were finally working, and the worst of the West Africa Ebola outbreak appeared to be over. Governments in the region, donors, and staff generally viewed Save the Children's willingness to take on such a risk as a brave, values-driven act of solidarity. But in all the years of working on emergencies, I'd never been involved in one with so much political pressure. Though SCUK could rightly be proud that it had stepped up when it mattered most, insiders like me had never felt less like independent humanitarian actors.

By now, life at SCUK was an occasionally exhilarating, but often exhausting, rollercoaster ride of relentless drive to achieve ever greater impact for children and extend our reach. This came at the expense of other crucial considerations, most significantly, staff welfare and morale. The organisation was still very much in touch with its humanist foundations, but neomanagerialism was now the dominant culture. Staff felt increasingly overloaded and undervalued, their dignity and well-being eroded. Combined with controversies, such as the 2014 presentation of a Global Legacy Award by SCUS to Tony Blair, the effect was a collapse in leadership trust.[38] In late 2015, Forsyth stepped down as CEO and Alan Parker was replaced as SCUK Board Chair by Peter Bennett-Jones. In late 2016, after an interim period, Kevin Watkins, an SCUK trustee with a long career in the aid sector, took charge as CEO. This seemed to signal the start of a new leadership era that would expressly place staff well-being at its core.

In February 2018, a scandal broke in the UK press relating to safeguarding in the aid sector. Allegations that former senior staff within SCUK had sexually harassed colleagues were widely reported. In response to concerns about the internal handling of these allegations, SCUK commissioned an independent review of workplace culture. Then, in April 2018, the Charity Commission announced a statutory inquiry into the charity, at which point SCUK temporarily suspended all bids for DfID funding. Changes were made at board level, with several long-serving trustees stepping down in favour of more sector-facing expertise. This in turn brought a more diverse range of people to the table. In April 2019, at the SCUK centenary conference, 'Politics, Humanitarianism & Children's Rights', Charles Steel, the new interim Board Chair, committed to rebuilding trust between staff and the board, and to strengthening organisational accountability. In 2020, initiatives to address workplace and leadership culture seemed to signal that an essential rebalancing was underway. The drive to acquire is a less dominant feature of organisational discourse. As Kevin Watkins put it in an email to staff in May 2020, 'ambition and kindness are not mutually exclusive'.[39]

Remaining true to humanist values and a sense of purpose has been a real challenge for me, as it has been for other colleagues in the aid sector in recent decades. But, as a humanitarian realist, I have willingly stayed involved, and, indeed, I encouraged many others to do the same, as SCUK charted its deliberately economistic course. I have keenly felt the 'shifts and drifts' in organisational 'nature'—even as I have contributed to them. My recourse has always been to go back to foundational inspiration and strategise from there.

Any organisation that hosts gala dinners for billionaire supporters and has a Bulgari jewellery line in its name should accept that it will be seen as part of the elite. Of course, it should reflect critically and continuously on its relationship to economic and political power. But it should also seek to influence the privileged milieu in which it exists, just as forthrightly as the Jebb sisters did in their day. Maintaining its establishment credentials makes good business sense for SCUK. The organisation does not stand among the poor, as its marketing rhetoric would often have the world believe. Rather it stands among the rich and powerful in an effort to further the cause of the poor. At its best, it poses as a plausible insider, mindful of risks and thresholds, while holding to an outsider worldview. Through words and actions, it has often cast a critical light on the excesses of capitalist development. And yet, since its very beginnings, it has worked to prevent these excesses from disordering society, at home and abroad, in the cause of a fairer capitalism. Even when attending to the most basic needs of children affected by disaster, it has acted in accordance with an ideal of political order. But there is always a risk that this ideal—not entirely fixed—can be distorted through the organisation's pragmatic association with those who would champion other visions of order. Save the Children experienced such a distortion during what might be looked back on as a period of liberal humanitarian order, when NGOs were in the limelight.

Now, the influence of NGOs seems to be waning, temporarily at least, amid widespread political challenges to humanitarian morality. In June 2020, the UK government folded DfID into the Foreign and Commonwealth Office. Five months later, as a second wave of the COVID-19 pandemic forced the UK into lockdown, Chancellor Rishi Sunak used emergency measures to cut the aid budget from 0.7 percent to 0.5 percent of national income. On the one hand, I am troubled by the politics behind these decisions, and I feel a certain trepidation about their implications for people affected by conflict and disaster abroad. On the other hand, they might force humanitarian agencies to delink from state power and adapt their financial models for the better, to reassess the balance between humanist values and apparent economic imperatives. Perhaps they will offer Save the Children an opportunity to reassess institutional dependencies and to build an organisational culture that prioritises staff well-being and dignity—one that, true to foundational beliefs, makes a virtue out of 'high ambition with kindness', in pursuit of children's rights.[40] My hope is that, as the world changes, forcing pragmatic adaptation to new circumstances, the organisation, and the people within it, can remain true to their humanitarian heart.

4

A PESTILENTIAL WORLD

PROMISES OF PROTECTION

Nimmi Gowrinathan

According to its inscription, an original copy of *Toto and the Goats, and Tales from Ceylon* was gifted to Joan Barry in Upton Cross for Christmas, in 1953. When it made its way into my hands, I was struck by the tattered cover image, captioned 'a "lazy" dark-skinned boy' sleeping among animals.

Africa and Sri Lanka are swiftly interchangeable backdrops, and the reader arrives on the western shores of the South Asian island alongside a 'big fellow'—a sailor escaping the demands of private schooling in Europe. A strange presence, 'the people of the jungle village called him the White Giant of Norway', and the monkeys mock the 'big and lazy' character searching for sunshine with fruits that ripened of their own accord.[1]

The looming figure of whiteness would appear decades later, in poetic echoes from the Caribbean—those of Aimé Césaire—in a conversation with colonialism that warns of both recognition and rebellion:

ECHO:

[...]

Blue-eyed architect
I defy you
beware architect, for if the Rebel dies it will not be without making
everyone aware that you are the constructor of a pestilential world

architect beware
who crowned you? During what night did you exchange compass
for dagger?[2]

* * *

There is a line to meet the chief of this block. The camp is divided
into quadrants, then halves. One half to UNHCR,[3] the other to IOM,[4]
the chief explains. Each letter of the acronymed organisations falls
heavy as the exhaustion of a moment somehow karmically recycled
in my adult life settles in.

He is the third such Big Man we have encountered on this trip,
puffed up to fill out an office chair that is ornate relative to its bland
surroundings. Underlings hover anxiously beside, behind, outside—
waiting to serve a new master in a colonial image retouched for
colour, not reconfigured for power.

He has just come from the daily coordination briefing we attended
in the neighbouring tent. I am transported back to a past life under
tarp ceilings, as a clipboard-wielding aid worker, wandering through
the tsunami-devastated shores and earthquake-cracked mountains of
South Asia. A decade has passed, and every scene from that afternoon
in Bangladesh embeds deeper a sense of personal defeat at the hands
of humanitarianism.

Foreign women wear emblazoned vests over locally purchased
tunics, sitting with hands crossed on their laps, mimicking modesty.
Local men stand around in pressed salwars, hands clasped behind their
backs, projecting authority. An optical illusion of gendered power
that dissipates as quickly as the men plead for the funds that flew these
women in.

The Chief is pleased that my level of education might transfer
Western credit to his efforts. 'This must be the most organised camp

you've ever seen, Professor, no? Isn't it beautiful?' The view from the vantage point of hovering drones and military aircrafts matches his own: clear lines, an ode to order. Beautiful, to some.

It is the kind of order that, after the summits and pleasantries, the liberal imaginary expects the humanitarian industry to enforce. And, under the cover of neutrality, it reproduces a worldview divided, as scholar Mahmood Mamdani notes, 'into two unequal parts: one privileged, the other subjugated'.[5]

To me, there has always been something sinister about these spaces, each of us tripping over ourselves to avoid the dark shadow of the camp. Had the Big Man been kind, thoughtful, and charismatic (he was not), I would have hated him just the same. The performance of humanitarian purity didn't interest me anymore.

* * *

In a crisis, a political moment is captured in still frame—even as its fractures continue to spread, separating the dispossessed from power.

In 1983, a violent pogrom left thousands of Tamils dead in the capital city of Colombo. It sent my grandmother into hiding in a neighbourhood home. It pushed thousands offshore, across the Palk Strait. Others sought refuge in temple courtyards.

Severed from a complete, complex existence by political violence, entire cosmopolitan neighbourhoods would be reduced to the bare life of refugeedom. It is inside the granular view of these branded tents, not the myopic vantage-point of a tax shelter, that the organic impulse to aid is an affirmation of multifaceted existence—a rejection of collapsed political personhood.

The Tamil Rehabilitation Organisation (TRO) began, as many collectives do, embedded inside forgotten populations. Refugees for whom this latest dislocation was still believed to be temporary. Now labelled mutual aid, then 'self-help', the work of the organisation took form in the void left by the state. TRO established institutional structures and delinked itself from rebel activity to inspire donor confidence—but it remained committed, internally, to a new political order.

TRO did not operate on the premise of a hollowed humanity, carved out by a liberal international order that, Mamdani notes, 'turns citizens into wards'.[6] 'We were always with the people', Ravi, the director, told me, pulling TRO out of the jumble of acronyms he saw as representative of one monolithic white invasion. The Tamil people were 'rights-bearing citizens' inside an explicit bid for permanent political protection. 'We were there from when the baby is born to the coffin', Ravi told me. Sometimes, he noted, for the very brief time between the two.

He recalls the early days when the white NGOs wanted to work with a scrappy little 'local' group. Even over the phone, his satisfaction at the reflective gleam of whiteness seen from abroad was audible. 'You know, Nimmi, they liked that we were efficient, always on time, and our numbers of microcredit programme returns were higher than everyone else's.' The group had brought in a senior consultant from McKinsey Consulting to ensure that they mimicked the development metrics of the West.

In the case of Ravi and others like him, who unabashedly articulate their political positioning, it is always difficult to gauge whether the performance is concession or subversion—the incessant resistance of a subaltern consciousness. As I followed the field workers of the organisation into Tamil villages, I noted that they acted with a clarity of intent, a 'refusal to fall for the ruses of incorporation and exclusion that say all we can and should desire is citizenship and subjectivity'.[7] They were, quietly, drawing from the well of humanitarian assistance to challenge the imposition of a liberal order that bartered basic protections for political aspirations.

It was a balancing act that suddenly collapsed when lofty theories of apolitical change met the air-bombardments of political violence, severing the happy ties between TRO and the West. 'When the shelling was every day, the outside organisations could not operate, they left. It was only the Tigers who gave us logistical support in the jungle.'

* * *

In a crisis, need becomes stark, naked: inequality has no cover, democratic façades lose their sheen. Race divides territories between the living and the damned.

Sara is conscious that she is a singular loathed being inside the collective 'these people', in Myanmar. She is from the Kachin community, but grew up amidst the Rohingya. Her childhood memories included camps of a different kind, temporary dwellings for family members moving through a base for the Kachin Independence Army. For some communities, the cover of camouflage is a generational adaptation for survival.

This iteration of a crisis was woman-made. It should have been expected, but was unnatural to those invested in assumptions of gender and ideology, those not following the politics of an idol. Aung San Suu Kyi, then-arrested pro-democracy activist, temporarily dimmed the bright orange of her Buddhist nationalism to blend into a background of red, white, and blue. The predator, too, can adapt.

In the latest exodus, a tinderbox of aggrieved minorities asking for the minimal political recognition of a laminated identification card, set off a militarised Buddhist nationalist fervour. A loyalist to the pro-democracy counsellor, Daw, as she was called, would tell me over an early morning coffee and dumplings that she suspected the news of mass exodus of Rohingya to be largely based on 'rumours and WhatsApp groups'. She dismissed the fact that the fire started inside village homes had been lit by a military general who had recently donated US$300,000 dollars to the hardline Buddhist Nationalist party.

Aung San Suu Kyi herself is known, a collective of activists in the capital whisper, to dislike civil society when it presents a political challenge beyond 'charity for poor people'. Even those inherently enraged grassroots activists like Sara found themselves swept up by a 'neoliberal push' in Yangon to fit into contained boxes of human rights, service delivery, or religious engagement in marginalised communities.

Slightly distanced, a Bangladeshi researcher recognises that 'racism is rampant' amongst the amalgam of internationalised aid groups in Myanmar's 'civil society'. Up-close, Sara gives in, temporarily, to the dark line of delineation: 'In the end, I am just a brown girl. How can I challenge them?' An internalised experience of race, alongside a reckoning with the violence it breeds around her, akin to the young slave daughter in Toni Morrison's novel, *A Mercy*: 'She learned the intricacy of loneliness: the horror of color, the roar of soundlessness and the menace of familiar objects lying still.'[8]

Sara asks: 'What if you are an IDP all the time? What are you called?' A person displaced, internally. Growing up inside a rebel family, the fight to survive was ingrained. 'Why is nationalism seen as an illegitimate struggle—why is it a bad word?' Sara asks, assuming I might have an answer. If the Buddhists can exist inside a Buddhist nation, surely the Kachin and the Rohingya had a right to their own line of control? 'Instead, we, my people, are in IDP camps, moving all the time. We cannot be nationalists. We are all reduced to being monkeys—dancing for the NGOs for food.'

* * *

In a crisis, soft, privileged hands cover the sight of suffering, block the muffled cries of the not-yet-dead. Privilege is preserved if you see no, hear no, speak no evil.

Monkeys are playful. Child-like. Pests, at times. They are both the impish cartoons in the moral dilemmas of nursery tales and the per-fect caricatures to justify grown-up narratives of violence.

Although monkeys can mimic human behaviours, in the sixteenth century European philosophers would declare them fundamentally irrational, incapable of feeling or suffering.

The dark metaphor for lives in the global South spread as quickly as colonising British overlords absolved an entire race from moral consideration.

* * *

In a crisis, a partially developed consciousness seeks complete validation; the not entirely apathetic are moved to action.

For most, humanitarianism is a profession: a network of organisa-tions enamoured of corporate efficiency models, bidding against each other to be the lucrative chosen one. Inside the super-sized letters are individuals who were pulled towards crisis—the human suffering carried in the newspapers that crossed their doorsteps. It is this small number that felt the need to *do something*, whom I would ask to read carefully, while exempting them from the challenge levelled further up, at large overheads.

Barbara Harrell-Bond would infamously ask such actors, *can humanitarian work be humane?* A pioneering scholar, organiser, and deeply empathetic being, Barbara would accept an invitation I once extended—to reimagine the refugee camp. A description of my steps through camps around the world always eluded me on the page—everything trite, nothing profound. Perhaps I could fill the inarticulable void if I organised a conference, a gathering to address the gross inhumanity of it all. And perhaps the words of this collection of beings would be reinforced, elevated, by the stature of the Rockefellers—industrial magnates, tax-deductibly dedicated to the well-being of humanity.

Not unlike the sorting of a middle-school cafeteria, each group congregated around its own rectangular desk. The architects who had designed eco-friendly collapsible structures to increase the standard of living. The United Nations actors working through governments who relied on malnutrition to control rebellion. The scholars unveiling the complicity that wound its way through this very room. The lifetime humanitarians who stood defensively on the goodness of their intentions and believed their own commitment to neutrality.

The growing indignation of the last cohort would seem to challenge the presumption of critics like Michael Barnett, that humanitarian actors 'recognised that humanitarianism was the offspring of politics, that their activities had political consequences, and that they were inextricably part of the political world'.[9]

On the page, Barbara's words were soft; in person her voice was harsh. She spoke through one corner of her mouth, the other closed around an indoor cigarette. Her comments are a scathing indictment of an industry built on human suffering.

It was a point of tension that I had witnessed, even created, many times before: when professed humanitarian intent is forced to reckon with evident political impact. It was there in the frenzied working group sessions gathered on the putatively neutral ground of the UN Church Center. In the final phases of the war in Sri Lanka, in 2009, I was part-expert, part-aid-director, part-suspicious-diaspora-native, managing the collective demands of the humanitarians compiled in the lines of a letter to an elevated bureaucrat.

In those days, I did not understand why a request to disarm paramilitary Tamil groups was apolitical to liberal sensibilities, while the release of civilians from illegal internment by the government was a demand too political for humanitarians to make. The question in itself would pierce our fragile collegiality, built, as it was, on the shared assumption of purity of intent.

The next year, further uptown, while still within the sterile blocks that border the United Nations, there would again be no consensus, only contention. The polite veneer of professionalised voluntarism quickly disintegrated when integrity was questioned, deeper incentives revealed. 'How can you suggest we are invested in keeping people in these conditions?' An actual fist bangs the table. Barbara smiles, unsurprised at the postcolonial fragility that is 'triggered by discomfort and anxiety; born of superiority and entitlement'.[10]

To be inhumane is to lack qualities of compassion and mercy. To border on the cruel and barbaric. A secular compassion is, of course, built into the mission statements of charitable groups—some taking care to cover the directives drawn directly from God or the American President.

In the aftermath of moments when the earth shook across war-ravaged South Asian landscapes, my younger self would bear witness to scientologists guiding confused preschoolers in chants, Korean church groups integrating the gospel and 'play therapy', American government-funded aid groups exchanging food for information. The kind of contemporary interventionism 'legitimised in terms of a moral obligation, rather than a political principle'.[11]

The bewildered, mourning, and dispossessed are at the mercy of the intervenor's intent.

* * *

A crisis is politically incorrect: entire populations are bacterialised, dehumanised, animalised.

'We ate grass and leaves', one Rohingya refugee would tell me of running from a homeland on fire, in 2012. Even bananas, 'the poor man's apple', were priced out of their reach.

It was a gritty glimpse of suffering that men like The Chief had purposely blocked. His worldview relied on the far-sighted ideology of the big picture. While their close-up view of reality was narrowed by casting a vacuum around human suffering.

The Chief mentioned them once, 'these people', only to acknowledge the violence that happened inside their temporary domestic spaces—only the darkest cultural markers imprint on the mind of the oppressor. A hotel driver in Dhaka would make reference, unprompted, to Rohingya people as 'so ugly', his own face contorting in disgust.

Unphased by a feeling person's shock, he would go on to clarify, 'Madam. You do not understand. These people are filthy... they are not really human.' He pauses. 'Sub-human', he adds, revealing a wide grin of self-satisfaction for locating the correct word in English.

The Big Man was right that Cox's Bazar was the logical extreme of organisational tidiness that I may have expected, but had never seen, in my years of humanitarian work. Squares. Distribution Graphs. Boxes. A humanitarianism so enamoured of its own precise geometry it need not ever even mention the not-quite-human beings inside the lines.

* * *

In a crisis, 'the urgency of the situation and the danger to victims—both of war and of disaster—justified the exception of intervention, which then needed no further justification, least of all in law'.[12]

October 2015 marked almost a full decade since I had seen him, and even back then, I never really got a full view. In 2005, Ravi sat hunched over in front of an army of scattered cell phones in the corner of an office in Colombo that had the energy and anxiety of a bunker too close to the front lines. A programme officer for the Tamil Rehabilitation Organisation whispered, 'That's *Anna* [*older brother*].' Even distant blood lines linked us as family in the struggle.

Ravi reaches out over LinkedIn, a platform I assumed to be a largely defunct form of interaction, save for the occasional South Indian engineer with a one-line marriage proposal. 'I hope you remember me, Nimmi. I need your help for my asylum case.'

The Skype feed places me in between the stern British judge and the frayed brown lawyers, their white wigs not entirely covering black hair, lined up in defence of their brethren. Again, Ravi is blurry, I can make out only an outline.

Over time, I would learn that these white Anglo-American court rooms were the looking glass through which the conventional view of darker nations would occasionally be challenged, but most often reinforced. As Atiya Husain notes, on the classification of colonised peoples as 'terrorists':

> This is not an inadvertently racist label that can be peeled off of brown men and stuck onto white men. Rather, the racial history and significance of the concept is constitutive of terrorism. The terrorist is a racial, epistemic, ideological, and material *other*.[13]

The questioning would move in contortions of power, legal language casting the net to catch a native. Was the defendant affiliated with a terrorist organisation? Were funds used to purchase arms? How often did I visit to check on these 'local' aid workers whose postcolonial capacity had not yet built trust? As Michael Barnett would note, I am asked to reaffirm an existing order, parsing politics from humanitarianism:

> Humanitarianism plays a distinctive role in the international sacrificial order. All international orders have winners and losers and thus require their quota of victims. Humanitarianism interrupts this selection process by saving lives, thus reducing the number of sacrifices. However, it does not aspire to alter that order; that is the job of politics.[14]

I heard my own voice speaking their language. Methodology. Monitoring and Evaluation. I am constructing a quantifiable case for his humanity through their tools of measurement. To do otherwise would be to strip the desperate camouflage from every brown person in the room reliant on the façade of humanitarianism to relieve liberal anxieties.

The judge is unyielding, growing hostile in a battle against the image of a terrorist inside his own limited imagination. 'Did the organisation have ties to the Tigers?' My own emotions build slowly behind a deadpan façade until they break through, still calibrated to stay within the Most Excellent Order of the British Empire. 'The Tigers created a state. The non-governmental organisation operated in Tiger-controlled territory. How else does a non-governmental organisation work if not in direct coordination with the governing state?'

I temporarily inhabit Césaire's character, the Narratress, pulled by the pain of a people and performing in the theatre of empire: 'Here I am, I, I: a woman obsessed by big words—toward the elementary smell of cadavers I swim amidst gladiolas and Jericho roses.'[15]

One never really knows what sways an officer, a judge, executioners of the liberal order's will: empathy, judicial precedence, or a bad day. For some, a British-Tamil scholar told me once, the decision to deport often results from a desire not to become that month's 'head monkey'. We were entering the evening hours of an increasingly rowdy pub and I was certain I had misheard him.

He shook his head. 'One asylum officer revealed to me that a stuffed monkey is placed on the desk of the Home Office officer who lets in too many asylum cases.' A distinction that comes with departmental derision.

This particular judge decided in favour of leniency: Ravi was a refugee and not a rebel.

* * *

A crisis is, almost always, created.

'Rohingya are a lazy people, they don't have our morality', the Big Man explained to me. In the jungles, the Rohingya befriended elephants and relied on their protection. TRO actors took cues from the Tigers' animal-adaptation in order to survive, climbing trees for surveillance, gathering coconut flakes for sustenance against blockades, sensing the movements of a predatory state. A real-life deployment of what Neel Ahuja calls the 'animal mask' device in fiction—a temporary embrace of animality that 'unveils a historical logic of animalization inherent in processes of racial subjection'.[16]

Inside the order of primates, monkeys are very attuned to the needs of their group—for survival and protection. 'On the beaches there were more dead bodies than living people.' Three years and 3,000 miles apart, a Rohingya and Tamil refugee recall the same image, the same failure to protect, that haunts collective memories and provokes political demands.

Those who work from the inside to alleviate suffering see, with clarity, that need is created by state violence. They would begin to rebel, recognising that every modicum of performed moderation was a concession to their own sub-status in the naturalised order of the world. TRO's cooperation and blood ties to the governing rebel movement would be weaponised against it, as the state invited the West to reinstate order through a renegade War on Terror, not bound by the rules of international law or even humanitarian principle.

Still adjusting to life between a successful asylum claim and a defeated political struggle, Ravi recalls that 'TRO was shut down with no evidence. The US, the UK, nobody ever found any evidence of misuse of funds. Still, we are done.' A young Rohingya man, offered a branded vest to operate in the camps, whispers, 'All of this, this aid, is just so they can pretend they don't want us all gone. They will never change unless we force them to see us as human, too.'

Soon after we meet, he will join the rebels in the jungle, banished from the aid world—for being too political. Césaire foresaw this certain death. As, too, he saw the beauty in short-lived life: the rebellious days of a fully human, politicised being:

> ECHO: [...] For sure the rebel is going to die... in this crippled world: upheld and a prisoner of itself.

> [...]

> architect deaf to things [...] Each of your steps is a conquest and a spoliation and a misconception and an assassination.

> [...]

> LOVER: Embrace me: life is *right here*, out of its own tatters the banana tree polishes its violet sex [...] my life is surrounded by threats of life, promises of life.[17]

5

THE MODERNITY AND LIBERAL VALUE
OF HUMANITARIAN THINGS

Bertrand Taithe

COVID-19 and the Globalisation of Pandemic

In the intervening weeks between writing the first draft of this paper,
falling ill with COVID-19, and revising this paper, a number of striking realignments occurred to this story of humanitarian goods and
their market. The first significant realignment was that humanitarian
aid from the North became deployed in the North, as field hospitals
sprang up in Central Park, or Nightingale wards inspired by the
Crimean War were opened in all large cities of the United Kingdom—
returning humanitarian workers to the field in which they began.[1]
Interestingly, the reference point in this surge of hospital capacity was
not the field hospital of the humanitarians but of the military, tying us
back to the origins of our story.[2] The second realignment was the
considerable focus on the logistics of aid and on competitive forces
disrupting the supply chains of goods, both humble and sophisticated.[3]
This rush for goods set health services, NGOs, states, and pooled

multinational purchasing efforts in competition with one another. Shortages of all sorts multiplied. Deficiencies in the procurement of gloves, masks, visors, and other PPE equipment made headlines, while governments pondered the limits of sovereignty when most manufacturing takes place away from their shores.[4] Meanwhile, laboratories, universities, and humanitarians have joined forces and received state funding to consider clinical trials of new and old medicines. One of the most publicly debated was a colonial-era compound dating from 1934. Chloroquine and hydroxychloroquine were promoted by Donald Trump despite being generic drugs barely produced in the North any longer.[5] In a manner very reminiscent of the empirical reuse of pharmaceuticals promoted by the Drugs for Neglected Diseases initiative (DNDi), a medical repurposing of an old compound found a new and controversial life in the COVID-19 pandemic. Meanwhile, many public and private resources were poured into finding a vaccine for the coronavirus which would deliver the much-needed herd immunity and, potentially, immense profit and reputation enhancement for the winning laboratory.[6] It has been a long time since so much public hope and state resources were vested into pharmaceutical research, and 'Big Pharma' appears to have restored some of its dented reputation. Once again this forefronting of pharmaceutical research as first response to an emergency recalled days gone by. The deployment of screening tests, validated treatments, and ultimately mass vaccination will involve partnerships between states and industry, industry and non-governmental actors in a manner that has not been seen since the Second World War. The market forces that lay dormant in this debate will no doubt reawaken once this crisis is over, but the prospect of new pandemics may infer a new alliance of interests, such as the one Victorian humanitarians imagined to be progressive. This paper investigates how humanitarians have engaged with their material world, industrial partners, and commercial outlets to develop their own liberal marketplace of humanitarian goods.

While the literature has proved prolix and somewhat indulgent on the historical origins and justifications of 'humanitarian principles'—which no one articulated precisely until the 1940s[7]—there has been a relative silence on the world of humanitarian goods and how they became 'actants', agency free actors, in the defining of what humanitarianism was or what humanitarians might be, or how objects might define what could be deployed in terms of aid.[8] This paper will thus consider them in turn as objects at the heart of humanitarian trade fairs, as actants in negotiations and normalisation of aid, and as tradeable objects within a 'liberal' marketplace which sat at the heart of the humanitarian endeavour.[9] Beyond the consumption patterns underpinning early humanitarianism, this paper is focusing on specific aspects of the humanitarian market: its capitalistic modes of production and diffusion of 'innovative' products originating from the encounter between industrial and humanitarian concerns.[10]

Though this paper begins with a brief historical vignette, its intention is to be thematic and bring issues to the present. In order to keep this discussion within reasonable boundaries I will primarily discuss it from the perspective of medical humanitarian response, which has the longest genealogy and the clearest humanitarian mandate.[11]

The Liberal Origins of Humanitarian Objects

When what would later became the International Red Cross movement contributed for the first time to a universal exhibition, in Paris in 1867, it did so among some 50,000 other exhibitors.[12] Universal exhibitions had begun in London in 1851, and were fast becoming the most significant sites of exchange, demonstrations of might, and commercial arenas for industrialised nations.[13] The prizes were held in great esteem and added value to the winning products. It was thus a competitive industrial environment which combined with a universalist desire to promote modern civilisation and the arts. The 'movement', which later rebranded itself as the Red Cross and Red Crescent, arranged its exhibits thematically at the behest of the main organisers and in order to fit into a grand normative pedagogical project imagined by the sociologist Frédéric le Play.[14] The aim of the exhibit was:

> to establish in each group of similar items a model type which could be adopted in principle by all the national societies, each retaining the right to adapt it according to the specific circumstances of its climate. In view of this aim and in order to facilitate the judgement and comparison, we have distributed our exhibition in five sections, each of

them collecting the objects of a similar nature and in the alphabetical order of the committees.[15]

At the heart of the humanitarian exhibits, beyond the relics of the American Civil War or the terms of new societies (which later became the national Red Cross societies) organised to relieve the sufferings of the wounded and sick in war, was a crucial deployment of physical demonstrations of ingenuity: medicines and bandages, shock-absorbing carriages and stretchers. Beyond educating the public in the modern arts of war medicine (the display was hosted in the French national quarter of the park by the Ministry of War), the exhibition was meant to serve a grander purpose. It served as the foundational trade fair of humanitarian goods and heralded a procurement market for 'model types' which could be 'adopted in principle' or purchased from the exhibiting manufacturers and inventors. The exhibition itself was centred around the weights and measures (metre and kilogram), of which the French intended to be recognised as custodians. The main aim of the universal exhibition itself was to order and recognise common international standards of aesthetics and material quality. The humble humanitarian display, like much of the exhibition, set out to define humanitarian aid as a normative process legally *and* practically; a process grounded not so much in some noble but potentially vacuous declaration of intents, but in the displaying and retailing of advanced technical objects defined by their humanitarian intent and values. The volume of devices and tools, surgical implements and first aid kits, embodied the new spirit of humanitarianism borne out of industrial societies. In an era of armament race and build-up—the stars of the exhibition were probably the steel guns exhibited by Krupp—humanitarians displayed their ingenuity and sought a share in growing military markets.[16]

Subsequent humanitarian exhibitions of the long nineteenth century, up to 1914, continued on a similar track and combined exhibitions of manufactured goods, supplies, and logistical solutions along with prizes awarded for the 'best improvised responses'. Meanwhile, the proponents of the Geneva Convention led by Gustave Moynier, a lawyer rather than a medical practitioner or inventor, forged ahead along the legal and 'dogmatic lines' which soon defined the international humanitarian identity and 'mandate' of the Genevan committee of the Red Cross. Their emphasis was primarily to promote the neutrality of humanitarians in wartime and the duties of warring nations towards wounded and sick soldiers. The Red Cross movement thus claimed to be a legally binding new system in wartime. Made up of independent national societies emulating each other to provide new practices and techniques, it sought to help the wounded and sick in the midst of war and disaster. Thus from its historical origins within the Red Cross movement—origins that included the Ottoman empire from 1867 and later the Japanese, who were also present at the exhibition in 1867—the exhibitionary complex of goods, to embrace Tony Bennett's definition,[17] mingled with the wider sociodicy that became part of what Didier Fassin calls 'humanitarian reason'.[18]

The Objects of Humanitarian Trade Fairs

From the exhibition of 1867 onwards, humanitarians participated in and organised a multitude of events which sought to bring their work to public attention: educating and lecturing in turn, persuading and challenging—often with a view to raise funds, but more often than not with the purpose of broadening horizons, encouraging empathy, and stimulating political responses.[19] These events might be part of other gatherings with which they shared only some objectives: a celebration of pan-American trade; a universal exhibition devoted to the advancement of civilisation; a public health event; or even an insurance summit in San Francisco, in which humanitarians represented only one amongst the many forms of aid delivery deployed following a catastrophic event.[20] Between the world wars, Red Cross societies were regularly invited to the military medicine summits that took place and which represented the finest examples of 'humanitarian medicine'.[21] Civilian first aid helpers and humanitarians remained implicit adjuncts of the armed forces, even though Red Cross societies had diversified their work into public health, disaster response, and even epidemic control since the 1880s. Wartime humanitarian work remained the most noble and urgent form of humanitarianism, and the one that fitted best with the Geneva Convention. These military medicine congresses brought together the Allies of 1918, and had limited universalist aims.[22] They assembled scientific papers, memorandums on war-related medical interventions, and the best tools to mend, cut, repair, and treat soldiers—who remained one of the main humanitarian subjects, despite a growing awareness that children, women and civilians, refugees and stateless people represented a greater mass of needs in wartime and in the aftermath of wars.

Following the Second World War, there were a few instances of humanitarian medicine summits which took stock of the difficult alliance between military medicine and humanitarian work in the troubled conflicts of decolonisation. Thus, three international congresses of the 1960s (the third and last one in Rome in 1968)[23] took stock of the need to develop the principles enunciated afresh at the XXth Red Cross Conference in Vienna in 1965 (the conference at which the principles of humanitarianism became enshrined in the form that is commonly understood today).[24] At the congress of 1968, the ICRC worked with the World Medical Association and the International Committee of Military Medicine and Pharmacy (created in 1921, and operating throughout the interwar period on issues of neutrality) to ask for international medical ethics to be given legal protection, and for the creation of an international penal court whose remit would cover the violations of the laws of war by 'states, organisations or groups of individuals and persons, whether military or civilian'.[25] This renewed emphasis on medical ethics on the one hand and neutrality on the other, came after over a decade of irregular warfare and counter-insurgency practices, which both instrumentalised access to health and denial of access for political purposes. Despite the dominance of legal and moral debates, all humanitarian gatherings contained some material dimension, and brought mementos of action as well as model types of the range of humanitarian goods and temporary infrastructure.

Yet one had to wait until the 1970s for a genuine humanitarian trade fair, once again clearly branded as such, in which the debates on principles would only occupy the plenary sessions. In the 1990s and 2000s, humanitarian trade fairs were developed professionally and became networking and procurement events, such as those held in Brussels and Dubai.[26] The first World Humanitarian Summit, in 2016 in Istanbul, thus contained, within its heavily policed walls, a trade fair and an 'innovation marketplace'.[27] The latter invited 'UN

Member States, intergovernmental organizations, international and non-governmental organizations, UN agencies, civil society, NGOs, corporations/companies, foundations, innovators, and other stakeholder organizations' to showcase their goods in a specific arena, which would 'feature practical applications of innovations, new or improved products, services and processes in the humanitarian sector/context'.[28] This shift of interest to the new products of humanitarian ingenuity—processes, services, and apps—was set up in competition with the hardware exhibited in the larger, and much better attended, traditional trade fair a floor below.[29]

Exhibitions were often dominated by images, visual representations, and multi-media experiences (from films to immersive re-enactments) which have attracted the most scholarly attention, but the collections of objects which formed the bulk of what was exhibited have received less attention. From 1867 onwards, the display cases contained prostheses mimicking human limbs or machine parts, sometimes demonstrated by a war amputee. Humanitarian associations such as the 1868 Association pour l'Assistance aux Mutilés Pauvres (association for the relief of mutilated paupers) collaborated closely with the main prosthetic manufacturer in France, Weber, and promoted its goods.[30] At the Lyons national exhibition of 1885 devoted to labour and technology, spectators 'watched with great interest the automated artificial arm which a mechanism keeps moving and the lovely little artificial hand which could lift a weight of ½ a kg, put it down, leave it and pick it up again'—the manufacturer Weber provided the machinery and the Association pour l'Assistance aux Mutilés Pauvres collected the funds.[31] The industrial providers and their humanitarian clients merged their interests in promoting their 'forgotten' humanitarian cause in exhibition after exhibition.[32] Ultimately, the convergence of viewpoint was such that goods could bear humanitarian emblems and become vehicles of the new sensibility. From the earliest exhibitions onwards, display cabinets contained polished steel tools, first aid kits, military equipment, and the necessities of physical and mental health. Attached to each type of equipment was the name of an inventor and that of a manufacturer. The fairs played on the considerable ingenuity these objects demonstrated. Until the First World War, virtually no one objected to seeing them listed alongside evermore advanced killing machines and sophisticated weapons. In 1867, field guns were displayed alongside field ambulances. Humanitarian objects were produced along with other medical or war supplies as part of the more efficient delivery of war. Admittedly, this applied first and foremost to the medical implements, including many specula, forceps, and surgical knives, as well as the casts that helped reset wounded and maimed bodies and contraptions to correct and restore the bodily functions of the main humanitarian subjects of the pre-1914 era: the soldiers enlisted in mass conscript armies.

The market for these humanitarian objects was multi-layered. While armies might have been the main purchasers of kits, organisations set up to respond to wars, such as the Stafford House Committee, active in the United Kingdom in the 1870s, which raised more resources and sent more medical staff during the Russo-Turkish wars of 1877–8 than the Red Cross and Red Crescent, also procured supplies for themselves directly from the manufacturers. The procurement market gained directly from prior advertising efforts as well as the prizes harvested during these humanitarian trade fairs.[33] Industrialists and inventors were engaging in a genuinely international competition, based on the virtues of emulation and ingenuity (the term innovation was also used, primarily in relation to objects: ingenuity implied a broader viewpoint which might also invite the novel deployment of old equipment for new purposes or improvisation).[34]

At a more modest level, in the same way that soldiers and officers would have been able to trade up their equipment, families were able to purchase humanitarian first aid kits to supplement or replace the ones distributed by the military. In a manner more reminiscent of what is often proposed at these fairs today, the public could subscribe to support the purchase of an entire ambulance or field hospital—ready kitted out and corresponding to the ideal types specified at the fair. Thus, newspaper subscriptions during the wars that took place between 1870 and 1914 could embrace this marketing opportunity by raising funds for humanitarian hardware.[35] The market for such goods remained relatively unregulated and was also international, crossing boundaries and borders. It included a number of food supplements which all predated the Plumpy'nut 'fetish' so well analysed by

Tom Scott-Smith.[36] The great food supplement of 1867 was the Liebig cube—beef stock produced from South American cattle— which was intended to provide the food supplement essential for post-surgical recovery. Later on, as Lola Wilhelm has shown, dried milk supplements, chocolates, and other Nestlé products, could be promoted for their humanitarian purpose.[37] Even though Liebig stock cubes were eventually dismissed as of little measurable nutritional value during the siege of Paris in 1871, and for being a 'little too salty', the humanitarian embrace ensured their position within the food supplement market.[38] As many have since pointed out, the objects in these trade fairs were not simple commodities awaiting customers in a growing market; they also helped shape this market and condition it for growth.[39] The humanitarian identity of a brand or of its objects—in particular when the commodities crossed into the mainstream consumer market—proved invaluable to the development of international brands associated with humanitarianism. The development of the Red Cross emblem cannot be separated from its display on first aid kits, manuals, and a veritable panoply of goods associated with humanitarian relief. The commercial use of trademarks and copyrighted emblems arose at the same period as the development of modern humanitarian organisations. Objects mattered, and their identifiable origin or association with a cause granted them a meaning beyond the ordinary.

Actants of Aid

In this sense, humanitarian-labelled products were actants of aid— objects with agency serving different but complementary markets. In the same way that humanitarian causes defined an expansive sociodicy[40]—expanding through their causes the range of what could be done and to whom by a wider range of people, while not challenging in any meaningful way the society in which they operated—objects of aid could also define the nature of aid. The deployment of tools and treatments, medicines and their administration, shaped what could be undertaken and how humanitarian aid might reach out.

Moving away from the purely military domain that had long been at the centre of humanitarianism, access to new medicine and new medical processes to prevent and cure what were called the 'great' endemic diseases in the interwar period, became a humanitarian objective in itself.[41] The term itself was the title of a series of medical conferences in Paris, in 1931–3, which brought together the key specialists of colonial medicine to engage medical students to follow in their humanitarian tracks.[42] Treatments for diseases uncommon in the North became the object of humanitarian representations which often focused on colonial doctors and their forcible administration of treatments.[43] The growth of a medical economy around these diseases involved medical research in often state-owned or charitable laboratories, medical manufacture in the North and occasionally in colonised territories, and a chain of distribution and logistics mirroring the 'arteries' of colonial power, as Frederick Cooper would have it.[44] Products defined the causes, and it would be difficult to comprehend interwar and immediate postwar colonial humanitarianism without mentioning a litany of medical treatments which each defined a new priority, whether it was guinea-worm disease or sleeping sickness.[45] DDT and malaria eradication went alongside each other, and made the fortunes of chemical companies until widespread insecticide use was finally banned in 2004.[46] The development of pharmaceutical industries and the expansion of humanitarian colonial medicine as the expression of the 'civilising mission', combined with a colonial desire to develop a disease-free workforce, did not proceed without challenges and contradictions.[47] The role that American foundations played in this history highlights the direct connection between capitalism, science, and the demands of operationalising medico-scientific interventions abetment across the world.[48] Historians have shown how these entangled objectives could fail, and how local politics might impair grand humanitarian campaigns or bring some realism in relation to unattainable objectives.[49]

Crucially, the terms of this association of increasingly complex technical objects, products, laboratories, and medicine entailed equally complex networks of exchange and supply, cold chains, and procurement. These networks matched in complexity the increasingly specialised and technical health networks of the interwar era.[50] The costs of these infrastructural demands could only be satisfactorily controlled when they were backed by the largesse of institutions like the Rockefeller Foundation, which would select a number of causes to support, or by the priorities of imperial powers often under international scrutiny. The immediate aftermath of the Second World War was probably the golden age of this convergence of interests and resources.[51] The later years of empires were the ones in which most aid targeting specific diseases and making use of pharmacopoeia deployed massively during the war, could be heralded as the expression of humanitarianism.[52] The mass deployment of medicine and preventative measures at the end of the Second World War, such as the delousing powder and epidemic management policies organised through the United Nations Relief and Rehabilitation Administration set up in 1943, aimed to address the humanitarian needs of war-torn territories. Agencies working closely with the military[53] undoubtedly played a major part in preventing outbreaks such as the ones which had decimated Eastern and Central Europe after the First World War.[54] Of course, this 'command supply discipline' approach enlisted the humanitarians as adjuncts and subordinated manufacturers to the war effort. The postwar period witnessed a radical loosening of both imperial projects and disciplined logistics of aid.

The humanitarian aid that was deployed outside of mass military operations (such as the Korean and Vietnam wars) in the 1950s and 1960s, had to reinvent its relationship with supply chains and pharmaceutical industries with which it could only work sporadically. On the one hand, pharmaceutical industries in the North had fewer state incentives to develop treatments for diseases in countries with limited purchasing power; on the other, humanitarian actors often confronted crises in an ad hoc manner, and resorted to seeking local suppliers in often underdeveloped markets. The crises of the 1970s and 1980s brought about a new focus on ideal type responses, particularly in relation to refugee camps.

By the early 1980s, in response to the growth of large refugee camps in the Horn of Africa, as well as at the Afghan and Thai borders, the WHO eventually produced long lists of products in collaboration with MSF, which were intended to respond to the needs of groups of 10,000 refugees held in camps. The lists were the subject of considerable revisions and consultations in 1989–90.[55] The items on these lists were systematically neutral in terms of the origins of the products—leaving it to the local purchasers to source them in a globalised market with often complex tax and licensing regimes. There were some debates on the classification when some of the items were too closely identified to one manufacturer, and where the products had to be suitable for austere contexts. Thus, a representative from UNICEF contested the recommended stove on the grounds of its type, brand, and suitability: 'kerosene stove Gemiol 36 type. This type is unknown to us and therefore we would like more detailed specifications. If it is a Primus/ Optimus model we hope it can operate on low purity kerosene without the nozzle clogging.'[56] Much of the effort was in seeking a common generic terminology and minimum standards of production, which would enable some degree of consistency whatever the circumstances. From the early 1980s onwards, medical NGOs started to develop specific response packs based on military experience, as Jacques Pinel, founder of MSF Logistique, and Claudine Vidal testified.[57] In order to discipline supply chains and control objects, source medications, and develop medical processes aligned with the most rational use of resources, a considerable ordering of humanitarian aid took place. On the one hand, some large humanitarian NGOs developed 4x4 fleets and, in the case of MSF, even became a registered Toyota dealership, on the other, as Lisa Smirl and Roger Mac Ginty point out, white Land Cruisers and their ilk became identity signifiers in the congested streets of humanitarian emergencies.[58] The response kits themselves developed an agency of sorts when they limited the type of response that might be taking place. Sociologists of humanitarian aid noted how the kits deployed to the initial visit or exploratory mission then defined the response, at least until some of the initial misunderstandings of the situation had been corrected.[59] At the international level, WHO's list of essential medicines, expressed in their international non-proprietary names, thus forms the basis of a generic pharmaceutical supply chain. These lists of essential medicines were also the core of guidelines published by MSF in white and green handbooks. A large medical NGO thus developed purchasing centres which could negotiate prices and monitor quality—very much like a chain of private pharmacies might do.[60] In 2008, within the international context of MSF, 'Any purchase on the local market can only take place with the formal authorization of the headquarter medical director'.[61] But no more than a chain of pharmacies might do—and indeed potentially in competition with other distribution channels.[62]

In this respect, as in many others, the humanitarian marketplace resembled the mainstream world, and was submitted to the same logistical constraints, competitions, and attempts at regulation.[63] The procurement of goods and their dispatch for humanitarian purposes might compete with other logistical demands at times of significant emergencies.[64] In 2010, following the earthquake in Port-au-Prince in Haiti, supply flights were thus deprioritised to allow the planes of celebrities to land. Collecting old supplies of medicine and out of date products for humanitarian purposes—upcycling pharmaceuticals—were notable features of humanitarian efforts in the 1990s and early 2000.[65] The provision of the global South with the unused pharmaceuticals of the North proved to be a logistical nightmare, and rightly became the object of considerable criticism. Yet the gift of medicine was merely intended as matching other in kind, humanitarian gifts. Unlike blankets and used clothing, these humanitarian objects were potentially lethal, themselves requiring considerable resources for their triage or destruction. Local markets might be unreliable and their products of low quality.[66] Humanitarian aid in this instance could not function purely through the distribution of surpluses and waste products—it required to be integrated into an international chain of values focusing on the development of a fair, liberal, market-based economy of health.[67]

Liberal Marketplaces and their Objectors

Yet, historically, humanitarians have functioned best within market forces when the latter were clearly tied to them through common objectives or command and control chains.[68] The liberal humanitarianism of the late nineteenth century was targeting northern humanitarian subjects who would be integrated for the long run in the same markets in which humanitarian goods' producers intervened. The sustainability of the market for medicine, for instance, was by no means assured when medical insurance did not cover its costs. From the 1980s onwards, and particularly around the market for HIV treatments, humanitarians found themselves torn between the danger of having to become lifelong suppliers of drugs to insolvent humanitarian subjects on the one hand, and by the profit margins that medical suppliers were intent on extracting from the pandemic on the other. The response that humanitarians heralded was to challenge the suppliers to lower their prices and license their drugs to manufacturers in the global South. Since 2000, humanitarians have called for an ethical approach to the supply of the goods they need in order to operate.[69]

Far from being a radical act, one could argue the humanitarians were set to globalise the trade of drugs in a manner resembling the importers of cloned electronics or designer clothes. They were seeking to re-route the supply chains to take advantage—in their patients' name—of the lower costs enabled by the threat of open copyright infringements. From a purely capitalist perspective, this set the humanitarian actors in a very different relationship with their suppliers. Humanitarian actors berated the pharmaceutical companies for their obscene profiteering, but when they challenged monopolistic and trust market behaviour they unwittingly employed many of the classic liberal arguments in favour of a more open market.

At the same time that they confronted profit-making pharmaceutical industries, they also condemned them for neglecting research into diseases that were deemed to be unprofitable. The cost of pharmaceutical research without strong political incentives could not be met in a market in which the consumers were unlikely ever to be able to repay the investment. Arguably, the pharmaceutical industry of the later twentieth century had itself become habituated to high returns and profit levels that only lifestyle drugs could provide.

Throughout the 2000s and 2010s, 'Big Pharma' thus became the enemy of effective humanitarian deployments of generic treatments. Pharmaceutical industrial concerns were accused of being simultaneously the monopolistic holders of effective treatments and the agents of medical obscurantism by blocking new research into unprofitable diseases. In contrast with the common purpose of the origins or of the colonial period, the market forces of liberal humanitarians were confronted by the twisted priorities of highly distorted medical markets in the North and under-protected medical markets in the South.[70]

The net result today is that, by hook or by crook, some NGOs can organise with state pressure groups to lower the cost of treatment in some countries—making, for instance, the very effective treatment for hepatitis C 400-times cheaper to buy in Cambodia from MSF than in the US, where the product was developed by Gilead.[71] Supply chains of generic treatments now bypass the Northern routes and source their goods in the South.[72] Better than any delocalisation discourse or World Humanitarian Summit commitment, the market forces of humanitarian supplies are reshaping its global footprint. They do not yet address the research gap: this means that Northern pharmaceutical companies and other producers of goods retain significant advantage in the production of new compounds or products. Nevertheless, the alliance of Southern industrialists and humanitarians can at least research the best use of existing compounds for new therapeutic uses.[73] The liberal order of medical innovation is not yet profoundly challenged by contenders who are not content with delivering minimal standards of care in 'austere environments'. Furthermore, these humanitarian disrupting agents of aid do not often have lasting power. Left to itself, the market they contributed to transform will have to endure past their departure.[74] If anything, the insistence of humanitarian actors to access complex and costly copyrighted compounds in order to deliver them cheaply to emerging markets opens up these markets to pharmaceutical companies.[75] Concessions on price can be countered by growth in market shares, and the enemies of monopolies may yet extend their reach. The displacement of humanitarian work from the hinterland of pharmaceutical concerns split them apart—at least for a time. Recent humanitarian concerns with non-communicable diseases such as diabetes or hypertension might lead to a new common ground being found, since many treatments are relatively cheap but have the potential, through high volume of sales, to generate big returns for industrialists while meeting the low-cost ideals of humanitarians.

Conclusion

The critique of humanitarian goods has often been limited to that of the exaggerated claims made (often by journalists or communication officers) for new model stoves, Plumpy'nut or MUAC armbands.[76] Critiques were able to highlight how technology fetishes could prevent the close investigation of market forces or political agents.[77] Yet if one considers more broadly the market forces and the objects of humanitarian aid, one gets a sense of a complex history which entangled capitalism and humanitarianism. It is a story in which the state played a role at different stages, sometimes forcing together industrial concerns and humanitarians, sometimes encouraging an approach inspired by the deregulating of the markets in which humanitarians sourced their tools. The world of goods exhibited in 1867, along with Dr Louis Appia's armband, was made up of products competing for market share. The command-and-control approach to colonial humanitarianism profoundly instrumentalised—in the literal sense— humanitarians in delivering products and extracting progress from unequal political structures. The moment of liberalisation of humanitarian aid, arguably corresponding to the structural adjustment era of the 1980s, witnessed the development of new markets for NGOs and industries working in a disharmonious symbiosis. A world traversed by pandemics and commensurable experiences of deprivation which ignore North–South or East–West polarities, may become a very different environment for humanitarians and industrial providers of humanitarian goods. Non-communicable diseases as objects of humanitarian interventions invite a closer alignment of humanitarian aid with public health and social policies. Meanwhile, pandemics have the potential to return durable power to the state from the market— putting sovereignty concerns back at the heart of debates on supply, logistics, and humanitarian ingenuity.

6

THE CONSCIENCE OF THE ISLAND?

THE NGO MOMENT IN AUSTRALIAN OFFSHORE DETENTION

Eleanor Davey[1]

In March 2014, the Melbourne-based newspaper *The Herald Sun* ran a biting satire of Scott Morrison, then Australian Minister for Immigration and Border Protection, later to become Prime Minister. The sweating minister, practising his ducking moves in between press conferences, thinks back over allusions to Christian kindness and honesty in his first speech to parliament. 'Had he really said all that?' he wonders, obsequious aides hovering beside him to prepare his next round of rebuttals.[2]

The News Corp daily, part of Rupert Murdoch's press empire, is not known for its promotion of refugee and asylum-seeker interests, but the piece appeared in the aftermath of a savage outburst of violence against men in detention on Manus Island, Papua New Guinea (PNG). The camp where they were confined was one of the so-called 'regional processing centres' (RPCs) of the Australian asylum frame-

work: from 2001 to 2008, and again since 2012, Australian governments have exiled thousands of men, women, and children to PNG
and Nauru as part of hardening the borders against asylum seekers
arriving via boat. Morrison faced the press as the relevant, if not
responsible minister, his statements blending inaccuracy, deflection,
and accusation, blaming the men for the violence to which they were
subjected.[3] 'Don't these people know how good they've got it on
Manus Island?' muses one of Morrison's aides in the *Herald Sun* satire.
The second concurs: 'Three meals a day and a tent over their heads.
And we've got Save the Children looking after the kiddies.'

By this time Save the Children Australia (SCA) was no longer on
Manus Island, as the families they were there to support had been
transferred to other detention centres. But the organisation had
indeed been in that role, 'looking after the kiddies' on Manus Island
from November 2012 to June 2013, and it took on similar work
with a larger remit on Nauru from July 2013 until October 2015.
SCA provided education, child protection services, welfare and casework assistance, initially to families only and later also to adults
without children. Under similar contracts, the Salvation Army (TSA)
also provided recreation, welfare, and casework for adults on both
islands from October 2012 until February 2014. A complex ecosys-
tem of contractors and subcontractors, many of them private companies, sustains and depends upon Australia's immigration detention
system, including a number of non-governmental organisations
(NGOs).[4] Amongst these contracts, however, the programmes of
Save the Children and the Salvation Army on Manus Island and
Nauru stand out as a short-lived experiment in the management of
offshore detention.

Without downplaying the harm caused by other components of
the asylum framework, the presence of NGOs in this system requires
particular consideration. Australian immigration detention, whether
onshore or offshore, causes extreme suffering. Its violence has historical continuities, as Suvendrini Perera explained: 'Forms of
racialised confinement and separation combined with the denation-
alisation and deterritorialisation of certain racialised subjects link
immigration policy and the domestic programs imposed on
Indigenous people.'[5] Further, offshore detention has enacted a neo-

colonial power relationship between Australia and the smaller, poorer, aid-hungry nations that agreed to host RPCs—both of which were previously subject to Australian colonial rule. It created and exploited legal gaps and grey zones. Its opponents—including those imprisoned within it—have condemned it in the harshest terms, as a 'laboratory for the exploration of human suffering', 'singularly dangerous and shameful environments', 'an enormous cage deep in the heart of the jungle', a 'nation-sized spit hood'.[6] To have this system be implemented—even only partially, even only temporarily—by organisations founded on humanitarian values raises profoundly uncomfortable questions. As the refugee-led association RISE: Refugees, Survivors and eX-detainees asked, '[k]nowing that the arbitrary detention of asylum seekers and the refoulement of asylum seekers to Manus and Nauru is illegal, anti-refugee and unhumanitarian, why did Save the Children sign a contract to work for and accept money from the very government that was violating basic human rights laws, including the rights of children?'[7]

This chapter plots the trajectory of Save the Children Australia's programmes in these offshore prisons. It focuses on SCA due to the duration and scale of their operations, their position as part of an influential international humanitarian organisation, and the particular place of children as figures in debates about asylum. The chapter starts by outlining the offshore sites and their return to use in 2012. It then explains the context of SCA's first contract, for Manus Island, as well as the experiences of the Salvation Army. The third section traces SCA's decision to renew its work through a contract on Nauru, and the fourth section recounts the organisation's reaction after the Australian government and others accused its staff members of fabricating abuse claims.

Beyond the organisations involved, this episode shines a light on two dark corners of democratic societies: on the one hand, the limits of 'humanitarian' responses when governments undermine the values they profess; on the other, the exclusion of certain types of people from the supposedly universal benefits of those values. The chapter therefore maps the proximate history while making the case for considering the longer historical arcs to which the NGO moment in Australian offshore detention belongs.

Offshore

On Manus Island, the detention centre sat within Lombrum naval base. 'Manus' (the byname that rolls the site and island into one) is a place of unrelenting heat and humidity, nourishing mosquitoes, malaria, termites, and the tropical vegetation that overgrew the facilities during their period of disuse. When it rained the site stank of sewage. Though families were there for a time, PNG is most associated with the detention of unaccompanied men, who slept in accommodation of varying standards across several compounds, including the 'P Dorm', an unventilated 40-metre-long shed with a curved tin roof that warehoused more than 100 men. In April 2013, the Australian Department of Immigration and Citizenship (DIAC) informed a parliamentary committee that by its own assessment the facilities entailed 'problematic living arrangements' that caused physical and mental health problems.[8] The most feared part of the site was the solitary confinement area known as 'Chauka'. It did not appear on official maps.[9]

On Nauru, the detention site was known as Topside. The first people in the recommissioned Topside camp lived in tents that were mouldy with damp, regularly flooded by tropical storms, and infested with insects and rats. The ground cover was blinding white gravel. Phosphate dust caused constant illness.[10] One teacher, struggling to explain the combined effect of the heat and the facilities, described the accommodation as equivalent to 'standing, sitting or sleeping inside an industrial strength garbage bag in the middle of the Australian desert from dawn to dusk'.[11] Where PNG is an archipelago of islands, with Manus towards the top of its northern arc, Nauru is one tiny dot: Disney World in Florida is about five times its size.

Something other than 'stopping the boats' is required to explain why, as the number of people held offshore declined through transfers (including due to ill health), resettlement, and premature deaths, the extraterritorial exile of thousands has calcified into an irrational punishment of a smaller group of individuals. Since the end of 2013, a naval blockade has been largely responsible for preventing asylum seekers from reaching Australian territories via boat.[12] This approach is described by David Scott FitzGerald as the 'most extreme form of the externalisation of the borders' amongst the interlocking measures that place 'refuge beyond reach'.[13] While the United States under President Ronald Reagan was the first to intercept and return boats, in that case carrying Haitians, and many other countries have contributed to the criminalisation of asylum, Australia's combination of legislative creativity, regional burden-shifting, overt messaging, and bureaucratic violence has brought it particular notoriety.[14] The criminalisation and securitisation of asylum have sustained and drawn energy from portrayals of people on boats as 'queue-jumpers', untrustworthy, selfish, or of bad character.

Hospitality has long been racialised in Australian policies on immigration and asylum. In 1950, as governments were preparing their responses to the draft United Nations (UN) Convention Relating to the Status of Refugees, an official from the Australian Department of Immigration noted that provisions to protect non-European refugees from discrimination 'would be a direct negation of the immigration policy followed by all Australian Governments since Federation'.[15] Refugees in the mid-century decades largely entered Australia as migrants, accepted under immigration policy rather than for humanitarian reasons; this mattered, as historian Klaus Neumann indicated, because the rationale affected which people the government selected.[16] The desire to preserve an asserted European character in Australia, an image of it as 'a country of Western European background living alongside an Asian country', to quote another official, drove Australia's approach to immigration and asylum alike.[17]

These policies are inseparable from histories of violence directed towards First Peoples during colonisation, and of dispossession and discrimination since. Survivors of immigration detention have been at the forefront of advocacy that recognises this link. Solidarity between Indigenous people, refugees, and asylum seekers is a key position for RISE, which links past and present violence:

> The systemic abuse of Aboriginal and Torres Strait Islander peoples is a result of over 200 years of discrimination and continues to this day. The template is now being used against our own refugee communities who are coming on boats. It is impossible to dismantle refugee torture built within and outside detention without addressing the root cause of this ongoing criminal abuse of Aboriginal and Torres Strait Islander peoples.[18]

This analysis highlights both the racialised politics that tolerate or justify harm and the particular techniques and practices that enact it, a combination that Anne McNevin captured as 'the conditions of possibility for offshore detention, as one among other forms of violent policing—conditions that include enduring forms of racial and colonial division'.[19] The function of exclusion common to missions, reservations, protectorates, refugee camps, internment camps, and quarantine stations is integral to 'regulating membership to the community' of the whole.[20] Tropes of invasion, protection, and (settler) identity have also characterised reactions to Indonesian fishermen, for instance, who have criss-crossed the waters north of Australia for centuries, and who have since the 1970s also been the objects of intimidation and criminalisation, their boats turned around and destroyed.[21] As Perera wrote in 2002, '*Not-Australia*'s isolated detention camps cannot be disowned as anomalies in an otherwise healthy, democratic society, nor disconnected from a global system of xeno-racism.'[22]

Immigration detention is a costly business. Since 1996, private security firms and prison operators have held contracts for the running of Australian immigration detention facilities despite the latter officially being administrative, not correctional, in nature.[23] Originally rationalised as a cost-saving measure, the immigration department has repeatedly issued contracts to service providers without following procedures or justifying the ballooning costs.[24] Alongside a larger number of for-profit contractors, NGOs have provided welfare and recreational services in onshore detention and on Christmas Island (an Australian territory with centres used for transit and detention), including the Forum of Australian Services for Survivors of Torture and Trauma (FASSTT), the Coalition for Asylum Seekers, Refugees and Detainees (CARAD), Youth with a Mission (YWAM), and SCA itself. The Australian Red Cross has also held contracts to provide relief and family tracing, and to implement community detention, while describing itself as 'independent' in its role as monitor of conditions in detention.[25]

The use of offshore detention is just one part of the asylum policy framework, but one that encapsulates its rights violations, cultivated vulnerability, and long-term damage. While the Australian immigration detention system has in general lacked transparency and account-ability, the remoteness and overlapping sovereignty regimes of the neocolonial offshore arrangement have further inhibited scrutiny.[26] During its 2014 review of the impact of immigration detention on children, representatives of the Australian Human Rights Commission (AHRC) were denied access to offshore centres on the grounds that their jurisdiction did not extend to foreign countries. Later, Amnesty International resorted to sneaking a researcher onto Nauru after six requests to visit were either ignored or refused.[27] As successive governments have sought to deny responsibility for the offshore prisons, minimise scrutiny and transfer risks, their contracts have bound organisations and individuals alike through confidentiality clauses. And, with the Border Force Act of mid-2015, they made disclosures of information punishable by two years in prison.[28]

'Hard-headed but not hard-hearted', was how the Expert Panel appointed by Julia Gillard's Labor government characterised its asy-lum proposals in August 2012, recommendations that saw the Gillard government hastily recommission the mouldering offshore prisons. The deployment of NGOs on Manus Island and Nauru fit with that government's attempt, as Brett Neilson highlighted early in its term, to project 'a certain humanitarianism that might be claimed by polic-ing borders according to UN protocols or observing principles of human rights'.[29] International organisations have also at times facili-tated offshore processing and, more deeply, the state-centric nature of international law underpins border protection regimes even as some of the associated practices violate international law.[30] While the 'humanitarian imperative' of caring for others provided a rationale for the NGOs' role, their presence also manifested the pattern in which, to quote Neilson again, 'human rights play just as much a role in establishing the conditions under which border crossing can be blocked or slowed as those under which it is facilitated'.[31]

Getting In

Within only two months of the Expert Panel issuing its recommenda-tions, two household names connoting child well-being and com-munity welfare had accepted lucrative contracts to manage the imprisonment of asylum seekers and refugees. 'The off-the-record view of most of the Australian aid sector', according to a rare acknowledgement of this issue in the press, 'is that the two charities are effectively colluding with the government and lending their good name and reputation, and therefore implicit imprimatur, to the detention regime and more particularly, the mandatory detention of children.'[32] This claim requires more interrogation, particularly as it is not clear what proportion of the public knew or cared that NGOs were 'looking after the kiddies'. Put another way, since the NGOs left offshore detention, there has been little sign in mainstream public discussion that their absence has made the policy less palatable. And, indeed, there were few public ripples in the early days of their off-shore contracts, although more criticism emerged over time.

Save the Children Australia had been expanding its humanitarian operations, and its public statements suggested a willingness to add offshore detention to the list. In August 2012, CEO Suzanne Dvorak responded to the Expert Panel with a commentary suggestively titled 'Making the Best of Nauru'.[33] She positioned SCA as 'an aid agency that works in so-called "source", "transit" and "destination" countries' of global forced migration, the piece resembling nothing so much as a hopeful candidate's cover letter. Dvorak had taken up her post in 2009, along with a new Chair of the Board and five new Directors. The consolidation of the separate state-based Save the Children committees into a single, nationwide organisation had only been completed in 2004.[34] Annual reports from that period indicated SCA's focus on development work. From 2009 onwards, 'emergencies' featured in annual reports as their own section, re-energised by the recruitment of British aid entrepreneur Mike Penrose as SCA's Emergency Program Director.

Penrose's role in Australia channelled locally some of the expansionist trends that were driving the Save the Children movement internationally. In 2010, the movement created a new organisation, Save the Children International (SCI), and appointed as its head Jasmine Whitbread, outgoing CEO of Save the Children UK (SCUK). As SCUK Humanitarian Director Gareth Owen explains in this volume, Whitbread had overseen the rapid growth of SCUK and was applying the same commercial, expansionist approach to SCI. With Dvorak at the helm and Penrose pushing humanitarian programmes, SCA's strategies embraced this mentality of growth. In 2011, SCA landed an immense AU$35.7 million grant from AusAID, the Australian government's development agency, for work in Afghanistan.[35] The contract was to run health and education programmes in Uruzgan province—where Australian troops were stationed.

SCA's large contracts in Afghanistan and offshore detention came in the context of a precarious Australian aid sector, where funding is unpredictable and usually scarce. This point was underscored in December 2012, when the Gillard government diverted AU$375 million from the foreign aid budget to help pay for offshore detention.[36] In its international make-up, each member of Save the Children is financially independent: SCA needed to manage its own income in order to stay afloat, and there was little room for complacency. In 2012, SCA adopted a three-year plan to increase income by 60 percent.[37] With the contract to provide services to children and their families on Manus, it won an initial AU$8 million towards that goal. Over time its offshore contracts amounted on paper to AU$160 million, though by late 2016 (a year after its contracts finished), SCA had received a total of AU$76 million, according to the national auditor.[38]

The NGOs arrived offshore in haste and amidst ambiguity. The experience of the Salvation Army strikingly illustrates this. TSA met with the Department of Immigration and Citizenship on 1 September 2012. The following day it contributed to an ecumenical statement expressing concern at the return of offshore processing, and on 10 September it issued its own statement explaining why it had taken on work in the centres: 'We are a people of action who stand with the vulnerable and oppressed, and therefore commit ourselves to give our very best to serve those who will be transferred for off-shore processing.'[39] The government transferred the first asylum seekers to Nauru just four days later, only one month after the Expert Panel had issued its recommendations.[40] At that time, Nauru had no capacity to assess refugee claims.

Provisions for families took shape slightly later. In late September, Minister for Immigration Chris Bowen conceded in a radio interview that the department was trying to secure accommodation 'appropriate' for families. The accommodation on Nauru was not adequate, so work was underway on Manus Island. He insisted on the importance of sending children offshore: 'Everybody wants to do the right thing by children, but you can't have a rule that says, well if you send children they can stay and everybody else goes—you just create a loophole for the people smugglers, as tough as that sounds.'[41] On 12 October 2012, the department issued a letter of intent, thanking SCA representatives for attending a 'PNG service provider workshop' the previous day and authorising it to commence planning and spending, pending confirmation of a full contract.[42] The first flight to bring asylum seekers to PNG on 21 November included several families. At the minister's request, young-looking children were specifically selected in order to hide the medical advice against children under the age of seven being exposed on Manus Island to diseases against which they could not be safely vaccinated.[43] Families lived in 'dongas' (portable containers with marginally more privacy than the accommodation for men), adjacent to the men's compound, though able to witness any distress the men experienced. Save the Children issued a statement to explain its role: 'While we do not want children sent to offshore processing centres, we are committed to providing services of support to the world's most vulnerable children—wherever they are.'[44]

There is evidence that the organisations faced criticism early on. Major Paul Moulds, who along with Major Robbin Moulds, his wife, led TSA's offshore operations, addressed this explicitly in November 2012. 'It has deeply saddened me to hear the attacks by some people in the community on our organisation and our people', he wrote, continuing that '[i]t astounds me that some people who oppose this policy, and say they care for the refugees, have decided to attack one of the organisations that is prepared to go into the heat and harshness of this environment to be with the people.'[45] The Refugee Action Coalition (RAC), a Sydney-based campaigning organisation, was one of the channels for what TSA perceived as 'attacks', both in communicating views of prisoners and in its own right. An undated Save the Children release was less explicit, but started its own Q&A asking: 'Are you saying it's ok for children to be detained on Nauru or Manus Island?'[46] While one cannot assume that all supporters of aid organisations would oppose offshore detention—and one certainly cannot assume that all opponents of detention would support large NGOs—it is not difficult to imagine this concern arising for a significant group pursuing social or cosmopolitan engagement on both fronts.

As the prompt about whether offshore detention is 'ok for children' highlights, SCA's focus on children particularly, and problematically, sharpened hierarchies of tolerance for detention. Children have been a focus of immigration debates in several countries, with the motif of generosity towards children set against the need to defend borders.[47] In Australian parliamentary debates since 2010, the idea of rescue has been directly linked to the deterrence approach, as encapsulated in former Liberal Treasurer Joe Hockey's claim that as a result of his party's policies 'there are no children floating in the ocean between Australia and East Timor'.[48] This rhetoric alludes to the deaths of fifteen children on 15 December 2010, when, along with fifty adults, they drowned after an asylum-seeker boat broke up on the rocks of Christmas Island. In these arguments, historian Jordana Silverstein wrote, children 'are differentiated, understood to carry some distinct significatory power and are used discursively—and materially—to produce a particular set of national emotions'.[49] Since the return of offshore detention, several mobilisations around the plight of children have achieved tactical successes, their consensus-building approach summed up in one appeal by a former SCA teacher on Nauru, that '[n]o matter what your political view—the indefinite detention of children is astoundingly cruel'.[50] But as their repetition shows, these concessions for certain young innocents carry no guarantee of systemic change, and they have pernicious undertones, allowing the inference that the detention of others (especially men of colour) is less inhumane, more justifiable, more necessary.

What to make of the NGOs' early commitments? On the one hand, those making the decision could not have known precisely how the return of offshore detention would unfold, who would be held there, or how long it would last. On the other hand, there could be no ignorance of its extreme human toll. When the Expert Panel recommended returning to offshore processing, respondents had warned of the cost to human rights, with Amnesty International Australia issuing a dire prediction: 'we know that it will leave vulnerable refugees languishing in limbo for years'.[51]

Staying In

In 2012, Save the Children Australia and the Salvation Army had certain shared experiences: of rapid contracting, dealing with contentious politics, and discovering harsh and volatile environments. As their programmes continued, their trajectories began to diverge more noticeably. In Save the Children's case, the offshore work was split into two distinct phases: the first, on Manus, ended in mid-2013; the second, on Nauru, began only weeks later and continued for more than two years. The Salvation Army's offshore operations ended in February 2014.

According to analysis by *The Guardian*, the Salvation Army's contracts for services in immigration detention (three offshore and one for community detention on the mainland) came to AU$113.2 million.[52] When starting out, TSA had claimed 'extensive frontline experience' in emergency response and social work, including with asylum seekers and refugees in Australia and other communities in the Pacific region.[53] Its magazine proclaimed their offshore work as a Christian mission.[54] However, Paul Moulds also admitted that he and Robbin Moulds didn't 'know anything much' about Manus Island and had 'never worked with global poverty before'.[55] In April 2013, workers from the centres began to speak out, including Moulds himself, who featured in a TV reportage along with two former TSA workers.[56] In December, TSA announced that its contract would not be renewed beyond February 2014. It gave no reason, nor did Scott Morrison—minister of a portfolio by then recast as 'Immigration and Border Protection'—elaborate on why the government had decided not to retain it.[57]

Within a month of the TSA contract finishing, former employee Mark Isaacs published a book on his experience as a 'Salvo' on Nauru.[58] Though Isaacs clearly attributed responsibility for suffering in the centres to the Australian government, he described chaotic improvisation in the TSA operations. Several months later, in mid-2014, two other Salvos joined Isaacs in publicly describing how the insufficient recruitment and induction process placed them in a situation for which they were unqualified and untrained.[59] *The Saturday Paper*, which reports regularly on asylum issues, broke allegations that TSA did not adequately support staff following their return from the traumatic postings, a criticism which has also been directed to other offshore service providers through press coverage and compensation claims.[60] For individuals in many agencies, the offshore detention centres constituted a singular and taxing environment: not free spaces, but not emergency settings; created by a wealthy nation, but under-resourced in contexts of poverty and limited health facilities; with overlapping compliance regimes, but underdeveloped legal frameworks; distressing experiences on a fly-in-fly-out roster.

Save the Children operations that had started very modestly on Manus Island became much larger in the second phase on Nauru. The Department of Immigration and Border Protection (DIBP) transferred families, including thirty-four children, to Manus in 2012, but the first part of 2013 saw no more families brought to PNG (the transfers in 2013 were unaccompanied adults).[61] When the ailing Labor government removed families from Manus Island in mid-2013, contracts of SCA staff members there ended. However, the organisation soon found itself recruiting for offshore work again with a new contract worth over AU$36 million as children and their parents went on to Nauru. DIBP officials were transferring more and more people into offshore detention. In February 2014, SCA picked up welfare services on Nauru (formerly a TSA caseload) and its number of 'clients' rapidly went from 167 to 679.[62] In 2014 and 2015, SCA had more full-time employees on Nauru than in its other international programmes combined.[63]

Though conditions did change over time, it is important not to oversimplify the situation on Nauru as 'better'—for children or anyone else—than on Manus Island, simply because families ended up there. In the weeks between SCA's departure from Manus and its establishment on Nauru, the announcement that no one in offshore detention would ever be granted settlement in Australia had provoked unrest leading to a riot and the destruction of facilities in the Nauru centre. Families, and with them Save the Children, arrived in the aftermath of a fire. It took until April 2014 to secure air-conditioned facilities for children to attend school in. One day that September, six boys, all unaccompanied minors, attempted to kill themselves with the same single blade.[64]

Conditions and procedures in the camps defied professional standards. An anonymous former NGO worker on Nauru, writing with activist academic Linda Briskman, described how principles of social work such as empowerment and trauma-based practice were impossible to implement in the context of offshore detention.[65] The practice of removing at-risk children from the source of harm—in this case their ongoing detention—was impossible. Child protection frameworks such as domestic legislation or local working-with-children checks were missing or incomplete. Legal guardianship of unaccompanied children was contested.[66] An inquiry found gaps in the Nauruan authorities' capacity to investigate allegations of abuse or assault.[67] Indeed, certain democratic standards in Nauru have actually regressed since 2012, with Australia's quiescence.[68]

SCA frequently and clearly stated its opposition to the detention of children and to indefinite detention more broadly. Paul Ronalds, who became CEO of Save the Children Australia in July 2013, has indicated that one of its Trustee Board's conditions for the Nauru phase of operations was that the organisation retain the right to publicly advocate on asylum policy.[69] The Not-for-profit Sector Freedom to Advocate Act 2013, passed in the last days of the Gillard government, nominally ensured NGO freedom of expression, but there was no blueprint for how to reconcile its limited protections with the secrecy measures enacted to shield the offshore apparatus from scrutiny.[70] SCA submitted to public inquiries into offshore detention, taking the opportunity (under parliamentary privilege) to place on the record its concerns with the fact and conditions of detention. An increase of disclosure is apparent when reviewing these submissions over time: from a 2013 document focusing on the effects of detention; to a similarly geared document in 2014, accompanied by testimony at a public hearing describing conditions; to a 2015 document that for the first time acknowledged allegations of abuse in the centres.[71]

Statements by staff members outstripped SCA's evolving organisational positions. Employees of the two NGOs, along with medical staff and to a lesser extent security company personnel, have been significant contributors to official inquiries into offshore detention. Their testimonies are difficult documents, catalogues of despair and damage made all the more powerful by their rhetorical restraint. Beyond the cover of official inquiries, there have also been less sanctioned forms of witnessing. There is anecdotal evidence that leaks to press outlets have come from NGO employees, as well as other individuals working or confined in the detention centres.[72] A determination not to 'collude' with the system's abuses was explicit in an open letter from detention centre staff in 2015, challenging the government to prosecute them under the Border Force Act.[73] Such forms of secondary witnessing interact in complex ways with the protests of people in detention: where protest and self-harm converge, care responses in detention and the language used to describe the acts can seem to encourage silencing or victim narratives over political recognition.[74]

The difficulties this practice created for SCA can be seen in Submission 183 to the AHRC inquiry of 2014, a particularly controversial example. The submission described its authors as 'some Save the Children Australia (SCA) staff employees past and present'.[75] It stated that 'not only are children routinely exposed to episodes of violence, threats and self-harming attempts by others, but they have also been the victims of abuse, assault, bullying, and threats of violence by both staff and community members'.[76] It asserted that SCA management (though did not specify the level or location of that management) 'actively discouraged' staff members from advocating for individual children to be taken off the island, 'because SCA management indicates that DIBP will not remove children and therefore any advocacy will not make a difference and will be a waste of time'.[77] It included over a hundred operational documents and the Australian Federal Police investigated the possibility of charging the authors with confidentiality breaches.

SCA leadership have generally expressed sympathy for whistleblowers' choices while casting them as detrimental to the organisation's operations. SCA legal counsel, Simon Miller and Sophie Coleman, argued that 'current and former personnel who "spoke out" undoubtedly negatively impacted Save the Children's relationship with the government during the contract term, which in turn undermined Save the Children's targeted advocacy and capacity to achieve operational change'.[78] A subsequent SCA brief acknowledged that it was 'in the public interest' that information to which its personnel were party and which had been suppressed due to secrecy provisions be made known.[79] The situation placed a heavy burden on individual ethics and organisational decision-making alike; speaking out is one of the ways aid organisations seek to enact and demonstrate their independence, which in turn sustains an identity as 'humanitarian'.

It is not clear how the experience on Manus informed the choice to take on the Nauru programmes, but a decision to continue has a different momentum from a decision to begin. It is possible that the removal of families from PNG after several months raised expectations that the same would happen again once the point had been made. But, by that time, the Labor government had declared that no one transferred offshore would ever be settled in Australia, before losing power to a Liberal–National Party coalition that ran an even grimmer line on asylum. In an extraordinary admission that these governments had created an environment that defied principled conduct, when interviewed about SCA's role offshore, a DIBP official observed: 'it's not a stretch for me to think that somebody who bases their professional career around their moral and ethical base, would… let that drive their behaviour in terms of how they would respond'.[80] As had become clear, a commitment to humanity got you sent home.

Falling Out

The Herald Sun's satire of Morrison in March 2014 implied that the presence of NGOs 'looking after the kiddies' and others in offshore detention offered the authorities a fig leaf for abuses. In October 2014, however, Morrison came out swinging against Save the Children Australia in an episode that suggested his government no longer found their presence useful. A short report from a security firm alleged that SCA staff members working on Nauru had been stoking protests and falsifying complaints. 'If people want to be political activists, that's their choice', Morrison blustered, 'but they don't get to do it on the taxpayer's dollar and working in a sensitive place like Nauru.'[81] Far more than the departure of the Salvation Army, this confrontation signalled the beginning of the end of the NGO moment.

Like other sectors including the media, research, and public service, NGOs have been subject to government pressure since at least the 1990s. 'The attempts by the Australian Government to close down or marginalise all but the tamest NGOs stand in stark contrast to developments in the role of civil society in other liberal democracies, where frameworks for NGO-government relations are being built or rebuilt', claimed two scholars in a 2007 book called *Silencing Dissent*.[82] And, though Morrison's clash with Save the Children was unusually dramatic, he was not alone in his desire to sideline humanitarian or human rights critiques. Pronounced hostility to rights-based discourses has periodically marked Canberra's attitudes since at least the 1990s.[83] In the period this chapter covers, governments from both sides of the aisle have brushed off criticism of offshore conditions, from then Labor Minister Chris Bowen sneering that 'Amnesty International opposed the Nauru processing facility before they got there, they oppose it after they leave', to Liberal Party leader Tony Abbott, Prime Minister at the time, claiming that 'Australians are sick of being lectured to by the United Nations.'[84]

Tensions between DIBP and Save the Children had been increasing in the second half of 2014. Ronalds identified several drivers: SCA's public statements, those of SCA employees, unattributed leaks, and ongoing private negotiations.[85] When Mat Tinkler, SCA Head of Public Affairs, gave testimony to the AHRC in April 2014, he received a call from DIBP threatening to withdraw the contract.[86] Around the middle of the year, Ronalds also received a call, requesting that SCA stand down five staff members about whom DIBP officials claimed to have concerns. At that time, the organisation undertook its own investigation, cleared the individuals of any wrongdoing, and confirmed with the government their return to work.[87] Throughout this period, SCA was still negotiating the terms of its contract, with points of friction including the costs of the contract as well as confidentiality clauses. The contract was ultimately signed in September 2014, over a year into its second phase of work.

The deteriorating relationship also reflected increasingly hostile conditions. As lawyer Madeline Gleeson indicated, the Abbott government had doubled down on the 'security focus on immigration matters', and it had 'ushered in an era of unprecedented secrecy around the offshore processing of asylum seekers'.[88] Following this change, according to Miller and Coleman, the interpretation and implementation of contracts and procedures hardened and the new government showed far less interest in seeking SCA's advice on child protection or other welfare issues.[89] As DIBP's and service providers' approach toughened, as asylum seekers' hope died, the suffering, protest, and self-harm increased, and Save the Children found itself in a position that Tinkler later described as 'the conscience of the island'.[90] In the words of one SCA worker, 'you can't treat someone for trauma when they're living, when they're actually living the trauma on a day-to-day basis [...] we really were there in the end just to get them through each day'.[91]

Notwithstanding some public statements, the majority of SCA's advocacy to government was being done behind closed doors. Incident reports represented a first, and official, mechanism for conveying concerns. In SCA's 'Holistic Support Approach' to Nauru, they are amongst the steps to find resolutions on-island, supporting the maintenance of lists of particularly 'vulnerable' individuals whose cases were discussed at cross-agency meetings. The Holistic Support Approach described advocacy as being 'about drawing attention to issues and influencing decision-makers to achieve lasting, positive change', while recognising tensions between this goal and the status of service provider.[92] It provided a process for escalation of issues up to ministerial level, and cautioned that 'where individuals take matters into their own hands and do not follow formal organisational processes, it can potentially have a negative impact on beneficiaries, the individual and the effective delivery of program services'.[93]

As indicated above, however, the practice of whistle-blowing showed that for some workers the formal processes were a constraint on personal ethics that they could not tolerate. In humanitarian organisations, especially large ones, disconnects can develop between headquarters and frontline staff, or between operational staff and those with other roles, including advocacy. In one instance in 2015, in the context of the SCA-run school within the Nauru detention centre being closed down, the operations manager emailed staff to caution against their speaking out amidst 'a sense of anger and desire for retribution'.[94] The Border Force Act was due to come into force soon after, though the email claimed it was already in operation. Managers who stress confidentiality obligations of field staff can coexist institutionally with advocacy colleagues seeking to influence government, but the acts of the former might understandably fuel doubts about the approach of the latter. In any case, the use of back channels could do little to assuage aid workers' concerns that the presence of recognised aid agencies would misleadingly imply the conditions in the centres, or even their very existence, were acceptable.

The Australian government and Save the Children Australia fell out with an intense altercation in which the former had the upper hand, followed by a slow vindication for the latter. By late September 2014, Morrison had become worried about the risk of an outburst of violence on Nauru. The incidence of self-harm had risen after he screened a video telling people they would not be resettled in Australia, according to leaked transcripts from a subsequent inquiry, and the DIBP went looking for a list of Save the Children staff members to whom it could attribute the tensions.[95] Having triggered a flimsy report from Wilson Security, on 2 October the department demanded that SCA take ten named staff members off Nauru. Unlike the previous instance, it would not await an investigation (though one of the ten nominated individuals had already resigned and left). The next day, the News Corp-owned *Daily Telegraph* ran a story based on the report, accusing SCA and its staff members of fabricating abuse, encouraging self-harm, and 'using children as a human shield in protest activity'.[96] Bizarrely, no one at SCA could access the contents of this report until March the following year when a Green Party senator read it on to parliamentary record.[97]

Powerless to prevent the removal and blind to the substance of the allegations, SCA leadership nonetheless came out strongly in defence of their staff. Morrison spoke of 'tactical use of children' in orchestrating protests, 'coaching and encouragement of self-harm for people to be evacuated off the island and fabrication of allegations as part of a campaign to seek to undermine operations and support for the offshore processing policy of the Government'.[98] These smears also implicated the children's parents, tapping into Howard-era accusations that asylum seekers had thrown children into the water to bring about their own rescue, demonising refugees as inhuman, selfish, fanatical.[99] Indeed, the *Daily Telegraph*'s headline 'Truth Overboard' explicitly evoked this 'children overboard' scandal, showing the continuing currency of those accusations despite their proven groundlessness. Ronalds responded, in the same paper: 'We reject strongly the allegations that our staff would fabricate cases of abuse or encourage children to hurt themselves, much less coach them in doing so.'[100] Later, one of the ten staff members, social worker Poppy Browne, described how '[t]his experience impacted every part of me—my personal life, my professional capacities, my relationships and my daily functioning'.[101]

One way of reading this episode is through the logic of offshore prison administration: how the Australian government applied to its own contractor the techniques it used to keep detainees in insecurity. Denied access to accusations or a process to respond to them, obliged to comply with unseen orders, delegitimised through a concurrent media campaign, SCA was confronted with the full weight of the unequal power dynamics inherent in its service provision contract. Another reading (complementary rather than contradictory) is through the logic of silencing witnesses: how the Australian government responded to pressure from humanitarians by removing them from the site of the abuse and pointing the finger back at them. This was a tactic seen in Ethiopia, when the Derg under Mengistu Haile Mariam expelled the outspoken French section of Médecins Sans Frontières (MSF); or in Sudan, when Omar al-Bashir expelled thirteen international NGOs and closed three domestic NGOs after the International Criminal Court issued a warrant against him with war crimes charges.

An independent investigation led by Philip Moss cleared SCA and its employees of any wrongdoing, but the relationship with the DIBP could not be repaired. Moss finalised his report in early February 2015; the government released it in late March, on the day that former Prime Minister (and refugee advocate) Malcolm Fraser died; in June a second report recommended the staff members receive compensation.[102] This period also marked the official transformation of the RPC into an 'open centre', allowing freedom of movement around the island—though no escape from it. As the end date neared, intimidation of SCA staff members increased. The Nauruan police twice raided the organisation's offices in October 2015, with Australian Border Force officials reportedly watching on as they searched staff and premises and confiscated computers and phones.[103] At the end of that month, SCA's contract ended. DIBP subsequently changed the offshore tender rules, effectively barring NGOs from bidding as direct contractors.

In their offshore operations, Save the Children Australia encountered ethical compromises, created internal tensions, came into conflict with its own staff, and may well have ended up in positions that contradicted its stated principles. The pragmatic approach of the Save the Children movement, its culture of engagement over denunciation, shaped this response to offshore detention. SCA became one of the cogs of the detention machine; but it also sought to influence it with an approach that did not aim solely (like some of its counterparts) to accumulate profit or perpetuate detention. SCA cultivated expertise, lobbied for improved conditions, fuelled public debate, and enabled the presence of individuals who, after witnessing the conditions, spoke out. Looking back on the experience, Ronalds affirmed SCA's decisions on Nauru as acting 'in the best interests of children'.[104] Notwithstanding other objections and incentives, there is no doubt that many people across leadership and frontline positions believed that it was better for SCA to be in those camps than some other contractor. Which is to say: after nearly a century of Save the Children's humanitarian activities, its Australian chapter could see no better way to defend refugee children's rights and lives than to become a part of their detention.

Conclusion

In August 2016, *The Guardian* published a leaked dossier of incident reports from offshore detention known as the 'Nauru Files': 2,116 reports dating from May 2013 to October 2015—a disturbing catalogue of abuse and self-harm.[105] More than half of the incidents involved children, including thirty incidents of children self-harming, fifty-nine reports of assault on children, and seven of sexual assault of children. Former SCA staff members stepped forward to contextual-ise, humanise, and authenticate the short, redacted texts.[106] The files showed that Wilson Security frequently downgraded the severity rating of incidents as originally submitted by NGO workers.

While the Nauru Files provided insight into SCA's unpublicised attempts to influence conditions in the centres, they also sharpened accusations of complicity. None of the abuse revelations in the Nauru Files implicated SCA staff members. But the violence and suffering, the extent and the severity, fuelled questions about whether SCA had made enough noise about what it was witnessing. Viktoria Vibhakar, a former employee and whistle-blower, criticised SCA's handling of the issue.[107] RISE questioned the extent of SCA's reporting to over-sight bodies, putting the problem starkly: 'We are appalled by the apparent hypocrisy in the actions of your organisation publicly con-demning the detention of children, while accepting lucrative sums of money from DIBP, the very same abusers of both adults and children from our community, with the children under your care being caged and abused, rather than being saved'.[108]

Reduced to its most basic terms, this a familiar dilemma for humanitarian organisations. In the words of Rony Brauman, the influ-ential former president of MSF:

> [t]he very object of humanitarian action—both constituting its main strength and setting its structural limits—is to try to combat suffering directly, irrespective of its political roots or historical context. Yet humanitarian workers are under a compelling moral obligation to mistrust this premise, to be aware of the risk that any such program may rebound against those for whom it was intended.[109]

As Brauman went on to explain, a drive for action frequently dis-places this moral obligation, 'since the humanitarian movement seems largely oblivious of the positive ethical implications of refusing to act'.

Reflection on this ethical dilemma and its manifestations in the last few decades has often focused on mass violence outside the global North. The complicity of aid organisations after the genocide in Rwanda is perhaps its most emblematic illustration, which Jennifer Rubenstein called the 'problem of spattered hands'.[110] As *génocidaires* regrouped amidst the Rwandan refugees in neighbouring countries, aid agencies became a resource for the militias and provided (unwilling) cover for their exploitation of and attacks upon civilians. In these analyses, in contrast with Rwanda's *génocidaires*, Ethiopia's Derg, or Myanmar's military regime, Northern states figure more as invaders and occupiers abroad than persecutors at home. The primary cases of the latter are Iraq and Afghanistan, where—like SCA in Uruzgan province, alongside Australian troops—aid organisations have been folded into military interventions.

The securitisation of asylum in the West presents a counterpoint, creating harm not only beyond or at the threshold of Western states but inside them. By creating barriers to journeys for asylum, increasing dangers and deaths, by penalising with detention, isolation, and deprivation those who make such journeys, through mechanisms that keep people vulnerable even after release, denying them livelihoods and healthcare, fortress states like Australia have undermined expectations of democratic governments. When the SCA aid workers were summarily evicted from Nauru, Paul Ronalds observed that this was 'certainly not something we would expect in a country like Australia, a member of the OECD and a functioning democracy'.[111] Nor, of course, is indefinite detention of people seeking asylum—but this has been legal in Australia since 1992, when the government legislated to remove limitations on the length of immigration detention. Humanitarian organisations working in the resulting spaces of exclusion must confront their contribution to this decline in expectations.

This questioning must be informed by recognition of the deep implication of Western humanitarianism in the management of those whose full humanity is denied. Racialised and paternalistic foundations informed the 'humanitarian' practices of colonial administrators, for instance, and aid organisations rooted in empire often channelled those views and interests through their relief work in anti-colonial conflicts. In the 1950s, these two faces of imperialist humanitarianism found expression in different parts of the Save the Children movement. The earliest roots of Save the Children Australia date to 1919—the founding year of the original Save the Children Fund in England—but these initial committees died away in the interwar period and new networks were mobilised during the 1940s and 1950s. This period of revival was marked by a new interest in care for Indigenous children, establishing schools to counter state neglect, and giving health, parenting, and sewing instruction for Aboriginal mothers.[112] In another part of the empire, Save the Children projects for children and women sought to win support for imperialist rule and 'enabled colonial brutality' during the independence uprisings of the Kenyan Emergency.[113]

If offshore detention was intended to send a message of deterrence, the offshore imprisonment of children was especially pointed: a punishment of the figure of innocence intended to show that none would be exempted. Yet Australia's approach to territorial asylum, like those of other fortress states, relies upon a system of exceptions firmly knotted into its modern society, racialised exclusions from benefits and protections that nominally apply to all. Childhood in these debates shows a devastating promiscuity: not sacred enough to prevent the imprisonment of children on Manus or Nauru (or in onshore detention), but still sufficiently unique to support campaigns that leave adults locked up. To recognise these dark histories and conflictual presents provides an opportunity for reflective action—a challenge for the conscience of the larger island, Australia, not just the aid workers whose jobs took them to Manus and Nauru as proxies for our claimed goodwill.

7

RIGHTS-BEARING MIGRANTS AND THE
RIGHTFULNESS OF THEIR RESCUE

THE EMERGENCE OF A 'NEW MODEL OF
HUMANITARIAN ENGAGEMENT' AT EUROPE'S BORDERS

Klaus Neumann[1]

Nicholas is a former commercial diver. In 2017, he volunteered for a search and rescue (SAR) mission conducted by SOS MEDITERRANEE in the Central Mediterranean. When asked what he liked most about his assignment, he said: 'Giving people a chance. If we were not out here, I think most people would die. We are not necessarily giving them a better life, but they get a chance of having one. A chance of living.'[2] His statement suggests that his impulse was humanitarian, pure and simple—all he was trying to do was to respond to an emergency and save lives. As I hope to show in this chapter, however, the intentions and practices of Nicholas and the NGO he worked for mark a departure from traditional humanitarianism defined by the principles of humanity, impartiality, neutrality, and independence.

'As liberal humanitarianism is challenged in its European heartland', observes Juliano Fiori, introducing an interview with Caroline Abu Sa'Da, Director General of SOS MEDITERRANEE Suisse, '[NGOs like hers] are developing—through practice—a new model of humanitarian engagement.'[3] I shall explain why I believe Fiori's assessment to be apt—with the proviso that we are not witnessing the emergence of a model that is, or could be, emulated by many other humanitarian agencies across a range of operational settings. NGOs like SOS MEDITERRANEE do indeed represent a phenomenon that is exemplary and qualitatively new. That begs the question: what are its enabling factors and distinctive features? I argue that this new model is specific, as it has emerged in contexts in which the recipients of humanitarian assistance are asylum seekers and other irregularised migrants on the move.[4] I explore why the delivery of assistance to them, specifically, might prompt NGOs to position themselves in particular ways. I argue that the humanitarian engagement practised by SOS MEDITERRANEE and similar organisations is marked by a commitment to an expansive understanding of human rights that necessarily puts these organisations in conflict with European governments as it challenges nation-states' prerogative to control the borders of their territory.

Humanitarian Interventions at European Borders

SOS MEDITERRANEE was set up in May 2015. Since February 2016 it has conducted SAR missions: first with the *Aquarius* (2016–18) and then with the *Ocean Viking* (since 2019).[5] On its website, the organisation declares: 'Our vision is of a world where every person in distress at sea is rescued and treated with dignity.'[6] While this statement suggests a broad remit, SOS MEDITERRANEE has had in fact a much more specific aim: to rescue migrants who are trying to cross the stretch of sea separating North Africa from Europe. In recent years, the Central Mediterranean crossing—from Libya and Tunisia to Italy and Malta—has been used by hundreds of thousands of migrants in an attempt to circumvent European border controls.[7] But that same crossing has also become the deadliest migrant route in the world. The International Organization for Migration (IOM) confirmed

16,324 migrant deaths in the Central Mediterranean between 1 January 2014 and 31 December 2019 alone, almost half of the global total of 35,186 for the same period.[8] Because many deaths remain unreported, the actual number of fatalities is likely to be substantially higher.[9]

Migrant deaths in the Mediterranean have attracted attention particularly since 3 October 2013. On that day, at least 366 people died when a boat carrying mainly migrants from Eritrea sank near the Italian island of Lampedusa. Following these deaths, and the sinking of another boat near Lampedusa eight days later, the Italian government launched a one-year SAR mission, *Operation Mare Nostrum*. In its course the Italian military and police rescued some 150,000 migrants.[10] After the conclusion of this Italian operation on 31 October 2014, the European Union's border control agency, Frontex, coordinated a follow-up mission, *Operation Triton*. Unlike *Mare Nostrum*, *Triton* was conceived primarily as a border security operation; it would draw on far fewer resources and cover a much smaller area.[11] The number of drownings in the Central Mediterranean initially increased.[12] On 13 and 19 April 2015, two boats sank off the Libyan coast, and more than 1,200 people perished. These disasters once again raised public awareness about the humanitarian crisis at Europe's southern sea border and motivated civil society initiatives to take a stance against the perceived indifference of European governments.

Since 2014, up to ten NGOs at a time have carried out monitoring and/or SAR missions in the Central Mediterranean; others have been active in the Aegean Sea.[13] They vary significantly in terms of their SAR capabilities, the size of their operations, and their approach.[14] Long-established agencies MSF and Save the Children initiated operations in the Mediterranean in 2015 and 2016 respectively. Migrant Offshore Aid Station (MOAS), founded and initially funded by entrepreneurs and philanthropists Christopher and Regina Catrambone, ran operations out of Malta between August 2014 and August 2017. Other NGOs—including SOS MEDITERRANEE, Sea-Watch, Jugend Rettet, Sea-Eye, Mission Lifeline, Mediterranea, and Proactiva Open Arms—entered the scene only after the end of *Mare Nostrum*; they have emerged out of European civil society and rely on private donations.[15] Here, I am primarily interested in this latter type of organisation: NGOs that have been set up by private citizens to carry out monitoring and/or SAR missions in the Mediterranean, and whose vessels are largely staffed by people who identify as activists and have usually volunteered as crew. At the time of writing, in early 2020, all NGOs still conducting SAR missions in the Central Mediterranean, except for MSF, largely fit this description. MOAS and Save the Children, which do not, terminated their missions in the Mediterranean in the second half of 2017.[16]

MOAS and Save the Children were primarily, if not exclusively, concerned with responding to a humanitarian emergency and saving the lives of migrants attempting to cross the Mediterranean. NGOs that are the result of grassroots initiatives, such as SOS MEDITERRANEE and the German NGO Sea-Watch, have similarly tried to make the Mediterranean crossing safer, both by monitoring the waters between North Africa and Southern Europe and by rescuing migrants at risk of drowning. But they have also challenged policies of the European Union and its member states that have aimed at the securitisation of Europe's southern maritime border, which have arguably been responsible for the high death toll of migrants trying to reach Europe.[17] This challenge has been an important dimension of their identity. SOS MEDITERRANEE, for example, states on its website that the organisation 'was founded... in response to the deaths in the Mediterranean and *the failure of the European Union* to prevent these deaths'.[18] The Spanish NGO Proactiva Open Arms says it specialises in 'boats carrying people who need help in the Aegean and Central Mediterranean sea, as well as *raising awareness of all the injustices* that are happening which have been untold'.[19] Sea-Watch lists three aims: it 'provides emergency relief capacities, demands and pushes for rescue operations by the European institutions and *stands up publicly for legal escape routes*'.[20] Because of the organisations' emphasis on public awareness raising, many rescue missions carried out by activist NGOs are accompanied by journalists.

The politics of organisations such as Sea-Watch has much in common with that of anti-deportation activists and support networks working with migrants crossing borders within Europe. The latter include, for example, civic networks that have supported migrants trying to enter France from Italy.[21] Their assistance has been likened to the 'underground railroad' that, in the first half of the nineteenth century, helped African American slaves from the southern states of the United States escape to free states in the North, Canada, or Mexico.[22] On the Italian side of the border, No Border activists have set up 'free-spots' where migrants might camp; they have provided information about the logistics of the border crossing; and they have arranged safe places to stay in France. On the French side, local residents in the Roya Valley have provided food and accommodation to migrants who make it across the border; some of them have also picked up migrants in Italy and taken them across the border.

Non-governmental Rescuers vs. European Governments

The initial impetus to assist irregularised migrants in the Mediterranean has often been prompted by a humanitarian concern for the alleviation of suffering. For two reasons, however, NGOs quickly moved beyond a strictly humanitarian approach, and engaged in political advocacy, if not political activism. The first is that they have been compelled to fill a gap left by agencies of the EU and of its member states. They have often done so under protest, arguing that maritime search and rescue should be the responsibility of states, rather than that of the crews of fishing trawlers, merchant ships, or NGO vessels. They have lamented that although the EU maintains a presence in the Mediterranean through its border agency Frontex, its own SAR activities are extremely limited, while it has entrusted search and rescue operations to militias acting under the guise of a Libyan 'coastguard' funded by Italy and the EU. In fact, several of the NGOs that were initially set up to denounce the EU's inaction, became prominently involved in rescuing migrants at sea only at a later stage. For example, Harald Höppner, the founder of Sea-Watch, at first merely wanted to force governments to act: 'It was obvious to me that in the end only the politicians would be able to stop the dying in the Mediterranean', he wrote in a 2016 memoir.[23] Four years later, Sea-Watch claims on its website that its 'goal remains to make itself redundant'.[24] It was only after it became apparent that European governments could not be shamed into playing a greater role in rescuing migrants that Sea-Watch and other NGOs increased their SAR capabilities.[25] Here, the approach of SAR organisations in the Mediterranean differs from that of traditional humanitarian NGOs, which often willingly perform roles that states prefer to outsource.

The second reason why individuals assisting migrants at the border, activist networks, and NGOs, as well as their supporters, adopt a more politicised and antagonistic stance towards the EU and European governments, is that irregular border crossings and humanitarian assistance provided to migrants attempting such crossings have been criminalised. An annual report by Roya Citoyenne, an association of residents in the Roya Valley assisting migrants in transit, illustrates how humanitarian and political aspects have become intertwined in responses to irregularised migration. Under the heading 'Humanitarian or political?', the report suggests that '[t]his question arises from the start':

> some try to make up for the shortcomings of Italy and France in terms of reception [for the migrants], and to provide exiles with basic necessities (meals, clothing, care, shelters…), while others think that it is also necessary to wage a political battle. Politics is quickly catching up, however, with the humanitarian, it is there every evening, with the presence of the police, the checking of the papers of the 'marauders', the decrees of the mayor of Ventimiglia that prohibit the provision of meals to refugees…[26]

On the French side of the Italian–French border, several locals have been accused of committing a *délit de solidarité*, a 'solidarity offence', for assisting migrants. The best-known of these locals internationally, French farmer Cédric Herrou, has ferried migrants from Ventimiglia to France and invited them to camp at his property and at a disused railway station he and other activists occupied. He has been arrested numerous times, and in 2017 received a four-month suspended prison sentence for aiding migrants to cross the Italian–French border. However, in 2018, the Constitutional Council ruled that the law under which Herrou was convicted did not conform with the constitutional principle of *fraternité*; parliament subsequently changed the law, and a court of cassation annulled Herrou's prison sentence.[27]

In recent years, across Europe, activists assisting irregularised migrants have been taken to court for a variety of offences.[28] Three examples must suffice to demonstrate the range of cases: In 2016, locals in Kirkenes in Norway's far north were prosecuted for trying to prevent the forcible return of asylum seekers who had entered the country from Russia.[29] In 2018, a group in England known as the Stansted 15 were charged with 'endangering airport security' after attempting to stop a deportation flight from London Stansted Airport to West Africa by chaining themselves to the plane.[30] That same year, eleven Belgian citizens, who had hosted or otherwise assisted migrants, were tried for human smuggling offences.[31]

The criminalisation of assistance rendered to irregularised migrants is covered by the EU's controversial Facilitation Directive of 2002, which compels member states to sanction 'any person who intentionally assists a person who is not a national of a Member State to enter, or transit across, the territory of a Member State in breach of the laws of the State concerned on the entry or transit of aliens'.[32] That courts have often thrown out charges levelled at those assisting irregularised migrants is beside the point; public prosecutors' insistence on criminalising solidarity, even though prosecutions often fail, illustrates how aggrieved state authorities have been about such solidarity activism. Also beside the point is the Facilitation Directive's provision that member states 'may decide not to impose sanctions… where the aim of the behaviour is to provide humanitarian assistance to the person concerned',[33] because precisely such assistance has been criminalised even in countries that legislated a humanitarian exception clause.[34]

Of the individuals and groups supporting irregularised migrants at European borders, those involved in private SAR missions in the Mediterranean have been particularly affected by the criminalisation of their activities.[35] NGOs such as Sea-Watch have been accused of deliberately or unwittingly assisting people smugglers and of providing an incentive for migrants to risk the dangerous sea crossing.[36] In Italy, Greece, and Malta, vessels used in SAR missions have been impounded, and captains and crew members indicted for a range of criminal offences, including people smuggling. Consequently, SAR missions have become more complex, time-consuming, and costly, and several NGOs have either suspended their activities or terminated them altogether.

At the same time, the criminalisation of humanitarian activities has motivated some organisations and activists to persevere. Sometimes it has prompted a groundswell of public support, boosting fundraising campaigns. For example, in June 2019, after the arrest in Italy of Carola Rackete, the captain of the *Sea-Watch 3*, a campaign launched by two German television presenters raised more than €1 million in donations for the NGO Sea-Watch, which operated that vessel, within twenty-four hours.[37] The previous year, German activists formed the Seebrücke network to coordinate public support for NGOs that operate SAR vessels in the Mediterranean. They then organised public rallies in most German cities, as well as many smaller towns, in protest against the Italian and Maltese governments' criminalisation of SAR missions and the EU's unwillingness to accommodate rescued migrants.[38]

The criminalisation of humanitarian assistance for irregularised migrants has stoked the antagonism of activists and activist NGOs towards the EU and its member governments, but criminalisation does not sufficiently explain the doggedness with which organisations like Sea-Watch and individuals like Herrou have persisted with their activities. After all, other NGOs, including Save the Children and MOAS, abandoned their SAR missions in the Mediterranean when they were exposed to legal risks. In the next section, I dig deeper to identify the fundamental disagreement at the heart of both certain NGOs' perseverance, and ongoing attempts to criminalise private rescue missions.

Invoking and Recovering International Law

In support of their position, NGOs involved in maritime SAR operations have invoked two bodies of international law.[39] The first is the international law of the sea, as codified in the 1974 International Convention for the Safety of Life at Sea (the so-called SOLAS Convention), the 1979 International Convention on Maritime Search and Rescue (SAR Convention), and the 1982 UN Convention on the Law of the Sea (UNCLOS). These conventions commit all states to ensuring that ships flying their national flags rescue persons in distress; coastal states to providing adequate SAR services; and masters of vessels to rendering assistance to save lives at sea. Although they were drafted only in the past fifty years, the rescue provisions are often portrayed as representing a 'long-standing maritime tradition' (United Nations High Commissioner for Refugees),[40] an 'age-old duty' (Council of Europe Commissioner for Human Rights),[41] an 'ancient custom'[42] or a 'time-honoured rule'.[43] NGOs have put forward three arguments based on the law of the sea: European states are duty-bound to rescue migrants in the Mediterranean; NGO vessels (which operate only because states do not provide adequate SAR services) are similarly obliged to come to the rescue of migrants; and coastal states must allow NGO vessels to disembark those they rescue at a 'place of safety'.[44] The second body of international law that NGOs cite is human rights law, specifically the right to life as enshrined in Article 6(1) of the 1966 International Covenant on Civil and Political Rights (ICCPR): 'Every human being has the inherent right to life. This right shall be protected by law. No one shall be arbitrarily deprived of his life.' NGOs argue that the relevant stipulations of both the law of the sea and international human rights law amount to a right to be rescued.

The European Commission and European governments have side-stepped these accusations. They have neither challenged the supremacy of the right to life—after all, this right also features prominently in relevant European human rights instruments[45]—nor have they disputed that the law of the sea ought to govern the maritime conduct of state and non-state actors. Instead, they have offered two responses. In relation to their own duty to carry out SAR operations, they have suggested that they would always meet their obligations to save lives at sea and had done so in the past. However, such a commitment is immaterial, because since the end of *Mare Nostrum*, European governments have refused to be proactive. Whenever feasible, the EU member states and Frontex have employed planes and drones rather than ships to patrol the relevant areas of the Mediterranean. From March 2019, the EU's *Operation Sophia*, although nominally a *naval* operation tasked with disrupting human smuggling, no longer used naval assets to perform its task.[46] On 17 February 2020, the EU's foreign ministers agreed to launch a new operation that would replace *Sophia* to implement the arms embargo imposed by the UN Security Council in relation to the civil war in Libya. Called *Irini*, this operation commenced on 31 March 2020. It does include navy ships, but 'Ministers agreed that the potential impact on migration flows would be monitored carefully and could, in some cases, lead to the withdrawal of maritime assets from the relevant area.'[47] In other words, as soon as *Irini* incidentally results in the rescue of migrants at sea, its ships may be redeployed in an area away from the routes used by migrant boats, or withdrawn altogether.

The EU's reluctance to become involved in SAR activities does not mean that such activities are outsourced to NGOs. On the contrary, as discussed above, the European Commission and individual governments have impeded the very activities of NGOs that could be a substitute for operations conducted by EU or government agencies. When criminalising NGOs' SAR operations by using domestic legislation, even in cases in which it conflicts with international law, governments have pointed to their commitment to the UN Protocol Against the Smuggling of Migrants (2000), which supplements the UN Convention Against Transnational Organised Crime (2000), and to the EU's resultant policy objectives as formulated in its 2015 Action Plan Against Migrant Smuggling.[48] However, the validity of their argument in relation to the UN Protocol hinges on evidence proving that NGOs rescuing migrants *are* aiding and abetting people smugglers, and so far, governments and state prosecutors have failed to produce such evidence.[49] This means that the only non-domestic legal justification for criminalising SAR operations is the EU's 2002 Facilitation Directive, which, unlike the 2000 UN Protocol, does not specify that the assistance rendered to migrants must be sanctioned *only* if it is done in pursuit of a direct or indirect 'financial or other material benefit'.[50]

The Facilitation Directive and its interpretation by various European governments suggests that for the EU the combating of 'illegal immigration'—and hence also of the 'aiding of illegal immigration'—is a paramount objective.[51] In the context of Europe's southern maritime border, Article 2(1) of the EU's Charter of Fundamental Rights—'Everyone has the right to life'—is an abstract notion; at most, it would come into play now if one of *Irini*'s ships chanced upon migrants at risk of drowning and for some reason could not delegate their rescue to the so-called Libyan coastguard.

The crews of NGO vessels conducting SAR missions do not rely on such chance encounters. They *look for* boats in distress. This is crucial. Itamar Mann has identified the 'legal energy field' created by the prospective rescuer.[52] By looking for boats in distress, the rescuer comes into proximity with the person to be rescued, who otherwise enters a 'maritime legal black hole':[53]

> [C]ome closer to the person at risk, and your privilege to rescue them will transform, due to the rules of the law of the sea, into a duty to do so; the drowning person's *de jure* rightlessness becomes a relationship of rights and duties. The drowning person has a claim upon you.[54]

While the prospective rescuer deliberately seeks proximity to the migrant at risk of drowning, the migrant is also purposefully on the move: away from home or a transit country (and either could mean away from persecution) and towards Europe and a place of safety. Unlike supra-national and national agencies such as the Maltese and Italian coastguards or Frontex, private rescuers do not query migrants' decision to attempt the perilous crossing to Europe, nor do they value some motives (for example, persecution) more highly than others. I suggest that in doing so they are tacitly recognising two other rights that are anathema to European governments. For the NGOs conducting SAR operations, the right to life (and, in turn, the right to be rescued) comes into play only once a migrant has exercised her right to free movement, possibly in order to claim the right to asylum. Neither of the latter has been enshrined in international law. Rather than being recognised as a right, free movement is a privilege accorded to citizens of the global North. Citizens of refugee-producing countries in the global South are least likely to be able to cross international borders freely. According to the authoritative Henley Passport Index, in 2020 a citizen of Japan may travel to 191 countries without a visa, while for citizens of Syria, Afghanistan, and Iraq, visa-free travel is possible only to fewer than 30 countries.[55] There is also no right *to* asylum in international law beyond the non-*refoulement* provisions of the 1951 Refugee Convention.[56] International law recognises only a right *of* asylum, that is, the right of nation-states to grant asylum as they see fit.[57]

The ambit of human rights—encompassing civil and political rights, as well as social, economic and cultural rights—expanded substantially in the last quarter of the twentieth century. It was only in the twenty-first century that the seemingly unstoppable expansion of the human rights agenda came to a crashing halt, reversing some of the gains of the 1980s and 1990s. However, this widely acknowledged account of human rights' progress and decline is complicated by the fact that the two human rights mentioned above—the right to asylum and the right to free movement—never became part of the breakthrough of the human rights agenda in the 1970s. The former featured in an early draft of the 1948 Universal Declaration of Human Rights (UDHR) and it was included in the watered-down text finally approved by the UN General Assembly in December 1948, only to be omitted from the 1966 ICCPR. The push for a convention that would enshrine the right to asylum in international law continued from the 1940s until the 1970s, but eventually failed in 1977, when a conference of plenipotentiaries could not agree on a text.[58] Rather than including a right to free movement, the UDHR and the ICCPR feature a right to leave, and return to, one's country, and a right to free movement within the borders of each state;[59] but neither instrument makes reference to the right to enter a country of which one is not a citizen.[60]

For both rights, the UDHR represented a watershed. The discussions of the draft Universal Declaration suggest that the omission of these rights was not a foregone conclusion. Advocates of the rights to free movement and asylum were eventually outvoted, but not until after they had made their case. For example, during the discussion of the right to emigrate, the Chilean delegation said that a broader freedom of movement was 'the sacred right of every human being', while the Haitian delegate stressed that the world belongs to all humankind; also speaking against any restrictions, the Belgian representative said that 'The ideal would be a return to a time when men could travel the world armed with nothing but a visiting card.'[61] While for most other human rights the UDHR marked the beginning of their codification in international law, for the rights to free movement and asylum the UDHR represented a step back, because previously (and particularly before the advent of the modern nation-state and the introduction of effective border controls), both had been widely, albeit informally, recognised.

At stake here is the question of whether—to use Liisa Malkki's words—the 'national order of things' is the 'natural order of things', or whether the primacy of the nation-state's sovereignty is recognised as a comparatively recent innovation.[62] The claims of NGOs performing SAR operations derive their traction from a history according to which the obligations vis-à-vis people at danger of drowning, the right to asylum, and the right to free movement, have a tradition eclipsing that of the modern nation-state.

'Disobedience for Human Rights!'

In March 2020, Seebrücke, the German network that has advocated on behalf of NGOs engaged in SAR activities and demanded that Angela Merkel's government accept migrants rescued in the Mediterranean and from camps in Libya and Greece, published a statement under the heading 'Open the borders! Save lives! Disobedience for human rights!' It called on its supporters to engage in civil disobedience if the German government did not heed the call to evacuate migrants from Greece: 'picket the Greek consulates and party offices, disrupt traffic, disturb the racist everyday life in German ministries!'.[63] I suspect Seebrücke took its cue from former *Sea-Watch 3* captain and Extinction Rebellion activist Carola Rackete, who dedicated her book about the events that led to her arrest in June 2019 'to all victims of civil obedience'.[64] The book highlights the role that civil *dis*obedience can play. 'We are living at a time when the existing order is wrong and destructive. It *has* to be disrupted, because otherwise people die', Rackete writes.[65] She encourages her readers to act, rather than to hope 'that we will get our right and our future, if only we please those who are at this point still in power'.[66]

The civil disobedience of private rescuers operating in the Mediterranean can take various forms. For example, they may disregard instructions from a particular government not to enter its country's territorial waters or not to disembark rescued migrants. Rackete's decision to disobey the Italian authorities on both those counts led to her arrest in 2019. But involvement in search and rescue efforts in the Mediterranean more generally, once considered the responsibility of national governments and EU agencies, could now

119

also qualify as a form of civil disobedience. Maurice Stierl has made this point with regard to WatchTheMed's Alarm Phone initiative, set up by private citizens as an emergency hotline for migrants trying to reach Europe by sea. Drawing on Lorenzo Pezzani's and Charles Heller's discussion of 'Forensic Oceanography', Stierl writes that the founders of WatchTheMed regarded it as 'a tool that would open up the ambivalent and often violent Mediterranean borderzone and sub-ject it to a "disobedient gaze", one that could potentially democratise a highly undemocratic space'.[67]

The decision to call for and practise civil disobedience is prompted by the perception that there is an emergency and that people might die at sea or at Europe's borders, and the belief that governments are not just wrong but that they are violating human rights and interna-tional law. Opposition to government policies in such circumstances can be seen as legitimate even if it falls foul of domestic law. In her book, Rackete writes that public debate often treats the legitimacy of search and rescue as a 'matter of opinion'.[68] 'This is fundamentally incorrect', she argues; referring to Article 98 of UNCLOS, she sug-gests that search and rescue is mandated by international law.[69] Elsewhere she rejects interpretations of her disobedience of Italian government edicts as either a crime or an act of heroism; she insists that she merely carried out her duty to save lives.[70] NGOs claim to have justice, if not the law, on their side—to the extent that they anticipate that history will prove them right. In that sense, the com-parison with the 'underground railroad' is particularly apt: with the benefit of hindsight we know that slavery was eventually to become not only illegitimate but also unlawful. NGOs can also claim that their activities are informed by principles, values, and rights that may have been temporarily suspended by states but have not lost their validity; such as the principle of *fraternité* in France, the value of solidarity that is foundational to the European project, or the right to asylum which was recognised as far back as in ancient Greece.[71]

In his 1971 *A Theory of Justice*, John Rawls, drawing on the philoso-pher Hugo Bedau, defines civil disobedience as a 'public, nonviolent, conscientious yet political act contrary to law usually done with the aim of bringing about a change in the law or policies of the govern-ment'.[72] For Rawls, this act is 'guided and justified by… the principles of justice which regulate the constitution and social institutions generally'; it 'expresses disobedience to law *within the limits of fidelity to law*, although at the outer edges thereof'.[73] This latter idea was also shared by political theorists who did not subscribe to the 'circumscribed reformism' inherent in Rawls' account, where civil disobedience 'served as a corrective to violations of basic civil and political but not social or economic rights'.[74]

William Scheuerman observes that for Rawls, '[f]idelity to the law meant fidelity to the legal order of specific "nearly just" (nation-state) constitutional democracies' and that in fact his 'exposition directly reproduced the Westphalian premise of a strict divide between domestic and international affairs'.[75] The 'transnational maritime civil disobedience'[76] practised by Rackete and other solidarity activists is still guided and justified by what Rawls calls 'principles of justice'—but these can no longer be located within the legal framework of a particular nation-state. Disobedient private rescuers are in fact able to play off international law—including the 'ancient customs' of the international law of the sea, and human rights that derive their traction not from their codification but from their extensive pedigree—against domestic law. That allows them also to dispense with the reformist strictures inherent in Rawls' understanding of civil disobedience, and to pose a fundamental challenge to nation-states' legal order.

In the previous section I have suggested that in order to appreciate the significance of the encounter in the Mediterranean between the private rescuers and the migrants in distress, it is important to keep in mind that both parties are on the move: the former looking for and approaching the migrants, and the latter trying to reach a place of safety.[77] The migrants' right to be rescued can be brought to life because of the rescuers' proximity; the rescuers' embrace of, and advocacy for, an expansive notion of human rights is informed by the migrants' agency in a world where a right to free movement is considered a 'natural' impossibility. The rescuers' civil disobedience may also be inspired by the preparedness of migrants—people who embark on the hazardous journey across the Mediterranean in the hope of entering Europe without a visa, or those who move between European countries in defiance of the Dublin Regulations—to violate

European laws. Admittedly, many migrants risk their lives as well as break the law for lack of choice, but neither implies a lack of initiative. Besides, government authorities rarely perceive migrants' crossing of Europe's external and internal borders as an involuntary act. Their strong and at times hysterical response to undocumented migration—and to assistance provided to irregularised migrants— suggests that they tend to view the unauthorised crossing of the Mediterranean as a wilful violation of Europe's borders, and as a real threat to the sovereignty of nation-states.

The agency of migrants on the move, as well as their defiance of the borders meant to keep them out, shapes the relationship between rescuer and rescued, and between givers and recipients of humanitarian assistance. Migrants who are perceived as people with agency are less likely regarded as victims dependent on the benevolence of a potential saviour. Rather than responding to irregularised migrants with compassion (which always implies a hierarchical relationship between those extending it and its object), humanitarian actors in the Mediterranean, as well as in the Roya Valley, respond with solidarity. It is significant, and a result of the politics that informs their activism, that NGOs such as Sea-Watch and SOS MEDITERRANEE draw on the discourses of solidarity, rights, and justice when soliciting donations and political support, and avoid conventional humanitarian appeals to compassion.

Luis Cabrera, among others, has claimed that migrants' legal transgressions, including their violations of the integrity of borders, also amount to civil disobedience.[78] This is certainly true for transgressions that take place in full public view. A good example here is the walk of migrants from Budapest towards Austria at the height of the so-called refugee crisis of 2015.[79] Many public protests by irregularised migrants also qualify as civil disobedience.[80] The covert crossing of a border, on the other hand, while a violation of laws that are unjust, should not be regarded as an act of civil disobedience.[81] It could be argued, however, that the rescue of migrants by private search and rescue missions turns a covert action into a public (and often well-publicised) event; that is, qua their rescue, migrants retrospectively engage in civil disobedience. This argument could be taken one step further. If, as Hannah Arendt has suggested, civil disobedience is associative—that is, if it not only requires a group of like-minded individuals but also is constitutive of the group—then an act such as the violation of Italian law by the *Sea-Watch 3* in June 2019 unites rescuers and rescued in a performance of civil disobedience.[82]

Conclusion

I began this chapter with a note of caution, which I would like to reiterate: The 'model of humanitarian engagement' discussed here is specific to those groups that assist irregularised migrants as they attempt to cross national borders. It is also new—at least as new as the securitisation of the borders of the global North, irregularised migrants' assertion of their rights, and the emergence of a cosmopolitanism that recognises these rights; the 'radical humanism' of those conducting SAR missions in the late 1970s and early 1980s in the South China Sea was qualitatively different from the humanitarianism of organisations such as SOS MEDITERRANEE.[83] This is not to say that it all began with Cédric Herrou and Carola Rackete. In the Central Mediterranean, Sea-Watch and SOS MEDITERRANEE were preceded by the crew of the *Cap Anamur*. In 2004, although working for a conventional humanitarian NGO, they saved the lives of thirty-seven migrants trying to cross the Mediterranean. Their ship was impounded, and they were tried before an Italian court.[84]

The humanitarianism of SAR activists is specific also because it is shaped by their encounter with irregularised migrants. The fact that they are purposefully moving away from places of persecution or despair and towards places of safety, their agency, and their violation of national laws determine the nature of humanitarian assistance offered by activist NGOs. At the same time, the rescuers' proactive approach, which makes them look for migrants in distress, activates migrants' right to be rescued, and the act of rescue turns a covert activity into an act of civil disobedience. More broadly, I would like to suggest that we may want to think of the relationship between rescuer and rescued not only as one between a humanitarian actor and a (passive) recipient of humanitarian assistance, but also in terms of its associative and productive qualities.

By assisting migrants who cross national borders without authorisation, NGOs such as Sea-Watch are—correctly—perceived by European governments to be challenging the prerogative of nation-states to regulate access to their territory. Governments, regardless of their political persuasion, hold that national sovereignty, which finds its expression in states' right to control their borders, trumps other rights claims, whereas NGOs undertaking SAR missions in the Mediterranean argue that the prerogative of nation-states to deal with non-citizens as they see fit is curtailed by international law, specifically the law of the sea and human rights law. The positions of NGOs and European governments—about the extent and nature of human rights, but also about the legitimacy of an international system of territorially bounded nation-states—are, in the last instance, irreconcilable. The 'new model of humanitarian engagement' thus challenges a fundamental tenet of this system.

The new model of humanitarian engagement may also allow us to rethink some taken-for-granted 'truths', whereby the 'national order' gets confused with the 'natural order'. 'The state system under which we live is one based on and produced by such distinctions: between domestic and foreign, inside and outside, us and them, here and there', Jenny Edkins observes in *Change and the Politics of Certainty*. 'To take these distinctions for granted is already to frame the whole debate in a way that leads inexorably towards a solution supportive of state sovereignty.'[85] The case of NGOs like SOS MEDITERRANEE seems to suggest that the reverse might also hold: once state sovereignty is challenged 'from below', it becomes easier not to rely on these binary categories mentioned by Edkins, to approach strangers not as others, and to practise solidarity rather than extend compassion.

PART TWO

THE PRACTICE OF HUMANITARIAN POLITICS

8

THE LEGITIMATION CRISIS
OF THE LIBERAL ORDER

POLITICAL MINIMALISM, HUMANITARIANISM,
AND THE GOVERNMENT OF INEQUALITY

Simon Reid-Henry

Introduction

The international order constructed after the Second World War was intended to promote and protect 'liberal' values. Free enterprise was to be underpinned by individual liberties and property rights. The sovereign integrity of national states was to be upheld by international law. Rules-based international institutions were to govern these political and economic relations. Yet as numerous critics have pointed out, the liberal order that resulted always turned more on the 'order' part than on its ostensible 'liberalism'. And when push came to shove, as often it did during the Cold War, it was international authority—and US hegemony in particular—that mattered more than any counterpart commitments to human rights. Arguably, therefore, the liberal international order has never been either as liberal or as openly internationalist as its proponents like to claim—even during the post-Cold War years of the so-called 'democratic peace' when a 'real new world order' of transnational cooperation briefly surfaced as the focus of liberal international thought.[1]

But rather than critique liberal internationalism for what it is not, or for what it has failed to be, I want in this chapter to take the normative aspirations of liberal internationalism at face value. In particular I want to enquire into the roots of liberalism's 'vision' for the world in the post-1945 era. Doing so opens up a rather different vista onto the present crisis of the liberal international order: one focused less on what has risen to 'challenge' it in recent years (to wit, a now lengthy literature on the rise of illiberal democracies and the decline of multilateralism) and more on the contradictions and tensions that emerged within liberalism as it engaged with a changing world.[2] In particular I want to examine how a more conservative—'defensive'—form of liberalism, that feared and opposed such projects as the redistribution of wealth and political power, but which equally stood firm on the need to promote the interests of democracy (understood narrowly as political freedom) abroad, emerged to shape the post-1945 international order. I propose that we understand this more reductive disposition within liberalism as an ethos: the ethos of 'political minimalism'.

By adopting the term 'ethos' I mean to highlight that at stake here is something less coherent than a doctrine, or a fixed ideological position, or even the sort of 'intellectual style' of Richard Hofstadter's imagining; and yet the shadow that political minimalism has cast upon liberal thinking is real and can be found in some of the most influential ideas and intellectual currents of the twentieth century.[3] For reasons that we shall see, political minimalism is most clearly articulated in American liberal thought and practice, and as part of the mid-century reimagination of liberalism that took place during these years of greatest American hegemony.

Political scientists have sometimes adopted the term political minimalism as shorthand for the 'nightwatchman state' itself, protecting a core set of human rights such as to property and civil and political liberties.[4] But here I am thinking more specifically of the normative or ethical sentiments that underpin such liberal claims as these, and out of which more formal concepts and ideological positions are subsequently constructed, either by individuals or within groups. Hence, an ethos: in this case an ethos whose dispositions lean towards minimising the risks of governmental authority. One of political minimalism's characteristic features, for example, is a rejection of the view that personal freedom must be balanced in some way by the demands of equality.[5] Since such a narrowed vision of 'the good' requires actively defending, the result is often paradoxically a defensive antagonism. A concrete example of this, in the US context, would be Cold War Liberalism: that body of conservative thought which advanced the idea that to make America safe at home required defending it actively abroad. But in what follows I want to explore political minimalism as something that in fact feeds into a range of liberal '-isms'.

To examine how this ethos took shape in the post-1945 era in particular, the remainder of this essay takes the form of three short sketches that together, I hope, trace out something of the arc of political minimalism's emergence and influence within liberal thought, and allow us to say something about its role in the crisis of liberal internationalism today. The first sketch reconsiders the triumphalist narrative of the post-1945 moment via the writing of one of the postwar era's clearest-thinking liberals, Judith Shklar. Through Shklar's eyes we see political minimalism begin to take shape amidst the crisis of liberalism in the early to mid-twentieth century, as an intellectual project formed in response to totalising theories of political life elsewhere, notably fascism and communism. Political minimalism can be approached, via this first sketch, as a distinctive element of the postwar liberal rejection of utopia. Tracking forward to the late Cold War and immediate post-Cold War moment (broadly speaking the 1970s to 1990s) our second sketch sees political minimalism receive its institutional moment of breakthrough: both domestically on the back of the retrenchment of New Deal liberalism and the welfare state, and internationally on the back of the dramatic rise of a plethora of international courts and tribunals based upon human rights and international law (via the emergence of what is sometimes called 'humanity law').[6] Both developments were geared to the protection of political rather than economic freedoms: to weeding out political, not socioeconomic violence in the world, in other words. Our third sketch examines some of the basic challenges to this entrenched politically minimalist approach to international order today. What I hope we may by then be able to see is the extent to which the current moment of crisis is not simply a crisis of liberal internationalism's protagonists and institutions; it is also a crisis of liberal intentions, beliefs, and ideas more broadly.

I. Political Minimalism Ascendant

At the close of the Second World War, the Western powers and the US in particular were granted the opportunity to reimagine liberalism and liberal institutions on a new, transnational scale. Victory in the war, for all that it relied upon the assistance of Soviet and colony forces, was understood (perhaps above all in the US) to represent a universal, global victory for liberal democratic regimes: an understanding soon mobilised through the building of an Atlantic-centred postwar architecture.[7] That architecture took the form of the newly christened United Nations system, and the organisations of international economic rule centred upon the Bretton Woods institutions. This institutionalisation of postwar liberal internationalism took place (and it was also contested) on a variety of fronts, from the Havana Charter (1948) addressing questions of world trade, to the mutual defence pact enshrined in NATO (1949), to the Treaty of Rome (1957) establishing the European Economic Community (EEC), to the Yaoundé Convention (1963) establishing a free trade agreement between that recently formed EEC and newly independent African nations, and more besides. In such ways, the Atlantic-based liberal international order articulated the victor nations' desire to spring forward into economic prosperity and to thereby also leave behind the upheavals and destruction of the recent past.

While much writing has focused on the first of these two impulses, and the so-called 'golden age' of economic growth and rising prosperity that ensued, the work of Judith Shklar (1928–1992) gives us good reason to focus also on the latter: at least if we want to understand what particular elements of 'liberalism' it was that placed themselves at the heart of that emergent international order. Born in Latvia, from where she was forced to emigrate at the start of the war, Shklar studied first in Montreal and then at Harvard in the late 1940s and early 1950s. Along with the likes of France's Raymond Aron and Isaiah Berlin in Great Britain, Shklar is often, and rightly, thought of as a 'Cold War liberal'. Her liberalism was certainly world-weary and negatively inclined: a 'liberalism of fear' as she would later put it, geared most strongly, and understandably, to the defence of the individual and minorities—a politics of pluralism as against conformist majoritarianism and the state, we might say. But perhaps more than any other liberal thinker, and certainly more so than her Cold War liberal confrères, including Hannah Arendt, Shklar was well attuned to the limitations of liberalism's political prescriptions: at least at the beginning of her career, and perhaps also at its end. Indeed, it is Shklar's first book, *After Utopia* (1957), that first cracks a self-conscious window onto political minimalism in the ascendant.

Written amidst the early years of the liberal international order's founding, Shklar's book provides a penetrating critique of the post war moment as one of 'general political fatigue'.[8] *After Utopia* is not a book about the Cold War itself, however, nor even really about the early twentieth-century's 'age of extremes' that gave onto it. It is a book about what liberalism—and liberals—think they believe: and above all, what they don't. In particular it is an effort to understand why they no longer believe in utopia.[9] For Shklar, as Samuel Moyn has noted,

> Liberalism was at fault for approximating and indeed incorporating the hatred of Enlightenment of its own historic adversaries. It was most of all to blame for the Cold War syndrome of renouncing the Enlightenment, treating the state as congenitally oppressive and democracy as a recipe for totalitarianism unless the first was minimized and the second qualified.[10]

As Shklar herself put it: [L]iberalism has become unsure of its moral basis, as well as increasingly defensive and conservative.' And it is not long after this that Shklar's own 'bare bones' liberalism would go on to encapsulate this Cold War liberalism of restraint. As she later put it in her essay 'The Liberalism of Fear', there is no *summum bonum* in human life, all we have is 'the *summum malam* which all of us know and would avoid if only we could. That evil is cruelty and the fear it inspires'.[11] And yet: prior to her joining the ranks of the Cold War liberals, Shklar is adamant too, at least at this early point in her thinking, that 'without a minimum of utopian faith, no radicalism is meaningful'—and moreover that, possessing no such faith, liberals in particular have given over to an inward and defensive-oriented conservatism.[12] Why then, we might ask, as she did, were liberals now—at this very point, postwar—presenting themselves as the beacon of political progress internationally if they did not really believe in it themselves?

The tempting answer, of course, would be the usual chessboard reckonings of geopolitical punditry: in this case, the felt need of US liberals in particular to counter the 'rise' of the Soviet Union. But this takes our eyes away from developments within liberalism itself when, like Shklar, we should be keeping them there. For what Shklar's account of nineteenth-century liberalism ultimately reveals is a political tradition so concerned to define itself against the previous era's wayward projects of emancipation that it ended up rejecting a positive vision of politics altogether in favour of a narrower, negative focus on the defence of liberty as the primary task of any legitimate political system: and no more. Such a minimalist vision was inherently vulnerable to alternatives that sought to do 'more', however, and so required 'securing' by means of force as well. Hence Truman's 'four freedoms' speech of 1945, delivered just a few months before war's end, which framed this new internationalism as a largely negative enterprise based upon the core freedoms (of speech and of religion, and from want and from fear). Truman's international agenda also fired a starting gun for a newly internationalist policy waged by the United States in pursuit of those four freedoms: which, in turn, would lead the United States into escalating security commitments spanning the globe. Development and militarism thus went hand in hand, crucially—and this is often overlooked—with liberal freedoms prioritised over democratic equality in both. Hence, as the night-watchman state went looking for spectres to slay in the dark, a conservative counter-movement to the New Deal era's progressivism thus now also gained its mobilising mission: to wit, on the domestic front, the passing of the National Security Act (in 1947) to protect Americans' political freedoms—a complement, but also a notable contrast, as the coming era of McCarthyism would show, to the earlier Social Security Act (1935) of the post-Depression era, which set out to improve their socioeconomic status.

Shklar's identification of this defensive turn at the heart of postwar liberal thinking, for all she does not focus on the making of postwar internationalism herself, thus helps us to locate the ground that political minimalism would come to occupy. Not least she is attuned to the fact that, in order to uphold the primacy of a negative form of liberty as the only acceptable social end for politics (an understanding that Isaiah Berlin would, the very next year, in 1958, provide the requisite terminology for), an emergent, inward-looking, and defensive form of liberalism needed actively 'securing', both at home and abroad—and via force when need be. Here, the emergent Cold War struggle between the 'empire of justice' and the 'empire of liberty' as Odd Arne Westad has put it, did indeed supply a fitting vehicle.[13] Political minimalism, in other words, emerged as something of a *paradox* at the heart of US political liberalism, and this was why it could only ever really exist *as* a disposition—as a *sense* of what the political should be—rather than a reasoned ideological standpoint. As we shall see, more overtly ideological standpoints soon emerged in its image. But what drove this ethos itself forward, in the context of the deepening Cold War, was mid-twentieth-century US liberalism's need to colour its otherwise near complete rejection of utopia with the most minimal level of 'ought'. And this ought was centred upon a philosophy of liberty shorn of the encroachments of equality.[14]

The term ethos was a favourite of another important figure in our story: Reinhold Niebuhr (1892–1971), a theologian and public intellectual born a generation before Shklar. For Niebuhr, an ethos was 'a combination of dispositions, temperament and perceptions… determining the quality of political action'.[15] It was a shared and usually implicit inclination, in other words, reflected in his view that there was no Christian political system per se so much as a Christian attitude *to* political systems.[16] Niebuhr's thought and career was itself the product of his Christian-inflected liberal standpoint. But he became ever more pragmatic in the manner in which he sought to ringfence what he saw as liberal democracy's achievements in America, by the projection of force to secure the basic and fundamental good of liberty (even if this came at the expense of the more emancipatory project of equality). In contrast to Shklar, therefore, Niebuhr does not so much allow us to see political minimalism as he embodies it.

In many respects, in fact, it is Niebuhr's growing influence in the interwar era that offers a first glimpse of the ethos of political minimalism in the making. Writing in 1932, during the tumultuous interwar years, with fascism, Nazism, and communism ascendant in Europe, Niebuhr made it clear that liberal democracy was the best of all available political systems—certainly the most likely to achieve real social justice—and, given that, he was of the view that political violence may need to be entertained in its defence. 'It may be necessary at times to sacrifice a degree of moral purity for political effectiveness', as he put it in his *Moral Man and Immoral Society* that year.[17] Niebuhr had long kept a close eye on developments in Europe and he found himself lecturing in Great Britain when war broke out in 1939. Soon afterwards he returned to a United States that he could scarcely believe was committed still to non-intervention, resigned his membership of the (still pacifist) Socialist Party, and by 1941 'had renounced both radicalism and pacifism in pursuit of an achievable, moral foreign policy—achievable because of its limited goals, and moral for its recognition that the US, with its vast power and resources, could be an effective agent for good in securing it'.[18]

Here, in effect, was the ethos of political minimalism in action: a prioritisation of the need to protect and support liberty within liberalism before even the equality that Niebuhr had previously argued was freedom's necessary twin (as he still did, when pragmatism did not forbid it, and 'vital interests' were not at stake). From this point on, Niebuhr's increasingly defensive commitment to democracy outweighed his earlier pacifist reluctance to defend it through force, culminating in the carefully qualified support he offered in defence of the nuclear bombing of Hiroshima, and his later argument justifying the use of nuclear arms against the Soviet Union.[19] In the process, the moral grounds for subsequent reincarnations of 'just war' doctrines and responsibility-to-protect mandates could be glimpsed emerging within the contemporary liberal imagination. This is hardly undermined by Niebuhr's later antipathy to the war in Vietnam: indeed, it was Niebuhr's historically informed conviction that Vietnam was neither a just nor a necessary war that led him to be critical of it.

Until President Obama announced him to have been his favourite philosopher some years ago, few people had paid much attention to Niebuhr in recent decades. But in the early to mid-century, his ideas exerted considerable influence on American domestic politics. This was the man, after all, who in the words of Kenneth Thompson 'helped shape a whole generation of political observers and practitioners' in America, including foreign policy heavyweights like George Kennan and Hans Morgenthau.[20] In a manner that some of these other thinkers shared, Niebuhr thought it short-sighted to focus only on the national imperative, and in such ways concerns about the international sphere were incorporated into political minimalism from the start. Hence, he favoured America having a *limited* engagement with the world internationally: limited, we are to presume, not in the meaning of 'restrained' (though as his 1930 *Atlantic Monthly* essay, 'Awkward Imperialists', made clear, he was no devotee of the doctrine of American exceptionalism) but in the meaning of 'narrow in scope'. By the end of the Second World War, then, and before Shklar's encapsulation of the problem in *After Utopia*, figures like Niebuhr were manning the ramparts of a defensive liberalism that had consciously relinquished utopia (as politically dangerous), yet which sought to retain the use of political violence more specifically to support a newly expansive politics of liberalism's recently narrowed definition of freedom. Consider, for example, the primary contribution of another Niebuhr acolyte, Paul Nitze—lead author of the influential NSC-68 (1950), which pushed the US towards its policy of containment of the USSR's 'hostile design' and its countervailing 'building up of the political, economic, and military strength of the free world'.[21] Niebuhr, via his Christian commitment to democracy, had in effect provided the conservative and anti-utopian liberalism insightfully identified by Shklar's account with a distinctly more interventionary mandate and a normative tinge.

Niebuhr is a pivotal character in the development of political minimalism. But this ethos was also powerfully expressed within some of the new liberal intellectual currents and ideological movements that took shape at around this time. Two of the most influential of these give us a sense of the intellectual and political range across which political minimalism held. First was the postwar school of thinking about international relations known as political realism, embodied by liberal foreign policy thinkers such as Hans Morgenthau (the author, amongst other works, of *Politics Among Nations*: a landmark publication in US foreign policy circles), who argued that interest and power are the primary concerns of international relations and national states the principal actors. In the United States, political realism was to become the establishment position throughout the Cold War. Political realism traded on its 'rationalist' credentials and made the 'hard decisions' of statesmen (callous though they may have been) seem like the height of political virtue. Yet statesmen, no less than political realism's own leading figures, such as Morgenthau, were hardly free of moral commitments, which meant that political minimalism's foregrounding of freedom as an 'apolitical' political value was useful here. Might may be right, in other words, but if it was to be responsibly wielded, if a liberal democracy such as America was legitimately to lay claim to the use of political violence at the 'end' of the age of empires, in the aftermath of the Second World War, and as a counterpart to the totalitarian state, then that violence would need to be severed from anything that looked like being an ideological programme; instead its normative girding could be founded upon a narrow and formal commitment to freedom.

The other doctrine within which the ethos of political minimalism gained concrete expression at this time was neoliberalism. One of the celebrated figures in early 'neo' liberal thought, the Austrian economist F. A. Hayek, argued for the moral primacy of individuals as against centralised visions of 'society' and the removal of intrusive state regulations on the economy. Despite what is often assumed and written about him, however, Hayek never really called for a 'minimal state'.[22] He did not call for a laissez-faire order either, and, along with many other neoliberals, he was against social liberalism too. In fact, what Hayek and the early neoliberals sought to pursue was precisely a way out of what they perceived as liberalism's then current impasse, caught between a laissez-faire variant that had proven futile before totalitarian alternatives in the interwar era, and a social liberalism, embodied in Roosevelt's New Deal programme in the US, that sought to extend the benefits of liberal freedoms to greater numbers of people.[23] Hayek was more interested in building a pro-market legal and political architecture that would itself sustain purely market-based social relations (relations based upon competition between private interests): and *that* project required the whip hand of the state and the power of the law when need be. The history of what these 'neo' liberals around Hayek did about this impasse—their effort to renew liberalism by taking it in a new direction via the work of the Centre International d'Études pour la Rénovation du Libéralisme (CIRL), established after the influential Walter Lippmann Colloquium in Paris in 1938—is another, and a well told story.[24] The point I want to make here is simply to note how the construction of 'neo' liberalism at this moment also gave concrete expression to the ethos of political minimalism.

Indeed, Hayek's justificatory armature in much of his writing conforms to political minimalism no less than does Niebuhr's writing from across the political aisle. Niebuhr sought to protect social liberalism; Hayek to do away with it. But the two figures shared an anti-totalitarian commitment and each characteristically—if for different reasons—sought to strip away ambitions of equality in favour of a (supposedly) ideologically denuded, and so politically 'safer', account of freedom. Niebuhr and his political realist acolytes fretted over how to reimagine the liberal state; Hayek and his neoliberal confrères fretted over how to reimagine the market (largely by countenancing a shift from markets as mechanisms of allocation *within* society to markets as a medium *for* society rooted in the principle of competition). Shklar had in fact picked up on precisely this in the 1950s. For, as she laid out in *After Utopia*, neoliberals like Hayek (she mentions both Hayek and Wilhelm Röpke), no less than the likes of Niebuhr, saw twentieth-century totalitarianism as the product of a wayward nineteenth-century liberalism, and they intended to rectify this by a flattening of political space in which law and economics—not the moral critique that leads to utopia—would shepherd individuals towards a political order free of the contusions of democratic politics. Their mistake was to succumb to an 'intellectual determinism' that ruled out the very pluralism upon which democracy depends.[25] At the same time, as the international relations scholar Nicolas Guilhot has observed, her mentor Carl Friedrich was saying more or less exactly the same of political realists.[26] The effect, as Guilhot goes on to say, was an increasingly influential metanarrative which assumed that 'public opinion was essentially irrational' and that freedom was best preserved not by maximising those popular capacities but through the measured action of experts.[27] Thus did political minimalism's anti-democratic instincts find concrete expression through the twin political programmes of political realism and neoliberalism.[28]

Revisiting Shklar's work directs us towards recognising the grounds upon which neoliberalism and political realism could align during these years (each being, as Guilhot notes, and as we have seen, a reaction to their nineteenth-century forebears and the crisis of liberalism in the 1930s): grounds which had less to do with the promotion of real individual autonomy for persons than with freedom itself as an anti-utopian teleological value. Neoliberalism thus becomes important as a body of thinking not just for what it sought to do to democracy in the name of the economy, but for what it helped do to transform the place of utopian thinking in mid-century liberalism; likewise, political realism matters as a body of thinking not simply for the way it influenced US foreign policy over half a century, but for what it *also* did to put liberalism's new relationship to utopia into practice. These were two predominantly conservative movements. But the terms of political minimalism were conveyed on the liberal-progressive side as well, including by Niebuhr's Christian ethics—rendering it something that both sides of the political centre ground could converge around.

Indeed, for all that it was Christian thought which had helped animate the ethos of political minimalism, a more secular (and self-styled centre-progressive) variant soon also began to spring up in domestic liberal thinking, thanks to the role played, amongst others, by another figure that Niebuhr influenced, Arthur Schlesinger, Jr. As Richard Aldous writes in his biography of Schlesinger, this historian of the Kennedy years, and intellectual-at-large within that decisive and fateful administration, was drawn to Niebuhr's writings for their 'arguments about... how man's wickedness made government both essential and dangerous'. Schlesinger himself was soon arguing, not for 'the creation of an ideal society in which there will be uncoerced and perfect peace and justice, but a society in which there will be enough justice, and in which coercion will be sufficiently *non-violent* to prevent [our] common enterprise from issuing into complete disaster'.[29] On this basis Schlesinger constructed his hugely influential notion of *The Vital Center*, published as the book of that name in 1949: one of the founding documents of postwar US domestic liberalism.

Here, then, we find a further expression of the ethos of political minimalism as I am trying to understand it, this time on the domestic political stage and via Schlesinger's attempt to *secure* liberty at large by minimising the state interventions required to ensure liberty is maintained. As the Cold War steadily took hold of the liberal political imagination in the United States, this desire to 'secure' a narrower vision of freedom, once again excised from its counterpart of equality, became more and more dogmatically pursued, because it was taken to be fundamental to the very survival of liberal democratic politics itself. With Schlesinger, any such dogma was hidden under the rubric of 'consensus'. But he was far from the only mid-century liberal intellectual peddling such a line. The likes of Hofstadter, Arendt, and others too felt this line was in just the right place, amidst a deepening great power struggle between communism and capitalism internationally. In such ways the global Cold War struggle inflected the national political scene as well (Schlesinger's *Vital Center*, for example, was premised in part on the idea that saving the achievements of the New Deal required the *exclusion* of the radical left at home as well as abroad).[30]

Political minimalism as it emerged, then, was about a good deal more (and perhaps also less) than simple sufficientarianism, as political philosophers would later label the philosophy of providing a base level of social protections but nothing more. On my reading, it was—and still is—a prioritisation of a specifically negative form of liberty on the grounds of avoiding the worst of all possible outcomes: the tyranny of the state and the erosion of the individual as the moral centre of political life. In other words, taken to its extremes, political minimalism must ultimately pitch liberalism against democracy itself, while to justify its deployment of the very powers of the state it claims to distrust in its defence of liberty, it must remain resolutely anti-utopian. In liberal thought, the scalpel of political violence must be wielded cleanly, too, and that means taking it out of the hands of the people to decide. This three-fold characteristic defines the essence of political minimalism today.

139

And yet, ironically, all this was first being consolidated at the very moment that new social forms, from new social movements to non-governmental and civil society sector actors, were emerging as a new and dynamic element to democratic politics domestically. These alternative voices too were instinctively reaching out internationally at this moment: their future being to some extent overwritten by a defensive and increasingly hegemonic liberalism's projection onto the world of its own fears born of the past. In such ways, then, was America's early twentieth-century promise to make the world safe for democracy realised in practice, by the mid-twentieth century, as a programme in fact geared towards making democracy safe for America, by curating its adoption elsewhere in the world. The result was indeed more about 'order' than it was about 'liberalism': it was about consolidating political authority in the name of freedom.

II. Political Minimalism Between the National and the International Stage

The foregoing outlines the emergence of political minimalism as a mid-century current in liberal political thinking. The second task I set for this essay was to examine how this ethos of political minimalism, as a retrenchment of liberal utopianism in the domestic United States wedded to the effort to restrain social liberalism within its representative (liberal democratic) national form, later becomes an organising framework, paradoxically, for the *re-enchantment* of liberalism at the international scale. To illustrate the switch between the two we might usefully here refer to another influential liberal, John Rawls. In particular, his 1971 *Theory of Justice* provides, I think, a way to understand how political minimalism connects the domestic and the international scales in liberal thinking. In particular, it will be useful here to approach Rawls while keeping Shklar's critique still in mind. For while Shklar may have been sceptical of such efforts as by Rawls to find an 'overlapping consensus' within whose bounds all reasonably pluralist individuals might come to accept the same basic institutions for the regulation of society,[31] Rawls' effort to institutionally prioritise the defence of what he called 'the basic liberties' chimed with Shklar's own later 'negative egalitarianism' and the generally more defensive direction in which US liberal political thought had been travelling since the war. Shklar may not have had much time for expansive talk about 'the popular will' and deliberative reason, or for the legal formalism that characterises procedural accounts of justice, but she agreed with Rawls that political institutions ought to be directed towards reducing the negative effects of inequality.[32] The real reason for turning to John Rawls, however, is to uncover how the early to mid-century ethos of political minimalism was, in the 1970s, refashioned once more and projected out on to the international context. Rawls, who had begun his studies focusing on Christian thought, thereby bringing to his *Theory of Justice* some of the same preoccupations as Niebuhr, provides us with an illuminating bridge between the two moments.[33]

There are two basic observations to make here. The first concerns the fact that Rawls seems to operate in his *Theory of Justice* largely *without* a reckoning with forms of violence. More than that, he does not really even consider violence in any great depth. Rawls uses the word violence five times in the original text of *A Theory of Justice*. One of those times he is quoting Locke on the matter. Another is in his relatively well-known discussion of civil disobedience, and another is when he is speaking of just war: in both cases he merely seeks to outlaw a particular form of (political) violence. The rest of his uses are metaphysical statements: 'injustice is a kind of violence', and so forth. This is not an etymological sleight of hand. The word 'violent' appears only once as well.

Of course, Rawls might reply that his theory of justice is one that explicitly seeks the *avoidance* of violence through reasoned deliberation. He would also likely point out that he fundamentally *is* interested in violence, since the heart of his theory is famously a discussion of how to arrange inequalities so that, to the extent they are permitted, they work to the benefit of the least well-off—in effect, taking the pressure cooker of an uneven society off the boil just a little. But this boils down in turn to deciding which inequalities can be justified and when. And Rawls' 'difference principle', which deals with economic inequalities, is also the second, *least prioritised* part, of the second, *less prioritised* of Rawls' two principles of justice. It forces him to downplay the possibility that a proliferation of economic inequalities may be sufficiently systematic and burdensome as to comprise a form of 'violence' in itself. Rawls' attempt to outlaw violence at the level of the basic liberties is thus ultimately defined in such narrow terms as to be capable of re-admitting it through the back door of the difference principle. Here is just one point, I would suggest, where Rawls reveals his own perhaps unacknowledged commitments to a form of political minimalism, and not just political liberalism.

Like Shklar, Rawls too was sceptical of the state (it remains little remarked upon that he was a member of the Mont Pèlerin Society— co-founded by Hayek—for three years from 1968, after having been proposed by Milton Friedman, though he let his membership lapse in 1971 before the publication of *A Theory of Justice*).[34] But while Shklar is open about her scepticism of the state, in Rawls this is less explicit, for it is ultimately to be found not within the terms of his theory but in its starting point: that is to say in an already existing, minimally intrusive liberal democracy.[35] Brian Barry was on to something important here when he wrote to Rawls already in 1967 to point out that one problem with his famous 'veil of ignorance'—the thought experiment at the heart of his theory—is that from behind that veil, given the question you are posed, you have no choice *but* to choose a utilitarian society.[36] The problem 'of' the state is in that sense circumvented to all practical effect.

That may not be entirely fair to Rawls' efforts to secure the grounds of an overlapping consensus, but it is true that you can but choose a certain sort of liberal democratic society in his account, just as his later upscaling of that theory to the global domain presupposes a world of functioning liberal democratic societies upon which to build an international order. For Rawls, as indeed for Kant before him, a just world is thus ultimately imagined as a consequence of the extension of his own ethical starting point: peace (for Kant) and justice (for Rawls) will exist when Republican/Liberal principles are accepted by all. Here was political minimalism's second, more consequential opening onto the international scene. In place of its providing a minimal normative standpoint from which to assert the justness of US deployments of power in the name of keeping the world safe for democracy, this second opening gave on to a more universal application: the expansion of liberal internationalism and its accompaniments of 'humanity law' today. For this is indeed the 'just' world we have inherited: one in which Responsibility to Protect doctrines seek to justify the deployment of Western military power abroad; where poverty reduction and levelling up the poor to a minimal 'poverty line' come before taxes on wealth and redistribution between regions and classes.[37] This is not a vision of the world that Rawls really intended. So how are we to explain it? Here I would suggest the answer turns less on Rawls' theory itself—as political philosophical debate has for so long centred—but on the changing *context* within which the theory was developed.

Rawls' political theory was framed, we are frequently reminded, beneath the sign of Vietnam, of civil rights. But it was also framed under the more promising star of maximal equality. The 'intolerable choices' that Shklar saw liberal democracy to have banished were thus most likely banished not by liberalism's own moral commitments, which Shklar and Rawls alike took to be the essential building blocks of any just theory, but by the particular constraints on liberalism enforced by a Cold War political order (not least its encouragement of the welfare state). In other words, the 'stability' that Rawls took to be the very measure of success of his theory was nothing if not a Trojan horse within it (as he himself, in *Political Liberalism*, in fact comes close to saying). Hence at the end of the day it is not the much-discussed 'scale' of Rawls' theory that is the problem (why does it only speak to bounded national societies, and so on) but its *temporality*. Rawls' *Theory of Justice* was devised in an era when political mini-malism could realistically claim to provide a workable vision of social harmony under the conditions of mid- to late twentieth-century welfare; but it came into life at the peak of that era of welfare and relative social harmony, and was carried forward in an increasingly inegalitarian world that ever since has required something more. The early 1970s, after all, are the moment when the long downwards arc of inequality across the twentieth century bottoms out and begins to head back up again.[38]

This then raises a second observation about Rawls and political minimalism, which is less about Rawls and more about his followers.[39] It seems fairly uncontroversial to say that the sheer ambition and the aspiration of Rawls' vision is what stands behind a veritable re-enchantment of US liberals after the 1970s: as the likes of Michael Walzer, Charles Beitz, Robert Nozick, and others variously set about trying to transpose or to rework Rawls' vision of justice in light of the international scale they believed *he* had neglected and their *country* had affronted in its postwar reordering of the world. Here, in many ways, is the thrust of formal political thought and theory that lies behind the development at this moment of a new and legalistic vision of world order: the 'humanity law' of Ruti Teitel's telling description, a world of International Courts and Tribunals, of a formalised infrastructure of global humanitarianism and 'emergency response', patching up the world's problems without unduly concerning itself with why they come about. And here too is where political minimalism is refashioned for a new career at the international scale. For as this re-enchantment got underway, a fact Shklar credited Rawls with having precipitated, the liberalism which is transposed to the international domain in the process is also, in the way I hope to have shown, one whose potential economic safeguards have already been defanged by Rawls in order to prioritise political equality with regard to the basic liberties.[40]

It is a politically minimalist form of liberalism, in other words, which now ascends to the international realm amidst the upheavals of the 1970s: this time not as a global hegemon's assumed responsibility to defend freedom abroad during the Cold War in order to secure liberal democracy at home, but as a self-proclaimed vision of global emancipation. Emancipation in the form of humanitarian redress, that is: emancipation from the worst consequences of socioeconomic neglect and political mistreatment alike, without the need for a progressive and 'welfarist' politics. The trope of (national) security now merged with the growing need internationally for (socioeconomic) security, just as it had done domestically a generation before. Solidarity was deprived of its political commitments in favour of a watered-down form of empathy. And, ideally, that empathy would produce its own return: for as humanitarian organisations now learned to explain, every 'life saved' or 'improved' was to be documented as evidence of the rightfulness of the mission. Political minimalism's earlier defensive anti-utopianism was thus now reframed as a vision for improving the world in its own right. And this was a task for which the political realists and neoliberals were well attuned.

Indeed, political realism (with its concern for power) and neoliberalism (with its concern for competition), as they began to be adopted within the international institutional architecture chiefly designed by the US at the close of the war, helped to effect a shift in US 'globalism' at this point on just these terms: away from a hegemony based on the military and towards a hegemony based on exploiting, what Barry Eichengreen once called, the 'exorbitant privilege' of the dollar. The effects of this shift proved to be far-reaching: be it as the institutional framework of the liberal international order was reconstructed between states and non-governmental organisations, or as human rights instruments, courts, and humanitarian agencies began to take over the work of promoting liberal freedoms abroad, all under the sign of the value of human life as distinct from its wider 'social shell'.[41] We see this shift at work too in the rejection of the UNCTAD-sponsored programme for a New International Economic Order (NIEO) by the US; in the turn towards 'Basic Needs' in development policy, the reinvention of the World Bank and the IMF as disciplinary agents within the Washington Consensus, and the emergence of rational choice theory and trickle-down economics.[42] If today the liberal international order demonstrates a remarkable tolerance for structural as opposed to political violence, it is in no small part owing to the transformation of the ethos of political minimalism from a domestic retrenchment of utopian liberalism in the early to mid-twentieth century to an international programme of anti-democratic emancipation by the mid- to late twentieth century.

III. The Crisis of the Liberal International Order Today

What, then, of political minimalism and the liberal order today? In locating the emergence of political minimalism as an ethos centred in the early to mid-twentieth-century US, and further tracing its mid- to late twentieth-century projection onto the international domain, it becomes possible to see how a basic and consequential rejection of utopia was consolidated at the heart of the modern liberal project *in such a way* as to ultimately turn that project into something else. This anti-utopianism developed across successive eras and in response to some of those eras' defining political challenges, at the same time as it was worked out across the twentieth century's primary geographical tension between the domestic and the international stage. The first era saw liberalism respond to the problem of *state excess* (often reduced to, and misunderstood as, a problem of 'totalitarianism') in the era of post-imperial international relations. Political realism and neoliberalism were two concrete expressions of this emergent ethos. The second saw it responding to the problem of *state failure* in the era of the individual and (still apparently 'his') global universal rights. An international architecture of state obligations to the individual now provided those earlier expressions of political minimalism with a concrete form. The third, which is what I want briefly to consider now, is forcing liberalism to respond today to the problem of *state re-articulation* in an era of heightened national and international inequality alike. What is different about the present moment, however, is that the challenges are today brought about by the collision of this prior internal history of liberalism's defensive antipathy towards utopia and its effort to inoculate the global liberal order against the excesses of utopian visions by restraining democracy both at home and abroad.

The heart of the problem today, in other words, turns on the way that the consequences of the political and economic inequality occasioned by the liberal international order require, in the first place, a considerable degree of international cooperation to resolve; and yet, at the same time, the escalation of domestic political uncertainty brought about by that same inequality (as registered in the rise of populist movements and the far-right backlash against immigration, for example) makes such cooperation almost impossible to achieve. The only cooperation states do in fact seem willing to enter into today concern ongoing projects for retrenching, rather than reforming, the liberal order—be these economic, such as trade agreements, or political, such as the 'unending war' that the war on terror has become. Political minimalism's concern to root out the problem of *political evil* in the world (articulated on the international scene through R2P mandates, through the doctrine of state failure and peace and conflict resolution, through the prosecution of political malfeasance at the international courts, and so on) seems therefore to have created a blind spot in thinking about international affairs when it comes to the *structural violence* of the economy. The seventy-year project of international development does not counteract this argument; it is part of what has helped to occlude it while justifying liberal projects of order elsewhere. Today it is this blind spot that is the underlying cause (rather than the presenting behaviour) of the problems that proponents of the liberal order confront.

It is here that we might finally turn our attention, more fully, to the matter of humanitarianism specifically. Humanitarianism, no less than development, can hardly be said to be a driver of state disorder and crisis, though with refugee camps having become near permanent fixtures in parts of the world, it may prevent its effective resolution. As with development, however, it *has* been a useful ally of the projection of this US-centred 'politically minimalist' liberal order, through its offering a means of legitimising the response to international 'emergencies' with legalist fiat, and by its creating a useful condition of Western liberal engagement in the world—sometimes forcibly so (as twice in Iraq, in Haiti, Mogadishu, and elsewhere).[43] At the same time, it began to dawn that freedom alone did not, in fact, suffice to secure either democracy (as had been tried by 'democracy promotion' initiatives in the 1980s) *or* liberalism (as was now envisaged through various forms of a 'new world order' of cooperative cross-border technocrats). Between these two extremes, and with the promise of global protection against communism no longer a credible means of justifying its interventions around the world, the US increasingly promoted instead a 'humanitarian' logic of engagement in the post-Cold War years. And yet, the more it did so, the more the limits of that logic revealed themselves. George H. W. Bush used humanitarianism as a reason to leave the Kurds to their own fate after the first Iraq war in 1991. The Clinton administration then turned quite explicitly to 'armed humanitarianism' as a tool of liberal policing internationally in Kosovo, in 1999.

The denouement followed swiftly after and was accelerated by the 'twin crises' of the early twenty-first century: the long tail of the war on terror and the bloody conflicts in Afghanistan and Iraq (which by now have easily become more expensive and more costly, although not in US service lives, than Vietnam), and the financial crisis of 2008/9 with *its* long tail of the Great Recession. Linking the two was the administration of George W. Bush, which pursued the conflation of militarism with humanitarianism to its limits. At the close of the first decade of the twenty-first century, therefore, a more aggressive international politics now resumed, as the trope of 'security' trumped that of 'prosperity', and in many ways returned liberalism to the very crises that political minimalism had sought to avoid for it in the first place: a failure to stem the rise of totalitarianism (now in the form of a broad 'populist authoritarian' front), and a failure to address the incursions of 'the system' (now an avowedly politically realist and neoliberal system) upon the freedom and autonomy of individuals under liberalism. These freedoms were, however, stripped down to the level where technological improvements converged with the ability to combine life more easily with work.

Liberal humanitarianism (by which I mean to denote the modern humanitarian system, not the transcultural ethics of care that may also be assembled under the term) thus becomes, in its own way, the last redoubt of political minimalism at home as well as abroad. Following on from the global financial crisis, with its intensification of the racial and class contradictions of US capitalism, humanitarian gestures (be it immigration amnesties, or philanthropic endeavours) have become an important counterweight to the failure of domestic politics and social policy in liberal democratic regimes, just as much as they have internationally. The 'humanitarianism' of Europe's southern rim of refugee camps is likewise now used both to manage and to ward off an inflow of desperate souls fleeing the scorched earth of the previous decades' front lines of the war on terror: up to and including European leaders' recent calls to get the 'right balance between solidarity and responsibility' in their humanitarianism: a politically minimalist phrase if ever there was one, and one quickly criticised by numerous humanitarian NGOs, from Save the Children to Amnesty International.[44]

All of this was falling into place long before Trump had faced off with Kim Jong-un and flirted with the idea of deploying the nation's nuclear arsenal; before he had granted political concessions to Russia and wrought diplomatic havoc in the Middle East. It does, however, help us to understand what often seems too chaotic in the former president's support base to conform to any sort of pattern at all. For example, if we want to understand not only why Trump may have wanted to reduce US payments to NATO, or retract his nation's contributions to WHO, we would do well to look beyond the diplomatic and media circus that accompanied his tweeted policies, to the reasons why he was able even to tap into a language of 'fiscal sovereignty' in the first place. Or to why Trump's Republican Party fellow-travellers (perhaps even more so than his active supporters) believe that justice is only worth considering for others when the justice in question is one that does not hinder the way that inequalities have tended to be arranged to the benefit of the most well-off in recent decades. Rawls may not have stood for this. But take up of his arguments within a politically minimalist ethos makes it almost as if he would have.

Understanding the ways in which this ethos of political minimalism plays out allows us to see, finally, just in what way the current moment of crisis of liberal internationalism is, as suggested in this chapter's title, in many ways a crisis of legitimation. The term was coined by Jürgen Habermas in 1976 in a somewhat different context: referring as he was to the gnawing away of 'mass loyalty' to domestic political systems, and specifically with reference to the challenges confronted by capitalist democracies that promote democratic inclusivity, despite their own complicity in the exclusions and marginalisations of the capitalist system.[45] To talk of the contradictions between capitalism and democracy in this way is hardly new then: at least at the domestic level. But the underlying problem we have been considering here is distinct from this. It is that this effort to reimagine liberalism through the ethos of political minimalism, in addition to fostering a convergence of capitalism and democracy at the domestic scale, was also influenced by the way it sought to project this arrangement internationally. This required in turn a normative vision for the world.[46] But the specific challenge for liberalism here, as we have seen, was that such a normative vision also needed to avoid the temptations of utopianism. A vision for global 'society' thus needed holding in abeyance; a vision for liberal 'order' took its place—the world should be well ordered rather than, say, fair or just. Order first, then, equality second. It was the same mantra, an inversion of the Brechtian insight ('grub first, then ethics') internationally, as was preached at the domestic scale in Europe and America alike after the war: order first, then democracy.[47] For much of the postwar era, the Cold War supplied the moral imperative that this global order required. Post-Cold War, something else—namely humanitarianism—was required as a salve to ward off global *dis*order. Hence, yes to an international architecture for economic stability, went the logic; yes to international courts; and yes to the Responsibility to Protect; but no to the General Assembly as a meaningful international decision-making body; no to health systems research and the social protectionism of the UN Conference on Trade and Development (UNCTAD), the UN Industrial Development Organization (UNIDO), and the International Labour Organization (ILO)—all underprivileged elements of the UN system—and no to the New International Economic Order (NIEO). The needs of liberal order were foregrounded; demands for a more democratic distribution of power were turned down. Political violence was outlawed and socioeconomic violence was permitted: both in the name of liberal order.

Political minimalism, understood as this impulse to secure freedom without equality, was the underlying legitimatory device that made this paradox—offering to protect the world while refusing to provide for it—seem possible. It provided what was essentially a liberal will-to-order with a minimum of normative façade as could be obtained from a (negative) notion of freedom alone. If this was implicit before the 1970s, it became explicit afterwards. And it is this legitimatory function which is undergoing a crisis today: because the letter of the law, if not the substance of many of our supposedly 'liberal' international institutions, rules, and principles—be it membership in the UN, international human rights regimes, IHRL and international courts, or even just compliance with the WTO—is just as easily conformed with by the illiberal and undemocratic states that commentary today so often focuses upon, and who have little interest in either equality *or* freedom. The problem is not that these regimes are advancing. It is that liberalism now, as in the interwar era, offers no substantive alternative with which to contest their desultory visions. Political minimalism's trump card has come back to haunt it. It is now this historically narrowed ideal of liberal freedom as an (ostensibly) non-ideological, anti-utopian teleology that is itself today in crisis in liberal democracies the world over. For too long that ideal has been deprived of the countervailing political architecture of equality, such that professed commitments 'to' liberty, be it by neoliberals, political realists or others, have been too easily performed as little more than loudly trumpeted lip service. In such conditions, the mass loyalty of a global public of liberal democratic citizens to the liberal order begins to wane. At the very least, people will need to be convinced that liberty is something all can share in if they are to be won back to the cause.

Here, I think, is the final insight into the current moment that political minimalism affords us. For someone like Shklar, liberalism might embrace egalitarianism domestically not because it was desirable (or utopian) in itself, but because it offered a means of checking power run amok: the root cause of infringements on peoples' freedoms and of everyday evil. But this also required political institutions capable of ensuring things didn't tip over the other way *and* the background condition of socioeconomic growth making it less likely that things would. The same held true for John Rawls' take on egalitarianism: his desire to arrange inequalities so that they were to the benefit of the least well-off made sense only given the capacities of a functioning 'basic structure' of liberal *democratic* institutions and a generally *benign* economic outlook. Political minimalism thus was always an easier commitment to sustain at the national scale, during a relatively benign era in liberalism's history, than it ever was internationally and certainly than it is today, because of what its protagonists could take for granted: because, in other words, of democracy and economic growth. And to return to where we started, the refusal to acknowledge this, when the ground has shifted beneath us, is one reason why liberalism—and the liberal international order in particular—is experiencing such turbulence today.

Conclusion

In this chapter I have tried to outline an account of 'political minimalism' as a distinctive ethos emerging out of the crisis of liberalism in the early to mid-twentieth century, and in response to totalising theories of political life elsewhere. That ethos, I have tried to suggest, later becomes a characteristic trait of domestic postwar political liberal ideas, before achieving its institutional breakthrough (and eventual comeuppance) in the post-Cold War era at the international scale. In other words, political minimalism as first and perhaps most reflectively articulated by Reinhold Niebuhr, was normalised and secularised in postwar progressive liberalism in the form of the cross-party defensive liberalism of the vital centre. In a different world, such commitments to combating political excess as the first and prioritised step towards the amelioration of socioeconomic violence might have been well and good. But in *our* world, this narrowing of liberal commitments around a more defensive vision occurred, fatefully, at just the moment the sort of well-ordered political societies John Rawls in particular sought to account for were becoming de-bounded internationally, and at just the moment the domestic conditions for their existence—namely democratically bulwarked welfare and political moderation—were beginning to fragment. Shklar is therefore correct that (liberal) political thought regained its compass and its direction with the normative theories of the 1970s (such as Rawls' *Theory of Justice* and Habermas' theory of communicative action), but she never really addressed their international implications, nor what some of the flaws in that new compass were—as she herself had earlier detected them.[48]

And they were considerable. For here were anti-utopian accounts of a liberal order, largely shorn of democratic equality, ready and waiting for a career at the international scale. Yet if these accounts were ahead of their time in some respects, they were also behind it in others: for these were also nationally oriented *political* philosophies at a time of extensive *economic* globalisation. It is this political brew that accounts, I would argue, for the expansions and contradictions of liberal internationalism in the later twentieth century: bringing into play a series of arguments bent on enforcing peoples' right to have rights, while ignoring the matter of their capability for doing so. This may not have gone unchallenged. Far from it in fact, as we have noted via the calls for a New International Economic Order in the 1970s or, as more recently, at the Battle of Seattle WTO protests in

1999. But those challenges were, for a long time, successfully ignored.[49] And it is along this trajectory that we arrive at the legitimation crisis liberal internationalism is experiencing today: where 'liberal norms and institutions *have* been challenged by a visceral and affective politics', as one of the editors to this volume has noted, and where even their traditional constituents have grown sceptical of the project.[50] If humanitarianism has played a role in this, it has been not only as the redemptive façade of liberalism's politically minimalist ethos, but as the limit point—and perhaps even the last redoubt—of liberalism's willingness to conceive of a better version of itself: to embrace the challenge of thinking through utopia, or for Shklar, perhaps, simply thinking around it. Against its tendency to avoid the dilemmas of identity politics and calls for social justice, it is on these terms that liberalism today will need to rediscover, as Mark Lilla puts it, what it wants to stand 'for' rather than 'against'. And that will ultimately require thinking through internationally as much as nationally if the current moment of crisis is to be overcome.[51]

9

NOTES ON OUR MELANCHOLY PRESENT

Juliano Fiori[1]

Requiem for a Dream

In 1904, British political and social theorist L. T. Hobhouse bemoaned a 'wave of reaction' that for thirty years had washed across the 'civilised world', invading 'one department after another of thought and action'.[2] The 'great humanising movement' of the mid-nineteenth century, to which he attributed responsibility for social reforms, trade liberalisation, and the advance of 'moral sciences', had entered a period of lassitude, leaving the minds of the people—'empty, swept, and garnished'—to be taken by 'bad teaching and spurious philosophy'.[3] For Hobhouse, as for fellow 'new liberal' J. A. Hobson, the old *laissez-faire* liberalism that had produced this humanising movement was defunct. Liberal doyens, such as Bentham, Cobden, Mill, and Gladstone, left important legacies, but their ideas had been unable to protect the moral authority of Western civilisation and colonial empire from the onslaught of an expansionist 'new imperialism'—the primary expression of the political reaction—which provoked 'endless frontier wars', legitimated a burgeoning militarism, and reinforced the racist subjugation of foreign peoples.[4]

From the 1870s onwards, totems of liberal ideology had been challenged across Europe and the United States. The Panic of 1873 and subsequent depression checked economic liberalisation on both sides of the Atlantic, as governments increased trade tariffs and attended to the clamour for easy money. Movement of labour was restricted—for example, through the Chinese Exclusion Act in the United States, in 1882, and the Aliens Act in the UK, in 1905—in response to an upsurge in ethnonationalist sentiment, which also fuelled widespread anti-Semitic violence. To progressives in Britain, a decade of Conservative rule, straddling the turn of the century, seemed to confirm liberal decline. But, of course, liberalism had not disappeared as a political force. In the 1870s and 1880s, Gladstone had passed liberal reforms of electoral law and poverty relief. The rise of collectivism in this period reflected disaffection with individualism but by no means a categorical disavowal of liberal ideals.[5] And, unlike Hobhouse and Hobson, many British liberals were sympathetic towards new imperialist adventures. In 1906, a radical liberalism asserted itself over British politics, following the election of Henry Campbell-Bannerman.

Hobhouse believed that the close of the nineteenth century had distanced the 'civilised world' from the humanitarian morality he associated with an evolved rational self-development. But his expressions of anguish also performed a rhetorical function in the revision of liberal history through which he justified the incorporation of socialistic methods into liberal political theory. In 1911, he affirmed that '[i]f liberals had been defeated, something much worse seemed about to befall liberalism. Its faith in itself was waxing cold.'[6] His questionable pronouncement of defeat would seem to have followed from the fluctuation of his own faith. In its very contrivance, then, this formulation betrays the role of imagination in Hobhouse's liberal declinism.

The long-drawn-out requiem offered for liberal norms and institutions over recent years suggests a similar collapse in faith. Indeed, although comparisons with the 1930s have become a mainstay of conjunctural analyses in our 'disorderly moment', the late nineteenth century is arguably more instructive for reflections on contemporary liberal disillusionment.[7] There are significant theoretical differences between the new liberalism and the Rawlsian egalitarianism that has dominated philosophical liberalism over the last half-century.[8] (There are those who would even question the liberal credentials of new liberal theory.)[9] But like disillusioned progressives in *fin de siècle* Britain, self-defined liberals who now perceive grave challenges to liberalism expose in their lamentation assumptions about its boundaries.[10] That such challenges often emerge from within liberal politics raises questions about the reality of liberal decline—about possible, if not necessarily wilful, conflation of *the real* and *the ideal*. It is arguably in the moment of liberalism's putative decline that the extent of its dominion is revealed, and that the struggle for its soul is vigorously renewed.

Conservatives, such as Patrick J. Deneen and R. Emmett Tyrrell, Jr., have also been quick to pronounce liberalism's downfall.[11] But the doomsayers overlook the intrinsic function of liberal ideology in the unfolding, and indeed the unravelling, of capitalist modernity—not its promotion of 'free markets' or individual rights or rule of law, but, through adumbration of politics, its ordering of social expectations. Emerging with capitalist modernity, liberal ideology extends the promise of freedom in a *real world* whose limits and possibilities are determined by the bourgeois order of civil society. From the Coup of 18 Brumaire onwards, it has promised revolution without revolutionaries.[12] As elements of liberal utopia are realised—through social struggle within civil society and the pressure it exerts on the state—the gap between liberal expectation and experience closes. But no sooner is politics negated than liberal capitalism itself alters society's material base, undermining hopes of a liberal millennium. Liberal utopias are autophagic.

Over the last decade or so, politics seems to have resurfaced in the West, impelled *from below* and demagogically beckoned *from above*, stubbornly refusing the subjugation to humanitarian ethics envisaged by the acolytes of liberal eschatology. Of concern here is not the extent to which this represents a crisis of liberalism, nor the prospects for the reassertion of liberal hegemony. Rather: How has the dialectic of liberal capitalism contributed to the frustration of liberal hopes? What is the role of the liberal humanitarian imagination in the rise and fall of humanitarian society? And what are the political implications of diminishing social expectations in the West?

At the turn of the twentieth century, liberal despondency opened on to a vast horizon of possible futures. Substantial economic and cultural geographies were yet to be colonised by capitalism and would become objects of a dispute for a world not yet determined. Socialists and fascists would proffer their own utopian visions of modernisation, stretching and contorting liberal imaginaries of orderly civilisation. But as capitalism has reached its worldly limits, it has rebounded to recolonise its heartlands. The post-capitalist horizon has long since faded. And humanitarian minimalism—extolled by the Panglossian proponents of billionaire philanthropy as proof of progress—has minimised expectations of even its own possibilities. Now, liberal disillusionment folds inwards to a melancholy present.

Utopia after Ideology

In May 1984, the General Assembly of the French branch of Médecins Sans Frontières (MSF) resolved to establish the Fondation Liberté Sans Frontières (LSF), a think tank that would soon project humanitarians to the forefront of French debates about 'human rights and development' in the Third World. Under a second generation of leaders—less swashbuckling than the first, but no less media savvy—MSF had become the most iconic aid agency in an emboldened humanitarian movement. Towards the end of the previous decade, censure of the Khmer Rouge and the government that replaced it had done at least as much to boost the organisation's profile as had operations to assist Cambodian and Vietnamese refugees. During the early 1980s, MSF had publicly protested against Soviet attacks on foreign aid workers and journalists in Afghanistan. Now, it was in the midst of the most widely televised famine relief campaign to date, in Ethiopia; and, the following year, it would be expelled from the country after accusing the Derg—the ruling junta—of using food aid to induce mass relocation. If speaking out in this way demonstrated a commitment to the *sans-frontiériste* principle of *témoignage* ('bearing witness'), it was also motivated by an evolving interpretation of humanitarian action as necessarily anti-totalitarian and, more specifically, anti-communist.

Rony Brauman and Claude Malhuret—respectively, president and director of MSF-France at this time—were the driving force behind LSF. Brauman had been a member of the Gauche Prolé-tarienne; Malhuret, of the Parti Socialiste Unifié. Both were *soix-ante-huitards*. But they had abandoned their *gauchisme* and their hopes of Third World revolution in Southeast Asia. And they had then sought to cast *sans-frontiérisme* as a practical rejoinder to their own previous utopian ideas.[13]

By the 1980s, leftist *auto-critique*—galvanised by the Padilla affair in Cuba and then the publication of Aleksandr Solzhenitsyn's *The Gulag Archipelago*—had been channelled into a stream of invective against *tiers-mondisme*.[14] LSF, as Brauman would later admit, was con-ceived as a way to 'get involved in the fight'.[15] And yet Malhuret, in particular, took care to present the new initiative as ideologically neutral and grounded in the practical expertise of humanitarian med-ics. This was not so much deceit as an opportunistic radicalisation of humanitarian neutrality, as a political posture.[16] Humanitarianism now demanded not just the disavowal of third-worldist ideology, but the total substitution of ideological politics for a moral politics.[17] '[LSF] is a product of the immediate knowledge of generous men, free from all political, religious, and philosophical affiliation', Malhuret wrote in *Le Monde*, in late January 1985.[18]

A few days earlier, LSF had hosted its inaugural conference, which had courted controversy by lining up polemical critics of Third World developmentalism and anti-imperialism. Peter Bauer, a prominent neoclassical economist, vituperated development aid and redistribu-tion.[19] Jacques Broyelle, a journalist, former Maoist, and LSF council member, lamented the American defeat in Vietnam, arguing against the denunciation of injustices where this might lead to communist rule.[20] The LSF statute, drafted the year before, had rejected struc-turalist theories that attributed responsibility for under-development to capitalism and the West; it had even rejected 'the idea of a Third World'.[21] Blaming oppression and suffering on 'human error and bad local political decisions', LSF demonstrated a technocratic preference for neoliberal political economy, representative democracy, and human rights.[22] Claims that LSF was unsullied by ideology belied its captivity to the counter-revolutionary *zeitgeist*.

In *Idealism Beyond Borders*, historian Eleanor Davey discusses the emergence of *sans-frontiérisme* in the moment of disillusionment with *tiers-mondisme*. The relationship between the two movements, she argues, was '[p]art legacy, part continued dialogue'.[23] There has been much dissension within MSF regarding the nature and implications of this legacy; for many, it was not the place of a humanitarian organisation to take a political stance against *tiers-mondisme*. MSF-Belgium severed relations with MSF-France over the creation of LSF. But even those counter-revolutionaries who explicitly renounced past ideals did not renounce moral idealism.[24] Moreover, their deconstruction of past utopias did not necessarily divest them of a utopian imaginary.[25] Political energies once expended in revolutionism were transferred to the pursuit of an alternative utopia—unlike previous humanitarian utopias, a negative utopia, to the extent that it was articulated as a negation of the past, of utopian projects and their pathologies. (*Sans-frontiéristes* particularly mobilised Holocaust memory in their advocacy to prevent genocidal violence.)[26] It was also a negation of the future, in so far as it permitted of no further positive contestation. The only acceptable remaining utopia was a world free of utopianism.

In his address to the LSF conference, Brauman discussed the demise of political messianism.[27] But the 'morality of *urgence*' that he saw emerging in its place would also become the object of messianic faith. Political scientist Olivier Roy provided the conference with a telling reflection on the ebb of *tiers-mondisme*: 'the critique of history led to a refusal of history, a refusal of the historical perspective, and withdrawal to an ethical position'.[28] The morality of *urgence* bore the promise of universal humanity—preservation of life and freedom from suffering—which represented a historical resolution.[29] 'Human rights and development', primary concerns of LSF, were conceived in accordance with this humanitarian imagination; indeed, Brauman disapproved of Rousseau's 'maximalist conception' of human rights as progeny of a general will.[30] Liberalism, Malhuret argued, had 'proven itself'—not because it produced idyllic societies, but because it was least likely to produce mass atrocity, and likely to produce least want.[31] The negative utopia of counter-revolutionary *sans-frontiéristes* amounted to the totalisation of a humanitarian present that Western liberal democracies came closest to producing.

LSF was effectively deactivated in 1989. In the decades since, the capability of liberal democracies to attend to human necessity has periodically been called into question, in spite of increasingly sophisticated technologies to manage recurrent crises of the present. Meanwhile, attempts to universalise the society of the humanitarian minimum, through pacification, cultural conversion, and commercial expansion, have produced grisly hellscapes in capitalism's borderlands and, subsequently, floods of desperate humanity on the shores of its metropolis. MSF generally abstained from the militarised humanitarian adventurism of the 1990s. Brauman became increasingly critical of the exportation of liberal democracy, humanitarian wars, and the contribution of aid workers to Western security strategies.[32] Malhuret became François Mitterrand's Secretary of State for Human Rights in 1986.

In the 1980s, aid agencies rooted in the less radical Anglo-American philanthropic tradition, such as Save the Children, Oxfam, and CARE, were generally less zealous advocates of counter-revolution than MSF-France, even though many had been faithful allies of Cold War anti-communism. But their millenarian enthusiasm became apparent as a new decade dawned. Capitalising on histories of close association with Western governments, they positioned themselves at the forefront of efforts to impose liberal peace on the periphery; more developmentally focused than their francophone counterparts, they were readily integrated into stabilisation strategies. While MSF's commitment to independence and critique usually distanced it from multi-agency initiatives, Anglo-American agencies collaborated to accelerate professionalisation in the aid sector, ultimately becoming vectors in the globalisation of neoliberal management technologies.[33]

As Davey points out, the dominance of anglophone accounts of humanitarian history has focused attention on the end of the Cold War as a moment of rupture.[34] Through her study of *sans-frontiérisme*, she instead emphasises the 1970s as formative of the new moral politics.[35] This periodisation allows for closer consideration of the ideological and intellectual interdependencies between contemporary humanitarianism (as it merged with human rights) and neoliberalism. But its primary value, here, is in highlighting the relationship between counter-revolution and social expectations. Samuel Moyn's identification of human rights as the last utopia is relevant in this regard, even if his iconoclastic assertion that they emerged in the 1970s 'seemingly from nowhere' surely exaggerates their originality.[36] Moyn notes that this utopia became 'powerful and prominent because other visions imploded'.[37] Its power and prominence have arguably been more dependent on the structuring function of human rights in neoliberalism's moral economy than Moyn admits.[38] More to the point, if human rights 'emerged historically as the last utopia', it is not only because of the exhaustion of past utopian projects. It is, more specifically, because they reflected an idealism defined by the negation of other utopias, albeit not always with the ardour of LSF. Moreover, as they drew support from disenchanted utopians—*sans-frontiéristes* being only the most striking and cohesive example—their success would constitute a reduction in social ambitions, a closing in of the horizon of social change. Relief from necessity became a utopian maximum in more and more spheres of social life; the realm of freedom would be sought within the realm of necessity.[39] The proximity of expectation to experience seemed to extinguish the future. *Urgence* accelerated passage through continuous presents towards a historical synthesis that nonetheless remained elusive.

Diminishing Expectations in a Colonised World

LSF had almost been named 'Fondation Raymond Aron pour le Tiers Monde'. Raymond Aron's writing on industrial society and the end of ideology had influenced the post-historical sensibility of many former *tiers-mondistes*, including members of LSF's council. 'I continue to believe a happy outcome [is] conceivable, well beyond the political horizon', Aron wrote in his memoirs, published shortly before his death in 1983.[40] But by the turn of the 1980s, a broad consensus had formed within the French intelligentsia, if not on the ills of ideology, at least on an anti-political interpretation of human rights. Aron was joined by intellectuals of different political persuasions—most notably, his rival Jean-Paul Sartre—in the vanguard of campaigns to 'rescue' Vietnamese 'boat people', in 1979, and boycott the Moscow Olympics, in 1980. In 1981, Michel Foucault, a contributor to these campaigns, addressed the UN in Geneva with a speech on 'confronting governments'—something of a human rights manifesto. He referred to an 'absolute right to stand up and speak to those who hold power' and a 'new right... of private individuals to effectively intervene in the sphere of international policy and strategy'.[41] This seemed in contradiction to his earlier criticism of rights discourse for obscuring systems of social domination.[42]

By now, Foucault had turned his attention to governmentality— the 'art of government'—a central concept in the philosophy of his final years. He had used a lecture series at the Collège de France, in 1978–9, to analyse and historicise an emerging neoliberal governmentality. He criticised 'state-phobia', a suspicion of the state's 'intrinsic and irrepressible dynamism', fomented by an earlier generation of neoliberals, who bracketed welfarism and totalitarianism as related forms of state control.[43] But Foucault's work on governmentality reflected a growing scepticism of state authority that perhaps explains his turn towards the rights of 'private individuals'. Sections of the postmodern left, influenced by Foucault, particularly in the Anglosphere, would be led by this scepticism back around to defence of market freedoms and competition.[44] And while others would remain distrustful of the new individualism, postmodern critique of the neoliberal government of bodies would supplant analysis of historical capitalism from the field of critical theory. Left-wing politics in the West would increasingly focus on culture and identity, rather than transformation of the social relations of production.

In art and literature, as well as theory, postmodernism was characterised by an 'inverted millenarianism' that suggested the disappearance of a post-capitalist imagination.[45] In 1979, historian H. Bruce Franklin accused J. G. Ballard of 'mistaking the end of capitalism for the end of the world'.[46] Ballard's apocalyptic New Wave fiction disconcertingly explores 'the postmodern condition'. Ballard dissociated himself from the postmodern novel, which he saw as a 'dead-end'; but if his surrealist literary experiment sought to recover historicity and subjectivity, it nonetheless reaffirmed the limits imposed by postmodernity.[47] According to Fredric Jameson, the 'deepest vocation' of the literary utopias produced by science-fiction writers from the 1960s onwards had not been 'to keep the future alive' but 'to demonstrate and to dramatise [an] incapacity to imagine the future'.[48] By the end of the 1970s, acknowledgement of the postmodern condition, by detractors and enthusiasts alike, seemed to signal not just a dislocation of the utopian horizon, but a fundamental alteration in Western societies' relationship to Time.

In 1979, historian and social critic Christopher Lasch published an influential book on 'American life in an age of diminishing expectations'. He attributed the 'waning of the sense of historical time' to a new narcissistic culture, which, derived from the 'disintegration of public life', turned individuals inwards to attend to their personal psychic survival.[49] In more recent years, Brazilian philosopher Paulo Arantes has drawn loosely on Lasch's thesis, in his conceptualisation of our contemporary historical period: 'the new time of the world'.[50] Heralded by the Great War of 1914–18—the first systemic crisis of Progress—and definitively inaugurated in the 1970s, this *new Time*, according to Arantes, is characterised by diminishing expectations. More specifically, it was begotten through erasure of the 'difference between experience and expectation', identified by Reinhart Koselleck as 'history in general' and the condition of modernity.[51] Presentism has then made of the new time of the world an age of emergency. Like Lasch, Arantes associates the endless extension of the present with survivalism, as a basic mode of existence. But whereas Lasch's culturalist analysis presents Time as a function of psychology, Arantes offers a more dynamic, materialist explanation of historical closure.

Arantes draws a connection between the two meanings of the term *emergência*. With capitalism's global expansion, the *emergence* of economies on the periphery of the world system indicates that a somewhat dystopian future has arrived for everyone: the periphery has not 'caught up'; rather, economies of the capitalist core have developed pathologies of the periphery.[52] '[E]veryone is running, although they have nowhere left to go', and so acceleration occurs in the present, a time of flux and crisis, according to conventional modern conceptions.[53] *Urgence* then becomes not only a mode of government and a moral disposition, but also a unit of temporal measurement, giving the impression of a permanent *emergency*.

The temporal horizon, here, is also a spatial horizon: in modernist terms, the future only appears possible while there are territories—'worlds', *topias*—yet to be colonised by capitalist modernity. Europeans have long imagined utopias forming where their own civilisation is yet to have imposed itself fully: the New World, distant settler colonies, the Third World. Capitalism's approximation to its outer limits, then, truncated historical Time, diminishing expectations of a world beyond the present. Approximation to its inner limits, meanwhile, compressed Time, contributing in turn to the destruction of spatial barriers and, ultimately, accelerating historical closure.[54]

Hopes of permanent growth and rising employment following the Second World War were undone by a rapid drop in the rate of profit across the largest capitalist economies, beginning in the 1960s. Automation, though as yet limited, promised to reduce the participation of labour in industrial production and restrict surplus-value. The tendency towards over-capitalisation produced surpluses of capital, which, with dwindling opportunities for productive investment, were channelled into an expanding services sector. International concentration and centralisation of capital corresponded with the redirection of metropolitan capital away from decolonising states, where anti-imperialist resistance accelerated the decline of colonial surplus profits. Undermining a return to previous profit rates, the conditions of 'late capitalism', perspicaciously analysed by Ernest Mandel, also threatened the command exercised by the imperialist bourgeoisie over the cadence of History through its ordering of the production process.[55] Historical representation itself was commodified as late capitalism generalised exchange-value. The fate of this old bourgeoisie then became tied, as Guy Debord recognised, to the 'preservation of a new immobility *within history*'.[56] Thus, if the counter-revolution of the 1970s—an implosion of the social state and the collective sense of society—was most immediately aimed at restoring profitability, its strategic function was 'preventive': in the absence of active revolt, it erased social expectations that could undermine the bourgeois monopoly on irreversible Time.[57]

Amidst the atrocities of a war that was never cold, the collapse of modern ideologies, the fragmentation of universal identities, and the 'refusal of History' accompanied and were precipitated by the historical development of late capitalism. Once expectations had been reduced from freedom beyond the present to survival within it, History would not be 'temporalised' again merely through the formation of new mentalities.

The End (i)

'The end of history will be a very sad time', cautioned Francis Fukuyama, in 1989.[58] Yet the time in question has been inscribed in the collective memory of the West as one of triumph, if not triumphalism. Among Western aid workers, the end of the Cold War generated hope of a reduction in the geopolitical conditioning of 'humanitarian space'. In the late 1980s and early 1990s, the UN General Assembly adopted a number of resolutions emphasising the role of aid agencies within the national borders of states affected by disaster. In 1992, UN Secretary-General Boutros Boutros-Ghali affirmed that 'the time of absolute and exclusive sovereignty... has passed'.[59] State refusal of foreign aid was increasingly seen as a moral transgression.

In the apparent absence of alternatives to neoliberal globalisation, the moralisation of politics transformed humanitarians into protagonists of a story told by the West about itself. The aid industry remained minuscule in relation to commercial industries with comparable workforces. But having garnered media attention through participation in spectacular relief campaigns—Live Aid, in particular—aid agencies became subcontractors for the West's moral conscience. Changes in the political economy of humanitarianism allowed aid agencies to use their moral capital to promote the spread of humanitarian reason, in turn further boosting their profile and income. Private and government funding for emergency relief increased from the late 1980s onwards. This enabled professionalising reforms in the aid sector, initiated in response to donor government demands for closer evaluation of overseas aid impact, then accelerated following perceived failures in inter-agency coordination and technical proficiency.[60] Most notably, a critical evaluation of aid operations in the aftermath of the Rwandan genocide, published in 1996, produced a torrent of reform activity.[61]

Initiatives to improve 'humanitarian effectiveness' in the 1990s were heavily influenced by the neomanagerial reorganisation of

Western government bureaucracies over the previous decade. Professional performance in the aid sector would increasingly be defined according to business imperatives, such as value for money and productivity. Human rights, now widely recognised as providing the moral rationale for disaster relief, also inspired advocacy for minimum standards and 'community participation' in aid operations— which were to be secured through accountability in a 'humanitarian marketplace'.[62] As aid agencies expanded fundraising and marketing departments, the quest for effectiveness simultaneously contributed to the commercialisation of Western humanitarian cultures. And it contributed to a humanitarianisation of professional cultures. With greater opportunity for the development of professional careers in charity, aid agencies also exported professional expertise imbued with humanitarian morality. As such, they became preeminent, if often unsuspecting, missionaries for the society of the humanitarian minimum. By the turn of the millennium, as a consequence of the fusion of charitable and commercial cultures, aid agency executives were no more out of place in the world of business than Bill Gates was in the aid sector.

The End (ii)

Perhaps the most remarkable thing about Fukuyama's pronouncement of the end of history is the stir it caused. Fukuyama epitomised liberal hubris as the Soviet Union disintegrated. He became the emblematic intellectual of that moment—something of a herald for a new order. Yet his thesis—first articulated in an essay, published in July 1989, then developed in a book, published three years later— was almost universally rejected. Political scientists have eagerly pronounced the end of the end of history at various moments since, often unwittingly reproducing the 'endism' they seek to discredit.[63] But Fukuyama's critics, on the left in particular, have often mistaken opportunism for naïveté.

The sense of historical closure given expression in pop culture in the 1960s and 1970s had been growing for a number of decades. A couple of months before the publication of Fukuyama's essay, German historian Lutz Niethammer completed a study on the post-historical turn of a group of twentieth-century European intellectuals with radically divergent politics.[64] Unfulfilled ambitions of social transformation during the interwar period caused them to become profoundly disillusioned with the historical process. Inverting the progressivist optimism of the nineteenth century, they speculated that History had reached a dead-end, in so far as the world's meaning had been exhausted. Among them was Franco-Russian Hegelian philosopher Alexandre Kojève, who argued that history had ended with the formation of a 'universal and homogenous state', which had resolved the master-slave dialectic.[65] He ultimately situated this moment in 1806, with Napoleon Bonaparte's victory at Jena, arguing that what had happened since then was 'but an extension in space of the universal revolutionary force actualised in France by Robespierre-Napoleon'.[66] He saw the two world wars as having brought 'backward civilisations... into line with the most advanced'. And, despite his earlier Stalinist sympathies, he conceded that, in the postwar period, this Hegelian resolution of history had tended to the right, in favour of capitalism.

Fukuyama reproduced Kojève's argument that, domesticating nationalism and nurturing consumerism, capitalist democracy had come to embody a state of 'universal recognition'. Unlike Kojève, he also adopted Hegel's liberal constitutionalism and optimism regarding the end-time. This synthesis, as Perry Anderson notes, was not just original, but it also transformed the philosophical discourse on the end of history into a potent political expression.[67] At the moment of Soviet communism's collapse, Fukuyama attributed the presumptive victory of capitalist liberal democracy to the irresistible force of universal History. Moreover, by reclaiming an idealist basis for History—placing Hegel back on his feet, so to speak—he sought to dismiss once and for all materialist challenges to liberal capitalism. Jacques Derrida referred to his book as a 'new gospel... on... the death of Marxism'.[68]

There was more than a hint of Judeo-Christian eschatology in Fukuyama's scheme. '[T]he good news has come', he affirmed; 'modern natural science guides us to the gates of the Promised Land of liberal democracy', he continued.[69] Of course, the majority of the world's population did not live in this Promised Land. So the attribution of universal meaning to its consumer culture implied that their passage towards it was not just an inevitability, but also a moral obligation. Fukuyama thus revived an optimistic civilisational discourse, joining the dots between neoconservative evangelism and neoliberal progressivism.[70] Abandoning the Eurocentricity of civilising missions of the past, he elaborated a concept of 'the Western idea' exemplified by the United States. A State Department official in 1989, he provided intellectual ballast for the 'American universalism' through which, over the following decade, the United States constructed an international ethical order, promoting liberal humanitarian ideas to expand its power.[71] But as the twentieth century drew to a close, this universalism was undermined by the very exceptionalism that had begotten it. In order to consolidate its hegemony, the United States increasingly exempted itself from the rules-based multilateralism it had promoted for others, exercising sovereign power over the inter-state system.

The Great Introflection

'Thirty-five years after its best formulations', remarked cultural critic Mark Greif, in 2019, '"postmodernism" has become an essentially historical term'.[72] Notwithstanding the paranoid vulgarisations of alt-right pop intellectuals, few commentators today regard it as a living movement. At one point representative of an aesthetic vanguardism, postmodernism in the arts was swallowed up by the culture industry, which commodified what it could and spat out the rest.

If, at the turn of the millennium, certain conditions of postmodernity remained, they were shaping new aesthetic and moral sensibilities, epistemic postures, and even master narratives. Hyperreality itself—which, according to Jean Baudrillard, transformed simulacra into truths—seemed to put an end to postmodern irony.[73] As *the subjectivised real*, in its most banal form, became an object of popular consumption (through reality TV shows, and then social media), new boundaries to authentic experience were etched into the depthless surfaces that Jameson had identified as constitutive of the postmodern.[74] Today, the affirmation of such boundaries to protect hard-won subjectivities has little to do with the open-ended play of deconstruction or the fluidity of identities. With the revindication of an inside–outside distinction, the language of 'self-expression', exalted by the massification of reflexive therapeutic practices and well-being products, has contributed to a new spectacle of affect, reproduced in politics, academia, and the arts. At the same time, the postmodern sense that everything connects—that *there is no outside*—has inflected the ideological imagination of a new messianic right. Responding to overwhelming complexity, the conspiratorialism of QAnon and the alt-right roots expectation of a final victory in a mythical truth;[75] and, as such, it sets up a closed historical narrative. But, already at the beginning of the 2000s, conspiracy theory filled in the gaps of a new meta-narrative. Reference to 'unknown unknowns' provided not only a pretext for the invasion of Iraq, but also an indication of the epistemology that justified expansive neoconservative strategy in the Global War on Terror.

For many sceptics of the 'inverted millenarianism' that reached apotheosis with Fukuyama, the launch of a totalising war in the wake of 9/11 provided confirmation that History was very much alive.[76] Claims of an emerging consensus on liberal democracy, leading to a stable peace, had been at least premature. Societies across the world would now increasingly be haunted by the spectre of catastrophe (terror, climate change, economic collapse, pandemic disease).[77] If postmodernism had expired as an intellectual movement, postmodern conceptions of crisis—as endogenous to human society—had nonetheless become embedded in a late capitalist common sense.[78] Broad resignation to the ubiquity of risk reflected a preoccupation not with the future, as Anthony Giddens argued, but rather with securitisation of the present.[79] The radical uncertainty presumed to result from global interconnectedness and technological complexity portended only the imminence of loss, not the possibility of social advancement, from which a future could be born. Uncertainty was invoked in denial of a decisive resolution of the historical process; but it did not imply a historical opening.

Nor did the development of late capitalism itself produce such an opening, contrary to Ernest Mandel's hopeful dialectic. Mandel had argued that a 'third technological revolution' would bring about 'generalised universal industrialisation', intensifying the contradiction between productive forces and the social relations of production.[80] Although he recognised the possibility that long-term mass unemployment could fragment and demoralise the working class, he eagerly predicted a 'new epoch of social revolution'.[81] The counter-revolution initiated in the 1970s was resisted by labour—think of the miners' strikes in Britain, the mobilisation of communist parties in continental Europe—but it was Theodor Adorno's suggestion that late capitalism would dampen proletarian revolutionism that was ultimately borne out, not Mandel's stubborn optimism.[82] Technological change has been less profound than Mandel imagined it would be amid revolutionary class struggle (and, without rupture from existing relations of production, it is unlikely to prove as socially transformative as today's left-wing enthusiasts of automation propose).[83] Western economies have de-industrialised, albeit without exactly vindicating prophecies of post-industrial society—which Mandel rejected.[84] Industry was moved offshore, where greater surplus-value could be extracted from labour. And, although the proportion of manufacturing jobs in peripheral labour markets has declined—Brazil, South Africa, and Mexico provide notable examples—the global industrial workforce has steadily risen.[85]

In the decades following the Second World War, the Western bourgeoisie, dependent on colonisation for its own reproduction, had sought new frontiers for accumulation. If de-industrialisation in those countries that had begotten industrial capitalism was arguably an inevitable consequence of the tendency of the rate of profit to fall, it can also be understood as reflecting a particular directionality in the process of capitalist development.[86] In the 1980s, banking deregulation and import-promotion, particularly in the United States, led to a rapid expansion of the financial sector. The development of new financial derivatives and the advent of 'fast trading' enabled the exponential growth and circulation of fictitious capital, to the detriment of productive investment. Generally associated with the *opening outwards* of globalisation, financialisation provided the Western bourgeoisie with a new frontier for an accelerated *expansion inwards*. As government and finance consolidated their old alliance, the pursuit of monopoly rent enabled and required the imposition of a new capitalist discipline for Western workers.[87] Domestic manufacturing industries were abandoned to ruination and prominent unions were dismantled. A new precarity was introduced into labour markets and wages were progressively suppressed. The threat of under-consumption was then addressed through the provision of credit, by deregulated banks, but also by the state, which was placed at the service of neoliberal technologies of accumulation.

Something akin to what Hannah Arendt called the 'boomerang effect of imperialism' is in play here.[88] The expansion inwards of Western capital 'brings home' social conditions of underdevelopment imposed upon the periphery: extreme disparities of income, chronic underemployment, urban informality and violence.[89] In the 1990s, a generalised reproduction of the periphery was recognised by scholars who spoke of 'Brazilianisation'.[90] But many overlooked the double movement in this process.[91] If Brazil has become constitutive of the world, the world has also produced Brazil. The peripheral pathologies for which Brazil becomes a representation are born of the dialectic of capitalist development; Brazil, as periphery, is conditioned by its insertion in the world economy; its fitful modernisation then becomes the reinvention of modernity itself. And so we return to Arantes' discussion of the *emergence* of the periphery as capitalism approaches its worldly limits. His suggestion that 'there is nowhere left to go' can be taken as figurative of the limits of outwards expansion. But acceleration in the present results from continued dialectical movement, from the systemic logic that demands the accumulation of power and capital. And it is this movement that compels expansion inwards— not only as recolonisation of liberal capitalism's Western heartlands, but also as recolonisation of people's minds, first through the installation of a new common sense based on self-reliance, and then through the pre-cognitive, cybernetic determination of consumer and voter behaviour.

Koselleck uses the term *Sattelzeit* ('saddle time') to conceptualise the period of transition to modernity, which he sees as having given rise to 'history in general'.[92] Italian historian Enzo Traverso tentatively suggests that, producing 'a radical change of our general landmarks, of our political and intellectual landscape', the years between the late 1970s and 9/11 brought about a comparable transition.[93] 'Old and new forms merged together', he argues. But, if this period did indeed inaugurate a new Time, it was precisely because reduction of the time and space of the yet-to-be-determined constrained the possibility of the new.[94] Much of what appeared to be new on the 'political and intellectual landscape' had *emerged* from immanent tensions of the old, as inversion or simulacrum, as a lustreless response to the old, folding into a temporal no man's land. Approximately spanning the lifetime of postmodernism, the last quarter of the twentieth century was not so much a period of transition to the substantively new as it was a period of turning inwards—a *point of introflection* into the present.

This introflection was apparent in the social disposition of the Western bourgeoisie, and that of a growing professional–managerial class broadly submissive to its interests. Christopher Lasch's identification of a new narcissism is relevant here. Lasch associates a turning inwards—from the public sphere towards the Self—with a 'cult of consumption' and the 'glorification of the individual'.[95] But he provides little insight into its function in the self-reproduction of capital. Betraying a traditionalist and curiously choleric aversion to progressive cultural politics, he aims his censure at the subjective turn itself.[96] He thus dismisses the emancipatory opportunity that subjective morality seemed to represent for many of those historically oppressed in the name of universalisms. And he understates the embeddedness of the bourgeois Self in class consciousness and ideology. If, as Lasch suggests, the new narcissism was produced by a 'disintegration of public life', it nonetheless allowed those with privileged access to the political realm to reaffirm a collective Self, protect cultural capital, and propagate a moral politics of the present.

Progressive elements among the neoliberal bourgeoisie and the professional class incorporated rights claims of the oppressed into this moral politics. Assuming custodianship for inclusion, they would more readily neutralise concomitant challenges to neoliberal political economy.[97] The promise of a universal right to life became an expression of this arrangement. But the right to life for some depends upon the disposability of life for others. In addition to inequalities of economic and political power, unequal treatment of life would ultimately contribute to sprawling social rebellion and provide opportunity for a new preventive counter-revolution.[98]

Beyond the End

Essayist Pankaj Mishra proposes that we are living in an 'age of anger'.[99] He sees a violent resurgence of religious fanaticism, ethnonationalism, and cultural supremacism across the world as expressive of widespread *ressentiment*—'[a]n existential resentment of other people's being, caused by an intense mix of envy and sense of humiliation and powerlessness'.[100] Directed in particular towards the idols and gatekeepers of modernity, *ressentiment*, he argues, is born of modernisation itself. Mishra's history of the present cannot quite sustain his identification of ostensibly disparate contemporary political phenomena—European xenophobia, Hindu nationalism, ISIS, Trumpism, American shooters—with canonical European intellectuals. But he provides an elegant and arresting account of the contradictory logic through which capitalist modernity forces a historical protagonism on the underclass it produces.

Following Nietzsche, Mishra understands *ressentiment* as generating moral claims on society by those who lack the power to transform it materially.[101] Over the last decade, such claims have been enunciated in the West with growing urgency—and, indeed, anger. French geographer Christophe Guilluy associates this with a process that is now commonly recognised: the hollowing out of the Western middle class.[102] With broad brushstrokes, Guilluy paints a picture of social division in France that is nonetheless amply representative of other Western societies. The 'upper classes'—those who have profited from the globalisation of capitalism, or who have at least been able to protect themselves from its fallout—have increasingly hunkered down in private enclaves, from which they unironically cast moral aspersions on the reactionary 'lower classes' raging against the 'open society'.[103] They call for multiculturalism from below while extolling the urban homogenisation that disproportionately expels poor ethnic minorities to the periphery. What Guilluy calls the 'gentrification of social struggles' reflects the turning inwards through which upper classes have appropriated a morality of the oppressed while politically disarming it. The reaction of the lower classes exposes a moral distance that itself becomes indicative of a more structural emptying of the middle.

That a paroxysm of moral reaction on 'the periphery' of Western societies became the spark for a new counter-revolution depended not only on the decades-long dissolution of working-class solidarity, but also on a sufficient realignment of elite interests. Following 9/11, warnings of an inimical Other increasingly conditioned the humanitarian rhetoric of governments and news media. The debacle of the Iraq War precipitated the political decline of American neoconservatives, whose Evangelical Christian base drifted away from the neoliberal establishment. In Britain and Spain, the decision to go to war despite historic popular protests contributed to a growing sense of disenfranchisement. A few years later, when the stock market crash thrust the West's financialised economies into recession, increasing inequalities, elite appeals to stoic frugality were sufficient to create an electoral basis for austerity, but they could not suppress the albeit ambiguous clamour for more democracy. Mobilisations of *indignados* initially tended to the left: Movimiento 15-M in Spain, Amesi Dimokratia Tora! in Greece, Occupy Wall Street in the United States. But movements of the right also articulated grievances with the course of capitalist democracy, and, eliciting nostalgic fantasies of national grandeur, they would ultimately exercise a greater pull on the disaffected and on the political centre ground: in the United States, the Tea Party drew support from libertarians and religious conservatives, and it played to a white identity politics; in Europe, anti-immigrant groups animated and built outwards from the undead forces of fascism. Following the sudden surge in forced migration to Europe and North America in 2015, debates about border control and national identity exposed and accentuated moral polarisation. With the help of billionaire investments in psychographic profiling and audience segmentation, and an acute sense of the moment, unashamedly authoritarian politicians of the right mobilised moral reaction as a political force, offering not a democratic future, but vindication in the present.

Even before the financial crisis of 2008, the competitiveness of Western corporations was in decline. Productivity and reinvestment lagged behind the rate of profit. Wages had been more or less stagnant for more than three decades. After the crash, the flight of jobs— notably to China—left dwindling sources of surplus value. Western economies entered a state of low-intensity capitalism from which they have not since emerged. Once governments had bailed out the banks, the financial bourgeoisie doubled down on its neoliberal fundamentalism. But some other segments of capital—residual oligarchs of heavy industry, in particular—cheered on an apparent neomercantilist revival. The coalition that placed Donald Trump in the White House was forged through a pledge to restore both national industry and the 'cultural sovereignty' of white America.[104]

Political commentary now insists that the rise of the authoritarian, nationalist right necessarily undermines neoliberal strategies of order and accumulation—as if neoliberalism depended on democratic politics and open borders. In fact, owing its hegemony to brazen and sometimes sanguinary states of exception, neoliberal reason has always been in tension with the democratic principle.[105] And free movement of labour is not a prerequisite to the movement of goods, wages, and capital.[106] Trump introduced new trade tariffs and threatened to impose capital controls, as well as restricting immigration. But he reduced corporate taxes, cut social security, and pursued a more ambitious programme of deregulation than his predecessors, enabling a massive expansion of the gig economy. In doing so, he reinforced the role of the state in the creation of risk.[107] (It is unsurprising, then, that, despite early opposition, the libertarian Club for Growth warmed to him.)

Rather than a reversion towards some national capitalism of the past, the rise of Trumpism has portended an acceleration of capital's expansion inwards through generalisation of the gig economy's logic of *self-exploitation*.[108] For Trump, dollar devaluation was to serve not to rebuild blue-collar America, but to 'nationalise' the returns from increasing precarity. Its mere suggestion also intensified geoeconomic competition. On account of vain posturing and incoherence, as much as political strategy, Trump became a wrecking ball in the inter-state system, bringing to a destructive climax the institutional fragmentation initiated under George W. Bush and continued, despite cosmopolitan rhetoric, under Barack Obama.[109] Withdrawing the United States from the UN Human Rights Council and the World Health Organization, and cutting aid to Palestinian refugees, he disavowed humanitarian multilateralism. As he undermined state protection of the right to life at home and abroad, he offered a reminder of the role American power played in the idealisation and reproduction of the society of the humanitarian minimum.

A shift in the state's relationship to the right to life became clear during the COVID-19 pandemic. Brazilian philosopher Rodrigo Nunes proposes that the Trump administration's fatal neglect during the pandemic be seen as initiating a formal rupture with the prevailing biopolitical pact.[110] (That Brazilians, as Nunes points out, have also been subjected to such a social experiment—indeed, arguably a more extreme version—suggests that Brazil might once again be showing Western societies their future.) But rupture is not a spontaneous response to the pandemic. Rather, the arrival of the pandemic society, itself a product of capitalist expansion, precipitates a rupture already in course. And it produces new opportunities for accumulation: between early March and early August 2020, as COVID-19 killed 150,000 people in the United States, American billionaires added US$637 billion to their personal wealth. Not only in the United States, but in Britain, Hungary, Poland, and elsewhere, the pandemic has provided signs of substantive change in the relationship between state and society through the normalisation of autocratic but conspicuous management of death.[111]

In mid-2020, Samuel Moyn argued that Trump would be rendered 'an aberration whose rise and fall says nothing about America', were he to fail in his bid for re-election.[112] But, despite the outpouring of relief from progressives following Trump's defeat in November 2020, the election results suggested a consolidation of Trumpism's base. More to the point, even if Joe Biden were to initiate a restoration of the erstwhile consensus on progressive neoliberalism, the last five years have had an irreversible impact on political imagination in the West. Epitomised and emboldened by Trump, the popular authoritarianism that has swept the West continues to disrupt liberal modes of ordering society—for now. But its direct assault on a morality of *urgence*—its flagrant denial of relief from necessity, for the working poor, for refugees—has put paid to illusions of gradual and continuous inclusion in the humanitarian present. The last utopia of a moral society unencumbered by ideology has thus dissipated.

In agreement with Friedrich Hayek, Judith Shklar recognised the necessary role of 'utopian impulses' in the development of liberal theory and politics.[113] But the renewal of liberal utopianism relies on more ambitious visions of the future, which raise expectations and inspire actions that sustain belief in progress within capitalism. Unless stretched by revolutionary hopes, liberalism folds inwards into a moralism readily exploited by forces of annihilation that lurk impatiently in the matrix of modernity.[114] Despite the statistical sophistry of Steven Pinker and other late prophets of the Enlightenment, belief in progress, as J. B. Bury famously pointed out, is 'an act of faith'.[115] It depends on the imagination of movement beyond the present. Once such imagination was extinguished, the last utopia of a *real world* free from utopianisms then succumbed to the logic of diminishing expectations. Without a utopian horizon, there is no obvious route for a *fuite en avant* from the dejection produced by fallen ideals.

This predicament has brought on a profound and enduring sense of loss, now most immediately detectable in the political and cultural expression of those well-meaning meliorists morally invested in the society of the humanitarian minimum—bourgeois liberals of the compassionate left and compassionate right, who might not have believed that History had ended, but hoped that it had. Their revanchism—on widespread display in the moment of Biden's election—is no less indicative of melancholia than the lament it defers.

In what remains the most influential commentary on melancholia, published in 1917, Freud described the condition as 'related to an object-loss which is withdrawn from consciousness'.[116] That is, the melancholic 'cannot see clearly what it is that has been lost'. For Giorgio Agamben, this is because the object was never possessed.[117] The melancholic's sense of loss is specifically induced by an act of imagination that, paradoxically, appropriates an unobtained object. And this act of imagination is provoked by realisation or confirmation of a *lack*.[118] Accordingly, liberal melancholy now interprets as a lost object a social ideal that was never fully realised. In other words, an act of imagination treats as lost what was never more than an object of imagination—a utopia.

Freud speculated that the melancholy disposition depends on 'narcissistic identification' with an object.[119] This would seem to provide a neat explanation for the particular anguish projected by those who, over recent decades, turned inwards, away from political contestation, exalting a society made in their own image. But other, albeit more ambiguous displays of melancholia have also contributed to the contemporary politics of affect. Nietzsche believed *ressentiment* to be caused by a 'yearning... to *anaesthetise* a tormenting, secret pain... with a more violent emotion'.[120] He associated it with scapegoating by those suffering from a personal affliction—and, to be sure, the concept betrays a certain haughtiness and, indeed, resentment, however it is deployed.[121] The contemporary diagnosis of *ressentiment* downplays the responsibility of capital and government for anger among the downtrodden. However, this anger, surging tempestuously, but soon abating, reduced through cooption to an impotent rumble, also serves to suppress pain—the pain of injustice and the pain of hardship, but also the pain of loss. For many of those who rebelled against an amorphous establishment in the years following the 2008 financial crisis, the non-realisation of the last utopia's inclusive promise had already caused dejection. The anger identified by Mishra is symptomatic; melancholia is the affective condition structuring the political temperament of our age.

In the absence of competing visions of the future, the ideal of the humanitarian society appealed to different political persuasions. It became an object of identification for those who maintained faith in progress, as well as those who believed aspiration and hard work would improve their lives. If the impact of its frustration is thus widespread, its most trenchant opponents generally appear to have been mired in melancholia for much longer: those on the left remain attached to lost utopias of the past; those on the right, to collapsed empires, vanquished deities, decapitated monarchs, or the 'traditional family'. Collective expressions of hope now seem to emerge only from struggles for rights and subjectivities that are themselves imbued with melancholy. Almost seventy years ago, Frantz Fanon denounced the European demand for black colonial subjects to '*turn white or disappear*'.[122] Today, mimicry of hegemonic identities remains both a tactic and a precondition of assimilation, imposed by the powerful, whose own appropriative mimicry has contributed to the erasure of the past futures of the historically oppressed. Every demand for the abolition of racist institutions or the revision of colonial histories, indeed every assertion of anti-racist and anti-colonial progress, is also a melancholy statement on the loss of histories and identities that might have been. The construction of normative subjectivity would seem to establish as constitutive of othered identities an experience of loss that, paradoxically, becomes more pronounced as they are assimilated into bourgeois society.[123]

For French sociologist Alain Ehrenberg, melancholia, once 'the elective illness of the exceptional man', is now 'the situation of every individual in Western society'.[124] As *the exceptional* has been democ-ratised through the modern development of individualism, melancho-lia has been generalised as depression, a 'pathology of grandeur'. Ehrenberg's contention rests on an understanding of melancholia as an 'exacerbation of self-consciousness'.[125] The imposition of expecta-tions on the autonomous individual and the destruction of traditional references would seem to bear on the 'expansion of the diagnosis of depression' over the last fifty years, as, of course, would the massive growth of the psychotherapy industry. But the sense of loss at the end of the last utopia resides not so much in the individual psyche as in a *space between*: between subjective experience and social process, between the intimate and the public. It interacts with and aggravates contemporary depressive conditions—the chronic inferiority com-plexes nourished by social media, the 'solitary tiredness' resulting from pressure to perform and produce.[126] However, it cascades out-wards from the individual, with insufficient uniformity to shape a common sense or *conscience collective*, but with an affective force abun-dant enough to alter the grammar of social life and expose latent antagonisms. Melancholia, sustained by the apparent impossibility of utopia, comes to define a social mood, a change in the 'structures of feeling', which precedes and conditions political thought and action in the current conjuncture.[127]

Freud initially defined melancholia as a pathological mode of mourning.[128] And the option of societal suicide seems in recent years to have contributed to the appeal of politicians who flaunt their will to extreme violence, or at least their disregard for life. ('Annihilation', as Adorno strikingly affirmed, 'is the psychological substitute for the millennium.')[129] But, in 1923, Freud revised his concept of melan-cholia, recognising its necessary role in the formation of the ego, and, indeed, in the completion of mourning.[130] Melancholia is also given a productive function in Carl Jung's theory of individuation. Like Freud, Jung believed that, demanding conformity, civilisation caused a state of discontent in individuals. However, he differed from Freud in his suggestion that this was a melancholic state, which enabled individuals to differentiate themselves from the collective and overcome the impositions of 'civilised reason'.[131] On the one hand, melancholia becomes instrumental in the process of modern fragmentation that produces individuals as such. On the other, it becomes instrumental to the incorporation of elements of the unconscious through which the individual can overcome the modern conditioning of life as a fragment, stripped of feeling, intuition, and meaning.

Inherent to the logic of modernity, fragmentation—of societies, polities, economies, identities—has accelerated with the dissolution of utopias. If it has facilitated the generalisation of capitalist culture, it has also facilitated cultural differentiation, within capitalism, from the European project of civilisation. This invites Western societies to 'unlearn' Progress, which has served as sociodicy for all modern ideologies—to take heed of historical opposition to the submission of humanity and nature to the imperatives of political economy.[132] And it reveals the 'unconscious colonialism' of past utopian projects.[133] In a world without expectations, reinventing the future now demands a collective incorporation not only of lost fragments of the utopian imagination, but also of fragments of the unconscious, the ignored, the repressed. A product of dejection, the present melancholia nonetheless provides opportunity for this.

And reinventing the future is necessary. The pursuit of *mésure* in the present will not suffice for the majority who have experienced relative decline over the last fifteen years—not only precarious workers and the unemployed, but also small business owners and professionals, many of whom initially benefited from the neoliberal counter-revolution.[134] To project towards the future is not to postpone change in the present; rather, a utopian horizon is prerequisite to such change. Moreover, in a world in which the human quest for reason is constantly undermined by the contingent and the inexplicable, the struggle that produces an illusion of meaning—albeit necessarily ephemeral—is a more potent force of life than hedonistic abandon or meditative stasis. In a here and now pregnant with pandemic disease and apocalyptic climate change, the struggle for a future becomes a necessary defence against extinction. And that requires rupture from the presentist status quo.

Previously justified as an antidote to totalitarian violence, presentism is now complicit in the precipitation of the world's end. So too is nostalgia—for an imaginary golden age, but also for past imaginations of a brighter future.[135] The left, for which the loss of utopia is a recurrent and constitutive experience, is particularly prone to the latter variety.[136] But, as Wendy Brown has argued, its attachment to 'formations and formulations' of the past 'installs traditionalism in the very heart of its praxis, in the place where commitment to risk and upheaval belongs'.[137] Nostalgia prevents the sublimation of melancholia. It reifies past struggles as articles of indulgence and comfort. It thus neutralises their revolutionary potential in the present, producing the sort of 'negativistic quiet' Walter Benjamin associated with 'left-wing melancholy'—a literary mood, exemplified in the work of 'left radical publicists' of the New Objectivity. Taking pride in 'the traces of former spiritual goods', these writers had become disconnected from political action.[138] Despite this critique, Benjamin attributed to melancholia a revolutionary function.[139] In *The Origin of German Trauerspiel*, he argued that its 'persevering absorption takes the dead things up into its contemplation in order to save them'.[140] For Benjamin, the suffering of the past was incomplete.[141] The possibility of 'redemption' then lay amidst the debris produced by the passage of History—which came to represent unfinished business, to be taken on by the revolutionary class.[142]

Maintaining its destructive force, late capitalist Time is now nonetheless unable to propel History into the future. And so it piles its wreckage not in History's wake, but around us, in our conjuncture, crafting a wretched terrain over which we scramble just to stay still. Amidst the debris of the present lie fragments waiting to be born anew and charged with political meaning—fragments of different volume and character, fragments of thought and experience, of past certainties and meaning, of histories and totalities, of lost hopes and unconscious images, fragments which do not neatly fit together. But which of them can serve a rupture that revives struggle for the future? Is there a predetermined combination? Fragmentation disorientates.

NOTES ON OUR MELANCHOLY PRESENT

But perhaps *the real* was never more than a fragment. Perhaps modernity strips us back to what is necessary or—dare we say it—essential. Nude to the world, we are compelled to change our relationship with it. In search of a collective historical subject, a guarded gaze is cast upon those whose very survival is threatened by the capitalist present. The possibility of a future can only emerge from their claim to a necessity that, previously promised, is now precluded yet radically available: life. For if History is written by the victors, it is made by the vanquished.

November 2020

10

WARFARE ON WELFARE IN THE AGE OF EMERGENCY

Mark Duffield

For those who glaze over at the mention of 'neoliberalism', Quinn Slobodian's recent book, *Globalists*, provides a timely restorative.[1] Instead of the dominant Anglo-American position, he focuses on neoliberalism's neglected Geneva School. Its message subverts much of what usually passes as 'neoliberalism'. It is more than a market fundamentalist rationale. The thrust of Slobodian's argument is that the early neoliberals both reinforced, and went beyond, liberalism's originary fear and distrust of the popular masses. In the aftermath of the First World War, and in a world changed by the Russian Revolution and the establishment of the League of Nations, they tasked themselves with renewing liberalism's defence of private property against democracy in the new circumstances of an age without empire.

The challenge was to protect the 'world economy' from political demands for redistributive justice that would emerge from the coming 'world of states'. From the beginning, the neoliberals were globalist and, like Keynes, believed that the market cannot take care of itself. Since a world without empire was a challenge that classical liberalism could not have foreseen, the prefix 'neo' was added towards the end of the 1930s in recognition of this novel global responsibility.

For social democrats, the question of world order was resolved in the early twentieth century in favour of decolonisation and national self-determination. The Geneva School, however, stood apart from this developmental narrative. The passing of empire created a more pressing problem. It was imperative that new nation-states remained embedded within global institutions that safeguarded capital's inviolability. Rather than freeing markets, as such, during the latter half of the twentieth century, neoliberals largely focused on creating extra-economic supranational means to legally 'encase' the world market from political agitation for economic redistribution and social justice. They were associated with crafting opaque institutional rule-makers like the IMF, World Bank, and European Central Bank, together with governance structures such as the EU, NAFTA, and WTO.

Drawing on Carl Schmitt, the Geneva School developed a distinct 'two world' imaginary of world order to frame its concerns. Instead of cleaving the world into political East/West or developmental North/South divisions, they saw each world overlapping, nesting within, and transcendentally permeating the other. Rather than two separate halves of an orange, world order was more like its pith and peel.[2] The ideal world was one of bordered territories governed by sovereign states (*imperium*) together with an intermeshing world of privately owned property and resources scattered around the globe (*dominium*) that was quietly protected by opaque supranational legal arrangements.

During the 1990s, the legal insulation between *dominion* and *imperium* began to weaken. Rather than as feared, however, it was not the world of states encroaching on the world economy. It was the opposite. Unleashed by a capitalism now free of its social democratic fetters, the privatising, deregulating, and internationalising forces of globalisation reversed, if you will, the relationship between the two worlds. Instead of being distant or invisible, the violent operation of the world economy became an increasingly harsh reality for the majority world. Coupled with dangerous climate change, rather than being transcendental, capitalism, and the vulnerabilities it has created, is currently amid a *crisis of visibility*. This crisis has called forth new world reordering technologies of redirection, concealment, and disappearance.

Taking the *re*-encasement of an exposed global capitalism as a starting point, this essay critically explores the neoliberal theory of the welfare/warfare nexus and secessionism—including its populist new-right dimensions of belonging, identity, and culture.[3] Using Europe and its southern security frontier as a point of reference, it interprets this nexus as a war on social reproduction. The expulsion of reproduction from the modernist social commons has been achieved through interconnected processes of privatisation and, where resisted, the deliberate destruction of vital infrastructure and societal de-development. It concludes with a discussion of the emergence of a digital workhouse as a global technology for disappearing the resulting poor and precarious lives.

The Southern Frontier

Europe's external security frontier comprises those adjoining and contiguous countries that form the current limit of its declining ability to manage threat at a distance. This frontier emerged with the breakup of Yugoslavia: especially, moves to contain irregular migration through a combination of *in situ* humanitarian assistance and the alignment and tightening of Europe's refugee regimes. In 2003, on the heels of the US-led War on Terror and invasion of Iraq, the EU launched its defensive 'European Neighbourhood Policy' (ENP) strategy. Future security was vested in developing cooperative relations with bordering countries to the east and south. Of interest, here, is Europe's southern frontier.

Buffered from the 'mainland' by the Mediterranean and the Balkans, today this deep frontier zone curves from North Africa and the Sahel, through the Horn of Africa to the Middle East and Afghanistan. Together with the growing numbers of refugees moving north, its consolidation was prompted by the Iraqi debacle, the Arab Spring uprisings, and the collapse of Libya and Syria into civil war. In the mid-2000s, the EU forged a new policy consensus along its southern frontier known as the Khartoum Process. Irregular migration was criminalised in order to facilitate subcontracting Europe's frontier security to the participating states and their armed auxiliaries. In return for implementing a punitive regime of migrant interdiction and deterrent encampment, participants are compensated with security and development funding.

Compared to the expansionary logic of the twentieth century, the emergence of a deep European security frontier marks a structural break. It suggests a defensive inward retreat, as it were.[4] This frontier, moreover, gives a few suggestions regarding the emerging world order. Changes in international aid practice are suggestive.

The 1990s was a highpoint of direct humanitarian assistance and attempts at grounded UN peacebuilding. Indeed, for a few years, it looked as if a human security-based system of global governance was in the offing. As a result of political push-back and growing insecurity, however, Western aid agencies have retreated or relocated to safer neighbouring countries. Direct engagement has given way to remote management involving combinations of satellite surveillance, digital technology, and, importantly, local subcontracting. Now reliant upon local cooperative security agreements, earlier European human rights diplomacy has more or less disappeared.

The 'new wars' are wars within states where non-state and regional actors exploit the cross-border self-provisioning opportunities created by globalisation. They were instrumental in founding Europe's security frontier. Compared to their earlier incarnations, however, today's new wars differ in several ways. The direct humanitarian access and Western political leverage that existed in the 1990s, albeit limited and contingent, is absent. Modes of internationalised and protracted civil conflict have erupted that destroy vital reproductive systems and inflict horrendous civilian suffering and mass displacement as a *deliberate* war aim. Despite an open disregard for humanitarian norms, these urbicidal terror-wars now attract little international condemnation.

Fuelled by declining international media coverage and NGO safeguarding scandals, public indifference and antipathy to such violence and suffering is intrinsic to the reordering process underway. The outlawing of the internationalism once central to social democracy in favour of patriotism is evident. At the same time, a formative inter-dependence between this violent frontier and Europe's internal hostile environment engulfing the motley ranks of a new servant class of working poor, ethnic minorities, and migrants is taking shape.[5] The common denominator across this zone is capital's war on welfare or, more precisely, its war on social reproduction.

The Warfare / Welfare Nexus

Although plenty has been written about the new wars, Georgio Agamben has argued that, as a body of work, it falls short of a theory of civil war.[6] Rather than theorising, it leans towards uncritical problem-solving; for example, trying to make existing humanitarian practice more effective. In working toward a critical theory, Agamben distinguishes revolution from *stasis*, as the civil wars that disturbed the Greek *polis* where known. Revolutions, like love, create beginnings. Civil wars, on the other hand, rather than something new, appear more like quasi-natural progressions, or recurring clashes of established interests.

In Agamben's reading, the *stasis* of civil war marks a threshold of politicisation. *Stasis* lies between *oikos* (the family/household/economy) and *polis* (the city/political community). It is usually assumed that classical thought understood *polis* as overcoming *oikos* once and for all. He argues, however, that the relationship is complicated and unresolved. *Stasis* is a threshold through which *oikos* is politicised into *polis*, and, conversely, *polis* is depoliticised into *oikos*. Rather than a one-way ticket, *stasis* is a recurrent cycle of the politicisation *and* depoliticisation of *oikos*.

That Western political culture emerged from the classical world is axiomatic. As a heuristic exercise, *stasis* is here transposed onto the Geneva School's two-world imaginary of world order. Neoliberalism also presupposes a threshold of politicisation separating the word of states (*polis*) from the world economy (*oikos*). That liberalism takes the household as the basic model of economic behaviour adds some support for this anachronistic transposition. For much of the twentieth century, neoliberalism sought to *prevent* the politicisation of the world economy by arguing its transcendental unknowability, at the same time as protecting it by legal encasement. Given the activist backlash against globalisation, health inequality, and climate change, however, recent struggles have stripped this veil away. The world economy as a wrecking ball is more visible and politicised than at any time in recent history.

Attempts to *re*-conceal capitalism have usually been explored in relation to the Hayekian embrace of resilience and complex adaptive systems theory. Here, the focus is on the Geneva School, especially its American new-right strand and its understanding of modern warfare and secession; in particular, the welfare/warfare nexus first mooted by Murray Rothbard, in 1967.[7] For Rothbard, there are two pathways for acquiring wealth. Either the legitimate production of goods and services for voluntary exchange (the economic means), or, dispensing with this, the illegitimate appropriation of the labour and wealth of others (the political means).

Modern inter-state warfare has allowed the state to *politicise* the economy. It is this fear of political control, rather than any progressive or humane sentiment, that shapes neoliberalism's otherwise anti-war stance. Given the extraordinary resourcing and human sacrifice needed to wage the total wars of the twentieth century, the warfare state is regarded as susceptible to pressure for liberal welfare reforms. By calling for public welfare at home to offset the societal demands of global-hegemonic wars, it is argued that social democrats used the state to gain control over private property, thus 'distorting' the economy. This process culminated in what Rothbard mockingly calls liberalism's mid-twentieth-century Great Society.

The relationship between militarism and welfare deserves further analysis. One could say that the interconnection is intrinsic to modernism. On this point, however, the neoliberal analysis of the welfare/warfare nexus is wanting at several levels. The nexus, for example, has both European *and* non-European variants.[8] With the countries that form Europe's southern frontier as examples, rather than associated with global-hegemonic warfare, non-European welfare variants were the result of wars of national liberation and, more recently, the anti-liberal struggles of political Islam. Not only is this history occluded; European variants of the modernist welfare state did not just appear like a political cancer as Rothbard suggests. Rather than being given, they were *taken*. Besides struggles for universal suffrage and national liberation, the politicisation of the economy, so to speak, required decades of violent resistance, mass strikes, civil protest, and democratic contestation *from below*.

The Centrality of Social Reproduction

The question of social reproduction is also missing from the neoliberal account of the welfare/warfare nexus. The threshold of politicisation between economy and politics is occupied by the 'zero point' of social reproduction. The 'economic means' for acquiring wealth requires the free production and exchange of goods and services. Wealth, however, is dependent upon the social reproduction of the labour to both produce and consume it.[9] Although men help, social reproduction is reliant upon women and much of their lifetime labour. For the majority world, besides birthing, it involves nurturing the young, and caring for the old and sick. Crucially, however, social reproduction goes beyond these household functions and moral reciprocities to encompass a whole range of societal structures, including ancillary employment, health, and educational activities, necessary to reproduce day-to-day life.

Importantly, there is an antagonism between production (profit-making) and reproduction (life-making). As the history of liberalism and slavery attests, capital prefers the latter activities to be as cheap and transactional as possible.[10] Like American self-employed gig workers or the World Bank's Community-Driven Development (CDD) programmes in Africa, ideally, social reproduction should be external to capital and free, or as good as.

Integral to the growth of modern welfare states was the creation of insurance and tax-based national institutions to support social reproduction. Asserted rather than granted, *oikos*, if you will, was politicised during the mass social-democratic and nationalist struggles of the twentieth century. Together with trade union representation, it was enclosed within a mesh of bureaucratised education, health and employment benefits, rights and protection. This modernist 'social commons' was predictably condemned by (neo)liberals as economic distortion. To be frank, however, it was no utopia. The social commons was patriarchal, racialised, and hardly universal. Nonetheless, by the 1970s, this temporary accommodation had fostered a belief that political progress *was* possible. It had also helped author historically low levels of global inequality.

If welfare emerged from warfare during the twentieth century, *warfare is now being waged on welfare*. More precisely, for the last four decades war has been waged on social reproduction. Reflecting the *stasis* of civil war, following the politicisation of social reproduction (the creation of a modernist social commons), the effect of the conservative backlash has again been to *depoliticise* social reproduction. Apart from a workfare residuum, reproductive responsibility has been purged from the economy, freeing it from the 'distortions' capital was forced to suffer. The destruction of the social commons is tantamount to the *re*-individualisation of reproductive liability. And this has depoliticised social reproduction, reducing its political visibility at a time when austerity has plunged reproduction into a deepening global crisis.

There is more to reindividualisation, however, than the counter-revolutionary destruction of the social commons. Already present when the idea of the warfare/welfare nexus was first mooted, there is an aspect of 'warfare' that has not only outlived the social-democratic welfare state but, arguably, is only today coming into its own. That is, the systems-based, cybernetic 'science of warfare' that, since the 1960s, has grown into a vast techno-infrastructure for coding, surveilling, and remotely managing the poor and precarious lives that capitalism is now producing in abundance. This is discussed below in relation to the digital workhouse.

Privatisation and Destruction

It is uncanny how the British warfare state, in imaginatively enacting how to survive nuclear war, anticipated the emerging post-social world. In 1972, the British government changed the name of its national war preparations from Civil Defence to *Home* Defence. Official thinking had moved away from earlier commitments to mass shelter construction and other universalistic measures. Instead, only vital war-fighting infrastructure was to be protected while the sinews of a secret deep-state were, quite literally, buried. Apart from advice, the public was abandoned to its fate.[11]

The government went on to covertly game the survival of a nuclear attack. This culminated in the ultimately aborted 1982 Hard Rock exercise. Assuming extensive destruction and loss of life, these games were imaginative enactments of proto-resilience. Among other things, they explored the transition to new post-attack equilibria. Cities were left to burn out and, as radiation levels dropped, the anticipated civil breakdown and lawlessness was played out. Re-establishing equilibrium involved, for example, the triage of survivors. Diseased and irradiated 'zombies' were denied what limited food and care was available. Dictated by the technical knowledge or skills required to work the salvageable infrastructure, the healthy were themselves ranked and prioritised.

These imaginative enactments anticipated a new relationship to reproductive infrastructure. Rather than a modernist social commons, with its open and universal pretensions, people were profiled according to the requirements of the vital systems themselves. With the welfare state destroyed, the masters of the surviving post-attack infrastructure assumed the power to delineate the 'useful' and 'useless'; the 'inside' and 'outside'; and the 'visible' and 'invisible'. This new and subordinate relationship to critical infrastructure entered the real world with the privatisation of the social state that gathered speed in the 1980s.

In relation to the expulsion of social reproduction from the social state and its reindividualisation, the gaming of nuclear war suggests two main processes: the *privatisation* and the *destruction* of vital infrastructure. While different, these processes are interconnected. Across Europe and along its deep security frontier, the war on social reproduction has been relentlessly prosecuted through both modalities.

Since the 1980s, through processes of privatisation, deregulation, and internationalisation of erstwhile public services and utilities, both European and non-European variants of modernism have been subject to their own forms of 'structural adjustment'. Both, for example, have experienced austerity and variants of the voluntarisation or NGO-isation of welfare provision.

Where this globalising process has been resisted or obstacles encountered, vital reproductive systems have, quite literally, been destroyed. While European trade unionism figures here, in terms of public health systems, this is mainly associated with the southern frontier and the new wars. Recalcitrant modernist states or resistant organisations have been violently *de*-developed. The example of Iraq is discussed below.

Having different speeds, scales, and temporalities, privatisation and destruction are part of the same world reordering dynamic. Together, they have had the effect of blurring the developmental gap between the global North and South, creating a motley middle ground of poverty, inequality, and precarity.[12] In the age of emergency, the world is pulling apart politically while, in terms of capitalism's border-hopping social, health, and environmental crises, it is drawing closer together. The destruction of the social state along Europe's security frontier is intrinsic to this crisis.

New Wars Redux

The breakup of Yugoslavia at the beginning of the 1990s into ethno-separatist parties was the ground on which the 'new wars' thesis took root.[13] Happening on the doorstep of Europe, such nation-state fragmentation was an existential shock to its metropolitan elite. From a liberal left perspective, globalisation's blurring of national boundaries exposed and encouraged existing ethnic and cultural tensions. It created new extra-legal transborder connections able to realise the financial, weapons, and combatant flows to sustain and reward these divisions. Globalisation encouraged the internationalisation of national disintegration. For the liberal left, the new wars were a negative expression of backward nationalism, human rights abuse, and international criminality.[14] For a decade or more, they were the evil genie that humanitarian actors, UN state-builders, and affronted cosmopolitans tried to put back in the bottle.

The emerging new right, however, saw things differently. Rather than condemning ethno-separatism, Hans-Hermann Hoppe imagined it as 'potentially the most progressive historical force'.[15] Instead of dismay, the breakup of Yugoslavia was a positive opportunity. National warfare states had grown, it was argued, through subsuming hundreds of former small countries, independent principalities and free cities. The centralising nation-state dynamic had everywhere ridden roughshod over former independent economic entities, ethnic groups, and cultural preferences. The many had been corralled into a pressure-cooker world of the few. The upsurge of Eastern European secessionism at the end of the Cold War was not only inevitable, it was welcome. The new right saw in it a long-suppressed desire for autonomy and consumer freedom; a demand to take back control that was forecast to spread to Western Europe.

Within this new-right iteration of neoliberalism, identity, and culture are forces able to *un*-distort the economy, so to speak. This required a rewriting of the twentieth-century two-world thesis in favour of a *de*-globalising populism. Processes of political integration (centralisation) among the world of states and the economic (market) integration of the world economy are different and *opposed* phenomena.[16] Political integration is proscribed as it encourages taxation, property regulation, and, as indicated above, it expands the social state. However, world market integration, or economic circulation, is positive.

Economic circulation makes it possible for interpersonal relations, interregional divisions of labour, and local forms of market participation to interpolate the world of states. No longer transcendental or invisible, political economy is now manifest in visible ethnic and cultural networks that operationalise dispersed economic conglomerations. The new wars are one example of the 'progressive historical force' of economic circulation to transcend the world of states and unlock suppressed majority identities within them. New-right populism envisions a world that is pulling apart into its 'natural' constituencies while still retaining a liberal faith in private property.

For the new right, globalisation makes the 'freedom' of uniculturalism possible. It gives the lie to multiculturalism and the belief that states can bind different ethnic or cultural groups together. Not only are multicultural states destined to fragment; decentralisation through secession is also argued to offer economic advantages. Just as the relative surface area of a sphere increases as its size decreases, secession creates smaller and more efficient economic units.[17] Greater surface area, so to speak, exposes the latent interpersonal linkages and networking power that secessionist groups embody.

Such views underpin neoliberalism's opposition to imperialism. It is a politically hegemonic project. Given this objection, the new right is more sympathetic to settler colonialism. As long, that is, as clear lines of separation divide newcomers from indigenous peoples—as in, for example, the nineteenth-century Boer Republics of South Africa.[18] For similar reasons, there is support for the emphatic spatial divisions of apartheid states. Held up as an example of small-is-efficient, Somalia also holds a special fascination. Although a tiny country, beset by insecurity and without an effective state, its economic diversification to become a regional telecommunications hub, for example, is regularly cited as a libertarian success story.[19]

Two Sides of the Same Coin

The liberal left and the new right are the conjoined heirs of liberalism. While capable of strongly opposed views, they also have much in common. As Domenico Losurdo argues, liberalism and illiberalism were irredeemably fused at birth. Many of liberalism's founding fathers were share-holders, apologists, and supporters of chattel slavery in the Americas. With such help, this most abhorrent form of slavery 'triumphed in the golden age of liberalism and at the heart of the liberal world'.[20] The burden of living with this original sin has rendered liberalism incapable of voicing freedom without having to justify and delimit the conditions of unfreedom.

This ill-starred settlement has important consequences for the unfinished business of emancipation. It draws attention to liberalism's proscription of the political. In defining what sort of life is capable of political freedom, thus creating space for that which is not, liberalism seeks social agreement. Driven by capital's enduring paradox of wealth and freedom amidst poverty and slavery, liberalism is preoccupied with spreading the net of culpability. Since the age of revolution, delimiting the political is no longer a sovereign act. It needs the agreement of the left and right persuasions, if you will, that constitute the liberal canon. Denying political voice to those deemed incapable of freedom requires social consensus. Liberal hegemony is thus all the more complete and chilling.

In order to make contestation and agreement possible, liberalism needs an agreed set of ontological building-blocks that unite left and right. It requires a common lens through which the capacities that make freedom possible can be debated and ranked. Having supplanted biological race, since the mid-twentieth century a key assumption uniting left and right has been the causal primacy of cultural difference. And, consequently, the centrality of the registers of ethnicity and religion that follow from this.[21]

During the 1960s and 1970s, these were the agreed categories that both left and right used to rework issues of race and immigration.[22] By the 1990s, the same common lens was being directed toward the new wars.[23] Both the liberal left and the new right accepted the importance and explanatory power of cultural difference. They also shared the same worst case scenario: left to itself, ethnonationalism can easily spiral into intolerance, violence, and social breakdown. Where they differed was on *outcomes*. For the liberal left, breakdown could be avoided through, for example, conflict resolution programmes, multi-actor peace-building, and equal opportunity measures. For the new right, however, violence was inevitable. As we have seen above, secession and cultural separation was the only viable solution and should, at least, be allowed. As well as fuelling the intolerance the liberal left opposed, the new right saw the necessity for external equality and state-building measures as a vindication of its position.

Our main interest in liberalism's left–right dialectic is not the opposing programmes that each side can generate from the same ontological building-blocks. More importantly, a common lens facilitates a continual process of political elision. A revolving door, if you will, allowing one side to turn into the other, and then move back again. In times of emergency, left–right canonical divisions blur into consensus. The waving through by progressives and conservatives alike, on grounds of national security, of a rapidly expanding security state following the 9/11 attacks is a paradigmatic example.[24] Another case, discussed below, is the fragility of the liberal left promotion of refugee rights.[25]

Since the latter half of the twentieth century, the left–right syndrome has expanded its basic conceptual building-blocks together with its field of operation. Culture, ethnicity, and identity still remain central. Now, however, they are refracted through the circulatory and biological registers of social reproduction. Whereas the new right and liberal left agree, for example, that globalisation has accelerated inequality and social exclusion, their differences now lie at the heart of the West's culture wars.[26] While this is beyond the scope of this chapter, one connection is important. As the austerity-driven hostile environment has engulfed Europe's working poor, benefit claimants, ethnic minorities, and migrants, the new wars have morphed into the deliberate destruction of reproductive infrastructure along its security frontier.

Shock & Awe

Europe's southern security frontier did not emerge, it was created. Faced with bordering or contiguous autonomous modernist regimes, Europe has been involved with, or complicit in, their removal. This has occurred either through privatisation or, if resisted, the destruction of their reproductive infrastructure and allied professions and trades. One obvious consequence has been the growing migrant and refugee crisis.

Regarding destruction, drawing on the first Gulf War and the breakup of Yugoslavia, Zygmunt Bauman, writing in 2001, argued that, whatever their stated intention, the structural effect of 'wars in the globalising era' has been the removal of obstacles to privatisation.[27] Only launched if there was a low-risk, high probability of success, the outcome was an opening of otherwise closed areas to the free circulation of finance, capital, and commodities. Rather than armies pitched against each other on a battlefield, globalising wars did this by one-sidedly destroying the recalcitrant party's ability to resist through the deliberate elimination of national reproductive and public health capacity.

Omar Dewachi's account of the creation of Iraq's modern public health system and, following the 1991 Gulf War, its relatively quick destruction, is instructive.[28] Iraq's health system had its origins in the Ottoman empire. Its professionalisation, centralisation, and internationalisation developed further under British colonial rule. The postcolonial socialist and Ba'athist regimes continued to expand public health capacity, reaching a high point during the militarism of the Iran–Iraq war in the 1980s. Reliant on the mobilisation of women, infant and child mortality halved as primary healthcare was extended to Iraq's periphery. At the time, this strengthening of national reproductive capacity was widely celebrated by the UN as a development success.

In the case of a recalcitrant Iraq, decapacitation and the creation of a post-social wild was rapidly imposed by the brutal hammer-blows of the Gulf War aerial assault, years of crippling UN sanctions and, finally, the devastating 2003 US-led occupation. A century in the making, in little more than a decade Iraq's proven public health system lay in ruins, its doctors and nurses scattered throughout the Middle East and Europe. Iraq is now incapable of providing anything but basic care within its borders. The few remaining doctors have gone from being icons of modernity to targets for assassination, kidnapping, and the reparational violence of patients' families.

In the mid-1990s, when Yugoslavia was in the midst of its own abrupt admittance to the post-social world, buoyed by the 'success' of the Gulf War, US military analysts were consolidating a doctrine of rapid dominance known as *Shock & Awe*. This envisaged the quick and comprehensive degrading of a society's vital systems, just shy of total destruction, such that all enemy resistance—physical, mental, and reproductive—becomes impossible.[29] Soon, however, this highly mimetic and easily subcontracted terror-war genie would be out of the bottle.

As the subsequent state/non-state actor demolition of the existing reproductive capacities of Libya, Syria, Somalia, South Sudan, and Yemen suggests, the civil horror of Yugoslavia and Iraq would be endured by many others.[30] By the mid-2000s, not only the US, its allies, and opponents, but all sides and persuasions along Europe's southern frontier—internal and external, local and regional—would be pulling the levelling levers of terror-war with impunity. Given the secrecy precedent set by first movers in these fields, this includes the unregulated global proliferation of cheap surveillance and drone warfare technologies.

As Middle Eastern states fractured with the internationalisation of internal antagonisms, globalising wars have pulverised and scattered to the winds the skilled, professional, and cultural classes that previously defined what, by common consent, were educated, scientifically proficient, middle-income countries. Following their violent expulsion from the social commons, the remaining inhabitants of these states have typically been rediscovered and reclassified in terms of their more 'authentic' premodern tribal and religious indigeneity. As if they had been masquerading all along.

The idea of 'collateral damage' has seamlessly occluded such terror, transforming it into an unfortunate but necessary by-product of making the world a safer place. Liberal sensibility is thus shielded from culpability with the most heinous acts of recent times. Critical theorists have struggled to throw this normalised mayhem into relief. Gaining fresh traction as Yugoslavia disintegrated, the idea of urbicide, *or the killing of cities*, for example, attempts to puncture such complacency and capture the gravity of the event.[31] Urbicide, however, is but one descriptor of the transformation of the old modernist biopolitics of 'make live', into the new necropolitics of 'let die'.[32]

The new-right acceptance of the inevitability, indeed, the desirability of secession, including the pulling apart of nation-states, is part of the political ascendancy of necropolitics. Violent and purposeful de-development through the destruction of urbanity along Europe's southern frontier is tantamount to the dehumanisation of those on the receiving end. Indeed, their ejection from modernity. The increasing militarisation of Europe's borders and stripping of migrants and refugees of all rights—except that of dying—marks a new left–right convergence.

As long as the 'resilience' of refugees remained within approved limits of adaptation, innovation, and acceptance, their rights could be defended. During the refugee crisis however, resilience has morphed into threatening autonomy, defiance, and anger. Through the 'discovery' of criminality and extremism, a new left–right consensus regarding unworthiness has emerged. As the official indifference and complicity with the mass drownings in the Mediterranean suggests, supporting the deep frontier as a 'shield' for the preservation of European 'values' is something that all now agree on.[33]

Recalcitrant states were remnants of a modernist past. Following their destruction, they have been replaced by a disaster capitalism that reproduces itself through precarity.[34] Hidden from view by the technological veil of remote humanitarian management and arm's-length news gathering, Europe's security frontier anticipates the future.

The Digital Workhouse

For those who care to look, capitalism is more visible now that at any time in recent history. The violence of globalisation, the crisis of social reproduction, and depth of the climate crisis have changed everything. There is a dialectical relationship between visibility and invisibility. The one requires the other; they cannot exist alone. Capitalism is visible because its old extra-economic means of supranational legal encasement have broken down. Since the world has changed, however, rather than a repair exercise something new is required. While growing authoritarianism is significant, it does not exhaust the new forms of redirection, manipulation, and disappearance that are rising to the challenge.

Data is not knowledge. It is optimised for immediate operationality. Knowledge, in contrast, requires a long process of contact, refinement, and maturation. It sits awkwardly with demands for speed, productivity, and efficiency. Big Data contains little knowledge. Algorithms look for patterns and correlations. If X happens, expect Y but not Z. This is a valid and actionable correlation. As such, it is unnecessary to know the causal relationship between X, Y, and Z. Thought thus becomes unnecessary.[35] If the computer 'says no', the question 'why' is irrelevant. In all likelihood, no one knows; and few have the authority to override the decision. Rather than creating closeness, smart technology's abolition of distance prevents it, creating instead a digital 'gaplessness' into which all types of distance and proximity collapse—along with the history, struggles, and knowledge of digitally coded lives.[36] The conventional view of smart technology is that it either acts as a force-multiplier for human agency or, more narcissistically, it is rewiring our brains as we become cyborgs. The reality is more mundane and chilling: it is *indifferent* to the human condition.

The poorhouse in America, like the workhouse in Britain, predates the modernist welfare state. Both were stark punishment regimes designed to deter the destitute from seeking relief. The poor have traditionally been among the most surveilled in society. It has already been mentioned that besides 'welfare', the mid-twentieth-century warfare state also gave us cybernetics, computer simulation, geospatial surveillance, and systems management. In other words, the 'science of warfare'. Gathering pace in the 1960s, the war on welfare involved attempts to extend this new computational science direct to social problems. Initially, this was the 'war on poverty' in American cities.[37] Through the RAND corporation, new technology was harnessed to resolve capitalism's paradox of poverty amidst plenty.[38]

While achieving little or nothing on the ground, the main effect was to radically change the institutional management and understanding of welfare at a time when political pressure to close the social commons was growing. Over the past three or four decades, as part of the reindividualisation and depoliticisation of social reproduction, computer technologies have become increasingly used to sorting, classifying, and ranking the residual poor. The workfare state that has emerged looks backwards as well as forwards. As Virginia Eubanks has argued, premodern contempt for the habits, behaviour, and household dynamics of poor lives has returned. Now, however, this contempt is wired into the system.[39] The tension between the long history of struggle for welfare rights, and the disappearance of political support for those rights, was resolved by the logic of smart technology.

From the early days of the 'war on poverty', techno-science helped depoliticise reproduction by promising new efficiencies that circumvent the need for wasteful notions of universalism. Able to 'zoom in', even from space, and 'objectively' differentiate agglomerated populations, the new welfare managers favoured more textured targeting rather than blanket prescriptions. Smart welfare weapons rather than dumb redistribution bombs. This is the welfare of special needs, cultural difference, behavioural change, and choice. Little pleasure is gained from observing that, over the intervening decades, social breakdown, urban fragmentation, and inequality have gone off the scale. For the first time in a century, even life expectancy is declining among the 'disadvantaged'.[40] It also misses the point. There is no comeback, no redress, no responsibility. The capture of welfare by the science of warfare laid the foundation for the digitalisation of poor and precarious lives and, with the automation of welfare, the 'gapless' disappearance of a whole swathe of global society.

As suggested by Britain's 'digital-by-design' universal credit reforms, an unaccountable and punitive digital workhouse is emerging.[41] Kept at arm's length through spatial segregation and the automation of workfare benefits, the depth of social breakdown and immiseration is hidden. Helped by the levelling effects of privatisation and the globalising wars, with little public debate or scrutiny, the digital workhouse is being rolled out across the world of states.[42] Billions of low-income households, working poor, the destitute, and irregular migrants are having their interactions with state authorities automated and enclosed within opaque systems of biometric identification and predictive algorithms. Their reproductive lives are being decided and managed by anonymous systems of artificial intelligence protected from accountability by competition law.

The digital workhouse also subsumes humanitarian assistance. Indeed, since the 1980s, the sector has been an important site of workfare innovation linked to the introduction of smart technology in partnership with the private sector.[43] Innovations include automated needs assessment, mobile cash-transfer, and the medicalisation of nutrition. Refugees and irregular migrants have long been a testbed for remote cross-border tracking. From London to New Delhi via Lagos, the global digital workhouse is being rolled-out amid a deafening celebration of smart technology by policymakers, academics, and humanitarians.

Across the world of states, huge amounts of money are being spent to push through digital-by-design workfare systems. There has been a massive increase in biometric registration by stealth amidst lack of data protection, limited legislative oversight, and political function creep. This is compounded by the absence of human instrumentality in assessment, adjudication, and monitoring. The digital workhouse amounts to a punitive regime of endless access difficulties, entitlement mistakes, missed payments, and lack of redress, in exchange for nugatory benefits and intrusive surveillance by a system that never forgets. At a time of increasing precarity and the normalisation of otherwise high global levels of malnutrition, against expectations, the figures suggest that the transition has produced steep reductions in global welfare spending and beneficiary numbers.[44] Like the refugees who avoid 'biometric tattooing' as they move towards Europe, even desperate people keep out of the digital workhouse.

Concluding Remarks

In an age of permanent emergency, it is vital to occupy a political position outside liberalism's left–right dialectic. Without such a refuge, life will be wracked by endless cycles of virtue and hate within what Mark Fisher calls the vampire castle—a site of condemnation and the propagation of guilt.[45] An alternative requires confronting liberalism's proscription of the political. We cannot look to the established order of political acceptance and liberal recognition for salvation. Emancipation is not within the gift of liberalism's community of the free. This community fully acknowledges, even documents and teaches, the barbarity around us, yet continues to identify European values as our best hope.

A different and radical phenomenology of power is required; one that accepts that the interlocutors of change are those that the community of the free render invisible, worthless, and disposable. A radical perspective is one that is open to revolution from below. It identifies and denounces barbarism 'in those responsible for, and complicit with, the most macroscopic violation of the rights and dignity of man'.[46] The hostile environment currently directed at the working poor, benefit claimants, and immigrants within Europe, the militarisation of its borders, and the violent de-development and terror that has engulfed its deep security frontier drives a stake through the dead heart of European values.

The fashioning of a surveilled servant class from the expanding global precariat irredeemably brands the society we live in.

The left–right nexus, however, is wider than liberalism's proscription of the political. For Keynesians and neoliberals alike, the state and the market fill the entire space of the social. They cannot 'conceive of a world in which there are multiple social fields, other spaces in which organisational or allocative work is possible'.[47] Despite the new-right support of secession and the pulling apart of nation-states, unicultural and apartheid societies still need a state. At the same time, since the 2008 financial crisis, the prospect of the return of the state has been greeted by the liberal left with optimism. Consequently, within the nexus, the political novelty of the new wars remains unrecognised. Namely, that, emerging in the shadow of globalisation, they revealed reproductive possibilities beyond the state.

Given the privatisation and destruction of the modernist social commons, criminalised by the liberal left and paraded by the new right, the new wars were examples of emerging forms of politicised *self*-reproduction outside of states. As a response to the post-social world, they were 'new' in pioneering modes of asymmetric warfare that were also independent of the mass support deemed necessary for earlier revolutionary and national liberation struggles. They typically entail leveraging illicit resources and shadow markets to pursue political agendas and meet welfare needs. Rather than the wars themselves, however, it is their underlying *modus operandi* that is important: the possibility of modes of autonomous off-grid reproduction capable of supporting local recalcitrance in the name of political change. Thus, from the Battle of Seattle through the Arab Spring to the Sudanese Revolution, local and community life-making activities have been able to assume different scales, degrees of internationalisation, and longevity in the struggle against authoritarianism and austerity.[48]

In the context of the new subaltern struggles for recognition that the age of emergency is generating, the return of the state cannot be uncritically accepted. It is possible, perhaps likely, that the disposable ranks of capital's new servant class—*those destined to circulate while elites connect*—will disappear within an expanding digital workhouse. The repoliticisation of social reproduction is more necessary than ever—and it will depend on the voices of change from below.

11

THE WHITE MODERATES

EUROPE AND THE RETURN OF THE STATE IN MALI

Fernando Espada

When, in January 2013, President François Hollande authorised *Opération Serval*, he insisted that France had no interests in Mali other than 'protecting an ally country and fighting terrorists'.[1] A seemingly selfless Hollande talked about supporting Mali's sovereignty and territorial integrity, respect for the UN Charter, and France's support for the Security Council's resolution mandating the deployment of an African-led mission in the Sahelian country.[2] However, aside from these reasons of *big politics*, Hollande did not explain during the televised speech why his countrymen should rally behind what would soon become a fairly large military operation. Perhaps he thought that a vague reference to the terrorist threat emanating from the Central Sahel and confidence in the performance of the French army in the *pré carré* of the Francophonie would be enough to persuade public opinion that, in fact, *Opération Serval* was not such a big deal. The positive media coverage of the presidential announcement,[3] followed by a modest uptick in Hollande's approval ratings, seemed to prove him right.[4] It did not seem to matter that the images of thousands of Malians greeting 'Papa Hollande' on the streets of Bamako only a few days later suggested that France's game in Mali was not as straightforward as it seemed.[5] A game that would lead Hollande, an unlikely advocate of a revived *Françafrique*, to open the doors to France's largest foreign military deployment since the Algerian war of independence.[6]

While *Opération Serval* was not a departure from a less interventionist French policy in Africa—when Europeans send troops to Africa 'it is essentially a French intervention'[7]—it would also be wrong to reduce Hollande's decision to just another postcolonial adventure. As Roland Marchal explains, there was hardly a consensus within the French government about whether and how to intervene in Mali.[8] France considered several options, from building an African-led coalition with international support to *smart* military operations. A large-scale operation was not among their preferred options in the absence of the prerequisites that, Stephen Smith argues, led to other military adventures decades earlier:

> Hollande would enjoy a cosy relationship with the 'big man' in power in Bamako, who would have secretly funded the French Socialist Party; thousands of French expats would be making a good living in the former colony; Mali's mineral or agricultural resources would be firmly in the hands of French companies; and the country's diplomacy would follow the French lead as unerringly as a sunflower follows the daystar.[9]

'Protecting an ally country and fighting terrorists' was an uncontroversial justification, even though in 2013—and perhaps still today—French public opinion would not consider the Central Sahel a terrorist hotspot of the same scale as the Middle East or the Maghreb. The message was that *Opération Serval* was the right thing to do to protect a weak country, not what had to be done to protect France. Neither Hollande nor his government openly admitted that they were, indeed, worried that Mali could become a direct threat if the authorities in Bamako collapsed. According to the assessment of security officials, the Malian diaspora would be receptive to jihadist propaganda in that scenario:[10] 'If we don't fight today in Mali, we will fight tomorrow in Marseille'—or so some in circles close to the Palais de l'Élysée argued.[11] Despite that assessment, Hollande and his government probably thought that the domestic threat argument would have looked far-fetched. Or perhaps they thought that it was too real to be disclosed. It was one thing to say that fighting terrorism was an objective for *Opération Serval*—and for *Opération Barkhane*, its offshoot from 2014—and another thing to go public with an assessment of the potential impact of the crisis in Mali on France's internal security.

For those who see Marseille as the quintessential 'lost territory of the Republic',[12] the French city is not only poor—26 percent of the population, according to official figures—but not French enough.[13] It is estimated that, as a proportion of its population, Marseille hosts the largest number of Muslims in the country—many of them, presumably, of Malian origin.[14] And so follows the fear that Marseille is constantly on the brink of social violence, a threat to the rest of France. It matters little that there is less ethnic tension in Marseille than in other French cities, as the small number of violent incidents during the civil unrest in 2005 showed.[15] The counterpoint of a prosperous and liberal France, Marseille is a space believed to require policies and policing to tackle marginalisation, crime, and corruption in the hope that it will eventually catch up with the rest of the country and the European average.

All these factors were probably enough justification for security officials to conclude that the Mediterranean city was vulnerable to the spill-over effect of the collapse of state authorities in Mali, another lost territory of the Republic. However, could the feared contagion effect of the jihadists' success in the Central Sahel or the expeditionary fantasies of the grand strategists in the Élysée alone justify the substantial cost and risks of such a large-scale military deployment?

As a *ghost-chasing* strategy, the Global War on Terror—'an expensive, exhausting, bewildering, chaotic and paranoia-inducing process'—has proven elastic enough to accommodate all sorts of geostrategic impulses, including putting boots on the ground.[16] Moreover, military interventions have long been part of the toolbox that liberal democracies—and other less liberal states such as Russia or Turkey— have at their disposal to fix, tweak, or kick down the road issues of concern, whether for selfless or selfish reasons, or a blurring of the two. So, according to that familiar logic, the costs and risks of a large French military deployment were not completely out of place, or scale, as a preventive measure.

What makes the *Mali–Marseille connection* particularly interesting is that it displays a mindset that permeates the European liberal project at home and abroad, making Hollande's decision less of a tactical miscalculation. The Mali–Marseille connection that this chapter explores is not defined by the threat of radical Islamist propaganda and terrorist plots travelling from Africa to Europe, through a modern version of the gate left unlocked in Constantinople's wall of Theodosius. On the contrary, this imagined connection is relevant for what it tells us about the liberal impulse to order; what Martin Luther King, Jr., described in his 'Letter from a Birmingham Jail' as:

> the white moderate who is more devoted to 'order' than to justice; who prefers a negative peace which is the absence of tension to a positive peace which is the presence of justice; who constantly says: 'I agree with you in the goal you seek, but I cannot agree with your methods of direct action'; who paternalistically believes he can set the timetable for another man's freedom; who lives by a mythical concept of time and who constantly advises the Negro to wait for a 'more convenient season'.[17]

In recent times, white moderates have responded with the same agreement on the goals, and disagreement on the direct-action methods, of Black Lives Matter protesters. And they now express hope that Joe Biden's electoral victory can bring about a return to normality. The airtime that has been given to images of violence on American streets, and to debates about whether demonstrations would end up helping Trump's re-election and a further populist backlash elsewhere, show the same preoccupation with order.[18] The white moderates' devotion to order was plain to see in the French President's determined announcement of the deployment of thousands of soldiers to Mali, without much consideration as to what had caused instability and what it entailed. The Mali–Marseille connection worked well as the trigger of France and Europe's intervention in Mali. However, without dismissing the validity of the security concerns, this chapter proposes a more nuanced explanation of Europe's policies in so-called 'fragile contexts'.[19]

The liberal democracies that in 2013 went 'to the rescue' of Mali did so with a strategy but without purpose. That seven years later an increasing number of European countries continue to deploy significant human and material resources to contain the spread of terrorism and the criminal activities of human and drug traffickers, and funnel hundreds of millions of euros-worth of humanitarian and development aid to an ever-growing number of people affected by violence, hunger, or forced displacement, reinforces the illusion of collective commitment to a goal that, while difficult, is achievable and worthwhile. Yet, as I argue in this chapter, the European intervention in Mali is defined and sustained by what it lacks rather than by what it tries to achieve. This is not a design failure but a symptom of a malaise that affects Western liberal societies.

Taken at face value, Europe's policies in Mali are still driven by what John Gray defined as the *central myth of apocalyptic religion*: 'The end of history, the passing of the sovereign state, universal acceptance of democracy and the defeat of evil.'[20] Indeed, the hope of an unprecedented change in human affairs that shaped global politics in the past three decades permeates European discourse and practice in the so-called 'surrounding regions'. Little does it seem to matter that promises of transformation through the Global War on Terror, humanitarian interventions, or the Millennium Development Goals vanished amidst the generalisation of instability: wars in Iraq and Syria, and a global financial crisis which blew open the cleavage between the richest and the middle classes, such that it was no longer possible to pretend that it did not exist or that it did not matter.

Western liberal-democratic governments claim to seek social and political transformation in fragile and conflict-affected countries. Their actions, however, undermine that claim. This is not cynicism but a genuine inability to imagine an alternative way of doing politics, to tackle growing inequality and marginalisation, and to promote social change at home and abroad. It is not just that by obsessing about border management, counterterrorism, and a particular understanding of good governance Europe is arguably making the situation worse in Mali. Brussels, Paris, and Berlin are replicating there the limits for change and the obsession with order that have resulted in the fracture of their own societies. So, before going back to Mali, we will interrogate the consequences for Europe's policy in fragile and conflict-affected countries of what is one of the clearest symptoms of the implausibility of the liberal project at home and abroad: the rise in inequality and the resulting decline of the Western middle classes.

Interlude: 'A Few People in the Middle'

The growing income inequality in Western countries has received increasing attention over recent years, particularly since the global financial crisis of 2008. Economists such as Thomas Piketty have shown that far from being a recent phenomenon, inequality has been steadily rising in developed economies since the 1970s, reversing a trend that started after the Second World War with the reconstruction of Europe.[21] In the US and Europe, the top decile of the population is receiving an ever-growing share of the national income either through very high salaries—configuring what Piketty calls 'the society of supermanagers'—or, in the case of the top 1 percent of the population, primarily through capital income.[22] In Europe, the richest 10 percent's total income amounts to 45 percent of national wealth, compared to only 40 percent for the 'middle class' and 25 percent for the 'lower class'. In the US, the 'upper class' gets 50 percent of total national income; that will become 60 percent in 2030, leaving the middle 40 percent with a quarter and the bottom 50 percent with just 15 percent.[23] With differences between developed economies, the 1970s was the decade when productivity and wages parted ways after growing in parallel since the end of the Second World War. It doesn't matter how much the economies of rich countries have grown for the last fifty years; the wages that 80 percent of the population rely on have stagnated.

As Peter Temin argues in *The Vanishing Middle Class*, 'we are on our way to become a nation of the rich and the poor with only a few people in the middle'.[24] Although Temin's analysis focuses on the US, his argument that the middle class is vanishing as a result of a process of dualisation of the economy similar to that of developing countries—as theorised by the British economist W. Arthur Lewis—can be applied to Europe as well.[25] What Temin calls the FTE sector (finance, technology, and electronics) employs 20 percent of the population. The remaining 80 percent works in the low-wage sector. Whites dominate both the FTE and the low-wage sector. African Americans and Latinos are almost entirely concentrated in the low-wage sector. Middle-wage jobs—factory workers, administrative staff, or even civil servants—have all but disappeared or are in decline. Those on low wages sell services—cooking, cleaning, delivering parcels, driving taxis, etc.—to those in the FTE sector. The wages of the former are prices that the latter pay until they find a cheaper, more convenient alternative which only workers on even lower pay and protection levels can provide. Similar to the Lewis model, Temin describes the efforts of the FTE sector 'to keep incomes low in the low-wage sector, and that includes lowering the quality of public services in the low-wage sector'[26] to the point of criminalising those who depend on a shrinking welfare system—for example, the *welfare queens*[27]—after years of austerity-driven fiscal policies.

In *Le Crépuscule de la France d'en haut*, French geographer Christophe Guilluy describes a similar socioeconomic landscape.[28] In an account that foreshadowed the combativeness of the *gilets jaunes*, and the anti-immigration and anti-elitist sentiment of populists movements across Europe, Guilluy argues that in France, 'an American society like the others', the middle class is disappearing as the social and territorial inequalities between the big cities and the periphery accelerate. His version of Lewis–Temin's dual economy is a country torn between the winners of globalisation—those living in well-off neighbourhoods of the big cities and employed by the FTE sector—and those who lost their jobs in factories and offices and are excluded from the prosperous 'ville-citadelles'. Guilluy has little sympathy for the open multicultural societies that new elites—*hipsters* and *bobos*, as he calls them—hold dear but don't experience in their daily lives, the neighbourhoods where they live, or the schools their children attend. The new bourgeoisie is the face of cool, multicultural France, while the lower classes, the unemployed, and immigrants are condemned to live in precarious invisibility.[29]

Unquestionably, the economic, social, and political implications of a vanishing middle class are a direct threat to the politics that have dominated Western liberal democracies since the 1970s, once, as

Simon Reid-Henry notes, 'collective obligations and political compromise were out[, and] self-reliance and political minimalism were in'.[30] It would be naive to assume that, somehow, this crisis has not permeated Europe's strategy in the *surrounding regions*. In fact, the intervention in Mali offers an opportunity to understand how.

'C'est le retour de l'état'

Eight years on, 5,000 French soldiers are still stationed in Mali, now under *Opération Barkhane*. Together with them are 15,000 members of the United Nations Multidimensional Integrated Stabilization Mission (MINUSMA), the G5 Sahel Joint Force (an experiment in cross-border military coordination between Burkina Faso, Chad, Mali, Mauritania, and Niger), the European Union's Training Mission and its Capacity Building Mission in Mali (EUCAP Sahel Mali), and, in fewer numbers, US forces.[31] Individual European countries are scaling up their direct involvement in the Central Sahel: the German Defence Minister recently said that they could not continue to duck out of their responsibility in the region, suggesting a stronger presence of the *Bundeswehr*;[32] while Spain recently doubled its military contingent and appointed a Special Envoy to the Sahel 'to gain influence'.[33] The European Union continues to approve funding packages for the Sahel; Brussels' aid envelope reached €4.5 billion between 2014 and 2020, half of which was direct budget support, and over €1 billion in humanitarian assistance. It also continues to deploy military and police advisors to support the G5 Sahel.[34] Despite all that, the security and humanitarian situation in Mali and the rest of the Central Sahel is only worsening after the first quick wins of *Opération Serval*. The multiple diplomatic initiatives, summits, alliances, integrated strategies, special forces, and drone operations are yet to show positive results.

Mali, the 'donor darling', has become a donor headache, and other countries in the Central Sahel are moving in the same direction.[35] As Isaline Bergamaschi explains, for years international donors rewarded the appearance of democracy and good governance because it brought stability to the country. Or perhaps they hoped that the appearance of stability would eventually bring democracy and good governance. Regardless of what the Malian government and its inter-national partners thought or wanted, an increasing number of Malians grew frustrated with a culture of 'political consensus' that blocked all attempts to address their demands and the deep-seated ethnic grievances in one of the poorest countries of Africa.[36] But it wasn't until the widening of the gap in Mali between the basic func-tion of the state—law and order—and that of the government—to sustain the basic conditions of life using international aid—that France decided to intervene militarily.[37]

Bruno Charbonneau and Jonathan M. Sears point out that 'the use of terms such as Islamist, jihadist, Salafist and terrorist to express security considerations legitimizes international military violence and is legitimized by the ontological priority given to the Malian state'.[38] The fact that the rapid collapse of the state authorities in Mali led to a similarly quick and resolved military response from France was hardly a surprise, but another example of their symbiotic relationship. However, focusing on the scale of *Opération Serval* and *Barkhane*, and on the multiple security and aid interventions that followed, as evidence of both the dimension of the problem and the determination to tackle it, presupposes that terrorism is the disease and order the cure. The challenge becomes how to achieve order, even if it is just to 'secure the limits of Malian politics' or that of other countries in the region.[39]

At the G5 Sahel summit in Nouakchott, in June 2020, President Emmanuel Macron stated that, in addition to winning the war against the terrorists, the objective is the return of the state.[40] That the offi-cial Twitter account rephrased Macron's original words—from 'sta-biliser la population' to the more palatable 'stabiliser la région'—is a good example of what France and its European and regional allies think the real challenge is. No wonder the French President praised the Sahel Alliance (a group of eight European governments, the EU, multilateral development banks, and the UN)[41] for their support to bring police, judges, and *préfets* back to Mauritania, Mali, Niger, Burkina Faso, and Chad to 'reverse the situation.'

The return of the state is proving more problematic than Macron's words suggest. Human rights violations, killings of villagers, elders, and religious leaders, and extrajudicial executions of insurgents and militants by security forces in the Central Sahel have been extensively reported.[42] In 2019, a government official in the Mopti region of Mali told Human Rights Watch:

> There is a new logic for ending the violence in central Mali, which is to prioritize social cohesion, or dialogue, between communities and armed groups, to get them to commit to ceasefires and desist from violence against each other. This is where everyone's attention is going. This effort has been carried out through high-level visits to central Mali by the prime minister and others and is done with the support of civil society and international organizations.[43]

In the first half of 2020, the streets of Bamako, where 'Papa Hollande' was greeted not long before, were the setting for demonstrations led by the *Mouvement du 5 juin—Rassemblement des Forces Patriotiques* (M5-RFP) against President Ibrahim Boubacar Keïta, accused of corruption and nepotism.[44] He had been criticised for being too close to Paris—80 percent of Malians have a negative view of France—and incapable of ending the violence in the country.[45] Some were quick to suggest that the *Mouvement du 5 juin* was being used by Imam Mahmoud Dicko to take power. A former president of the High Islamic Council of Mali, Dicko had become the most notorious leader of the protests. It did not matter whether they were wrong,[46] the possibility of a putatively illiberal, Islamist government in Bamako shifted the attention from those who advocated for a political alternative in Mali to those who would rather wait for a more convenient season, even if that meant deepening the social fracture. On 18 August 2020, a military coup overthrew President Keïta and his government, altering political calculations.

Europe's Surrounding Regions

> Not many people may know, but right now the EU has around 5,000 women and men working for 16 crisis management missions and operations deployed on three continents—soon to become 17 with the new civilian mission to be launched in the Central African Republic. They are the beating heart of the EU's common security and defence policy and often the face of the EU in crisis-zones around the world.[47]

Josep Borrell, High Representative of the EU for Foreign Affairs and Security Policy, is right. Not many European citizens know what the EU Common Defence and Security Policy looks like on the ground. However, considering that the popular support for a European common defence and security policy has remained constant since 1992 (ranging between 61 percent in 2012 and 72 percent in 2007),[48] the EU and its member states are probably fine with whatever citizens know (or ignore) about the outcomes of the integrated approaches to conflict and crises in the so-called 'surrounding regions'.[49] Therefore, it is of limited public relevance that interventions that should promote local ownership, reinforce state institutions, provide long-term solutions, and be conflict sensitive and needs-driven, end up being designed in Brussels, negotiated with political and economic elites, vulnerable to the changing political agendas of EU member states. Such interventions generally prioritise measures to control and deter migration, and are increasingly militarised and focused on short-term conflict management, as a recent review of Europe's crisis response showed.[50]

The Sahel Alliance, in which the Europeans are the dominant players, is not only about security. Running until 2022, its 730 projects, worth €11 billion, address agriculture, rural development and food security, decentralisation and basic services, education and youth employment, energy and climate, very much in the spirit of the EU Global Strategy and the now almost forgotten UN Sustainable Development Goals. The largest state-building effort in the region, the Sahel Alliance is predicated upon the long-standing focus on good governance and the role of the state in ensuring peace, and on the central role of Europe in designing, funding, and measuring its success.

Regardless of funding and alliances, the multi-phased, multidimensional, multilevel and multilateral approach of the European Global Strategy does not seem to be working in the Central Sahel.[51] According to the UN, more than 23 million out of a total population of 120 million are in need of humanitarian assistance in the region.[52] Across Mali, Niger, and Burkina Faso the number of internally displaced people rose from 70,000 in 2018 to 1.2 million in 2020, and food insecurity is expected to reach its highest level in a decade.

Violence against civilians jumped from 54 incidents in 2016, to 823 in 2019.[53] In Mali, between 2017 and 2020, violence doubled and the number of internally displaced people is four times higher.[54] The common explanation is that the roots of the conflict in the Central Sahel are too deep, and yet 'the crisis that engulfed Mali in early 2012 surprised many policymakers and analysts'.[55] How these two arguments can be true at the same time is a mystery, unless we interrogate how Europe sees the world and its role in it.

Europe's integrated approach in Mali reproduces the four structural features of international interventions that Meera Sabaratnam describes in *Decolonising Intervention*: *protagonismo*, disposability, entitlement, and dependency.[56] Europe shows a need for presence, effect, and significance in Mali. This *protagonismo* is not limited to deploying thousands of soldiers to Mali, but to the performance of that presence, effect, and significance when Hollande visited Bamako in 2013; or when, in January 2020, Macron *summoned* the heads of state of G5 Sahel to the South of France 'to discuss the situation in the region'.[57] Of course, the 'situation in the region' dates back only to 2012, when the conflict in North Mali threatened the collapse of the government in Bamako and Europe *rediscovered* the Central Sahel. Anything that happened before the Tuareg uprising in 2012 is jammed in the background section of dozens of reports produced by Western think tanks and experts to support decision-making in European capitals, reinforcing the sense of 'disposability of the target state and society compared to the interveners'.[58] As for Europe's sense of entitlement, Josep Borrell's call for Europe 'to develop an appetite for power',[59] Germany's appetite for more responsibility in the region, and Spain's interest in the Sahel Alliance as soon as instability reached Mauritania—its preferred partner in the Central Sahel[60]— can be added to Macron's demand for 'clear-cut answers' from the G5 Sahel heads of state in response to growing anti-French 'movements and comments' in Mali and Burkina Faso.[61] Dependency on Western aid influenced every decision of governments in the region. As Charbonneau and Sears explain:

> These political elites oversaw the past two decades of Mali's tutelage by the International Monetary Fund, World Bank and major bilateral donors such as France, a period marked by excessive executive domi-

nance and a minimalist and procedural vision of democratization as electoralism to support 'good governance' for international financial institutions-mandated economic liberalization and development initiatives. Thus, liberalizing governance in Mali prior to the events of 2011–13 had further centralized power, concentrated wealth and intensified socio-economic cleavages, especially between rural and urban populations, but also among classes within urban areas.[62]

Europe's relationship with Mali is hindered by its own exceptionalism.[63] Meanwhile, the maximalism of the EU integrated approach conceals an inability to imagine an alternative future and unwillingness to let others do so; moreover, it conceals an assumption that stability in Mali depends on Europe's actions. As long as the goal is to secure a liberal project that never took roots in Mali, there is little hope that an integrated approach will help 'translate "thin" liberal democratic peace into more meaningful moral and political authority'.[64]

Democracy Must Be Accepted

In June 2020, tens of thousands participated in protests on the streets of Bamako. They joined the *Mouvement du 5 juin* in demanding the resignation of President Keïta and the release of Soumaïla Cissé, the opposition leader kidnapped while campaigning for the March parliamentary elections. Protests went on in July despite the President's offer to appoint new judges to the constitutional court, a rerun of the parliamentary elections that the constitutional court partially annulled, and a government of national unity.[65] Anti-terrorism forces killed 14 protesters and injured 124 others.[66]

Mali was stuck between the *Mouvement du 5 juin* calls for civil disobedience and the efforts from the government and its international allies to restore order. While for some the concern was the security situation, protesters saw an opportunity for political change in a country where security, jobs, and political representation have been lacking for too long. As Gregory Mann explained:

> Virtually the whole political class is widely considered corrupt, as is the game of politics itself. Keita himself has no small part in this. A proud, exacting and fiercely intelligent septuagenarian, Keita excels at immobilizing his political opponents by pulling them close. This

includes the most competent of them. Moussa Mara, former mayor of one of Bamako's districts? Make him Prime Minister, let him burn his own fingers by grabbing for Kidal, nominal capital of the rebellious North. Tiébele Dramé, long-time critic, early human rights activist, man taken seriously in diplomatic circles? Make him Foreign Minister, inside the tent pissing out, as L[indon] B J[ohnson] would have said, but into one of Mali's torrential rainstorms. The effect of this strategy in the long-term is to clip the wings of contenders and to try to shred their legitimacy. Put differently, one rotten peanut and you'll spit out the mouthful.[67]

'Democracy must be accepted', said the US ambassador to Mali; 'you cannot force the departure of a democratically elected president.'[68] Dialogue is the answer proposed by the US, France,[69] the EU,[70] and other international actors that hoped the mediation of a delegation of the Economic Community of West African States would bear fruit. The five West African former heads of state that made up the ECOWAS delegation failed to convince the *Mouvement du 5 juin* to drop their main demand: Keïta's resignation.[71] The untold fear across capitals in the Central Sahel and Europe was that the presidential election could result in the victory of Imam Dicko. The sequence of demands for justice, activism, protests, and political Islam made the prospect of a Salafist imam sitting in the presidential palace too real in the minds of regional and international actors that analyse the Central Sahel based on their experiences in the Middle East and the Maghreb. Perhaps some even imagined an *Iraq/Syria–Mali connection*, misunderstanding the long tradition of activism and political engagement of religious leaders in the country,[72] reviving 'the French identification of Islamic leaders as either loyal or seditious'[73] during the colonial years.

And then a military coup took place on 18 August 2020, ousting Keïta from the presidency. With the tacit support of the international community, ECOWAS swiftly imposed a political and economic blockade on Mali, demanding the dissolution of the military junta and the reinstatement of Keïta.[74] As expected, the UN, the European Union, France, and the US, condemned the coup. Brussels even decided to put on hold the civil and military missions in Mali. A month later, a transitional president and a prime minister were sworn into office, and the *Comité national pour le salut du peuple*—the official name of the military junta—was still visibly in charge. Although their demands had not been fully accepted, ECOWAS sent a delegation to the swearing-in ceremony. At the time of writing, the sanctions remained in place and the military junta was still in power, although as part of a transitional government in which the *Mouvement du 5 juin* was not offered any position.[75]

It is difficult to understand what Europe is hoping to achieve or what tools the integrated approach and the hundreds of projects funded by the Sahel Alliance offer. In a striking intervention after a meeting of EU defence ministers, Josep Borrell said to the press:

> Well, we do not train the armies to be putschists. 90% of the Malian army has been receiving training from our mission, but I checked and none of the four most important and prominent leaders of the military movement against the President [of Mali] IBK [Ibrahim Boubacar Keïta] has been trained by our mission [...] But we do not feel responsible; this coup d'état has been by no means related to the training that we are offering to the Malian soldiers.[76]

At least until the military coup, European governments saw the armed forces and the government of Mali as natural counterparts in bringing back the state, as a precondition for peace and stability. This assumption ignores two important and interconnected realities. First, the Malian Armed Forces would need more than training and logistics support to become a functional and accountable army. Even then, their international counterparts would still disregard their capacities, entrenching a mutually dismissive relationship and a spiral of self-interested assistance to a sceptical audience.[77] Second, the Malian state had retreated from what foreign analysts call *ungoverned spaces* in the North and the Centre of the country long before the Tuareg uprising, the attacks of the jihadists, or the intensification of intercommunal violence.[78] As Catriona Dowd and Clionadh Raleigh wrote, in 2013, instability in the Central Sahel 'is the result of state policy, not state failure'.[79] Indeed, the idea of the inevitability of widespread violence in Mali and the Sahel because of the retreat of the state implied the direct intervention of Western countries and the securitisation of 'underdevelopment, climate change, democratic change and territory itself'.[80]

If, as Charbonneau and Sears rightly argue, 'liberal peace is a radical impossibility given the contested politics and political narratives about what ought to be Mali, the state and peace', what could Europe possibly aspire to achieve in the Central Sahel?[81] Moreover, that 'the Malian state is mimicked more than it is built and its reconstruction imagined more than it is implemented', as Catriona Craven-Matthews and Pierre Englebert explain, tells us more about European assumptions than about the flaws of countries in the *surrounding regions*.[82]

Reiteration and Re-Permutation

Without a workable path towards progress and social harmony through equality and justice, Europe's alternative for its own societies and the *surrounding regions* evokes Zygmunt Bauman's retrotopia: the negation of utopia's negation.[83] While seeking to ensure the levels of stability and self-assurance of the previous liberal utopia—product of the apocalyptic religion identified by John Gray—retrotopia implies no longer seeking the ultimate perfection promised by progress. Instead, backward-looking repetitions through integrated approaches offer donors and recipients, trainers and trainees, a space of certainty through order, even in the midst of instability and unsatisfaction with the outcomes.

Coherently with the idea of retrotopia, the lack of results of Europe's intervention and the failure of the Malian state to do its part do not seem to weaken the push for emulating France's political and administrative structures. Regardless of whether Paris has neocolonial plans in Mali or not, 'the French aspirations of the Malian state have endured', reinforcing a nostalgia through which civil society cannot shape its future because a fantasised liberal past is the only accepted aspiration.[84] The promise of a liberal dream for the *surrounding regions* is not different from the experience of the vanishing European middle classes that Guilluy describes. In fact, they are part of a mutually reinforcing dynamic in which the real *Mali–Marseille connection* is one in which those outside the top decile in Europe, and all except elites in Mali, endure the deterioration of their lives and react, sometimes rebelliously, to the constant demand for individual flexibility and responsibility (resilience, in aid-sector-speak) and the abandonment of the future for the past.[85]

Europe will continue to do just enough to avoid a deterioration of the situation in Mali and the Central Sahel, putting in place improved adaptations of its integrated approach to conflict and crisis. However, with the passing of what Pankaj Mishra describes as the 'curious global conjuncture in which neoliberal capitalism and technological leaps forward guaranteed endless progress, and a tiny elite passed off its interests as universal norms', demands for equality and justice in both rich and poor countries are harder to silence with lamentations about the lost past or empty promises to prevent the future from taking shape.[86] The white moderates will only engage with those demanding change in the streets of Bamako or Marseille to ask them to wait for a more convenient season—even if postponement, as Mark Fisher deduced, would confirm 'the suspicion that the end has already come, the thought that it could well be the case that the future harbours only reiteration and re-permutation'.[87]

London, November 2020

12

DEPLORABLE LIBERALISM

WHITENESS, TRUMP, AND THE ANTI-HUMANITARIAN
SOCIAL CONTRACT

Stephanie Reist

On 11 January 2018, the 45th President of the United States allegedly labelled El Salvador, Haiti, and some unspecified African nations 'shithole countries'. Speaking with several senators in a closed-door Oval Office meeting about foreign nationals living under Temporary Protected Status (TPS), he was reported to have asked: 'Why are we having all these people from shithole countries coming here?' When the comment made headlines, Trump did not initially deny making it. Instead, the White House issued an official statement doubling down on the hardline anti-immigrant rhetoric that defined his constantly campaigning policy agenda: 'Certain Washington politicians choose to fight for foreign countries, but President Trump will always fight for the American people.' In this instance and in others, the Trump administration was making clear its aim to restrict immigration to those perceived as able to 'contribute to our society, grow our economy and assimilate into our great nation'.[1] Such immigrants, the President allegedly suggested during the meeting, would come from places like Norway.

Ever since Trump announced his candidacy by descending a gilt escalator to declare Mexicans rapists, liberal commentators of different political stripes from David Frum to Robert Reich have characterised his bigoted rhetoric and political agenda as an aberration—an assault on bourgeois norms of decorum and civility, on American values and institutions. Many believed his America First platform, which vilified existing trade agreements and strategic alliances, represented a threat to the future of the liberal world order. Beyond trade and national security, Trump's hostility towards much of the rest of the world threatened the (however partial) cosmopolitan, multicultural order promised by the acolytes of globalisation. In defiance of elite promises of a globalised world, in which goods and people could cross borders, Trump's very agenda was one of rejecting the claims of migrants, asylum seekers, and refugees, not just to a new home, but to their very humanity. Indeed, the people he belittled as being from 'shithole countries' had been granted Temporary Protected Status because they were in the United States when a humanitarian crisis occurred in their home country.

With the alleged utterance, Trump, as he was wont to do, had crossed yet another line. Though he would face few tangible consequences, his comments were considered outside the bounds of the civil diplomacy that has been celebrated as the bedrock of the liberal order since the end of the Second World War. But were his comments really such a departure from the existing racialised hierarchies of the liberal order? This is, obviously, not to suggest that these countries are in fact backwaters that produce nothing more than irredeemable, welfare-draining immigrants, but rather that a geographically conceived racial deservedness has been a hallmark of the liberal order itself. For example, though Trump allegedly insulted El Salvadorians and Haitians and moved to strip TPS holders of their status, the Clinton State Department backed the post-coup government in Honduras, deepening the violence in Central America's Northern Triangle, and pressured the Haitian government to suppress the minimum wage for fabric workers tied to major US brands even after the 2010 earthquake.[2] The difference, thus, may be more a matter of style than of material consequences for non-white people within and outside the West. As philosopher Charles W. Mills has maintained since his publication of *The Racial Contract* in 1997— arguably the high point of the end of history—racial liberalism, which in his formulation is liberalism itself, is best understood as a 'white contract to regard one another as moral equals who are superior to nonwhites and who create, accordingly, governments, legal systems and economic structures that privilege them at the expense of people of colour'.[3]

Clearly, Trump, whose conception of a deserving humanity is manifestly bounded, said the small print of that contract out loud. Spawned in the Birther movement, his campaign to 'Make America Great Again' following the first black president sounded an audible dog-whistle to white Americans. Tapping into 'alternating moods of optimism and *ressentiment*', Trump's successful campaign mobilised a cross class, exurban 'aggrieved whiteness' purportedly produced by the interlocking false promises of globalisation and multicultural-ism.[4] Characterised even by his opponents as someone who is 'willing to tell it like it is', Trump positioned himself as the heir to Nixon's Silent Majority; except now he had given this group of so-called ordinary (read white) Americans the courage to openly chant for a border wall.

But the historic continuity of this racial deservedness is not simply evident in the way Trump took post-Civil Rights Movement Republican white grievance politics to their reality TV-show extreme. Nor in how Trump's most controversial policies and fail-ures of government—the Muslim ban, proposed border wall, family separation border policy, and mishandling of Hurricane Maria in Puerto Rico—were not so much departures from, but explicitly white-nationalism-infused escalations of policies and practices estab-lished in the previous administrations of Clinton, Bush, and Obama. As I will argue, the racial deservedness of the white contract is inte-gral to liberal ordering. At the national level, it has historically con-ferred authentic, unquestionable citizenship status to whites deemed fit to rule themselves—hence Obama's perceived illegitimacy, but also the emergence of the Black Lives Matter movement demanding an end to racist police violence during his tenure. At the international level, development and humanitarian aid have marked the collective 'unfitness' of non-white subjects to do the same—hence widespread backlash against immigrants, despite the proliferation of trade deals and international human rights treaties that purportedly codified the global adoption of a Western consumer lifestyle and acceptance of its values.

I contend that racialised liberal ordering undergirds criticism of Trump and his supporters for being insufficiently liberal—which is to say Western. Even before the Trump administration's fatal mishandling of the COVID-19 pandemic and support for repressive policing during anti-racist protests in 2020, commentators in outlets like *World Politics Review*, *The Guardian*, and *New York Magazine* riffed on the idea of the United States as a failed state in need of humanitarian intervention.[5] The perceived uniqueness of Trump's illiberalism has been enough to unironically muse on the idea of the US as a banana republic, ignoring how the US has backed, if not outright installed, such regimes for economic profit.[6] For liberal thinkers like Francis Fukuyama, Trump animated and was animated by the pathologies of the white working class, whose voting preferences represented 'the democratic part of the political system [rising up] against the liberal part'.[7] In trying to explain Trump almost exclusively through the 'angry nationalism' of the white precariat, racialised geography has ostensibly come home to roost. The political dysfunction and economic instability that the US once pointed to as evidence of the developing world's inability to rule itself were rendered new abnormalities within the American body politic that must be exorcised by making either America or American liberalism great again.

Hence the impasse between Trump and liberals when it came to what he called 'American carnage' in his inauguration speech. Trump was several steps ahead of his detractors in declaring the United States a failed state, or, as he would say, a loser. In the Trumpian worldview, stewardship over the liberal order had left the American white man overburdened: lopsided trade deals and international aid were detracting from investment at home, while Democrat representatives of 'rat-infested' cities with high black and Latino populations had spurred crime and disorder and encouraged an 'immigrant invasion'.[8] Although Trump promised to restore if not factory jobs then at least cultural sovereignty to the white precariat of the American heartland, the mainstream media's myopic focus on the tens of thousands of Obama-to-Trump voters insidiously obfuscated his cross-class appeal, especially among white male voters. This was in part because Trump's rhetoric and politics did not reject American liberalism wholesale. Rather, he renounced an abstract liberal internationalism that he saw as subverting US interests. Trump disavowed the notion of American exceptionalism—in part because Obama espouses *and* embodies it—believing that hegemony is achieved primarily through brute force and extraction, as well as good genes.[9] If universalism disguises the racial premises of Western liberal politics, the 'Trump Doctrine' is overtly racialised. China, for example, was presented as a unique threat because it is, as a State Department official affirmed, 'a great power competitor that is not Caucasian'.[10] At the same time, the American liberal establishment continues to fear that the potential loss of US leadership and hegemony wrought by Trump's single term in office will leave the door open for the rise of an authoritarian China they claim lacks scruples and values because it is not Western.

In the hope of re-election, Trump continued to sell himself as a dealmaker-cum-president renegotiating a new global contract that would reorder the failed state of American whiteness, without the faux universalist ideological baggage of liberalism. Meanwhile, liberal revanchism betrayed an indifference to the racial prejudices that have structured global order by default and design. Trump's explicit rejection of universal humanity—his anti-humanitarianism—thus provides an entry point for critical exploration of the relationship between Trumpism and liberalism.

Racial Liberal Ordering

In 2013, the conservative standard bearer *The National Review* published an article by Kevin D. Williamson about Appalachia—a region that has since become synonymous with impoverished white Trump supporters. Entitled 'The White Ghetto', the article describes white working-class residents primarily through their morally depraved behaviour and cyclical dependency on the state—'the federally funded ritual of trading cases of food-stamp Pepsi for packs of Kentucky's Best cigarettes and good old hard currency, tall piles of gas-station nachos, the occasional blast of meth, Narcotics Anonymous meetings, petty crime, the draw, the recreational making and surgical unmaking of teenaged mothers, and death'.[11] As if one racist geographic metonymy was not enough, he closes this caricature with another: 'If the people here weren't 98.5 percent white, we'd call it a reservation.' Williamson's central argument is that 'if you go looking for the catastrophe that laid this area low, you'll eventually discover a terrifying story: Nothing happened.' In fact, according to Williamson, the biggest problem facing Appalachia, beyond, again, perverse government incentives, is decades of 'adverse selection' whereby the best and brightest 'get the hell out as fast as they can' taking with them stable institutions and social networks, and that ever-illusive fuel of progress—'enterprising grit'. The only thing that happened to the Big White Ghetto was a bunch of do-nothings.

Williamson returned to this argument three years later at the height of the Republican primary. In another *National Review* article, he blamed poor whites not only for their own plight but for their foolish corollary desire to make a reality TV star the nominee. An ardent small-government, family values conservative, who identifies as a 'classical liberal' lest he be confused with someone who does not revere the US constitution, Williamson despises Trump's populism because he believes it to be based on a lie—not that Trump is a champion of the poor, but that poor white people, with their 'selfish culture', are worthy of the concern:

> It wasn't Beijing. It wasn't even Washington, as bad as Washington can be. It wasn't immigrants from Mexico, excessive and problematic as our current immigration levels are. It wasn't any of that. *Nothing happened to them.* There wasn't some awful disaster. There wasn't a war or a famine or a plague or a foreign occupation. Even the economic changes of the past few decades do very little to explain the dysfunction and negligence—and the incomprehensible *malice*—of poor white America... The truth about these dysfunctional, downscale communities is that they deserve to die. Economically, they are negative assets. Morally, they are indefensible.

According to Williamson, the people of 'Trump country' should be left to die because their plight is an obvious consequence of broken homes and subsequent drug use and their support of Trump an irresponsible and reprehensible 'longing for Daddy'. Thus, instead of government intervention 'they need real opportunity, which means that they need real change, which means that they need U-Haul'.[12]

Williamson takes issue with the attribution of Trump's election to his appeal to 'unionised workers who had been hit by deindustrialisation'.[13] If the *New York Times* and *Washington Post* profiles are any indication, Trump was the president of the invariably white left-behind, whose habitat is the local diner, a short pick-up truck drive away from the shuttered factory.[14] For Williamson, however, white blue-collar workers weren't alienated by globalisation and political correctness, but by their own dysfunction.

What does it mean for something to happen to a *them*, to a collective? In calling for the death by U-Haul of the Big White Ghetto, Williamson presents an ideological argument about personal responsibility in defence of what Stephen Hopgood calls 'liberal space', which 'could [in principle and does in practice] tolerate suffering and death from poverty'.[15] A fundamental claim about liberal space is that it 'exists above and beyond political space, a space where, regardless of one's identity, nationality, ethnicity, religion, gender, sexuality or citizenship, one retains a set of private rights and personal freedoms that no collective authority can interfere with legitimately'.[16] In principle, liberal institutions safeguard the rights of individuals and sovereign nations from the arbitrary abuses that happen in absolute and imperial systems. Champions of liberal space contend that these institutions are most realised through Western democracy, which fosters stability, economic growth, and respect for universal values. This liberal *place*, as Fukuyama has argued, is evident in the way, prior to the election of Trump, 'America symbolised democracy itself'.[17]

In providing a list of things that did not happen to the Big White Ghetto, Williamson is describing 'humanitarian space'. Humanitarian space tends to be narrowly conceived: a space of disaster, conflict, and mass, *collective* suffering, and thus a space requiring robust, 'neutral' interventions that, at the very least, preserve lives. In this sense, humanitarian space could emerge anywhere, even in liberal place.

231

However, the perceived need for and legitimacy of extra-national intervention is precisely what renders the liberal place of the West and humanitarian place of the Rest distinct within liberal ordering. This paternalistic ordering does not simply stem from the fact that liberal democracies have sufficient wealth, infrastructure, or technocratic knowledge to handle disasters within their borders (a 'fact' now questioned by the gross mismanagement of the coronavirus pandemic in the US and much of Europe), but rather that *only* disasters, which is to say exogenous and largely 'natural' events, take place in the West. Within the rest of the world, the world of humanitarian *place*, crises occur, exacerbated by underlying incompetence such that even when the initial thing that 'happened' is also a natural disaster, as was the case with the 2010 earthquake in Haiti, international intervention is not only legitimate but necessary. Whether through a 'civilising mission' or 'capacity building', liberal ordering *produces* humanitarian space through an imagination of non-Western and insufficiently liberal states as perpetually on the brink of failure.[18]

Racial ordering also takes place within liberal place, hence Williamson's description of poor white Appalachia as a ghetto and a reservation. Though Fukuyama and Williamson disagree on the existence of structural explanations for Trump's victory, they agree that the white poverty of now looks a lot like the black poverty of, well, always. In an article on Trumpism for *Foreign Affairs*, Fukuyama outlines this comparison:

> Back in the 1980s, there was a broad national conversation about the emergence of an African American underclass—that is, a mass of underemployed and under-skilled people whose poverty seemed self-replicating because it led to broken families that were unable to transmit the kinds of social norms and behaviours required to compete in the job market. Today, the white working class is in virtually the same position as the black underclass was back then.[19]

This narrative casts the white working-class 'deplorables' as the wretched protagonists of a twenty-first-century counter-revolution, through what Daniel Martinez HoSang and Joseph E. Lowndes call 'racial transposition': 'explanations of dependency, behavioural pathos, family breakdown, and cultural dysfunction that have long been used to contrast black failure with white success [… are] summoned and deployed to discipline white workers around privatised market logics'.[20] Poor white people are imagined as living like black people, in one-parent households, choosing drugs over a college education. Faced with the reality of white downward mobility, exponents of this narrative draw from the genealogy of *The Negro Family: The Case for National Action*—a now infamous report written in 1965 by sociologist Daniel Patrick Moynihan when he was Lyndon B. Johnson's Assistant Secretary of Labor. (Appalachia was also a central focus of Johnson's Great Society and War on Poverty.) For Fukuyama and Williamson, white poverty has become an inherited and inheritable 'tangle of pathology' similar to that of black families in 1960s Harlem described by Moynihan. After decades of social scientists attributing black poverty to black pathology, they now turn to racial transposition to preserve liberalism's racialised and individualistic social contract. That the white working class 'tangle' is assumed to include racist white nationalism is, of course, of great convenience to the elitist politics of both Fukuyama and Williamson.

The presumption, then, is that, as with the white ghetto, nothing happened to form the black ghetto or the American Indian reservation. As Mills contends, conceived within an 'ideal-theory framework', liberal space necessitates the 'massive and willful ignoring of the actual history' of liberal *place*; that is, the history of the West, of 'European expansionism, colonialism, white settlement, slavery, apartheid, and jim crow [sic]'.[21] The contractual promise of nothing happening within the liberal place of the West depends on a belief that nothing has happened. Though racialised geography animated these at times competing and divergent projects of global white supremacy, what Mills calls a wilful 'global white ignorance' allows liberal place to be historically conceptualised as categorically different from humanitarian place, with a universal respect for human life and rights routinely deployed as a justification for Western hegemony.[22] Indeed, the geography of racial liberalism connects Williamson's white ghetto with Trump's shithole countries. Despite advocating personal responsibility, Williamson imbues the racialised places of the ghetto, the reservation, and now Trump country with the same truncated agency of the shithole: they may not produce the people who live there, but they certainly reproduce them—and their festering could contaminate order itself. These are 'failed places', akin to those states that Fukuyama posited as representing the final impediment to the durability of the liberal project.

In this 'ideal-framework' liberal space, Williamson can, for example, argue against writer Ta-Nehisi Coates' 'Case for Reparation'—centred not on slavery but on the legacy of twentieth-century federally sanctioned housing segregation that created black ghettos—with recourse, as always, to principle: 'it is not a persuasive case for converting the liberal Anglo-American tradition of justice into a system of racial apportionment'; and yet, Williamson admits that it 'was a system of racial apportionment, and a brutal one at that, for centuries'.[23] According to the now dominant American libertarian conception of negative rights, any social programmes, but especially racially targeted programmes, are understood as interference. For Williamson, the dysfunction of the white ghetto self-perpetuates in part because of *illegitimate* federal food assistance, an argument against welfare programmes popularised by Reagan's infamous invocation of the black 'welfare queen'. However, even what Williamson might describe as overreaching social engineering policies like housing don't *happen to a collective* (though they do unduly happen to individual taxpayers); they are simply part of a rule-based system. Racial liberalism thrives not at the end of history, but in the experimental headspace where history never existed and the future need only exist in principle.

Trump was fully invested in the white contract, but divested of the liberal white man's burden, taking the geography of racial liberalism to its most extreme.[24] Recourse to the geography of racial liberalism and non-white pathology enabled Trump in 2018 to discursively pass off the federal government's negligent response to the previous year's Hurricane Maria—by all accounts a genuine humanitarian emergency—as the incompetence of a 'corrupt' tropical government. As he told it, his administration's response to the hurricane, to the thing that happened, was an 'incredible, unsung success', because the initial death toll of sixty-four was not a 'real catastrophe like Katrina'. In the following years, Trump continued to insist that the recovery was a success, given the difficulty of transporting goods to the island and an electrical grid that was allegedly 'dead' before the storm hit, projecting the higher death toll of over 3,000 onto the island's failing infrastructure and political dysfunction—a recourse to political dys-function that itself ignores the ongoing colonial relationship between the US and Puerto Rico.[25] In some ways, Trump was correct that Maria differed from other catastrophes: due to a combination of his well-known indifference towards non-white lives and the failures of previous humanitarian responses in the Western Hemisphere—to Hurricane Katrina in 2005, and the Haitian earthquake in 2010—expectations were very low. Viral photos of Trump throwing paper towels during a press conference while 90 percent of the island, including hospitals, still did not have electricity, evoked memories of Bush, after Hurricane Katrina, telling FEMA Director Mike Brown that he was doing a 'heckuva job', while hundreds of people were still stranded on their roofs and in the Superdome.[26] Unsurprisingly, Trump was particularly callous: rather than mourning the lives lost, he lamented that the response effort had 'thrown our budget a little out of whack'.[27] Yet this was simply a vulgar articulation of how accounting has increasingly structured American liberal notions of deservedness, with the real tragedy being state redistribution of resources—even when something as predictable though damaging as a hurricane happens.

Conceptually unmoored from the legacies of European colonial-ism, segregation and global supply chains predicated on resource extraction and labour exploitation, the underdevelopment of humani-tarian place is claimed to produce crises that threaten to 'spill over' into liberal place.[28] Migrants literally embody this 'spill over', such that the migrant 'crises' are said to be happening on and to the US border with Mexico and the European shores of the Mediterranean rather than within nations and regions increasingly destabilised by climate change, the US-led War on Terror and War on Drugs, and recurrent economic crises originating in the West. Migration has long been a conundrum for the liberal order, not simply due to the seem-ing contradiction between unrestricted flows of capital and goods with restricted flows of people and their labour, but principally because masked in technocratic language and legal statuses like Temporary Protected Status, Western conceptions of migration are inseparable from histories of colonisation and ideas of whose move-ment orders and whose disorders.[29] This is why Williamson's solution for residents of the Big White Ghetto—or at least those with 'enter-prising grit'—is simply to get out, to pursue the American Dream. Free marketeers often link spatial and social mobility, positing both as individual choices. Although there is a legislative difference between domestic mobility and international migration, in the American experience both are intertwined with the idea of making a better life for oneself and the nation: America, it is said, was built by European immigrants with grit.[30] However, simultaneously reifying and ignoring this history of mass European settler-colonialism and migration, stalwarts of the liberal order largely discuss contemporary migration as an inversion of the white man's civilising burden—save for the bronzed expat—with the only authentic migration being 'the movement of millions of people from poorer countries to richer ones', as Fukuyama himself put it.[31] This redemptive interpretation of migration from the Rest to the West is undergirded by a racial geography consolidated by liberal political scientists in the immediate post-Cold War period. (Foremost among them was Fukuyama, who revived a civilisational discourse by distinguishing the enlightened, multicultural West, where universal recognition had been achieved, from 'backwards' countries like Albania and Burkina Faso, which he deemed irrelevant to the course of history.)[32] Yet, migration teeters on the liminal space where racial liberal space accommodates humani-tarian space. In recent years, ethnonationalist politicians, including Trump, have reproduced this racial geography, drawing on long-standing media narratives about the encumbrance of immigration to justify discriminatory policies and demonise forced migrants and even the very concept of asylum.

Granted, there is a significant difference of degree between Trump's Muslim ban or border wall and liberal calls to better regu-late immigration, with commentators like Fukuyama suggesting a limited amnesty law, as was passed by Reagan in the 1980s and attempted by Obama. However, both Trump and his liberal oppo-nents present immigration as a threat—to security and culture—while detaching it from 'global conflicts, wars, political interests, and economic dynamics'.[33] Committed to not only nationalism but a hierarchy of nations, liberals routinely deploy the migrant against the 'left-behind', rather than reckon with a system of global capitalism that disorders the lives of both. To appease emboldened white nationalists, Fukuyama proposes an 'assimilation agenda' grounded in 'creedal national identities'. Promoting 'core values and beliefs' through public policy, he argues, will 'encourage citizens to identify with their countries' foundational ideals'.[34] Though this is, especially in the European case, an argument against ethnicity as a basis for citizenship, his solution to the migrant 'crisis' is a nativism of principles that puts the burden of subduing white nationalism on individual immigrants' capacity to assimilate. Coupled with a call for obligatory national service, Fukuyama's solutions significantly align with Trump's pledge to 'fight for the American people' by ensuring that immigrants 'contribute to our society, grow our economy and assimilate into our great nation'.[35]

Aggrieved Liberalism

For many liberal thinkers, Trump's victory represented an encroachment of the Big White Ghetto into an erstwhile liberal space. The problem is not the poverty, increased rates of mortality or incarceration that people in the Big White Ghetto face, but racist populism spilling over. However, though these dominant liberal narratives pathologise the white working class as chronically uneducated at best and inherently racist at worst, the vast majority—Williamson not included—argue that the future of American liberalism lies in this group's redemption, re-enforcing the foundation of the white contract.

Therein lies the quintessentially liberal perversion in blaming the white working class for a populist backlash against American liberalism itself despite Trump losing the popular vote. Firstly, and most obviously, though it bears repeating, invocations of the white working class as a distinct socioeconomic category more or less confined to 'fly-over country' obfuscates Trump's cross-class appeal, especially among white men. Both Fukuyama and Williamson assume the readers of the *National Review* and *Financial Times* to be Reagan-Republican 'Never Trumpers', who either abstained from casting a ballot or whose tacit electoral support of Trump was strictly motivated by tax cuts and the appointment of conservatives to the federal courts. Accordingly, the lack of a college degree is fundamental to how both Fukuyama and

Williamson conceive of the white precariat. Fukuyama accepts that some 'better-educated and more well-off voters' also joined the nationalist white poor in voting for Trump because 'their communities were filling with immigrants', and 'politically correct language' had placed 'ordinary Americans' in a situation in which 'one could not even complain about the problem'. However, white workers remained the principal protagonists of Trump's rise in Fukuyama's analysis: they were the left behind, with no other choice but revanchist nationalism. Politically, they had been abandoned by a Democratic Party that had not only adopted the corporate friendly policies of the Republican Party, but, more egregiously, 'had become the party of identity politics: a coalition of women, African-Americans, Hispanics, environmentalists, and the LGBT community'.[36]

As numerous post-election analyses have argued, however, not only did Trump win the majority of white votes across income brackets in both the primaries and the national election, but a majority of his non-college-educated supporters lived in households earning above the national median income of US$50,000 a year.[37] In this way, the insidious myopia of racial liberalism is exposed when thinkers like Fukuyama use educational attainment as a proxy for social class, ignoring the historical segregation that has enabled white upwards social mobility, particularly for white men without a college degree. What's more, due to a combination of disillusionment with both political parties and the difficulties of voting in many states, not to say anything of outright voter suppression, the majority of low-income people across races do not vote, and overall turnout in 2016, 58 percent of eligible voters, was in line with previous years. In fact, more white Americans have voted for the Republican candidate in every election since Jimmy Carter's narrow victory over Gerald Ford in 1976, or since Nixon in 1964, if one considers Carter's single term the death rattle of the New Deal coalition. Trump's share of the white vote (57 percent) was in line with those of Romney in 2012 (59 percent) and McCain in 2008 (55 percent).[38]

White workers are indeed facing downward mobility after decades of union busting, stagnant wages, and cuts to social welfare programmes. The foreclosure crisis exacerbated this by forcing millions of Americans from their homes. Yet, though Fukuyama and others primarily date the anger of the white working class to the 2007–8 financial crash, liberals have long highlighted the social mobility of the white worker as the basis for the legitimacy of American racial liberalism, a social mobility that reciprocally justified racial liberalism since black poverty was attributed to 'a tangle of pathology'. The white working class as a singular, geographically ambiguous socioeconomic category is relatively new within national discourse, though there has long circulated a common refrain that in joining wealthier whites in voting Republican they chronically, though individually, vote against their own self-interests. Politicians, their consultants, and the media creating a category of citizens tacitly connected to whiteness has long been a staple of national politics—from Nixon's 'silent majority' to the 'soccer moms' of the 1990s to Fukuyama's evocation of the timeless 'ordinary Americans'. These categories by and large gain relevance in the US context only in so far as they can be construed as the most significant voting bloc to win over: the assumption being that this elusive but representative and decisive constituency already manifests the 'core values and beliefs' exalted by Fukuyama, unlike Occupy Wall Street, immigrant rights, or Black Lives Matter activists who 'undermine the legitimacy of the American national story', or even unionised public servants who unpatriotically live off dwindling public coffers.[39] But these categories differ from the white working class. Not only is their whiteness typically obscured; they are also imagined as individuals, not a cultural collective.

Because there is a long US tradition of eliding class politics that even Tocqueville famously observed, the reification of the Appalachian white working class wreaks of present-day liberals applauding themselves for taking the question of class seriously. Yet, they deploy a particular construct of the white worker that, we are repeatedly told, 'doesn't want any hand outs' or feels that women and non-white others are cutting ahead in the line to the 'American Dream'—as sociologist Arlie Russell Hochschild argues in her provocatively titled book, *Strangers in Their Own Land*.[40] Actual receipt of welfare benefits (or tax subsidies) notwithstanding, the liberal caricature of the white working class—and white people more broadly—presents people who, purely out of their own liberal principles, might support humanitarian causes elsewhere—or at least used to—through their individual donations, but generally would prefer not to receive government benefits in order to preserve that same individualism.[41] As sociologist Andrew Perrin argues, 'the white working class was made, not found; deployed, not discovered'.[42]

The liberal identification of the white working class serves two functions. Firstly, as discussed earlier, racial transposition creates a debased identity of uneducated, angry white workers to shoulder the blame for the Republican Party's overt racism under Trump, as HoSang and Lowndes argue. White workers are white because of their support for Trump. However, since 'those narratives are only legible because they have been long deployed to construct "the abject black other"', the hardworking white voter is still redeemable.[43] In effect, these narratives suggest they can stop being *white*, that is, part of a collective, if they vote correctly and stop rebelling against their own core, identity-politics-free liberalism. Thus, this preserves the supposed non-whiteness of American liberal ordering and its relative innocence in creating the conditions for Trump (not to say anything of Bush, Reagan, or Clinton, each of whom had their own dog whistle). In implicit refutation of W. E. B. Du Bois' famous 1903 observation that 'the problem of the twentieth century is the problem of the color line', Fukuyama argues that the political disputes of the past century were largely economic until the emergence of identitarian social movements from the 1970s on. That the white working class 'overwhelmingly supported the Democratic Party from the New Deal, in the 1930s, up until the rise of Ronald Reagan, in the 1980s', supposedly evidences a progressive party that sought to appeal to 'larger collectives' rather than 'ever-smaller groups that found themselves marginalised in specific and unique ways'. This ignores how non-whites were excluded from New Deal and GI Bill redistributive programmes, and how that very exclusion—through documents like the Moynihan report—was used to advance the idea that 'redistributive programs were creating perverse incentives that discouraged work, savings, and entrepreneurship, which in turn shrank the overall economic pie'.[44] While it is generally true that the Democratic Party has embraced a tokenistic multiculturalism, many scholars in the Black Radical Tradition have rebuked this politics of 'black faces in high places' as cover for aggressively gutting social welfare programmes—often in the name of appealing to the media-exalted, fis-cally conservative, independent white voter.[45] Obama is the obvious example, with his colour-blind policies (except when it came to deportations and drone strikes) and rhetoric fine-tuned to assuage white fears. In this way, the misappropriation and denigration of the term 'identity politics'—a term coined by queer black women in the 1970s to express their practice of left-wing intersectional organising and coalition-building—by people across the political spectrum, ulti-mately serves to negate the history of mobilised whiteness in order to reinscribe the idea that 'nothing happened' to create the black ghetto or the American Indian reservation, and thus situate the white person as the truly legitimate citizen, just as Trump did.[46]

Ultimately, this simultaneous disparaging and upholding of the white working class leads liberals to oversimplify Trump's victory and neglect its roots in racial liberalism. To claim, as Fukuyama does, that 'the white working class is in virtually the same position as the black underclass was back then' is to perform two socio-historical sleights of hand in one sentence: it presents widespread white poverty as a recent defect, much like Trump himself, and it at best overlooks the fact that the 'black underclass' experiences *in the present* the same 'strained circumstance of those [white] left behind'.[47] Black poverty is both a constant and a thing of the past, such that the systematic targeting of black families with predatory sub-prime bank loans before the 2008 crash is not written about as a 'staggering loss of black wealth' but as a latent cause of white nationalism years later.[48] Thus, not only did nothing that happened to white people in 2008 happen to black people, but black people also did nothing in response. Both the contemptuous narrative of Williamson and the pitying nar-rative of Fukuyama attribute Trump's victory to racially or economi-cally or nationally or selfishly motivated white voters, and white voters alone. Gone from such narratives is, as attorney and writer Malaika Jabali argues, 'the uncomfortable fact... that black voter turnout in 2016 was down in over half the country', especially in key states like Wisconsin.[49] Fukuyama blames the Democrats' supposed embrace of multiculturalism for abandoning the white working class, but fails to acknowledge how Hillary Clinton *lost* black voters due to her continual attempts to decouple black people's economic concerns from structural racism. As Jabali contends, this was epitomised by Clinton's 'shamefully disingenuous' rhetorical question directed at Bernie Sanders: 'If we broke up the banks tomorrow... would that end racism?'[50] Both Clinton's question and Fukuyama's analysis wilfully overlook how the banks that were bailed out had referred to predatory sub-prime mortgages as 'ghetto loans', or how much of the GOP resentment towards Obama's presidency, manifested in the Tea Party movement well before Trump, sprang from cable news commentator Rick Santelli's 2009 rant calling Obama's stimulus package a plan to subsidise 'losers' mortgages'.[51]

Trump simply and explicitly mobilised this white racial political subjectivity—of being entitled to but ultimately above benefits—more effectively across classes. He did not invent the narrative that the Guatemalan family fleeing a confluence of US-backed labour exploitation, drought, and paramilitary and sexual violence is not motivated by grit—despite traversing thousands of miles—but by the pull of scarcely existing government benefits to the detriment of the white left behind. Nor was he the first to claim that black demands for reparations and to end police violence or indigenous struggles for land rights—like resistance to the Keystone XL pipeline—were mere undue race-based benefits rather than material concerns. He merely capitalised on how racial liberalism upholds white grievance as articulating an underlying universal claim. With government provisions at home and abroad the province of the non-white undeserving, Trump vowed to do away with welfare and aid while simultaneously resignifying any benefits received by white Americans as both redress for politically correct policies and the spoils of 'winning'.

From the Big White Ghetto to the Big Easy and Back Again

The post-Cold War American political class has not only used racial deservedness as a pretext to dismantle government-funded social programmes. It has also abandoned its responsibility to respond to even its own narrowly defined humanitarian space. Trump's 'American carnage' seized on this abandonment, promising that the racial, if not the liberal order would be restored. However, the seeds of Trump's mishandling of Hurricane Maria and the COVID-19 pandemic were sown long before his politics of pettiness led him to become the leader of the 'free world'. Hurricane Katrina and its aftermath offer perhaps the most heartbreakingly explicit demonstration of racialised liberal capitalism's role in leaving more and more poor and working-class people behind—be they from the Big Easy or the Big White Ghetto.

On 24 August 2015, the ten-year anniversary of Hurricane Katrina, liberal media darling Malcolm Gladwell published a piece in *The New Yorker* titled 'Starting Over: Many Katrina Victims Left New Orleans for Good. What Can We Learn from Them?' In what is more a homage to social science research than a reflection on the legacy of Hurricane Katrina, Gladwell argues that, because Katrina 'happened to hit one of the most dysfunctional urban areas in the country', when many of the black victims were displaced, '[t]heir lives got better'.[52] As Glen Ford pointed out shortly after the piece's publication, Gladwell's 'reasoning is genocidal: the elimination—rather than mere deconcentration—of "bad" populations'.[53] Death by U-Haul, supported by the data of a natural experiment.

Yet, amid the Panglossian celebration of the disintegration of black neighbourhoods lies an even sadder, more twisted irony: the piece is about black displacement as a testament to social mobility, and yet the initial response to hundreds of thousands of black people being made homeless overnight was a toxic mix of government negligence and surveillance with white vigilantism. Sociologist Margaret Somers refers to the mostly black victims of Katrina as the 'left-behind', and though hardly an original turn of phrase, in the context of humanitarian space it speaks to how they were left for dead, by drowning, insulin shortage, or even bullet, despite the storm warnings and media coverage that evidenced that something had happened to them. Somers believes that 'something qualitatively more terrible was at work in those scenes of abandonment and terror, something even more than the inflictions of racism's second-class citizenship'.[54] For Somers, the negligence was a denial of citizenship by all levels of government, which, guided by market fundamentalism, rendered the poor, black, and disabled residents of New Orleans 'contractually malfeasant', and, in turn, freed government officials from any liability to act. Right-wing news media revelled in this simplified contract, with Fox News' most popular pundit at the time, Bill O'Reilly, advocating that 'American middle and high school students everywhere should be required to watch the video tape of the poor people stranded by Hurricane Katrina.' Teachers were to underscore the lesson that the poor black left-behind 'wound up floating face down in a river' due to their own lack of interest in social mobility, since 'millions of poor people from all over the world sneak into America because they can make money here if they work hard'. This way, students would learn the virtues of not being poor.[55]

Rather than much needed medical supplies or bottled water, what circulated most amid the delta heat of the late summer of 2005 were rumours of looters and marauding gangs of young black men— armies of the dispossessed. (This too was a difference between hurricanes Katrina and Maria: there was little threat of Puerto Rico's island residents immediately 'invading'.) While the police murder of unarmed James Brissette and Ronald Madison on Danziger Bridge gained national attention, media and law enforcement agencies alike rarely investigated the widespread accounts of white vigilantes murdering black men who were seeking shelter, food, and other survivors—loved ones and strangers alike. Indeed, instead of evacuating survivors and helping to distribute supplies, government resources went towards the National Guard and Blackwater contractors controlling the 'insurgency' in 'little Somalia': the threat of black gangs spilling over into the less affected suburbs provided a pretext for turning the War on Terror on to US citizens victimised by the humanitarian disaster.[56]

'Like elites when they panic', writes Rebecca Solnit, in reference to post-hurricane New Orleans, 'racists imagine again and again that without them utter savagery would break out, so that their own homicidal violence is in defense of civilisation and the preservation of order.'[57] Neither Somers nor Solnit reflect on Hurricane Katrina and its aftermath through the lens of humanitarianism. Solnit's concern is not a professionalised aid sector, but the mutual aid groups and communities that forge themselves in the wake of disasters. If this reflects a humanitarian ethos, for Solnit it is driven by a 'sense of immersion in the moment and solidarity with others caused by the rupture in everyday life', rather than a global abstract humanity. Without entirely escaping neoliberal conceptions of community resilience, Solnit dwells not on overcoming hardship but on the *enjoyment* of consolidated 'friendship and love' as a basis for collective responses to disaster.[58]

Somers, on the other hand, does interrogate the liberal tradition, drawing on Hannah Arendt's discussion of 'the right to have rights' as a basis for a state recognition of citizenship that rejects a *quid pro quo* social contract. But at work in both readings of Hurricane Katrina is an implication that it happened outside of humanitarian *place*. Residents of the Louisiana Gulf were left behind by the putative guardians of liberal order. And they were recognised as neither citizens nor neighbours—indeed they were referred to as refugees—precisely for this reason. For, although liberal ideology promotes 'respect *in principle* for each individual human life', in practice this respect is limited by a racial contract imposed by the custodians of order.[59] Obscured beneath the defence of the universal equality of individual life is a white collective's contractual right to administer death, be it by negligence, militia, or displacement.[60]

Fifteen years after Hurricane Katrina, right-wing militias emerged as a central part of Trump's botched response to the co-pandemics of COVID-19 and police violence, as well as his re-election strategy. Overtaking state legislatures to demand the 'reopening of the economy' against public health lockdown mandates and patrolling the streets with the blessing of police departments that brutally repressed the multi-racial BLM uprisings calling for an end to the racist, classist carceral state in the wake of George Floyd's public lynching in May 2020, it is clear that these groups had signed on to the white contract. But it is also clear that neither the pandemic response—which varied across states—nor police violence and mass incarceration—which is tolerated by Democrat and Republican mayors and governors alike—were due to the supposed disaster that was Trump. This partially explains why Trump's election produced so much panic among liberals. With an ideology grounded in a 'wilful ignorance' of its own past, liberals have turned the geography of racial liberalism onto itself. They deemed the very symbol of liberal democracy's legitimacy, once socially mobile white people, as the force that had disordered liberalism itself: the 'left behind' releasing in their wake angry white nationalism. The racism and jingoism of MAGA is undeniable. Yet so too are the chronic crises of the American project, crises that do not manifest only as devastating financial recessions, but also as an entire political class' inability and unwillingness to respond to the largest US protest movement since the Civil Rights struggle with anything other than curfews, rubber bullets, targeted arrests, and even more death: a slightly tempered, less deadly version of how it has responded to a great number of humanitarian crises elsewhere, often provoked by the US. Trump declared the political elite the true contractual mal-feasants for pretending that fortified whiteness was not the appropri-ate response to an already encroaching humanitarian place.

With #pleasevote and Joe Biden as the Democratic nominee, the liberal elite's political project amounted to an attempt at recapture. To construct a creedal national identity that could combat Trump's racist revanchism, Fukuyama proposed 'constitutionalism, the rule of law, and human equality'.[61] His solution to the crisis of liberal democracy is more liberal democracy. However, in denouncing the 'identity politics' of black and brown social movements that decry white supremacy as a if not the cause of white supremacists, he ignores how the Confederate-flag-waving, gun-toting white 'worker' supported Trump in the name of defending other central creeds of liberal space: individual autonomy and the sanctity of private property.[62] These creeds have historically justified the liberal order's violent incursions into humanitarian place—from Watts to Jakarta.[63] Moreover, Fukuyama does not explain how such an identity would be disseminated beyond civics lessons in schools and immigration exams—those already deemed sufficiently American, white adults, are assumed to believe and practice this creed already, despite their voting preferences. One clear answer is through the media and the stories nations repeatedly tell themselves about themselves. And if that is the case, there is hardly anything more American than the story of black pathology, even when redressed in exurban white face. '[F]rom the president on down there is an accepted belief in America—black and white—that African American people, and African American men in particular, are lacking in the virtues in family, hard work, and citizenship', wrote Ta-Nehisi Coates, referring not to Trump's but to Obama's penchant for imploring black Americans to take responsibility for their own lives and communities.[64] Well before Trump, communi-ties conceived of as outside of liberal space were denied the resources, rights, and agency to order their own place, to claim their own home.

November 2020

13

REQUIEM FOR A MOST VIOLENT
HUMANITARIAN ORDER

José Luís Fiori[1]

So long as human culture remains at its present stage, war is therefore
an indispensable means of advancing further, and only when culture
has reached its full development—and only God knows when that
will be—will perpetual peace become possible and of benefit to us.

Immanuel Kant, 'Conjectures on the Beginning of Human History'[2]

One often hears about the acceleration of historical time. While it is
never exactly clear what this means, nor why it happens, everyone is
aware of those periods in which important facts and decisions suddenly converge, altering the course of history; and it is generally
accepted that something of the sort occurred around the end of the
1980s, radically upsetting the geopolitical panorama. It began at dawn
on 9 November 1989, when the wall dividing the city of Berlin and
separating the 'liberal West' from the 'communist East' was brought
down, and the borders opened. However, it was what followed that
was most important: a chain reaction of regime change across the

socialist countries of Central and Eastern Europe, leading to the dissolution of the Warsaw Pact, the reunification of Germany on 3 October 1990, and the break-up of the Soviet Union in December 1991. The West celebrated this as a definitive victory for democracy, the market economy, and a new 'international ethical order', with a focus on the defence of human rights. Exercising almost global power, the United States claimed a right to intervene to protect this order. Only a decade-and-a-half later, at the 2005 United Nations World Summit, was this right consecrated, when 150 heads of state and government formally recognised a responsibility to 'protect populations from genocide, war crimes, ethnic cleansing and crimes against humanity'.[3] But, by then, the global political landscape had changed, and a new calculus was shaping US strategy.

Thirty years after the end of the Cold War, the old geopolitics of nations once again serves as a compass for the inter-state system, the major powers once again extol nationalism and protectionism, and the humanitarian objectives of the 1990s appear to have been relegated to the bottom of the international agenda. The world has seen the vertiginous economic ascension of China, the resurgence of Russia's military ambition, and the splintering of the European Union. But perhaps most surprising of all, in recent times, is the way in which the United States has pivoted away from its old liberal allies, turning its back on the values and institutions it had itself previously promoted—in rhetoric, at least.

None of this happened overnight; rather, there was a slow unravelling of *Pax Americana*, which eventually exposed its ambiguities and contradictions. Without the restraint of rival powers, the US lacked the limits that might prevent its descent into arbitrariness.[4] While the Western world was still celebrating the fall of the Berlin Wall, Kuwait was invaded by Iraqi troops. This prompted a violent response, with the creation of a twenty-six-nation-strong military coalition led by the US, which destroyed Iraq in the first 'humanitarian war' of the 1990s. That same Gulf War served as a testing ground for a new kind of remote warfare, with minimal loss of American lives and maximum destructive power against American enemies.[5] Forty-two days of aerial attacks were followed by a rapid and vigorous territorial invasion, resulting in a few hundred American casualties and around

150,000 Iraqi deaths. That same style of warfare was later employed in the Yugoslav wars—the most violent episode in European history since the Second World War.

The central hypothesis of this chapter is that the humanitarian order of the 1990s was undone by the limitless expansion of the global power of the US. The imperial advance of the US towards absolute power went largely uninterrupted until it created conditions for the emergence of new rival powers, at the beginning of the twenty-first century. At this point, humanitarian rhetoric offered less strategic value, and geopolitics once again became overtly expressive of the old Westphalian paradigm. The culmination of a process of strategic repositioning, rather than a clean break, the 'America First' policy of Donald Trump after his election in 2016, then represented the definitive abandonment of humanitarian order. Briefly addressing the contradictions of 'ethical war' in the 1990s, this chapter goes on to consider the gradual relegation of humanitarian ideas in American strategy, through discussion of the four wars of greatest geopolitical significance in the first two decades of the twenty-first century.

Humanitarian Interventions in the 1990s: 'Ethical War'

The Cold War did not end with a peace treaty, nor, after the dissolution of the Soviet Union, did the great powers define a new world 'constitution'—as they had in Westphalia in 1648, Vienna in 1815, Versailles in 1918, or, indeed, in Yalta, Potsdam, and San Francisco in 1945. Rather, the military and economic strength of the US was accepted by its allies as a source of international stability. But no sooner had the Group of Seven (G7) met to discuss economic issues at the end of the Cold War than the US launched Operation Desert Shield in the Persian Gulf, in August 1990. The aerial bombardment of Iraq the following year played a role similar to that of the atomic bombing of Hiroshima and Nagasaki in 1945: it established a new ethical order and a new 'sovereign power', responsible for defining and arbitrating right and wrong in the inter-state system. A major difference in this regard, however, was that in 1991—unlike in 1945—there was no other power capable of questioning the will of the US. And yet, US foreign policy often appeared ambiguous.

During the General Debate of the UN General Assembly in 1990, President George H. W. Bush's speech seemed to echo Woodrow Wilson's proposals in 1918:

> We have a vision of a new partnership of nations that transcends the Cold War. A partnership based on consultation, cooperation, and collective action, especially through international and regional organisations. A partnership united by principle and the rule of law and supported by an equitable sharing of both cost and commitment. A partnership whose goals are to increase democracy, increase prosperity, increase the peace, and reduce arms.[6]

At the same time, US Secretary of Defense Dick Cheney established a working group to reimagine US foreign policy and defence for the post-Cold War world. He was joined by fellow neoconservatives Paul Wolfowitz, Lewis Libby, and Eric Edelman, among others. Based on a report by this group, Bush made a different kind of speech to US Congress in August 1990, in which he defended a policy of 'active containment' of any regional powers that might undermine the global power of the US.

The same tension was notable in the foreign policy of Bush's successor. Speaking at the opening of the UN General Assembly in 1993, Democratic President Bill Clinton reproduced elements of Bush's UN speech of three years earlier, almost word for word:

> In a new era of peril and opportunity, our overriding purpose must be to expand and strengthen the world's community of market-based democracies. During the Cold War, we sought to contain a threat to survival of free institutions. Now we seek to enlarge the circle of nations that live under those free institutions, for our dream is of a day when the opinions and energies of every person in the world will be given full expression in a world of thriving democracies that cooperate with each other and live in peace.[7]

If this epitomised the idealistic discourse of the 1990s, in practice Clinton continued the project to forge a 'new American century' with even greater zeal and violence than his predecessor. '[T]he world needed the United States', argued Madeleine Albright, Clinton's Secretary of State. And this was deemed to justify the active militarism that Clinton exercised during eight years in office. According to Andrew Bacevich, the US participated in forty-eight military interventions during the 1990s, many more than during the whole Cold War.[8] These included its 'humanitarian interventions' in Somalia in 1992–3, Macedonia in 1993, Haiti in 1994, Bosnia-Herzegovina in 1995, Yugoslavia in 1999, Kosovo in 1999, and East Timor, also in 1999. The US also bombed military and industrial targets in Iraq in 1998.

In this period, the US strengthened NATO (even, in some cases, against European wishes); and it increased its own military presence in around 130 countries, including many previously under Soviet control: starting in 1991, in Latvia, Estonia, and Lithuania; then in Ukraine, Belarus, the Balkans, and the Caucasus; then in Central Asia and Pakistan. As observed by Chalmers Johnson, a political scientist and former CIA consultant:

> From 1989 to 2002, there was a revolution in America's relations with the rest of the world. At the beginning of that period, the con- duct of foreign policy was still largely a civilian operation... By 2002, all this had changed. The United States no longer had a 'foreign pol- icy'. Instead it had a military empire... a vast complex of interests, commitments, and projects... consist[ing] of permanent naval bases, military airfields, army garrisons, espionage listening posts, and stra- tegic enclaves on every continent of the globe.[9]

This 'vast complex' allowed the US to establish an effective 'cordon sanitaire' separating Germany from Russia, and Russia from China. Meanwhile, financialisation of the global economy reinforced the primacy of the dollar. In the wake of the Cold War, it was primarily through military and economic dominance that the US consolidated its global power and its position as an arbiter in the inter-state system. But into the new millennium, its ethical order would come under increased pressure as unconstrained expansion itself created condi- tions for the emergence of rival powers. Imagining plausible threats to its hegemony, the US supplanted humanitarian rhetoric with a new discourse of total war, which exposed the tensions between apparent idealism and militaristic expansionism.

The Global War on Terror: An Imperial War

Reading the history of the 1990s in this way—through the tensions of ethical order—can provide a better understanding of how the project of humanitarian hegemony became explicitly imperial under the administration of George W. Bush. With the immediate declaration of war following the attacks of 11 September 2001, Bush, spurred on by his vice, Dick Cheney, sought to reinvigorate the construction of a 'new American century'. While his 'war on terror' began with the invasion of a single country—Afghanistan—one month later, its reach became clear over the coming years, as the US bombed countries in the Middle East, Central Asia, and North and East Africa. And yet, its geographic expansiveness could not hide the fact that all of the countries targeted were predominantly Muslim, as had been the countries targeted by European humanitarian interventions in the nineteenth century. As such, even as humanitarian idealism faded—reappearing only occasionally, in the form of pretext—Bush's war on terror took on the character of a civilisational clash with the Islamic world, despite the latter's own notable contribution to Western modernity.[10]

At the same time, the enemy of the war on terror was imagined as ubiquitous. The US adapted its military doctrine. Donald Rumsfeld, Bush's Secretary of Defense, spoke of a shift from a 'threats-based' approach to a 'capabilities-based' one.[11] In accordance with the new approach, any possible vulnerability required a strategic response. The notion that there were 'unknown unknowns' to contend with implied that the US could be vulnerable always and everywhere. This compelled a total response that would override claims to national sovereignty. Those countries allying themselves with the US in the war on terror thus submitted to its imperial power of arbitration within the inter-state system. While they feared terrorist attacks in their own territories as a consequence of this alliance, they gradually became more wary of the impact that American responses to these attacks might have. And they were right to be wary, for, as the US demonised those peripheral states it deemed to be sponsoring terrorism, it also ramped up tensions with potential rivals that might challenge its global power. Immediately after the 11 September attacks, the Bush administration announced the withdrawal of the US from the Anti-Ballistic Missile Treaty negotiated with the Soviet Union in 1972. It later announced the installation of an anti-ballistic missile defence system in Polish and Czech territories, on the edge of Russia's sphere of influence, justifying this as a way of protecting Europe from terrorist attacks from the Middle East—and in particular from Iran.

Through the war on terror, the US announced, not only to terrorist groups, but primarily to other states, its determination to extend its technological and military dominance. But the imperial character of this war produced resistance from states within the nucleus of the inter-state system, which now felt compelled to take greater risks, drawing on their latent power: first, militarily, Russia, and then, through primarily economic means, China.

The Georgian War: The Reappearance of Limits

It was in Georgia, in 2008, that limits to the sovereign power of the US appeared for the first time since the end of the Cold War. The Russo-Georgian War was brief, but its geopolitical significance should not be overlooked. In April 2008, in the city of Bucharest, NATO began the process of incorporating Georgia as a member state, despite the reluctance of Germany and the explicit objection of Russia. On 11 June 2008, Russian fighter jets flew over the territory of South Ossetia, on the eve of US Secretary of State Condoleezza Rice's arrival in Georgia for 'Immediate Response 2008'—a joint military exercise involving US forces, as well as those from Georgia, Ukraine, Armenia, and Azerbaijan. The joint exercise was to be conducted at the Vaziani Military Base, which had belonged to the Russian Air Force until 2001. On 8 August 2008, the Georgian Armed Forces attacked the province of South Ossetia and captured the capital, Tskhinvali. Somewhat unexpectedly, the Russian Army then intervened, and within a few hours it surrounded the Georgian territory, in an emphatic demonstration of resistance to NATO's eastwards expansion.

In *Politics Among Nations*, published in 1948, American political scientist Hans Morgenthau introduces his influential theory of political realism. He describes the possible responses of the vanquished when the victorious seek imperial power:

> [...] the very status of subordination, intended for permanency, may easily engender in the vanquished a desire to turn the scales on the victor, to overthrow the status quo created by his victory, and to

change places with him in the hierarchy of power. In other words, the policy of imperialism pursued by the victor in anticipation of his victory will be likely to call forth a policy of imperialism on the part of the vanquished. If he is not forever ruined or else won over to the cause of the victor, the vanquished will want to regain what he has lost and to gain more if possible.[12]

The Soviet Union did not suffer military defeat in 1991; Russia was not forced to dissolve its Armed Forces, nor were its leaders punished. But throughout the 1990s, the US and the EU encouraged and, in many cases, sponsored the 'Westernisation' of post-Soviet states. In 1890, the Russian empire, constructed in the eighteenth century by Peter the Great and Catherine II, had spanned 22,400,000 square kilometres, with a population of almost 130 million. It was the second largest contiguous empire in history and one of the five major European powers. A century later, the Soviet Union covered the same territory, its population had reached almost 300 million, and it had spent the best part of half a century as the second most powerful country in the world in military and economic terms. But, with the dissolution of the Soviet Union, the territory under Russian control was reduced to approximately 17,000,000 square kilometres, inhabited by half the number of people. Russian attempts to build closer relations with the US at the beginning of the new millennium were then rejected. And so it was a resentful government of a mutilated state, which nonetheless maintained the world's largest nuclear arsenal, that set out to revive Russia's standing in the world, as the US overstretched in pursuit of absolute power.

The Libyan War: The Curtain Call

The NATO-led intervention in Libya in 2011, initiated the last of the humanitarian wars waged in the name of protecting civilians and authorised by the UN Security Council. NATO had been instrumental in drawing the countries of the Warsaw Pact towards the West, incorporating them as members—first Poland, Hungary, and the Czech Republic, and then post-Soviet republics of Eastern Europe. Some of these countries participated in the US-led coalition during the Gulf War, years before joining NATO. NATO carried out its first major military intervention in Bosnia-Herzegovina, in the early 1990s. But it was more patently mobilised as an instrument of US interests during the Kosovo War. Without sanction from the Security Council, the US used NATO as a surrogate for the UN, to legitimise intervention.[13] This crucially undermined the performance of humanitarian multilateralism. NATO played an increasingly important role in US geostrategy beyond Europe from the middle of the 1990s onwards. In 1994, it launched the Mediterranean Dialogue, a security forum involving mostly Middle Eastern and North African countries. A decade later, it built on this, involving other Arab countries in the Istanbul Cooperation Initiative. By then, it had joined US troops in the occupation of Afghanistan. NATO thus became a protagonist in the war on terror and in US efforts to transform the 'Greater Middle East'.

When NATO intervened in Libya, it was still credible to speak of an 'Arab Spring'. But conflict in the country would be brutal and protracted, as the intervention intensified the struggle between long-standing enemies inside the country. Within the UN, activity to institutionalise the 'responsibility to protect' had been intensified. And Western apologists claimed the intervention demonstrated the maturity of this norm. But the humanitarian rationale for war appeared as an anachronism, a vestige of an exhausted idealism. After a decade of imperial war, the appeal to humanitarian concern was unconvincing, as was the presentation of NATO as a humanitarian actor. Humanitarian discourse also jarred against invocation of the war on terror. NATO Supreme Allied Commander James G. Stavridis, for example, claimed that intelligence pointed to 'flickers' of Al-Qaeda in Libyan territory.[14]

Libya remained locked in conflict until late October 2020, when a permanent ceasefire was agreed between rival factions. It was just one more case of Western intervention leaving a legacy of deadly instability. Once the militarised humanitarianism of the 1990s appeared for its curtain call, chaos would ensue behind the curtain long after the lights shone by Western media were dimmed.

The Syrian War: The Watershed

Beginning in 2011 with a popular revolt against the government of Bashar al-Assad, the Syrian War soon developed an international character, placing great powers in more direct conflict than at any time in the previous two decades. In 2013, after allegations that Assad had used chemical weapons, the US government threatened to intervene. The British government failed to gain support in parliament for intervention, despite its humanitarian appeals. The conflict worsened still in 2014, when the Islamic State began its own war against the Syrian government, with the intention of creating a caliphate with a territorial base in Syria and Iraq. The first aerial attacks by a US-led coalition began almost at the same time, without UN Security Council authorisation. Initially focused on destroying Islamic State, the coalition then began targeting Syrian government forces and their allies within Syria; but Assad maintained the upper hand over his opponents.

Russia, meanwhile, began direct military action in Syria in September 2015, following requests for support from the Syrian government. In doing so, it took a decisive step beyond the defence of its sphere of interest, which it assertively exercised in Georgia in 2008, and then in Ukraine in 2014. Directly challenging US strategic interests in Syria, Russia also demonstrated greater effectiveness than Western forces in driving Islamic State from its Syrian strongholds; Russian President Vladimir Putin often adopted humanitarian language and invoked the idea of civilisational struggle against jihadi terrorism. With the US bypassing multilateral institutions, Russia exercised its power of veto through military intervention. But it also asserted a right to arbitrate in international conflicts, against enemies, and in the name of values, shared by the West. It thus demonstrated a willingness not only to dispute territories of strategic interest to the US, but also to include itself within the cultural community of a 'Greater Europe', and pursue hegemony from the inside.

By the time President Trump announced the withdrawal of US troops from Syria in 2018, the war had already left half a million people dead and 1.5 million injured. Around 7 million had left the country as refugees, for neighbouring countries, but also for Europe and North America. As the Syrian War became a turning point in geopolitics, the exodus it caused also accelerated the advance of authoritarian nationalism in the West, the growth of xenophobic far-right movements, and the feeble concession of liberal politicians to challenges from within. The challenge provoked by the resurgence of

Russia goes some way to explaining Trump's unexpected election in 2016, and his aggressive assault on 'globalism', a catch-all term for the project of the 1990s that foregrounded humanitarian morality.[15]

Trump took office disqualifying rules and institutions developed under the aegis of US power in the twentieth century, particularly after the Second World War. The rejection of established norms was then confirmed in the new national security doctrine, published by the White House in December 2017.[16] After more than a decade in which US governments emphasised the threat of terrorism, this doctrine identified the primary strategic threats to the US as coming from nation-states, and in particular from rival powers, such as Russia and China, but also from North Korea and Iran. But perhaps of most note was the repudiation of American universalism—a denial that the 'American way of life... [is] the inevitable culmination of progress' and that it should be imposed on other cultures, societies, and civilisations. As such, the implication was that, under Trump's policy of 'America First', the US would abdicate its moral hegemony and more brazenly pursue national interests.

It is not possible to know the extent to which Joe Biden, elected in November 2020, will revert to previous doctrine. But that the moral discourse decisively abandoned by Trump had already been fading for more than a decade suggests that the humanitarian politics of the 1990s is unlikely to make an immediate return. The mobilisation of liberal humanitarianism as a strategic force marked a moment of violent expansionism, in which the US pursued imperial power. In a world of intensified inter-state rivalry, in which the great powers contest each other's claims to a right of moral arbitration, universalisms are exposed as reflecting particular interests—and the violence that underwrites their propagation is laid bare.

November 2020

14

ORDERS AND DISORDERS OF REFUGEE
HUMANITARIANISM IN THE ARAB MIDDLE EAST

Tamirace Fakhoury

What do we know about refugee humanitarian orders and disorders in the Arab Middle East? What are the defining policy instruments and practices shaping these (dis)orders? And how have external actors shaped the politics of refugee humanitarianism in the Arab region?

Building on the case of cooperation between the European Union (EU) and regional refugee-hosting states in the context of Syria's conflict, which has led to the displacement of 6.7 million individuals, this chapter explores how cooperation on refugee humanitarianism has evolved into a geostrategic deal built on a 'new grand compromise' in the context of refugee flight.[1] Key regional refugee-hosting states that received displaced Syrians, such as Lebanon and Jordan, attempted to leverage their open borders. In their cooperation with the EU, they also sought to strategically capitalise on its member states' fear of refugee influx to the European continent, with a view to making their refugee response a key pillar at the heart of the international refugee regime. In return, the EU has provided these host states not only with refugee aid, but with an elevated status of cooperation on refugee protection.[2] This 'new grand compromise', however, has had various backlash effects on humanitarian protection. Negotiated refugee instruments set to alleviate the suffering of displaced individuals and to strengthen local protection regimes have seen an encroachment of economic and security agendas on humanitarian protection.[3] Colliding policy approaches on the issue of protracted displacement have further turned the issue of EU–Arab refugee diplomacy into a matter of leverage and friction.[4] Instrumentalising refuge as a source for geopolitical and economic rent has led to an erosion of refugee rights on the ground. Additionally, divergent policy expectations between the EU and host states over asylum prompted local governing powers to either overtly or covertly contest the refugee deals that the EU has negotiated with them.

Setting the context, the first part of this chapter gives a general overview of the politics of forced migration in the Arab region. It sheds light on key institutional and geopolitical factors that have shaped the politics of refugee reception in the region. It further shows how a myriad of power brokers, formal and informal institutions, legal and informal norms have created refugee (dis)ordering processes that remain enshrined through immobility and emergency.[5] The second part turns to the specific case of cooperation between the EU and key refugee-hosting states in the Arab Middle East, with examples derived from Lebanon and Jordan. It explores how cooperation on refugee humanitarianism has privileged models of a so-called 'resiliency humanitarianism'.[6] The latter shifts the gaze from rights-based humanitarianism to conceptions portraying refugees as actors who ought to develop survival strategies, adapt to adversity, and bounce back in the face of crises. This part also shows how cooperation on refugee humanitarianism has become mired in geopolitical leverage and clashing policy logics.

The Arab region is no exception when it comes to understanding how refugee humanitarianism is subject in practice to a continuum of economic, security, and geostrategic interests. Rather, it is emblematic of a global production of precarity in which the political economy of displacement has favoured the transformation of 'refugees from recipients of humanitarian aid to highly exploitable workers'.[7] It is also indicative of broader trends, whereby refugees are instrumental-ised as geopolitical 'pawns' in the politics of asylum.[8] From this per-spective, this chapter contributes to the broader literature on the political economy and geopolitics of asylum. Regional analysis is important to understanding how 'expressions, experiences and understandings of power' at the heart of the global refugee regime materialise on the ground.[9]

Setting the Context: Refugee (Dis)Ordering Processes

Throughout history, the Arab Middle East has been a key terrain for exploring the multiscalar forms of power shaping the politics of asy-lum and forced migration.[10] The region represents 5 percent of the world's population, yet accounts for 32 percent of global displace-ment.[11] Most countries in the region have concomitantly produced and hosted refugees, making the notion of *refugeeness* intertwined with overlapping conflicts and narratives of threat to state security. In this context, forced displacement and population movements have occurred in the framework of colonial, postcolonial, civil war, as well as post-conflict contexts,[12] making legacies of refugee governance extremely complex.[13] Key examples of displacement span several periods, and most of them remain protracted. They range from the post-1948 wave of Palestinian displacement, to more recent waves of forced migration in the wake of the first Gulf War, the post-2003 US-led invasion in Iraq, and the post-2011 Arab upheavals.

The governance of forced migration has been a matter of concern for the Arab regional system. Examples range from the Arab Charter to the Arab Declaration on Belonging and Legal Identity, the Protocol for the Treatment of Palestinians in Arab States (the Casablanca Protocol of 1965), and the Convention on Regulating Status of Refugees in the Arab Countries in 1994. Still, regional conflicts, stra-tegic interests, and identity politics have sidelined a rights-based approach to refugee displacement.[14] Very few states in the region have signed the 1951 Refugee Convention and its 1967 Protocol, or have endeavoured to develop rights-based asylum regimes. Though they have hosted large, forcibly displaced populations, they have treated them as guests or *duyuf*. The notion of 'guesthood' inscribes itself into a longstanding historical legacy whereby the Arab national state has opened its borders, favouring regional mobility and free exchange without necessarily institutionalising such practices. Notwithstanding informal traditions of hospitality, authoritarian governance has to a large extent curbed refugees' rights and access to service provision and justice.[15] Since most refugees come from the region itself, issues of local integration have been heavily politicised, evolving often into instruments to shape the regional balance of power. Analysts have captured host states' politics of refugee reception through the lens of a behavioural paradox.[16] In the context of such conflicts as the 2003 US-led invasion of Iraq and Syria's 2011 war, states have displayed a seemingly receptive attitude to hosting refugees at the outset of a conflict, only to close their borders later and adopt restrictive policies that have cast displaced individuals in a state of illegality.[17] In their management of displacement, states such as Lebanon, Jordan, and Egypt have adopted hybrid governing strategies, alternating from open borders to border closures and policy crackdowns.[18] Within this climate, a myriad of state and non-state actors ranging from ministries, landowners, local powerbrokers, and international aid agencies have governed refugee stay.[19] It is safe to say here that the politics of refugee governance has established itself as an assemblage of inconsistent and often informal responses that are not anchored in legal frameworks. These responses fluctuate in response to changing geostrategic and economic interests.

Against this background, the Arab region has mostly relied on external entities such as UN agencies, international non-governmental organisations (INGOs), and supranational organisations such as the European Union to cater to refugee needs, livelihoods, and rights.[20] Indeed, the international humanitarian order—defined as a set of norms, discourses, as well as formal and informal institutions that motivate intervention to protect vulnerable populations—has taken key interest in the Arab refugee landscape since the outbreak of the Palestinian–Israeli conflict.[21] In this context, external actors have sought to provide services and protection to displaced individuals and host communities within the region. Notwithstanding the proliferation of external initiatives, refugee governance has been predicated on emergency, securitisation, and eroded protection.[22] Here, intersecting policy dilemmas have been at play.

As underscored, given that most refugees come from the region itself, Arab states have perceived refugee governance as a tool for settling political scores and deriving geopolitical pay-offs.[23] In this landscape, governments have embraced the narrative of a host state under massive strain, arguing that refugees represent exogeneous threats to their economies and security.[24]

Against this backdrop, and as noted earlier, governing powers have outsourced refugee aid and protection to external entities. They have largely relied on supranational organisations and externally sponsored initiatives to cater to refugee livelihoods and rights. At the same time, though supranational organisations have set up quasi-permanent structures in the region, humanitarian programming has had low effectiveness in improving the living conditions and rights of refugees on the ground.[25] In general perspective, refugee humanitarianism, built on short-term solutions to displacement, has enshrined as Brun puts it 'emergency, temporality and protracted displacement'.[26]

On the one hand, endemic challenges in host polities such as authoritarian governance and an entrenched reluctance to reform asylum laws have made the work of international humanitarian agencies extremely challenging. The UN Refugee Agency (UNHCR), a major international humanitarian actor in the Arab region that has provided vital services and protection to refugees, has had in most cases to conform to host governments' strategic imperatives and to mitigate its calls for asylum reform in the light of local contestation.[27] Recently, in the context of forced displacement from Syria, UNHCR has initiated large-scale Regional Refugee and Resilience Plans (the so-called 3RP) that stressed the necessity of synchronising humanitarian relief with development and protection. It has also sought to play an important 'normative role' in advocating for refugee rights. However, the Agency has had to acquiesce to states' restrictive refugee policies.[28] In practice, it has gradually shifted from a purely protection-driven to a pragmatic agenda negotiating livelihoods, relief, and temporary protection measures.[29]

Notwithstanding the difficulties that international humanitarian actors have faced in enforcing protection norms in the region, their strategies have often been based on standardised, normative, or liberal policy templates.[30] International humanitarian proposals have clashed with the region's historical legacies, and refugee voices. Context-specific situations have also altered their implementation.

Adding to this, external aid strategies have been inextricably intertwined with security interests and bordering practices. As many have already argued, external aid has often provided a geopolitical terrain for catering to the security interests of the affluent global North. For instance, the EU's cooperation on migration in the Mediterranean has served the broader interest of externalising border controls and discouraging refugees from leaving the first countries of asylum.[31] At the heart of such a matter is the pragmatic 'grand compromise' upon which the international refugee regime is predicated: states of the global South host most refugees in the world. In return, richer countries of the global North allocate funding to refugee hosting states, yet they resettle few refugees.[32] This grand compromise has encouraged the rise of a political economy of displacement whereby financial incentives dispensed by richer states incentivise host states to become refugee rentier economies.[33] In return for hosting refugees on their soil, governments leverage their position as buffer zones to derive national revenue and gains, often at the expense of refugee rights. They also instrumentalise their politics of hospitality to upgrade their negotiating powers or derive benefits in regional conflicts.[34] In this context, analysts have deplored the fact that state-centric agendas of deterrence and geostrategic leverage have encroached on rights-based refugee humanitarianism.[35]

It is within this mutually reinforcing dynamic that histories of refugee humanitarianism have unfolded in the Arab region: Weak local protection systems compounded by external aid strategies privileging refugee containment have made the policy field of refugee humanitarianism highly contested.[36] On the one hand, Arab states have sought through border management and asylum strategies to keep the displaced in check and to extract geostrategic pay-offs.[37] On the other, donor states and organisations have provided relief to the 'distant others', often with the underlying intent of creating offshore borders.[38] In this context, it is no exaggeration to say that cooperation on refugee rights has evolved into a minefield.

*EU–Arab Refugee Humanitarian Diplomacy: The Politics
of Refugee Resilience and Deterrence*

In this landscape of contested refugee humanitarian legacies, how
have the EU and Arab host states cooperated on refugee flight? What
conceptions of refugee humanitarianism have they advocated? And
how have divergent logics on refugee cooperation and norms affected
refugee rights?

As Arab organisations have seen their vitality and effectiveness
erode across the decades, the EU has stepped in, evolving into a
prominent yet contested transregional actor in the landscape of refugee humanitarianism.[39] In the context of the 1995 Barcelona Process
and the 2004 EU Neighbourhood Policy (ENP), two key policy platforms that have regulated the interactions between the EU and its
so-called 'Southern Neighbourhood', the EU has strengthened its
cooperation on migration governance with Arab countries. Through
various instruments, the EU has adopted an intersectoral policy
approach, linking cooperation on migration with development and
support for human rights and local institutions. Literature, however,
often portrays this cooperation through the lens of the EU's search
for regional stabilisation and security.[40] References to Fortress
Europe, extraterritorial migration management, and remote controls
have abounded in describing the EU's perspective on migration policies in the Middle East and North Africa Region (MENA).[41] In 2011,
the cascading Arab revolts that called for the dismantling of governmental autocracies caused the EU to depart, at least rhetorically, from
its previous focus on stability and security. Calling for cooperation on
democracy deepening, the EU adopted several Arab Spring documents that ambitiously aim to upgrade the partnership between the
EU and its neighbours. Still, this shift has remained largely cosmetic.[42]
In the wake of the Arab uprisings, that in some cases turned into
upheavals, the EU redeployed a pragmatic policy approach focusing
on stabilising the region and boosting its capacity to adapt to threats
and adversity.[43] Following widespread displacement from Syria, the
EU has devised a variety of external refugee tools with Syria's neighbouring host states. These instruments strengthen the capacity of host
states to accommodate refugees and provide them with services. At

the same time, they reflect to a large extent the various ways through which the EU seeks through its funding power to contain refugees where they are, extraterritorialising migration control.

In the context of largescale displacement from Syria, the EU has considerably upscaled its refugee diplomacy efforts with neighbouring countries that have taken in more than 5 million displaced Syrians. 'Resilience-building' in the context of displacement—understood here as the capacity to provide refugees with opportunities that allow them to withstand adversity—arises as a key pillar characterising the EU–Arab diplomacy approach on forced migration.[44] A case in point are the EU's 'resilience-building' efforts in Jordan and Lebanon, two states that have received large refugee populations from Syria and that the EU has framed as priority countries in its external migration policy.[45] In this context, the EU has negotiated refugee instruments such as the 2016 Jordan and Lebanon Compacts, which provide financial and trade facilitation incentives in exchange for the temporary integration of refugees in the respective states and their labour markets. According to the EU, these policy instruments aim to strengthen the capacity of local refugee protection regimes, and to foster the economic resilience of refugees as close as possible to their country of origin.[46] At the same time, as many analysts argue, such instruments—'under the guise of resilience' or the ability to cope with adversity—serve broader containment strategies.[47] By providing extraterritorial opportunities for livelihoods and protection, the EU shrinks avenues for asylum in Europe, encouraging 'non-departure' from the region of origin.[48] These opportunities, set to withstand adversity in the first countries of asylum, are, however, predicated on temporariness. In the face of governments that dispute asylum as a permanent condition, the EU has had to publicly acknowledge that host states such as Lebanon consider the stay of displaced individuals only as a temporary state of affairs.[49]

In the section below, I explore how the EU has consolidated cooperation in refugee humanitarianism with Lebanon and Jordan. I argue, however, that cooperation in this policy field has led to several tradeoffs that have diluted rights-based humanitarianism. First, cooperation has entrenched a so-called 'resiliency humanitarianism' that sidelines protection as the core concern, shifting the gaze to temporary economic opportunities and temporary adaptation to adversity.[50] Second, colliding norms between the EU and national governments have turned the field of refugee humanitarianism into a platform for friction and geopolitical as well as economic rent.[51] Refugee-hosting states have sought to capitalise on the EU's fear of 'refugee waves' to lobby for more aid. They have also either explicitly or implicitly disputed the EU's conception of 'resiliency humanitarianism' on the grounds that it imposes strains and risks on their society and economy. Against this backdrop, the field of refugee humanitarianism has evolved into a contentious terrain where actors clash on conceptions of humanitarian protection and burden sharing.

The EU–Lebanon Case

Since the eruption of Syria's full-scale conflict in 2011, Lebanon has hosted more than 1 million displaced individuals. The EU has been one of the main funding powers that has provided refugee aid since then. At the beginning of the conflict, the Lebanese government adopted an open-border policy. Soon, however, this policy, that was commonly framed as the policy of no-policy, shifted into containment. In 2015, Lebanon closed its borders and asked UNHCR to stop registering refugees. In the last few years, politicians have consistently portrayed refugees as security and economic threats, and mostly as threats to Lebanon's sectarian power-sharing arrangement, which relies on a demographic equilibrium between Christians and Muslims.[52] As soon as the Syrian regime regained control of most of its territory, various political parties have been vociferously lobbying for Syrian refugee return, stressing Lebanon's overstretched capacity and blaming the displaced for many of the country's problems. Municipalities and security forces have enforced practices that have significantly restricted Syrians' access to employment and housing. In parallel, key political executives have scaled up calls for refugee repatriation. In coordination with Syrian authorities, the Lebanese government has been processing applications for return.

Following Lebanon's 2019 October uprising, which broke out in the context of a full-scale financial crash,[53] the Lebanese government started implementing crackdown measures against displaced individuals working in the informal sector and not in possession of a labour permit.[54] In reality, the country's restrictive labour market and its inconsistent procedural policies have created fluctuating and constantly changing 'migrant' statuses for displaced individuals. This situation has severely restricted displaced Syrians' ability to obtain work permits. Prior to 2016, Syrians who registered as refugees with UNHCR had to sign a pledge not to work. Conversely, Syrians who found a local guarantor to renew their legal residency could apply for a labour permit only in extremely restricted professions such as agriculture and construction.

In this landscape, the EU has scaled up its refugee diplomacy with Lebanon's successive governments since 2011, negotiating instruments that seek to boost the resilience and protection of both refugee and host communities. In 2016, it renewed its partnership priorities with the government of Lebanon, stressing that it aims to deploy various forms of financial assistance, grants, and loans so as to reduce the impacts of Syrian displacement on Lebanon's economy and host communities while providing various economic opportunities for the displaced.[55] In practice however, many of these policy packages remained in the realm of declaratory diplomacy. The 2016 Lebanon–EU Compact, which is at the core of these renewed partnership priorities, is a case in point.

In the context of the 2016 London conference for 'Supporting the Future of Syria and the Region', the EU negotiated with the Lebanese government a Compact which promised funding in return for the Lebanese government easing Syrians' temporary stay and employment. In the wake of these negotiations, the Lebanese government pledged to embark on some asylum reforms. It announced its decision to waive the US$200 refugee residency fee, enabling Syrian refugees to renew their legal stay. It also adopted measures allowing Syrian parents to register the birth of their children born in Lebanon. It further pledged to simplify refugee documentation requirements, and to facilitate Syrian refugees' access to work.[56] In the context of the Brussels conferences on 'Supporting the Future of Syria and the Region' that have been co-hosted by the EU since 2017, the debate on optimising refugee rights in Lebanon continued. However, these pledges and conversations on improving asylum governance have not had much traction on the ground. The much-celebrated policy rhetoric on refugee resilience paled in the face of deteriorating refugee livelihoods and rights. UNHCR reports that more than 70 percent of surveyed Syrians do not have legal status.[57] In the wake of Lebanon's financial collapse that spawned a large-scale wave of contention, the UN Refugee Agency declared that 75 percent of Syrian refugees in Lebanon slipped below the poverty line in 2020, in contrast to 55 percent in 2019.[58]

Over the years, the Lebanese government has recurrently argued that obstacles such as an extremely overstretched capacity and massive economic strains, as well as a spike in national unemployment, have obstructed the spelt-out pledges of refugee inclusion. In practice, however, analysts concur that the Lebanese state, that insists on safeguarding its status as a no-asylum country, intends to maintain legal ambiguity towards asylum as the desired policy.[59]

Within this context, the EU's approach, which seeks to incentivise Lebanon to create opportunities for refugee 'resilience-building', has not seen any progress towards the declared objectives. Despite a proliferation of high-level meetings between EU officials and their Lebanese counterparts, governing elite cartels have not given much weight to the EU's refugee diplomacy.[60] Instead, some political parties have vociferously contested the EU's approach of resiliency humanitarianism, decrying it as a subterfuge for keeping refugees at bay.[61] They have also doubted the approach of keeping refugees in the first countries of asylum when the host state has succumbed to major strains.[62] The motives for contesting the EU's conception of refugee resilience go beyond mere divergences on refugee norms. Rather, contestation is anchored in geostrategic ends. Through such a rhetoric of contestation, the government has sought to evade responsibility to craft rights-based asylum policies. In its dealings with the EU, it has repeatedly buttressed the country's position as a no-country asylum. It has also sought to leverage refugees as geopolitical rent with the EU, albeit with little success.[63]

Most importantly, the EU's refugee diplomacy with Lebanon remained disconnected from an understanding of Lebanon's deeply polarised perceptions over the Syrian conflict and the issue of displacement.[64] Since the outbreak of Syria's war, Lebanon has shied away from developing a unified policy stance—either towards Syria's war or towards the refugee issue. Some Lebanese factions have backed the Syrian regime in the face of its rivals. Others have viewed the conflict as an opportunity to weaken Syria's control over Lebanon. Amidst domestic tensions, most political factions have started portraying the extended stay of Syrian refugees, who are mostly Sunni, as a threat to Lebanon's system of sectarian power-sharing. Additionally, Lebanese politicians have instrumentalised the issue of Syrian refugee stay and return as a geopolitical card in the international relations of the Syrian conflict. Political executives who are staunch allies of the Syrian regime hoped that, by advocating refugee return, they would contribute to rehabilitating the legitimacy of the Syrian regime within the international system.[65] In this context, the EU's humanitarian scripts relating to refugees have become deeply entangled in the complex geopolitics of Lebanese–Syrian relations. On the one hand, the EU has indefatigably promoted the narrative of refugee 'resilience-building', as long as a political settlement in Syria remains out of sight. On the other, some Lebanese politicians have called for the prompt return of refugees, irrespective of a political settlement.[66] In 2020, the Hassan Diab government that was appointed in the context of Lebanon's large-scale 2019 protests, hurried to discuss a comprehensive Syrian refugee return draft plan, even though conditions are not propitious for return in safety and dignity to Syria.

Further to this, given local resistance, some of the EU's policy proposals on increasing refugees' economic opportunities have remained only ink on paper. For instance, the EU attempted to negotiate trade facilitation schemes in return for the better integration of Syrian refugees into Lebanon's labour market.[67] Rashly advocating the return of refugees, Lebanese governments have, however, perceived this as political liability. Political factions have argued that the EU's approach to entice refugee employment in first countries of asylum, does not take account of complex historical legacies and local strains.

The EU–Jordan Case

Jordan represents yet another case of mixed success in the field of cooperation with the EU on refugee humanitarianism. For decades the country has welcomed various refugee populations.[68] Framing refugees as guests, however, the Hashemite Kingdom has developed a complex politics of asylum that accommodates refugees while seeking to control their mobility and access to rights. Leveraging its politics of hospitality in the international system, it has branded itself as an important pillar of the global refugee response.[69] In this context, Jordan has sought to leverage this politics to extract revenue and consolidate its international relations.[70] Its cooperation with the EU on migration management, development, and security has provided a key channel for consolidating Jordan's refugee-hosting value in the international system.[71] Unlike Lebanon, which has contested the EU's rhetoric on resilience-building in the first country of asylum, Jordan has welcomed the EU's aid and diplomacy on refugee humanitarianism. Notwithstanding this, it has not altered its stance on refugees as *duyuf*, or guests. Its cooperation on refugee 'resilience-building' with the EU has led to various reforms that have, however, not engaged with the deeper causes and roots of dispossession and refugee vulnerability.

At the outbreak of Syria's war, Jordan opened its borders to displaced Syrians, hosting more than 600,000 refugees. By 2014, just like Egypt and Lebanon, invoking the heavy economic strains brought about by the costs of hosting refugees and referring to the transborder challenges that Syria's conflict posed for its security, the Hashemite Kingdom closed its borders. In an attempt to regulate refugee displacement on its soil, Jordan severely restricted refugee mobility until 2016. Refugees who wanted to exit camps have had to provide 'bail out' documents that were extremely hard to obtain and that entailed restrictive procedures.[72] Though Jordan grants the right to employment to Syrian refugees who possess a labour permit, reports confirmed that prior to the adoption of the Jordan Compact, few Syrians were able to do so.[73] In 2016, in the context of the Supporting Syria and the Region conference in London, the EU's negotiations on the Compact were hailed as a turning point for Syrian refugee rights in the Hashemite Kingdom. The Compact promised to unlock various trade facilitation schemes, grants, and concessions in return for Jordan providing 200,000 work permits for Syrian refugees and facilitating Syrian refugee access to education and healthcare.[74] Initially, it stipulated that Jordanian companies that were located in the country's eighteen Special Economic Zones (SEZ) could benefit from relaxed Rules of Origin (RoO), provided that Syrian refugees represented 15 percent of the company's workforce in the first two years. In other words, companies that allocated 15 percent of their job positions to Syrian refugees could export commodities to the EU. Once the target of 200,000 jobs was reached, trade facilitation schemes could be extended. This deal was hailed as a win-win solution in the sense that economic and employment opportunities would trickle down both to Jordanians and Syrians.[75]

In the context of these positive incentives, Jordan embarked on a series of reforms with the aim of facilitating refugee stay and access to its labour market. For example, it waived the fee that Syrians incurred in exchange for a work permit.[76] The government also sought to facilitate the obtention of short-term and flexible work permits which accommodated various situations. Moreover, it enabled Syrians living in refugee camps to work outside, toning down the previous criticism that Jordan attracted when it came to restricting refugee mobility through encampment. The government also facilitated the enrolment of Syrian refugees in education, and substantially reduced obstacles preventing access to healthcare; steps that the EU lauded in the last 2020 Brussels conference for Supporting the Future of Syria and the Region.[77]

In practice, however, reforms have seen an encroachment of the logic of 'extractivism' in humanitarian agendas.[78] They have neither led to overhauling Jordan's asylum system, nor have they created sustainable pathways to employment or integration. In diplomatic circles, a conception of refugee humanitarianism set on creating as many work permits as possible and celebrating refugees as entrepreneurs has instead prevailed.[79] The Compact could also not reach the primary objective of creating 200,000 work permits. An ILO study suggested that by 2018, as little as 13 percent of the Syrian working-age population had obtained a work permit.[80] Also, there was no clarity as to whether the number of work permits reflected the number of Syrians who had actually found a job opportunity. Arguing that work permits are about opportunities and not people, it was possible for the government to increase the number of labour permits by granting them to the same individuals year after year; or by granting the same individual more than one labour permit.[81] Civil society decried the process of reducing employment to the number of issued work permits, and argued that it overshadowed the debate on sustainable and dignified employment.[82] Research further denounced non-compliance with labour rights and standards of decent work.[83]

Various obstacles relating to the segmentation of Jordan's labour market—bureaucratic hurdles, such as the necessity for a refugee to submit adequate documentation and have a guarantor, together with a lingering mistrust in formal institutions—hampered the spelt-out objectives of the Compact.[84] Also, a mismatch between refugee preferences and available employment opportunities discouraged Syrians from applying. Asked about their preferences, refugees communicated their reluctance to work in remote Special Economic Zones under unattractive conditions.[85] They also underlined that available work opportunities did not necessarily reflect the skills that they had acquired or practised in their country of origin.[86] Highly skilled Syrians could not apply to professional sectors restricted to Jordanians, such as education, medicine, or business management.[87]

In the light of these limitations, the EU and the Jordanian government agreed by 2018 to review the Jordan Compact. In parallel, to make refugee employment more attractive, the Jordanian government has devised a variety of measures such as providing home office opportunities and flexible work permits outside the Special Economic Zones. Nonetheless, the economic gains promised to both Jordanian companies and refugees remain limited. Most importantly, the adoption of trade preferences in return for refugee employment in migration policy was vociferously debated in the literature that cautions against commodifying refugee protection.[88]

Jordanian policymakers have not refuted the EU's policy proposals as openly as some of their Lebanese counterparts have done.[89] Yet the state's policy behaviour has to a large extent shaped the outcomes of negotiated refugee instruments. As stated, the Hashemite Kingdom has not altered underlying conditions obstructing Syrians' access to protection and to the labour market. Some academics have suggested that the low performance of the Compact must be read in the context of the Jordanian government's pragmatic strategy to prevent Syrian refugees from competing with the Jordanian labour force.[90] Prioritising a policy of containment, Jordan has refused in various instances to welcome Syrians trapped at the borders. Instead, it has called for their return despite the raging conflict.[91] In this context, the government has stressed the narrative of a host state under massive strains, and has criticised the limited attempts at burden-sharing of the global refugee regime. Additionally, large-scale mass protests in 2018 drew the government's attention towards prioritising the management of social and economic tensions rather than accommodating international proposals of refugee resilience-building.[92] Unlike Lebanon, which has expressed overt contestation, Jordan has through various subtle strategies stressed the kingdom's limited capacity, lobbying for more aid while stressing limited efforts at international burden-sharing. In the latest Brussels conference for Supporting the Future of Syria and the Region in 2020,[93] Jordan highlighted its efforts at hosting refugees and underlined the massive strains that it has incurred as a consequence.[94]

Conclusion: Refugee Humanitarianism as an Arena for Frictional Encounters

The assumption that the international humanitarian order is key to socialising host states into refugee norms has historically prevailed.[95] It is often thought that reluctant host states may yield to reform pressures in the light of positive incentives such as financial aid and soft coercion such as reputation or conditionality. What is, however, under-researched is how refugee humanitarianism may evolve into an arena for frictional encounters often with negative implications for refugee rights. Multiple forms of governmentality negotiate clashing policy aspirations and expectations that lead to crafting diluted versions of humanitarianism. On the one hand, affluent states of the global North look to offshore borders to buttress their own state-centric interests.[96] On the other, first countries of asylum in the global South bypass commitments to protection while lobbying for refugee aid. In this context, the refugee humanitarian order has come to refract broader 'expressions and experiences of power' at play within the broader international system.[97] It is against this backdrop that B. S. Chimni makes a case for studying the geopolitics of asylum in the world order.[98]

Building on the case of cooperation between the EU and select Arab refugee-hosting states, this chapter has shown how the dynamics of refugee cooperation have forged precarious orders of refugee humanitarianism. The EU has approached displacement in its 'near abroad' through a crisis governance imaginary (MAGYC 2020), privileging hybrid approaches combining aid and protection with the power of trade and economy. This political economy of refugee aid has, however, promoted short-termism, failing to engage with the causes and consequences of dispossession. In the absence of underlying protection environments, refugee deals such as the proposal to integrate refugees in return for trade facilitation schemes, or projects focusing on refugee self-reliance and technical capacity-building, failed to address refugees' aspirations for dignified livelihoods and future options. Far from generating a fleeting reality, such aid paradigms create and enforce new policy scripts. They encourage the marketing of refugees as active entrepreneurs and downplay the rights-based implications associated with *refugeeness*.[99] By shifting the debate from fully fledged humanitarian protection to the search for economic opportunities, they advocate a version of humanitarian governance predicated on strengthening coping mechanisms, ensuring triumph over adversity, and bouncing back in the face of crises. In that regard, they risk turning refugees into migrants in search of economic survival.[100] As Lewis Turner argues, framing refugees as 'entrepreneurs' in search of economic opportunities is revelatory of the patterns of continuity and change at the heart of humanitarian orders.[101] Such practices represent one of the latest manifestations of a long-standing emphasis in humanitarianism on self-reliance. At the same time, they attest to the shifting nature of humanitarianism, which prioritises resilience instead of recreating 'the severed connection between state and citizen that refugeehood represents'.[102]

For their part, the neighbouring countries of Syria have not been compliant borrowers of this 'resiliency humanitarianism' script that international actors have advocated. Cooperation with international actors such as the EU has turned into an opportunity to bargain for leverage and contest refugee norms. Host states have leveraged their so-called hospitable economies to extract more revenue, while reaffirming (no-)asylum as a matter of national sovereignty. In this context, clashing conceptions of humanitarian protection and burden-sharing have abounded. The EU has favoured solutions that encourage the 'non-departure' of displaced individuals from the region of origin, seeking to provide relief and temporary protection in the first countries of asylum. Conversely, host states have decried the massive strains that the politics of refugee hospitality brings along, flagging limited international burden-sharing and asymmetries of power in the international system.

Divergent expectations of what refugee humanitarianism entails on the ground carry along with them complex implications. They yield consequences for constructing and reconstructing the norms and practices in which humanitarian protection is anchored. First, clashing narratives lead to portraying refugees through a crisis governance lens that privileges quick fixes or solutions that are not harmonised with local contexts.[103] Second, the EU's approach to displacement as an opportunity to boost refugee resilience may provide an opportunity for hosting states to resist and contest refugee rights—either more vociferously or in more covert forms.[104] In Lebanon, as noted in this chapter, the government perceived the EU's diplomacy on refugee humanitarianism as an opportunity to reassert its limited capacity, and to leverage the EU's fear of new migrant waves rather than to consolidate the rights-based bond between the refugee and the host state. In diplomatic circles, discussions between the EU, Jordan, and Lebanon on refugee inclusion have led to promoting supposedly 'innovative', albeit atrophied, versions of humanitarianism confined to temporary inclusion and self-reliance. In Jordan, economic opportunities that have revolved around granting labour permits, reaching numerical targets, and devising flexible working permits have arguably diluted debates on refugee rights. They have also cast refugees into more precarity and uncertainty over future options, as work permits have not paved the way to sustainable employment. Borrowing from Marianne Fotaki, such policy scripts end up branding 'a type of humanitarianism that does not consider the causes of dispossession'.[105] Rather, they entertain 'a temporary illusion' that precarity can somehow become liveable and bearable, albeit with no fully fledged solutions in sight.

In this landscape, refugees and host communities—as actors in their own right—have not remained idle. They have sought to shape these (dis)orders, critically interrogating notions of 'resiliency humanitarianism' amidst waning rights and scarce livelihoods. Lebanon is a case in point. In October 2019, mass protests erupted in Lebanon, decrying the government's corrupt politics. Activists highlighted interrelated struggles embracing various social causes ranging from workers' to refugees' rights. Protest framings have discredited the political narrative of the refugee as a liability, shifting rather the gaze to Lebanon's political regime as the key threat to citizen well-being. In the context of these protests, civil society activists have particularly questioned the EU's cooperation with the Lebanese state, and the unintended consequences that such cooperation yields on the ground.[106] By cooperating with corrupt governments under the guise of humanitarian crises, international actors end up legitimising their rule, often at the expense of ordinary citizens' aspirations and refugees' needs. A couple of months after the outbreak of Lebanon's protests in October 2019, Syrian refugees have staged a daily sit-in at the UN Refugee Agency in Tripoli, a city on the northern coast of Lebanon. They have flagged deteriorating rights, scarce funds, and limited options for resettlement.[107]

Notwithstanding its veneer of stability, Jordan has also witnessed grassroots unrest. In 2018, large-scale protests in Jordan targeted the government's politics that, despite extracting international revenue and attracting concessions and loans, has failed to curb unemployment and social tensions. In the wake of signing the 2016 EU–Jordan Compact, refugees residing in Jordan have expressed their dismay at job opportunities that do not match their aspirations and preferences.

Amidst loose or crumbling social contracts between the state and the individual, it is worth exploring whether, and if so how, refugee humanitarian models which promote an imaginary of 'resiliency humanitarianism' rather than fully fledged protection, may end up creating more instability and precarity in the very contexts that they seek to 'stabilise'.

PART THREE

HUMANITARIANISM AFTER LIBERALISM?

15

VIOLENCE IN A POST-LIBERAL WORLD

Brad Evans

End of Liberal Times

We are certainly living in turbulent times. From the internal strife tearing apart the European Union and the rise of authoritarian populists, to the general sense that democratic 'entitlements' are crumbling, we are a world away from the liberal optimism of Fukuyama.[1] But it is not simply political malaise and the will to despotism that cast doubt over 'progress'. Neither can this turn be neatly explained by pointing to the ineptitude of the uneducated poor. A clue lies amid the ruins of liberalism itself: its narcissistic impulses, which produced ill-fated wars of conversion, and which ontologised insecurity, paving the way for the liberation of prejudice and the normalisation of besieged mentalities only *they* were meant to experience. That we may all be 'going South' is the spectre now haunting the liberal imagination.[2]

We can present a stark reading of the history of the liberal encounter by diagnosing its violence. Whilst liberalism is a complex political ideology, of concern here is less the claim to universal rights, security, and justice, than the regime of power that from Kant onwards has sought to govern planetary life. Liberalism in this regard is a bio-political regime shaped by a moral conception of life as something both autonomous and in need of governance. In short, it connects the human with the planetary in a way that is fully in keeping with the logics of capitalism.

This account of liberalism recognises its historical mutations, even though the will to govern planetary life has remained consistent. Thus, whilst early liberalism was integral to the onset of the global slave trade and the civilising mission, it has gone through a number of effective reinventions, reconstructing its own past through the violence of organised forgetting.[3] Covering the past with the cloak of idealism, liberals bind themselves to a universal history of rights and justice.[4] Undoubtedly, the Second World War was a watershed moment, as liberal regimes positioned themselves as the victors over ideological fascism, often erasing the contribution of communists to achieving the same ends.[5] The black rain that fell over Japanese skies initiated a new phase of liberal revivalism. Notwithstanding a few direct and disastrous interventions during the Cold War, most notably in Vietnam and Cambodia, Western liberal regimes largely subcontracted their violence to proxy actors (as did the Soviet Union)— the aim being to control popular uprisings in former colonial territories at an effective distance. This would provide them with re-entry points in the global South. But it would take the fall of the Berlin Wall to create conditions for conversion to 'liberal democratic principles'. The notion that underdevelopment is dangerous could be used to justify a range of coercive measures, from the denial of aid to outright annihilation.[6] Yet, this period following the Cold War can be seen as a final chapter in the liberal will to rule planetary life. Its emblematic moment was the crossing of the Mogadishu line in Somalia, in 1992, which made explicit the willingness to go to war in the name of peaceful cohabitation. And it ended with the violent assault on Libya, in 2011, a decade after the fateful attacks on New York's Twin Towers. During this 'Twenty-Year War', liberal regimes steadily retreated from the world of peoples, abandoning conversion in favour of containment. But as forced migrants sought Europe (often driven from territories ravaged by liberal war), they demonstrated that this world of people would not accept containment, reasserting their political right to flee.[7]

At the beginning of this period, liberals revived the claim that their ideas could free the world from conflict. Kant's concept of perpetual peace made a come-back, notably disassociated from his racial anthropology; so, belatedly, did Just War theory, confirming the theological character of liberal mission.[8] Some still argue that a reduction in conflict represents the principal benefit of liberal apotheosis—that we have never lived in more secure and less violent times. And they point to fewer deaths, or some other Steven Pinker equation, to prove it.[9] But such statistics were always ethically dubious, reflecting a Eurocentric concept of conflict and ignoring the pernicious forms violence takes as it is pushed to the margins. In the 1990s, the liberal claim of an approximation to planetary peace was itself indicative of the unlimited war that was being waged by other means through 'full spectrum domination'.[10] And the longer this low-intensity global war played out, the more liberal regimes normalised a state of vulnerability that would be capitalised upon by a post-liberal fascism.

Liberalism has thus placed in check the pursuit of its own stated objectives of freedom and tolerance. Populist nationalism has emerged from the Open Society to question globalisation. But we cannot explain the break-up of the liberal world order as a retreat to neat sovereign divisions. Another form of fragmentation is taking place within societies, accelerated by the multiplicity of crises produced by liberal capitalism. No longer able to lay claim to the world, the entitled classes of the North frantically seek to preserve what they have, except for an elite few, who accumulate wealth with greater voracity. Meanwhile, an ignored underclass expands, experiencing an existential precarity increasingly comparable to that of the poor of the South—those on whose subjugation the provision of welfare previously depended. To understand violence in an emerging post-liberal world, and to consider an appropriate response, there is a need to account for the resentment, anxiety, and opportunism produced by the recent history of liberal hegemony.

Liberalism: The Final Chapter

Following the end of the Cold War, liberal regimes presented military intervention in the global South as the surest evidence of a humanitarian commitment to saving the lives of distant peoples. However, colonial legacies had already brought distance into question, and these peoples had not always asked to be saved. Imagined as incorporating illiberal subjects into the liberal order, humanitarian warfare would blow back on Western populations in multiple ways: terror attacks on the streets of metropolitan capitals, the domestic application of war technologies of surveillance and pacification, and the demonisation of ethnic minorities, not least by far-right nationalist groups that grew as forced migrants reached Western shores in greater numbers.

That doesn't mean to suggest there was an absence of tensions within liberal thought. In the final decade of this war, two distinct yet overlapping visions of battle emerged, which proved instructive. The first was premised on the supreme logic of liberal technology, where it was assumed that high-tech sophistry and digital advancement could replace the need to suffer casualties (at least on the part of interventionist forces);[11] the idea here being that violence could be carried out at a distance by soldiers working in the post-industrial shadowlands. The second was premised upon a more humanitarian ethos, which demanded local knowledge and engagement with dangerous populations. For a brief period in the 1990s, for example, the UN attempted to use the humanitarian plight of war-affected populations to foster peace among state and non-state perpetrators, by utilising local brokers and anthropological expertise.[12] The narcissistic violence of the Global War on Terror would place this secondary vision in lasting crisis, as the violence of liberal encounter fatefully exposed any universal commitment to rights and justice. Not only did liberal regimes appear to be the principal authors of violence in the borderlands of the world, thereby challenging the notion that underdevelopment or poverty was the true cause of planetary endangerment, but populations within liberal consumer societies would become increasingly critical of the war efforts, regardless of the moral sentiments. The wars, in fact, would lead liberalism to ethical ruin, and the investment of the economic resources required would add to the pain felt during years of austerity. Indeed, post-Iraq, if there has been one notable casualty of the wars on terror, it has been precisely the belief that we might engage and transform the world and its peoples for the better.

The reluctance to put any forces on the ground in the battles authored in Libya and Syria was most instructive in this regard. Metaphysical hubris had, therefore, been displaced by phased withdrawal from the world of peoples, as liberalism was coming to terms with its failed humanism and the limits to its territorial will to rule.

After Libya was literally left in ruins and at the mercy of the new mercenaries who profited from such devastated conditions, the nature of liberal warfare would become increasingly invisible and distanced from the public imaginary. As the vocabulary of the New Wars would be subsumed within narratives of insurgency, popular uprising, and criminality,[13] what became of the Global War on Terror would discursively evaporate into the political ether, devoid of political currency and yet normalised to its veritable occlusion. Iraq and Afghanistan would be given focus primarily on their ongoing anniversaries, to remind us that the violence was, in the end, simply without ending. And Guantanamo Bay would be handed over to the lawyers, who in a world beyond Netflix, captured very little public interest except for the purpose of academic study. At the same time, conscript armies had given way to professional soldiers of fortune and, arguably as a result, recorded battlefield deaths relentlessly declined.[14] The very location of war had disappeared into the background, while in the same movement, this disappearing act rendered landscapes unreadable, as if all meaning and certainty had now collapsed into the complexity void. As a result, domestic constituencies in the global North could no longer fully understand the nature of the warfare being conducted, let alone question with any authority the legitimacy, objectives, or legality of the violent acts still carried out in their names. Indeed, it seemed however much information was being leaked about what was taking place in the atmospheric shadows, the more populations became desensitised to the atrocities that were immediately broadcast before their eyes and digitally rendered in the palms of their hands.

Physically separated from a world they could no longer understand or control with any political and ethical surety, liberal regimes increasingly relied upon the digital recoupment of distance through strategies of targeted assassination, surveillance, and containment, which at least still allowed them to continue to make an atmospheric bonfire of sovereign principles. Just as liberal agents in the dangerous borderland areas increasingly found themselves operating within fortified protectorates[15]—which now proves to be revealing of a great separation *from* the world—this was matched, albeit in ways that initially appeared disconnected, by new forms of violence and orchestration that also took place *at a distance*.[16] The political and philosophical significance of this should not be underestimated. The strategic confluence between the remote management of populations and new modes of violence-at-a-distance, proved to be indicative of the narcissism of a liberal project that reeked of the worst excesses of technological determinism and its full abandonment of any serious claim to humanism. How could you ever possibly claim to be humanist if the prevailing mantra proceeds from the assumption that humans are fallible and can no longer be trusted? However, instead of looking with confidence towards a post-liberal commitment to transforming the living conditions of the world of peoples, what has taken its place is an intellectually barren landscape offering no alternative other than to live out our catastrophically fated existence with ever greater speed and intensity; a condition where instead new forms of fascism are appearing through the cracks, as the globally vulnerable—notably refugees and migrants—have been wagered in outright political warfare against the locally precarious, notably those in broken white communities. This should be instructive regarding how we envisage the end of liberal times as marked out and defined by an incommensurable sense of planetary siege. It also demands new thinking about the human subject and what it means to live more affirmatively beyond the catastrophism of a deathly liberal rule.

Populations in more prosperous metropolitan districts have not in any way been exempt from this drama and the imminent collapse of the liberal order of things. Citizens and professionals who, it was said, had nothing to hide have been expected to enact their innocence by living openly in the electronic gaze. To be connected has meant to have access to the only rights that seemingly matter—the smart rights of digital passage and consumer spending privileges. Disconnection, on the other hand, would not only be presented as pathologically inexplicable; it would be a form of political and social nihilism and self-harm. Hence, while liberal forms of violence, both from aerial assaults and ground interventions, would be continually repackaged for Western media consumption, we had reached the point where any possible distinction between the realms of civil and militaristic order was blurred, such that the interconnected subject would be one who actively embraced a technological mindset that privatised everything—violence included. The call to violence, but a 'like click' away from the composition of a digitalised frame, that would be less about content than the immediacy and potency of affective registers which defy more considered deliberation. Drone violence would be particularly diagnostic here, also revealing of a shift in the liberal worldview that increasingly took place in the atmospheric shadows—literally the place in the clouds, above our heads, and in the invisible virtual domains.

Drone technologies were not simply a new tool of warfare. They would prove to be paradigmatic to late liberal rule. They also further radicalised the very idea of the territorial front line, such that any Schmittean notion of inside/outside appeared like some arcane remnant of an out-dated past. By definition, there was no existential enemy to be vanquished as the outside had all but vanished. There were no fixed lines to be drawn in the sand. No sovereign integrities to claim and be protected. Geopolitics would be firmly displaced by complex and dynamic atmospheric geographies, whose forms of hostility we are still yet to fully comprehend. Drone violence would therefore usher in a post-territorial phase in the liberal way of war, in the sense that territorial integrities simply no longer concerned the deliverance of violence. While masquerading as a form of civilised advancement that confirmed the oft-touted modernist mantra that technological supremacy automatically bestowed ethical providence, they proceeded on the basis that everybody, everything, and everywhere was a source of perpetual endangerment. And it was only a matter of time before they were also called into action over metropolitan skies. Such is the nature of the colonial boomerang. And human presence only made things worse. Displacing the primacy of human agency from the act of killing represented more than the realisation of the military's dream of zero casualties. Post-traumatic stress disorder (PTSD), after all, still remained an afflicted curse, even for those who engaged in violence at a 'safe distance'. What was more fully revealed by this weaponry was the lack of confidence permeating the entire liberal system. The military would appear just as fragile and untrustworthy as anybody or anything else. Helping heroes was a broken-hearted cry to help the vulnerable, helping the victims. All soldiers were now soldiering with misfortune, demanding forms of training that authenticated ontological vulnerabilities, thereby paving the way for a truly post-human sensibility wherein the task of policing the global borderlands could no longer be left to military agency.

We saw this most clearly in the deployment of the resilience doctrine within military academies. Resilience promoted forms of life tasked with mastering the art of living dangerously.[17] Abandoning any foundational claims to security and truth, its ontological premise would be that all things were fundamentally insecure by design. What is more, as the future was deemed to be a terrain of unavoidable disasters already in the making, the doctrine both normalised catastrophes, while demanding a certain exposure to their very possibility even before the violence materialised. Resilience as such was situated within the order of battle, as the promise of violence would be the surest guarantee that life was permanently under siege, from terror to weather and everything in between. Our societies, so we were told, were 'built to be vulnerable'. And so, it was imperative that we learned to adapt to 'whatever threat' might be looming on the horizon of uncertainty, to be prepared for the catastrophic event which was always and already there in the making. What was at stake here was more than simply accepting the inevitability of future catastrophe; it was all about the necessity of liberal societies to encourage their citizens to be on a permanent war footing for a war that nobody even mentioned. The War on Terror would not come to an official end. There would be no victory parade. No time and date to memorialise its passing. It would instead become so normalised that very few felt compelled to mention its existence or even afford it discursive acknowledgement.

Retreating from the World of People

In its response of catastrophe and crisis, modernism, it was claimed, banished God from the world. While this was certainly disputable, as the enduring presence of political theology remained integral to the modern political canon (see below), it proved to be more prescient in the move from apocalyptic to catastrophic narratives of endangerment.[18] Disasters would become random accidents rather than divine punishment or retributive actions by vengeful deities for human failings. But such randomness would be increasingly nuanced, as human agency was gradually introduced into the disaster zone. Emergencies would be intrinsically related to society and the complexity of human activity. This found graphic expression in the notion of the Anthropocene, which denoted a new geological age in which cumulative human activity was seen to impact, potentially and catastrophically, on all planetary systems. Humans thus became the principal authors of their own potential extinction. And since their activity had unintended consequences of an interconnected and truly immense scale, it had to be governed accordingly. But the way it had to be governed, however, would be radically altered as a result of past failures to tame and socialise the global borderlands. Whilst action and engagement were the prevailing mantras until the late 1990s, following the ethical failures of the Global War on Terror there was a notable shift towards governing at a distance through technological means. In fact, as a result of a notable separation from the world, global governance was increasingly concealed, arbitrary, and beyond democratic control. This would reveal the fundamental paradox of the 'information age'. Rather than knowing more, liberal regimes that had embraced epistemological uncertainty as part of their allegiance to risk analysis and the complexity sciences, replaced people-based knowledge enquiries with an algorithmically fuelled politics of anxiety: a politics based around stabilising cultural and consumption-based walled gardens, while much of the world, in terms of direct experience, became an ethnographic closed area.

The more connected we appeared, in all aspects of our electronically trafficked and autonomously mated lives, the more distanced we became from ourselves and our worldly fellows. Such separation, even before the physical walls that were retrenching Europe and the United States were more eagerly set, reflected the *final act* in the decade's long reversal of half a millennium of expansionary and territorially globalising European political action. It also found an important expression in humanitarianism and its experimental practices.

Liberal interventionism, as once reflected in the willingness of the aid industry to stay and expand humanitarian activity in politically challenging environments, contained a deepening paradox. Humanitarian 'presence' in zones of instability and crisis could only be maintained by the withdrawal of international aid workers into gated complexes and fortified compounds. Maintaining presence would be inseparable from a growing physical separation between aid workers and their operational environments. While liberals have long held that risk was essential to their commodified notions of creativity, enterprise, and the liberation of the individual subject, the accretion of postcolonial ethical inhibitions and demobilising sensibilities that defined late liberalism's problematisation of earlier forms of one-sided political action, gave rise to a compensatory politics of anxiety. The foregrounding of uncertainty as the defining principle of political inaction would inversely be related to a waning liberalism's inability to act territorially in a decisive, world-changing manner. The resulting attempt to govern security through insecurity would become synonymous with a pervasive culture of anxiety that encapsulated a fear of *the Other* within an inclusive imaginary that had little curiosity, understanding, or tolerance for the outside.

Fuelled by periodic and politically directed attacks on aid workers in the global South, the dominant perception among international actors was that aid work was increasingly dangerous and demanded a certain phased withdrawal for its own protective sake. Since Katrina, moreover, and reflecting the default practice of borderland states, there would be a growing tendency to define disasters, even so-called natural ones, as primarily breakdowns in public order, and therefore as security problems which demanded a militarised response.[19] Disaster zones became sites that had to be first secured before any humanitarian help could be given. Fear of beneficiaries, in terms of their unpredictable potential for violence or the contagious effect of the trauma marking them, would be widespread among international aid workers. At the same time, however, this fear was not entirely irrational, especially once ISIS emerged on the scene and made a notable spectacle of violence against those once tasked with delivering a 'war by other means'. Uncoupled from the protective shield of one-sided European political action, aid agencies increasingly found themselves hostage to a wide range of hostile state and non-state actors, fundamentalist groups, men with guns, and machete-wielding killers. Within the humanitarian sphere, global rebalancing through localising agendas became synonymous with political push-back, the reassertion of local sovereignties, access denial, and the growth of international no-go areas.

In places like Iraq, Afghanistan, Sudan, Libya, Pakistan, the Central African Republic, and Syria, to name just a few headline cases, hard-to-reach areas for aid workers and ungoverned liberal spaces were expanding and opening up in the borderland zones, refugee camps, and burgeoning urban slums of the global South. Rather than containing the promise of riches, fame and religious redemption for those who dared, these new spaces of concern now harboured and concentrated the anxieties, uncertainties, and demoralisation of a territorially inhibited liberalism. The international aid industry was a good example of liberalism's wider operational withdrawal from the chaotic and chance-affected world of people. Linked by secure transport corridors, the industry's gated complexes and fortified aid compounds came together to represent archipelagos of privileged international space that outlined the boundaries of the ungovernable spaces they sought to contain. More than anything else, this reflected the demoralisation and political bankruptcy of liberal humanism that, as is now plain to see, was ultimately incapable of doing anything other than shore-up and massage an unsustainable debt-driven and increasingly jobless consumer society, while protecting the interests of the economic and political status quo. That did not, however, mean to say that the global South could be left to chance or its own autonomous proclivities. It was too dangerous to be left to its own devices. And besides, they were now coming to us, by whatever precarious means, in their thousands. Whilst the one-sided action that drove forward Anglophile visions of globalisation was lost and in its liberal guise never to be recovered, the ungovernable spaces of the world, which could still be observed in far greater clarity, detail, and depth of aesthetic projection, nevertheless required continued surveillance, mapping, and policing. Although taking place more remotely and relying heavily on satellites, computers, and algorithms, what took its place was a digital and atmospheric remapping which proved to be just as one-sided and expansive as terrestrial cartography ever was. At the same time, new digital and surveillance technologies would offer a territorially inhibited liberalism an irresistible Faustian bargain as it choreographed its final deathly dance. Besides allowing capitalism to wring the last dregs of profit from an unsustainable consumerism, they would be seduced by enticing ways to eavesdrop and remotely recoup lost ground, with all their futuristic fetishisms. And from secure bunkers, they also provided concealed ways to reach out and strike any place on the globe; even in an age that was for all intents and purposes *beyond war*, for it was no longer even declared, in any conventional sense.

The Sacred Object for Violence

What binds together the history of Western metaphysics is a particular allegiance to the politics of sacrifice.[20] That we must give ourselves over to the order of the sacrificial in order to reclaim some form of earthly meaning is the truism that has consecrated all forms of allegiance. But while the sacrificial idea has remained a constant, the sacred object for power and violence has changed over time. Beginning with the sacrifice of Iphigenia, we might in fact chart the history of Western power through the sacrificial body. This would take us from the suffering of Christ as foundational to Christianity, to the advent of the hero as first depicted by Goya, who found its greatest expression in the sacrifice of nations, on to the crises of the sacrificial model, which Arendt recognised in the Holocaust, as the world found nothing sacred in the raw and abstract nakedness of human life. If the nation-state was a giant sacrificial machine, what became the sacred object for liberalism would be located in the body of the victim. For it would be precisely upon the body of the victim that universal meaning could be inscribed through justice carried out in their names.

It is no coincidence that, during the early stages of the twenty-year war waged in liberalism's name, Just War theory was revived.[21] Liberal violence was justified through the sacralisation of its victims. While the figure of the victim had appeared for some time prior as part of domestic liberal concerns, it is with the internationalisation of the victim that its onto-theological presence was fully announced. The sorrow of Iphigenia would be redramatised here as the innocent child became the defining motif for crystallising the moral sentiment at the heart of the liberal will to rule. The victim child would therefore be mercilessly marketed, and children's bodies appropriated in order to inscribe some form of meaning to their unnecessary deaths by condemning certain forms of conflict and yet justifying another in their names. The body of the desecrated innocent child became the ultimate sacred object, which demanded further sacrifice as humanitarian warfare went global. Such innocence would also be comported into the realm of gender politics, as unspeaking women, veiled and denied, would also see their bodies appropriated for the purpose of liberation. The woman behind the veil, in all her innocence, was the liberal subject-in-waiting, a source of reproductive power, and a means to the renewal of biopolitics.

As I have argued elsewhere, the liberal way of war was unashamedly faith-based.[22] Despite the embrace of complexity and uncertainty as part of the prevailing logic of security governance, it was nevertheless reasoned that the ends would justify the means. Even if war itself was the most uncertain of human activities, liberal leaders were sure in their beliefs and firm in the righteousness of their mission. And yet, in practice, liberal war proved completely incapable of answering the strategic question as to what constituted too much killing. There could be no answer to such a question, since the scope and temporality for power were unlimited. Liberal regimes therefore committed themselves to wars without the prospect of ending with a clear victory, or even with a strategy that might indicate a lasting cessation to hostilities. What did become clear was that the more violence was waged, the more the borderlands resisted. And the more the borderlands resisted, the more domestic populations questioned the commitment and integrity of the armed global liberal missionary.

So, while the metropolis played host to further terrorist atrocities in crowded areas through the continued weaponisation of transportation, those tasked with protecting the victim would soon become the victims themselves. And they would suffer literally at the hands of perpetrators that had emerged from the fires of the liberal wars in the early twenty-first century. Whilst the theological rage of 9/11 created the image of a global security crisis, it was nevertheless carried out by a number of nameable individuals, which revealed most fully the power now invested in the 'catastrophic individual' whose violence could have global effects. The appearance of ISIS in Iraq bore eerie similarities with the Khmer Rouge.[23] Radicalised in a ruined landscape mercilessly bombed for freedom's sake, they showed themselves all dressed in black, puritanical in the extreme, with violence to match. And yet whilst Al-Qaeda opted for the more spectacular violence against symbols of liberal power, the violence of ISIS was hyper-subjective, making it clear through the individualisation of sacrificial actions the very types of subjectivity which were to be literally severed. Beheading would serve a particular function as the journalist, aid worker, and humanitarian soldiers tasked with protecting the victim, became victims themselves to the most brutal ontological crimes and denied their humanity in the process. Such individualised attacks upon bodies which appeared alone and completely helpless in the middle of the open expanse, proved to be the ultimate example of intolerable violence.[24] And it would be the ultimate mimetic double for a system of divine violence, as the onto-theological tensions between the metropolitan city and borderland desert, sacred victims and sacrificial rage, entitled individualism and personalised slaughter, played out for our full viewing displeasure, again making us all forced witnesses to their occurrence.

A Return to the Mythical State?

It is tempting to view the subsequent arrival of new right-wing populist leaders, for whom the term fascism seemed particularly apt, as being a quintessential example of what Zygmunt Bauman called 'retrotopia'—romanticising a certain nostalgic past that seeks to resurrect some mythical glory in the here and now.[25] Amid attempts to reclaim some territorially bounded vision of a Paradise Lost, nostalgia returned through the resurrection of a retrospective imagination, which considered the present, in all too biblical ways, as fallen into some ruinous state. Rallying against the very idea of a globalising world and misguided foreign adventures, what appealed was a return to the more dogmatic ideas of the past. A world that was neatly divided and whose identities were made all too apparent through its protective walls and enclosures. Critics would be equally retrotopic. For many, what such nostalgia represented was a return back into a time when the world was truly dangerous, especially for the most entitled and educated metropolitan subject and member of the emerging liberal intelligentsia. And so, once again, it was claimed, we would encounter on the road back many shadowy figures thought to have been consigned to history: Carl Schmitt, Hobbes, Oedipus, and other mythical bodies who now appealed in landscapes where risk, complexity, uncertainty, and vulnerability once reigned supreme. René Girard was right when pointing out how the desire to reclaim some notion of a lost paradise would be essential to the consecration of myths, which could in turn sanction the most brutal and yet righteous forms of violence for the sake of reclamation.[26] Walter Benjamin was also astute when developing the idea of mythical violence and inserting its logic into the heart of the modern nation-state, which required its own myth making exercises to command allegiance and justify the violent sacrifice of millions in its name.[27] The new fascism of today is not, however, about some return to the past, even if the past can be invoked to create a certain mythical imaginary regarding belonging in the present. Nor is it simply about reclamation, even if the calls to material enrichment point to better days. It is about accelerating the forces of history, pushing them all to their point of exhaustion, running with the pure materiality of a nihilism that destroys all political difference in order to contain global life, whilst seeking to preserve something 'pure' and 'great' about the anglophone subject in the order of a world that's shrinking on every possible register, and its problems in such close proximity they are now too close to handle.

This invariably brings us to the contemporary rise of democratic authoritarianism and its neofascist advocates, such as the alt-right, which across the world have openly rejoiced in the collapse of liberalism. From the United States to Brazil, its leaders would mobilise the spectacle and the language of hatred to devastating effect. But there is something more pedagogical that these movements have done. Through an appeal to greatness, not only have they made a claim upon the politics of time, where the past is romanticised for the purpose of steering history in a particular direction, they would also mobilise ontological vulnerability to devastating effect. Positioning themselves as embodying the resistive force to a world of inevitable catastrophe and crises has not simply been about securitarian speak. It also provided an ontological and epistemological move; a counter to the perceived death of the white Promethean man, and the surety that comes with the ability to be secure about oneself and one's place in the world. It is perhaps no coincidence that the advent of such leaders would also result in a resurgence in criticism of theorists such as Foucault, where the shift towards post-truth would be neatly conflated with a certain post-Enlightenment disposition, devoid of the virtues of reason, rationality, and calm deliberation.[28] The betrayed liberal needed someone to intellectually blame for the demise. Leaving aside the nonsensical notion that Foucault, amongst others, disavowed all notions of truth (though clearly what had previously perturbed many liberals were their concerns with the brutalising violence of the Enlightenment and its deeply racialised images of thought), what became apparent were the ways orthodox liberal thinkers also recognised the alt-right as a condition of possibility for marking out their own authentic and dogmatic positions. We would see a response which forgetting even the recent history of liberal wars, also retreated back into a sort of liberal puritanicalism. Once again the world appeared for them in neat sovereign territories and clear dialectical markers of notable political (in)distinction.

Like unwitting students of history, leaders of the alt-right had also mastered the art of distraction by inducing and appropriating what Marxists would no doubt have termed 'false consciousness'. Their false consciousness, in an act of making what was unknowable apparent, was consciously dialectical. The nature of the *faux* retreat demanded it. Shifting the mode of perception back to times that never were great for the vast majority was illusionary in this regard, as they consciously invoked the terms 'fake' to create a consciousness of suspicion around all traditional sovereign markers (i.e. state, media, political elites—liberal or otherwise) which once appeared familiar, comforting, and secure in their monopolies over knowledge production. This is where these movements were different. The apparatus of state was both a friend and an enemy. It was duplicitous. It was to be trusted and distrusted. It was to be resisted and supported. It was to be drained and yet its walls built higher. Something that was made possible only through a mastery of the most advanced digital and social media platforms, which worked above and beyond the power of the state. And all the while the power of the free market economy would be unmediated, and its forces accelerated into every single aspect of human existence. This was never about sovereignty. It was about getting the masses to learn to desire their own containment and separations from one another. Conditions, we might argue, that were fully in alignment with the demands of global capitalism and the end of a particular phase of liberal globalisation, which already produced so many landscapes of disposability and now demanded total control over the mobility and containment of life. But the sacred object here still remains unclear.

Humanity at a Crossroads

Liberalism was able to withstand the terrifying violence of 11 September 2001. It could also deal with the violence and internal conflicts raging for many decades in parts of the global South. And when its own racialised communities were caught in the catastrophic crossfires, like New Orleans following Katrina it could still draw upon the necessary architectures of containment and militarised policing to withhold the flood of human misery. Such violence and catastrophe in fact proved time and again to be essential to its planetary ambitions, and provided with each crisis a renewed moral mandate to accelerate the liberal interventionist desire to incorporate all planetary life. What liberalism couldn't abide and contain, however, was the recalcitrance shown from its own domestic native white colonies of social abandonment and political neglect. For it was in these sites that the limits of liberal tolerance would be truly exposed and its duplicitous ontological claims on the vulnerability of the human subject revealed.

Like all great empires, liberalism didn't ultimately collapse because it was vanquished by some external force. The death of liberalism would be brought about through revealing the illusion of its myths, the fragility of its claims, the contingency of its eternal glory, and the exhaustion of its modes of subjectification, which destroyed from within. While the myth of universality would be fatefully wounded during its military adventures, which in the name of peace and security sanctioned war and torture, the final blows were realised through the breaking apart of its interconnected myths of democracy and entitlement, both of which also exposed its violence and prejudices. Liberal societies always had a suspect relationship with any viable notion of democracy. They had shown an active willingness to destabilise and overthrow any regime, especially the popularly elected, who had the temerity to present illiberal alternatives. From socialism in Latin America throughout the 1960s and 1970s, to the more recent and effective winning of elections in the Occupied Territories and Egypt, there was always a reason to claim the victory as a mere anathema, or misguided, and ultimately of dubious mandate. The problem, however, was that such denials of acceptance would unravel as broken white communities displayed their resentment and anger through the ballot. Liberal subjects would look on in a state of disbelief, unable to accept the collapse of their entitlement model. It simply couldn't be right that liberals in the United Kingdom could be stripped of their European citizenship because of the selfishness of the underclasses who had nothing to lose if the world went up in flames. And what injustice! Wasn't it simply time the United States had a female liberal president, regardless of the fact that she would be part of a family dynasty which openly called for war against the indigenous of Mexico and would embody the perpetuation of the liberal war machine?

The word 'entitlement' would gain popular international currency in the 1980s with Amartya Sen's pioneering study into conflict and famine.[29] It was a concept which immediately resonated with the liberal and could easily be worked into its understanding of multicultural tolerance without any disruption of the bourgeois social order. Entitlement never meant equality, but each afforded their dues so long as the bare necessities for survival were covered and the individual subject with all its normative reasoning reigned supreme. Some could quite rightly be more entitled than others to material well-being on account of their cultural acumen, appreciation of the rules and codes of the liberal game, and through following the correct pedagogical practices, which marked out in marketised ways the progressive from the regressive, the metropolitan from the borderland. Just as Brexit had taken a hammer to liberal entitlements, which were of very little benefit to broken working-class communities in the United Kingdom, the defeat suffered by Hillary Clinton was surely everything to do with her sense of entitlement to the presidency after so many years of dealing with a misogynistic husband, patriarchal oppression, and other forms of discrimination faced by the already materially entitled.

Through exercising their democratic right, broken underdeveloped communities in the United Kingdom and United States revealed most fully the illusion of a system of democracy which viewed any alternative as unjust and fraudulent. The figure of the imposter would appear here as a form of liberal Judas, the untrustworthy person who shouldn't even be on the stage of this worldly theatre. It is the syndrome which has always plagued and been inscribed upon the backs of the 'underclasses'. But the most important and revealing predicate here would be the question of tolerance. Liberalism had always accepted difference provided it could be absorbed, domesticated, and governed. Difference in itself would be intolerable, especially if its claims to autonomy challenged the liberal will to rule. But the idea of tolerance, which went to the heart of liberal multiculturalism, was never about creating a reciprocal ethical understanding and solidarity amongst the world of people. Tolerance was a limit condition, inclusively segregated, with cultured rules and social practices, which beneath the surface of politeness revealed the most pervasive violence and exclusions. And yet, whilst liberalism was able to tolerate racial differences by continually drawing upon the colonial memory of taming the noble savages of the world, the limits of that tolerance would be fully exposed as the liberal subject stared into the broken mirror and looked upon a cracked vision of whiteness, which was now screaming back. For what was being exposed in this doubling of white psychosis was the true nature of liberalism, like a retelling of the Emperor's new clothes; but on this occasion, it was the people who were all walking around naked in the most vulnerable of states. This liberalism was all about its material enrichment; it sought refuge in commodification, and its only salvation from all the world's ills was ultimately given over to the divine power of the market economy, which promised to rid the world of all its deadly sins.

The figure of the victim would again be central to this drama, even as those who believed in the system the most would be swallowed up and spat out in the most indiscriminate and public of ways. In the post-9/11 setting, the entitled subject was already under attack from forces it could no longer contain. The emergence of resilience would be a last desperate attempt at holding on to this ideal in the deluded hope that a bounce-back from personal tragedy would at least result in a return to some entitled landscape, with its material benefits reinstated: the proliferation of anxiety syndromes correlating to the proliferation of private insurance premiums and self-help guides for the resiliently minded. However, in order for this doctrine to have been sustained there was a need to ontologise vulnerability. Everybody could potentially be a victim, just as everybody could be a source of endangerment. This flattening of victimhood would again come up against its limits with the appearance of the resentment of broken white communities in the liberal homelands. It was simply unacceptable, indeed intolerable, to accept that the underprivileged white male subject could somehow be seen as a victim of history, let alone exercising political agency in a way that, according to conventional democratic mandates, ought to be respected.

The problem, of course, is that this is precisely where new forms of fascism would appear with such ferocity and dizzying speeds. Repackaging these concerns with the insecure order of things, they have been able to stoke greater divisions and author new forms of violence and exclusion. The advent of white terror is very real, very dangerous, and its fascistic face increasingly normalised as part of the mainstream. New fascism has become parasitic to white resentment and already proved its success in appealing directly to the duplicity of intolerance. It has also harnessed the crisis of subjectivity and fully exposed the poverty of the liberal political imagination, while continuing to have devastating political and social effects. Pitching the truly vulnerable of the world against the precarious and neglected from broken white communities, in the violent space vacated by liberalism, more explicit and openly prejudicial forms of violence and discrimination are being constantly affirmed, which having mobilised ontological vulnerability, repeat the promise to make those who never had any entitlement feel great again. It would be a grave mistake to see this as a simple return to twentieth-century ideological fascism. Fascism has always been a mutable beast, which has been capable of transforming and recreating the conditions of oppression without the need for ideological moorings. It is also painful and dangerous to watch the last remaining liberals trying to now fall back, without any safety nets, into an age of liberal purity, deploying their own retrotopic idealism of a once so-secure and entitled world—the liberal Paradise Lost—which was guided by the invisible hand of peace, truth, and justice.

What's needed in the present moment is a more sobering and honest reflection on the death of liberalism, its sacrificial violence, its duplicity, its tolerance thresholds, and its abandonment and neglect. And this needs to be matched by the continued need to fight fascism in all its forms, its sacrificial violence, its duplicity, its tolerance thresholds, and its abandonment and neglect. If we have entered into a post-liberal world, which has been accelerated by the myopic violence of the liberal wars for the past two decades, what is ultimately at stake here is the very idea of humanity and how it might be rethought in the twenty-first century. A post-liberal humanitarianism is possible, despite our physically locked down and humanely locked out conditions, which began some time before the planetary crisis of 2020. Humanity is at a crossroads; which road we choose will ultimately depend upon how we navigate and resist the violence and technological subjugations of the post-liberal disorder.

16

WHERE HUMANITY ENDS

DUBAI AND THE PERFORMANCE OF MODERNITY

Rafia Zakaria

Liberal Modernity and its Performances

The United Arab Emirates has worked long and hard at looking like the West—even better than the best. The world's tallest building, with its glistening spire, looms over Dubai's fake shoreline, proof of the Emiratis' technocratic zeal. The streets are clean; a brown or black person is always nearby to pick up any errant piece of litter. For entertainment, there are bars and clubs where liquor flows much like it does in New York or London or any place that draws the young and the affluent. Blazing lights shine from malls full of wares from around the world: perfumes that cost hundreds of dollars, couture houses that make their own statement by refusing to pin prices, cars that cost more than a small suburban home in the American Midwest.

There are many takers for Dubai's performance of modernity, gussied up as it is in the wrappings of abundance. You can see the glee on the faces of Western travellers as soon as they arrive, as they roam between duty-free stores full of candy and makeup and watches and so much else. Here they can play and buy and evade taxes and gather up goodies like never before. Whatever the condition of the consumer markets of their origins, here capitalism rules, and lays before them all the status symbols, all the gewgaws and gadgets, that their hearts desire. There are multiple Apple stores and Tesla dealerships too. If you've brought the cash—and the corrupt grifters and former dictators and dynastic rulers have—you can pour it into all this or into Dubai's internationally appealing estate market.

And even while the world, particularly the world still romancing liberal democracy, knows that Dubai's dalliance with modernity is a farce, the UAE continues to get a free pass. The well-worn list of Dubai's sins is proliferated with perfunctory regularity. A recent report by the Carnegie Endowment for International Peace considers it opportune for the incoming US administration to 'elevate and address widespread concerns about Dubai's role in enabling global corruption'—inevitably presented as an immoral impediment to capitalist development, rather than its immoral product.[1]

Enumerating Dubai's sins in as kindly a tone as possible, the report alleges that everyone from Afghan warlords to Nigerian kleptocrats to Russian mobsters and European money launderers are operating there, funnelling money in and out of Dubai's banks, which are only too happy to look away when it comes to the source of these amounts. Dubai is 'a magnet for tainted money', the report affirms. It has a thriving gold market with opaque business practices; its free trade zones are havens for trade-based money laundering. It is notable that the Carnegie report and others before it detailing the dark side of Dubai do not question the UAE's *de facto* admission into the ranks of neoliberal modernity.

Take, for instance, the fact that the summary of the report contains only one mention of Dubai's inhumane treatment of its migrant labourers, which doesn't appear until halfway down the page: 'Many migrant workers are also treated as commodities in Dubai through the *kafala* system, an exploitative migrant labour scheme that shares some characteristics with human trafficking.' Ironically, for a report trying to uncover corruption, this milquetoast characterisation of the tens of thousands of migrant workers who live a slave-like existence in the Emirate is itself a cover-up. Instead of emphasising the stunning abuses the system engenders, it normalises them as ones akin to, rather than equal to or even greater than, human trafficking. Later portions of the report try to cast a more in-depth look at particular financial crimes that go through the Emirate, noting that 'personalised institutions' and an unaccountable elite that is resistant to reform has exacerbated the proliferation of abuses within the Emirate.

The Carnegie report is but one example of how the developed world, the United Nations, and the post-Bretton Woods financial system have become used to turning their heads when it comes to the wrongdoings of powerful actors in places like Dubai. The diktats of neoliberalism, which crown *homo economicus* king, are, as the report shows, more concerned with financial crimes than with the welfare of actual human beings. Even when the report does indict one or another aspect of the UAE, it has the pronounced tone of a diffident shrug, a kind of resignation that seems to be in contrast to the valiant commitments to spreading democracy and the rule of law, which are central to the liberal order.

Liberal Order and the Threat of Dubai

The last Munich Security Conference, held in February 2019, was a glum affair.[2] The central quandary on the minds of those gathered there was 'Who can save the liberal order?' The reason for the question was simple: with the United States retreating from its usual role as rhetorical champion of liberal ideals, European nations, the other bastions of liberal democracy, were flummoxed. How would the rest of the world, large swathes of which had been forged in the image of Western liberal democracies, be saved from slipping into dictatorship and other illiberal systems? How would human rights regimes be enforced? How would the values on which their own societies were based be sustained with an isolationist and retrograde United States? 'What unifies us is the commitment to democracy, the rule of law, free elections, religious tolerance, equal rights for women and men', noted David McAllister of the Committee on Foreign Affairs of the European Parliament.

Liberalism had indeed taken a bashing. The years immediately preceding had seen the rise of the Islamic State, whose extremism presented the starkest contrast with what McAllister had outlined as liberal democratic values. But there was more: the decision by the United Kingdom to leave the European Union, the election of Donald Trump in the US, and the rise of right-wing populist movements in Latin America, Asia, and Europe itself.

And yet, glum as they may have been, the self-professed defenders of liberal democracy, gathered in Munich in February 2019, managed to assure themselves and each other that the liberal order would persist after all. At the end of the Conference they issued a 'Declaration of Principles', which reiterated their commitment to 'democracy, free, fair and open markets, and the rule of law'.[3] Like the lofty declarations issued when world leaders are ensconced at Davos, where the World Economic Forum meets, this Declaration of Principles seemed to have been crafted to keep up appearances, rather than actually ensure that the rule of law or even democracy accompany the commitment to free markets.

Indeed, while the Islamic State, Trump (until his electoral defeat in 2020), and the weakening of the European Union have represented overt threats to liberal order, little attention has been paid to the threat posed by places like Dubai, which have enticed the purveyors of liberal democracy, without signing on to either political and social liberalism or democracy. Performing liberal modernity, exalting the freedom to consume, Dubai exemplifies the partiality and inconstancy of Western commitment to liberal democracy—as well as the hollowness of the promise of liberal order itself.

Over the last decade, the UAE has become a leading donor of humanitarian aid, ostentatiously contributing to the international enterprise that has perhaps done most to provide the liberal order with moral legitimacy. But the UAE's humanitarian donorship places its inhumane domestic governance in particularly stark relief. As they welcome the UAE into the humanitarian international, Western governments expose their own humanitarian hypocrisies.

A Veneer of Humanity

I started receiving the letters in March 2020. Written by South Asian workers who were stranded in Dubai, they all told a similar tale.

After the onset of the COVID-19 pandemic, employers had disappeared, along with their workers' pay cheques. In one letter, a young man said he was so desperate that he was contemplating suicide. In others, wives asked for help for their forsaken husbands. In September 2020, an article in *The Guardian* described the dire conditions in a camp where at least 100 workers were living, dependent on the piecemeal assistance of ad hoc do-gooders.[4] There are thousands of workers living in such camps throughout the city. They include janitors and cab drivers, construction labourers and domestic servants; but many have been left begging on the street. Some are owed thousands of dollars by their employers. If they stay, they risk starvation and punishment for overstaying their visas. If they leave, they are unlikely ever to get the money that is owed to them.

On 17 May, the United Arab Emirates declared an amnesty for workers employed under the *kafala* system. According to this system, employers, acting as local sponsors, take on responsibility for employees' movement and residence. Often these employers keep the passports and other documents of employees, preventing sudden departure. The amnesty was to last until 17 November; it was then extended until the end of the year. In theory, this meant that those overstaying their visas would not have to worry about incurring fines. But the reality is much more complicated. Many workers had already been heavily fined before the amnesty—and their employers, who bore responsibility for their plight, had done nothing to advocate on their behalf.

In Dubai, the *kafala* system enables a form of slavery, which is particularly brazen in the construction industry.[5] Labourers, living in camps, work long arduous days in unbearable heat, with few breaks. The water provided to them is not desalinated properly and it often makes them sick. On account of the inadequate sanitation facilities in the camps, sewage overflows into the living areas. In one camp, it was reported that over 7,500 workers were sharing 1,248 rooms.[6] Female domestic workers also face harsh conditions. As with construction workers, these women have their passports confiscated. They are forced to work long hours, with no overtime pay and no way to escape. Living in the homes of their employers, they are subject to control all hours of the day and night. Beatings, rapes, and even torture occur often. I have come across many horrific stories. One woman was tortured so badly by her employer that she was disfigured for life. Another was slammed against a wall and beaten with broomsticks, after years of starvation. A Human Rights Watch report based on interviews conducted in 2013 noted that the UAE provided domestic workers with no employment safeguards, and that physical and sexual abuse is rampant.[7] Reports of such abuse are rarely published in the Emirati press and are suppressed by the UAE government.

One of the most astonishing aspects of the UAE, and Dubai in particular, is that even in the absence of state support, neither foreign aid agencies nor registered domestic charities are permitted to help foreign workers living in camps, destitute without wages. Such organisations cannot assess conditions in camps nor the needs of people living in them. They cannot even help with the payment of visa fees, the obtainment of travel documents, or passage to home countries. The UAE is intent on presenting itself as an aid donor, rather than an aid recipient.

In 2018, Dubai doled out more than 28 billion UAE dirhams (almost US$8 billion) in foreign aid, exceeding the United Nations target of 0.7 percent of national income and becoming the world's fifth largest aid donor. While the aid primarily went to Asia and Africa, the UAE has particularly emphasised its humanitarian role in responding to emergencies in the Arab world—not least Yemen, where it has also done its fair share to stoke conflict.

UAE's duplicity in Yemen is brazen. It offers aid with one hand, while, with the other, it smites the Houthis in the country's south. In February 2020, the UAE sent US$6 billion to Yemen, money that was to be used to build housing units and aid widows and orphans.[8] And yet the UAE has fuelled the war that produces these widows and orphans. Boosting an alliance seen as vital to its regional status, the UAE has provided military support for Saudi Arabia's warmongering in Yemen.[9] It withdrew its forces from Yemen in 2019, but it has continued to interfere in Yemeni politics. It has actively worked to undermine Yemen's Islah party—an offshoot of the Muslim Brotherhood—whose model of political Islam it sees as a direct threat to its own monarchy. It has also sought to weaken traffic in and out of the Yemeni port of Aden, in an effort to reduce Dubai's competition as a leading centre for Middle Eastern trade and commerce.

As its laws and institutions permit modern-day slavery, the UAE uses money that could rescue workers at home from destitution and debt burdens to purchase indemnity against foreign criticism. Some steal from the rich and give to the poor; the UAE steals from the poor and gives to other poor, in a crass laundering of its moral image. Foreign aid provides a veneer of humanity to the UAE's spectacle of modernity.

The UAE also recognises the power of paying empty homage to the concept of human rights. In 2014, for instance, the Middle Eastern website Jadaliyya exposed a dubious NGO that pretended to be a human rights organisation but was really a propaganda machine tasked with issuing 'reports' on human rights issues, such as the abuse of migrant workers. The 'International Gulf Organization' (IGO) was based in Geneva but 'operated a branch' in Dubai.[10] Its leadership included officials who were on very friendly terms with the Emirati rulers.

Just like Dubai's many banks, which slip in the illegitimate under the guise and trappings of the legitimate, the IGO produced documentaries and policy reports. However, instead of underscoring the abject condition of migrant workers or the torture of domestic workers, it parroted Emirati propaganda about the improvements being made in these realms. One of the IGO's first documentaries tried to prove the 'fairness' of trials under the Emirati justice system, according to which alleged Islamists have been jailed for up to fifteen years simply for criticising the government.[11] It also 'refuted' reports of torture, denial of legal representation for the accused, and prohibition of visits from family members.

The IGO's policy report, *Domestic Work Legislation in the GCC*, misleadingly labels pending or proposed legislation as proof of progress.[12] It incorrectly places hope in international frameworks and bodies like the International Labour Organization, despite the fact that most GCC countries have not ratified or adopted the ILO convention on decent work for domestic workers.[13] Other parts of the report obfuscate the reasons why the domestic work sector remains unregulated in Dubai, arguing that it is cultural precepts which produce this resistance, when it is those very cultural precepts that are actively promoted by the government, to ensure that there won't ever be regulation of the sector.

The example of the IGO reveals just how easy it is to talk the talk without any intention of ever walking the walk. If Dubai's banks can funnel money in illegal ways, then surely its fraudulent human rights organisations can do the same thing. After all, in the current age of liberal disenchantment and populist fervour, human rights organisations, even those with alleged enforcement powers like United Nations agencies, have been reduced to producing report after report that fail to move the powers that be or shame the governments that kill and enslave the most vulnerable.

In Dubai, we have a perfected performance of modernity embellished by the tokens of neoliberalism. The malls, the shops, the endless caverns of duty-free enterprises, all pay homage to *homo economicus*. The buying and selling are all interpreted as a commitment to freedom, where freedom means precisely the freedom to partake of frenzied economic activity. Aesthetics adds further credibility, the much-touted wonder of Dubai's metropolitan skyline offered up as the ultimate homage to technological achievement. (Art Dubai, one of the leading art fairs of the Middle East, attracts some 30,000 visitors annually.) In Dubai, slavery, the super-tall Burj Khalifa, and art from the Louvre coexist in happy union.[14] But while the UAE's spectacle of modernity is garnished with Prada bags and Ferraris, it only convinces wilful dupes by replicating the humanitarian motifs associated with Western liberalism and its civilising ambitions. That beneath the spectacle, beneath the imposing artefacts that would substantiate Dubai's pretensions, lie the bones of enslaved workers who toiled unto their death, can then be considered a footnote in the history of an accelerated passage to modernity—not so different to the passage of Western societies that now export bankers, brands, and moral duplicity to the UAE.

The UAE presents itself not just as an initiate to the club of developed countries, but a harbinger of capitalist civilisation's future. A burlesque portrayal of economistic modernity, Dubai is a product of the worst that capitalism has to offer. But maybe its pretentious claim on the future should be taken at face value. In a world in which the hollow performance of modernity is celebrated, what it means to be modern itself changes. Dubai, as showcase, might then not be just the case of a shady and ruthless city kingdom given to fraud. It perhaps instead offers a dystopian depiction of the post-liberal order, where capitalism savagely exacts profit and tramples the weak, and there is no way to rescue those it condemns as the detritus of its transactions. Dubai, this post-liberal necropolis, imposes its cruelties on hundreds of thousands because its rulers are aware that the values of human rights, of economic and gender equality, have all been reduced to nice words and policy briefs to be produced at regular intervals by frontline NGOs. The future, even the post-Trumpian future, promises many more Dubais. The UAE's legitimising veneer demonstrates the limits of shared humanity in such a future. Dubai offers us a vision of where humanity ends.

17

BILLIONAIRE PHILANTHROPY, WOMEN'S EMPOWERMENT, AND THE CURRENCY OF MODERNITY

Serene J. Khader

In September 2019, the Bill and Melinda Gates Foundation recognised Indian Prime Minister Narendra Modi with its Global Goalkeeper Award. Modi, who once earned the nickname 'Butcher of Gujarat' for presiding over a pogrom that killed thousands of Muslims,[1] may seem like an unlikely ally for an organisation that claims to be 'guided by the belief that every life has equal value'. In more recent years, the Modi government has arrested thousands of activists and critics,[2] placed the political leaders of Jammu and Kashmir under house arrest and cut off their access to outside media, and presided over an increase in caste violence against Dalits (members of the scheduled castes, once known as 'untouchables').[3] In February 2020, while Delhi burned in another anti-Muslim pogrom, Modi could be found proudly posing with Donald Trump. Nonetheless, in 2019, Bill Gates took to the stage to shake Modi's hand and congratulate him on his bravery in addressing what he claimed was a highly sensitive issue: sanitation. Modi dedicated his award to 'the Indian people', and he claimed that 'women benefited the most' from his campaign to end public defecation.[4]

Why is the world's largest philanthropic organisation publicly celebrating a right-wing ethnonationalist, and why is that ethnonationalist interested in portraying himself as a champion of women's empowerment? To answer this question, we need to recognise changes in the concept of women's empowerment. We need to ask what leaders like Modi have to gain by portraying themselves as advocates of empowerment. And we need to examine how billionaire philanthropists have contributed to changing conceptualisations. I argue in this essay that the Modi government's ability to violate human rights and call it 'women's empowerment' has been enabled by Western philanthropists, like the Gates Foundation, which thus boost its status in the global order. Technocratic philanthropists have redesigned women's empowerment so that it can ostensibly be achieved without women's collective agency, democracy, or increases in women's status. A depoliticised and minimalist conception of empowerment, which reduces it to a sort of humanitarian survivalism, is then more readily manipulated by leaders who wish to portray their countries as 'modern' and worthy of membership in the club of countries that dominate the globe, without having to adhere to liberal moral principles related to democracy, equality, and respect for individual and minority rights.

Curious Empowerment

In July 2018, the Modi government faced a vote of no confidence in the Indian parliament. The government responded by calling attention to 'its record on women's empowerment'.[5] In the words of one MP from Modi's Hindu nationalist Bharatiya Janata Party (BJP), the government's toilet-building project 'had improved the lives of millions of Indian "mothers and sisters"'.[6] This was far from the first time the Modi government had portrayed itself as an international leader on women's issues. At the 2015 Call to Action Summit, co-sponsored by the Gates Foundation and the World Health Organization (to which the Gates Foundation is the second largest donor, after the

United States government),[7] Modi offered to help other countries to develop programmes to improve maternal and child health outcomes.[8] He also touted his 'Beti Bachao Beti Padhao' ('Save the daughter, educate the daughter') programme, which aims to reduce sex-selective abortion and increase girls' access to social services.[9] In a 2018 speech, he said: 'After exploring various options in the last six to seven decades, women in the country reposed faith in the BJP. Previous governments did not do anything to provide even basic facilities to women and [they] just made promises.'[10]

Though the Modi government is quick to flash its women's empowerment credentials and make claims to international standing on the basis of them, there are important reasons to doubt its commitment to women. Women's empowerment, at least as understood by the activists from the global South who brought the term into widespread use, involves more than mentioning women. It means increasing women's control over material and ideological resources and fighting against power relations that subordinate women to men—typically through organised social movements led by women themselves.[11] Yet the Modi government often seems more interested in accruing reputational gains than doing anything to increase women's power and status. As of 2018, over 50 percent of the funding for the programme designed to reduce son preference was spent on advertising.[12] Similarly, in spite of promises to raise women's participation in parliament to 33 percent, only 8 percent of the BJP's nominated candidates were women.[13]

The Modi government also seems to be rebranding conservative ideas about women by calling them 'empowerment'. Indian women's groups note an emphasis on women's welfare, or even protecting women's role as mothers, over women's rights and equality.[14] Instead of increasing women's power in the home and increasing their opportunities outside of it, the Modi government describes providing toilets and cooking stoves as empowerment. More nefariously, the BJP explicitly redefines women's empowerment as part of a 'security paradigm', focusing its public conversations on how women (especially upper-caste Hindu women) need protection.[15] Modi introduced the death penalty for perpetrators of child rape, but his government has ignored calls from women's movements to improve the enforcement of existing rape laws, leading to speculation that the BJP is more interested in creating anxiety about Hindu women under attack than changing rape culture.[16] Many BJP members are publicly preoccupied with claims that Hindu women need to be saved from a 'love jihad' where Muslim men plot to marry them.[17] Modi and the BJP also seem to be using women's empowerment as a pretext for selectively criminalising Muslim men. The government publicly illegalised triple *talaq*, the practice of instant divorce.[18] However, at the same moment they were decrying Muslim divorce practices, BJP officials defended the murderers of a Hindu girl whose WhatsApp suggested she was dating a Muslim boy.[19]

Moreover, many Modi government policies that claim to empower women actively harm them—and disregard human rights more broadly. The same sanitation programme for which the Gates Foundation honoured Modi had previously attracted international opprobrium. A UN observer reported that Indian officials were meeting the targets that the Gates Foundation so prizes in its programmes by punishing people for defecating outdoors, sometimes taking away their ration cards or cutting off their electricity.[20] In the same week the Gates Foundation gave the award, two Dalit children were beaten to death for defecating in public in one of the villages the Swach Bharat programme had declared 'open-defecation free'.[21] The UN report also noted that the targets were being met by intensifying the caste-based practice of manual scavenging—that is, the practice of Dalits cleaning up human excreta by hand.[22]

But the tension between genuine women's empowerment and the Modi government's (and, as we shall see, the Gates Foundation's) characterisations of it, is at its starkest in the domain of reproductive health. The geographer Kalpana Wilson has documented the ways the Modi government and the Gates Foundation promote policies that amount to not just failed empowerment but, rather, gender-based violence.[23] Simply put, the current Indian government is promoting coercive sterilisation and long-acting contraception for poor women—and doing so in a political context replete with calls for Muslim, Dalit, and Adivasi (indigenous) women to stop reproducing.

During the 2002 anti-Muslim riots in Gujarat, mobs yelled 'take revenge and slaughter the Muslims', while cutting open the bodies of pregnant women and killing their babies.[24] In 2015, two BJP leaders publicly claimed that Hindu women should have at least four children, drawing on a popular Hindu supremacist argument that Muslims are reproducing at a rate that is going to cause them to outnumber Hindus.[25] Similar rhetoric has surrounded Dalit and Adivasi women, whose births are deemed undesirable because they will supposedly produce 'Naxalites' (revolutionary communists) and 'children who will become communists'.[26] According to Wilson, the Modi government—which, as we shall see towards the end of this essay, is greatly concerned with attracting Western investment—construes Dalit and Adivasi women as threats to development, because they are farmers who oppose corporate expropriation of land. Many government-led sterilisation programmes are concentrated in districts populated primarily by Dalit and Adivasi women.[27]

Indian government 'family-planning' policies, undertaken with the support of international organisations (most notably the Gates Foundation), prioritise two methods that are disfavoured in the North: sterilisation and long-acting contraception. The long-acting contraceptive drug currently being pushed is Depo-Provera, generally taken using the Sayana Press injection. The expansion of Sayana Press has been the centrepiece of the Gates Foundation's family-planning policy in India and sub-Saharan Africa since 2014;[28] and the foundation has made large investments in Pfizer, the American pharmaceutical company, to promote its diffusion.[29]

The Gates Foundation's stated rationale for pushing long-acting contraception in the global South is that women with inadequate healthcare access can inject it themselves. This not only overlooks the fact that improving healthcare infrastructure is an option for philanthropists, but also the reasons why Depo-Provera is not a popular method of contraception in the global North. Simply put, injectables can have significant side effects, like intermittent and heavy bleeding (which is especially likely to interfere with women's day-to-day lives in countries with poor sanitation) and an increased risk of developing osteoporosis. Until two years ago, it was thought that it increased women's risk of contracting HIV.[30] In fact, at the time of the Gates Foundation's investment in Pfizer, the World Health Organization did not even categorise Depo-Provera as a Category-1 contraceptive (whose use does not carry significant risks that need to be weighed against the benefits).

India has a long history of sterilisation abuse, and sterilisation continues to play a major role in the government's approach. Though the official recommendations of the Family Planning 2020 (FP2020) Summit—funded by the Gates Foundation—are to provide a wide range of contraceptive options, Indian women still disproportionately 'choose' sterilisation. India's 2014 update on its commitment to FP2020 cited over 4.5 million sterilisations, compared to 3.2 million new oral contraception users and 5.2 million intrauterine device (IUD) insertions.[31] In 2014, sixteen women died in a sterilisation camp in Chhattisarg.[32] Likely motivated by attempts to meet contraceptive use targets, some Indian NGOs report receiving incentives for each woman sterilised.[33] DAWN, a major collective of women's organisations in the global South, notes that in South Asia, the IUD, whose distribution the Gates Foundation and other international organisations are supporting, may be becoming the new sterilisation. Since women receive cash incentives to have babies in hospitals and are then pressured to have IUDs inserted immediately post-partum, the presence of choice from a wide menu of options is questionable.[34]

It is difficult to discuss Indian family-planning policy without discussing the role of international organisations and Western philanthropists. The coercive sterilisation camps that targeted men under Indira Gandhi's government in the 1970s are well known outside India. The Ford Foundation funded India's population control programmes to the tune of US$33 million in 1962, and the UN gave India US$40 million to implement a sterilisation programme in 1974.[35] Indian feminists have long believed the abusive application of these policies to be linked to the emphasis on reaching targets.[36]

Yet targets continue to be a key part of the Modi government's women's empowerment agenda and, as I'll discuss more directly in the next section, are central to the theory of change of the Gates Foundation. The FP2020 Summit organised by the Gates Foundation in 2012 hosted Modi as a major speaker. The goal was to get '120 million women on contraception by 2020', and the Indian government pledged to hit a target of 48 million.[37] The day after the summit, Human Rights Watch issued a report cautioning that the 48-million goal would lead to more human rights violations.[38] This worry is not only founded on evidence from the reproductive health domain; it is also exactly what the UN observer saw happening in the toilet programme funded and celebrated by the Gates Foundation.

Empowerment 3.0, Billionaire Philanthropy, and the Theory of Change

How did we get to a point where toilets, long-acting contraception, and moral panic about Hindu women's honour—all accompanied by human rights violations—could be touted as empowering to women? This is not a simple case of a good theory being implemented in unrecognisable ways. Instead, it is the result of two factors. The first, addressed in this section, is a technocratic reconceptualisation of women's empowerment by Western development actors. The second, which I will address in the final section, is a widespread presumption that these actors are morally progressive.

Women's empowerment was originally understood as the process by which women, usually acting in organised movements, demanded change to social practices and policies that treated them as inferior.[39] On this view, women's empowerment involved changing the contexts in which women operated, not just changing individual women. Also central to this original understanding was the idea that women's empowerment would enhance democracy by fostering social movements and treating women as possessed of intrinsic and equal value.

In the 1990s and early 2000s, in large part as a result of the advocacy of genuinely feminist organisations, women's empowerment drew the attention of mainstream development actors, such as the World Bank, which historically have been shaped by Western knowledge and interests. Although they recognised the detrimental impact on women of Structural Adjustment Programs (SAPs) in the 1980s, they nonetheless remained committed to neoliberal reforms. Rather than challenging cuts in social spending—to healthcare, for example—they often promoted the expansion of women's unpaid labour. By the 1990s, mainstream development organisations began to understand women's apparent inexhaustibility as a sign of their resilience.[40]

This neoliberal, technocratic conception of women's empowerment—what we might call 'empowerment 2.0'—proposed 'investing in women'.[41] It pushed the project of women's *collective* empowerment to the background; it was not so much about increasing the status of women as about targeting women to achieve other development goals more efficiently. One common argument was that 'investing in women' was 'smart economics' that would enable countries to achieve economic growth on the cheap. In other words, women's unpaid or low-paid labour could subsidise development.[42] The implication here was that work itself empowered women, even if they did not experience changes in household or social status.[43] For advocates of empowerment 2.0, targeting women also became a way to achieve better welfare outcomes for households and children.[44] Conditional cash transfer (CCT) programmes, which came to be seen as an effective technology of empowerment, promoted child health and literacy without compensating women for the labour of providing it.

By instrumentalising women's empowerment, this neoliberal conception disconnects it from social change. Power is a function of individuals' internal capacities and the conditions of the social world they occupy. A woman may have the skills to be an car mechanic but still lack the capacity to do so if there are no jobs, or if sexist social norms prevent her from being hired. Where empowerment was once about women's ability to change their contexts, empowerment 2.0 emphasised changing women, encouraging them to adapt to their social conditions. Indeed, as Sylvia Chant and Caroline Sweetman argue, neoliberal empowerment took changing women to be an *alternative* to changing their contexts.[45] Once again, conditional cash transfers are an example of this: women are treated as efficient service delivery vehicles to compensate a lack of health and education infrastructure.

Empowerment 2.0 complements technocratic approaches to development, which, according to Sanjay Reddy, pursue change through 'technical intervention from above'.[46] Such change is imagined as being reliant on 'the knowledge of experts as to "what works"', which can be applied in a modular form to create replicable models of intervention. Reddy continues:

> The presumption that there are near-universal and observable empirical regularities underlying the connection between inputs and outputs corresponds to a narrow engineering approach to causation in social

affairs. There is little room to take note of contextually variable social relations, let alone the role of political factors that undermine such a mechanistic image of society.

The Gates Foundation both continues a long legacy of technocratic approaches to development and adds a new flavour to technocracy. Older technocratic approaches to development, especially those that took root during the postwar era, emphasised Western nations sharing economic expertise and technologies relevant to infrastructure. Western philanthropic foundations worked largely as auxiliaries of the US government.[47] Philanthropists imagined themselves spreading liberal democracy. This self-representation was problematic in a number of ways—not least of which was that allowing foreign technocrats to make policy decisions for entire nations is not very democratic. At the same time, however, this older technocratic approach often directed policy towards broad-scale social goals, such as the restructuring of national economies.

In contrast, California Consensus philanthropists, such as Bill and Melinda Gates, have tended to function more independently of governments, and they see broad-scale social change as a pipe dream.[48] They adopt operational models on which 'donors are more heavily involved in beneficiary projects'.[49] Unlike the old philanthropists, California Consensus philanthropists assume much of their expertise is in the business and innovation side of service delivery.[50] These philanthrocapitalists, as they are sometimes called, exhibit a strong preference for technological solutions, metrics, and scalability. 'Rather than funding a medical clinic, for example, the new philanthropists invest in biotech companies working on tropical diseases. Rather than fund the distribution of drugs, the new philanthropists seek to invest in and create incentives for drug corporations to operate in poor regions.'[51]

The Gates Foundation, in particular, has a record of funding small, technical interventions over infrastructure—even the infrastructure necessary to support its own innovations. Public health scholar Heidi Morefield recounts a visit to a clinic in Congo, where she found high-tech coolers storing vaccines, funded by the Gates Foundation, but no electricity to power them.[52] In 2019, the Gates Foundation gave a US$40,000 prize to a team that designed a toilet that could produce clean water from human faeces, without the need for improved sewer systems.[53] The foundation invested in Pfizer's production of the Sayana Press injection, rather than investing in relevant healthcare infrastructure in the global South. California Consensus organisations regard themselves as alternatives to development business as usual— where the latter is concerned with context, politics, and society-wide change—and they focus on providing individuals with the minimum required for active participation in economic life.[54] This represents a reduction in the offer of foreign aid.

As Adam Fejerskov demonstrates in his extensive research on the organisational identity of the Gates Foundation, the incorporation of women's empowerment into the foundation's goals was highly controversial. According to Fejerskov, programme officers in the agriculture programme initially resisted Bill and Melinda Gates' insistence on including women's empowerment in every grant. These officers refused to incorporate gender concerns into their grant-making processes, or claimed that concern with gender constituted too much control by upper management.[55] An internal gender strategy drafted by the foundation's leadership had to go through fifty rounds of revision to receive anything resembling consensus support.[56]

To solidify women's empowerment within the organisation in the face of this resistance, the foundation hired a women's equality officer, who seems to have received uptake precisely by reframing women's empowerment as a vehicle for innovation and efficiency. In her formulation, women's empowerment was the only way to achieve 'impact' and 'measurable results'.[57] In reference to this incorporation of women's empowerment, one employee complained: 'I don't want this baloney about politically correct statements. I want efficiency and effectiveness.'[58]

Fejerskov notes that Bill Gates was initially opposed to the UN's Millennium Development Goals on the grounds that the ills of poverty had been declared without effective remedy many times throughout history. He only became a supporter when he learned of the MDGs' numerical time-bound targets.[59] He was vocally critical of the Sustainable Development Goals, which emphasised the intertwined character of health with other development goals, such as environmental preservation and democracy.[60]

This same conception of women's empowerment as a vehicle for efficient and effective development interventions has been used by the Modi government to legitimise its own policy agenda. This doesn't mean that the Gates Foundation intended to enable such policies, nor that efficiency and effectiveness have no role in development. Many feminists have been able to use instrumentalist arguments about women strategically, to generate support for women's empowerment.[61] Rather, the technocratic reconceptualisation has removed the teeth from women's empowerment. It has also fostered faith in the idea that increased access to technology should mean increased empowerment, irrespective of whether women themselves would choose relevant technology given other options.

If empowerment 2.0 instrumentalised women in the pursuit of other technocratic development goals, the conception of women's empowerment championed by the Gates Foundation—what we might call empowerment 3.0—subordinates women to programme optimisation. Empowerment 3.0 treats intended development beneficiaries as potential consumers, on whom new technologies can be tested. For the Gates Foundation, technological expertise contributes to learning about what works *through experimentation on people in the field*.[62] 'Failure is critical to success', as one Gates Foundation mantra goes.[63] Of course, it is not only philanthropists who imagine that the poor benefit from subjection to experimentation. The 2019 Nobel Prize in Economic Sciences was awarded to Esther Duflo and Abhijit Banerjee for work on randomised control trials and poverty. The Gates Foundation's promotion of Sayana Press can itself be seen as an experiment in how to deliver long-acting contraception in the absence of adequate health infrastructure.[64] A key reason for focusing so narrowly on this particular contraceptive is to see how rapidly it can be scaled up. Yet the risks involved in experimenting on poor women and other vulnerable populations are significant—particularly when a technology has side effects, is being tested in the absence of infrastructure that would help manage these side effects, and is being deployed in a context with a history of abuse of this type of technology.

If empowerment 2.0 prioritised changes to women over changes to social context, empowerment 3.0 begins from the assumption that projects aimed at contextual change are of lesser impact than 'high-leverage' interventions. One of the reasons the Gates Foundation favours Sayana Press is that it can be injected by a woman herself, or by a rural health worker with little training. Similarly, a reason for focusing on IUD availability is that it can be inserted during the same hospital visit in which a woman gives birth. Both strategies treat the absence of public health infrastructure as fixed—something irrelevant to women's empowerment, or something that a philanthropic organisation could do nothing about. Morefield, who has studied the Gates Foundation and its collaboration with the reproductive health technology organisation PATH, reveals its leaders' close personal associations with leaders of the 'appropriate technology' movement. This movement, whose founders were more likely to be hippies than billionaires, repeated the slogan 'small is beautiful' and claimed that inexpensive small-scale gadgets that people could easily operate were the future of development.[65] But what the appropriate technology movement shares with the Gates Foundation's high-tech approach is a lack of interest in trying to bring about a world in which the people of the global South have access to the same level of healthcare as those of the global North. In a very popular 2014 article in *Science*, Melinda Gates noted that it was *possible* that investments in health and other forms of social infrastructure would help empower women, but that we could not assume this, given the lack of evidence.[66]

That the Gates Foundation and other California Consensus philanthropists have pursued women's empowerment by experimenting on poor women and leaving their contexts untouched, does not mean that contraceptive access cannot play a role in women's empowerment. But we might question the validity of a concept of women's empowerment that legitimises interventions designed without input from poor women, interventions that expose them to risks that would not be accepted in the North.

The Ticket into the Post-Liberal Order?

These approaches seem a far cry from genuine women's empowerment. So why have they gained such currency? To begin to see how such conceptual drift can go unnoticed, we need to look beyond the

concepts themselves to questions about politics and background ideologies. A presumption of beneficence greets the Gates Foundation's
work, partly because of the type of political actor it is, and partly
because of the associations the ideas of women's empowerment,
development, and technology evoke in the Western imaginary. This
presumed beneficence is to some extent transferrable, and this enables
the Gates Foundation to confer a sense that the Modi government is
also to a large degree beneficent. Put simply, the redesign of women's
empowerment the Gates Foundation has enabled, and the projects it
has supported as a result, allow the Modi government to leverage
women's empowerment as a ticket into a reconfigured global order.

To associate oneself with women's empowerment is, in our political era, to lay claim not just to beneficence, but to a specific type of
legitimacy. The Western imaginary associates women's empowerment not just with goodness, but with moral *progress*. The notion of
moral progress, in turn, is difficult to separate from the idea that the
world is divided into a 'modern' West (that respects women's rights)
and a 'backward' rest. To understand the role the notion of moral
progress plays in shoring up the Western sense of cultural superiority,
it is helpful to consider a story that the West continues to tell itself
about its own role in human history. The essence of this story, which
I have elsewhere called 'the Enlightenment teleological narrative',[67]
goes something like this: the West has achieved civilisation because
its culture has evolved, whereas the cultures of other societies have
not. According to this narrative, we should expect trappings of
Western culture to accompany moral improvements, especially
improvements often thought to derive from liberalism, such as
respect for human rights, women's rights, and democracy. So, for
example, we should, according to this narrative, see scientific discov-
eries causing an increase in human rights, industrialisation leading to
roles assigned by custom, and so on. More relevant for our current
discussion, the Enlightenment teleological narrative sets the expectation that action by Westerners, technological progress, and increases
in the status of women should go together. In fact, combined with
widespread depictions of women in the global South as pathetic victims of their cultures, the narrative generates the view that *only*
Western intervention can change the status of women.[68]

To be clear, that this story is deeply embedded in the Western imaginary does not make it true. The idea that the West is a vanguard of moral progress simply misses the fact that the West became the West, and continues to be the West, through various forms of colonial power—ranging from slavery and genocide to economic exploitation and interference with democratically elected governments in the global South. The notion that women's empowerment accompanies Western intervention misses the fact that colonialism and Western intervention often exacerbate (and have exacerbated) gender inequality.[69] The idea that women's empowerment goes with technological progress misses the ways in which the rise of scientism seems to have been accompanied by a rise in scientific justifications of women's oppression.[70]

It is difficult to explain the popularity of the Enlightenment teleological narrative, and the view that women's empowerment comes from technology and the involvement of Western actors, without explaining how it serves Western *interests*. This narrative makes it seem as if Western domination of the globe is morally justified, because Western leadership brings about social justice. It now allows the level of women's empowerment in a society to signal how 'modern' a society is—in Western eyes, at least. But the barometer does not directly track women's empowerment. Instead, because the Enlightenment teleological narrative has always worked more to preserve Western interests than to recount the truth, what counts as women's empowerment shifts in accordance with what Western actors *do*; and the capacity of non-Western actors to lay claim to causing empowerment is limited. To put it in terms of the case at hand, what counts to most Western spectators as women's empowerment tracks what the Gates Foundation does more clearly than it tracks something that is independently morally meaningful.

Though my focus in this essay is on concepts, the Gates Foundation's ability to present itself as an agent of women's empowerment also derives from the organisation's role in global politics. At this point, the power of the Gates Foundation to set the international development agenda, and international health policy in particular, surpasses that of many states. As previously mentioned, it is the second largest donor to the World Health Organization—surpassed only by the US government.[71] It uses both wealth and celebrity power to broker influence over governments.[72] Western philanthropists are often thought to be morally unimpeachable because they are voluntarily 'giving' their money away, but (even brushing the tax benefits aside) the Gates Foundation is not, strictly speaking, in the business of giving gifts—unless we understand gift-giving to include 'retain[ing] control over what is given... reaping benefits in return', and attempting to influence the global context so that these gifts are the only ones available.[73]

The upshot of how the Gates Foundation's power and the Enlightenment teleological narrative work together, is that what looks like women's empowerment to Western audiences may have more to do with what the Gates Foundation says women's empowerment is than with what it actually is, or what feminist activists have thought it was for the last two generations.

In an era of global reordering, where the dominance of Western states has reduced and the importance of liberal ideals seems to be on the wane, the redesigned form of women's empowerment is an ideal political currency. Empowerment 3.0 allows an association with moral progress and modernity without taking on the baggage of liberal democracy; if women can be empowered by 'modern' toilets and contraceptives—irrespective of whether human rights and democracy are flouted in the process—then a country can gain the appearance of modernity while not embracing, even outwardly, liberal or democratic principles. This makes empowerment 3.0 an ideal vehicle for non-Western states to achieve Western-like status in the global order. Isis Giraldo has argued that associating oneself with women's empowerment facilitates what Walter Mignolo calls 'rewesternisation'.[74] In 'rewesternisation', states that would previously have been thought of as outside the West rebrand themselves as Western in order to stake a claim on their right to be part of the collection of states that now dominates the world.

The state of affairs in which Western democracies rule the world is commonly referred to in international relations theory as the 'liberal order'. It is important to note that this naming assumes that a version of the Enlightenment teleological narrative is correct: moral progress, it suggests, has been brought about through the activities and shared culture of Western nations. The use of the term 'liberal', rather than a term like 'American (or Western) hegemonic', trades on an equivocation that assigns moral legitimacy to the global order of the twentieth century. This is because of something I have alluded to at several points in this essay; the term 'liberal' refers in many contexts to a family of moral principles that includes democratic processes and respect for individual and minority rights. In international relations, the term 'liberal' has an additional moral meaning: namely, to describe states and orders that act on moral principles rather than out of pure self-interest. But the term 'liberal' also has a descriptive sense; international relations theorists and policymakers often use the word just to refer to governments who *call* themselves internally liberal, or to an international order ruled by Western nations.

The term 'liberal order' in itself suggests that a globe ruled by Western liberal democracies is also one in which peace, democracy, respect for human rights and the rule of law are achieved. Yet we know that Western nations, especially the United States, fall far short of respect for human rights (the US has failed to ratify most major human rights treaties, houses a quarter of the world's incarcerated people,[75] and so on), and that they continue to pursue their interests, especially abroad, but also at home, through violent means. So, the idea that a Western or US-led order is a liberal one is at best imprecise, and at worst obfuscating. It suggests that peace among Western nations is the same thing as peace, that Western nations are successfully functioning liberal democracies, and that the means by which Western nations are maintaining their global dominance are themselves in line with moral principles.

Once we see that the 'liberal order' was not necessarily liberal, we can see it for the political entity it was—a type of club, whose members' mutual non-aggression offered 'shared tools for moral and political advancement'.[76] The idea of liberal states refusing to go to war with each other originates in Enlightenment political philosophy. Immanuel Kant argued in the eighteenth century that liberal states should form a 'pacific federation' that would make decisions through discussion and debate rather than coercion.[77] Those who have adapted Kant's views to international relations theory have claimed that mutual interdependence, especially economic interdependence, among states would lead to peace. But in the version of the story that is prevalent in international relations theory, states can fall far short of the moral criteria for liberalism and yet still contribute to liberal order. They just need to be part of a powerful group of states that have intertwined economic and institutional activities, and not go to war with each other as a result.

If this analysis of the liberal order as a club is correct, we can see the current global stage as one in which the terms of membership are shifting. At one point, it seemed necessary to be a rich Western state to get into the club. However, as middle- and low-income countries, including non-Western ones, have gained economic and military power, they have sought to share markets and institutions with Western nations. Offering a sanguine assessment of this change in the global order, G. John Ikenberry argues that the rise to international prominence of countries like China and Brazil marks only a decrease in Western hegemony. In his words, Western hegemony over the order decreases 'while the liberal aspects persist'.[78] In my view, a more accurate way of looking at the contemporary global reordering would be to say that the function of 'Westernness' as a criterion for entering the group of countries who do not go to war because of shared markets and institutions is declining. But being 'modern' is important, and Western endorsement in this regard can be crucial.

Against this backdrop, the Modi government stands to gain significant benefits from winning the support of Western actors and associating itself with modernity. For even if Western states have never been liberal, their *self-conception* as liberal is alive and well—and intermingled with uninterrogated assumptions about Western cultural superiority. Empowerment 3.0 allows the Modi government to associate itself with moral progress and modernity while falling short of any liberal self-ascription. Liberalism dictates freedom of association and political disagreement and protection for minorities; yet Modi imprisons his detractors, requires Muslim citizens to 'register themselves', and perpetrates violence against women. Undermining the connections between women's empowerment and principles such as democracy and respect for women's own decisions allows the Modi government to gain a claim on moral legitimacy without becoming Western, and without even paying lip service to liberal principles.[79]

Moreover, redefining women's empowerment is not the only source of the Gates Foundation's complicity in the Modi government's ascent. The Gates Foundation is also complicit in disempowering an Indian civil society that wishes to hold Modi accountable to the moral principles associated with liberalism. Indian civil society organisations widely responded to the foundation's public honouring of Modi with an award as undermining their activism against him, as 'demoralising'.[80] In spite of nearly universal criticism from Indian civil society and the Indian diaspora in the United States, the Gates Foundation's official response was to defend giving the award, claiming that they were only narrowly focused on toilets. Though Western foundations have long tried to ignore political criticism of their actions, the Gates Foundation has a type of power in the global order that surpasses that of Ford and Rockefeller in the postwar era. Rather than being an agent of the US government, the Gates Foundation operates relatively independently of it. The foundation's sanitation award preceded President Trump's visit to India in 2020, and came after a period in which the US government had denied Modi a visa. Moreover, to analyse the responsibility the Gates Foundation has for conferring legitimacy on the Modi government, is not yet to begin to analyse its more direct responsibility for ignoring the rights violations directly involved in projects it promotes and funds, such as the violence against Dalits or contraceptive coercion.

It is difficult to isolate the causal role its association with the Gates Foundation and women's empowerment is playing in changing the Modi government's standing in the global order, but there are certainly indications that its association with women's empowerment, and with the Gates Foundation, is increasing India's global status. One business publication argues against claims that the Modi government's human rights abuses should lower India's standing in the international community, by first acknowledging that Modi wasn't always 'beyond reproach', but then mentioning the Gates Foundation's award to suggest that the government is now above board.[81] The article pivots from criticising those who opposed the award to discussing the 'strength of India's markets'. *The Economic Times* ran an article soon after Modi received the award, describing Bill Gates' own positive prognostications about the Indian economy

(India was actually in an economic slump at the time).[82] Multiple international media outlets, including *The Wall Street Journal*, seized on Modi's claim that he wanted toilets first, temples later, repeating a slogan designed to show that 'modernising' India was more central to Modi's goals than his Hindu nationalist agenda.[83] An op-ed columnist recently wrote that it has become difficult to call out Modi's human rights violations, because 'his supporters [will] instantly throw all his international awards and accolades in your face'.[84]

The Modi government is clearly waging a public relations war to be seen as a modern world power. Northern actors, most notably the Gates Foundation, are providing important tools for this war. By redefining women's empowerment so that it can be achieved without democracy and rights, and by funding, prioritising, and recognising projects that actively undermine them—as well as by wielding its status as an organisation associated with Western moral and technological progress—the Gates Foundation helps make the Modi government seem to be in its rightful place within the liberal 'club'.

As Indian civil society leader Suchitra Vijayan puts it, 'the narrative is India being the world's largest democracy, India being a great place to invest, India shining... All that only counts if the international community recognises these narratives.'[85] In this historical moment, we must move away from assuming that philanthropic organisations are apolitical, or that they are beyond moral question because they are 'giving away' their money. We must also recognise that the term 'women's empowerment' is no longer innocent in an era in which the term has been emptied of meaning, and the appearance of feminism is the currency of appearing 'modern'.

Though I have focused on a specific case here, we should expect these changes in the stakes, meaning, and politics of women's empowerment to affect global politics across a variety of global political domains. This goes for the field of humanitarian relief, in which women's empowerment is an increasingly explicit goal and the Gates Foundation is an important donor; but, in a sense, it is empowerment that has come into line with humanitarian reason, rather than the other way around. Unless we hold philanthropists morally and politically accountable, we can expect a world where the human rights of the poor, and of poor women in particular, are the collateral damage of a global political reordering.

18

HUMANITARIANISM AND
LIBERAL INTERNATIONAL ORDER

A NECESSARY RELATIONSHIP?

Jacinta O'Hagan

The spirit of humanitarianism can be found throughout societies and cultures across time. But, in the twentieth century, a network of actors, with particular institutional practices, gave shape to what Christina Bennett terms the 'formal international humanitarian system' (FIHS).[1] The birth, institutionalisation, and expansion of the FIHS coincided with the emergence of the liberal international order; indeed, Michael Barnett contends that it is a 'creature' of this order.[2] Understanding the relationship between the FIHS and liberal order is important at a time when the latter is perceived to be under threat. If the political turbulence of the last decade does really signal *the end* of liberal order—as many commentators have hastily suggested—what does it mean for the future of the FIHS, and for humanitarianism in general?

In this chapter, I address three key points. Firstly, I argue that the FIHS is not simply a *product* or 'creature' of the liberal international

order; humanitarian norms and practices also played a role in constituting that order. Secondly, I argue that some of the challenges faced
by the FIHS are not simply a knock-on effect of the crises in the liberal
international order; they rather demonstrate that the FIHS is a *site* in
which the crisis of liberal order plays out. Thirdly, I question whether
the relationship between the FIHS and liberal order suggests a necessary relationship between *humanitarianism* and that order.

Contemporary conceptions of humanitarianism tend to focus too
narrowly on the particular structures, ideas, and practices associated
with the FIHS. They overlook a broader complex of humanitarian
institutions and traditions that have taken form outside or on the
margins of the formal system. And they overlook 'parallel narratives'
of humanitarian action.[3] Adopting a more expansive concept of
humanitarianism adds necessary complexity to our understanding of
the implications of liberal ordering. And, in turn, this is crucial to the
development of a more inclusive international humanitarian system,
which is not necessarily tethered to the liberal international order.

The phrase *liberal international order* conjoins contested concepts.
Order can imply regularity and stability in contrast to turmoil.
However, I use this term in another sense, to describe a purposive
arrangement in pursuit of common objectives, goals, or values.
Political orders have three key elements: shared norms; key institutions; and relationships of authority and power. Shared norms reflect
common values and beliefs that shape the objectives of an order.
Institutions provide the rules and frameworks for interaction and
mechanisms through which authority is exercised. They regulate and
legitimate particular types of actors and practices; relationships of
power define who holds legitimate authority and how this can be exercised. They are embedded in institutions.[4] Power and authority are
related concepts but not synonymous. Power can be defined as the
capacity to direct or influence the behaviour of others or the course of
events. It can be based on material capacity but can also be social and
relational. Power can derive, for instance, from the capacity to shape
and influence institutions; from how actors are positioned in different
social or political structures; or from the capacity to produce knowledge or influence understandings. Authority can be defined as the
legitimate power that one person or group possesses and practises over

another. One can potentially exercise forms of authority, such as moral authority, without the predominance of material capacity.

Particularly over the last thirty years, politicians and academics have referred to liberal international order to characterise an inter-state system supposedly organised according to liberal principles. But there are multiple interpretations of what liberalism is, what its core values are, and how liberal ideas should be pursued in practice.[5] There is also the crucial question of how *liberal* the liberal interna-tional order and self-proclaimed liberal actors are in practice. Interpretations and evaluations of liberalism and liberal order are deeply contested.[6]

Here, however, I focus on a dominant conception of liberal order, according to which political authority is legitimated by the consent of those subject to it, and sovereignty resides in individuals.[7] According to this conception, liberal order—through the rhetoric of its cham-pions, at least, if not always through its institutions—promotes human rights, democracy, and market capitalism; and its intellectual foundations lie in the European Enlightenment, following which notions of universal humanity gave rise to struggles for rights and a burgeoning politics of compassion. Such notions also inspired the civilising missions that provided moral justification for empire. The implication of liberal ideas and politics in imperial histories has often been ignored in more celebratory accounts of liberal international order. The American international relations scholar G. John Ikenberry provides one of the most widely cited characterisations of liberal international order. He describes liberal internationalism as an 'ordering project' for the world.[8] And he identifies five *convictions* that underlie this project: international politics is not necessarily a realm of violence and power politics since '[p]ower politics can be tamed' through liberal ordering; the liberal international order is built on the conviction that openness in trade and economic exchange helps build mutual interdependence and cooperation; a commitment to a loosely rules-based set of relationships embodied in multilateralism; a com-mitment to some form of security cooperation; and the conviction that liberal democracy sits at the core of progress.[9]

Liberal internationalism was a key component of the order-build-ing projects that followed the First and Second World Wars. The centrepiece of liberal internationalism following the First World War was the League of Nations, a powerful expression of multilateralism. The Covenant of the League of Nations articulated a commitment to achieve a more peaceful world through open diplomacy, collective security, arms control, the promotion of international law, as well as multilateral bodies to enhance international cooperation in social and economic affairs. Importantly, the League's Covenant highlighted the centrality of self-determination and sovereign equality to international order. But the League also demonstrated the ambiguities of liberal internationalism, in that it continued to sustain imperial authority. Not only were the empires of the victors not dismantled, but under the Mandates system the governance of the former colonies of the defeated powers passed to these victors under the auspices of the *sacred trust of civilisation*. Hierarchy and liberal paternalism continued.

Despite the failure of the League of Nations to achieve a more peaceful world, liberal internationalism remained at the heart of the post-Second World War order-building project.[10] Commitments to liberal norms of democracy, freedom and equality, self-determination, and the maintenance of order through the rule of law were embodied in the UN Charter, where respect for state sovereignty sat alongside the promotion of human dignity and individual rights, later articulated in the Universal Declaration of Human Rights (1948). Multilateral organisations were created in the fields of trade (GATT and now the World Trade Organization), finance (the International Monetary Fund and the World Bank), the rule of international law (the International Court of Justice and more recently the International Criminal Court), health (World Health Organization), and development (UN Development Programme). This order was democratic in so far as all member states had an equal vote in the UN General Assembly. But it was also hierarchical in terms of the privileges given to permanent members of the UN Security Council, including the power of veto.

Whilst at one level this system projected a universalist set of norms and principles, it was also a project of building order amongst Western liberal democracies that was in antithesis to the alternative model pursued by the Soviet Union and communism.[11] The post-

Second World War liberal international order was not truly international during the Cold War, but reliant on the willingness of the US to underwrite it.[12] In Ikenberry's words, it was built on a set of bargains that were shaped by US power, ideas, and interests. In addition, whilst smaller states gained greater voice in the UN, the structures of economic, political, and institutional power continued to be balanced in favour of the rich and powerful states.

The dominant narrative frames the end of the Cold War and the demise of the Soviet bloc as the moment when the liberal international order did become global; as marking the triumph of Western ideas and the *ideological monopoly* of the liberal worldview.[13] It was lauded as promising *a new world order* in which multilateral institutions such as the UN could flourish in the absence of great power rivalry; an era of democracy promotion; and the globalisation of liberal market capitalism through deregulation of international trade and financial flows. But it was also a unipolar moment, with the US becoming the sole great power, determined to secure liberal international order through muscular means, including military intervention and state-building. In the words of then US Secretary of State Madeleine Albright, the US came to see itself as 'the indispensable nation'.[14]

The period between 1990 and 2004 has been described as 'the Golden Age' of the liberal international order, during which liberal internationalism appeared to thrive in a globalised world, despite the period seeing multiple conflicts and humanitarian crises such as those in Somalia, Rwanda, and the Balkans.[15] Tensions, fissures, and challenges to the liberal international order have become more pronounced since 2004. The US-led interventions in Afghanistan and Iraq and the NATO-led military intervention in Libya led to protracted conflicts and exacerbated instability, fuelling the emergence of armed non-state actors such as Al-Qaeda and ISIS. State-building in South Sudan has been stymied by civil conflict. The euphoria that greeted the pro-democracy movements of the Arab Spring in 2011 has been replaced by despondency in the face of the return to authoritarian rule in Egypt; the bitter and protracted conflicts in Syria and the system's inability to resolve the devastating war in Yemen, have led to disillusionment with multilateralist approaches to conflict resolution. The 2008 global financial crisis and Eurozone crisis shook belief in globalisation and liberal capitalism and laid bare the vulnerabilities of economic interdependence. They also undermined the notion that the US and the West were insuperable. But added to this is the growing awareness that globalisation has not produced greater economic equality; in fact, inequality has grown considerably.

The triumphalism of the early 1990s has been replaced by a narrative of crisis. The US National Intelligence Council's 2017 *Global Trends: Paradox of Progress* report observed: 'For better and worse, the emerging global landscape is drawing to a close an era of American dominance following the Cold War. So, too, perhaps is the rules-based international order that emerged after World War II.'[16] States such as China and Russia have been singled out by some Western commentators as *disruptors* of the international order.[17] In his remarks to the General Assembly on priorities for 2020, UN Secretary-General António Guterres warned of seeing '"four horsemen in our midst"—four looming threats that endanger 21st-century progress and imperil 21st-century possibilities'.[18] These *four horsemen* encompass the principal challenges to the liberal international order: geopolitical shifts and an increase in geostrategic rivalries with the rise of new actors who threaten to undermine the liberal order; a rise in populism, nationalism, and illiberal forces, fuelled by a growing mistrust of governments and discontent with globalisation; the challenges of new technologies, in particular digital technology and new forms of collective violence; and a range of complex transnational problems, such as climate change, migration and forced displacement, and terrorism. The severity of these challenges, combined with wavering support for multilateral institutions, is stretching the capacities of those institutions to the limits. The COVID-19 pandemic provides a vivid example of this. The pandemic has led to more emphatic assertions of sovereignty, the closing of borders, *vaccine nationalism*, and the WHO becoming a political football between the US and China.

Taken as a whole, the liberal international order is undoubtedly under significant pressure, which includes: criticism of the norms of liberal internationalism; a reduced willingness to accept the role of multilateral institutions; and challenges both to the distribution of power upon which the order had been built, and to the legitimacy of that authority. But how do these events affect humanitarianism and, in particular, the robustness of the FIHS?

A NECESSARY RELATIONSHIP?

Humanitarianism and the Liberal International Order

Some argue that we cannot speak of an international humanitarian system because it lacks the internal logic, cohesion, and functional coherence that the term *system* suggests. But despite its weak structures and leadership, I argue that there are sufficient shared values, principles, and common interests, and a sufficient degree of institutionalisation, to constitute a system.[19]

1. Humanitarian norms

Any discussion of the norms and values underpinning the international humanitarian system invariably leads to the four core principles of humanitarianism: humanity, impartiality, neutrality, and independence. First articulated in the Fundamental Principles of the Red Cross in 1965, these came to provide a normative framework of international humanitarian action that became integrated into the FIHS. Respect for these principles has dominated perceptions of who is a legitimate humanitarian actor. Whilst the ethics and feasibility of neutrality and independence are widely debated, the principles of humanity and impartiality remain at the heart of the humanitarian system. These norms resonate deeply with the liberal ideas of a common humanity and the obligation to respect the dignity and rights of our fellow humans. They also resonate with the Enlightenment values of sympathy and benevolence. These values were promoted by some of the pioneering movements of humanitarianism. The nineteenth-century British Anti-Slave Trade movement based its campaign on the premise that slaves were part of a common humanity and consequently had natural rights, including the right to liberty. Its public campaigns also invoked the ideas of compassion and benevolence. The belief that our common humanity generated a duty to alleviate suffering—even on the battlefield—was passionately appealed to by Henri Dunant, one of the founders of the Red Cross Movement. Save the Children's co-founder, Eglantyne Jebb, invoked the ideas of rights and compassion towards *all* children when drafting the Declaration of the Rights of the Child. Following the Second World War, the international community's responsibility to respond to humanitarian suffering was written into Article 1(3) of the UN Charter, and it remains a core part of the UN's mandate.

Even though the ideas of a common humanity, sympathy, and moral obligation to relieve the suffering of others—no matter who they are—resonate with liberal norms, organisations such as the Society for the Abolition of Slave Trade and other humanitarian movements of the colonial era were also deeply embedded in the normative frameworks of the imperial order. At the same time, these humanitarian movements were also sites in which liberal norms came to challenge and undermine the legitimacy of imperial hierarchies. In this respect, humanitarian movements were part of the process of transition from the normative frameworks of the imperial order to that of the liberal order.

2. The FIHS and institutions of the liberal international order

The evolution of the FIHS is also strongly linked to the institutionalisation of the liberal international order since the nineteenth century. The British government lobbied for the abolition of the slave trade at the Congresses of Vienna and Verona (1822), which was also—infamously—incorporated into the Berlin General Act (1884) and the Brussels Final Act (1890). Undeniably, pledges made in these conventions by European powers to wipe out the slave trade in Africa were not driven solely by a sense of compassion. They also served to project European power in Africa. Nevertheless, the way in which humanitarian movements promoted norms and objectives through multilateral mechanisms helped establish humanitarian issues as a legitimate concern of multilateral institutions.

Commitments to humanitarian obligations continued to be built into the mandates of multilateral institutions in the early twentieth century. For instance, the Covenant of the League of Nations included direct recognition of the importance of humanitarian work. In Article 25, members agreed to encourage and promote national Red Cross organisations having as purposes 'the mitigation of suffering throughout the world'. The League also instituted the Commission for Refugees, the forerunner of today's international refugee regime, as well as a range of mechanisms to further humanitarian protections in areas such as human trafficking, the protection of minorities, the abolition of slavery, and child welfare.

After the Second World War, the UN also established a range of specialised agencies with humanitarian mandates—such as the UN Relief and Works Agency for Palestinian Refugees (1949), UNICEF (1946), the UN High Commissioner for Refugees (1950), the World Health Organization (1948), and the World Food Programme (1961). Since the 1980s, the UN has taken on a more central role in coordinating international humanitarian action, with the creation, in 1991, of the roles of Under-Secretary-General for Humanitarian Affairs and Emergency Relief Coordinator, the Office for the Coordination of Humanitarian Affairs, and the Inter-Agency Standing Committee, all with mandates to lead, facilitate, and coordinate humanitarian assistance. Humanitarian issues have also been placed squarely in the ambit of the UN Security Council with a dedicated agenda item on Protection of Civilians.

Perhaps the most important site of overlap between the institution-building related to the FIHS and that of liberal international order is international law. The birth of International Humanitarian Law (IHL) represents one of the earliest instances of the embedding of humanitarian norms and practices into the structures of modern international order. Through the Geneva and Hague Conventions, states consent to bind themselves to certain rules where power politics plays out in starkest fashion: the field of war. These agreements codify customary law in multilateral conventions. They have expanded from commitments to humane treatment of wounded on the battlefield to encompass the protection of civilians in conflicts. They provide a means by which states commit to constrain the violence of war in the name of our common humanity. IHL institutionalises humanitarian commitments, but also gives expression to one of the key convictions of the liberal international order: the rule of law.

International refugee law is a second significant point at which multilateral institution-building in the FIHS and the liberal international order overlap. In agreements such as the 1951 Refugee Convention and its Protocols, and the Guiding Principles on Internal Displacement, states again have agreed rules, guidelines, and institutions through which to conduct their affairs with one another. In principle, by committing to these humanitarian conventions, states are agreeing to relinquish a small amount of their sovereign autonomy. Therefore, the establishment of a range of international institutions in the form of multilateral organisations, covenants, and agreements with humanitarian purposes has been a significant element of the constitution of the liberal international order. Sadly, in many respects, humanitarian aspirations of these institutions have not been met. International humanitarian institutions have a very mixed record of success, as they rely, for the most part, upon the voluntary compliance of states and have weak powers of enforcement. Nevertheless, they form an important dimension of the liberal international order and an important site at which the liberal international order has been constituted. They are mechanisms through which the normative aspirations of the order are expressed, and its institutional frameworks constituted. In other words, they are part of this order *and* have helped to build it.

3. The FIHS and structures of authority

The third important component of a political order is where power sits and how relationships of authority are configured. Again, we see important correlations here between FIHS and the liberal international order. Humanitarianism involves multiple forms of power and authority exercised by a complex range of actors. These actors include not only states and state-based international organisations, but also non-state actors. Non-governmental organisations (NGOs) and civil society groups play an influential role in the system as the principal actors who deliver humanitarian assistance and protection. The financial and material resources of humanitarian agencies provide them with a degree of material power, particularly in relations with recipients of assistance. This is particularly the case for large international NGOs, such as Oxfam, Médecins Sans Frontières, or World Vision. Humanitarian agencies and practitioners also gain a certain amount of power and authority from their status as experts within the field and their role in developing guidelines and mechanisms for humanitarian action. They also garner prestige as norm entrepreneurs. Finally, they exercise a degree of influence by monitoring the compliance of states and other actors with humanitarian norms and rules. By naming and shaming states, NGOs and civil society groups can hold states to account in the eyes of the public and their peers, which can affect a state's international reputation.

NGOs provide an interesting example of how power and authority, including moral authority, can diffuse to civil society in the liberal international order. However, their power remains very much subject to the principal holder of power and authority within the liberal international order: the state. States effectively control the parameters within which humanitarian action occurs. On the one hand, state support for humanitarian action and institutions is vital. States are the largest donors. Without state ratification and implementation, international humanitarian treaties and conventions have no meaning and little traction. On the other hand, states are the gatekeepers of humanitarian space, controlling the conditions under which humanitarian actors can enter and function in crisis zones. This includes the granting of permissions, visas and permits.[20] Through these means, state authorities can directly influence which areas of assistance and groups are prioritised. An increasingly important mechanism of state control over humanitarian actors is counterterrorism legislation. Many states have introduced regulations that can outlaw funding to agencies interacting directly or indirectly with groups designated as terrorist organisations, or may even make such agencies liable to prosecution.[21]

But whilst states can control humanitarian action, respect for humanitarian obligations has, to some degree, become one criterion for state legitimacy within the liberal international order. For instance, as Barnett observed, in the wake of the Indian Ocean tsunami of 2004, compassion became something of a status symbol for states.[22] The pull of humanitarianism as a marker of good international citizenship is also illustrated in the way in which many states, rhetorically at least, express commitments to humanitarian obligations and principles in their foreign policies. States once viewed primarily as aid recipients, such as India and Indonesia, are raising their profiles as humanitarian donors, even though they may avoid using the term humanitarianism, preferring that of disaster relief. From this perspective, humanitarianism has influenced how authority is legitimated in the liberal international order.

Perhaps the most important element in the parallels between structures of power and authority in the FIHS and in the liberal international order is the distribution of power between the global North and the global South. Institutional and material power within the FIHS is undoubtedly weighted towards traditional Western-based actors. Western states dominate the system, and the largest international humanitarian agencies, which receive a disproportionate percentage of funding, are all based or at least rooted in the West.[23] These powerful donors and agencies have significantly influenced the normative frameworks and institutions of the FIHS. This resonates powerfully with the power structures of the liberal international order. The imbalance of power and authority relationships that shapes the liberal international order, therefore, is echoed and played out in the FIHS.

Challenges to the FIHS

The FIHS is more extensive, more technically proficient and better funded than it has ever been. Yet there is a crisis of confidence in the system's capacity, with questions over whether it is 'fit for purpose'.[24] Here, I focus on three sets of challenges that resonate with those in the liberal international order: challenges to the efficacy and legitimacy of multilateral institutions; the challenge posed by emerging actors and perceptions of them as *disruptors* of the FIHS; and challenges to the legitimacy of relationships of authority and power.

The FIHS faces significant challenges to key institutions. IHL stands at the very heart of the FIHS but its enforcement powers are weak. Whilst compliance has never been universal, in recent conflicts the laws of war are being manifestly flouted. As the UN Secretary-General lamented in 2019, 'In many cases... respect for those bodies of law is at best questionable; in others... we have witnessed blatant violations.'[25] The distinction between combatants and civilians is increasingly blurred by the use of indiscriminate weapons and the deliberate targeting of civilians.[26] The Syrian government has used barrel bombs on civilian populations. Blockades, siege, and hunger have been used as weapons of war in Yemen, Syria, Afghanistan, and Iraq. Humanitarian assistance has been blocked; medical facilities, healthcare professionals, and patients targeted; populations enslaved;

and detainees tortured, abused, and summarily executed, their deaths broadcast on social media.

It would be naive to suggest that the flouting of IHL is new. Control of civilian populations and the use of indiscriminate weapons certainly has many precedents. But there seems to be a growing prevalence of such breaches: they are more pervasive, more codified, pursued as doctrine and practised by *rogue* and more established governments alike. Breaches of IHL have been perpetrated not only by actors who are not party to the Geneva or Hague Conventions—including armed non-state actors such as ISIS and Boko Haram—but also by ratifying states, such as Syria and the United States. Alex de Waal describes this as a form of *counter-humanitarianism*, 'a new political ideology and approach to conflicts that legitimizes political and military action that is indifferent to human life'.[27] Furthermore, other states often fail to hold to account those who breach IHL. This tolerance of lack of compliance constitutes complicity with these breaches.[28]

There are also challenges to the international refugee regime. Whilst the world faces the largest number of forcibly displaced people since the Second World War, almost 80 million people,[29] signatories to the Refugee Convention—particularly from the global North—are adopting increasingly narrow and restrictive interpretations of their obligations under the already narrow parameters of the Convention, or ignoring their obligations altogether. This includes the construction of fences, walls, or offshore processing centres and boat turn-backs. Rather than providing assistance, these actions generate more suffering through deaths at sea, the criminalisation of asylum seekers, and their indefinite detention. Paradoxically, this lack of compliance places greater strain on multilateral organisations, and on host states and transit countries that are often not signatories to the Refugee Convention.

Breaches of humanitarian treaty obligations are often justified by appeals to states' sovereignty, fuelled by the forces of populism and illiberal nationalism. Whilst state sovereignty is a key component of the liberal international order, these breaches demonstrate a retreat from commitments to the freedom and rights of individuals and humanitarian protection, and from internationalism.

A further challenge is provided by emerging humanitarian actors and the impact on the cohesion of the FIHS. As in the liberal international order, some see these emerging actors as *disruptors*. Whilst countries such as Saudi Arabia have long been amongst the twenty largest humanitarian donors, others such as China and Turkey have exercised greater influence over the last decade. For instance, in 2019, Turkey's hosting of Syrian refugees made it the world's largest government donor of humanitarian assistance.[30] China's rapid response to the 2014/16 Ebola crisis in West Africa and the 2015 Nepal earthquake, illustrate its growing profile as a humanitarian actor.[31] Similarly, Brazil took a prominent role in the 2010 Haiti earthquake response, although it has since taken an about-turn with respect to humanitarian assistance. Regional state-based organisations, such as the Organisation of Islamic Cooperation (OIC) and Association of Southeast Asian Nations (ASEAN), are developing specialised agencies to facilitate cooperation in disaster response amongst member states. Moreover, as noted above, states such as India and Indonesia that were previously viewed primarily as aid recipients are now becoming providers of assistance. There is also growing awareness of the important role non-Western NGOs and civil society organisations play in humanitarian responses. This includes social movements and faith-based organisations, such as the Indonesian Muslim social movement Muhammadiyah.

Many of these actors are not, in fact, new. Local communities, religious institutions, and civil society groups have long been at the heart of humanitarian responses to emergencies, and are often the first, and sometimes only, responders. However, many of these actors are weakly integrated into the structures of the FIHS. For example, few non-Western countries are members of the OECD Development Assistance Committee (DAC), the Good Humanitarian Donorship Principles, or party to the Refugee Convention. A number of NGOs and civil society organisations from the global South who undertake humanitarian action have not signed up to the ICRC's Code of Conduct.

There is also a perception that non-Western actors 'play by different rules' of humanitarian action.[32] Take China, for example. Although it is beginning to engage more in multilateral humanitarian responses, China's aid is channelled predominantly bilaterally to governments, rather than through multilateral organisations. Its humanitarian action is largely state-led rather than NGO-led, and has lacked a clear policy or central agency guiding humanitarian policy.[33] Consequently, China's humanitarian responses tend to be ad hoc, with the annual budget varying substantially.[34] Perhaps most significantly, China's humanitarian assistance is deeply integrated with other aspects of its longer-term development and economic programmes; official data does not clearly separate humanitarian assistance from other forms of development and economic expenditure. This has led to criticism that China's humanitarian policies lack financial transparency.[35] Moreover, China has been accused of failing to pull its weight in the humanitarian sphere despite being a rapidly growing global economy.[36] In short, China has been accused of instrumentalising aid. In Miwa Hirono's words, 'China's emergence as a global player often brings with it accusations that its humanitarian action will be used as a disguise, or a means, to expand its power '[37]

In a similar vein, civil society actors and NGOs from the global South do not always conform with conventional assumptions about non-state humanitarian actors. For instance, the lines between state and civil society organisations are not always clear. The Eid Foundation in Qatar and the King Khalid Foundation in Saudi Arabia are examples of this. Both are governed by members of the royal families, creating a hybrid form of state-controlled non-governmental humanitarian organisation. The religious affiliations of faith-based organisations have generated doubts as to whether these agencies can be independent and impartial, or whether they might favour assisting co-religionists. Furthermore, a number of states and non-state actors from the global South employ different vocabularies to define their overseas assistance. As noted above, the term disaster relief is preferred over humanitarianism. South–South assistance is often framed in terms such as 'solidarity and development cooperation based on the principle of mutual benefit and equality, not humanitarianisms'. This language of partnership and non-interference acts to distinguish Southern assistance from aid from Northern donors, 'that are perceived to be marked with dependency and inequity'.[38]

Taken together, these factors suggest the weak integration of alternative, non-Western approaches to humanitarianism into the FIHS.

The weak integration of such actors and the idea that they play by different rules fuels the perception of them as potential disruptors of the existing FIHS. But their weak integration is also a function of the fact that they have often not been recognised or adequately included in the decision-making mechanisms, funding, or coordination structures of the FIHS. In Bennett's words, they have been left 'outside the tent'. In order to be perceived as a legitimate humanitarian actor, to be brought into the tent, emerging and alternative actors have been expected to conform with existing normative and institutional frameworks of the FIHS: to be norm takers, not norm makers.[39]

There is, of course, more than a whiff of double standards lingering over some of these criticisms. Western donors also have a long history of instrumentalising humanitarian action, and many Western-based NGOs also have close links with governments. Western faith-based organisations have long played a significant role in humanitarian assistance. Whilst some are closely integrated into the FIHS, others stand very much apart. The core humanitarian principles are challenged not only by actors outside the formal system; they have been fiercely debated within the sector, with the ethics and feasibility of neutrality particularly contested.

The issues discussed above speak to a pivotal question of how genuinely universal the FIHS is: does it actually reflect the diversity of approaches to humanitarianism? Some have argued that the system, and indeed humanitarianism as a whole, is deeply Western-centric and a vehicle of Western power. Respected scholars such as Michael Barnett have argued that humanitarianism itself 'is rooted in Western history and globalized in ways that were largely responsive to interests and ideas emanating from the West'; whilst Antonio Donini maintains it is 'deeply embedded in a system of knowledge that professes to be universal but is in reality an extension of European and western hubris'.[40] Such critiques represent humanitarianism as a liberal global governance project with deep roots in the West's imperial past, which continues to sustain structures of unequal power that privilege the West.[41] Critics such as Michel Agier also highlight that such power imbalances are evident not only in the distribution of resources and influence within the FIHS, but also in how affected communities are perceived and represented as passive victims, rather than themselves humanitarian actors.[42] This has meant that the global South has long been perceived as the primary terrain of humanitarian action, whilst external actors are saviours helping those who cannot help themselves.[43]

These critiques are pivotal in highlighting structures of inequality in the FIHS operating at several levels. But at the same time, they perpetuate a discourse that treats humanitarianism as synonymous with the current FIHS. The binary of victims and saviours risks denying affected communities the status of political actors. It also leaves little space for alternative approaches to humanitarianism, masking what Elena Fiddian-Qasmiyeh describes as the 'plurality of communities of response'.[44] By treating humanitarianism as synonymous with the FIHS and an instrument of liberal governance, we risk perpetuating a discourse of humanitarianism as necessarily tethered to the liberal international order while failing to acknowledge the breadth of alternative approaches available to us.

Humanitarianism and Liberal International Order: A Necessary Relationship?

There are significant resonances between the sense of crisis in the FIHS and in the liberal international order. The growing disregard for IHL and refugee law presents a serious challenge to the efficacy, and even legitimacy, of institutions central to both the FIHS and liberal international order's commitment to the rule of law. Waning support for key humanitarian multilateral organisations adds grist to the mill of fears that we are seeing a retreat from liberal internationalism, even amongst actors seen as bastions of the liberal order. In both sectors we see perceptions of emerging actors as disruptors, who play by different rules and who increasingly assert themselves as norm makers rather than simply norm takers. Therefore, some of the challenges faced by the liberal international order are not simply replicated in the FIHS; they are played out there.

This leads us to a final question: Does a waning liberal international order necessarily mean a waning of the FIHS and of humanitarianism? The answer to this question is linked in no small part to how we conceptualise humanitarianism. As Elena Fiddian-Qasmiyeh and Julia Pacitto argue, if we conceptualise humanitarianism as simply synonymous with the structures and institutions of the FIHS, we neglect the complex heterogeneity of humanitarianism and humanitarian action.[45] To counter this, they argue, we need to 'write the other' into our analysis of humanitarianism to better encompass the variety of agents, conceptions, and practices that lie beyond the Western-dominated system.

Conclusion

This chapter has argued that there is a strong relationship between the evolution of FIHS and the liberal international order. The current FIHS is not simply a *product* of the liberal international order; it is also an important site at which this order was and is constituted. It is also the site at which the liberal international order is being challenged. A waning liberal international order means a waning FIHS and bodes ill for humanitarianism. But we often slip into treating humanitarianism as synonymous with the FIHS, masking the agency of both affected populations and alternative approaches to humanitarianism, and obscuring the complex heterogeneity of humanitarianism. Embracing this heterogeneity provides a more robust understanding of humanitarianism as a more variegated realm that owes much to, but is not necessarily bound to, the liberal international order. Rather than undermining the FIHS, this may provide a way forward and an opportunity to reconfigure the FIHS as more inclusive, robust, and better equipped to meet the challenges of international humanitarian action.

19

TOWARDS AN ANTI-RACIST HUMANITARIANISM
IN THE POST-LIBERAL WORLD

Patricia Daley

Introduction

In 2020, the coronavirus pandemic and the global Black Lives Matter (BLM) protests brought to the fore the pervasiveness of white supremacy and anti-blackness hidden within (neo)liberal states. They also challenged institutions and societies to think differently about the treatment of people racialised as black. The protesters were responding to the brutal police killing of George Floyd, a black man from Minneapolis, in the US. But debates ensuing from this murder have also exposed tensions in the global humanitarian regime. A major humanitarian donor country, the US has long denied the human rights of a segment of its own citizens. This apparent contradiction was accentuated when the United Nations Human Rights Council (UNHRC) issued a statement condemning 'the continuing racially discriminatory and violent practices perpetrated by law enforcement agencies against Africans and people of African descent'.[1] It was not the first time that the UNHRC had warned the US about its treatment of people of African descent.[2] But such admonitions have not brought about sufficient action. The sad truth remains: black lives are not deemed to matter even in the domestic politics of states that claim to support rights abroad.

Meanwhile, the conversion of the Mediterranean into a site of mass burial for forced migrants calls attention to Europe's long-standing racial politics of immigration and its criminalisation of asylum-seeking.[3] When not abandoned at sea, non-white migrants and refugees have often been detained by force or returned to persecution. Just as this exposes assumptions about which lives are superfluous, it also undermines facile Euro-American claims to an exalted ethics of responsibility.[4] Dissonance between the actions and humanitarian discourse of states of the global North can be traced back to colonialism.[5] If, today, contradictions appear as cracks in the liberal politics of the West, they are constitutive of capitalist modernity. Achille Mbembe, in a discussion of the persistence of anti-black racism, comments that 'liberal democracy has always needed a constitutive Other for its legitimation, an Other who is and is not at the same time part of the polis'.[6]

The unravelling of the geopolitical consensus that has shaped international institutions in the image of the global North suggests the possible emergence of a post-liberal world. Such institutional fragmentation could result in the intensification of humanitarian crises in the global South, but it could also provide an opportunity to rethink humanitarian action. Analysis of both these possibilities requires a racial lens rarely used in scholarship and policy discussions regarding humanitarian affairs, even since the growth of critical analyses of humanitarianism in the late 1980s. The lack of attention to the racialisation of humanitarian action is arguably due, as Alexander Weheliye notes, to 'white supremacy and coloniality still form[ing] the glue for the institutional and intellectual disciplinarity of western critical thought'.[7] This chapter, therefore, proposes the production of new decolonial histories of humanitarianism that might contribute to new meanings and practices. This is needed if *humanity* is to transcend narrow parochialisms, including Western universalisms, and foster planetary bonds of care that are relational and inclusive of all humans.

Re-historicising liberal humanitarianism in this way means shifting away from conventional understandings which associate it with benevolence, compassion, and humanity. Such critical examination can render visible humanitarianism's historical foundation, the ideologies that have emboldened it, and the economic and political structures that have given meaning to its practices, not least those institutionalised after the Second World War, with the establishment of a system of global governance.

This chapter will consider how colonial ideologies and assumptions of racial hierarchy are foundational to liberal humanitarianism's praxis. And it will propose that recent challenges to liberal humanitarianism from within the West and from beyond demand a critical reckoning with these foundations. The chapter draws on a conception of liberal humanitarianism as a Western mode of governance through the biopolitical differentiation between human beings. Born in Europe, its application was extended to the Americas and then Asia and Africa, as part of the colonial project that racialised and victimised non-white others, nonetheless saving them for the purpose of exploitation. Controlling racialised others became a matter of urgency for the guardians of the liberal international order at the height of anti-colonial struggle, in the two-and-a-half decades following the Second World War. Western governments and their citizens looked to humanitarian agencies—NGOs and UN agencies—to give a human face to efforts to postpone and then manage decolonisation. When these agencies came to codify the ethical principles upon which they acted, their imagination of the universal human was inevitably racialised.[8]

Coloniality and Liberal Humanitarianism

The origins of modern Western humanitarianism are often situated in the seventeenth century, with the development of early liberal thought, or in the following century, with the romantic 'revolution in compassion'.[9] But its globalisation can be considered to have begun in the moment of Europe's imperialist expansion, at the end of the nineteenth century, and to have accelerated in the aftermath of the First World War, as hegemonic Western states sought new modes of ordering a post-imperial world. It would thus be erroneous to consider it independent from the process of capitalist development and from the European wars that have shaped the world system. During the period of decolonisation and grand ideological conflict, humanitarian aid was often guided by the geopolitical interests of Western governments. After the end of the Cold War, humanitarianism became increasingly entangled with neoliberalism's minimalist politics, as well as the messianic ambitions to convert Southern countries to liberal democracy through military might. Recognising the political and economic dependencies of contemporary humanitarianism, the legal scholar B. S. Chimni understands it as 'the ideology of hegemonic states in the era of globalisation marked by the end of the Cold War and a growing North–South divide'.[10] 'The ideology of humanitarianism', he goes on to argue, mobilises ideas that 'sustain global relations of domination'—not least the incontrovertible 'unity of humankind'.[11] Notions of unity, he contends, are undermined by racialised humanitarian policies and practices.

Over the last twenty years in particular, critical scholars—not least historians—have rooted contemporary humanitarianism in the colonial past.[12] But, despite continued critique from the global South and diaspora populations in the global North,[13] Western humanitarian discourse still betrays Eurocentric assumptions of moral superiority. Southern and indigenous scholars have called for a recognition of how coloniality (socially, economically, epistemologically) has shaped existing unequal relations of power between the North and the South; and they have argued that decoloniality is a condition for liveable futures.[14] Coloniality refers to the contemporary continuation of systems that reproduce the dominance of Eurocentric modes of thought and capitalist modernisation. Maldonado Torres outlines the differences between colonialism and coloniality:

> Colonialism denotes a political and economic relation in which the sovereignty of a nation or a people rests on the power of another nation, which makes such a nation an empire. Coloniality, instead, refers to long-standing patterns of power that emerged as a result of colonialism, but that define culture, labour, intersubjectivity relations, and knowledge production well beyond the strict limits of colonial administrations. Thus, coloniality survives colonialism.[15]

The concept of coloniality poses a challenge to the facile presentation of Western humanitarianism as an unmitigated force for good—the well-meaning provision of material support to abject victims in the global South, whose underdevelopment derives from local corruption, 'tribal' feuds, or barbaric customs. Western humanitarian agencies have laid claim to neutrality—to independence from politics—in the hope that this will grant them access to contested spaces of conflict and disaster, and to the money of Western citizenries. However, they undermined this through their interactions with Western governments in the 1990s and early 2000s, supporting military interventions in the name of humanitarian concern and the responsibility to protect.[16] Their willing provision of services subcontracted by Western states also revealed an increasing embeddedness in neoliberal political economy. The blurred boundaries between humanitarian agencies and Western states became more apparent. Of the many critiques of the 'securitisation' of humanitarian aid,[17] few addressed the significance of racialisation; partly because critically engaging with racial ontologies would itself require stepping outside of Eurocentric frames of ethical analysis.

To go beyond the debates on relative ethics and to address racialisation, one can adopt a decolonial approach that critiques white supremacy and its methodological influence on how Western academics interpret colonial and postcolonial experiences, in particular the main tenets of colonisation: dominance and submission. In *Discourse on Colonialism*, Aimé Césaire argues that 'colonization = "thingification"':[18] the dehumanisation of the colonised, the destruction of cultures and economies, genocide, and other brutalities that accompanied colonisation mean that 'a nation which colonizes, that a civilization which justifies colonization—and therefore force—is already a sick civilization, a civilization that is morally diseased'.[19] Having committed colonial atrocities and needing to maintain its trade relations in the postcolonial era, Europe, Césaire argues, hoped to present itself as civilised/liberal, and so started 'the forgetting machine'. This was evident in the deliberate damage to colonial archives, where records of colonial repression and violence were destroyed. This colonial forgetting, or as Ann Stoler terms it, 'colonial aphasia',[20] was state-orchestrated, but permeated national consciousness to the extent that even in contemporary opinion polls, a significant proportion of Europe's population sees colonialism as beneficial. Stoler defined colonial aphasia as 'a dismembering, a difficulty speaking, a difficulty generating a vocabulary that associates appropriate words and concepts with appropriate things'.[21] A discussion of aphasia raises 'unsettling questions about what it means to know and not know something simultaneously, about what is implicit because it goes without saying, or because it cannot be thought, or because it can be thought and is known but cannot be said'.[22]

With the advent of the Rhodes Must Fall student protests in South Africa and the United Kingdom[23] and the global Black Lives Matter protests,[24] the reluctance of former colonial societies to revisit their racist histories reveals colonial aphasia as 'white supremacy'—a term that denotes the hegemonic dominance by people racialised as white of structures and institutions, to the extent that it is perceived as normative. Colonial aphasia is white supremacy covering its tracks. White supremacy was prevalent in the colonial discourse of elevating barbarians through Christianity and waged work; as part of the civilising mission promoted by some European explorers, Christian missionaries, and colonised authorities, and epitomised in the notion of the 'white man's burden'. Assumptions of white superiority explained the Othering of non-white peoples and provided justification for the perpetuation of atrocities and damages to colonised societies. The 'collective hypocrisy' of forgetting led Europe to represent its domination as delivering modernity—the rule of law, transport, and integration into the global economy. Such an idealised vision of encounter was taken up by development experts and upheld in institutions of global governance and international interventions, eliding the realities of racial domination. Humanitarians, in turn, sought to cure or provide palliative care to those suffering from the remaining vestiges of barbarism.

Michel Foucault theorised 'biopower' as the way in which modern Western states governed their citizens through a range of institutional and regulatory techniques for disciplining the body and controlling the population.[25] However, Weheliye, amongst others, has noted that Foucault did not engage explicitly with race and colonisation in his discussion of biopolitics, despite references to the necessity of hierarchies for the effective execution of biopower and arguing that Western societies were the only ones that had reached the level whereby the right to life could be regulated at such an intricate scale.[26] He did not dwell on how racialisation and enslavement in the European colonies enabled the perfecting of the biopolitical regulatory techniques. Extreme necropolitical power, the power over life and death, was exerted over people in the global South through the use of racialisation to justify their dehumanisation. For example, Africans, according to Frantz Fanon, were painted in zoological terms, representing their 'primitive' position on the evolutionary ladder, and were embodied as evil and destructive of nature and of others.[27] Fanon declares:

> The native is declared insensible to ethics; he represents not only the absence of values, but also the negation of values. He is, let us dare to admit it, the enemy of values, and in this sense he is absolute evil. He is the corrosive element, destroying all who come near him; he is the deforming element, disfiguring all that has to do with beauty and morality; he is the depository of maleficent powers, the unconscious and irretrievable instrument of blind forces.[28]

The 'uncivilised' native was constructed as a naturalised being, ruled by child-like emotions and thus capable of senseless, irrational destruction. The European 'civilising mission' necessitated the production of a knowledge system that would enable the regulation and control of the racialised 'natives' through health and other biopolitical interventions that later manifested in humanitarian interventions.[29]

To counter nationalist movements and the demands for equity from colonised and formerly enslaved peoples, Western states turned to the discourse of development and the humanitarian project partly as means of maintaining their hegemony and white supremacy in the global South. This was relatively easy, as they had control of the emerging international organisations in the United Nations system and the resources to back up their projects.[30] Consequently, the presence of white people in the former colonies was justified as not relating to domination but tutelage and supervision to enable newly independent countries to develop with regard for democracy and human rights. The underlying assumptions were that the material advancement of Europeans, supported by racist ideology, gave them the upper hand in aiding lesser humans. Whiteness and its privileges, that anti-colonialists contested, became the embodiment of progress and success and were promoted as universally desirable. As Makau Mutua notes, the assumption was that all 'human societies transform them-selves to fit a particular [Eurocentric human rights] blueprint'.[31] Such thinking was marked by the failure to include race equality in the Covenant of the League of Nations,[32] and the efforts by African Americans in the 1960s to get the human rights of black people in the United States addressed.[33] Even after considering Steven Jensen's recent historical study of the role Caribbean diplomats at the UN played in the universal application of international human rights law, it is still possible to argue that white supremacy was upheld in these institutions of global governance and international interventions, such that racial domination and hierarchies remain salient.[34]

The persistence of inequalities arising from the extraction of resources and unfair trade relations can only be justified by arguing that people in the global South, due to their inherent inadequacies, are solely responsible for the harrowingly inhumane conditions under which they live. Lawrence Summers, when Chief Economist for the World Bank, purportedly argued in 1991 that the World Bank should encourage the migration of dirty industries to less-developed coun-tries because 'under-populated countries in Africa are vastly UNDER-polluted' and life expectancy is shorter in contrast to the developed countries, where there will be greater 'demand for a clean environ-ment for aesthetic and health reasons' as people live longer.[35] While some might see this as reflecting economistic principles, the racial underpinnings cannot be overlooked.

Neoliberal humanitarianism led to the commodification of suffering. To compete for resources amongst the plethora of humanitarian agen-cies, aid recipients have to be marketed as needy, as vulnerable, help-less victims, without agential capacity to make changes to their own lives. Material deficits are then implicitly presented as cultural. Instead of using an overt racial lens, race is invisible, but present, where cul-tural differences are evoked to challenge what are represented as tra-ditional barbaric practices—this approach is sometimes evident in Western campaigns against gender-based violence and female genital mutilation (FGM) in African and Asian countries. Therefore, a question we might pose is what role have humanitarians played in reinforcing hegemonic discourses about race, in popularising notions of lesser humans subjected to conditions that are not acceptable to more 'evolved' human beings, and who, through practices of subjection, can benefit from humanitarian bountifulness?

White Privilege: The Elephant in the Room

The 2020 coronavirus pandemic's disproportionate impact on non-white peoples in the global North has put under the spotlight the racialised structural vulnerabilities that are embedded in global North societies, which are not addressed through the purview of human rights or humanitarian interventions.[36] In addition, the Black Lives Matter campaign pressured Western institutions to consider the effects of white supremacy in their organisations and to publish solidarity statements in support of black lives. Undoubtedly, in humanitarian spaces, normative actions and practices tend to reinforce hegemonic discourses about hierarchies of race and place. This is evident in the imagined geographies of humanitarian space, and how bodies racialised as white and non-white are treated as workers and as recipients of humanitarian largesse. For example, Lucy Mayblin shows the enduring influence of slavery and colonisation on asylum policy in the global North, but such connections are even more visibly displayed in the global South.[37]

Humanitarian discourse and practices produce their own imaginative geographies that correspond with colonial spatial Othering—'Aidland',[38] the camp, the compound, the protectorate[39]—that intersect with its own distinct power relations. Marked differences exist between the agency and the national and local state, the workers and the people they service; and humanitarian workers themselves are also differentiated according to geopolitical ordering and race. Coloniality and racialisation are implicit in the structure of these spaces and relationships. Within international institutions and in the formerly colonised world, the main actors in the humanitarian turn have been descendants of the colonial elites. Whether intended or not, white humanitarians have benefited from the privilege of whiteness that pervades postcolonial encounters in the global South. The salience of racial ideology and the unwillingness to discuss it constitutes the elephant in the room.

Humanitarian agencies tend to be white-led, despite the increasing sprinkle of 'natives'—the same way in which the bulk of the colonial staff were 'natives' but power was in white hands. In the contemporary period, white staff tend to be classified as 'international staff' and non-white staff predominantly as local 'national staff'.[40] This racialist geopolitical categorisation of humanitarian actors leads to different assumptions about capabilities and material differences in pay and benefits between the groups.[41] Even more insidiously, such differences reinforce the association of the white (foreign) face with improved well-being—and maintain superiority and inferiority complexes. Tajudeen Abdul-Raheem notes, in the context of African countries, that

> The racial imbalance is played out every day. Every white person is perceived and received as a boss with an obeisance that will nauseate any person with a conscience. Most expatriates have their huge houses with all the conveniences, house boys, house girls and a string of people to do their bidding, most of them at the cost of less than a week's travelling ticket on any subway in Europe. Anybody who ever wondered how the colonial staff live should visit Kampala, Kigali or Nairobi. The colonial mentality and its lifestyle are back. Colonial plunderers and marauding pirates like Christopher Columbus, Cecil Rhodes, Lord Lugard were eulogised as adventurers and nation-builders... their heirs of today are consultants, experts and the NGO community.[42]

As a response to the criticism of the absence of non-white and global South people amongst the staff in humanitarian agencies, some have developed initiatives to employ local staff or work through local NGOs, under the now popular discourse of building local capacity—a project that Amber Murrey and Nicholas Jackson describe as 'local whitewashing'.[43] While use of local staff (euphemistically termed 'partners') is a valid response,[44] the structural inequalities are left unaddressed and questions remain about the institutionalisation of white supremacy in the conceptualisation, design, and evaluation of projects, which are invariably conducted by external actors, and in the imbalance between the allocation of financial resources (more to international / white staff) and the distribution of the workload (bulk carried by local 'partners').

The use of racialised imagery in mediated campaigns has long been criticised and many agencies have adopted a more progressive stance, but the problem remains.[45] Murali Balaji, in a study of the role of the media in representations of the people affected by the Haitian earthquake, draws a distinction between evocations of empathy and pity.[46] He writes: 'empathy implies a sentiment based on equality. Pity, on the other hand, assumes the one pitying holds the power over the pitied.'[47] He contends that 'race is central to how pity is enacted... [in] the relationship between those who pity and those who are pitied... [and is] instrumental in creating the Other [since] poverty and famine have long been associated with a dark non-white world, where tragedy and hopelessness reign'.[48] Even if, as Lilie Chouliaraki argues in her analysis of the role of the media in the politics of pity, a paradigmatic shift has taken place in how solidarity is performed, the issue of racialisation remains prominent.[49] If relations of solidarity are individualised in the post-humanitarian world, then the new affective form is likely to focus narrowly on racialised criteria of vulnerable bodies.

Mutua uses the metaphors of 'savages, victims and saviours' to illustrate how the rhetoric of Western human rights advocates is informed by racialised categorisations of all those involved.[50] White humanitarians are portrayed as heroic individuals—'powerful white saviours'—irrespective of status and experience.[51] Such elevations allow for deceptions and malpractices to go unchallenged. White saviourism also requires the criminalisation of black (non-white people) to maintain its hegemony. Beverley Mullings et al., writing about relief after the Haitian earthquake of 2010, note the way in which 'racialized discourses of poverty and criminality [emerged] in the form of an almost pathological obsession with the issue of corruption'.[52] Narratives of looting and raping and black criminality lend credence to Western-supported reconstruction actors' attempts to bypass the state and local communities. Such external interventions are widespread; hence, the growing backlash from the global South against white saviourism.[53]

The psychological impact of persistent white supremacy in the global South affects both Western and non-Western subjectivities. In the global North, 'popular humanitarianism' means all white people, whether celebrities or school students, can see themselves as experts, able to provide services in the global South that local people are supposedly naturally deficient in.[54] Through the growth of voluntarism, students taking a gap year in their education volunteer to help Southerners by building schools, working in orphanages, teaching, and doing health work, as if local people lack the necessary knowledge and capacities to do such work, and, as Mary Mostafanezhad notes, reproducing colonial imaginaries and relations that 'resist introspection and historicization'.[55] In global South contexts, where local people have internalised white supremacy and their own inferiority, the expectation that whiteness will bring more resources, deliver better quality services and with no corruption, is often evident—thus undermining local dynamism and capacities for change.

In order to absolve themselves of responsibility for the dependent relationships that they created, humanitarians introduced concepts such as 'dependency syndrome' and 'compassion fatigue'; the former to denigrate and victimise the recipients and the latter to elevate the benevolence of the strained giver. Africans, for example, were said to be afflicted by characteristics that made them too dependent, lazy, and unwilling to take initiatives. Critics of the dependency syndrome argue that humanitarian actors can encourage dependency for the profitability and viability of agencies and individual careers. It is these humanitarians that A. M. Babu terms 'aid pushers', and Africans, especially those leaders who call for external assistance without first mobilising domestic resources, as 'aid addicts'.[56] Indebtedness and reliance on international financial institutions means that some states and elites have limited capacity to resist Western humanitarian action. If liberal humanitarian actors are increasingly constrained by their relationships with the state and the military, and continue to support militarism and securitisation, then it is imperative to rethink humanitarianism in the post-liberal era so that it challenges all the unspoken assumptions of the liberal era. This, I argue would require a decolonial turn.

Towards a Decolonial Humanitarianism for the Post-Liberal Era

A decolonial approach poses epistemic challenges to liberal humanitarianism and thus necessitates fundamental rethinking of its ideologies, histories, and politics. Already, critical scholarship has addressed the epistemologies underlying humanitarian policies and practices,[57] the colonial histories,[58] and the racialised biopolitics of humanitarian assistance.[59]

However, a more extensive engagement with Southern critique requires global North humanitarians to recognise that their conceptions of humanity and sociocultural life are Eurocentric in origin, and that the casting of non-white people in the binary of villain or victim must be viewed as prejudicial and destructive of human relations. Empathy and compassion exist in every society and every human being. Furthermore, as Mutua and others have argued,[60] there were clear articulations of human rights in anti-slavery campaigns and anti-colonial struggles in Africa, Asia, and Latin America before their universalisation as Western norms after 1945. What matters is how that empathy is performed, how it is institutionalised and promoted. White supremacy has led to the shrouding, in deathly ways, and the marginalisation of forms of empathy practised in the global South.

Modern Western cultural ways of empathy and care have been universalised as the norm. Such forms of empathy are classed, patriarchal, gendered, and individualised. Euro-American ideas about care form the ideologies that pervade humanitarian actions. Examples range from the biopolitical institutionalisation and segregation of those considered dysfunctional or potentially disruptive to the operations of capitalist societies. Such segregated spaces of care include orphanages, mental health institutions, and care homes for the elderly. These spaces of confinement and encampment have proliferated and are being marketed in the global South as good examples of liberal humanitarian care. The current trend for localisation has opened up spaces for the recognition of local, non-Western ways of caring.

However, even when local knowledges are sought, as Gabrielle Daoust and Synne Dyvik have shown with regards to the development of policies on safeguarding, they are valued mainly to contextualise previously developed policies and practices—rather than considered expertise in its own right and integral to developing global policies and standards.[61] Daoust and Dyvik call for rigorous attention to decolonial ethics that avoids tokenism and 'epistemic exploitation'. They urge humanitarians to reflect on '*whose* knowledge is recognized, valorised, and centred in developing "global" and "universal" standards', and on possibilities for informing more comprehensive understandings of the meaning and practice of safeguarding.[62]

Drawing on a non-Western ethics of caring that is familial and communal can provide legitimate knowledges about ways of living equitably that are urgently needed in the contemporary world, and particularly in this distinct, human-impacted geological period now termed the Anthropocene. In sub-Saharan Africa, for example, the tradition of hospitality and caring for others is often articulated in the concept of *ubuntu* (a philosophy of a common humanity). Even Berlinist postcolonial African states drew on *ubuntu* and anti-colonialism to mobilise support among African peoples for the anti-apartheid liberation forces of South Africa.[63] This support was spear-headed by African governments through the Organisation of African Unity (OAU) African Liberation Committee that was established in the 1960s. Ordinary Africans were united against the continued presence of oppression and exploitation across the continent, and provided support for refugees fleeing colonial domination and apartheid regimes. Here, the politics of care was not extracted from the wider politics of liberation that addresses the objective conditions under which oppression continues to exist.

In the twenty-first century, the hostility of states to refugees and migrants has led to the emergence of what some describe as 'everyday humanitarianism'[64] or 'subversive humanitarianism',[65] focusing essentially on individuals and rights groups in the global North who provide support to asylum seekers in their countries, in direct opposition to states and at the risk of being criminalised. While this is a welcomed shift, scholars of humanitarianism also need to recognise that such everyday acts of human kindness, obligations of mutuality, and forms of conviviality are also normative in the global South, in what Anne-Meike Fechter and Anke Schwittay now term 'citizen aid'.[66] Francis Nyamnjoh, in addressing violence against migrants in African countries, uses the concept of 'conviviality' to describe the non-violent practices that exist as part of human sociality. Conviviality, he explains, 'depict[s] diversity, tolerance, trust, equality, inclusiveness, cohabitation, coexistence, mutual accommodation, interaction, interdependence, getting along, generosity, hospitality, congeniality, festivity, civility and privileging peace over conflict, among other forms of sociality'.[67]

Throughout the 1970s and 1980s, a truism was propagated that the bulk of African refugees were self-settled—often relying on local communities, families, and friends. As the role of external actors increased in the 1990s, self-settled refugees were depicted by national governments and humanitarian agencies as unfair burdens and, by the time of the 'war on terror', a major security threat. Therefore, local acts of conviviality have been criminalised over time by the state and humanitarian interventions, as they confine and isolate destitute people in camps for purposes of security and efficient delivery of external aid.[68] Today, those seeking assistance within the boundaries of their countries or with kinfolk in neighbouring countries are labelled as either Internally Displaced Persons (IDPs) or refugees, and become the responsibility largely of external actors and their biopolitical regimes of governing. A similar situation is emerging with refugees in urban centres, who face stigmatisation and exclusion from the body politic, especially in contexts where belonging requires territorial and social rootedness in a community. Xenophobic violence against 'African foreigners' or non-citizens in parts of sub-Saharan Africa has to be understood as part of a history of marginalisation under a Western modernity that embodies ideas of the nation-state, hardens territorial boundaries, and constructs exclusive national citizenship, thus resulting in the creation of the social categories of *indigènes*, as well as aliens, immigrants, and refugees—people who are positioned as external from the body politic.[69]

While digital technologies might have changed the solidarity relationship between the Northern giver and the Southern receiver to one based even more on individual emotional satisfaction,[70] the growth in digital communication technologies has made it easier to challenge global North humanitarians and expose racialised malpractices, and has also facilitated communication between Southerners. While the West's geopolitical reach and humanitarian project may extend white supremacy, there are those subjected to coloniality within the global North who have experience of building solidarity between oppressed peoples. These diasporas have practised everyday transnational humanitarianism as part of their commitment to family and community—a form of humanitarian action that is often commoditised as remittance. These global diasporas have grown in size and will, no doubt, change the narratives on care, and play an increased role in relief efforts.

A decolonial turn in humanitarianism requires learning and working with new epistemologies of care that have the ultimate goal of uniting humanity in tackling the planetary challenges ahead. The decolonial turn is not to abandon principles of Western humanitarianism, even though its hegemonic manifestation has to be opposed. But, as Mutua suggests, it is necessary to recognise that 'in order ultimately to prevail, the human rights movement must be moored in the cultures of all peoples.'[71] This means, as Robtel Pailey argues in relation to the field of development, the liberal humanitarian white gaze has to be decentred.[72]

Conclusion

Even if liberalism does not die, there has been sufficient critique of liberal humanitarianism for it to take corrective steps. Certainly, its survival without any transformation would mean further embeddedness in a globally destructive Western military machine fuelled by xenophobic nationalism, Balkanisation, and a deep hostility to rights. The urgency of a planetary humanity consensus to tackle a range of climate change-induced environmental crises, necessitates moving beyond Western liberal humanitarianism. Transformation that is attentive to the critiques emerging from non-white others requires conducting historical analyses of its integration into global geopolitics and the prevalence of racialisation. Such analysis can draw on decolonial epistemologies and methodologies to reveal the relations, connections, peoplehood, and sociality existing beyond the humanitarian gaze. To do so also means challenging white supremacy by recognising, primarily, that whiteness accords privileges to humanitarians racialised as white, especially in the global South. But whilst we can ask individual white people to refuse those privileges, it is even more important to address the structures of white supremacy within which they operate. Institutional racism is often rejected by those working in humanitarian organisations as a direct personal attack against people who are 'doing good'. As an academic, my view is that humanitarians need to remember the histories of subjection that non-white peoples endured due to the promotion of racial hierarchies and confront white supremacy by unravelling its embeddedness in thinking about what it means to be human, how to organise the world of human beings, and how to empathetically care for global humanity.

20

WHAT'S THERE TO MOURN? WHAT'S THERE TO CELEBRATE?

DECOLONIAL RETRIEVALS OF HUMANITARIANISM

Olivia U. Rutazibwa[1]

Introduction

All over the globe, we have seen fascism, racism, and xenophobic nationalism resurfacing in what we once thought of as 'respectable' democracies. Following a particularly bleak weekend at the end of October 2018 (the election of Jair Bolsonaro in Brazil, reports of worsening famine in Yemen, Israeli bombardment of Gaza, the murder of eleven worshippers at a refugee-harbouring synagogue in Pittsburgh), my colleague Dr Sara Salem of the London School of Economics tweeted: 'It's difficult watching political scientists scrambling to understand what's happening around the world today as if there haven't been people... theorising racism, nationalism, empire and gender for a century and warning of exactly what we see now.' Today, the handling of the COVID-19 pandemic, and the reignited Black Lives Matter protests following the police killing of George Floyd, painfully underscore how a systemic disregard for *certain* lives continues to be the organising principle of the postcolonial world order.

Moulded by Eurocentric knowledge systems, most of us react with utter shock to such developments, as we do to the storming of the Capitol, the locking up of refugee children, separated from their accompanying family members, and the killing of unarmed black people. We—an imagined citizenry of respectable democracies—are horrified and appalled at how far we have been dragged from our liberal, more-or-less progressive self-image. 'This is not us; this is not who we are', someone will say. And we are invited to consider whether we might be witnessing the end of the liberal humanitarian order.

Eurocentrism has taught us to see the potential end of an era in every relative change in Western power.

Similarly, in reaction to the Capitol Hill insurrection on 6 January 2021, incoming president Joe Biden said: 'Let me be very clear. The scenes of chaos at the Capitol do not reflect a true America, do not represent who we are.'[2] His election was welcomed by many with a sigh of relief. With his presidency, things are expected to return to 'normal', return to 'decency'. There are many reasons to rejoice in the fact that Trump has not been re-elected. But the 'return to normalcy and decency', supposedly brought about by the Biden presidency,[3] offers an opportunity to critically engage with the coloniality of the liberal (humanitarian) order—that is, its systemic and uneven/targeted violence, its Death Project.[4] While it is still early days, the first few weeks of the Biden administration have shown the return of a US that is vocal about *other* nations' human rights violations.

Thinking critically about the role of humanitarianism today requires that we don't reproduce assumptions about Western-led order as a force for good by mourning the end of a history that never actually existed—or by celebrating its imagined continuation after a brief aberration. Given past and present non-Western experiences of liberal order, we might firstly ask: What's there to mourn? And secondly: How might we retrieve humanitarianism as a decolonial project of life?

In what follows, I point to avenues for engaging with these questions. Drawing inspiration from African (American) and decolonial thought, I also reflect on my personal and professional experiences. These avenues consist in (a) bearing witness and calling out what James Baldwin referred to as 'the lie',[5] and (b) confronting liberal humanitarianism's desire for, *jouissance* of,[6] and attachment to 'mastery',[7] by recentring the conversation around a project of indiscriminate life in dignity.

The Lie

Back when Trump was still president of the US, Harvard professor Eddie Glaude, Jr., stood out as one of the few voices in the centrist, progressive media who identified Trump not as an aberration, but as a crude embodiment of what America had always been. 'This *is* us', he proclaimed emphatically.[8] His perspective was formed through an intimate and long-standing relationship with the works of James Baldwin. His book *Begin Again: James Baldwin's America and Its Urgent Lessons for Our Own* (2020) is a powerful antidote to colonial amnesia and ignorance. It offers tools to think through the meaning and historical implications of white, liberal (world) order, amidst the debris of the present, from which it could once again take potent form. Glaude reminds us of the power with which Baldwin, a long time ago, told us about *the lie*.

The lie is best understood as 'several sets of lies with a single purpose': maintaining the 'value gap', 'the idea that in America white lives have always mattered more than lives of others'.[9] While Glaude speaks of the US context specifically, the lie is a powerful heuristic for understanding the postcolonial world order. One of the ways in which the lie is maintained is through white, liberal innocence—that is, the convenient disavowal of all those institutions and histories at the service of the 'value gap'.[10] It's what allows our cyclical consternation at the murderous features of liberal order when they're in fact 'hidden in plain sight'.[11] There is a merit in calling these out for what they represent: supremacy and racism. And there is a compelling simplicity to the label 'lie'. It tells of an impatience with the conceit of innocence and how it maintains the value gap. From Baldwin, we learn that bearing witness to the lie is a crucial aspect of dismantling it.

My personal experiences of research and knowledge production regarding humanitarianism have reinforced in me a desire to confront the lie, as well as an anti-colonial ethos—an intellectual opposition to coloniality, even in the most 'benign' of research and policy areas, like international aid and humanitarianism. Coloniality can be understood as the perpetuation of colonial systems and technologies of domination into the present. As discussed by scholars such as Quijano, Grosfoguel, Dussel, and Ndlovu-Gatsheni, the concept of decoloniality then encourages systemic and historical analysis of the organised (re)production of injustice and mass human suffering.[12]

Formal colonialism (which arguably existed from 1492 to the 1960s) and transatlantic enslavement are but two means through which Europeans made themselves the protagonists of global history. Europeans then rewrote their history, erasing the mass human suffering they had caused, promoting instead tales of white European innocence,[13] superiority, and exceptionalism. In its destruction of life, coloniality might be considered anti-humanitarian, and yet it is characteristic of the liberal humanitarianism whose possible end we now are invited to contemplate.

For over two decades, I have been struggling to make sense of humanitarian interventions. The topic was thrust upon me by events in Rwanda in 1994. As a teenage, second generation, Rwandan immigrant in Belgium, I was more personally affected than fellow classmates by the hypocrisy of the international community: the preaching of respect for human rights, followed by omission during 100 days of mass murder before the eyes of the world. It felt like there was more to the story than 'good intentions versus regrettable outcomes'.

Ever since, I have worried about the content and purpose of (Western) humanitarian research agendas. I became cognisant of the limited efforts to understand how good intentions coexist with a system of international aid and intervention that seems harmful not for the few but for the many. The silence of too many researchers simultaneously masks and normalises the harmful consequences of the aid system.

The scholarship and advice I was exposed to, as my early academic career developed, prompted me to explore the contradictory logic of international aid empirically: I set out to make a database of the EU's 'ethical' behaviour (sanctions, funding, declarations, military and humanitarian interventions, in relation to human rights and democracy) between 1999 and 2007 towards the countries of sub-Saharan Africa. I did not find any patterns that could fully explain the EU's action or inaction: not a country's size, its former colonial masters, nor its natural resources; not the member state presiding over the EU, nor even the African target country's human rights or humanitarian situation. After a stint at the European Commission's Directorate General of External Affairs, I also came to reject simplistic accounts about the absence of good intentions of the people devising and implementing aid policies.

I realised that I—and mainstream IR with me—had operated on an assumption that external involvement in the affairs of the 'developing world', if well-intentioned and effective, was desirable, indispensable even. Letting go of this assumption—confronting the lie—opens up a world of possibilities for the study of intervention. Doing so, I reconsidered the conventional narrative that attributes the genocide against the Tutsi in Rwanda to non-intervention, and came to see that the (post)colonial run-up to genocide was a story of too much intervention, in the name of democracy even.

During my doctoral research, I rediscovered the case of Somaliland. A self-declared independent republic in the north-western corner of Somalia, Somaliland had declined American and UN interventions at the beginning of the 1990s, apart from specific assistance (the clean-up of landmines, for example). Instead, it took care of its peace-building process internally and with its diaspora. Over the years, even though the international community had found its way to the capital, Hargeisa, Somaliland had arguably become the most stable democracy in the region, even as it awaited international recognition of its independence. It seemed to me, therefore, that the most salient question was not how intervention could be more effective and efficient, but whether it was necessary in the first place. Was Western presence itself constitutive of the problems facing 'host' countries?

Indiscriminate Life in Dignity

One could easily fill a lifetime exposing and bearing witness to *the lie* as it obfuscates the unwavering destructive force of coloniality (in the form of genocide, epistemicide, ecocide), racism, racial capitalism,[14] and the global colour line.[15] A decolonial ethos demands the imagination of afterlives and alternatives.

For now, in the context of this short chapter, I identify two mutually dependent endeavours that need attention if humanitarianism is to be retrieved from its instrumental role in liberal ordering and placed at the service of a *project of indiscriminate life in dignity*. The first is challenging Eurocentric epistemologies: interrogating how we know and learn, where we get out knowledges from, what we consider to be expertise, and who is considered to possess it. The second pertains to the dislocation of postcolonial power relations.

The epistemological question invites us to reckon with what Sabelo Ndlovu-Gatsheni, inspired by other African anti-colonial thinkers like Ngugi wa Thiong'o and Samir Amin, has called cognitive empire.[16] It is a reminder that empire, in its ongoing encounter with colonial legacies, causes not only material and bodily impositions, not only extraction and exploitation, but also the elimination of non-Western cultures, languages, and knowledge systems—their denial as *legitimate places from which to make sense of the world*. The violence of humanitarianism's own cognitive empire cannot be overstated. The details of the 'good life' and how we get there—whether it is how we understand sovereignty,[17] democracy, or good governance, or reduce the global South's problem to issues of corruption,[18] state failure, fragility, and neopatrimonialism[19]—all of these images continue to build on a mythological Western blueprint.

One antidote to such Eurocentrism is Meera Sabaratnam's 2017 book *Decolonising Intervention: International Statebuilding in Mozambique*, which offers a compelling feminist decolonial analysis of international state-building in the post-colony.[20] Sabaratnam foregrounds in-country critiques of foreign presence via the concept of *protagonismo*; and she reflects on *disposability* (of the 'beneficiaries'), *dependency* (on the interveners), and *entitlement* (of the interveners), as constitutive of interventions and not just technical glitches. If only I had had access to this work when I began my inquiry into humanitarianism.

I now include Sabaratnam's book as a core text for final-year undergraduate students reading International Development Studies and International Relations at the University of Portsmouth. My module on 'Rethinking Aid and Development' explores the implications of decolonial engagement with ideas and practices of international solidarity. Students have said: 'We should be assigned readings like this from year one.' So I ask the question here: 'What if we were to start our humanitarian conversation with Sabaratnam?'

Of course, other works have questioned the value of international intervention.[21] But it is necessary to reflect on the consequence of their marginality in the existing canon. Privileged research agendas shape academic career paths; and, increasingly, careers in 'the real world' shape academic disciplines. In this context, the marginalisation of critical decolonial perspectives in research and in practice becomes mutually reinforcing.

This is why attending to beyond-Western epistemologies 'of the South'[22] is a minimal, but never sufficient, condition for reinscribing humanitarianism into a project of life in dignity, indiscriminately. Stopping there, without addressing material power imbalances, would trap us in the multicultural lie of inclusion we see at work in Benetton commercials or in the World Bank or the UN, where everything looks more diverse yet remains the same, serving a neoliberal status quo.[23] Retrieving humanitarianism for a decolonial project of life requires an additional commitment to addressing the desire for mastery and control that, in spite of good intentions, has been a driving force of liberal humanitarianism.[24] Diversifying without unlearning this desire sustains humanitarianism as an instrument in coloniality's Death Project, adding to the sophistication of its lie.

Conclusion

In 1965, in the context of the march from Selma to Montgomery, Alabama, Martin Luther King, Jr., said: 'The only normalcy that we will settle for is the normalcy that recognises the dignity and worth of all of God's children.'[25] In a similar spirit, a decolonial retrieval of humanitarianism challenges Eurocentric analyses, foregrounding the experiences and knowledges of the intended targets of humanitarian aid.

Decoloniality poses questions not so much about the political will, operational implementation, and technical capabilities of humanitarians, but rather about the perpetuation of colonial power relations in seemingly benevolent activities.

Decoloniality asks: Where do we start the story? Who has the microphone and who usually doesn't? What are the implications of Eurocentric bias in knowledge production? Do our practices and knowledge systems contribute to the struggle against colonial power relations? And do challenges to Eurocentric discourse and knowledge result in a meaningful redistribution of power?

As we reflect on the potential end of liberal order, decoloniality questions what there is to mourn. As we reflect on its potential reassertion, decoloniality questions what there is to celebrate. With humanitarianism itself being redefined, black thought and decolonial perspectives can contribute to an understanding of the relevance of the good intentions of humanitarians to the aspirations of their intended 'beneficiaries'. They can provide an antidote to the lie—to 'colonial amnesia' and relentless 'moves to innocence'[26]—through which humanitarianism has served to sustain the liberal order's legitimacy. They can therefore provide a basis for the critical interrogation of, and contribution to, humanitarian endeavours in the service of life in dignity, and not merely survival. They can challenge not only the ideological character of a given order but also the power relations essential to it—something that the 'local turn' in humanitarian thinking has not done, despite discussion of 'shifting power'.

Without these perspectives informing research and policy agendas, whatever comes next is unlikely to be very different for those previously robbed of power and voice. Mourning the end, or celebrating the reassertion, of an order responsible for mass human suffering, while that suffering continues, then becomes an indulgent act of self-delusion.

NOTES

1. INTRODUCTION: HUMANITARIANISM AND LIBERAL ORDERING

1. Francine Prose, 'Catastrophe Has Been Averted. Let us all Breathe a Big, Long Sigh of Relief', *The Guardian*, 7 November 2020, https://www.theguardian.com/commentisfree/2020/nov/07/catastrophe-has-been-averted-let-us-all-breathe-a-big-long-sigh-of-relief (last accessed 15 November 2020).
2. Van Jones, 'Now We Can Breathe', CNN, 7 November 2020, https://edition.cnn.com/2020/11/07/opinions/the-election-is-a-huge-relief-van-jones/index.html (last accessed 15 November 2020).
3. Achille Mbembe, 'Le Droit universel à la respiration', *AOC*, 6 April 2020, https://aoc.media/opinion/2020/04/05/le-droit-universel-a-la-respiration/ (last accessed 22 November 2020).
4. Matt Stevens, 'Read Joe Biden's President-Elect Acceptance Speech: Full Transcript', *The New York Times*, 9 November 2020, https://www.nytimes.com/article/biden-speech-transcript.html (last accessed 25 November 2020).
5. Christophe Guilluy, *Le Crépuscule de la France d'en haut* (Paris: Flammarion, 2016).
6. Danny Sriskandarajah, 'REACTION: Oxfam Response to the Chancellor's Announcement to Cut Aid to 0.5%', Oxfam GB (blog), 25 November 2020, https://oxfamapps.org/media/press_release/reaction-oxfam-response-to-the-chancellors-announcement-to-cut-aid-to-0–5/ (last accessed 30 November 2020).
7. Kevin Watkins, 'Aid Spending Cut is a "Hammer Blow to British Impact"', Save the Children UK (blog), 25 November 2020, https://www.savethechildren.org.uk/news/media-centre/press-releases/aid-spending-cut-hammer-blow (last accessed 30 November 2020).
8. See, for example, G. John Ikenberry, 'The End of Liberal International Order?', *International Affairs* 94, no. 1 (January 2018): 7–23; Joseph S. Nye Jr., 'Will the Liberal Order Survive? The History of an Idea', *Foreign Affairs* 96, no. 1 (February 2017): 10–12; Francis Fukuyama and Robert Muggah, 'Populism is Poisoning the Global Liberal Order', *The Globe and Mail*, 29 January 2018, https://www.theglo

beandmail.com/opinion/populism-is-poisoning-the-global-liberal-order/arti-cle37777370/ (last accessed 15 November 2020); Richard N. Haass, 'Liberal World Order, R.I.P.', *Project Syndicate* (blog), 21 March 2018, https://www.proj-ect-syndicate.org/commentary/end-of-liberal-world-order-by-richard-n--haass-2018–03?barrier=accesspaylog (last accessed 15 November 2020).

9. Nye, 'Will the Liberal Order Survive?', 12.

10. Graham Allison, 'The Myth of the Liberal Order: From Historical Accident to Conventional Wisdom', *Foreign Affairs* 97, no. 4 (August 2018): 124–33.

11. Niall Ferguson, 'The Myth of the Liberal International Order', *The Global Times*, 11 January 2018, https://www.globaltimes.cn/content/1084413.shtml (last accessed 15 November 2020).

12. Michael Barnett, 'The End of a Liberal International Order that Never Existed', *The Global: Global Governance Debates* (blog), 16 April 2019, https://theglobal.blog/2019/04/16/the-end-of-a-liberal-international-order-that-never-existed/ (last accessed 15 November).

13. John Mearsheimer, 'Bound to Fail: The Rise and Fall of the Liberal International Order', *International Security* 43, no. 4 (Spring 2019): 7–50, 9. See, also, G. John Ikenberry, *After Victory: Institutions, Strategic Restraint, and the Rebuilding of Order after Major Wars* (Princeton, NJ: Princeton University Press, 2001), 23; and Nye, 'Will the Liberal Order Survive?', 11.

14. Wilhelm Röpke, 'The Economic System and International Order', in *International Order and Economic Integration* (Dordrecht: Springer, 1959), 69–93; Quinn Slobodian, *Globalists: The End of Empire and the Birth of Neoliberalism* (Cambridge, MA: Harvard University Press, 2018).

15. Nils Gilman, 'The New International Economic Order: A Reintroduction', *Humanity* 6, no. 1 (Spring 2015): 1–16.

16. Moyn offers a more apologetic reading of the relationship of human rights to neo-liberalism. Although human rights did not threaten neoliberal strategies, he argues, '[n]eoliberalism, not human rights, is to blame for neoliberalism'. Samuel Moyn, *Not Enough: Human Rights in an Unequal World* (Cambridge, MA: Belknap Press, 2018), 192.

17. Jeff Colgan and Robert Keohane, 'The Liberal Order is Rigged: Fix it Now or Watch it Wither', *Foreign Affairs* 96, no. 3 (June 2017): 36–44, 44.

18. 'A Manifesto for Renewing Liberalism', *The Economist*, 13 September 2018, https://www.economist.com/leaders/2018/09/13/a-manifesto-for-renewing-liberalism (last accessed 15 November 2020).

19. Patrick J. Deneen, *Why Liberalism Failed*, Politics and Culture (New Haven, CT: Yale University Press, 2018).

20. Fredric Jameson, 'Postmodernism, Or the Cultural Logic of Late Capitalism', *New Left Review* 146 (1984): 53–92.

21. Moyn develops his argument about human rights as the last utopia in Samuel Moyn, *The Last Utopia: Human Rights in History* (Cambridge, MA: Belknap Press, 2010).

22. Pankaj Mishra, 'The Economist and Liberalism', in *Bland Fanatics: Liberalism, Race and Empire* (London: Verso, 2020), 186–99, 199.

23. Jeremy Gilbert, 'Captive Creativity: Breaking Free from the Long "90s"' (blog), 2015, https://jeremygilbertwriting.files.wordpress.com/2015/09/the-end-of-the-long-90s1.pdf (last accessed 15 November 2020).

24. Bill Emmott, *The Fate of the West: The Battle to Save the World's Most Successful Political Idea* (London: Profile Books, 2017), 1.

25. Anne Applebaum, *Twilight of Democracy: The Seductive Lure of Authoritarianism* (New York, NY: Doubleday, 2020).

26. The 'new imperialism' characterises a period of accelerated imperial expansion from the late nineteenth century until the First World War. It is most commonly understood as having been driven by Europe's underconsumption, production of surplus capital, and technological development.

27. Emily Baughan, *Saving the Children: Humanitarianism, Internationalism and the British Empire, c.1918–1970* (Berkeley, CA: University of California Press, 2021).

28. Moyn, *Last Utopia*.

29. See, for example, Bertrand Taithe, 'Between the Border and a Hard Place: Negotiating Protection and Humanitarian Aid after the Genocide in Cambodia, 1979–1999', in *Humanitarianism and Human Rights*, ed. Michael Barnett (Cambridge: Cambridge University Press, 2020), 219–34.

30. Jean Pictet, 'The Fundamental Principles of the Red Cross: Commentary', *International Review of the Red Cross* 19, no. 210 (June 1979): 130–49, 144.

31. IFRC and ICRC, *Code of Conduct for the International Red Cross and Red Crescent Movement and Non-Governmental Organizations (NGOs) in Disaster Relief* (Geneva: IFRC, 1994), https://www.icrc.org/en/doc/assets/files/publications/icrc-002–1067.pdf (last accessed 15 November 2020).

32. Juliano Fiori, Fernando Espada, Jessica Field, and Sophie Dicker, *The Echo Chamber: Results, Management and the Humanitarian Effectiveness Agenda* (London: Save the Children, 2016), 10. This study was a product of collaboration between Save the Children's Humanitarian Affairs Team and the University of Manchester's Humanitarian and Conflict Response Institute.

33. Moyn, *Last Utopia*, 221.

34. See Didier Fassin, 'Humanitarianism as a Politics of Life', *Public Culture* 19, no. 3 (October 2007): 499–520.

35. Alexis Tocqueville, *Democracy in America* (New York, NY: Vintage, 1945), 275.

2. HUMANITARIANISM AND HISTORY: A CENTURY OF SAVE THE CHILDREN

1. A portion of the text that follows is drawn from Emily Baughan, *Saving the Children: Humanitarianism, Internationalism and the British Empire, c.1918–1970* (Berkeley, CA: University of California Press, 2021).

2. 'For German Babies', *Daily Herald*, 18 January 1919.

3. 'Report and Subscription List of German Babies' Rubber Teats Fund', YM/

MfS/FEWVRC/MISSIONS/10/2/3/1, Library of the Society of Friends (FHL), London.

4. The most striking example of this is MSF's Centre de Réflexion sur l'Action et les Savoirs Humanitaires (CRASH). See also Eleanor Davey, John Borton, and Matthew Foley, *A History of the Humanitarian System: Western Origins and Foundations*, HPG Working Paper (London: Overseas Development Institute, 2013); Juliano Fiori, Fernando Espada, Jessica Field, and Sophie Dicker, *The Echo Chamber: Results, Management, and the Humanitarian Effectiveness Agenda* (London: Humanitarian Affairs Team, Save the Children, 2016).

5. Justin Forsyth, 'We Must Not Turn Our Backs on Syria', *Daily Telegraph*, 31 August 2013; Plenary Session, Save the Children centenary conference, April 2019.

6. These allegations were addressed eventually in Suzanne Shale, *The Independent Review of Workplace Culture at Save the Children UK: Final Report* (8 October 2018), https://www.savethechildren.org.uk/content/dam/gb/reports/independent-review-of-workplace-culture-at-save-the-children-uk.pdf (last accessed 20 June 2020).

7. A conference report, *Politics, Humanitarianism & Children's Rights*, as well as video recordings of six witness panels and historical discussions of Save the Children, are accessible online at https://www.savethechildren.org.uk/conference100; see also, Mike Aaronson, '100 Years of Save the Children UK: What Have We Learned?', openDemocracy, 22 April 2019, https://www.opendemocracy.net/en/transformation/100-years-save-children-uk-what-have-we-learned/ (both last accessed 20 June 2020).

8. Plenary Session, Save the Children centenary conference, April 2019.

9. Didier Fassin, *Humanitarian Reason: A Moral History of the Present* (Berkeley, CA: University of California Press, 2011), 223–43; Panel 6, 'Iraq to Yemen: The Present Century', Save the Children centenary conference, April 2019; especially the comments of Gareth Owen.

10. Angus Urquart, *Global Humanitarian Assistance Report 2019* (Bristol: Development Initiatives, 2020), https://www.alnap.org/help-library/global-humanitarian-assistance-report-2019 (last accessed 26 June 2020).

11. Panel 6, 'Iraq to Yemen: The Present Century'.

12. Gregory Mann, *From Empires to NGOs in the West African Sahel: The Road to Nongovernmentality* (Cambridge: Cambridge University Press, 2015).

13. Andrzej Krassowski, *The Aid Relationship* (London: Overseas Development Institute, 1968); Teresa Hayter, *Aid as Imperialism* (London: Penguin, 1971); Gunnar Myrdal, *Asian Drama: An Inquiry into the Poverty of Nations* (London: Pantheon, 1968). More recently, see Corinna R. Unger, 'Postwar European Development Aid: Defined by Decolonization, the Cold War, and European Integration?', in *The Development Century: A Global History*, ed. Stephen Macekura and Erez Manela (Cambridge: Cambridge University Press, 2018), 240–60; Meera Sabaratnam, *Decolonising Intervention: International Statebuilding in Mozambique* (London: Rowman & Littlefield, 2017).

14. Plenary Session, Save the Children centenary conference, April 2019.

15. Karen Wells, 'Child Saving or Child Rights', *Journal of Children and Media* 2, no. 3 (2008): 235–50.

16. Children's Rights Workshop Session, Save the Children centenary conference, April 2019.

17. Ibid.

18. The United Nations Convention on the Rights of the Child (November 1989), at https://www.unicef.org.uk/what-we-do/un-convention-child-rights/ (last accessed 20 June 2020).

19. Save the Children, *A Practice Handbook: For Family Tracing and Reunification in Emergencies* (Save the Children Resource Centre, 2018), https://resourcecentre. savethechildren.net/library/practice-handbook-family-tracing-and-reunification-emergencies (last accessed 20 June 2020).

20. Shaheed Fatima, *Protecting Children in Armed Conflict* (London: Bloomsbury, 2018).

21. Save the Children, 'MPs Reject Dubs Amendment—Save the Children Response', London, 23 January 2020, https://www.savethechildren.org.uk/news/media-centre/press-releases/mp-reject-dubs-amendment-save-the-children-response (last accessed 20 June 2020).

22. My thinking has been influenced by Sophie Lewis, *Full Surrogacy Now: Feminism Against Family* (London: Verso, 2019).

23. Charlotte Riley, '"The Winds of Change are Blowing Economically": The Labour Party and British Overseas Development, 1940s–1960s', in *Britain, France and the Decolonisation of Africa: Future Imperfect?*, ed. Andrew W. M. Smith and Chris Jeppesen (London: UCL Press, 2017), 43–61.

24. Olivia Rutazibwa, 'What's there to Mourn? Decolonial Reflections on (the End of) Liberal Humanitarianism', *Journal of Humanitarian Affairs* 1, no. 1 (2019): 65–7.

25. Emily Baughan, 'Rehabilitating an Empire: Humanitarian Collusion with the Colonial State during the Kenyan Emergency, ca.1954–1960', *Journal of British Studies* 59, no. 1 (2020): 57–79.

26. This was covered in '"Prejudiced" Home Office Refusing Visas to African Researchers', *The Guardian*, 8 June 2019, https://www.theguardian.com/politics/2019/jun/08/home-office-racist-refusing-research-visas-africans (last accessed 20 June 2020).

27. Olivia Rutazibwa, 'On Babies and Bathwater: Decolonizing International Development Studies', in *Decolonization and Feminisms in Global Teaching and Learning*, ed. S. de Jong, R. Icaza, and O. U. Rutazibwa (Abingdon: Routledge, 2018), 158–80. See also https://medium.com/@aidreimagined (last accessed 20 June 2020).

28. Matthew Hilton, Emily Baughan, Eleanor Davey, Bronwen Everill, Kevin O'Sullivan, and Tehila Sasson, 'History and Humanitarianism: A Conversation', *Past & Present* 241, no. 1 (November 2018): 1–38.

3. THE RISE OF THE HUMANITARIAN CORPORATION: SAVE THE CHILDREN AND THE ORDERING OF EMERGENCY RESPONSE

1. Emily Baughan, *Saving the Children: Humanitarianism, Internationalism and the British Empire, c.1918–1970* (Berkeley, CA: University of California Press, 2021).

2. For comparison, Oxfam GB had an average annual turnover during the same period of £417.2 million.

3. John Francis Danby, *Shakespeare's Doctrine of Nature: A Study of King Lear* (London: Faber, 1948).

4. Ibid.

5. Juliano Fiori, Fernando Espada, Jessica Field, and Sophie Dicker, *The Echo Chamber* (London: Save the Children, 2016), 19.

6. John Borton, 'The Joint Evaluation of Emergency Assistance to Rwanda', *Humanitarian Exchange* 26 (March 2004): 14–18.

7. Fiori et al., *Echo Chamber*.

8. Ibid.

9. *Save the Children Global Programme Strategy* (London: Save the Children, 1997).

10. Ibid.

11. *SCUK Emergency Strategy 2000–2001* (London: Save the Children, 2000).

12. UK Government, *Iraq's Weapons of Mass Destruction: The Assessment of the British Government* (London, September 2002).

13. On 25 September 2002, *The Sun* newspaper ran the headline 'Brits 45 Mins from Doom' about the threat to troops in Cyprus.

14. SCUK press release, 13 September 2002.

15. Nicolas de Torrente, 'Humanitarian Action Under Attack: Reflections on the Iraq War', *Harvard Human Rights Journal* 17 (2004): 1–30.

16. US Secretary of State Colin Powell, 'Remarks to the National Foreign Policy Conference for Leaders of Nongovernmental Organizations' (Washington, DC: US Department of State, 26 October 2001).

17. As used by US General Tommy Franks in Qatar, March 2003, 'shock and awe' is the term for a military strategy based on achieving rapid dominance over an adversary by the initial imposition of overwhelming force and firepower.

18. Mike Aaronson, Internal memo to staff (SCUK, 25 March 2003).

19. Hugo Slim, 'How We Look: Hostile Perceptions of Humanitarian Action', Presentation to the Conference on Humanitarian Coordination, Wilton Park Montreux, 21 April 2004.

20. Ibid.

21. Ibid.

22. Michael Pirson, *Humanistic Management* (Cambridge: Cambridge University Press, 2017), 71.

23. The total raised was US$284 million. See https://www.savethechildren.org/content/dam/global/reports/emergency-humanitarian-response/tsunami-5yrs-09.pdf (last accessed 23 November 2020).

24. Clare Mulley, *The Woman who Saved the Children* (London: Oneworld, 2009).

25. Tony Waters, *Bureaucratizing the Good Samaritan: The Limitations of Humanitarian Relief Operations* (Oxford: Westview Press, 2001).

26. John Telford et al., *Joint Evaluation of the International Response to the Indian Ocean Tsunami* (London: Tsunami Evaluation Coalition, 2006).

27. Fiori et al., *Echo Chamber*.

28. SCUK, *Emergency Strategic Implementation Plan* (London: Save the Children, 2006).

29. Ibid.

30. Barney Tallack, *The Existential Funding Challenges for Northern INGOs* (Oxford: Averthur NGO Consulting, May 2020).

31. Timothy Heppell et al., 'The UK Government and the 0.7% International Aid Target: Opinion Among Conservative Parliamentarians', *British Journal of Politics and International Relations* 19, no. 4 (2017): 895–909.

32. Jasmine Whitbread, 'Protecting Aid is Good Politics and Good for Britain, it is also Right', *The Times*, 13 July 2009.

33. The Start Network, Elrha, and the Humanitarian Leadership Academy.

34. Richard Norton-Taylor, 'Mitchell v Fox, Armed Forces v Development Aid', *The Guardian*, 11 June 2011.

35. Heppell et al., 'The UK Government and the 0.7% International Aid Target'.

36. Lisa O'Carroll, 'World Leaders "Failing to Help" over Ebola Outbreak in Africa', *The Guardian*, 14 August 2014.

37. The MoD, DoH, DfID, FCO, UK Med, NHS, SCUK, and a Cuban Foreign Medical Team were all partners.

38. Harriet Sherwood, 'Save the Children Boss "Disappointed" Over Tony Blair Award Row', The Guardian, 28 November 2014.

39. Kevin Watkins, email to staff (SCUK, 22 May 2020).

40. Kevin Watkins, verbal comments to SCUK Corporate Senior Leadership Team (SCUK, 6 February 2020).

4. A PESTILENTIAL WORLD: PROMISES OF PROTECTION

1. Anon., *Toto and the Goats, and Tales from Ceylon*, Good Luck Series (London: Thomas Nelson & Sons, 1953), 141.

2. Aimé Césaire, 'And the Dogs Were Silent', in *Lyric and Dramatic Poetry, 1946–82* (Charlottesville, VA: University Press of Virginia, 1990), Act 1, p. 3.

3. United Nations High Commission for Refugees.

4. International Organization for Migration.

5. Mahmood Mamdani, 'The New Humanitarian Order', *The Nation*, 29 September 2008.

6. Ibid.

7. Fred Moten, *Black and Blur* (Durham, NC: Duke University Press, 2017).

8. Toni Morrison, *A Mercy* (London: Chatto & Windus, 2008), 90.

9. Michael Barnett, 'Humanitarianism Transformed', *Perspectives on Politics* 3, no. 4 (December 2005): 723–40.

10. Robin DiAngelo, *White Fragility* (Boston, MA: Beacon Press, 2018).

11. Didier Fassin and Mariella Pandolfi, 'Introduction: Military and Humanitarian Government in the Age of Intervention', in *Contemporary States of Emergency*, ed. Didier Fassin and Mariella Pandolfi (New York, NY: Zone Books, 2010), 9–27, 12.

12. Ibid.

13. Atiya Husain, 'Terror and Abolition', *Boston Review*, 11 June 2020, http://boston-review.net/race/atiya-husain-terror-and-abolition.

14. Barnett, 'Humanitarianism Transformed'.

15. Césaire, 'And the Dogs Were Silent', Act 1, p. 13.

16. Neel Ahuja, 'Postcolonial Critique in a Multispecies World', *PMLA* 124, no. 2 (March 2009): 556–63, 558.

17. Césaire, 'And the Dogs Were Silent', Act 1, pp. 1–2, 6.

5. THE MODERNITY AND LIBERAL VALUE OF HUMANITARIAN THINGS

1. Although this sudden surge in hospital capacity appears to have been largely under-utilised, as the hospital network redirected resources to meet the need in ICU beds.

2. Geoff Watts and Emma Wilkinson, 'What the NHS is Learning from the British Army in the Covid-19 Crisis', *BMJ* (May 2020), 369:m2055.

3. Alborz Shokrani et al., 'Exploration of Alternative Supply Chains and Distributed Manufacturing in Response to COVID-19: A Case Study of Medical Face Shields', *Materials & Design* 192 (July 2020): 108749.

4. World Health Organization, 'Shortage of Personal Protective Equipment Endangering Health Workers Worldwide', 3 March 2020, https://www.who.int/news-room/detail/03-03-2020-shortage-of-personal-protective-equipment-endangering-health-workers-worldwide (last accessed 2 June 2020).

5. 'Trump is Taking Hydroxychloroquine, White House Confirms', *The Guardian*, 20 May 2020, https://www.theguardian.com/us-news/2020/may/19/trump-hydroxychloroquine-covid-19-white-house (last accessed 2 June 2020).

6. T. T. Le, Z. Andreadakis, A, Kumar, R. G. Román, S. Tollefsen, M. Saville, and S. Mayhew, 'The COVID-19 Vaccine Development Landscape', *Nature Reviews Drug Discovery* 19, no. 5 (2020): 305–6.

7. Much of this definition work and some of its history was the work of Jean Pictet; see, inter alia, J. Pictet, 'The Formation of International Humanitarian Law', *International Review of the Red Cross* 34, no. 303 (1994): 526–31; J. Pictet, 'The Fundamental Principles of the Red Cross', *International Review of the Red Cross* 19, no. 210 (1979): 130–49.

8. Using actor network theory in this manner is not alien to humanitarians, and some at the heart of the humanitarian 'system' reflected in this way on the diffusion of information documents in the Federation of the Red Cross and Red Crescent. See William Hankey and Gabriel Pictet, 'Following Evidence from Production to Use at the International Federation of Red Cross and Red Crescent Societies: Where Does it All Go?', *Knowledge Management for Development Journal* 14, no. 1 (2019): 38–66.

9. In this sense, it is taking stock of the material turn identified by Frank Trentmann in 'Materiality in the Future of History: Things, Practices, and Politics', *Journal of British Studies* 48, no. 2 (2009): 283–307.

10. While Thomas Haskell has called for this broad interpretation, it is notable that later commenters focused most on consumption in his analysis of the market. See Thomas L. Haskell, 'Capitalism and the Origins of the Humanitarian Sensibility, Part 2', *The American Historical Review* 90, no. 3 (1985): 547–66.

11. This in contrast with so called multi-mandate organisations: see Dorothea Hilhorst and Eline Pereboom, 'Multi-Mandate Organisations in Humanitarian Aid', in *The New Humanitarians in International Practice*, ed. Zeynep Sezgin and Dennis Dijkzeul (Abingdon: Routledge, 2015), 85–102.

12. Édouard Vasseur, 'Pourquoi organiser des expositions universelles? Le "Succès" de l'exposition universelle de 1867', *Histoire, Économie et Société* 24, no. 4 (2005): 573–94.

13. Louise Purbrick, ed., *The Great Exhibition of 1851: New Interdisciplinary Essays* (Manchester: Manchester University Press, 2001).

14. Letter of Frédéric le Play, in Archives ICRC, AF 6–1–2 correspondance France 1863–73, 111; Volke Barth, 'Displaying Normalisation: The Paris Universal Exhibition of 1867', *Journal of Historical Sociology* 20, no. 4 (2007): 462–85.

15. Dr Gauvin, cited in *Exposition universelle de 1867 à Paris, catalogue général*, 2nd ed. (Paris, 1867), 1526.

16. C. H. Owen, 'Modern Artillery, as Exhibited at Paris in 1867', *Journal of the Royal United Services Institution* 12, no. 48 (1868): 90–104.

17. Tony Bennett, 'Exhibition, Truth, Power: Reconsidering "The Exhibitionary Complex"', in *The Documenta 14 Reader*, ed. Q. Latimer and A. Szymczyk (Munich: Prestel, 2017), 339–52.

18. Didier Fassin, *Humanitarian Reason: A Moral History of the Present* (Berkeley, CA: University of California Press, 2011).

19. David P. Forsythe, *The Humanitarians: The International Committee of the Red Cross* (Cambridge: Cambridge University Press, 2005).

20. Archives of ICRC, A, A, AF/24, 6 Exposition de San Francisco.

21. To be distinguished from disaster medicine, which has a more distinctly Cold War origin. See Cécile Stephanie Stehrenberger and Svenja Goltermann, 'Disaster Medicine: Genealogy of a Concept', *Social Science & Medicine* 120 (2014): 317–24.

22. A. Reverdin, 'Les Congrès de médecine et de pharmacie militaires', *Revue Internationale de la Croix-Rouge* 5, no. 56 (1923): 815–21.

23. De la Neutralité de la Médecine, 'Le Troisième Congrès International de la Neutralité de la Médecine, considérant que la coopération internationale est nécessaire pour apporter les garanties les plus sures d'efficacité en ce qui concerne la mission du médecin et de ses auxiliaires, et l'utilisation des moyens mis à leur disposition pour l'accomplissement de leur mission', in *Troisième Congrès International de la Neutralité de la Médecine* [1968], 418, https://international-review.icrc.org/sites/default/files/S0035336100140109a.pdf (last accessed 25 October 2020).

24. 'Congrès du Centenaire de la Croix-Rouge Internationale—Résolutions adoptées par le conseil des délégués', *International Review of the Red Cross* 45, no. 539 (November 1963): 541–67.

25. De la Neutralité de la Médecine 'Le Troisième Congrès International', 428; Hans-Ulrich Baer and Jacques Sanabria, 'History of the International Committee of Military Medicine', *Military Medicine* 167, suppl_3 (2002): 2–3.

26. DIHAD, which has run since 2004, claims to be the largest annual trade fair for the humanitarian sector: https://dihad.org/; meanwhile AIDex, which has been running since 2010 in Brussels, also claims to be the 'largest international event for the sector': https://www.aid-expo.com/visiting (last accessed 26 May 2020).

27. https://startnetwork.org/news-and-blogs/innovation-blockchain-and-world-humanitarian-summit; see also the following lists: https://www.agendaforhuman-ity.org/sites/default/files/resources/2017/Jul/ExhibitionFair-Participants-InnovationMarketplace-Booths.pdf; https://www.agendaforhumanity.org/sites/default/files/resources/2017/Jul/Exhibitor-List-WHS-2016.pdf (last accessed 25 October 2020). Thanks to Fernando Espada for these references.

28. https://hea.globalinnovationexchange.org/funding/world-humanitarian-summit-innovation-marketplace-showcase-application (last accessed 25 October 2020).

29. The World Humanitarian Summit's logistics were supported by a Turkish organisation close to President Erdogan. It had prior experience of humanitarian conferences and forums: https://www.aa.com.tr/en/turkey/turkish-first-lady-emine-erdogan-gets-changemaker-award/1455221 and https://www.whf.london/ (last accessed 25 October 2020). Thanks to Fernando Espada for these references.

30. *Association pour l'Assistance aux Mutilés Pauvres*, bulletin trimestriel (1878–85).

31. *Association pour l'Assistance aux Mutilés Pauvres*, no. 11 (October 1885).

32. Comte de Riencourt, *Les Blessés oubliés: les pensions militaires pour blessures et infirmités* (Abbeville: Paillart, 1882), 108–9.

33. Though one should be careful not to imagine the military marketplace to be orderly. See Richard V. N. Ginn, *The History of the U.S. Army Medical Service Corps* (Washington, DC: Office of the Surgeon General and Center of Military History, US Army, 1997), 21–4, on the collapse of procurement in the US army in 1899–1900, or the complexities arising again and again in subsequent conflicts: Albert L. Scott, 'The Procurement of Quartermaster Supplies during the World War', *Historical Outlook* 11, no. 4 (April 1920): 1–2; James C. Magee, 'Procurement of Medical Personnel and Matériel in the Present Emergency', *Journal of the American Medical Association* 117, no. 4 (1941): 253–5.

34. Archives CICR, AF35 1 Concours d'improvisation.

35. Bertrand Taithe, 'L'Humanitaire spectacle? Corps blessés et souffrance durant le siège de Paris', *Revue d'Histoire du XIXe Siècle* 60, no. 1 (2020): 177–90.

36. Katja Lindskov Jacobsen, *The Politics of Humanitarian Technology: Good Intentions, Unintended Consequences and Insecurity* (Abingdon: Routledge, 2015); Tom Scott-Smith, 'The Fetishism of Humanitarian Objects and the Management of Malnutrition in Emergencies', *Third World Quarterly* 34, no. 5 (2013): 913–28.

37. See Lola Wilhelm, '"One of the Most Urgent Problems to Solve": Malnutrition, Trans-Imperial Nutrition Science, and Nestlé's Medical Pursuits in Late Colonial Africa'. *The Journal of Imperial and Commonwealth History* 48.5 (2020): 914–933; and

Sébastie Farré, 'Sauver l'enfance de la faim (1914–1923): L'internationalisation des pratiques philanthropiques, *Relations Internationales* 161, no. 1 (2015): 13–26.

38. Bertrand Taithe, *Defeated Flesh* (Manchester: Manchester University Press, 1999), 116.

39. Thomas Richards, *The Commodity Culture of Victorian England: Advertising and Spectacle, 1851–1914* (Stanford, CA: Stanford University Press, 1990); Frank Trentmann, *The Making of the Consumer: Knowledge, Power and Identity in the Modern World* (Oxford: Berg, 2006).

40. Here, I wish to distinguish humanitarian sociodicy from the 'western sociodicy' associated with Christianity according to Fassin. See Nicolas Guilhot, 'The Anthropologist as Witness: Humanitarianism between Ethnography and Critique', *Humanity: An International Journal of Human Rights, Humanitarianism, and Development* 3, no. 1 (2012): 81–101, 98.

41. Jean-Paul Bado, *Médecine coloniale et grandes endémies en Afrique, 1900–1960: lèpre, trypanosomiase humaine et onchocercose* (Paris: Karthala Editions, 1996).

42. Institut de la Faculté de Médecine, *Les grandes endémies tropicales: études de pathogénie et de prophylaxie* (Paris: Vigot Frères, 1933).

43. Josiane Tantchou Yakam, 'Eugène Jamot: historiographie et hagiographie d'un médecin colonial', *Outre-Mers* 95, no. 360 (2008): 169–89.

44. Frederick Cooper, 'Conflict and Connection: Rethinking Colonial African History', *American Historical Review* 99, no. 5 (December 1994): 1516–45, 1533.

45. Maryinez Lyons, *The Colonial Disease: A History of Sleeping Sickness in Northern Zaire, 1900–1940* (Cambridge: Cambridge University Press, 1992); John Farley, *To Cast Out Disease: A History of the International Health Division of the Rockefeller Foundation (1913–1951)* (Oxford: Oxford University Press, 2004).

46. Marcos Cueto, *Cold War, Deadly Fevers: Malaria Eradication in Mexico, 1955–1975* (Baltimore, MD: Woodrow Wilson Center Press, 2007). On a positive reappraisal of DDT, see D. Roberts, R. Tren, R. Bate, and J. Zambone, *The Excellent Powder: DDT's Political and Scientific History* (Indianapolis, IN: Dog Ear Publishing, 2010).

47. Josiane Tantchou Yakam, 'De l'Impératif d'une "mise en valeur" à la sauvegarde des races indigènes? La lutte contre la maladie du sommeil au Cameroun français', *Canadian Journal of History* 44, no. 3 (2009): 411–34.

48. Inderjeet Parmar, *Foundations of the American Century: The Ford, Carnegie, and Rockefeller Foundations in the Rise of American Power* (New York, NY: Columbia University Press, 2012).

49. Guillaume Lachenal, 'Le Médecin qui voulut être roi: médecine coloniale et utopie au Cameroun', *Annales: Histoire, Sciences Sociales* 65, no. 1 (2010): 121–56.

50. Colin Jones, Paul Weindling, and Charles Rosenberg, eds., *International Health Organisations and Movements, 1918–1939* (Cambridge: Cambridge University Press, 1995).

51. Jessica Pearson-Patel, 'From the Civilizing Mission to International Development: France, the United Nations, and the Politics of Family Health in Postwar Africa, 1940–1960', PhD dissertation (New York University, 2013).

52. Jessica Pearson-Patel, 'Promoting Health, Protecting Empire: Inter-Colonial Medical Cooperation in Postwar Africa', *Monde(s)* 7, no. 1 (2015): 213–30.

53. Lee Kruger, *Logistics Matters and the U.S. Army in Occupied Germany, 1945–1949* (New York, NY: Springer, 2016); Frederick F. Aldridge, 'Contributions of the Sanitary Engineering Program of UNRRA to International Health', *Public Health Reports (1896–1970)* 62, no. 50 (December 1947): 1729–39.

54. Paul Weindling, 'Public Health and Political Stabilisation: The Rockefeller Foundation in Central and Eastern Europe between the Two World Wars', *Minerva* 31, no. 3 (1993): 253–67.

55. WHO archives, E17–374–2: *WHO Emergency Health Kit: Standard Drugs and Clinic for 10,000 Persons for 3 Months* (Geneva: World Health Organization, 1984).

56. WHO archives, E17–374–2: Letter from UNICEF to Dr Hogerzeil of WHO, 10 January 1989.

57. Bernard Pécoul et al., 'Access to Essential Drugs in Poor Countries: A Lost Battle?', *Journal of the American Medical Association* 281, no. 4 (1999): 361–7; Claudine Vidal and Jacques Pinel, 'MSF "Satellites": A Strategy Underlying Different Medical Practices', in *Medical Innovations in Humanitarian Situations: The Work of Médecins Sans Frontières*, ed. Jean-Hervé Bradol and Claudine Vidal (London: Hurst, 2011), 22–38.

58. Lisa Smirl, *Spaces of Aid: How Cars, Compounds and Hotels Shape Humanitarianism* (London: Zed Books, 2015); Roger Mac Ginty, 'A Material Turn in International Relations: The 4x4, Intervention and Resistance', *Review of International Studies* 43, no. 5 (2017): 855–74.

59. Marc Le Pape and Pierre Salignon, eds., *Une Guerre contre les civils: réflexions sur les pratiques humanitaires au Congo-Brazzaville, 1998–2000* (Paris: Karthala Editions, 2001).

60. Mustafa A. Ertem, Nebil Buyurgan, and Manuel D. Rossetti, 'Multiple–Buyer Procurement Auctions Framework for Humanitarian Supply Chain Management', *International Journal of Physical Distribution & Logistics Management* 40, no. 3 (2010): 202–27.

61. Médecins Sans Frontières, *Essential Drugs: Practical Guidelines* (Paris: MSF, 2008), 11.

62. Nidam Siawsh et al., 'Exploring the Role of Power on Procurement and Supply Chain Management Systems in a Humanitarian Organisation: A Socio-Technical Systems View', *International Journal of Production Research* (2019): 1–26.

63. Annet Blank and Gabrielle Zoe Marceau, 'A History of Multilateral Negotiations on Procurement: From ITO to WTO', in *Law and Policy in Public Purchasing: The WTO Agreement on Government Procurement*, ed. Bernard M. Hoekman and Petros C. Mavroidis (Ann Arbor, MI: University of Michigan Press, 1997), 31–55.

64. A. A. da Silva Lamenza, T. C. Fontainha, and A. Leiras, 'Purchasing Strategies for Relief Items in Humanitarian Operations', *Journal of Humanitarian Logistics and Supply Chain Management* 9, no. 2 (2019): 151–71.

65. Philippa Saunders, 'Donations of Useless Medicines to Kosovo Contributes to Chaos', *BMJ* 319, no. 7201 (1999): 11.

66. J. Schultz and T. Søreide, 'Corruption in Emergency Procurement', *Disasters* 32, no. 4 (2008): 516–36.

67. Timothy Edward Russell, 'The Humanitarian Relief Supply Chain: Analysis of the 2004 South East Asia Earthquake and Tsunami', thesis (Massachusetts Institute of Technology, 2005).

68. Aline Gatignon, Luk N. Van Wassenhove, and Aurélie Charles, 'The Yogyakarta Earthquake: Humanitarian Relief through IFRC's Decentralized Supply Chain', *International Journal of Production Economics* 126, no. 1 (2010): 102–10.

69. Nigel Wild and Li Zhou, 'Ethical Procurement Strategies for International Aid Non–Government Organisations', *Supply Chain Management* 16, no. 2 (2011): 110–27.

70. Jacques Pinel, 'Génériques, contrefaçon, qualité: quels médicaments pour les pays en voie de développement?', *Les Tribunes de la Santé* 1 (2005): 49–55.

71. Isabelle Andrieux-Meyer et al., 'Disparity in Market Prices for Hepatitis C Virus Direct-Acting Drugs', *The Lancet Global Health* 3, no. 11 (2015): e676–e677; Momoko Iwamoto et al., 'Identifying Optimal Care for Hepatitis C and Overcoming Barriers to Scale-Up: MSF Pilot Programme', *F1000Research* 7 (2018).

72. M. Jahre, L. Dumoulin, L. B. Greenhalgh, C. Hudspeth, P. Limlim, and A. Spindler, 'Improving Health in Developing Countries: Reducing Complexity of Drug Supply Chains', *Journal of Humanitarian Logistics and Supply Chain Management* 2, no. 1 (2012): 54–84.

73. Eric Chatelain and Jean-Robert Ioset, 'Drug Discovery and Development for Neglected Diseases: The DNDi Model', *Drug Design, Development and Therapy* 5 (2011): 175–81, 175.

74. Sharon Abramowitz, 'What Happens when MSF Leaves? Humanitarian Departure and Medical Sovereignty in Postconflict Liberia', in *Medical Humanitarianism: Ethnographies of Practice*, ed. Sharon Abramowitz and Catherine Panter-Brick (Philadelphia, PA: University of Pennsylvania Press, 2015), 137–54.

75. R. Lewin, M. Besiou, J-B. Lamarche, S. Cahill, and S. Guerrero-Garcia, 'Delivering in a Moving World... Looking to our Supply Chains to Meet the Increasing Scale, Cost and Complexity of Humanitarian Needs', *Journal of Humanitarian Logistics and Supply Chain Management* 8, no. 4 (2018): 518–32.

76. Tom Scott-Smith, 'Humanitarian Neophilia: The "Innovation Turn" and its Implications', *Third World Quarterly* 37, no. 12 (2016): 2229–51; Joël Glasman, *Humanitarianism and the Quantification of Human Needs* (Abingdon: Routledge, 2020), 92–122.

77. Jacobsen, *Politics of Humanitarian Technology*.

6. THE CONSCIENCE OF THE ISLAND? THE NGO MOMENT
IN AUSTRALIAN OFFSHORE DETENTION

1. This research was done independently. While it is based on published sources, I am grateful to all those who have helped me improve my understanding of the Australian

humanitarian and refugee sectors. I would like to thank Klaus Neumann, Gareth Owen, and the editors for their comments on earlier drafts. Special thanks are due to Juliano Fiori who was patient and generous, who kept faith in writing, while the world snarled and contracted under the weight of fire and fever.

2. Joanne McCarthy, 'Manus Machinations', *The Herald Sun*, 1 March 2014, 3.

3. Paul Farrell, 'Scott Morrison Contradicts First Account of Manus Island Unrest', *The Guardian*, 22 February 2014, https://www.theguardian.com/world/2014/feb/23/scott-morrison-contradicts-account-manus-island-unrest. (All URLs cited were last accessed 1 June 2020.)

4. Nick Evershed, 'Mandatory Immigration Detention is a Billion-Dollar Business—Analysis', *The Guardian*, 24 August 2015, https://www.theguardian.com/news/datablog/2014/aug/25/-sp-mandatory-immigration-detention-is-a-billion-dollar-business-analysis.

5. Suvendrini Perera, 'What is a Camp...?', *Borderlands* 1, no. 1 (2002), unpaginated [paragraph 21].

6. Guy Rundle, 'Offshore Detention is Sadism. The Camps are Labs for the Exploration of Human Suffering', *Crikey*, 21 August 2018, https://www.crikey.com.au/2018/08/21/offshore-detention-is-sadism; Niru Palanivel, in Helen Davidson, 'Nauru Files—Live', *The Guardian*, 10 August 2016 (accessed through NewsBank); Behrouz Boochani, *No Friend but the Mountains: Writing from Manus Prison* (Sydney: Pan Macmillan, 2018), 111; Richard Flanagan, 'Does Writing Matter?', *The Monthly*, October 2016.

7. 'Open Letter from RISE: Refugees, Survivors and Ex-Detainees to Save the Children-Australia and Overseas Board of Directors', 28 August 2016, http://riserefugee.org/open-letter-from-rise-refugees-survivors-and-ex-detainees-to-save-the-children-australia-overseas-board-of-directors/.

8. Department of Immigration and Citizenship, Manus Island Regional Processing Centre, Project Statement of Evidence, Submission 1 to Parliamentary Standing Committee on Public Works inquiry into 'Infrastructure and Upgrade Works to Establish a Regional Processing Centre on Manus Island, Papua New Guinea', 20 March 2013, 18, https://www.aph.gov.au/Parliamentary_Business/Committees/House_of_Representatives_Committees?url=pwc/regionalprocessing/report.htm.

9. See Madeline Gleeson, *Offshore: Behind the Wire on Manus and Nauru* (Sydney: NewSouth, 2016), 40–2, 144–7, and (on Chauka) 212–19.

10. Ibid., 24–33, 205–08.

11. Gabriella Sutherland, Submission 59 to Senate Legal and Constitutional Affairs References Committee inquiry into 'Serious Allegations of Abuse, Self-Harm and Neglect of Asylum Seekers in Relation to the Nauru Regional Processing Centre, and any like Allegations in Relation to the Manus Regional Processing Centre', March 2017, 2, https://www.aph.gov.au/Parliamentary_Business/Committees/Senate/Legal_and_Constitutional_Affairs/NauruandManusRPCs/Submissions.

12. Janet Phillips, 'Boat Arrivals and Boat "Turnbacks" in Australia since 1976: A Quick

Guide to the Statistics', Australian Parliamentary Library, last updated 17 January 2017, https://www.aph.gov.au/About_Parliament/Parliamentary_Departments/Parliamentary_Library/pubs/rp/rp1617/Quick_Guides/BoatTurnbacks.

13. David Scott FitzGerald, *Refuge Beyond Reach: How Rich Democracies Repel Asylum Seekers* (Oxford: Oxford University Press, 2019), 9.

14. Bill Frelick, Ian M. Kysel, and Jennifer Podkul, 'The Impact of Externalization of Migration Controls on the Rights of Asylum Seekers and Other Migrants', *Journal on Migration and Human Security* 4, no. 4 (2016): 190–220.

15. Tasman Heyes, cited in Klaus Neumann, *Refuge Australia: Australia's Humanitarian Record* (Sydney: UNSW Press, 2004), 82.

16. Neumann, *Refuge Australia*, 105.

17. Bob Furlonger, cited in ibid., 88.

18. 'RISE: Refugees, Survivors and eX-detainees Invasion Day Solidarity Statement—2020', 24 February 2020, http://riserefugee.org/rise-refugee-survivors-and-ex-detainees-invasion-day-solidarity-statement-2020/.

19. Anne McNevin, 'From Offshore Detention of Refugees to Indigenous Incarceration', Public Seminar, 18 December 2019, https://publicseminar.org/essays/from-offshore-detention-of-refugees-to-indigenous-incarceration/.

20. Amy Nethery, '"A Modern-day Concentration Camp": Using History to Make Sense of Australian Immigration Detention Centres', in *Does History Matter? Making and Debating Citizenship, Immigration and Refugee Policy in Australia and New Zealand*, ed. Klaus Neumann and Gwenda Tavan (Canberra: ANU Press, 2009), 65–80, 73.

21. Ruth Balint, '*Mare Nullius* and the Making of a White Ocean Policy', in *Our Patch: Enacting Australian Sovereignty Post-2001*, ed. Suvendrini Perera (Perth: Network Books, 2007), 87–104.

22. Perera, 'What is a Camp…?' [paragraph 36].

23. Public Interest Advocacy Centre, *Immigration Detention in Australia: The Loss of Decency and Humanity, Submission to the People's Inquiry into Immigration Detention* (Sydney, NSW: PIAC, 20 July 2006), https://piac.asn.au/wp-content/uploads/06.07-PIACSub-Peoples_Inquiry.pdf.

24. In the most recent iteration, immigration sits within the Department of Home Affairs. Australian National Audit Office (ANAO), *Procurement of Garrison Support and Welfare Services, Department of Home Affairs*, Auditor-General Report 37, 2019–20 (Canberra: ANAO, 2020), https://www.anao.gov.au/work/performance-audit/procurement-garrison-support-and-welfare-services.

25. See Zayne D'Crus, Kim Batchelor, and Vicki Mau, 'The Humanitarian Imperative to Assist Migrants', *Australian Outlook*, 11 January 2016, https://www.internationalaffairs.org.au/australianoutlook/the-humanitarian-imperative-to-assist-migrants/; ARC, 'Immigration Detention Monitoring', undated, https://www.redcross.org.au/about/how-we-help/migration-support/immigration-detention-monitoring-program.

26. Linda Briskman, 'Technology, Control, and Surveillance in Australia's Immigration Detention Centres', *Refuge* 29, no. 1 (2013): 9–19; Caroline Fleay, 'The Limitations

of Monitoring Immigration Detention in Australia', *Australian Journal of Human Rights* 21, no. 1 (2015): 21–46.

27. They also visited Manus Island in 2013. On unsuccessful requests, see 'Claims Probedo Brutal Conditions for Refugees on Island of Nauru', NPR Morning Edition, 11 August 2016, https://www.npr.org/2016/08/11/489584342/claims-probed-of-brutal-conditions-for-refugees-on-island-of-nauru.

28. See, for example, 'Contract in Relation to the Provision of Services in Regional Processing Countries, between the Commonwealth of Australia Represented by the Department of Immigration and Border Protection and Save the Children Australia', September 2014. Released under the Freedom of Information Act 1982 (FOI), https://www.righttoknow.org.au/request/2694/response/7582/attach/4/FA141000063%20Documents%20released.pdf.

29. Brett Neilson, 'Borderscape: Between Governance and Sovereignty: Remaking the Borderscape to Australia's North', *Local-Global: Identity, Security, Community* 8 (2010): 124–40, 127.

30. Sara Dehm, 'International Law at the Border: Refugee Deaths, the Necropolitical State and Sovereign Accountability', in *Routledge Handbook of International Law and the Humanities*, ed. Shane Chalmers and Sundhya Pahuja (Abingdon: Routledge, forthcoming), https://ssrn.com/abstract=3619656.

31. Neilson, 'Borderscape', 128.

32. Julie-Anne Davies, 'Abbott's New World Order', *The Age*, 15 November 2013, 16.

33. Suzanne Dvorak, 'Making the Best of Nauru', ABC News, 17 August 2012, https://www.abc.net.au/news/2012-08-17/woolverton-asylum-seekers/4205230.

34. SCA, *Save the Children Australia Annual Report 2004*, 4, https://www.savethechildren.org.au/getmedia/dbac74da-5438-4eb0-9c79-23580b32b056/2004_Annual_Report.pdf.aspx.

35. SCA, *Save the Children Australia Annual Report 2011*, 2, https://www.savethechildren.org.au/getmedia/39800cf6-5420-4104-9ed2-ff22d9b58bf9/2011 AnnualReport.pdf.aspx.

36. Joe Kelly and Ben Packham, 'Carr Confirms Aid Budget Shift', *The Australian*, 18 December 2012.

37. SCA, *Save the Children Australia Annual Report 2012*, 2, https://www.savethechildren.org.au/getmedia/f2e76952-16a0-4389-8944-6deef157ff10/2012_Annual_Report.pdf.aspx.

38. ANAO, *Offshore Processing Centres in Nauru and Papua New Guinea: Contract Management of Garrison Support and Welfare Services, Department of Immigration and Border Protection*, Auditor-General Report 32, 2016–17 (Canberra: ANAO, 2016), 23.

39. 'Joint Statement by Christian Leaders on the Passing of the Asylum Seeker Legislation', 2 September 2012, https://www.assembly.uca.org.au/news/item/1218-joint-statement-by-church-leaders-on-asylum-seekers; The Salvation Army, 'Statement on Involvement with Asylum Seekers in Nauru and Manus

Island', 10 September 2012 (henceforth TSA Statement), https://www.salvation-army.org.au/about-us/news-and-stories/media-newsroom/the-salvation-army-statement-on-involvement-with-asylum-seekers-in-nauru-and-manus-island/.

40. ANAO, *Offshore Processing Centres in Nauru and Papua New Guinea: Procurement of Garrison Support and Welfare Services, Department of Immigration and Border Protection*, Auditor-General Report 16, 2016–17 (Canberra: ANAO, 2016), 35.

41. Chris Bowen, 'Sri Lankan Voluntary Returns, People Smugglers, Regional Processing at Nauru', interview, John Laws Morning Show, 2SM, 25 September 2012, https://webarchive.nla.gov.au/awa/20130204000543/http://pandora.nla.gov.au/pan/67564/20130204–1043/www.minister.immi.gov.au/media/cb/2012/cb190051.htm.

42. Letter from Tracy Mackey to SCA Head of Humanitarian Emergency Response (Acting), 12 October 2012. Released under FOI, https://www.righttoknow.org.au/request/letter_of_intent_or_head_of_agre_2#incoming-17442.

43. Testimony of Gregory Lake, former employee at the Department of Immigration and Border Protection, Australian Human Rights Commission hearing, Sydney, 2 July 2014, https://www.humanrights.gov.au/sites/default/files/Mr%20Lake.pdf.

44. Save the Children Australia statement on 'Providing Support to Vulnerable Children on Manus Island', 21 November 2012, https://webarchive.nla.gov.au/awa/20130421032747/http://www.savethechildren.org.au/sites/noborders/provid-ing-support-to-vulnerable-children-on-manus-island/.

45. Paul Moulds, 'Response to Questions asked about the Involvement of The Salvation Army in Nauru and Manus Island', 6 November 2012, https://www.salvation-army.org.au/about-us/news-and-stories/media-newsroom/response-to-questions-asked-about-the-involvement-of-the-salvation-army-in-nauru-and-manus-island/.

46. SCA, 'Save the Children's Position on Children Being Detained in Nauru and Manus Island', undated, https://webarchive.nla.gov.au/awa/20150311053115/http://scasites.org.au/noborders/save-the-childrens-position-on-recommendations-from-the-expert-panel/.

47. Tony Kushner, 'Truly, Madly, Deeply... Nostalgically? Britain's On–Off Love Affair with Refugees, Past and Present', *Patterns of Prejudice* 52, nos. 2–3 (2018): 172–94.

48. Latika Bourke, 'Joe Hockey Refers to Asylum Seeker "Children Floating in Ocean" to Attack Labor's Border Protection Record', ABC News, 4 June 2014, https://www.abc.net.au/news/2014–06–04/labor-slams-asylum-seeker-com-ment/5500468. Other dynamics applied during earlier Pacific Solution debates.

49. Jordana Silverstein, '"Because We all Love our Country": Refugee and Asylum-Seeking Children, Australian Policy-Makers, and the Building of National Sentiment', *Australian Journal of Politics and History* 65, no. 4 (2019): 532–48, 539.

50. Gabby Sutherland, 'Appeal for the Children in Detention on Nauru', The Pen, 23 August 2018, http://the-pen.co/many-have-known-no-other-life/. See also, FAQ, #KIDSOFFNAURU campaign website, undated, https://www.kidsoffna-uru.com/faq.

51. 'Reaction to Australian Policy Reforms', *IRIN* [*The New Humanitarian*], 14 August 2012, http://www.thenewhumanitarian.org/news/2012/08/14/reaction-australian-policy-reforms.

52. Nick Evershed, 'Mandatory Immigration Detention is a Billion-Dollar Business—Analysis', *The Guardian*, 24 August 2015, https://www.theguardian.com/news/datablog/2014/aug/25/-sp-mandatory-immigration-detention-is-a-billion-dollar-business-analysis.

53. TSA Statement.

54. Peter McGuigan, 'An Open Door to Serve Desperate People', *Pipeline* 16, no. 10 (October 2012): 9–10.

55. 'Moulds Leave for PNG to Head up Asylum Seeker Ministry', www.mysalvos.org.au, 16 October 2012, https://my.salvos.org.au/news/2012/10/16/moulds-leave-for-png-to-head-up-asylum-seeker-ministry/.

56. 'No Advantage: Inside Australia's Offshore Processing Centres', ABC Four Corners, first broadcast 29 April 2013.

57. Oliver Laughland and Bridie Jabour, 'Salvation Army Humanitarian Work on Manus and Nauru to End', *The Guardian*, 13 December 2013, https://www.theguardian.com/world/2013/dec/13/salvation-army-humanitarian-work-on-manus-and-nauru-to-end.

58. Mark Isaacs, *The Undesirables: Inside Nauru* (Melbourne: Hardie Grant Books, 2014).

59. Tom Iggulden, 'Untrained Volunteers Become Counsellors to Detainees', ABC Lateline, first broadcast 12 June, 2014, https://www.abc.net.au/lateline/untrained-volunteers-become-counsellors-to/5520226.

60. Chris Shearer, 'Salvos Neglect Young Nauru, Manus Staff Suffering PTSD', *The Saturday Paper*, 14–20 February 2015; Nicole Hasham, 'Detention Centre Workers Suffering their own Trauma in Dealing with Asylum Seekers', *Sydney Morning Herald*, 26 February 2016.

61. Todagia Kelola, '40 Asylum Seekers Arrive', *PNG Post-Courier*, 14 January 2013, 5; SCA, Submission 4 to Parliamentary Standing Committee on Public Works inquiry into 'Infrastructure and Upgrade Works to Establish a Regional Processing Centre on Manus Island, Papua New Guinea', 19 April 2013, 9, https://www.aph.gov.au/Parliamentary_Business/Committees/House_of_Representatives_Committees?url=pwc/regionalprocessing/subs.htm.

62. SCA, Response to Submission 63 to Senate Select Committee inquiry into 'Recent Allegations Relating to Conditions and Circumstances at the Regional Processing Centre in Nauru', 29 May 2015, 3, https://www.aph.gov.au/Parliamentary_Business/Committees/Senate/Regional_processing_Nauru/Regional_processing_Nauru/Submissions.

63. SCA, *Save the Children Australia Annual Report 2014*, 52; SCA, *Save the Children Australia Annual Report 2015*, 57–8. Both at https://www.savethechildren.org.au/about-us/accountability/annual-reports. It is important to note that Save the Children International operates the majority of the network's humanitarian programmes, with SCA responsible for programmes in Australia and the Pacific.

64. Ben Doherty and David Marr, 'The Worst I've Seen—Trauma Expert Lifts Lid on "Atrocity" of Australia's Detention Regime', *The Guardian*, 20 June 2016, https://www.theguardian.com/australia-news/2016/jun/20/the-worst-ive-seen-trauma-expert-lifts-lid-on-atrocity-of-australias-detention-regime. Incident report of 26 September 2014, https://interactive.guim.co.uk/2016/08/nu-files/pdf/sca140775.pdf.

65. Linda Briskman and Jane Doe, 'Social Work in Dark Places: Clash of Values in Offshore Immigration Detention', *Social Alternatives* 35, no. 4 (2016): 73–9. Based on the indicated timeframe, this worker is likely to have been employed by TSA, but their description of conditions is applicable to all contracted employees.

66. Jordana Silverstein, '"I Am Responsible": Histories of the Intersection of the Guardianship of Unaccompanied Child Refugees and the Australian Border', *Cultural Studies Review* 22, no. 2 (2016): 65–89.

67. Philip Moss, *Review into Recent Allegations Relating to Conditions and Circumstances at the Regional Processing Centre in Nauru: Final Report* (6 February 2015), 76–80, https://www.homeaffairs.gov.au/reports-and-pubs/files/review-conditions-circumstances-nauru.pdf.

68. Stewart Firth, 'Australia's Detention Centre and the Erosion of Democracy in Nauru', *Journal of Pacific History* 51, no. 3 (2016): 286–300.

69. Paul Ronalds, *The Nauru Dilemma*, Development Policy Centre Discussion Paper 51 (12 December 2016), 10. Ronalds did not comment on the Manus phase, which predated his tenure.

70. See https://www.legislation.gov.au/Details/C2013A00056.

71. SCA submissions and testimonies to the following inquiries: Parliamentary Standing Committee on Public Works inquiry into 'Infrastructure and Upgrade Works to Establish a Regional Processing Centre on Manus Island, Papua New Guinea' (2013); AHRC, 'National Inquiry into Children in Immigration Detention' (2014); Senate Select Committee inquiry into 'Recent Allegations Relating to Conditions and Circumstances at the Regional Processing Centre in Nauru' (2015).

72. See allusions to this in Bec Zajac, 'More Australians Wanting to Blow the Whistle on Manus Island and Nauru Conditions', *The Citizen*, 23 January 2015, https://www.thecitizen.org.au/articles/more-australians-wanting-blow-whistle-manus-island-and-nauru-conditions; Shearer, 'Salvos Neglect Young Nauru, Manus Staff Suffering PTSD'; Q&A session following 'The Nauru Dilemma' public seminar with Paul Ronalds, Crawford School of Public Policy, Australian National University, 17 October 2016, https://soundcloud.com/devpolicy/the-nauru-dilemma.

73. 'Open Letter on the Border Force Act: "We Challenge the Department to Prosecute"', *The Guardian*, 1 July 2015, https://www.theguardian.com/australia-news/2015/jul/01/open-letter-on-the-border-force-act-we-challenge-the-department-to-prosecute.

74. On the Pacific Solution phase, see Kelly Jean Butler, *Witnessing Australian Stories: History, Testimony, and Memory in Contemporary Culture* (New Brunswick, NJ: Transaction Publishers, 2013), 151–84. See also Frederick M. Burkle, Jimmy

T. S. Chan, and Richard D. S. Yeung, 'Hunger Strikers: Historical Perspectives from the Emergency Management of Refugee Camp Asylum Seekers', *Prehospital and Disaster Medicine* 28, no. 6 (2013): 625–9; and Nicolas Fischer, 'The Management of Anxiety: An Ethnographical Outlook on Self-mutilations in a French Immigration Detention Centre', *Journal of Ethnic and Migration Studies* 41, no. 4 (2015): 599–616.

75. Anon., Submission to Australian Human Rights inquiry on 'Children in Detention', undated [2014], 1, https://humanrights.gov.au/our-work/asylum-seekers-and-refugees/submissions-made-inquiry.

76. Ibid., 9

77. Ibid., 18.

78. Simon Miller and Sophie Coleman, 'Legal Aspects of Managing Government Service Delivery Contracts in Complex Environments', *International In-House Counsel Journal* 8, no. 32 (2015): 9.

79. Mat Tinkler and Lisa Button, Submission 7 to Senate Legal and Constitutional Affairs Committee inquiry into 'the Australian Border Force Amendment (Protected Information) Bill 2017', 28 August 2017, 1, https://www.aph.gov.au/Parliamentary_Business/Committees/Senate/Legal_and_Constitutional_Affairs/ABFProtectedInfo2017/Submissions.

80. Max Chalmers, 'Nauru: You Don't Have to Be Indifferent to Work Here, But it Helps', *New Matilda*, 25 March 2015, https://newmatilda.com/2015/03/25/nauru-you-dont-have-be-indifferent-work-here-it-helps/.

81. Scott Morrison, 'Nauru, Burqa', press conference, Canberra, 3 October 2014, https://webarchive.nla.gov.au/awa/20141221233755/http://pandora.nla.gov.au/pan/143035/20141222–1032/www.minister.immi.gov.au/media/sm/2014/sm218347.htm.

82. Sarah Maddison and Clive Hamilton, 'Non-Government Organisations', in *Silencing Dissent: How the Australian Government is Controlling Public Opinion and Stifling Debate*, ed. Clive Hamilton and Sarah Maddison (Crows Nest, NSW: Allen and Unwin, 2007), 81.

83. Spencer Zifcak, *Mr Ruddock Goes to Geneva* (Sydney: UNSW Press, 2003).

84. 'Four Children Among Manus Island Transfers', Channel 9 News, 12 November 2012, https://www.9news.com.au/world/asylum-seekers-arrive-in-manus/899cec13-ef22-4b09-87e1-c250bfcbd8c5; 'Australians Sick of UN Lectures: Abbott', SBS News, 9 March 2015, https://www.sbs.com.au/news/australians-sick-of-un-lectures-abbott.

85. Ronalds, *The Nauru Dilemma*, 10.

86. 'What Happens when an Aid Group sees Abuse, But is Sworn to Secrecy?', NPR Morning Edition, 25 August 2016, https://www.npr.org/sections/parallels/2016/08/25/491311775/aid-worker-australian-treatment-of-migrants-in-nauru-is-a-stain.

87. Paul Ronalds, Testimony to Senate Select Committee on the Regional Processing Centre in Nauru, 19 May 2015, 48, https://parlinfo.aph.gov.au/parlInfo/

download/committees/commsen/9b9f7adf-e087-4332-a0b1-739986784d11/
toc_pdf/Regional%20Processing%20Centre%20in%20Nauru_2015_
05_19_3468_Official.pdf;fileType=application%2Fpdf#search=%22committ
ees/commsen/9b9f7adf-e087-4332-a0b1-739986784d11/0000%22.

88. Gleeson, *Offshore*, 124.

89. Miller and Coleman, 'Legal Aspects', 11.

90. Mat Tinkler, in 'What Happens when an Aid Group sees Abuse, But is Sworn to Secrecy?'.

91. Alyssa Munoz, in 'Nauru: In Conversation with Alyssa Munoz', Podsocs, hosted by Patricia Fronek, 23 November 2016, https://www.podsocs.com/podcast/nauru/.

92. SCA, 'Nauru—Holistic Support Approach', December 2014, 2. The original page hosting this document on the SCA website has expired and I am grateful to Simon Miller for sharing it and the SCA history cited in the conclusion.

93. Ibid., 3.

94. Paul Farrell, 'Nauru Detention Centre Staff Warned not to Speak about "Anything that Happens"', *The Guardian*, 6 July 2015, https://www.theguardian.com/australia-news/2015/jul/06/detention-centre-staff-warned-not-to-speak-out-nauru.

95. Chris Graham and Max Chalmers, 'Inside the Department: The Explosive Leaked Transcripts from the Moss Review', *New Matilda*, 13 March 2015, https://newmatilda.com/2015/03/13/inside-department-explosive-leaked-transcripts-moss-review/.

96. Simon Benson, 'Truth Overboard', *The Daily Telegraph*, 3 October 2014, 1.

97. Ronalds, *The Nauru Dilemma*, 13–14.

98. Scott Morrison, 'Nauru, Burqa', press conference, Canberra, 3 October 2014.

99. Perera, 'What is a Camp…?' [paragraphs 45–6].

100. Paul Ronalds, 'We Want the Truth to Come Out on Nauru', *The Daily Telegraph*, 8 October 2014, 21.

101. Adam Morton, 'Save the Children Staff Accused and Deported from Nauru Demand an Explanation', *Sydney Morning Herald*, 4 October 2015.

102. Moss, *Review into Recent Allegations*.

103. Alex McDonald, 'Save the Children Office Raided by Police in Nauru; Phones, Computers Confiscated', ABC News, 13 October 2015, https://www.abc.net.au/news/2015-10-13/save-the-children-nauru-office-raided-by-police/6850834.

104. Ronalds, *The Nauru Dilemma*, 17.

105. Nick Evershed, Ri Liu, Paul Farrell, and Helen Davidson, 'Nauru Files Interactive Database', *The Guardian*, 16 August 2016, https://www.theguardian.com/australia-news/ng-interactive/2016/aug/10/the-nauru-files-the-lives-of-asylum-seekers-in-detention-detailed-in-a-unique-database-interactive.

106. Helen Davidson, 'Former Save the Children Workers Say Nauru Files "Just the Tip of the Iceberg"', *The Guardian*, 10 August 2016, https://www.theguardian.

com/news/2016/aug/10/former-save-the-children-workers-say-nauru-files-just-the-tip-of-the-iceberg.

107. 'Ex-Aid Worker: Abuse of Refugee Children on Nauru was Mostly Ignored', NPR Morning Edition, 24 August 2016, https://www.npr.org/sections/parallels/2016/08/24/491170178/ex-aid-worker-abuse-of-refugee-children-on-nauru-was-ignored.

108. 'Open Letter from RISE: Refugees, Survivors and Ex-Detainees to Save the Children-Australia and Overseas Board of Directors'.

109. Rony Brauman, 'Refugee Camps, Population Transfers, and NGOs', in *Hard Choices: Moral Dilemmas in Humanitarian Intervention*, ed. Jonathan Moore (Lanham, MD: Rowman & Littlefield, 1998), 177–94, 192.

110. Jennifer Rubenstein, *Between Samaritans and States: The Political Ethics of Humanitarian INGOs* (Oxford: Oxford University Press, 2015).

111. Ronalds, Testimony to Senate Select Committee on the Regional Processing Centre in Nauru, 49.

112. *A History of Save the Children Australia*, undated [after 2005], 6–7.

113. Emily Baughan, 'Rehabilitating an Empire: Humanitarian Collusion with the Colonial State during the Kenyan Emergency, ca.1954–1960', *Journal of British Studies* 59, no. 1 (2020): 57–79, 58.

7. RIGHTS-BEARING MIGRANTS AND THE RIGHTFULNESS OF THEIR RESCUE: THE EMERGENCE OF A 'NEW MODEL OF HUMANITARIAN ENGAGEMENT' AT EUROPE'S BORDERS

1. I thank Fernando Espada, Juliano Fiori, Andrea Rigon, and Karina Horsti for their helpful comments on earlier versions of this chapter.

2. This and dozens of other first-person statements by crew members appear on the SOS MEDITERRANEE website: https://sosmediterranee.com/log/logbook-69-we-are-not-necessarily-giving-them-a-better-life-but-they-get-a-chance-of-having-one-a-chance-of-living/ (last accessed 31 March 2020).

3. Juliano Fiori, 'Rescue and Resistance in the Med: An Interview with Caroline Abu Sa'Da, General Director of SOS MEDITERRANEE Suisse', *Journal of Humanitarian Affairs* 1, no. 1 (2019): 62–4, 62.

4. I use the term 'irregularised migrant' to denote migrants with precarious legal status over that of the more common 'irregular migrant', because the passive form draws attention to the fact that a person's 'irregular' status is the outcome of nation-states' policies, rather than an intrinsic personal attribute.

5. Until April 2020, SOS MEDITERRANEE operated these vessels in partnership with Médecins Sans Frontières (MSF). The partnership ended in April 2020, because MSF wanted to continue patrolling the Central Mediterranean, while SOS MEDITERRANEE wanted to suspend operations due to the decision by European states to close their ports to vessels carrying rescued migrants because of the COVID-19 pandemic: 'Aid Group MSF Splits with Partner over Migrant Rescues', *The New York Times*, 17 April 2020, https://www.nytimes.com/aponline/2020/04/17/

world/europe/ap-eu-migrants-mediterranean-rescue-.html (last accessed 29 April 2020). SOS MEDITERRANEE resumed its operations on 22 June 2020.

6. https://sosmediterranee.com/about-us/ (last accessed 15 February 2020).

7. Simon McMahon and Nando Sigona, *Boat Migration Across the Central Mediterranean: Drivers, Experiences and Responses*, Unravelling the Mediterranean Migration Crisis (MEDMIG) Research Brief 3 (September 2016), https://www.fieri.it/wp-content/uploads/2015/02/research-brief-03-Boat-migration-across-the-Central-Mediterranean.pdf (last accessed 31 March 2020); Frontex Risk Analysis Unit, *Risk Analysis for 2019* (Warsaw: Frontex, 2019), https://frontex.europa.eu/assets/Publications/Risk_Analysis/Risk_Analysis/Risk_Analysis_for_2019.pdf (last accessed 31 March 2020).

8. The Missing Migrants Project of the International Organization for Migration (IOM) began counting the number of border-related deaths only in 2013: https://missingmigrants.iom.int/region/mediterranean (last accessed 15 February 2020). For fatalities in the Mediterranean in earlier years, see Gabriele Del Grande's blog, http://fortresseurope.blogspot.com/p/la-strage.html (last accessed 15 February 2020).

9. Paolo Cuttitta, Jana Häberlein, and Polly Pallister-Wilkins, 'Various Actors: The Border Death Regime', in *Border Deaths: Causes, Dynamics and Consequences of Migration-Related Mortality*, ed. Paolo Cuttitta and Tamara Last (Amsterdam: Amsterdam University Press, 2019), 35–51, 38.

10. On *Operation Mare Nostrum*, see Alessio Patalano, 'Night*mare Nostrum*? Not Quite: Lessons from the Italian Navy in the Mediterranean Migrant Crisis', *RUSI Journal* 160, no. 3 (2015): 14–19; and Stefania Panebianco, *The Mare Nostrum Operation and the SAR Approach: The Italian Response to Address the Mediterranean Migration Crisis*, EUMedEA Online Working Paper 3 (2016), http://www.dsps.unict.it/sites/default/files/files/panbianco_EUMedEA_JMWP_03_2016_.pdf (last accessed 15 February 2020).

11. Félix Vacas Fernández, 'The European Operations in the Mediterranean Sea to Deal with Migration as a Symptom: From the Italian Operation *Mare Nostrum* to Frontex Operations *Triton* and *Poseidon*, EUNAVFOR-MED and NATO's Assistance in the Aegean Sea', *Spanish Yearbook of International Law* 20 (2016): 98–101; see also Martina Tazzioli, 'Border Displacements: Challenging the Politics of Rescue between Mare Nostrum and Triton', *Migration Studies* 4, no. 1 (2016): 1–19.

12. The IOM's Missing Migrants Project recorded 2,036 deaths in the Central Mediterranean in the first six months of 2015, and 703 deaths in the first six months of 2014: https://missingmigrants.iom.int/region/mediterranean?migrant_route%5B%5D=1376 (last accessed 30 March 2020).

13. For a list of organisations active between 2016 and 2019, see https://fra.europa.eu/en/publication/2019/2019-update-ngo-ships-involved-search-and-rescue-mediterranean-and-criminal (last accessed 15 February 2020).

14. On individual NGOs and the differences between them, see Paolo Cuttitta, 'Repoliticization through Search and Rescue? Humanitarian NGOs and Migration Management in the Central Mediterranean', *Geopolitics* 23, no. 3 (2018): 632–60;

Özgün E. Topak, 'Humanitarian and Human Rights Surveillance: The Challenge to Border Surveillance and Invisibility?', *Surveillance & Society* 17, nos. 3–4 (2019): 382–404; and Maurice Stierl, 'A Fleet of Mediterranean Border Humanitarians', *Antipode* 50, no. 3 (2018): 704–24. On the approach of MSF, in particular, see Hernan del Valle, 'Search and Rescue in the Mediterranean Sea: Negotiating Political Differences', *Refugee Survey Quarterly* 35, no. 2 (2016): 22–40. On Proactiva Open Arms, see Gemma Álvarez-Jiménez and Maria Padrós-Cuxart, 'How Solidarity Influences Political Actors to Manage the Refugee Crisis: The Case of Proactiva Open Arms', *RIMCIS* 6, no. 2 (2017): 215–29. Some of the private vessels carrying out SAR operations have been jointly operated by two NGOs; for example, SOS MEDITERRANEE and MSF have teamed up to run first the *Aquarius* and then the *Ocean Viking*. Other NGOs have operated more than one vessel at a time. Most of these NGOs are from Germany, while others are based in Spain or Italy. SOS MEDITERRANEE is unusual in that it is a European organisation with branches in Switzerland, France, Germany, and Italy.

15. The Evangelische Kirche Deutschlands (EKD), a federation of twenty Protestant churches in Germany, has, however, been a major funder of SAR missions in the Mediterranean and is a key backer of United4Rescue, an alliance of organisations that has bought and will fund the *Sea-Watch 4* (which will be operated by Sea-Watch and patrol the Central Mediterranean from mid-2020): https://www.united4rescue.com/ (last accessed 15 February 2020).

16. MOAS is currently providing humanitarian assistance to victims of the civil war in Yemen and to Rohingya refugees in Bangladesh. In 2017, it was also assisting UNHCR in evacuating a small group of migrants from Libya to Niger. See https://www.moas.eu/about/ (last accessed 15 February 2020).

17. Thomas Spijkerboer, 'The Human Costs of Border Control', *European Journal of Migration and Law* 9 (2007): 127–39; Kira Williams and Alison Mountz, 'Between Enforcement and Precarity: Externalization and Migrant Deaths at Sea', *International Migration* 56, no. 5 (2018): 74–89.

18. https://sosmediterranee.com/about-us/ (last accessed 15 February 2020), emphasis added.

19. https://www.openarms.es/en/who-are-we (last accessed 27 April 2020). Here, the stance of MSF does not substantially differ from that of NGOs like SOS MEDITERRANEE and Open Arms. MSF believes its presence in the Mediterranean is needed not just to save lives but also 'to witness and speak out about the human costs of the policies and politics at play in the Mediterranean Sea' (http://searchandrescue.msf.org/, last accessed 15 February 2020). Since 2016, MSF has not accepted funding from the EU or individual EU member states, 'in opposition to their damaging deterrence policies on migration and their intensifying attempts to push people away from European shores' (https://www.msf.org/reports-and-finances#ifr, last accessed 15 February 2020).

20. https://sea-watch.org/en/ (last accessed 15 February 2020), emphasis added.

21. Luca Giliberti and Luca Queirolo Palmas, 'Solidarities in Transit on the French–Italian Border: Ethnographic Accounts from Ventimiglia and the Roya Valley', in

Migration, Borders and Citizenship: Between Policy and Public Spheres, ed. Maurizio Ambrosini, Manlio Cinalli, and David Jacobson (Cham: Palgrave Macmillan, 2020), 109–40.

22. For an example of this comparison, see Adam Nossiter, 'A French Underground Railroad, Moving African Migrants', *The New York Times*, 4 October 2016, https://www.nytimes.com/2016/10/05/world/europe/france-italy-migrants-smuggling.html (last accessed 15 February 2020). The historical analogy has also been used to refer to the movement of asylum seekers from Central America to the United States, and from the United States to Canada. See, for example, Jake Halpern, 'The Underground Railroad for Refugees', *The New Yorker*, 6 March 2017, https://www.newyorker.com/magazine/2017/03/13/the-underground-railroad-for-refugees (last accessed 21 April 2020). On these analogies, see also Maurice Stierl, 'Of Migrant Slaves and Underground Railroads: Movement, Containment, Freedom', *American Behavioral Scientist* 64, no. 4 (2020): 456–79.

23. Harald Höppner and Veronica Frenzel, *Menschenleben retten! Mit der Sea-Watch im Mittelmeer* (Köln: Eichborn, 2016), 20.

24. Sea-Watch, 'FAQ', answer to question #1, https://sea-watch.org/en/project/faq/#1549900776699–0f40b18b-577e (last accessed 25 April 2020).

25. Since 2015, Sea-Watch has successively increased the size of its rescue vessels. The first *Sea-Watch* was a 21-metre trawler; the most recent vessel, *Sea-Watch 4*, is a 60-metre former research ship, which is capable of accommodating hundreds of rescued migrants.

26. Roya Citoyenne, *Report d'activités 2017* (Saorge [2018]), 1, http://www.roya-citoyenne.fr/wp-content/uploads/2018/05/rc-rapport-dactivite-2017–1.pdf (last accessed 15 February 2020). In 2016, the municipality of Ventimiglia 'used food-hygiene concerns to prohibit food distribution to migrants': European Union Agency for Fundamental Rights, *Fundamental Rights Report 2019* (Luxembourg: Publications Office of the European Union, 2019), 134.

27. On the 'solidarity offence' in France, see Benjamin Boudou, 'The Solidarity Offense in France: Égalité, Fraternité, Solidarité!', *Verfassungsblog on Matters Constitutional*, 6 July 2018, https://verfassungsblog.de/the-solidarity-offense-in-france-egalite-fraternite-solidarite/ (last accessed 15 February 2020); Brigitte Bouquet, 'Le délit de solidarité en débat', *Vie Sociale* 27 (2019): 187–200; and Groupe d'information et de soutien des immigrées, 'Les délits de la solidarité', https://www.gisti.org/spip.php?article1399 (last accessed 31 March 2020). On Herrou, see the French documentary film *Libre* [*To the Four Winds*], directed by Michel Toesca, (SaNoSi Productions, 2018); and Janina Pescinski, 'Humanitarian Citizens: Breaking the Law to Protect Human Rights', openDemocracy, 28 August 2017, https://www.opendemocracy.net/en/mediterranean-journeys-in-hope/humanitarian-citizens-breaking-law-to-protect-human-/ (last accessed 25 April 2020).

28. For an overview of recent cases, see Liz Fekete, Frances Webber, and Anya Edmond-Pettitt, *Humanitarianism: The Unacceptable Face of Solidarity* (London: Institute of Race Relations, 2017); Sara Bellezza and Tiziana Calandrino, eds.,

Criminalization of Flight and Escape (Berlin: borderline-europe—Menschenrechte ohne Grenzen, 2017); Sergio Carrera et al., *Fit for Purpose? The Facilitation Directive and the Criminalisation of Humanitarian Assistance to Irregular Migrants: 2018 Update* (Brussels: Policy Department for Citizens' Rights and Constitutional Affairs, European Parliament, 2018); Yasha Maccanico et al., *The Shrinking Space for Solidarity with Migrants and Refugees: How the European Union and Member States Target and Criminalize Defenders of the Rights of People on the Move* (Amsterdam: Transnational Institute, 2018); Liz Fekete, Frances Webber, and Anya Edmond-Pettitt, *When Witnesses Won't Be Silenced: Citizens' Solidarity and Criminalisation*, Briefing Paper 13 (London: Institute of Race Relations, 2019); and Lina Vosyliūtė and Carmine Conte, *Crackdown on NGOs and Volunteers Helping Refugees and Other Migrants*, Final Synthetic Report (ReSOMA, 2019), http://www.resoma.eu/sites/resoma/resoma/files/policy_brief/pdf/Final%20Synthetic%20Report%20-%20Crackdown%20on%20NGOs%20and%20volunteers%20helping%20refugees%20and%20other%20migrants_1.pdf (last accessed 21 April 2020). See also Ana López-Sala and Iker Barbero, 'Solidarity under Siege: The Crimmigration of Activism(s) and Protest against Border Control in Spain', *European Journal of Criminology*, pre-print online publication (2019), https://doi.org/10.1177/1477370819882908; and Martina Tazzioli and William Walters, 'Migration, Solidarity and the Limits of Europe', *Global Discourse* 9, no. 1 (2019): 175–90.

29. Karina Horsti and Carolina S. Boe, 'Anti-Racism from the Margins: Welcoming Refugees at Schengen's Northernmost Border', in *Racialization, Racism, and Anti-Racism in the Nordic Countries*, ed. Peter Hervik (Cham: Palgrave Macmillan, 2019), 183–201.

30. Damien Gayle, 'Stansted 15: No Jail for Activists Convicted of Terror-Related Offences', *The Guardian*, 6 February 2019, https://www.theguardian.com/global/2019/feb/06/stansted-15-rights-campaigners-urge-judge-to-show-leniency (last accessed 15 February 2020); Fekete, Webber, and Edmond-Pettitt, *When Witnesses Won't Be Silenced*, 22. In January 2021, following an appeal, the convictions of the Stansted 15 were overturned.

31. Melissa Vida, '"Crimes of Solidarity" in Europe Multiply as 11 Stand Trial in Belgium for Helping Migrants', *Global Voices*, 17 September 2018, https://globalvoices.org/2018/09/17/crimes-of-solidarity-in-europe-multiply-as-11-stand-trial-in-belgium-for-helping-migrants/ (last accessed 15 February 2020).

32. Article 1(1a), Council of the European Union, 'Council Directive 2002/90/EC Defining the Facilitation of Unauthorised Entry, Transit and Residence' (Brussels, 28 November 2002). The Facilitation Directive needs to be read in conjunction with 'Preventing the Facilitation of Unauthorised Entry Council Framework Decision 2002/946/JHA' (Brussels, 28 November 2002); together, the two European Council documents form the so-called 'Facilitators Package'. For critical reviews that were commissioned by the European Parliament, see Carrera et al., *Fit for Purpose?* (2018); and Sergio Carrera et al., *Fit for Purpose? The Facilitation Directive and the Criminalisation of Humanitarian Assistance to Irregular Migrants*

(Brussels: Policy Department for Citizens' Rights and Constitutional Affairs, European Parliament, 2016).

33. Article 1(2), Council of the European Union, 'Council Directive 2002/90/EC'.

34. Carrera et al., *Fit for Purpose?* (2018), 40.

35. Fekete, Webber, and Edmond-Pettitt, *When Witnesses Won't Be Silenced*, 5–10.

36. The latter claim has been convincingly disproven: see, for example, Eugenio Cusumano and Matteo Villa, *Sea Rescue NGOs: A Pull Factor of Irregular Migration?*, Migration Policy Centre Policy Brief 2019/22 (European University Institute; Robert Schuman Centre for Advanced Studies, 2019), https://cadmus.eui.eu/bitstream/handle/1814/65024/pb_2019_22_mpc.pdf (last accessed 15 February 2020).

37. Klaus Neumann, 'The Appeal of "Civil Disobedience" in the Central Mediterranean: German Responses to the June 2019 Mission of the *Sea-Watch 3*', *Journal of Humanitarian Affairs* 2, no. 1 (2020): 53–61.

38. Klaus Neumann, 'Waving, But Also Drowning', *Inside Story*, 24 July 2018, https://insidestory.org.au/waving-but-drowning/ (last accessed 25 April 2020).

39. The question of how international law is relevant here has attracted a large body of scholarship; see, for example, Tullio Scovazzi, 'Human Rights and Immigration at Sea', in *Human Rights and Immigration*, ed. Ruth Rubio-Marín (Oxford: Oxford University Press, 2014), 212–60; Thomas Spijkerboer, 'Wasted Lives: Borders and the Right to Life of People Crossing Them', *Nordic Journal of International Law* 86 (2017): 1–29; Kristof Gombeer and Melanie Fink, 'Non-Governmental Organisations and Search and Rescue at Sea', *Maritime Safety and Security Law Journal* 4 (2018): 1–5; Giorgia Bevilacqua, 'The Right to Life at Sea: Seventy Years After the Proclamation of the Universal Declaration of Human Rights', *Europa Ethnica* 76, nos. 3–4 (2019): 149–54; and Giorgia Bevilacqua, 'Italy versus NGOs: The Controversial Interpretation and Implementation of Search and Rescue Obligations in the Context of Migration at Sea', *Italian Yearbook of International Law Online* 28 (2019): 11–27.

40. International Maritime Organization, International Chamber of Shipping, and Office of the United Nations High Commissioner for Refugees, *Rescue at Sea: A Guide to Principles and Practice as Applied to Refugees and Migrants* (UNHCR, January 2015), 4.

41. Council of Europe Commissioner for Human Rights, *Lives Saved. Rights Protected. Bridging the Protection Gap for Refugees and Migrants in the Mediterranean* (Strasbourg, 30 June 2019), 8.

42. Virginia Passalacqua, 'The 'Open Arms' Case: Reconciling the Notion of "Place of Safety" with the Human Rights of Migrants', *Ejil:Talk!*, 21 May 2018, https://www.ejiltalk.org/the-open-arms-case-reconciling-the-notion-of-place-of-safety-with-the-human-rights-of-migrants/ (last accessed 25 April 2020).

43. Irini Papanicolopulu, 'The Duty to Rescue at Sea, in Peacetime and in War: A General Overview', *International Review of the Red Cross* 98, no. 2 (2016): 491–514, 513.

44. On the 'place of safety' concept, whose interpretation in the context of private

SAR activities in the Mediterranean has been contentious, see Paolo Turrini, 'Between a "Go Back!" and a Hard (to Find) Place (of Safety): On the Rules and Standards of Disembarkation of People Rescued at Sea', *Italian Yearbook of International Law Online* 28 (2019): 29–46; and Kristof Gombeer, 'Human Rights Adrift? Enabling the Disembarkation of Migrants to a Place of Safety in the Mediterranean', *Irish Yearbook of International Law* 10 (2015 [2017]): 23–55.

45. Article 2(1), Convention for the Protection of Human Rights and Fundamental Freedoms (Council of Europe, 1950); Article 2(1), Charter of Fundamental Rights of the European Union (Brussels: European Commission, 2000).

46. Jennifer Rankin, 'EU to Stop Mediterranean Migrant Rescue Boat Patrols', *The Guardian*, 27 March 2019, https://www.theguardian.com/world/2019/mar/27/eu-to-stop-mediterranean-migrant-rescue-boat-patrols (last accessed 25 April 2020); Daniel Howden, Apostolis Fotiadis, and Antony Loewenstein, 'Once Migrants on Mediterranean were Saved by Naval Patrols. Now they have to Watch as Drones Fly Over', *The Guardian*, 4 August 2019, https://www.theguardian.com/world/2019/aug/04/drones-replace-patrol-ships-mediterranean-fears-more-migrant-deaths-eu (last accessed 25 April 2020); Daniel Howden, Apostolis Fotiadis, and Zach Campbell, 'Revealed: The Great European Refugee Scandal', *The Guardian*, 12 March 2020, https://www.theguardian.com/world/2020/mar/12/revealed-the-great-european-refugee-scandal (last accessed 25 April 2020).

47. Council of the European Union, 'Outcome of the Council Meeting, 3747th Council Meeting, Foreign Affairs' (Brussels, 17 February 2020), doc. 6117/20, https://www.consilium.europa.eu/doc/document/ST-6117-2020-INIT/en/pdf (last accessed 10 February 2020).

48. European Commission, 'EU Action Plan Against Migrant Smuggling (2015–2020)' (Brussels, 27 May 2015), https://ec.europa.eu/anti-trafficking/sites/antitrafficking/files/eu_action_plan_against_migrant_smuggling_en.pdf (last accessed 25 April 2020).

49. Much of the search for that evidence has been carried out in Italy, where several courts concluded that NGOs did not abet people smugglers and a Senate investigation found no link between non-governmental search and rescue operations and people smuggling: Senato della Repubblica, *Documento approvato dalla 4ª Commissione Permanente (Difesa) a conclusione dell'indagine concoscitiva… sul contributo dei militari italiani al controllo dei flussi migratori nel Mediterraneo e l'impatto delle attività delle organizzazioni non governative* (24 May 2017), http://www.senato.it/service/PDF/PDFServer/BGT/1023441.pdf (last accessed 23 April 2020).

50. Article 6(1), Protocol against the Smuggling of Migrants by Land, Sea and Air, supplementing the United Nations Convention against Transnational Organized Crime (Geneva: Office of the High Commissioner for Human Rights, 2000).

51. Council of the European Union, 'Council Directive 2002/90/EC'.

52. Itamar Mann, 'The Right to Perform Rescue at Sea: Jurisprudence and Drowning', *German Law Journal* 21, Special Issue no. 3 (2020): 598–619, 616.

53. Itamar Mann, 'Maritime Legal Black Holes: Migration and Rightlessness in International Law', *European Journal of International Law* 29, no. 2 (2018): 347–72.

54. Mann, 'The Right to Perform Rescue at Sea', 602.

55. Henley and Partners Passport Index, https://www.henleypassportindex.com/assets/2020/Q2/HENLEY_PASSPORT_INDEX_2020_Q2_INFOGRAPHIC_GLOBAL_RANKING_200407.pdf (last accessed 21 April 2020). These figures do not take into account temporary travel restrictions that were imposed to halt the spread of the COVID-19 virus.

56. Article 33(1), Convention Relating to the Status of Refugees (Geneva: Office of the High Commissioner for Human Rights, 1951).

57. Roman Boed, 'The State of the Right of Asylum in International Law', *Duke Journal of Comparative and International Law* 5, no. 1 (1994), 1–34.

58. Savitri Taylor and Klaus Neumann, 'Australia and the Abortive Convention on Territorial Asylum: A Case Study of a Cul de Sac in International Refugee and Human Rights Law', *International Journal of Refugee Law* 32, no. 1 (2020): 86–112.

59. Article 13, UDHR (1948); Article 12, ICCPR (1966).

60. See also Jane McAdam, 'An Intellectual History of Freedom of Movement in International Law: The Right to Leave as a Personal Liberty', *Melbourne Journal of International Law* 12, no. 1 (2011): 27–56; Kieran Oberman, 'Immigration as a Human Right', in *Migration in Political Theory: The Ethics of Movement and Membership*, ed. Sarah Fine and Lea Ypi (Oxford: Oxford University Press, 2016), 32–56.

61. UN General Assembly, 3rd session, Third Committee, 120th meeting, 2 November 1948, UN doc. A/C.3/SR.120.

62. Liisa Malkki, 'National Geographic: The Rooting of Peoples and the Territorialisation of National Identity among Scholars and Refugees', *Cultural Anthropology* 7, no. 1 (1992): 24–44, 26.

63. Seebrücke, 'Aufruf: Ungehorsam für Menschenrechte!', 4 March 2020, https://seebruecke.org/aufruf-ungehorsam-fuer-menschenrechte/ (last accessed 5 March 2020). The text was removed from the Seebrücke website one day after it was first posted. When questioned about this, a Seebrücke representative told me that this did *not* indicate that the organisation had second thoughts about the tenor of the statement.

64. Carola Rackete and Anne Weiss, *Handeln statt Hoffen: Aufruf an die letzte Generation* (München: Droemer, 2019), 5.

65. Ibid., 160.

66. Ibid.

67. Lorenzo Pezzani and Charles Heller, 'A Disobedient Gaze: Strategic Interventions in the Knowledge(s) of Maritime Borders', *Postcolonial Studies* 16, no. 3 (2013): 289–98; Maurice Stierl, 'The WatchTheMed Alarm Phone: A Disobedient Border-Intervention', *Movements* 1, no. 2 (2015): 10. See also Maurice Stierl, 'A Sea of Struggle—Activist Border Interventions in the Mediterranean Sea', *Citizenship Studies* 20, no. 5 (2016): 561–78; and Nina Violetta Schwarz and Maurice Stierl, 'Amplifying Migrant Voices and Struggles at Sea as a Radical Practice', *South Atlantic Quarterly* 118, no. 3 (2019): 661–9.

68. This is most likely a reference to the controversial publication on 12 July 2018 of articles by Caterina Lobenstein and Mariam Lau in the German weekly *Zeit*, Lobenstein's arguing for private search and rescue missions, and Lau's against, under the joint heading 'Oder soll man es lassen?' [Or should one refrain from doing it?], https://www.zeit.de/2018/29/seenotrettung-fluechtlinge-privat-mittelmeer-pro-contra (last accessed 25 April 2020). See also Neumann, 'Waving, But Also Drowning'.

69. Rackete and Weiss, *Handeln statt Hoffen*, 29–30.

70. Ibid., 52.

71. Article 2, Treaty of Lisbon (Brussels: European Council, 2007). For an example of the resonance of the right to asylum in debates about irregularised migration across the Mediterranean, see Alessandra Sciurba and Filippo Furri, 'Human Rights Beyond Humanitarianism: The Radical Challenge to the Right to Asylum in the Mediterranean Zone', *Antipode* 50, no. 3 (2018): 763–82.

72. John Rawls, *A Theory of Justice* (Cambridge, MA: Belknap Press, 1971), 364.

73. Ibid., 365–6; emphasis added.

74. William E. Scheuerman, *Civil Disobedience* (Cambridge: Polity Press, 2018), 52–3.

75. Ibid., 107.

76. Mann, 'The Right to Perform Rescue at Sea', 616.

77. Itamar Mann has termed this kind of encounter a 'human rights encounter'. See Itamar Mann, *Humanity at Sea: Maritime Migration and the Foundations of International Law* (Cambridge: Cambridge University Press, 2016), 54–5. I found his discussion of irregularised maritime migration particularly helpful when trying to think through the issues canvassed in this chapter.

78. Luis Cabrera, *The Practice of Global Citizenship* (Cambridge: Cambridge University Press, 2010), 132–46.

79. Ali Emre Benli, 'Refugees Traversing Borders: Disobedience as an Act of European Citizenship', in *Claiming Citizenship Rights in Europe: Emerging Challenges and Political Agents*, ed. Daniele Archibugi and Ali Emre Benli (Abingdon: Routledge, 2018), 47–61; Ali Emre Benli, 'March of Refugees: An Act of Civil Disobedience', *Journal of Global Ethics* 14, no. 3 (2018): 315–31.

80. Frédéric Mégret, 'Migrant Protests as a Form of Civil Disobedience: Which Cosmopolitanism?', in *Migration, Protest Movements and the Politics of Resistance: A Radical Political Philosophy of Cosmopolitanism*, ed. Tamara Caraus and Elena Paris (Abingdon: Routledge, 2018), 29–50.

81. William Smith and Luis Cabrera, 'The Morality of Border Crossing', *Contemporary Political Theory* 14, no. 1 (2015): 90–99, 90–4.

82. Hannah Arendt, 'Civil Disobedience', in *Crises of the Republic* (New York, NY: Harcourt Brace & Company, 1972), 51–102.

83. Patrick Merziger, 'The "Radical Humanism" of "Cap Anamur"/"German Emergency Doctors" in the 1980s: A Turning Point for the Idea, Practice and Policy of Humanitarian Aid', *European Review of History* 32, nos. 1–2 (2016): 171–92; Lorenzo Pezzani, 'The Two Lives of the Cap Anamur: Humanitarianism at Sea', in *Forensis:*

The Architecture of Public Truth, ed. Eyal Weizman et al. (Berlin: Sternberg Press, 2014), 685–92.

84. Elias Bierdel, *Ende einer Rettungsfahrt: Das Flüchtlingsdrama der Cap Anamur* (Weilerswist: Verlag Ralf Liebe, 2006); Silja Klepp, *Europa zwischen Grenzkontrolle und Flüchtlingsschutz: Eine Ethnographie der Seegrenze auf dem Mittelmeer* (Bielefeld: Transkript Verlag, 2011), 267–78; Tugba Basaran, 'The Curious State of the Good Samaritan: Humanitarianism under Conditions of Security', in *Governing Borders and Security: The Politics of Connectivity and Dispersal*, ed. Catarina Kinnvall and Ted Svensson (Abingdon: Routledge, 2014), 49–63; Tugba Basaran, 'Saving Lives at Sea: Security, Law and Adverse Effects', *European Journal of Migration and Law* 16, no. 3 (2014): 365–87.

85. Jenny Edkins, *Change and the Politics of Certainty* (Manchester: Manchester University Press, 2019), 79.

8. THE LEGITIMATION CRISIS OF THE LIBERAL ORDER: POLITICAL MINIMALISM, HUMANITARIANISM, AND THE GOVERNMENT OF INEQUALITY

1. Michael N. Barnett, 'The End of a Liberal International Order that Never Existed', *The Global* (blog), Graduate Institute of Geneva, 16 April 2019.

2. See, for example, Yascha Mounk's account of 'undemocratic liberalism' in *The People vs. Democracy: Why Our Freedom is in Danger and How to Save It* (Cambridge, MA: Harvard University Press, 2018); and Edward Luce's post-Cold War mise-en-scène in *The Retreat of Western Liberalism* (London: Little, Brown, 2017).

3. Richard Hofstadter, *The Paranoid Style in American Politics and Other Essays* (Cambridge, MA: Harvard University Press, 1964).

4. Rhoda. E. Howard, *Human Rights and the Search for Community* (Boulder, CO: Westview Press, 1995). For Rodríguez-Alcázar, for example, political minimalism concerns (and describes) the appropriate relationship between politics and ethics. For Shakman Hurd it is 'democratic individualism'. See Javier Rodríguez-Alcázar, 'Beyond Realism and Moralism: A Defense of Political Minimalism', *Metaphilosophy* 48, no. 5 (October 2017): 727–44; and Elizabeth Shakman Hurd, *The Politics of Secularism in International Relations*, Princeton Studies in International History and Politics (Princeton, NJ: Princeton University Press, 2008), 147.

5. See on this, Norberto Bobbio's *Liberalism and Democracy* (London: Verso, 2006), 90.

6. See Ruti Teitel, *Humanity's Law* (Oxford: Oxford University Press, 2013).

7. See Hans-Jurgen Pühle, 'Trajectories and Transformations of Western Democracies, 1950s–2000s', and Volker Depkat, 'Discussing Democracy in Western Europe and the United States, 1945–1970', both in *Transatlantic Democracy in the Twentieth Century: Transfer and Transformation*, ed. Paul Nolte (Berlin: Degruyter, 2016), 153–70 and 117–38, respectively. For a short account of the relative recency of the liberal democratic political form, see Adam Tooze, '1917—365 Days that Shook the World', *Prospect Magazine* (January 2017).

8. Judith Shklar, *After Utopia: The Decline of Political Faith* (1957; Princeton, NJ: Princeton University Press, 2016), ix.

9. For Shklar, this death of utopia in liberal thought needs to be traced back further into liberalism's past—to the French Revolution, in fact, 'not yesterday but two hundred years ago', as she put it in her later essay, 'The Political Theory of Utopia: From Melancholy to Nostalgia', chapter 9 in Judith N. Shklar, *Political Thought and Political Thinkers*, ed. Stanley Hoffman (Chicago, IL: University of Chicago Press, 1998), 161–75 (originally published in *Daedalus, Journal of the American Academy of Arts and Sciences* 94, no. 2 [Spring 1965]: 367–81).

10. Samuel Moyn, 'Before—and Beyond—the Liberalism of Fear', in *Between Utopia and Realism: The Political Thought of Judith Shklar*, ed. S. Ashenden and A. Hess (Philadelphia, PA: University of Pennsylvania Press, 2019), 24–46, 35.

11. Judith Shklar, 'The Liberalism of Fear', in *Liberalism and the Moral Life*, ed. Nancy L. Rosenblum (Cambridge, MA: Harvard University Press, 1989), 21–38, 29.

12. Shklar, 'The Political Theory of Utopia', 161, and Shklar, *After Utopia*, 219. Despite abandoning this more positive view for most of her career, Shklar returns to it somewhat towards the end of her life. As she writes in a late essay unpublished during her lifetime, she does not wish to join the ranks of those who see utopia as inherently a dangerous political form. But equally she sees no future in the concept, and therefore no meaningful use for it in the present. I am grateful here to Sam Moyn for, I think, really first drawing attention to the significance of *After Utopia* within (even against) Shklar's wider body of thought, initially in a lecture delivered at Queen Mary University of London. I have also here heeded Nicolas Guilhot's brilliant account of political realism for pointing out the route one would need to take in order to unravel the practical political implications of Shklar's insights, specifically with reference to neoliberalism and political realism. See Nicolas Guilhot, *After the Enlightenment: Political Realism and International Relations in the Mid-Twentieth Century* (Cambridge: Cambridge University Press, 2017), 6–7.

13. Odd Arne Westad, *The Global Cold War* (Cambridge: Cambridge University Press, 2007). The Cold War's great tragedy, Westad observes, was that it saw two originally fundamentally anti-colonial projects become part of a much older pattern of domination, continuing the work of the colonial powers through the projection of that bipolar struggle out onto the world at large. The open question in his account is in some senses, why this development? Shklar's account of liberalism's early to mid-century travails helps provide at least part of the answer to that.

14. Judith Shklar, *Legalism: Law, Morals, and Political Trials* (1964; Cambridge, MA: Harvard University Press, 1986), 5; contra Seyla Benhabib (see her 'Judith Shklar's Dystopic Liberalism', *Social Research* 61, no. 2 [Summer 1994]: 477–88). I see Shklar's relationship to utopia across the full spectrum of her career as 'non-utopian', at times even 'counter-utopian', but ultimately not 'anti-utopian', as Benhabib suggests. To wit Shklar's comment, at the end of her career, that while her view of utopianism may seem unkind, 'I do not wish to join the rather larger chorus that sees a great danger in utopian thought', an approach, she adds, which

'really does make positive political thought impossible' (Shklar, 'Political Theory of Utopia', 190.)

15. Joshua L. Cherniss, 'A Tempered Liberalism: Political Ethics and Ethos in Reinhold Niebuhr's Thought', *Review of Politics* 78, no. 1 (Winter 2016): 59–90, 59.

16. Daniel F. Rice, 'Reinhold Niebuhr on Democracy', in *Reinhold Niebuhr Revisited: Engagements with an American Original*, ed. Daniel F. Rice (Grand Rapids, MI: William B. Eerdmans, 2009), 123–38.

17. Cited in Ian E. Van Dyke, '"Serenity" in an Uncertain Age: Reinhold Niebuhr and America's Quest for Responsible Atomic Hegemony', *Eras Journal* 16, no. 2 (January 2015): 57–78, 63.

18. Van Dyke, '"Serenity" in an Uncertain Age', 67.

19. On Roosevelt, see ibid., 61; for the 'just war' account, ibid., 72.

20. Kenneth Thompson, 'The Forgotten Niebuhr', *Worldview* 14, nos. 7–8 (July–August 1971), 3–4, 3. See also Anatol Lieven and John Hulsman, 'Ethical Realism and Contemporary Challenges', *American Foreign Policy Interests* 28, no. 6 (2006): 413–20; though compare Daniel Rice, 'Reinhold Niebuhr and Hans Morgenthau: A Friendship with Contrasting Shades of Realism', *Journal of American Studies* 42, no. 2 (August 2008): 255–91.

21. On Nitze, see Van Dyke, '"Serenity" in an Uncertain Age', 74; see also Nicholas Thompson, *The Hawk and the Dove: Paul Nitze, George Kennan, and the History of the Cold War* (New York, NY: Henry Holt, 2009).

22. As suggested, for example, by Francis Fukuyama, in 'Friedrich A. Hayek: Big Government Skeptic', *The New York Times*, Book Review, 6 May 2011.

23. Ola Morris Innset, 'Reinventing Liberalism: Early Neoliberalism in Context, 1920–1947', PhD dissertation (European University Institute, Florence, 2017), 26–8; James L. Richardson, *Contending Liberalisms in World Politics: Ideology and Power* (Boulder, CO: Lynne Rienner, 2001). See also Mark Mazower, *Dark Continent: Europe's Twentieth Century*, new ed. (Harmondsworth: Penguin, 1999), chapters 1–2.

24. Among those in attendance were Ludwig von Mises, Wilhelm Røpke, Louis Rougier, and Alexander Rüstow.

25. See, for example, her discussion on the end of radicalism in Shklar, *After Utopia*, esp. 235–6.

26. See also Carl Friedrich, 'The Political Thought of Neoliberalism', *American Political Science Review* 49, no. 2 (1955): 509–25.

27. Guilhot, *After the Enlightenment*, 7.

28. My thanks to Joe Hoover for highlighting the extent to which political minimalism does indeed adopt an anti-democratic stance.

29. Richard Aldous, *Schlesinger: The Imperial Historian* (New York: W. W. Norton, 2017), 136.

30. Schlesinger was one of many such concerned liberals. Joseph Schumpeter, whose influential *Capitalism, Socialism and Democracy* (1942) was itself an expression of political minimalism, was another. A great many others also signed up to the same basic

rejection of a better world. After the war, Niebuhr was joined by the likes of Eleanor Roosevelt and Walter Reuther in establishing Americans for Democratic Action (ADA): an anti-communist left grouping whose specific aim was to make liberalism more fungible with this more conservative reading. And within a decade, of course, Isaiah Berlin had provided the requisite philosophical defence for much of this, with the prioritisation of negative over positive freedoms put forward in his 1958 *Two Concepts of Liberty*. By then the basic parameters of political minimalism are largely in place.

31. For Judith Shklar, Rawls' *Theory of Justice* was also the *only* really successful attempt to offer a normative vision for liberalism after the Enlightenment. It is true that, where Rawls sought to *resolve* social conflict, Shklar sought to defang the consequences of what she saw as the permanent and *irresolvable* nature of social conflict (Shklar was a 'member of the party of memory', as she once said; Rawls was of the party of hope). Shaun Young, 'Avoiding the Unavoidable? Judith Shklar's Unwilling Search for an Overlapping Consensus', *Res Publica* 13 (2007): 231–53, 234 and 240.

32. Katrina Forrester, 'Judith Shklar, Bernard Williams and Political Realism', *European Journal of Political Theory* 11, no. 3 (2012): 247–72, 252. Forrester rightly describes Shklar's own 'liberalism of fear' as a 'minimal liberalism, grounded in psychology rather than rights or nature' (252).

33. On Rawls' early religious thought, see Andrius Galisanka, *John Rawls: The Path to a Theory of Justice* (Cambridge, MA: Harvard University Press, 2019), 10. Rawls had likely read Niebuhr, who, according to Galisanka, was one of the assigned readings on a course he later identified as the most influential of all he had taken (19).

34. Avner Offer, *Self-interest, Sympathy and the Invisible Hand: From Adam Smith to Market Liberalism*, Oxford Economic and Social History Working Papers 101 (University of Oxford, Department of Economics, August 2012), 18.

35. Indeed, for Shklar, Niebuhr's fear of innate human evil, is *properly* transposed, in the modern era, to a fear of innate state evil under the watchful eye of her 'political scepticism'. See also Kerry E. Whiteside, 'Justice Uncertain: Judith Shklar on Liberalism, Skepticism and Equality', *Polity* 31, no. 3 (1999): 501–24, 507. For Rawls, it is also on these grounds that Hayek, for example, came to see much of what Rawls argued for as compatible with his own strong dislike of 'social justice': see Andrew Lister, *The 'Mirage' of Social Justice: Hayek Against (and For) Rawls*, CCSJ Working Papers Series SJ017 (Centre for the Study of Social Justice, Department of Politics and International Relations, University of Oxford, June 2011).

36. Brian Barry to Rawls, Rawls Archive, Widener Library, Harvard University, Box 19/F2, p. 3.

37. An example: in Rawls, civil disobedience represents the limit point when individuals may find themselves unable to be bound to fulfil their obligations to society; but this is reserved more strongly for the civic political rights pertaining to personal freedom than to the socioeconomic rights upon which those freedoms may also depend.

38. See, for example, the graphs on income inequality across the twentieth century provided by Thomas Piketty, in *Capital in the Twenty-First Century* (Cambridge, MA: Harvard University Press, 2014).

39. A distinction Shklar herself was always keen to maintain: she memorably called them his 'army of squabbling heirs'. See Judith N. Shklar, 'Injustice, Injury and Inequality: An Introduction', in *Justice and Equality Here and* Now, ed. Frank S. Lucash (Ithaca, NY: Cornell University Press, 1986), 13–33, 14.

40. Forrester, 'Judith Shklar, Bernard Williams and Political Realism', 261.

41. Gerry Kearns, 'The Social Shell', *Historical Geography* 34 (2006): 49–70.

42. Mark Mazower, *Governing the World: The History of an Idea, 1815 to the Present* (London: Allen Lane, 2012).

43. See Craig Calhoun, 'The Idea of Emergency: Humanitarian Action and Global (Dis) Order', in *Contemporary States of Emergency*, ed. Didier Fassin (Cambridge, MA: Zone Books, 2010), 29–58.

44. The phrase is that of the President of the European Commission, Ursula von der Leyen: https://www.bbc.com/news/world-europe-54249312.

45. Jürgen Habermas, *Legitimation Crisis*, trans. Thomas McCarthy (Boston, MA: Beacon, 1975); see also Alan Toplišek, 'Liberal Democracy in Crisis: Redefining Politics and Resistance through Power', PhD thesis (Queen Mary University of London, 2016), http://qmro.qmul.ac.uk/xmlui/handle/123456789/23844.

46. Westad, *The Global Cold War*.

47. See, for example, the argument in Martin Conway, *Western Europe's Democratic Age, 1945–1968* (Princeton, NJ: Princeton University Press, 2020). There are indeed some echoes here with what Marcel Gauchet calls a 'rights based minimal democracy' (in which the economy expands under the claim that human rights are a sufficient guardian and replacement of the political), but there is not the space to develop these ideas here. See Marcel Gauchet and Natalie J. Doyle, 'Democracy: From One Crisis to Another', in *Social Imaginaries* 1, no. 1 (Spring 2015): 163–87, 180–2.

48. Judith N. Shklar, 'What is the Use of Utopia?', chapter 10 in Judith N. Shklar, *Political Thought and Political Thinkers*, ed. Stanley Hoffman (Chicago, IL: University of Chicago Press, 1998), 175–91, 189.

49. One thinks here of Amartya Sen's and Martha Nussbaum's writings on capabilities.

50. Juliano Fiori, 'Humanitarianism and the End of Liberal Order', *Journal of Humanitarian Affairs* 1, no. 1 (2019): 1–3 (my emphasis).

51. Mark Lilla, *The Once and Future Liberal: After Identity Politics* (London: HarperCollins, 2017).

9. NOTES ON OUR MELANCHOLY PRESENT

1. I am very grateful for the generosity and critical engagement of those who read this chapter: Alba Asín Gázquez, Jorge Fiori, José Luís Fiori, Louis Amis, Paulo Arantes, Otília Fiori Arantes, José Gabriel Palma, Gareth Owen, Fernando Espada, Rafia

Zakaria, Bertrand Taithe, Andrea Rigon, Mark Duffield, Simon Reid-Henry, Klaus Neumann, Giuseppe Cocco, Lilie Chouliaraki, Stephanie Reist, Felipe Eugênio, Benjamin Fogel, Ana Naomi de Sousa, Brad Evans, Emily Baughan, Eleanor Davey, Antonio Donini, Elena Fiddian-Qasmiyeh, Olivia Rutazibwa, and Mandy Turner.

2. L. T. Hobhouse, *Democracy and Reaction* (London: T. Fisher Unwin, 1904), 2.

3. Ibid., 2, 58.

4. Ibid., 28.

5. As Stefan Collini points out, the opposition between individualism and collectivism was central to late Victorian political argument. See the first chapter of Stefan Collini, *Liberalism and Sociology: L. T. Hobhouse and Political Argument in England, 1880–1914* (Cambridge: Cambridge University Press, 1979).

6. L. T. Hobhouse, *Liberalism and Other Writings*, Cambridge Texts in the History of Political Thought (Cambridge: Cambridge University Press, 1994), 103.

7. For a recent discussion of the benefits and pitfalls of historical analogy, see Samuel Moyn, 'The Trouble with Comparisons', *The New York Review of Books*, 19 May 2020, https://www.nybooks.com/daily/2020/05/19/the-trouble-with-comparisons/ (last accessed 30 August 2020).

8. On the influence of Rawls' political philosophy, see Katrina Forrester, *In the Shadow of Justice: Postwar Liberalism and the Remaking of Political Philosophy* (Princeton, NJ: Princeton University Press, 2019).

9. Collini argues that, on account of its conceptions of state and society, Hobhouse's theory 'cannot easily be categorised as Liberal': Collini, *Liberalism and Sociology*, 96. Michael Freeden challenges this assertion in his review of Collini's book: Michael Freeden, 'Review of *Liberalism and Sociology* by Stefan Collini', *English Historical Review* 95, no. 377 (October 1980): 873–6.

10. See, for example, Yascha Mounk, *The People vs. Democracy: Why Our Freedom is in Danger and How to Save It* (Cambridge, MA: Harvard University Press, 2018); Edward Luce, *The Retreat of Western Liberalism* (New York, NY: Atlantic Monthly Press, 2017); and Bill Emmott, *The Fate of the West: The Battle to Save the World's Most Successful Political Idea* (New York, NY: PublicAffairs, 2017). In 2018, *The Economist* lamented that '[l]iberalism made the modern world, but the modern world is turning against it', in 'A Manifesto for Renewing Liberalism', *The Economist*, 13 September 2018, https://www.economist.com/leaders/2018/09/13/a-manifesto-for-renewing-liberalism (last accessed 13 July 2020).

11. Patrick J. Deneen, *Why Liberalism Failed*, Politics and Culture (New Haven, CT: Yale University Press, 2018); R. Emmett Tyrrell, Jr., *The Death of Liberalism* (Nashville, TN: Thomas Nelson, 2011). Tyrrell has been predicting the end of liberalism for more than three decades. See R. Emmett Tyrrell, *The Liberal Crack-Up* (New York, NY: Simon and Schuster, 1984).

12. Geoff Mann proposes that the promise of revolution without revolutionaries is at the heart of 'Keynesianism', which he understands as an immanent critique of liberal capitalism, first articulated by Hegel: Geoff Mann, *In the Long Run We Are All Dead: Keynesianism, Political Economy, and Revolution* (London and New York: Verso, 2017).

13. During an interview with Rony Brauman on 25 April 2020, he affirmed that, even as he turned away from Marxism, he maintained an appreciation for certain Marxian categories of analysis. I thank him for his generosity in speaking with me, candidly and at length.

14. See Eleanor Davey, *Idealism Beyond Borders: The French Revolutionary Left and the Rise of Humanitarianism, 1954–1988*, Human Rights in History (Cambridge: Cambridge University Press, 2015), chapter 7.

15. Laurence Binet, *Famine and Forced Relocations in Ethiopia, 1984–1986* (Geneva: Médecins Sans Frontières, 2013), 27.

16. Malhuret was clear that LSF could not be neutral in the struggle against communist ideology. Claude Malhuret, *Invitation de Liberté sans Frontières au Colloque des 23 et 24 Janvier 1985* (Médecins Sans Frontières, 11 January 1985).

17. Interview with Rony Brauman, 25 April 2020.

18. Claude Malhuret, 'À propos de "Liberté Sans Frontières"', *Le Monde*, 26 January 1985.

19. Peter Bauer, 'L'Aide au développement: pour ou contre?', in *Le Tiers-mondisme en question*, ed. Rony Brauman (Paris: Olivier Orban, 1986), 181–90, 188.

20. Jacques Broyelle, 'Commentaire', in *Le Tiers-mondisme en question*, ed. Rony Brauman (Paris: Olivier Orban, 1986), 70–5, 73–5.

21. Cited in Davey, *Idealism Beyond Borders*, 219.

22. Rony Brauman, 'Controverse sur l'aide humanitaire et ses utilisations politiques—tiers-mondisme: les intentions et les resultats', *Le Monde Diplomatique*, November 1985.

23. Davey, *Idealism Beyond Borders*, 7.

24. 'They are idealists', Malhuret affirmed, in the same *Le Monde* article. '[B]ut they are also men and women who are engaged and attentive.' Malhuret, 'À propos de "Liberté Sans Frontières"'.

25. Interview with Rony Brauman, 25 April 2020.

26. Davey, *Idealism Beyond Borders*, passim.

27. Rony Brauman, 'Ni tiers-mondisme, ni Cartiérisme', in *Le Tiers-mondisme en question*, ed. Rony Brauman (Paris: Olivier Orban, 1986), 11–19, 12.

28. This translation appears in Davey, *Idealism Beyond Borders*, 221. For the original transcript, see Olivier Roy, 'Commentaire', in *Le Tiers-mondisme en question*, ed. Rony Brauman (Paris: Olivier Orban, 1986), 76–81, 78.

29. For Brauman, 'man' was the end of the morality of *urgence*. Brauman, 'Ni tiers-mondisme, ni Cartiérisme', 12. Kant's categorical imperative, which casts humanity as an end in itself, provides the philosophical basis for the 'humanitarian imperative' frequently invoked by aid agencies in recent decades. In his commentary on the fundamental principles of the Red Cross, Pictet refers to the 'imperative element of humanity': Jean Pictet, *The Fundamental Principles of the Red Cross: Commentary* (Geneva: International Federation of Red Cross and Red Crescent Societies, 1979), 24.

30. Brauman, 'Ni tiers-mondisme, ni Cartiérisme', 13.

31. Cited in Binet, *Famine and Forced Relocations*, 26.

32. Brauman has nonetheless expressed sympathy for the Responsibility to Protect. Rony Brauman, *Guerres humanitaires? Mensonges et intox*, Conversations pour Demain (Paris: Textuel, 2018). See, also Rony Brauman and Pierre Salignon, 'Iraq: In Search of a "Humanitarian Crisis"', in *In the Shadow of 'Just Wars': Violence, Politics and Humanitarian Action*, ed. Fabrice Weissman (Ithaca, NY: Cornell University Press, 2004), 269–85.

33. Juliano Fiori, Fernando Espada, Jessica Field, and Sophie Dicker, *The Echo Chamber: Results, Management and the Humanitarian Effectiveness Agenda* (London: Save the Children, 2016).

34. Davey, *Idealism Beyond Borders*, 9.

35. Historians increasingly contest Malcolm Bradbury's characterisation of the 1970s as 'the decade that never was', emphasising the contribution of decolonisation and economic crisis to transformations of capitalist democracy. For a recent example, see Simon Reid-Henry, *Empire of Democracy: The Remaking of the West since the Cold War, 1971–2017* (New York, NY: Simon & Schuster, 2019). See also, Niall Ferguson, Charles S. Maier, Erez Manela, and Daniel J. Sargent, eds., *The Shock of the Global: The 1970s in Perspective* (Cambridge, MA: Belknap Press, 2010).

36. Samuel Moyn, *The Last Utopia: Human Rights in History* (Cambridge, MA: Belknap Press, 2010), 3. Robin Blackburn, among others, contests the newness Moyn attributes to human rights ideology in the 1970s, in Robin Blackburn, 'Reclaiming Human Rights', *New Left Review* 69 (May/June 2011): 126–38.

37. Moyn, *The Last Utopia*, 4.

38. See Jessica Whyte, *The Morals of the Market: Human Rights and the Rise of Neoliberalism* (London: Verso, 2019). Moyn argues that human rights became a companion to neoliberalism because they didn't threaten it, but that '[n]eoliberalism, not human rights, is to blame for neoliberalism'. Samuel Moyn, *Not Enough: Human Rights in an Unequal World* (Cambridge, MA: Belknap Press, 2018), 192.

39. For Marx, freedom from necessity specifically meant freedom from the capitalist condition of labour. In 1967, Herbert Marcuse inverted Marx's formulation, proposing that it had become possible to let 'the realm of freedom appear within the realm of necessity'. Herbert Marcuse, 'The End of Utopia', in *Five Lectures: Psychoanalysis, Politics, and Utopia* (London: Allen Lane, 1970), 62–82, 63.

40. Raymond Aron, *Mémoires: 50 ans de réflexion politique* (Paris: Juillard, 1983), 741.

41. Michel Foucault, 'Confronting Governments: Human Rights', in *Essential Works of Foucault, 1954–1984*, Vol. 3: *Power* (New York, NY: New Press, 1994), 475.

42. 'Right in the West is the King's right', he had asserted in 1976. See Michel Foucault, 'Two Lectures', in *Power/Knowledge: Selected Interviews and Other Writings, 1972–1977* (New York, NY: Pantheon Books, 1980), 78–108, 94. This contradiction is discussed in Jessica Whyte, 'Human Rights: Confronting Governments? Michel Foucault and the Right to Intervene', in *New Critical Legal Thinking: Law and the Political*, ed. Matthew Stone, Illan rua Wall, and Costas Douzinas (Abingdon: Routledge, 2012), 11–31.

43. Michel Foucault, *The Birth of Biopolitics: Lectures at the Collège de France, 1978–1979* (Basingstoke: Palgrave Macmillan, 2008), 189.

44. On Foucault and neoliberalism, see Daniel Zamora, ed., *Critiquer Foucault: les années 1980 et la tentation néolibérale* (Bruxelles: Éditions Aden, 2014).

45. Fredric Jameson, 'Postmodernism, Or the Cultural Logic of Late Capitalism', *New Left Review* 146 (1984): 53–92, 53.

46. H. Bruce Franklin, 'What are We to Make of J. G. Ballard's Apocalypse?', in *Voices for the Future: Essays on Major Science Fiction Writers*, Vol. 2, ed. Thomas D. Clareson (Bowling Green, OH: Bowling Green University Popular Press, 1979), 82–105, 103.

47. Paul Di Filippo, 'Ballard's Anatomy: An Interview with J. G. Ballard', *Science Fiction Eye* 8 (1991): 66–75, 71. On Ballard and historical recovery, see Jeannette Baxter, *J. G. Ballard's Surrealist Imagination: Spectacular Authorship* (Abingdon: Routledge, 2016).

48. Fredric Jameson, 'Progress versus Utopia; Or, Can We Imagine the Future', *Science Fiction Studies* 9, no. 2 (July 1982): 147–58, 153.

49. Christopher Lasch, *The Culture of Narcissism: American Life in an Age of Diminishing Expectations* (New York, NY: W. W. Norton, 2018).

50. Paulo Arantes, 'O Novo tempo do mundo', in *O Novo tempo do mundo e outros estudos sobre a era da emergência* (Sao Paulo, SP: Boitempo Editorial, 2014), 27–97.

51. For Koselleck, modernity constitutes an acceleration of the 'temporalisation of history', through which the 'horizon of expectation' was relocated in relation to the 'space of experience'. Reinhart Koselleck, *Futures Past: On the Semantics of Historical Time* (New York, NY: Columbia University Press, 2004).

52. Paulo Arantes, 'Entrevista com Marcos Barreira e Maurílio Lima Botelho', *Sinal de Menos* 2, no. 11 (May 2015): 9–47, 13–6.

53. Ibid., 15.

54. On 'time–space compression', see Part 3 of David Harvey, *The Condition of Postmodernity: An Enquiry into the Origins of Cultural Change* (Oxford: Blackwell, 1989).

55. Ernest Mandel, *Late Capitalism* (London: New Left Books, 1975).

56. Guy Debord, *The Society of the Spectacle* (Berkeley, CA: Bureau of Public Secrets, 2014), 77.

57. The notion that counter-revolution in this period was preventive is proposed by Herbert Marcuse in *Counter-Revolution and Revolt* (Boston, MA: Beacon Books, 1972). Arantes develops a similar argument on preventive counter-revolution and social expectations in, among others, Arantes, 'Entrevista', 45–6.

58. Francis Fukuyama, 'The End of History?', *The National Interest* 16 (Summer 1989): 3–18, 18.

59. UN Secretary-General Boutros Boutros-Ghali, *An Agenda for Peace: Preventive Diplomacy, Peacemaking and Peace-Keeping: Report of the Secretary-General* (New York, NY: United Nations, 1992).

60. Fiori et al., *Echo Chamber*.

61. The relevant section of the evaluation, known as the JEEAR, is John Borton, Emery Brusset, and Alistair Hallam, 'Study III: Humanitarian Aid and Effects, Joint Evaluation of Emergency Assistance to Rwanda' (Copenhagen: Danish Ministry of Foreign Affairs, 1996).

62. Fiori et al., *Echo Chamber*, 50–6.

63. Among others, see Fareed Zakaria, 'The End of the End of History', *Newsweek*, 23 September 2001, https://www.newsweek.com/end-end-history-152075 (last accessed 15 August 2020); and Robert Kagan, *The Return of History and the End of Dreams* (New York, NY: Vintage, 2009). There has been a rapid proliferation of such analysis since the election of Donald Trump in 2016.

64. Lutz Niethammer, *Posthistoire: Has History Come to an End?* (London: Verso, 1992).

65. Alexandre Kojève, *Introduction to the Reading of Hegel: Lectures on the Phenomenology of Spirit*, trans. James H. Nichols (Ithaca, NY: Cornell University Press, 1980).

66. Ibid., 160.

67. Perry Anderson, 'The Ends of History', in *A Zone of Engagement* (London: Verso, 1992), 279–376.

68. Jacques Derrida, *Specters of Marx: The State of the Debt, the Work of Mourning and the New International* (Abingdon: Routledge, 1994), 56.

69. Francis Fukuyama, *The End of History and the Last Man* (New York, NY: Free Press, 1992), viii, xv.

70. Brett Bowden argues that, although Samuel Huntington wrote *The Clash of Civilisations and the Remaking of World Order* (1996) as a critical response to *The End of History and the Last Man*, these works should be seen as 'two sides of the same coin': 'an attempt to impose Fukuyama's liberal democratic master plan across the globe will almost inevitably result in confrontations between Western civilisation and the peoples on which it is imposing this plan'. Brett Bowden, *The Empire of Civilization: The Evolution of an Imperial Idea* (Chicago, IL: University of Chicago Press, 2014), 4.

71. On the United States and ethical order, see José Luís Fiori, 'Guerra do Golfo: uma guerra ética', in *Sobre a guerra*, ed. José Luís Fiori (Petropolis, RJ: Editora Vozes, 2018), 23–46. On humanitarian ideas and ethical order, see Juliano Fiori, 'Humanitarian Wars and the Struggle for Ethical Order', *Medium*, 31 July 2018, https://medium.com/@julianofiori/humanitarian-wars-and-the-struggle-for-ethical-order-bafd382bf48f (last accessed 6 July 2020).

72. Mark Greif, 'The End of the World', *Chronicle Review*, 14 June 2019, https://www.chronicle.com/interactives/20190614-PoMoForum (last accessed 23 August 2020).

73. Baudrillard argued that hyperreality generates 'models of a real without origin or reality'. Jean Baudrillard, *Simulacra and Simulation* (Ann Arbor, MI: University of Michigan Press, 1994), 1.

74. Jameson, 'Postmodernism', passim.

75. Jameson's discussion of 'cognitive mapping' is of relevance here: he sees conspiracy as 'the poor person's cognitive mapping in the postmodern age'. Fredric

Jameson, 'Cognitive Mapping', in *Marxism and the Interpretation of Culture*, ed. Cary Nelson and Lawrence Grossberg (Champagne, IL: University of Illinois Press, 1988), 347–60. Moira Weigel relates this discussion to the cultural warriors of today's North American right, in Moira Weigel, 'You're so Paranoid, You Probably Think this Conspiracy is about You', *Chronicle Review*, 14 June 2019, https://www.chronicle.com/interactives/20190614-PoMoForum (last accessed 23 August 2020).

76. Given the association of Fukuyama with inverted millenarianism here, it is worth noting that he was himself fiercely critical of postmodernism. See Francis Fukuyama, 'Reflections on the End of History, Five Years Later', *History and Theory* 34, no. 2 (May 1995): 27–43.

77. Written in the months prior to 9/11, Jean-Pierre Dupuy's *Pour un catastrophisme éclaire: quand l'impossible est certain* (Paris: Éditions du Seuil, 2002), makes reference to a 'temps des catastrophes'.

78. On the postmodern 'internationalisation' of crisis, see Mark Duffield, 'Challenging Environments: Danger, Resilience and the Aid Industry', *Security Dialogue* 43, no. 5 (2012): 475–92.

79. Giddens describes 'risk society' as 'a society increasingly preoccupied with the future'. Anthony Giddens, 'Risk and Responsibility', *Modern Law Review* 62, no. 1 (1999): 1–10.

80. Mandel, *Late Capitalism*, 387, 570.

81. Ibid., 586. See also, Ernest Mandel, 'Marx, the Present Crisis and the Future of Labour', *Socialist Register: Social Democracy and After* 22 (1985/86): 436–54.

82. See, for example, Theodor Adorno, 'Spätkapitalismus oder Industriegesellschaft?', in *Gesammelte Schriften*, Vol. 8 (Frankfurt: Suhrkamp, 1987), 354–70. In his memoir, *An Impatient Life* (London: Verso, 2013), philosopher Daniel Bensaïd refers to a 'stubborn optimism of the will' that tempered Mandel's 'intermittent pessimism of reason'.

83. Against Mandel's warning in *Late Capitalism* (570), contemporary advocates of a post-work society seem to 'hope for the abolition of capitalist relations of production through the mere advance of automation'. See, for example, Nick Srnicek and Alex Williams, *Inventing the Future: Postcapitalism and a World Without Work* (London: Verso, 2015); and Aaron Bastani, *Fully Automated Luxury Communism: A Manifesto* (London: Verso, 2019). Anthropologist David Graeber challenges assertions of accelerating technological development, in his 'Of Flying Cars and the Declining Rate of Profit', *The Baffler* 19 (March 2012): 66–84, https://thebaffler.com/salvos/of-flying-cars-and-the-declining-rate-of-profit (last accessed 5 September 2020). With specific reference to the United States, Robert Gordon suggests that technological innovation has slowed since 1970: Robert J. Gordon, *The Rise and Fall of American Growth: The U.S. Standard of Living Since the Civil War*, with a new Afterword by the author (Princeton, NJ: Princeton University Press, 2017).

84. On post-industrial society, see, in particular, Daniel Bell, *The Coming of Post-Industrial Society: A Venture in Social Forecasting* (New York, NY: Harper Colophon

Books, 1974); and Alain Touraine, *The Post-Industrial Society: Tomorrow's Social History: Classes, Conflicts, and Culture in the Programmed Society* (New York, NY: Random House, 1971).

85. Drawing on data from the International Labour Organization, economist Michael Roberts notes that the global industrial workforce rose from 490 million people in 1991 to 715 million in 2012. Meanwhile, the industrial workforce in 'developed capitalist economies' dropped from 130 million people to 107 million. Michael Roberts, 'De-Industrialisation and Socialism', *The Next Recession* (blog), 21 October 2014, https://thenextrecession.wordpress.com/2014/10/21/de-industrialisation-and-socialism/ (last accessed 30 September 2020).

86. The much-debated thesis that the rate of industrial profit tends to fall, is set out by Karl Marx in *Capital: A Critique of Political Economy*, Vol. 3: *The Process of Capitalist Production as a Whole* (London: Penguin, 1981).

87. On the alliance between princes and financiers, see Fernand Braudel, *Civilisation matérielle, économie et capitalisme, xve–xviiie siècle*, Vol. 3: *Le temps du monde* (Paris: A. Colin, 1979).

88. Hannah Arendt, *The Origins of Totalitarianism* (London: Allen & Unwin, 1967), passim. Among others, Aimé Césaire, Jean-Paul Sartre, and Michel Foucault also discuss the use of technologies of imperial governance against domestic populations. Many nineteenth-century opponents of imperialism denounced its corruption of metropolitan morality, and of civilisation in general.

89. In this regard, it is the country that is less industrially developed that comes to show the more developed country 'the image of its own future', not, as Marx proposed, the other way around. Karl Marx, *Capital: A Critique of Political Economy*, Vol. 1: *The Process of Production of Capital* (London: Penguin, 1990), 91. Fukuyama expressed support for Marx's argument just as reality seemed to be contradicting it (Fukuyama, *End of History*, 68–70).

90. Brazil, here, ironically lives up to the epithet conferred on it by Stefan Zweig: 'country of the future'. The term 'Brazilianisation' seems to have been coined by Michael Lind in *The Next American Nation: The New Nationalism and the Fourth American Revolution* (New York, NY: Free Press, 1995).

91. Ulrich Beck, for example, offers a Eurocentric conception of Brazilianisation, with emphasis on the transformation of work in the West, in *The Brave New World of Work* (Cambridge: Polity Press, 2000). In contrast, Giuseppe Cocco refers to 'the becoming-world of Brazil and the becoming-Brazil of the world', in *MundoBraz: o devir-mundo do Brasil e o devir-brasil do mundo* (Rio de Janeiro, RJ: Record, 2009). Drawing on the work of Eduardo Viveiros de Castro, Cocco's book was a response to an essay by Arantes on the theme of Brazilianisation: Paulo Arantes, 'A fratura Brasileira do mundo', in *Zero à esquerda* (São Paulo, SP: Conrad Livros, 2004), 25–78.

92. See, for example, Reinhart Koselleck, 'Richtlinien für das Lexikon politisch-sozialer Begriffe der Neuzeit', *Archiv für Begriffsgeschichte* 11 (1967): 81–99.

93. Enzo Traverso, *Left-Wing Melancholia: Marxism, History, and Memory* (New York, NY: Columbia University Press, 2016), 3.

94. The postmodern argument that nothing new can happen was perhaps most starkly articulated by Baudrillard. See, for example, Jean Baudrillard, *Fatal Strategies* (Los Angeles, CA: Semiotext(e), 1990).

95. Lasch, *Culture of Narcissism*.

96. Among numerous critiques of Lasch's cultural conservatism, see Elizabeth Lunbeck, *The Americanization of Narcissism* (Cambridge, MA: Harvard University Press, 2014).

97. Brazilian sociologist Francisco de Oliveira uses the term 'hegemony in reverse' to define this process through which the dominant ostensibly accept the morality of the domination, on condition that the form of capitalist relations is not questioned. See Francisco de Oliveira, 'Lula in the Labyrinth', *New Left Review* 42 (December 2006): 5–22.

98. On unequal lives, see Didier Fassin, *Life: A Critical User's Manual* (Cambridge: Polity Press, 2018).

99. Pankaj Mishra, *Age of Anger: A History of the Present* (London: Allen Lane, 2017).

100. Ibid., 14.

101. Friedrich Nietzsche refers to 'the *ressentiment* of those beings who, denied the proper response of action, compensate for it only with imaginary revenge', in *On the Genealogy of Morals* (Cambridge: Cambridge University Press, 2006), 20.

102. Christophe Guilluy, *Le Crépuscule de la France d'en haut* (Paris: Flammarion, 2016); Christophe Guilluy, *No Society: la fin de la classe moyenne occidentale* (Paris: Flammarion, 2018).

103. For discussion of the implications of this social polarisation for humanitarian politics, see Juliano Fiori and Elena Fiddian-Qasmiyeh, 'Migration, Humanitarianism, and the Politics of Knowledge', *Migration and Society* 3 (2020): 180–9.

104. On cultural sovereignty, see Arjun Appadurai, 'Democracy Fatigue', in *The Great Regression*, ed. Heinrich Geiselberger (Cambridge: Polity Press, 2017), 1–12.

105. Quinn Slobodian points to a tension in neoliberal thought between, on the one hand, recognition of democracy's capacity to bring about 'peaceful change', and on the other, condemnation of its capacity to 'upend order'. Quinn Slobodian, *Globalists: The End of Empire and the Birth of Neoliberalism* (Cambridge, MA: Harvard University Press, 2018), 14.

106. This combination of freedom for the movement of capital with restrictions on the movement of labour was favoured by the early neoliberal economist Gottfried Haberler. See Gottfried Haberler, 'The Theory of Comparative Costs and its Use in the Defence of Free Trade', in *Selected Essays of Gottfried Haberler*, ed. A. Y. C. Koo (Cambridge, MA: MIT Press, 1985), 3–19.

107. For economist José Gabriel Palma, neoliberalism can be understood as a technology of power that reintroduces risk and uncertainty at the heart of the *welfarised* population. José Palma, 'Why Did the Latin American Critical Tradition in the Social Sciences Become Practically Extinct?', in *Routledge Handbook of International Political Economy (IPE): IPE as a Global Conversation*, ed. Mark Blyth (Abingdon: Routledge, 2009), 243–65, 257.

108. While it also seems to portend an acceleration towards climate apocalypse, it seems unlikely to bring about a sustained 'economic acceleration'.

109. José Luís Fiori, 'Babel Syndrome and the New Security Doctrine of the United States', *Journal of Humanitarian Affairs* 1, no. 1 (2019): 42–5.

110. Rodrigo Nunes, 'Necropolítica de Bolsonaro aponta para um futuro distópico', *Folha de São Paulo*, 18 June 2020, https://www1.folha.uol.com.br/ilustrissima/2020/06/vidas-de-negros-e-pobres-se-tornam-descartaveis-na-pandemia-afirma-professor.shtml (last accessed 5 September 2020).

111. On the relationship between biopolitics and necropolitics, see, in particular, Achille Mbembe, *Necropolitics* (Durham, NC: Duke University Press, 2019).

112. Moyn, 'The Trouble with Comparisons'.

113. Judith Shklar, *After Utopia: The Decline of Political Faith* (Princeton, NJ: Princeton University Press, 1957), 269.

114. With reference to the 1930s, Karl Polanyi argued that 'liberal utopianism' created conditions for the rise of fascism. Karl Polanyi, *The Great Transformation: The Political and Economic Origins of Our Time* (Boston, MA: Beacon, 2001).

115. Steven Pinker, *Enlightenment Now: The Case for Reason, Science, Humanism, and Progress* (New York, NY: Viking, 2018); J. B. Bury, *The Idea of Progress: An Inquiry into its Origin and Growth* (London: Macmillan and Co., 1920), 4.

116. Sigmund Freud, 'Mourning and Melancholy', in *The Standard Edition of the Complete Psychological Works of Sigmund Freud*, Vol. 14: *1914–1916: On the History of the Psycho-Analytic Movement: Papers on Metapsychology and Other Works* (London: Hogarth Press and the Institute of Psycho-Analysis, 1957), 243–58, 245.

117. Giorgio Agamben, *Stanzas: Word and Phantasm in Western Culture* (Minneapolis, MN: University of Minnesota Press, 1993), 20–1.

118. Following Agamben, Slavoj Žižek affirms that 'melancholy interprets… [a] lack as a loss'. Slavoj Žižek, 'Melancholy and the Act', *Critical Inquiry* 26, no. 4 (2000): 657–81, 659.

119. Freud, 'Mourning and Melancholy', 250.

120. Nietzsche, *Genealogy of Morals*, 93.

121. See Fredric Jameson, *The Political Unconscious: Narrative as a Socially Symbolic Act* (Abingdon: Routledge, 2007), particularly chapter 4.

122. Frantz Fanon, *Black Skin, White Masks* (London: Pluto Press, 1986), 100. On colonial mimicry, see also Homi Bhabha, 'Of Mimicry and Man: The Ambivalence of Colonial Discourse', *Discipleship: A Special Issue on Psychoanalysis* 28 (1984): 125–33.

123. David L. Eng discusses the melancholy condition of 'minoritarian subjectivities', in something of a rejoinder to Judith Butler's work on melancholy and same-sex gender identification. David L. Eng, 'Melancholia in the Late Twentieth Century', *Signs: Feminisms at a Millennium* 25, no. 4 (2000): 1275–81.

124. Alain Ehrenberg, *The Weariness of the Self: Diagnosing the History of Depression in the Contemporary Age* (Montreal: McGill-Queen's University Press, 2010), xxx.

125. In this regard, he follows Raymond Klibansky, Erwin Panofsky, and Fritz Saxl,

Saturn and Melancholy: Studies in the History of Natural Philosophy, Religion, and Art (London: Thomas Nelson & Sons, 1964).

126. On the impact of social media on depression, see Jonathan Haidt, 'More Social Media Regulation', *Politico Magazine* (blog), 28 September 2019, https://www. politico.com/interactives/2019/how-to-fix-politics-in-america/polarization/ more-social-media-regulation/ (last accessed 14 September 2020). The term 'solitary tiredness' is used by philosopher Byung-Chul Han in his discussion of the effects of 'achievement society', Byung-Chul Han, *The Burnout Society* (Stanford, CA: Stanford University Press, 2015).

127. 'Structures of feeling' is a concept developed in the work of Raymond Williams to enable a historical understanding of the affective elements of consciousness that, though emergent or pre-emergent, nonetheless 'exert palpable pressure and set effective limits on experience and on action'. Raymond Williams, *Marxism and Literature* (Oxford: Oxford University Press, 1977), 132.

128. Freud, 'Mourning and Melancholy'.

129. Theodor W. Adorno, *The Psychological Technique of Martin Luther Thomas' Radio Addresses* (Stanford, CA: Stanford University Press, 2000), 62.

130. Sigmund Freud, *The Ego and the Id* (London: Hogarth Press and the Institute of Psycho-Analysis, 1926).

131. Jung sees melancholia as the product of an encounter with what he calls 'the shadow': unconscious elements not recognised by the ego, or indeed the entire unconscious. See, for example, Carl G. Jung, *Mysterium Coniunctionis: An Inquiry into the Separation and Synthesis of Psychic Opposites in Alchemy* (Princeton, NJ: Princeton University Press, 1970), particularly chapters 3 and 6.

132. Following Hannah Arendt's association of the 'law of movement' with terror, Ariella Aïsha Azoulay, in *Potential History: Unlearning Imperialism* (London: Verso, 2019), proposes that unlearning the movement of Progress is necessary to unlearning imperialism.

133. Enzo Traverso associates the restricted epistemic horizon of Marx and many of his disciples, specifically those of the Frankfurt School, with a 'colonial unconscious'. Traverso, *Left-Wing Melancholia*, 175.

134. Albert Camus' 'philosophy of limits' proposed living in the present and pursuing *mésure* ('measuredness' or 'balance'), rather than projecting hopes to change the world into the future. See, for example, Albert Camus, *L'Homme révolté* (Paris: Gallimard, 2013).

135. On nostalgia as a form of imagination, see Felipe de Brigard, 'A Nostalgia reimaginada', *Piauí*, September 2020, https://piaui.folha.uol.com.br/materia/ a-nostalgia-reimaginada/ (last accessed 5 October 2020).

136. 'Melancholy', as Jürgen Habermas—of all people—points out, 'is inscribed in the revolutionary consciousness.' Jürgen Habermas, *Between Facts and Norms: Contributions to a Discourse Theory of Law and Democracy* (Cambridge, MA: MIT Press, 2001), 471.

137. Wendy Brown, 'Resisting Left Melancholy', *Boundary (2)* 26, no. 3 (1999): 19–27, 25.

138. Walter Benjamin, 'Left-Wing Melancholy (On Erich Kästner' New Book of Poems)', *Screen* 15, no. 2 (1974): 28–32, 29–30.

139. On the antinomy in Benjamin's writings on melancholia, see Traverso, *Left-Wing Melancholia*, 45–8. Max Pensky discusses the centrality of melancholia in Benjamin's thought in *Melancholy Dialectics: Walter Benjamin and the Play of Mourning* (Amherst, MA: University of Massachusetts Press, 2001).

140. Walter Benjamin, *Origin of the German Trauerspiel* (Cambridge, MA: Harvard University Press, 2019), 162.

141. In *The Arcades Project*, Benjamin quotes a letter sent to him by Max Horkheimer, in 1937: 'Past injustice has occurred and is completed. The slain are really slain… Perhaps… only the injustice, the horror, the sufferings of the past are irreparable. The justice practised, the joys, the works, have a different relation to time, for their positive character is largely negated by the transience of things.' He offers a rejoinder: that history be viewed as a form of remembrance, such that the incomplete (happiness) be rendered complete, and the complete (suffering) be rendered incomplete. 'That is theology', he affirms. See Walter Benjamin, 'On the Theory of Knowledge, Theory of Progress', in *The Arcades Project*, trans. Howard Eiland and Kevin McLaughlin (Cambridge, MA: Belknap Press), 471 (N8.1).

142. In his celebrated interpretation of Paul Klee's painting *Angelus Novus*, Benjamin describes the 'angel of history' being propelled 'into the future to which his back is turned, while the pile of debris before him grows skyward'. Walter Benjamin, 'Theses on the Philosophy of History', in *Illuminations*, ed. Hannah Arendt (New York: Schocken Books, 1986), 258.

10. WARFARE ON WELFARE IN THE AGE OF EMERGENCY

1. Quinn Slobodian, *Globalists: The End of Empire and the Birth of Neoliberalism* (Cambridge, MA: Harvard University Press, 2018).

2. Ibid., 10.

3. Quinn Slobodian, 'Anti-'68ers and the Racist-Libertarian Alliance', *Cultural Politics* 15, no. 3 (2019): 272–86.

4. For a comparison with America's similar dynamic, see Greg Grandin, *The End of the Myth: From the Frontier to the Border Wall in the Mind of America* (New York, NY: Metropolitan Books, 2019).

5. Ruben Anderson and David Keen, *Partners in Crime? The Impacts of Europe's Outsourced Migration Controls on Peace, Stability and Rights* (London: Saferworld, 2019).

6. Georgio Agamben, *Stasis: Civil War as a Political Paradigm (Homo Sacer II,2)* (Stanford, CA: Stanford University Press, 2015).

7. Murray Rothbard, 'The Great Society: A Libertarian Critique', Mises Institute, 30 January 2008 (original 1967), https://mises.org/library/great-society-libertarian-critique (last accessed 7 August 2020).

8. Dipesh Chakrabarty, *Provincializing Europe: Poscolonial Thought and Historical Difference* (Princeton, NJ: Princeton University Press, 2008).

9. Alessandra Mezzadri, 'On the Value of Social Reproduction: Infomal Labour, the Majority World and the Need for Inclusive Theories and Politics', *Radical Philosophy* 2, no. 4 (2019): 33–41, https://www.radicalphilosophy.com/article/on-the-value-of-social-reproduction (last accessed 7 August 2020).

10. Domenico Losurdo, *Liberalism: A Counter-History* (New York, NY: Verso, 2014).

11. Mark Duffield, 'Total War as Environmental Terror: Linking Liberalism, Resilience and the Bunker', *South Atlantic Quarterly* 110, no. 3 (2011): 757–69.

12. The fieldwork for my anthropology PhD was completed in Sudan. Lying south of Sennar on the Blue Nile, I arrived in the village of Maiurno in January 1974, where I stayed for the next fourteen months. At the time, my hometown of Dudley in the West Midlands was a thriving Black Country municipality. Its busy High Street offered a range of shops and services. There was plenty of work, and the surrounding factories paid some of the highest manual labour wages in the country. A tangible development gap existed between working-class Dudley and peasant Maiurno.

    Maiurno lies about 200 miles south of Khartoum. In the 1970s, a tarmac road extended half the way. At the best of times, travelling between the two was an uncomfortable dawn-to-dusk journey in an open-sided bus. During the rainy season the unsurfaced section of the journey became a quagmire. Maiurno was a sprawling agricultural village with a central marketplace. With the exception of a handful of brick-built compounds belonging to leading merchant families, it was constructed of mud and thatch. There was no electricity, save for the merchant compounds. Water was drawn directly from the river and sold from donkeys by the jerry-can. It was culturally conservative, and married women were seldom seen in the street. With no telephones, external communication was via the post office in Sennar, 10 miles away. Dudley was, at best, a three-week letter cycle.

    I returned to Maiurno in 2014, almost forty years to the day after first arriving. In the intervening years, Dudley has changed. If not boarded up, the run-down High Street has surrendered to thrift-shops, pawnbrokers, and takeaways. The department stores and factories went decades ago. In their place, if anything, are anonymous warehouses and empty car parks. The young people that are able to move have done, accentuating the lack of education, precarious employment, and benefit-dependency among those remaining. At night, the bus station resembles a refugee transit centre. In the 2019 general election, Dudley returned a Conservative MP.

    Maiurno has also changed—in a different way, however. While Dudley has moved 'down' in many respects, Maiurno has gone from a mud and thatch village to a small brick-built town. Three-wheel scooter taxis now ply Maiurno's lanes. It is linked to Khartoum by an all-weather road, allowing air-conditioned buses to complete the journey in five hours. The whole town has electricity and piped drinking water is pumped from the ground. Everywhere, there are cheap satellite TV sets, refrigerators, freezers, and washing machines imported from Asia. The market has also grown. Some old trades have declined as new services have appeared. Practically everyone has a mobile telephone. Indeed, telecom masts outnumber and stand taller than the minarets. A marked liberalisation of gender relations has also occurred. Increased educational opportunities within Maiurno have accompanied a more visible and active presence of women.

　　If a development gap separated Dudley and Maiurno in the mid-1970s, today it feels less certain, more contradictory and difficult to locate. There is now more of a 'sameness' regarding the issues and problems facing people in both places: youth unemployment, debt, rising costs, stagnant wages, intergenerational poverty, and bad government.

13. Mary Kaldor, *New and Old Wars: Organised Violence in a Global Era* (Cambridge: Polity Press, 1999).

14. For example, UN Secretary-General Boutros Boutros-Ghali, *An Agenda for Peace: Preventive Diplomacy, Peacemaking and Peace-Keeping: Report of the Secretary-General* (New York, NY: United Nations, 1992).

15. Hans-Hermann Hoppe, 'Nationalism and Secession', *Chronicles* (November 1993): 23–5, http://www.hanshoppe.com/wp-content/uploads/publications/nationalism_chronicles.pdf (last accessed 7 August 2020).

16. Ibid.

17. Llewellyn H. Rockwell, 'Iraq and the Democratic Empire', Mises Institute, 17 February 2006, https://mises.org/library/iraq-and-democratic-empire (last accessed 7 August 2020).

18. Murray Rothbard, 'The Vital Importance of Separation', *Rothbard-Rockwell Report* 5, no. 4 (1994): 1–10., http://www.rothbard.it/articles/vital-importance-separation.pdf (last accessed 7 August 2020).

19. Yumi Kim, 'Stateless in Somalia, and Loving It', Mises Institute, 21 February 2006, https://mises.org/library/stateless-somalia-and-loving-it (last accessed 7 August 2020).

20. Losurdo, *Liberalism*, 37.

21. Samuel P. Huntington, 'The Clash of Civilizations?', *Foreign Affairs* 72, no. 3 (1993): 22–49.

22. Martin Barker, *The New Racism: Conservatives and the Ideology of the Tribe* (London: Junction Books, 1981). For an exposition in relation to Asian foundry workers during the 1960s and 1970s, see Mark Duffield, *Black Radicalism and the Politics of De-Industrialisation: The Hidden History of Indian Foundry Workers* (Aldershot: Avebury, 1988).

23. Mark Duffield, 'The Symphony of the Damned: Racial Discourse, Complex Political Emergencies and Humanitarian Aid', *Disasters* 20, no. 3 (1996): 173–93.

24. At the time of editing this chapter, the coronavirus pandemic gripped the world, deepening further the state of exception.

25. For analysis of the left–right dialectic in relation to the Taliban in pre-invasion Afghanistan, see Mark Duffield, *Development, Security and Unending War: Governing the World of Peoples* (Cambridge: Polity Press, 2007), 133–58.

26. Angela Nagle, *Kill all Normies: Online Culture Wars from 4chan and Tumblr to Trump and the Alt-Right* (Alresford, Hants: Zero Books, 2017).

27. Zygmunt Bauman, 'Wars of the Globalization Era', *European Journal of Social Theory* 4, no. 1 (2001): 11–28.

28. Omar Dewachi, *Ungovernable Life: Mandatory Medicine and Statecraft in Iraq* (Stanford, CA: Stanford University Press, 2017).

29. Harlan K. Ullman and James P. Wade, *Shock and Awe: Achieving Rapid Dominance* (Washington DC: National Defense University, 1996), http://www.dodccrp.org/files/Ullman_Shock.pdf (last accessed 7 August 2020).

30. The World Peace Foundation, working in collaboration with Global Rights Compliance, has produced recent reports on starvation crimes in Syria, Yemen, and South Sudan. These reports detail the deliberate destruction of critical infrastructure as an all-party war aim. See https://sites.tufts.edu/wpf/accountability-for-mass-starvation/ (last accessed 7 August 2020).

31. David Campbell, Stephen Graham, and Daniel Bertrand Monk, 'Introduction to Urbicide: The Killing of Cities?', *Theory & Event* 10, no. 2 (2007): 1–8.

32. Achille Mbembe, 'Necropolitics', *Public Culture* 15, no. 1 (2003): 11–40.

33. Jennifer Rankin, 'Migration: EU Praises Greece as "Shield" after Turkey Opens Border', *The Guardian*, 2 March 2020, https://www.theguardian.com/world/2020/mar/03/migration-eu-praises-greece-as-shield-after-turkey-opens-border (last accessed 7 August 2020).

34. Besides the waves of irregular migration, globalising wars have also given life to a raw, unfettered capitalism. They have revealed the systemic link between disaster and economy that social democracy sort to contain. There is, for example, a dark side to the new right's celebration of Somalia. Following the internationalised destruction of the state, over several decades an indigenous capitalism has expanded in response to changing global market opportunities. This has gone together with the systematic dispossession and uprooting of subordinate clans and communities, making them akin to slaves in their own country. Economic innovation spans mobile financial services, telecommunications, and high-end cash-crop production, through to the comprehensive capture of the aid economy, including transport, food retail, and cash-transfer programmes. IDP camps function as reserves of bare labour supporting opportunistic elite economic ventures. Humanitarians have been complicit with the creation of a post-social plantation economy. See Susanne Jaspars, Guhad M. Adan, and Nisar Majid, *Food and Power in Somalia: Business as Usual?* (London: Conflict Research Programme, LSE, 2020).

35. For my discussion of *homo inscius*, as the embodiment of the necessary ignorance of the neoliberal subject, see Mark Duffield, *Post-Humanitarianism: Governing Precarity in the Digital World* (Cambridge: Polity Press, 2019), 155. *Homo inscius* is now a central player in how crisis informatics reconfigures the cognitive landscape of disaster zones. Due to an overload of stimuli, so it is argued, necessarily ignorant humans would be at a loss without new sense-making tools.

36. Byung-Chul Han, *The Expulsion of the Other: Society, Perception and Communication Today* (Cambridge: Polity Press, 2018), 4.

37. Jennifer S. Light, *From Warfare to Welfare: Defense Intellectuals and Urban Problems in Cold War America* (Baltimore, MD: Johns Hopkins University Press, 2003).

38. Created in 1948 by Douglas Aircraft Company, the RAND Corporation is a US global policy think tank. Financed by government and private donors, it specialises in using applied science and operations research across a range of defence and non-defence issues.

39. Virginia Eubanks, *Automating Inequality: How High-Tech Tools Profile, Police, and Punish the Poor* (New York, NY: St Martin's Press, 2018).

40. Michael Marmot et al., *Health Equity in England: The Marmot Review 10 Years On* (London: Institute of Health Equity, Feburary 2020), https://www.health.org. uk/sites/default/files/upload/publications/2020/Health%20Equity%20in%20 England_The%20Marmot%20Review%2010%20Years%20On_full%20report. pdf (last accessed 7 August 2020).

41. Office of the High Commissioner for Human Rights, 'Statement on Visit to the United Kingdom, by Professor Philip Alston, United Nations Special Rapporteur on Extreme Poverty and Human Rights', London, 16 November 2018, https:// www.ohchr.org/Documents/Issues/Poverty/EOM_GB_16Nov2018.pdf.

42. Based on submissions from thirty-four countries: see, Philip Alston, *Digital Welfare States and Human Rights*(Geneva: Office of the High Commissioner for Human Rights, 11 October 2019), UN Doc. A/74/48037, https://www.ohchr.org/en/ issues/poverty/pages/srextremepovertyindex.aspx (last accessed 7 August 2020). Also see the *Guardian* investigative series on 'automating poverty', *The Guardian*, 'Automating Poverty', October 2019, https://www.theguardian.com/technol-ogy/series/automating-poverty (last accessed 7 August 2020).

43. Duffield, *Post-Humanitarianism*.

44. Helen Young and Anastasia Marshak, *Persistent Global Acute Malnutrition* (Boston, MA: Feinstein International Centre, Tufts University, 2017); Alston, *Digital Welfare States and Human Rights (A/74/48037)*.

45. Mark Fisher, 'Exiting the Vampire's Castle', openDemocracy, 22 November 2013, https://www.opendemocracy.net/en/opendemocracyuk/exiting-vampire-cas-tle/ (last accessed 7 August 2020).

46. Losurdo, *Liberalism*, 169.

47. Joel Wainwright and Geoff Mann, *Climate Leviathan: A Political Theory of our Plantary Future* (London & New York: Verso, 2018), 125.

48. Fiona Jeffries, 'Social Reproduction and Politics: Overcoming the Separation', *Sociological Review* 66, no. 3 (2018): 577–92.

11. THE WHITE MODERATES: EUROPE AND THE RETURN OF THE STATE IN MALI

1. 'Après les menaces des islamistes Maliens, François Hollande renforce le plan vigip-irate', France 24, 12 January 2013, https://www.france24.com/fr/20130112-intervention-mali-hollande-annonce-renforcement-plan-vigipirate-securite-france-armee-ansar-dine. (Unless otherwise stated, all URLs cited were last accessed 14 November 2020).

2. United Nations, 'Security Council Authorizes Deployment of African-Led International Support Mission in Mali for Initial Year-Long Period', Meetings Coverage and Press Releases (New York, NY, 20 December 2012), https://www. un.org/press/en/2012/sc10870.doc.htm. (last accessed 7 April 2020).

3. 'Mali: Pour la presse, Hollande a gagné sa stature présidentielle', LExpress.fr, 4 February 2013, https://www.lexpress.fr/actualite/politique/mali-pour-la-presse-hollande-a-gagne-sa-stature-presidentielle_1216470.html.

4. 'Sondage. Hollande, l'état de disgrâce', leparisien.fr, 11 April 2013, http://www. leparisien.fr/politique/sondage-hollande-l-etat-de-disgrace-11-04-2013-2717687. php.

5. Rémi Carayol, '"Papa Hollande" au Mali', JeuneAfrique (blog), 2 February 2013, https://www.jeuneafrique.com/172393/politique/papa-hollande-au-mali/.

6. According to Tony Chafer, 'La Françafrique testified to a symbiotic relationship in which Africa is experienced in French representations as a natural extension where the Francophone world and Francophilia merge.' See Tony Chafer, 'Chirac and "la Françafrique": No Longer a Family Affair', Modern & Contemporary France 13, no. 1 (February 2005): 7–23, 7, https://doi.org/10.1080/0963948052000341196.

7. Catherine Gegout, Why Europe Intervenes in Africa: Security Prestige and the Legacy of Colonialism (Oxford: Oxford University Press, 2018), 5.

8. Roland Marchal, 'Military (Mis)Adventures in Mali', African Affairs 112, no. 448 (2013): 486–97, https://doi.org/10.1093/afraf/adt038.

9. Stephen W. Smith, 'In Search of Monsters', London Review of Books 35, no. 3 (7 February 2013), https://www.lrb.co.uk/the-paper/v35/n03/stephen-w.-smith/in-search-of-monsters.

10. Malians constitute the largest group of sub-Saharan diaspora in France. See, Ministère de l'Europe et des Affaires étrangères, The African Diaspora in France (France Diplomacy—Ministry for Europe and Foreign Affairs, February 2019 update), https://www.diplomatie.gouv.fr/en/country-files/africa/the-african-diaspora-in-france/ (last accessed 8 April 2020).

11. Isabelle Lasserre and Thierry Oberlé, Notre guerre secrète au Mali: les nouvelles menaces contre la France (Paris: Fayard, 2013), 27.

12. Claude Askolovitch, 'Marseille, territoire perdu de la république', Marianne, 15 September 2012, https://www.marianne.net/societe/marseille-territoire-perdu-de-la-republique.

13. Insee, Comparateur de territoire—commune de Marseille, 22 September 2020, https://www.insee.fr/fr/statistiques/1405599?geo=COM-13055.

14. In France it is illegal to collect data on ethnicity and religion.

15. For example, during the civil unrest of 2005, there were few instances of violence in Marseille compared to other big cities in France. See Katharyne Mitchell, 'Marseille's Not for Burning: Comparative Networks of Integration and Exclusion in Two French Cities', Annals of the Association of American Geographers 101, no. 2 (2011): 404–23.

16. John E. Mueller and Mark G. Stewart, Chasing Ghosts: The Policing of Terrorism

(Oxford: Oxford University Press, 2016), 2. See also John Mueller, *Overblown: How Politicians and the Terrorism Industry Inflate National Security Threats, and Why We Believe Them* (New York, NY: Simon & Schuster, 2006).

17. Martin Luther King, Jr., 'Letter from a Birmingham Jail', 16 April 1963, https://kinginstitute.stanford.edu/king-papers/documents/letter-birmingham-jail.

18. Charles Sykes, 'Why Trump Thinks Statue-Toppling Activists Will Save Him in Wisconsin', *Politico*, 29 June 2020, https://www.politico.com/news/magazine/2020/06/29/trump-statue-toppling-activistswisconsin-343910.

19. Organisation for Economic Co-operation and Development, *States of Fragility 2018* (Paris, 2018), https://www.oecd.org/dac/states-of-fragility-2018-9789264302075-en.htm.

20. John Gray, *Black Mass: Apocalyptic Religion and the Death of Utopia* (London: Penguin Books, 2007), 259.

21. Thomas Piketty, *Capital in the Twenty-First Century*, trans. Arthur Goldhammer (Cambridge, MA: Belknap Press, 2014).

22. Ibid., 265.

23. Ibid., 249.

24. Peter Temin, *The Vanishing Middle Class: Prejudice and Power in a Dual Economy*, ePub Version 1.0 (Cambridge, MA: MIT Press, 2018), 84.

25. W. Arthur Lewis, 'Economic Development with Unlimited Supplies of Labour', *Manchester School* 22, no. 2 (May 1954): 139–91.

26. Temin, *The Vanishing Middle Class*, 968.

27. Jhumpa Bhattacharya, Aisha Nyandoro, and Anne Price, 'If Black Lives Matter, the "Welfare Queen" Myth Must Go', *The Nation*, 10 June 2020, https://www.thenation.com/article/society/black-lives-welfare-queen/.

28. Christophe Guilluy, *Le Crépuscule de la France d'en haut*, ePUB, Champs Actuel (Paris: Flammarion, 2014). There is an English edition: *Twilight of the Elites: Prosperity, the Periphery and the Future of France* (New Haven, CT: Yale University Press, 2019).

29. Christophe Guilluy, 'France is Deeply Fractured. Gilets Jaunes are Just a Symptom', *The Guardian*, 2 December 2018, https://www.theguardian.com/commentisfree/2018/dec/02/france-is-deeply-fractured-gilets-jeunes-just-a-symptom.

30. Simon Reid-Henry, *Empire of Democracy: The Remaking of the West Since the Cold War, 1971–2017*, e-book (London: John Murray, 2019), 2851.

31. Helene Cooper et al., 'Pentagon Eyes Africa Drawdown as First Step in Global Troop Shift', *The New York Times*, 24 December 2019, https://www.nytimes.com/2019/12/24/world/africa/esper-troops-africa-china.html.

32. 'Germany Ponders Bigger Troop Mandate in Africa's Sahel', *Deutsche Welle*, 29 December 2019, https://www.dw.com/en/germany-ponders-bigger-troop-mandate-in-africas-sahel/a-51828723.

33. Lucía Abellán and Miguel González, 'España redobla su esfuerzo militar en el Sahel para ganar influencia', *El País*, 19 July 2020, https://elpais.com/espana/2020-07-19/espana-redobla-su-esfuerzo-militar-en-el-sahel-para-ganar-influencia.html.

34. EEAS/European Union, 'L'Union européenne et le G5 Sahel un partenariat plus que jamais d'actualité' (Brussels, 28 April 2020), https://eeas.europa.eu/head-quarters/headquarters-homepage/78009/l%E2%80%99union-europ%C3%A9enne-et-le-g5-sahel-un-partenariat-plus-que-jamais-d%E2%80%99actualit%C3%A9_fr.

35. Isaline Bergamaschi, 'The Fall of a Donor Darling: The Role of Aid in Mali's Crisis', *Journal of Modern African Studies* 52, no. 3 (September 2014): 347–78, https://doi.org/10.1017/S0022278X14000251.

36. Ibid., 357.

37. Gregory Mann, *From Empires to NGOs in the West African Sahel* (Cambridge: Cambridge University Press, 2015).

38. Bruno Charbonneau and Jonathan M. Sears, 'Fighting for Liberal Peace in Mali? The Limits of International Military Intervention', *Journal of Intervention and Statebuilding* 8, nos. 2–3 (3 July 2014): 192–213, 200, https://doi.org/10.1080/17502977.2014.930221.

39. Ibid., 206.

40. Emmanuel Macron on Twitter: 'Au-delà de l'effort militaire, c'est le retour de l'État, des administrations, des services publics, que nous allons poursuivre au Sahel. Ce sera notre priorité pour stabiliser la région', 30 June 2020, https://twitter.com/emmanuelmacron/status/1278066814388445186 (last accessed 17 July 2020).

41. 'The Sahel Alliance', Alliance Sahel, https://www.alliance-sahel.org/en/sahel-alliance/ (last accessed 28 July 2020).

42. See, for example, Human Rights Watch, *Mali: Unchecked Abuses in Military Operations* (New York, 8 September 2017), https://www.hrw.org/news/2017/09/08/mali-unchecked-abuses-military-operations; Amnesty International, *'They Executed Some and Brought the Rest with Them.' Human Rights Violations by Security Forces in the Sahel* (London, 2020), https://www.amnesty.org/download/Documents/AFR3723182020ENGLISH.pdf; Human Rights Watch, *Burkina Faso: Residents' Accounts Point to Mass Executions* (New York, 8 July 2020), https://www.hrw.org/news/2020/07/08/burkina-faso-residents-accounts-point-mass-executions.

43. Corinne Dufka, *'How Much More Blood Must Be Spilled?': Atrocities against Civilians in Central Mali, 2019* (New York: Human Rights Watch, February 2020), 69–70, https://www.hrw.org/report/2020/02/11/how-much-more-blood-must-be-spilled/atrocities-against-civilians-central-mali.

44. Alex Thurston, 'Mali: Recent Developments Connected with the June 5 Movement', Sahel Blog, 6 July 2020, https://sahelblog.wordpress.com/2020/07/06/mali-recent-developments-connected-with-the-june-5-movement/.

45. 'Sondage: Plus de 80% de la population ont une opinion défavorable de la France', Bamada, 14 December 2019, http://bamada.net/sondage-plus-de-80-de-la-population-ont-une-opinion-defavorable-de-la-france (last accessed 22 July 2020).

46. Boubacar Haidara and Lamine Savane, 'Les Religieux sont-ils en train de prendre le pouvoir au Mali?', *The Conversation*, 24 June 2020, http://theconversation.com/

les-religieux-sont-ils-en-train-de-prendre-le-pouvoir-au-mali-141085 (last accessed 22 July 2020).

47. Josep Borrell, 'Taking Risks for Peace: EU Crisis Management in Action' (EEAS/ European Union blog, 23 January 2020), https://eeas.europa.eu/headquarters/ headquarters-homepage/73386/taking-risks-peace-eu-crisis-management-action_en.

48. European Commission, *Europeans' Opinions about the European Union's Priorities— Fieldwork November 2019*, Standard Eurobarometer 92 (Brussels, 2020), 102, https://ec.europa.eu/commfrontoffice/publicopinion/index.cfm/Survey/get-SurveyDetail/instruments/STANDARD/surveyKy/2255.

49. European Union, *The European Union's Global Strategy: Three Years On, Looking Forward* (Brussels, 2019), https://eeas.europa.eu/sites/eeas/files/eu_global_strategy_2019.pdf.

50. Ingo Peters et al., *European Union's Crisis Response in the Extended Neighbourhood: Comparing the EU's Output Effectiveness in the Cases of Afghanistan, Iraq and Mali* (Berlin: EUNPACK, 2018), http://www.eunpack.eu/sites/default/files/publications/ WP%207%20Comparative%20for%207.1._final%20version%2010.03.18.pdf.

51. EEAS/European Union, *EU Global Strategy* (Brussels, 2019), https://eeas.europa. eu/topics/eu-global-strategy_en.

52. UN Office for the Coordination of Humanitarian Affairs, *Sahel Crisis: Overview of Humanitarian Needs and Requirements* (New York, NY: United Nations, May 2020), https://reliefweb.int/report/nigeria/sahel-crisis-overview-humanitarian-needs-and-requirements-may-2020.

53. ACLED, *Dashboard*, 28 August 2019, https://acleddata.com/dashboard/.

54. José Luengo-Cabrera on Twitter: 'Mali: violence & displacement—Between mid-2017 & mid-2020, countrywide reported violent events more than doubled. Meanwhile, the number of IDPs increased fourfold.—Central Mali, where 62% of violent events have been reported so far in 2020, currently hosts 51% of IDPs', 3 July 2020, https://twitter.com/J_LuengoCabrera/status/127910067801 1531269 (last accessed 30 July 2020).

55. Sergei Boeke and Giliam de Valk, 'The Unforeseen 2012 Crisis in Mali: The Diverging Outcomes of Risk and Threat Analyses', *Studies in Conflict & Terrorism* (29 March 2019): 1, https://doi.org/10.1080/1057610X.2019.1592356.

56. Meera Sabaratnam, *Decolonising Intervention: International Statebuilding in Mozambique* (London: Rowman & Littlefield, 2017).

57. Ministère de l'Europe et des Affaires étrangères, 'G5 Sahel—Pau Summit— Statement by the Heads of State', 13 January 2020 (France Diplomacy, Ministry for Europe and Foreign Affairs), https://www.diplomatie.gouv.fr/en/french-for-eign-policy/security-disarmament-and-non-proliferation/news/news-about-defence-and-security/article/g5-sahel-pau-summit-statement-by-the-heads-of-state-13-jan-2020.

58. Sabaratnam, *Decolonising Intervention*, 134.

59. Pauline Bock, 'EU Must Develop "Appetite for Power" Says Foreign Policy Chief

Josep Borrell', Euronews, 16 February 2020, https://www.euronews.com/2020/02/16/eu-must-develop-appetite-for-power-says-foreign-policy-chief-josep-borrell.

60. Miguel Hernando de Larramendi and Ana I. Planet, *España y Mauritania: Sáhara, pesca, inmigración y desarrollo en el centro de la agenda bilateral*, Documentos CIDOB Mediterráneo y Oriente Medio (Barcelona: CIDOB, 2009), https://www.cidob.org/publicaciones/series_pasadas/documentos/mediterraneo_y_oriente_medio/espana_y_mauritania_sahara_pesca_migraciones_y_desarrollo_en_el_centro_de_la_agenda_bilateral.

61. Aïssatou Diallo and Benjamin Roger, 'French "Summons" on Operation Barkhane Raises Hackles in Mali and Burkina Faso', *Africa Report*, 9 December 2019, https://www.theafricareport.com/21022/french-summons-on-operation-barkhane-raises-hackles-in-mali-and-burkina-faso/.

62. Charbonneau and Sears, 'Fighting for Liberal Peace in Mali?', 201.

63. Sabaratnam refers to Europeans' belief that they are 'historically, economically, culturally and politically distinctive in ways which significantly determine the over-all character of world politics'. Sabaratnam, *Decolonising Intervention*, 20.

64. Charbonneau and Sears, 'Fighting for Liberal Peace in Mali?', 205.

65. 'Mali President Offers Concessions to End Political Stalemate', Reuters, 9 July 2020, https://uk.reuters.com/article/uk-mali-politics-idUKKBN24A1JE.

66. 'UN Urges Inquiry into Violence by Anti-Terrorism Force against Malian Protestors', Voice of America—English, 19 July 2020, https://www.voanews.com/africa/un-urges-inquiry-violence-anti-terrorism-force-against-malian-protestors (last accessed 30 July 2020).

67. Gregory Mann, 'Ça chauffe à Bamako de', *Africa Is a Country*, https://africasacountry.com/2020/07/ca-chauffe-a-bamako-de (last accessed 30 July 2020).

68. Dennis Hankins, US Ambassador to Mali, on Twitter, 23 June 2020, https://twitter.com/MaliEmbassyUSA/status/1275663755960094720 (last accessed 30 July 2020).

69. 'Déclaration du Quai d'Orsay—Situation au Mali', *La France au Mali*, https://ml.ambafrance.org/Declaration-du-Quai-d-Orsay-Situation-au-Mali (last accessed 30 July 2020).

70. Délégation de l'Union européenne en République du Mali, 'Mali: Déclaration du Haut Représentant/Vice-Président Josep Borrell sur la crise politique', 22 June 2020, https://eeas.europa.eu/delegations/mali/81261/mali-d%C3%A9claration-du-haut-repr%C3%A9sentantvice-pr%C3%A9sident-josep-borrell-sur-la-crise-politique_fr (last accessed 30 July 2020).

71. Alex Thurston, 'ECOWAS Leaves Bamako Empty-Handed; M5-RFP in the Driver's Seat by Holding Firm', Sahel Blog, 20 July 2020, https://sahelblog.wordpress.com/2020/07/20/ecowas-leaves-bamako-empty-handed-m5-rfp-in-the-drivers-seat-by-holding-firm/.

72. Andrew Lebovich, *Sacred Struggles: How Islam Shapes Politics in Mali*, Policy Brief (London: European Council on Foreign Relations, November 2019).

73. Robert Launay and Benjamin F. Soares, 'The Formation of an "Islamic Sphere" in French Colonial West Africa', *Economy and Society* 28, no. 4 (January 1999): 497–519, 513, https://doi.org/10.1080/03085149900000015.

74. European Community of West African States, 'Declaration of ECOWAS Heads of State and Government on Mali', 28 August 2020, https://www.ecowas.int/declaration-of-ecowas-heads-of-states-and-governmenet-on-mali-2020/.

75. For an overview of Mali's transitional government, see Andrew Lebovich, 'Mali's Transitional Government: The Dangers of the Junta Clinging to Power', Commentary, European Council on Foreign Relations, 6 October 2020, https://ecfr.eu/article/commentary_malis_transitional_government_the_dangers_of_the_junta_clinging/.

76. EEAS/European Union, 'Informal Meeting of EU Defence Ministers: Remarks by the High Representative/Vice-President Josep Borrell at the Press Conference', Berlin, 26 August 2020, https://eeas.europa.eu/headquarters/headquarters-homepage/84441/informal-meeting-eu-defence-ministers-remarks-high-representativevice-president-josep-borrell_en.

77. Denis M. Tull, 'Rebuilding Mali's Army: The Dissonant Relationship between Mali and its International Partners', *International Affairs* 95, no. 2 (1 March 2019): 405–22, https://doi.org/10.1093/ia/iiz003.

78. See, for example, Robert B. Lloyd, 'Ungoverned Spaces and Regional Insecurity: The Case of Mali', *SAIS Review of International Affairs* 36, no. 1 (12 July 2016): 133–41, https://doi.org/10.1353/sais.2016.0012.

79. Catriona Dowd and Clionadh Raleigh, 'The Myth of Global Islamic Terrorism and Local Conflict in Mali and the Sahel', *African Affairs* 112, no. 448 (July 2013): 498–509, 506, https://doi.org/10.1093/afraf/adt039.

80. Ibid., 508.

81. Charbonneau and Sears, 'Fighting for Liberal Peace in Mali?', 208.

82. Catriona Craven-Matthews and Pierre Englebert, 'A Potemkin State in the Sahel? The Empirical and the Fictional in Malian State Reconstruction', *African Security* 11, no. 1 (January 2018): 1–31, https://doi.org/10.1080/19392206.2017.1419634.

83. Zygmunt Bauman, *Retrotopia* (Cambridge: Polity Press, 2017).

84. Craven-Matthews and Englebert, 'A Potemkin State in the Sahel?', 15.

85. Zygmunt Bauman elaborates this idea in *Liquid Modernity* (Cambridge: Polity Press, 2012).

86. Pankaj Mishra, *Bland Fanatics: Liberals, Race and Empire* (London: Verso, 2020), 172.

87. Mark Fisher, *Capitalist Realism* (Winchester: Zero Books, 2009), 3.

12. DEPLORABLE LIBERALISM: WHITENESS, TRUMP, AND THE ANTI-HUMANITARIAN SOCIAL CONTRACT

1. Josh Dawsey, 'Trump Derides Protections for Immigrants from "Shithole" Countries', *The Washington Post*, 12 January 2018.

2. Dan Coughlin and Kim Ives, 'WikiLeaks Haiti: Let Them Live on $3 a Day', *The*

Nation, 1 June 2011, https://www.thenation.com/article/archive/wikileaks-haiti-let-them-live-3-day/; Greg Grandin, 'A Voter's Guide to Hillary Clinton's Policies in Latin America', *The Nation*, 15 April 2016, https://www.thenation.com/article/archive/a-voters-guide-to-hillary-clintons-policies-in-latin-america/. (Unless otherwise stated, all URLs cited were last accessed 25 October 2020.)

3. Charles W. Mills, 'Racial Liberalism', *PMLA* 123, no. 5 (2008): 1380–97, 1386.

4. Greg Grandin, 'The Strange Career of American Exceptionalism', *The Nation*, 6 December 2016, https://www.thenation.com/article/archive/the-strange-career-of-american-exceptionalism/; Mike King, 'Aggrieved Whiteness: White Identity Politics and Modern American Racial Formation', *Abolition*, 5 May 2017, https://abolitionjournal.org/aggrieved-whiteness-white-identity-politics-and-modern-american-racial-formation/.

5. Judah Grunstein, 'Will the World have to Learn to Live with the U.S. as a Failed State?', *World Politics Review*, 15 February 2017, https://www.worldpoliticsreview.com/articles/21226/will-the-world-have-to-learn-to-live-with-the-u-s-as-a-failed-state; Heather Hurlburt, 'Is America Becoming a Failed State?, *New York Magazine*, 12 May 2017, https://nymag.com/intelligencer/2017/05/is-america-becoming-a-failed-state.html; Moustafa Bayoumi, 'My Fellow Americans, It's Time to Intervene in Our Failed State', *The Guardian*, 3 August 2017, https://www.theguardian.com/commentisfree/2017/aug/03/my-fellow-americans failed state-trump-united-states-must-invade-usa.

6. David Rothkopf, 'Is America a Failing State?', *Foreign Policy*, 10 May 2019, https://foreignpolicy.com/2017/05/10/is-america-a-failing-state-trump-fires-comey-fbi/.

7. Francis Fukuyama, 'US Against the World? Trump's America and the New Global Order', *The Financial Times*, 11 November 2016, https://www.ft.com/content/6a43cf54-a75d-11e6-8b69-02899e8bd9d1.

8. Martin Pengelly, 'Trump "Rat-Infested" Attack on Elijah Cummings was Racist, Pelosi Says', *The Guardian*, 27 July 2019, https://www.theguardian.com/us-news/2019/jul/27/donald-trump-elijah-cummings-democrat-house-oversight-bully-rat-rodent.

9. David Corn, 'Donald Trump says he Doesn't Believe in "American Exceptionalism"', *Mother Jones*, 7 June 2016, https://www.motherjones.com/politics/2016/06/donald-trump-american-exceptionalism/; Marina Fang and J. M. Rieger, 'This May Be the Most Horrible Thing that Donald Trump Believes', *HuffPost* (blog), 28 September 2016, https://www.huffpost.com/entry/donald-trump-eugenics_n_57ec4cc2e4b024a52d2cc7f9.

10. Tara Francis Chan, 'State Department Official says China Threat is the First Time the U.S. has a Great "Competitor that is Not Caucasian"', *Newsweek*, 2 May 2019, https://www.newsweek.com/china-threat-state-department-race-caucasian-1413202. For a critique of Western universality, see, for example, Sylvia Wynter, 'Unsettling the Coloniality of Being/Power/Truth/Freedom: Towards the Human, after Man, its Overrepresentation—An Argument', *CR: The New Centennial Review* 3, no. 3 (2003): 257–337.

11. Kevin D. Williamson, 'The White Ghetto', *National Review*, 16 December 2013, https://www.nationalreview.com/2013/12/white-ghetto-kevin-d-williamson.

12. Kevin D. Williamson, 'Chaos in the Family, Chaos in the State: The White Working Class's Dysfunction', *National Review*, 17 March 2016, https://www.nationalreview.com/2016/03/donald-trump-white-working-class-dysfunction-real-opportunity-needed-not-trump/ (emphasis added).

13. For an articulation of this interpretation, see Francis Fukuyama, 'US Against the World?'

14. Eduardo Porter, 'How the G.O.P. Became the Party of the Left Behind', *The New York Times*, 27 January 2020, https://www.nytimes.com/interactive/2020/01/27/business/economy/republican-party-voters-income.html; Terrence McCoy, 'How Does it Feel to be White, Rural and in the Minority?', *The Washington Post*, 30 July 2018, https://www.washingtonpost.com/news/local/wp/2018/07/30/feature/majority-minority-white-workers-at-this-pennsylvania-chicken-plant-now-struggle-to-fit-in/.

15. Stephen Hopgood, 'When the Music Stops: Humanitarianism in a Post-Liberal World Order', *Journal of Humanitarian Affairs* 1, no. 1 (January 2019): 4–14, 7.

16. Ibid., 6.

17. Fukuyama, 'US Against the World'.

18. Michael Barnett, *Empire of Humanity: A History of Humanitarianism* (Ithaca, NY: Cornell University Press, 2011).

19. Francis Fukuyama, 'American Political Decay or Renewal?', *Foreign Affairs* 95, no. 4 (July/August 2016): 58–68, https://www.foreignaffairs.com/articles/united-states/2016-06-13/american-political-decay-or-renewal (last accessed 15 March 2020).

20. Daniel Martinez HoSang and Joseph E. Lowndes, *Producers, Parasites, Patriots: Race and the New Right-Wing Politics of Precarity* (Minneapolis, MN: University of Minnesota Press, 2019), 64.

21. Mills, 'Racial Liberalism', 1387, 1386.

22. Charles W. Mills, 'Global White Ignorance', in *Routledge International Handbook of Ignorance Studies*, ed. Matthias Gross and Linsey McGoey (Abingdon: Routledge, 2015), 217–27.

23. Kevin D. Williamson, 'The Case Against Reparations', *National Review*, 25 May 2014, https://www.nationalreview.com/2014/05/case-against-reparations-kevin-d-williamson/.

24. Cheryl I. Harris, 'Whiteness as Property', *Harvard Law Review* 106, no. 8 (June 1993): 1707–91.

25. Lauren Gambino, 'Donald Trump Attacked for Calling Hurricane Maria Response an "Incredible Success"', *The Guardian*, 12 September 2018, https://www.theguardian.com/us-news/2018/sep/11/trump-hurricane-maria-puerto-rico-success; Yarimar Bonilla and Marisol LeBrón, *Aftershocks of Disaster: Puerto Rico Before and After the Storm* (Chicago, IL: Haymarket Books, 2019).

26. Mychal Denzel Smith, 'The Rebirth of Black Rage', *The Nation*, 13 August 2015, https://www.thenation.com/article/archive/the-rebirth-of-black-rage/.

27. Roberta Rampton and Gabriel Stargardter, 'Trump Praises Response to Puerto Rico, Says Crisis Straining Budget', Reuters, 4 October 2017, https://www.reuters.com/article/us-usa-puertorico-idUSKCN1C80DO.

28. Roberto Belloni, 'The Trouble with Humanitarianism', *Review of International Studies* 33, no. 3 (2007): 451–74.

29. Encarnación Gutiérrez Rodríguez, 'The Coloniality of Migration and the "Refugee Crisis": On the Asylum-Migration Nexus, the Transatlantic White European Settler Colonialism-Migration and Racial Capitalism', *Refuge: Canada's Journal on Refugees* 34, no. 1 (2018): 16–28.

30. Stewart E. Tolnay and E. M. Beck, 'Black Flight: Lethal Violence and the Great Migration, 1900–1930', *Social Science History* 14, no. 3 (1990): 347–70.

31. Fukuyama, 'US Against the World?'

32. Francis Fukuyama, 'The End of History?', *The National Interest* 16 (Summer 1989): 3–18, 9.

33. Gutiérrez Rodríguez, 'The Coloniality of Migration and the "Refugee Crisis"', 19.

34. Francis Fukuyama, 'Against Identity Politics', *Foreign Affairs* 97, no. 5 (September/October 2018): 90–114, https://www.foreignaffairs.com/articles/americas/2018–08–14/against-identity-politics-tribalism-francis-fukuyama.

35. Dawsey, 'Trump Derides Protections for Immigrants'.

36. Francis Fukuyama, 'US Against the World?'.

37. Nicholas Carnes and Noam Lupu, 'It's Time to Bust the Myth: Most Trump Voters Were Not Working Class', *Washington Post*, 5 June 2017, https://www.washingtonpost.com/news/monkey-cage/wp/2017/06/05/its-time-to-bust-the-myth-most-trump-voters-were-not-working-class/.

38. Roper Center for Public Opinion Research, *How Groups Voted* (Ithaca, NY: Cornell University, 2016), https://ropercenter.cornell.edu/how-groups-voted-2016.

39. Fukuyama, 'Against Identity Politics'; HoSang and Lowndes, *Producers, Parasites, Patriots*.

40. Arlie Russell Hochschild, *Strangers in Their Own Land* (New York, NY: New Press, 2016), quoted in Andrew J. Perrin, 'The Invention of the "White Working Class"', *Public Books*, 30 January 2018, https://www.publicbooks.org/the-invention-of-the-white-working-class/ (last accessed 25 October 2020).

41. HoSang and Lowndes, *Producers, Parasites, Patriots*.

42. Perrin, 'The Invention of the "White Working Class"'.

43. HoSang and Lowndes, *Producers, Parasites, Patriots*, 14.

44. Fukuyama, 'Against Identity Politics'.

45. Keeanga-Yamahtta Taylor, 'Black Faces in High Places', *Jacobin* (May 2015), https://jacobinmag.com/2015/05/baltimore-uprising-protests-freddie-gray-black-politicians/.

46. The Combahee River Collective, 'A Black Feminist Statement', *Women's Studies Quarterly* 42, nos. 3–4 (2014): 271–80.

47. Fukuyama, 'American Political Decay or Renewal?'.

48. Nathalie Baptiste, 'Staggering Loss of Black Wealth Due to Subprime Scandal

Continues Unabated', *American Prospect*, 13 October 2014, https://prospect.org/api/content/c5278216-cb68–540e-b41f-522696be117c/.

49.　Malaika Jabali, 'The Color of Economic Anxiety', *Current Affairs*, 3 October 2018, https://www.currentaffairs.org/2018/10/the-color-of-economic-anxiety.

50.　Ibid.

51.　Eric Etheridge, 'Rick Santelli: Tea Party Time', *The New York Times | Opinionator*, 20 February 2009, https://opinionator.blogs.nytimes.com/2009/02/20/rick-santelli-tea-party-time/.

52.　Malcolm Gladwell, 'Starting Over', *The New Yorker*, 24 August 2015, https://www.newyorker.com/magazine/2015/08/24/starting-over-dept-of-social-studies-malcolm-gladwell.

53.　Glen Ford, 'Katrina: The Logic of Genocide', *Black Agenda Report*, 27 August 2015, http://www.blackagendareport.com/new_yorker_katrina_logic_of_genocide.

54.　Margaret Somers, *Genealogies of Citizenship: Markets, Statelessness, and the Right to Have Rights* (Cambridge: Cambridge University Press, 2008), 101.

55.　Bill O'Reilly, 'Katrina and the Poor', 8 September 2008, https://www.billoreilly.com/b/Katrina-and-the-Poor/19095.html.

56.　James Ridgeway, 'The Secret History of Hurricane Katrina', *Mother Jones*, 28 August 2009, https://www.motherjones.com/environment/2009/08/secret-history-hurricane-katrina/. The line between military intervention and humanitarian response had already been blurring for decades since the end of the Cold War, but the response to Katrina seemed novel given that this was a natural disaster on US soil. See Barnett, *Empire of Humanity*.

57.　Rebecca Solnit, *A Paradise Built in Hell: The Extraordinary Communities that Arise in Disaster* (Harmondsworth: Penguin, 2010), 259.

58.　Ibid., 5.

59.　Hopgood, 'When the Music Stops', 7, original emphasis.

60.　Achille Mbembe, trans. Libby Meintjes, 'Necropolitics', *Public Culture* 15, no. 1 (25 March 2003): 11–40; Mills, 'Racial Liberalism'.

61.　Fukuyama, 'Against Identity Politics'.

62.　Mainstream commentators rarely discuss the class composition of militias. However, American gun culture, expensive as it is, is routinely characterised as rural, if not working class.

63.　Vincent Bevins, *The Jakarta Method: Washington's Anticommunist Crusade and the Mass Murder Program that Shaped Our World* (New York: PublicAffairs, 2020).

64.　Ta-Nehisi Coates, 'The Secret Lives of Inner-City Black Males', *The Atlantic*, 18 March 2014, https://www.theatlantic.com/politics/archive/2014/03/the-secret-lives-of-inner-city-black-males/284454/.

13.　REQUIEM FOR A MOST VIOLENT HUMANITARIAN ORDER

1.　Translated from Portuguese by Ana Naomi de Sousa.

2.　Immanuel Kant, 'Conjectures on the Beginning of Human History [1786]', in *Kant:*

Political Writings, ed. H. S. Reiss (Cambridge: Cambridge University Press, 2007), 221–34, 232.

3. Juliano Fiori, 'Guerras humanitárias e ordem ética', in *Sobre a guerra*, ed. José Luís Fiori (Petrópolis: Editora Vozes, 2018), 232.

4. José Luís Fiori, 'A Guerra pérsica: Uma guerra ética', *Cadernos de Conjuntura* 8 (Rio de Janeiro: Instituto de Economia Industrial/UFRJ, April 1991), 5.

5. In truth, this 'military revolution' began much earlier. America's defeat in Vietnam was followed by setbacks in US foreign policy during the 1970s: the victory of the Islamic Revolution in Iran; the Sandinista victory in Nicaragua; the growing Soviet presence in Africa and the Middle East; and, finally, the Russian invasion of Afghanistan. This series of humiliations contributed to the election of Ronald Reagan, and to legitimising his project to reignite the Cold War in the early 1980s, leading the US government to increase its military expenditure. Reagan's 'Strategic Defense Initiative', often referred to as the 'Star Wars' programme, brought about the development of new information systems to improve battlefield control and command; high-precision remote-controlled carriers and bombs; and sophisticated stealth attack systems. See José Luís Fiori, 'Império e pauperização', *Folha de São Paulo*, 16 October 2001.

6. George H. W. Bush, 'Address Before the 45th Session of the United Nations General Assembly in New York, October 1, 1990', in *Public Papers of the Presidents of the United States: George Bush*: Book 2: *July 1 to December 31, 1990* (Washington, DC: Government Printing Press, 1990), 1332.

7. William J. Clinton, 'Remarks to the 48th Session of the United Nations General Assembly in New York City, September 27, 1993', in *Public Papers of the Presidents of the United States: William J. Clinton*: Book 2, *August 1 to December 31, 1993* (Washington, DC: Government Printing Press, 1993), 1614.

8. Andrew Bacevich, *American Empire* (Cambridge, MA: Harvard University Press, 2002), 143.

9. Chalmers Johnson, *The Sorrows of Empire* (New York, NY: Metropolitan Books, 2004), 22–3.

10. On the contribution of the Islamic world to Western modernity, see, for example, Samir Amin, *Eurocentrism* (New York: Monthly Review Press, 1989); and John M. Hobson, *The Eastern Origins of Western Civilisation* (Cambridge: Cambridge University Press, 2004).

11. Donald Rumsfeld, 'Transforming the Military', *Foreign Affairs* 81, no. 3 (May/June 2002): 20–32, 20.

12. Hans J. Morgenthau, *Politics Among Nations: The Struggle for Power and Peace* (New York, NY: McGraw Hill, 1993), 66.

13. Juliano Fiori, 'Guerras humanitárias e ordem ética', 239.

14. Missy Ryan and Susan Cornwall, 'Intelligence on Libya Rebels Shows "Flickers" of Qaeda', Reuters, 29 March 2011, https://www.reuters.com/article/us-libya-usa-intelligence-idUSTRE72S43P20110329 (last accessed 20 September 2020).

15. José Luís Fiori, 'Babel Syndrome and the New Security Doctrine of the United States', *Journal of Humanitarian Affairs* 1, no. 1 (2019): 42–5.

16. Presidency of the United States, *National Security Strategy of the United States* (Washington, DC, 2017).

14. ORDERS AND DISORDERS OF REFUGEE HUMANITARIANISM IN THE ARAB MIDDLE EAST

1. R. Arar, 'The New Grand Compromise: How Syrian Refugees Changed the Stakes in the Global Refugee Assistance Regime', *Middle East Law and Governance* 9, no. 3 (2017): 298–312, 299, https://doi.org/10.1163/1876337500903007. (All URLs cited were last accessed 15 October 2020.)

2. T. Fakhoury, *The European Union and Arab Refugee Hosting States: Frictional Encounters*, Working Paper 1 (University of Vienna, Centre for European Integration Research, 2019), https://eif.univie.ac.at/downloads/workingpapers/wp2019–01.pdf.

3. R. Anholt and G. Sinatti, 'Under the Guise of Resilience: The EU Approach to Migration and Forced Displacement in Jordan and Lebanon', *Contemporary Security Policy* 41, no. 2 (2020): 311–35, https://doi.org/10.1080/13523260.2019.169 8182.

4. T. Fakhoury, 'Leverage and Contestation in Refugee Governance: Lebanon and Europe in the Context of Mass Displacement', in *Resisting Europe: Practices of Contestation in the Mediterranean Middle East*, ed. R. A. Del Sarto and S. Tholens (Ann Arbor, MI: University of Michigan Press, 2020), 142–63; J. C. Völkel, 'Fanning Fears, Winning Praise: Egypt's Smart Play on Europe's Apprehension of More Undocumented Immigration', *Mediterranean Politics* (2020), https://doi.org/10.1 080/13629395.2020.1758450.

5. C. Brun, 'There is no Future in Humanitarianism: Emergency, Temporality and Protracted Displacement', *History and Anthropology* 27, no. 4 (2016): 393–410, https://doi.org/10.1080/02757206.2016.1207637.

6. Lewis Turner, '"#Refugees Can be Entrepreneurs Too!" Humanitarianism, Race, and the Marketing of Syrian Refugees', *Review of International Studies* 46, no. 1 (January 2020): 137–55.

7. G. Ramsay, 'Humanitarian Exploits: Ordinary Displacement and the Political Economy of the Global Refugee Regime', *Critique of Anthropology* 40, no. 2 (2019): 1–25, 1, https://doi.org/10.1177/0308275X19840417.

8. B. S. Chimni, 'The Geopolitics of Refugee Studies: A View from the South', *Journal of Refugee Studies* 11, no. 4 (1998): 350–74, 371, https://doi.org/10.1093/jrs/11.4.350-a.

9. J. Milner, 'Power and Influence in the Global Refugee Regime', *Refuge: Canadian Journal on Refugees* 33, no. 1 (2017): 3–6, https://refuge.journals.yorku.ca/index.php/refuge/issue/view/2316.

10. D. Chatty, 'Special Issue Introduction', *International Journal of Middle East Studies* 49, no. 4 (2017): 577–82, https://doi.org/10.1017/S002074381700059; D. Chatty, 'The Syrian Humanitarian Disaster: Understanding Perceptions and Aspirations in Jordan, Lebanon and Turkey', *Global Policy* 8, no. 1 (2017): 25–32, https://doi.org/10.1111/1758–5899.12390.

11. United Nations Educational, Scientific and Cultural Organization, *Arab States: Migration, Displacement and Education: Building Bridges, Not Walls*, Global Education Monitoring Report (Paris: UNESCO, 2019), http://gem-report-2019.unesco.org/arab-states/#:~:text=No%20part%20of%20the%20world,people%20internally%20displaced%20by%20conflict.

12. S. Hanafi, 'Forced Migration in the Middle East and North Africa', in *The Oxford Handbook of Refugee and Forced Migration Studies*, ed. E. Fiddian-Qasmiyeh, G. Loescher, K. Long, and N. Sigona (Oxford: Oxford University Press, 2014), 585–98, https://doi.org/10.1093/oxfordhb/9780199652433.013.0029.

13. K. Lenner, '"Biting Our Tongues": Policy Legacies and Memories in the Making of the Syrian Refugee Response in Jordan', *Refugee Survey Quarterly* 39, no. 3 (2020): 273–98, https://doi.org/10.1093/rsq/hdaa005.

14. H. Thiollet, 'Migration as Diplomacy: Labor Migrants, Refugees, and Arab Regional Politics in the Oil-Rich Countries', *International Labor and Working-Class History* 79 (2011): 103–21, https://www.jstor.org/stable/41306911; S. Khallaf, *Refugee Movements in the Middle East: Old Crises, New Ideas*, MENARA Working Papers 29 (2019), 1–12, https://www.iai.it/sites/default/files/menara_wp_29.pdf; P. Fargues, 'International Migration and the Nation State in Arab Countries', *Middle East Law and Governance* 5, nos. 1–2 (2013): 5–35, http://apps.eui.eu/Personal/fargues/Documents/MELG_005_01_01Fargues.pdf; AKM A. Ullah, 'Geopolitics of Conflicts and Refugees in the Middle East and North Africa', *Contemporary Review of the Middle East* 5, no. 3 (2018): 258–74, https://doi.org/10.1177/2347798 918776751.

15. Fargues, 'International Migration'.

16. L. Mourad, 'Open Borders, Local Closures: Decentralization and the Politics of Local Responses to the Syrian Refugee Influx in Lebanon', PhD dissertation (University of Toronto, 2019); Fargues, 'International Migration'; T. Fakhoury, 'Refugee Return and Fragmented Governance in the Host State: Displaced Syrians in the Face of Lebanon's Divided Politics', *Third World Quarterly* 42, no. 1 (2020): 162–81, https://doi.org/10.1080/01436597.2020.1762485.

17. T. Fakhoury, 'Multi-Level Governance and Migration Politics in the Arab World: The Case of Syria's Displacement', *Journal of Ethnic and Migration Studies* 45, no. 8 (2019): 1310–26, https://doi.org/10.1080/1369183X.2018.1441609; L. Hilal and S. Samy, *Asylum and Migration in the Mashrek*, (Euro-Mediterranean Human Rights Network, 2008), https://ec.europa.eu/migrant-integration/index.cfm?action=media.download&uuid=2A9339E1-E12B-E824-A57C5AEF-9CF4F31D.

18. Mourad, 'Open Borders, Local Closures'; L. Achilli, *Syrian Refugees in Jordan: A Reality Check*, Migration Policy Centre Briefs 2 (2015), https://cadmus.eui.eu/bitstream/handle/1814/34904/MPC_2015–02_PB.pdf?sequence= 1&isAllowed=y; Al-Monitor Correspondent in Egypt, 'Syrian Refugees Arrested, Race Deportation from Egypt', *Al-Monitor*, 25 October 2019, https://www.al-monitor.com/pulse/originals/2019/10/egypt-syria-arrest-refugees-human-rights-violations-illegal.html.

19. D. Sullivan and S. Tobin, *Security and Resilience Among Syrian Refugees in Jordan* (Middle East Research and Information Project, 14 October 2014), https://merip.org/2014/10/security-and-resilience-among-syrian-refugees-in-jordan/.

20. Fakhoury, 'Multi-Level Governance'.

21. M. Barnett, 'Refugees and Humanitarianism', in *The Oxford Handbook of Refugee and Forced Migration Studies*, ed. E. Fiddian-Qasmiyeh, G. Loescher, K. Long, and N. Sigona (Oxford: Oxford University Press, 2014), 241–52, 242, https://doi.org/10.1093/oxfordhb/9780199652433.013.0026.

22. Brun, 'There is No Future in Humanitarianism'; Chatty, 'Special Issue Introduction'.

23. R. Sayigh, 'Palestinian Refugees in Lebanon: Implantation, Transfer or Return', *Middle East Policy Council* 8, no. 1 (2001): 94–105, https://mepc.org/journal/palestinian-refugees-lebanon-implantation-transfer-or-return; G. Tsourapas, 'The Syrian Refugee Crisis and Foreign Policy Decision-Making in Jordan, Lebanon, and Turkey', *Journal of Global Security Studies* 4, no. 4 (2019): 464–81, https://doi.org/10.1093/jogss/ogz016.

24. Achilli, *Syrian Refugees in Jordan*; M. Janmyr, 'No Country of Asylum: "Legitimizing" Lebanon's Rejection of the 1951 Refugee Convention', *International Journal of Refugee Law* 29, no. 3 (2017): 438–65, https://doi.org/10.1093/ijrl/eex026; P. Seeberg and J. C. Völkel, 'Introduction: Arab Responses to EU Foreign and Security Policy Incentives: Perspectives on Migration Diplomacy and Institutionalized Flexibility in the Arab Mediterranean Turned Upside Down', *Mediterranean Politics* (2020), https://doi.org/10.1080/13629395.2020.1758451.

25. Chatty, 'The Syrian Humanitarian Disaster'; M. Yahya and M. Muasher, *Refugee Crises in the Arab World*, (Washington, DC: Carnegie Endowment for International Peace, 2018), https://carnegieendowment.org/2018/10/18/refugee-crises-in-arab-world-pub-77522

26. Brun, 'There is No Future in Humanitarianism'.

27. M. Janmyr, 'UNHCR and the Syrian Refugee Response: Negotiating Status and Registration in Lebanon', *International Journal of Human Rights* 22, no. 3 (2017): 393–419, https://doi.org/10.1080/13642987.2017. 1371140; C. Geha and J. Talhouk, 'From Recipients of Aid to Shapers of Policies: Conceptualizing Government–United Nations Relations during the Syrian Refugee Crisis in Lebanon', *Journal of Refugee Studies* 32, no. 4 (2019): 645–63, https://doi.org/10.1093/jrs/fey052.

28. Fakhoury, 'Multi-Level Governance'; Fakhoury, 'Refugee Return and Fragmented Governance in the Host State'.

29. D. Stevens, 'Rights, Needs or Assistance? The Role of the UNHCR in Refugee Protection in the Middle East', *International Journal of Human Rights* 20, no. 2 (2016): 264–83, https://doi.org/10.1080/13642987.2015.1079026.

30. Chatty, 'The Syrian Humanitarian Disaster'; S. Hoffmann, 'International Humanitarian Agencies and Iraqi Migration in PreConflict Syria', *International Journal of Middle East Studies* 48, no. 2 (2016): 339–55, https://doi.org/10.1017/S0020743816000076.

31. J-P. Cassarino and R. A. Del Sarto, *The Governance of Migration and Border Controls in the European–North African Context*, MENARA Working Papers 13 (2018), https://www.iai.it/en/pubblicazioni/governance-migration-and-border-controls-european-north-african-context; S. Lavenex, *Instruments, Methods, Mechanisms of Externalisation: Trajectory and Implications*, Draft Working Paper for the Comparative Network on Refugee Externalization Policies (CONREP, 2019).

32. M. F. Cuéllar, 'Refugee Security and the Organizational Logic of Legal Mandates', *Georgetown Journal of International Law* 37, no. 4 (2006): 583–723, 622.

33. Tsourapas, 'The Syrian Refugee Crisis'.

34. Arar, 'The New Grand Compromise'; Fakhoury, 'Leverage and Contestation in Refugee Governance'.

35. B. Lauten and S. Nelson-Pollard, *Lessons from Responsibility Sharing Mechanisms: For an Ambitious and Strong Global Compact on Refugees*, Briefing Note (Norwegian Refugee Council, August 2017), https://www.nrc.no/globalassets/pdf/briefing-notes/lessons-fromresponsibility--sharing-mechanisms/lessons-from-responsibility-sharing-mechanisms.pdf.

36. Chatty, 'The Syrian Humanitarian Disaster'.

37. Tsourapas, 'The Syrian Refugee Crisis'.

38. Sandra Lavenex and Tamirace Fakhoury, 'Trade Agreements as a Venue for Migration Governance? Potential and Challenges for the European Union', Seminar presentation, Delegationen för migrationsstudier (Delmi), Stockholm, 2019.

39. Fakhoury, 'Leverage and Contestation in Refugee Governance'.

40. H. Darbouche, 'Decoding Algeria's ENP Policy: Differentiation by Other Means?', *Mediterranean Politics* 13, no. 3 (2008): 371–89, https://doi.org/10.1080/13629390802386770; Fakhoury, *The European Union and Arab Refugee Hosting States*.

41. L. Mourad and K. P. Norman, 'Transforming Refugees into Migrants: Institutional Change and the Politics of International Protection', *European Journal of International Relations* 26, no. 3 (2019): 687–713, https://doi.org/10.1177/1354066119883688; David Scott FitzGerald, *Refuge Beyond Reach: How Rich Democracies Repel Asylum Seekers* (Oxford: Oxford University Press, 2019).

42. D. Huber, 'Ten Years into the Arab Uprising: Images of EU's Presence, Practices, and Alternatives in the Mediterranean Space', *European Foreign Affairs Review* 25 (2020): 131–50; A. Teti, P. Abbott, V. Talbot, and P. Maggiolini, *Democratisation against Democracy: How EU Foreign Policy Fails the Middle East* (London: Palgrave Macmillan, 2020).

43. Fakhoury, 'Leverage and Contestation in Refugee Governance'.

44. R. Anholt and G. Sinatti, 'Under the Guise of Resilience: The EU Approach to Migration and Forced Displacement in Jordan and Lebanon', *Contemporary Security Policy* 41, no. 2 (2020): 311–35, https://doi.org/10.1080/13523260.2019.1698182; Fakhoury, *The European Union and Arab Refugee Hosting States*.

45. Fakhoury, 'Leverage and Contestation in Refugee Governance'.

46. European Economic and Social Committee, *Establishing a New Partnership Framework with Third Countries under the European Agenda on Migration* (Brussels, 6 June 2011),

COM (2016) 385 final, https://www.europarl.europa.eu/RegData/docs_autres_institutions/commission_europeenne/com/2016/0385/COM_COM (2016)0385_EN.pdf; European Commission, *Lives in Dignity: From Aid-Dependence to Self-Reliance—Forced Displacement and Development* (Brussels, 24 April 2016), COM (2016) 234 final, https://ec.europa.eu/echo/files/policies/refugees-idp/Communication_Forced_Displacement_Development_2016.pdf.

47. Anholt and Sinatti, 'Under the Guise of Resilience'.

48. Lavenex, *Instruments, Methods, Mechanisms of Externalisation*.

49. Delegation of the European Union to Lebanon, 'Syrian Refugees in Lebanon', Beirut, 29 November 2019 (Brussels: EEAS press release), https://eeas.europa.eu/delegations/lebanon/71235/node/71235_pt.

50. Turner, '"#Refugees Can be Entrepreneurs Too!"'

51. Arar, 'The New Grand Compromise'; Tsourapas, 'The Syrian Refugee Crisis'; Fakhoury, *The European Union and Arab Refugee Hosting States*; Fakhoury, 'Leverage and Contestation in Refugee Governance'.

52. Fakhoury, 'Refugee Return and Fragmented Governance in the Host State'.

53. C. Cornish, 'Bankers "Smuggled" $6bn Out of Lebanon, Says Ex-Finance Chief', *The Financial Times*, 13 July 2020, https://www.ft.com/content/df234c78-a945-4199-befe-0272259dc755.

54. 'Labor Ministry begins Crackdown on Foreign Labor', *The Daily Star Lebanon*, 15 July 2020, http://dailystar.com.lb/News/Lebanon-News/2020/Jul-15/509015-labor-ministry-begins-crackdown-on-foreign-labor.ashx.

55. The European Union and Lebanon Association Council, 'Decision No 1/2016 of the EU-Lebanon Association Council agreeing on EU–Lebanon Partnership Priorities' (Brussels, 11 November 2016), UE-RL 3001/16, https://ec.europa.eu/neighbourhood-enlargement/sites/near/files/eu_lebanon_partnership_priorities_2016-2020_and_their_annexed_eu-lebanon_compact.pdf.

56. Lavenex and Fakhoury, 'Trade Agreements as a Venue for Migration Governance?'

57. UNHCR, UNICEF, WFP, and Inter-Agency Coordination Lebanon, *VASyR 2019: Vulnerability Assessment of Syrian Refugees in Lebanon* (Reliefweb, 2019), https://reliefweb.int/sites/reliefweb.int/files/resources/73118.pdf.

58. P. Khoder, 'La communauté internationale espère lever 2.6 milliards de dollars pour le Liban', *L'Orient-le-Jour*, 30 June 2020, https://www.lorientlejour.com/article/1224000/la-communaute-internationale-espere-lever-26-milliards-de-dollars-pour-le-liban.html.

59. N. Stel, *Hybrid Political Order and the Politics of Uncertainty: Refugee Governance in Lebanon* (Abingdon: Routledge, 2020).

60. Fakhoury, 'Leverage and Contestation in Refugee Governance'.

61. Fakhoury, 'Multi-Level Governance and Migration Politics in the Arab World'.

62. 'Interview with Lebanese President Michel Aoun on the Eve of the Elections', BBC News Arabic (translated), 5 May 2018, https://www.youtube.com/watch?v=v2AlDCu61cI, details/transcript in Arabic: http://www.presidency.gov.lb/Arabic/News/Pages/Details.aspx?nid=24822; 'EU, Lebanon Call for

Political Solution in Syria', Kuwait News Agency, 18 July 2017, https://www.kuna.net.kw/ArticleDetails.aspx?id=2624280&Language=en.

63. I. Diwan, 'Lebanon's Dysfunctional Political Economy', *Project Syndicate*, 27 July 2020, https://www.project-syndicate.org/commentary/lebanon-economic-crisis-perverse-incentives-by-ishac-diwan-2020–07.

64. Lavenex and Fakhoury, 'Trade Agreements as a Venue for Migration Governance?'

65. Fakhoury, 'Refugee Return and Fragmented Governance in the Host State'.

66. 'Bassil from Brussels: Syrian Displacement Crisis Biggest Challenge to All of Us', National News Agency, 4 February 2019, http://nna-leb.gov.lb/en/show-news/100232/Bassil-from-Brussels-Syrian-displacement-crisis-biggest-challenge-to-all-of-us.

67. Lavenex and Fakhoury, 'Trade Agreements as a Venue for Migration Governance?'.

68. C. Brun 'There is No Future in Humanitarianism: Emergency, Temporality and Protracted Displacement', *History and Anthropology* 27, no. 4 (2016): 393–410, https://doi.org/10.1080/02757206.2016.1207637; G. Chatelard, 'Jordan: A Refugee Haven', *Online Journal of Migration Policy Institute* (31 August 2010), https://www.migrationpolicy.org/article/jordan-refugee-haven.

69. Arar, 'The New Grand Compromise'.

70. Tsourapas, 'The Syrian Refugee Crisis'.

71. Arar, 'The New Grand Compromise'; Fakhoury, *The European Union and Arab Refugee Hosting States*.

72. Achilli, *Syrian Refugees in Jordan*; Tsourapas, 'The Syrian Refugee Crisis'; Sullivan and Tobin, *Security and Resilience*.

73. Lavenex and Fakhoury, 'Trade Agreements as a Venue for Migration Governance?'

74. European Commission, 'EU–Jordan Partnership: The Compact' (Brussels, March 2017), https://ec.europa.eu/neighbourhood-enlargement/sites/near/files/jordan-compact.pdf.

75. M. Schubert and I. Haase, 'How to Combat the Causes of Refugee Flows: The EU–Jordan Compact in Practice', *Konrad Adenauer Stiftung*, 16 April 2018, 98, 100, https://www.kas.de/c/document_library/get_file?uuid=7c25eba0-342f-b05a-7022-212b042ebffe&groupId=252038.

76. E. Grawert, *The EU–Jordan Compact: A Model for Burden-Sharing in Refugee Crises?* Policy Brief 3 (Bonn International Center for Conversion, 2019), 1, 4, https://www.bicc.de/uploads/tx_bicctools/BICC_Policy_Brief_3_2019.pdf.

77. Council of the European Union, 'Brussels IV Conference on "Supporting the Future of Syria and the Region": Co-Chairs' Declaration' (Brussels, 30 June 2020), https://www.consilium.europa.eu/en/press/press-releases/2020/06/30/brussels-iv-conference-on-supporting-the-future-of-syria-and-the-region-co-chairs-declaration/.

78. Julia Morris, 'Extractive Landscapes: The Case of the Jordan Refugee Compact', *Refuge: Canada's Journal on Refugees* 36, no. 1 (2020): 87–96.

79. Lenner, '"Biting Our Tongues"'.

80. V. Barbelet, J. Hagen-Zanke, and D. Mansour-Ille, *The Jordan Compact: Lessons Learnt*

and Implications for Future Refugee Compacts, Overseas Development Institute Briefing Paper (London: ODI, 2018), 4, https://www.odi.org/publications/11045-jordan-compact-lessons-learnt-and-implications-future-refugee-compacts.

81. Tsourapas, 'The Syrian Refugee Crisis', 9.
82. Lavenex and Fakhoury, 'Trade Agreements as a Venue for Migration Governance?'.
83. Grawert, *The EU–Jordan Compact*, 1.
84. Barbelet, Hagen-Zanke, and Mansour-Ille, *The Jordan Compact*, 4.
85. C. Huang and K. Gough, *The Jordan Compact: Three Years on, Where Do We Stand?* (Center for Global Development, 11 March 2019), https://www.cgdev.org/blog/jordan-compact-three-years-on
86. Schubert and Haase, 'How to Combat the Causes of Refugee Flows', 100.
87. Grawert, *The EU–Jordan Compact*, 4.
88. Morris, 'Extractive Landscapes'.
89. Fakhoury, *The European Union and Arab Refugee Hosting States*.
90. Schubert and Haase, 'How to Combat the Causes of Refugee Flows'; Grawert, *The EU–Jordan Compact*.
91. A. Alrababa'h and S. Williamson, 'Jordan Shut Out 60,000 Syrian Refugees—and then Saw a Backlash. This is Why', *The Washington Post*, 20 July 2018, https://www.washingtonpost.com/news/monkey-cage/wp/2018/07/20/when-jordan-closed-its-border-to-refugees-the-public-protested-heres-why/.
92. Lavenex and Fakhoury, 'Trade Agreements as a Venue for Migration Governance?'.
93. See, the Hashemite Kingdom of Jordan Ministry of Foreign Affairs and Expatriates, Speech, Brussels IV Conference on the Future of Syria and the Region, 30 June 2020.
94. Council of the European Union, 'Brussels IV Conference… Co-Chairs' Declaration'.
95. Barnett, 'Refugees and Humanitarianism'.
96. FitzGerald, *Refuge Beyond Reach*.
97. J. Milner and K. Wojnarowicz, 'Power in the Global Refugee Regime: Understanding Expressions and Experiences of Power in Global and Local Contexts', *Refuge: Canada's Journal on Refugees* 33, no. 1 (2017): 7–17, https://refuge.journals.yorku.ca/index.php/refuge/article/view/40444
98. Chimni, 'The Geopolitics of Refugee Studies'.
99. Lauten and Nelson-Pollard, *Lessons from Responsibility Sharing Mechanisms*; Morris, 'Extractive Landscapes'.
100. Mourad and Norman, 'Transforming Refugees into Migrants'.
101. Turner, '"#Refugees Can be Entrepreneurs Too!"'
102. Ibid., 137.
103. Chatty, 'The Syrian Humanitarian Disaster'.
104. Fakhoury, 'Leverage and Contestation in Refugee Governance'.
105. M. Fotaki, 'A Crisis of Humanitarianism: Refugees at the Gates of Europe', *International Journal of Health Policy and Management* 8, no. 6 (2019): 321–4, https://dx.doi.org/10.15171/ijhpm.2019.22.
106. Author's conversations with civil society activists, 2019 and 2020.
107. Fakhoury, 'Refugee Return and Fragmented Governance in the Host State'.

15. VIOLENCE IN A POST-LIBERAL WORLD

1. F. Fukuyama, *The End of History and the Last Man* (New York, NY: Free Press, 1992).

2. See M. Duffield, 'Post-Humanitarianism: Governing Precarity through Adaptive Design', *Journal of Humanitarian Affairs* 1, no. 1 (2019): 15–27.

3. On this, see D. Losurdo, *Liberalism: A Counter-History* (New York, NY: Verso, 2014).

4. Here, I am borrowing terms used by Henry Giroux. See, in particular, H. A. Giroux, *The Violence of Organized Forgetting* (San Francisco, CA: CityLights, 2014).

5. This claim is made to the point of monotony by liberal thinkers and politicians alike. For the most recent treatment on this, see M. Albright, *Fascism: A Warning* (New York, NY: Harper Collins, 2018).

6. M. Duffield, *Global Governance and the New Wars: The Merging of Development and Security* (London: Zed Books, 2001).

7. B. Evans, 'Dead in the Waters', in *Life Adrift: Climate Change, Migration, Critique*, ed. A. Baldwin and G. Bettini (Lanham, MD: Rowman & Littlefield, 2017), 59–78.

8. For an overview of liberal war, see B. Evans, 'The Liberal War Thesis: Introducing the Ten Key Principles of Twenty-First-Century Biopolitical Warfare', *South Atlantic Quarterly* 110, no. 3 (2011). 747–56.

9. S. Pinker, *The Better Angels of Our Nature: A History of Violence and Humanity* (London: Penguin: 2011).

10. On this see, in particular, M. Dillon and J. Reid, *The Liberal Way of War: Killing to Make Life Live* (Abingdon: Routledge, 2009); B. Evans and M. Hardt, 'Barbarians to Savages: Liberal War Inside and Out', *Theory & Event* 13, no. 3 (2010).

11. Whilst the idea of technological supremacy was at the heart of the revolution in military affairs, with its idea of zero-casualty wars, and the inspired shift towards what many called 'network-centric warfare' (notably promoted and developed by the RAND Corporation and its principle advocates, John Arquilla and David Ronfeldt), the idea that technological advance leads to 'smarter and more civilised violence' has been well established since the dropping of the atomic bombs on Hiroshima and Nagasaki, which invariably required a redemptive narrative. For a compelling history of the more recent links between technology and war, see A. Bousquet, *The Eye of War: Military Perception from the Telescope to the Drone* (Minneapolis, MN: University of Minnesota Press, 2018).

12. See M. Duffield, *Development, Security and Unending War: Governing the World of Peoples* (Cambridge: Polity Press, 2007).

13. D. Kilcullen, *The Accidental Guerrilla: Fighting Small Wars in the Midst of a Big One* (London: Hurst, 2017).

14. For a considered history on the role of the mercenary, see T. Geraghty, *Soldiers of Fortune: A History of the Mercenary in Modern Warfare* (New York, NY: Pegasus, 2011). See also S. McFate, *The Modern Mercenary: Private Armies and What they Mean for World Order* (Oxford: Oxford University Press, 2014).

15. M. Duffield, 'Risk-Management and the Fortified Aid Compound: Everyday Life in Post-Interventionary Society', *Journal of Intervention and Statebuilding* 4, no. 4 (2010): 453–74.

16. M. Duffield, *Post-Humanitarianism: Governing Precarity in the Digital World* (Cambridge: Polity Press, 2019).

17. B. Evans and J. Reid, *Resilient Life: The Art of Living Dangerously* (Cambridge: Polity Press, 2014).

18. I have developed the idea of 'the catastrophic topography of endangerment' in both B. Evans, *Liberal Terror* (Cambridge: Polity Press, 2013), and Evans and Reid, *Resilient Life*.

19. See H. A. Giroux, *Stormy Weather: Katrina and the Politics of Disposability* (Abingdon: Routledge, 2006).

20. Developing on from the work of René Girard, amongst others, this is the focus of a new comprehensive study: B. Evans, *Ecce Humanitas: Beholding the Pain of Humanity* (New York, NY: Columbia University Press, 2021).

21. The most prominent in this regard would be M. Walzer, *Just and Unjust Wars: A Moral Argument with Historical Illustrations*, 5th ed. (New York: Basic Books, 2015). For an important critique of Just War and how it links to liberal theology, see J. Gray, *Black Mass: Apocalyptic Religion and the Death of Utopia* (New York, NY: Penguin, 2007).

22. B. Evans, 'Liberal Violence: The Benjaminian Divine to the Angels of History', *Theory & Event* 19, no. 1 (2016).

23. This comparison would be made by a number of authors and commentators, notably John Pilger. See http://johnpilger.com/articles/from-pol-pot-to-isis-the-blood-never-dried (last accessed 10 October 2020).

24. B. Evans and H. A. Giroux, 'Intolerable Violence', *Symploke* 23, nos. 1–2 (2015): 197–219.

25. Z. Bauman, *Retrotopia* (Cambridge: Polity Press, 2017).

26. R. Girard, *Violence and the Sacred* (London: Athlone Press, 1988).

27. W. Benjamin, 'Critique of Violence', in *Reflections: Essays, Aphorisms, Autobiographical Writings*, ed. P. Demetz (New York, NY: Schocken Books), 198, 277–300.

28. On the debates surrounding this, see S. Prozorov, 'Why is there Truth? Foucault in the Age of Post–Truth Politics', *Constellations* 26, no. 1 (2019): 18–30.

29. A. Sen, *Poverty and Famines: An Essay on Entitlement and Deprivation* (Oxford: Oxford University Press, 1981).

16. WHERE HUMANITY ENDS: DUBAI AND THE PERFORMANCE OF MODERNITY

1. M. Page and J. Vittori, *Dubai's Role in Facilitating Corruption and Global Illicit Financial Flows* (Washington, DC: Carnegie Endowment for International Peace, 7 July 2020).

2. B. Knight, 'Munich Security Conference 2019: Who Will Save the World Liberal Order?', *Deutsche Welle*, 18 February 2019, https://www.dw.com/en/munich-

security-conference-2019-who-can-save-the-liberal-world-order/a-47547868. (All URLs cited were last accessed 14 November 2020.)

3. P. Porter, *The False Promise of Liberal Order* (London: Polity Press, 2020), 10.

4. K. McQue, 'We are Starving: The Migrant Workers Abandoned by Dubai Employers', *The Guardian*, 3 September 2020, https://www.theguardian.com/global-development/2020/sep/03/i-am-starving-the-migrant-workers-abandoned-by-dubai-employers.

5. N. Cooper, 'City of Gold, City of Slaves: Slavery and Indentured Servitude in Dubai', *Journal of Strategic Security* 6, no. 3 (2013): 65–71.

6. Ibid.

7. Human Rights Watch, *'I Already Bought You': Abuse and Exploitation of Female Migrant Domestic Workers in the United Arab Emirates* (New York, 22 October 2014), https://www.hrw.org/report/2014/10/22/i-already-bought-you/abuse-and-exploitation-female-migrant-domestic-workers#.

8. UAE Government Press Release, 'AED 22 bn in Assistance Provided by UAE to Yemen Between 2015–2020', *Reliefweb*, 10 February 2020, https://reliefweb.int/report/yemen/aed22-bn-assistance-provided-uae-yemen-april-2015-through-2020.

9. Thomas Juneau, 'The UAE in Yemen: From Surge to Recalibration', *Lawfare* (blog), 11 October 2020, https://www.lawfareblog.com/uae-yemen-surge-recalibration.

10. 'UAE-linked NGO Whitewashes Migrant Abuse', *Jadaliyya Reports*, 15 August 2014, https://www.jadaliyya.com/Details/31104.

11. The documentary was fake, in that it misrepresents the condition both of Emirati dissidents but also of migrant workers. It is available at: https://www.youtube.com/watch?v=HGs5ThGnBiQ

12. IGO, *Domestic Work Legislation in the GCC*, Policy Report (2014), 9.

13. The text of the ILO Convention is available at: http://www.ilo.org/dyn/normlex/en/f?p=NORMLEXPUB:12100:0::NO::P12100_ILO_CODE:C189%255C%2522%20data-mce-href=.

14. There is an outcropping of the famous French Museum in nearby Abu Dhabi, which is one of the Emirates. See https://www.louvre.fr/en/louvre-abu-dhabi.

17. BILLIONAIRE PHILANTHROPY, WOMEN'S EMPOWERMENT, AND THE CURRENCY OF MODERNITY

1. Dibyesh Anand, 'Indian Fantasies about Gujarat and Narendra Modi', *The Guardian*, 28 December 2012, https://www.theguardian.com/commentisfree/2012/dec/28/india-fantasy-gujarat-modi-hindus. (Unless otherwise stated, all URLs cited were last accessed 24 September 2020.)

2. Nigam Prusty and Shilpa Jamkhadandikar, 'Hundreds Arrested in India During Days of Protests over Citizenship Law', Reuters, 21 December 2019, https://www.reuters.com/article/us-india-citizenship-protests-idUSKBN1YP03E.

3. Neha Therani Bagri, 'India's Lower-Caste Dalits, Who Helped Elect Modi, Now

Threaten to Oust Him', *Los Angeles Times*, 17 May 2019, https://www.latimes.com/world/asia/la-fg-india-elections-caste-dalits-20190517-story.html.

4. '"Women Benefited the Most": PM Modi Receives Award for Swachh Bharat Campaign', *Hindustan Times*, 25 September 2019, https://www.hindustantimes.com/india-news/pm-modi-receives-award-for-swachh-bharat-abhiyan-by-bill-and-melinda-gates-foundation/story-DiqTOu90IqPyoQ6bXQgAgP.html.

5. Maria Thomas, 'Modi's Government Claims it's Improved the Lives of Women. But Here's the Reality', Quartz India, 23 July 2018, https://qz.com/india/1333614/has-the-modi-government-improved-the-lives-of-indian-women/.

6. Ibid.

7. Sophie Harman, 'The Bill and Melinda Gates Foundation and Legitimacy in Global Health Governance', *Global Governance* 22, no. 3 (2016): 349–68, 355.

8. Prime Minister Narendra Modi, 'PM's Address at the Global "Call to Action" Summit 2015', 27 August 2015, https://www.narendramodi.in/pm-s-address-at-the-global-%E2%80%98call-to-action-summit-2015-282780.

9. Ibid.

10. 'Women's Welfare was Never Priority of Previous Governments: PM Modi', *The Economic Times*, 22 December 2018.

11. Srilatha Batliwala, 'The Meaning of Women's Empowerment: New Concepts from Action', in *Population Policies Reconsidered: Health, Empowerment and Rights*, ed. G. Sen, A. Germain and L. C. Chen (Cambridge, MA: Harvard University Press, 1994), 127–38, https://www.eldis.org/document/A53502; Andrea Cornwall, 'Women's Empowerment: What Works?', *Journal of International Development* 28, no. 3 (2016): 342–59, https://doi.org/10.1002/jid.3210.

12. Aarefa Johari, 'How Much has the Modi Government Done for Women's Empowerment?', DAWN, 10 April 2019, https://www.dawn.com/news/1475163.

13. Ibid.

14. Kavita Krishnan, 'Gendered Discipline in Globalising India', *Feminist Review* 119, no. 1 (17 July 2018): 72–88, https://doi.org/10.1057/s41305-018-0119-6; Thomas, 'Modi's Government Claims it's Improved the Lives of Women'.

15. Modi, 'PM's Address at the Global "Call to Action" Summit 2015'; Krishnan, 'Gendered Discipline in Globalising India'.

16. Aarefa Johari, 'Fact Check: Are Rapists Now Getting Hanged Between Three and 30 Days, as Modi Claimed?', *Scroll-in*, 31 January 2019, https://scroll.in/article/911536/fact-check-are-rapists-now-getting-hanged-between-three-and-30-days-as-modi-claimed (last accessed 1 May 2020).

17. Krishnan, 'Gendered Discipline in Globalising India'.

18. Johari, 'How Much has the Modi Government Done for Women's Empowerment?'; Ajaz Ashraf, 'Narendra Modi: A False Crusader for Women's Rights', Al Jazeera, 25 January 2018, https://www.aljazeera.com/indepth/opinion/narendra-modi-false-crusader-women-rights-180118112500013.html.

19. Johari, 'How Much has the Modi Government Done for Women's Empowerment?'; Ashraf, 'Narendra Modi: A False Crusader for Women's Rights'.

20. Léo Heller, 'End of Mission Statement by the Special Rapporteur on the Human Rights to Safe Drinking Water and Sanitation', New Delhi, 10 November 2017 (New York, NY: United Nations, 2017), https://www.ohchr.org/EN/NewsEvents/Pages/DisplayNews.aspx?NewsID=22375 (last accessed 1 May 2020).

21. Saurabh Sharma, 'Two Lower Caste Children in India Beaten to Death for "Open Defecation"', US News and World Report, 26 September 2019, https://www.usnews.com/news/us/articles/2019–09–26/two-lower-caste-children-in-india-beaten-to-death-for-open-defecation.

22. Heller, 'End of Mission Statement'.

23. Kalpana Wilson, 'For Reproductive Justice in an Era of Gates and Modi: The Violence of India's Population Policies', Feminist Review 119 (17 July 2018): 89–105, https://doi.org/10.1057/s41305–018–0112–0.

24. Dexter Filkins, 'Blood and Soil in Narendra Modi's India', The New Yorker, 2 December 2019, https://www.newyorker.com/magazine/2019/12/09/blood-and-soil-in-narendra-modis-india.

25. Johari, 'How Much has the Modi Government Done for Women's Empowerment?'; Aarefa Johari, 'BJP Leader asks Hindu Women to have Five Babies, but Hindutva Fears of Being Outnumbered are Unfounded', Scroll.in, 13 January 2015, http://scroll.in/article/700251/bjp-leader-asks-hindu-women-to-have-five-babies-but-hindutva-fears-of-being-outnumbered-are-unfounded.

26. Morrison, cited in Wilson, 'For Reproductive Justice in an Era of Gates and Modi'.

27. Wilson, 'For Reproductive Justice in an Era of Gates and Modi', 92–3.

28. Ransdell Pierson and James Dalgleish, 'Pfizer, Gates Foundation, Expand Contraceptive Access in Poor Nations', Reuters, 13 November 2014, https://www.reuters.com/article/us-pfizer-gates-contraception-idUSKCN0IX1WF20141113.

29. A common criticism of the Gates Foundation is that its corporate investments are self-enriching. See Mark Curtis, Gated Development: Is the Gates Foundation Always a Force for Good? (London: Global Justice Now, June 2016), https://www.globaljustice.org.uk/sites/default/files/files/resources/gjn_gates_report_june_2016_web_final_version_2.pdf.

30. S. Madhok, A. Phillips, K. Wilson, and C. Hemmings, eds., Gender, Agency, and Coercion (London: Palgrave Macmillan, 2013).

31. Family Planning 2020, 'India Official Report', 28 August 2015, http://www.familyplanning2020.org/news/india-official-report.

32. 'Robbed of Choice and Dignity: Indian Women Dead after Mass Sterilization: Situational Assessment of Sterilization Camps in Bilaspur District, Chhattisgarh: Report by a Multi-Organizational Team, December 1, 2014', Reproductive Health Matters 22, no. 44 (2014): 91–3, https://doi.org/10.1016/S0968–8080(14)44823–7.

NOTES

33. Wilson, 'For Reproductive Justice in an Era of Gates and Modi', 93.

34. Sapna Desai, *Regional Advocacy Tool: Sexual and Reproductive Health and Rights Advocacy in South Asia* (Suva, Fiji: DAWN, 2015), 6, 30, https://dawnnet.org/wp-content/uploads/2016/04/RAT_SouthASIADAWNPaper_2015.pdf.

35. Lizzie Tribone, 'Reproducing Injustice', *Jacobin*, 17 May 2016, https://jacobin-mag.com/2016/05/reproductive-health-sterilization-modi-contraceptives-population-control/.

36. Wilson, 'For Reproductive Justice in an Era of Gates and Modi', 94.

37. Ibid., 95.

38. Ibid.

39. Cornwall, 'Women's Empowerment'; Batliwala, 'The Meaning of Women's Empowerment'; Srilatha Batliwala, 'Taking the Power out of Empowerment: An Experiential Account', *Development in Practice* 17, nos. 4–5 (2007): 557–65.

40. Batliwala, 'The Meaning of Women's Empowerment'; Batliwala, 'Taking the Power out of Empowerment'; Cornwall, 'Women's Empowerment'.

41. Sylvia Chant and Caroline Sweetman, 'Fixing Women or Fixing the World? "Smart Economics", Efficiency Approaches, and Gender Equality in Development', *Gender & Development* 20, no. 3 (1 November 2012): 517–29, https://doi.org/10.1080/13552074.2012.731812.

42. Ibid., 521.

43. Ibid.

44. Maxine Molyneux, 'Mothers at the Service of the New Poverty Agenda: Progresa/Oportunidades, Mexico's Conditional Transfer Programme', *Social Policy & Administration* 40, no. 4 (2006): 425–49, https://doi.org/10.1111/j.1467-9515.2006.00497.x; Serene J. Khader, 'Global Gender Justice and the Feminization of Responsibility,' *Feminist Philosophy Quarterly* 5, no. 2 (25 July 2019), https://doi.org/10.5206/fpq/2019.2.7282.

45. Chant and Sweetman, 'Fixing Women or Fixing the World?', 524.

46. Sanjay Reddy, 'Randomise This! On Poor Economics', *Review of Agrarian Studies* 2, no. 2 (2013), http://ras.org.in/randomise_this_on_poor_economics (last accessed 28 April 2020); see also William Easterly, *The Tyranny of Experts* (New York, NY: Basic Books, 2014).

47. See Nelson A. Rockefeller, 'Widening the Boundaries of National Interest', in *What Was the Liberal Order?*, Foreign Affairs Anthology Series (New York, NY: Council on Foreign Relations, 2017), https://www.foreignaffairs.com/articles/united-states/1951–07–01/widening-boundaries-national-interest?fa_anthology=1119541; Easterly, *The Tyranny of Experts*.

48. Raj Desai and Homi Kharas, 'The California Consensus: Can Private Aid End Global Poverty?', *Survival* 50, no. 4 (2008): 155–68.

49. Ibid., 156.

50. Ibid.

51. Ibid., 158.

52. Heidi Morefield, 'If We Really Want to Eradicate Diseases such as Ebola, We Need

a New Strategy', *The Washington Post*, 9 July 2018, https://www.washingtonpost.com/ (last accessed 29 April 2020).

53. Heidi Morefield, 'Developing to Scale: Appropriate Technology and the Making of Global Health', PhD dissertation (Johns Hopkins University, 2019).

54. Adam Moe Fejerskov, *The Gates Foundation's Rise to Power* (Abingdon: Routledge, 2018), 116.

55. Ibid., 110–14.

56. Ibid., 11.

57. Ibid., 112.

58. Ibid., 113.

59. Ibid., 165.

60. Ibid., 46.

61. See Chant and Sweetman, 'Fixing Women or Fixing the World?', 525–6.

62. Fejerskov, *The Gates Foundation's Rise to Power*, 133.

63. Ibid., 133.

64. Daniel Bendix et al., 'Targets and Technologies: Sayana Press and Jadelle in Contemporary Population Policies', *Gender, Place & Culture* 27, no. 3 (March 2019): 351–69, https://doi.org/10.1080/0966369X.2018.1555145.

65. Morefield, 'Developing to Scale', 15.

66. Melinda French Gates, 'Putting Women and Girls at the Center of Development', *Science* 345, no. 6202 (12 September 2014): 1273–5, https://doi.org/10.1126/science.1258882.

67. Serene J. Khader, *Decolonizing Universalism: A Transnational Feminist Ethic*, Studies in Feminist Philosophy (Oxford: Oxford University Press, 2018), 25–6.

68. Serene Khader, 'Why are Poor Women Poor?', *The New York Times*, 11 September 2019, https://www.nytimes.com/2019/09/11/opinion/why-are-poor-women-poor.html; Chandra Talpade Mohanty, 'Under Western Eyes: Feminist Scholarship and Colonial Discourses', *Boundary (2)* 12, no. 3 (1984): 333–58, https://doi.org/10.2307/302821; Uma Narayan, *Dislocating Cultures: Identities, Traditions, and Third World Feminism* (Abingdon: Routledge, 1997), https://www.routledge.com/Dislocating-Cultures-Identities-Traditions-and-Third-World-Feminism/Narayan/p/book/9780415914192.

69. See, for example, Khader, *Decolonizing Universalism*; Judith van Allen, '"Sitting on a Man": Colonialism and the Lost Political Institutions of Igbo Women', *Canadian Journal of African Studies* 6, no. 2 (1972): 165–81, https://doi.org/10.2307/484197; Narayan, *Dislocating Cultures*; Bonita Lawrence, 'Gender, Race, and the Regulation of Native Identity in Canada and the United States: An Overview', *Hypatia* 18, no. 2 (2003): 3–31, https://doi.org/10.1111/j.1527–2001.2003.tb00799.x.

70. Joan Scott, *Sex and Secularism* (Princeton, NJ: Princeton University Press, 2017), https://press.princeton.edu/books/hardcover/9780691160641/sex-and-secularism.

71. Harman, 'The Bill and Melinda Gates Foundation', 35.

72. Fejerskov, *The Gates Foundation's Rise to Power*, 94–5.

73. Carl Rhodes and Peter Bloom, 'The Trouble with Charitable Billionaires', *The*

Guardian, 24 May 2018, https://www.theguardian.com/news/2018/may/24/the-trouble-with-charitable-billionaires-philanthrocapitalism.

74. Isis Giraldo, 'Coloniality at Work: Decolonial Critique and the Postfeminist Regime', *Feminist Theory* 17, no. 2 (28 May 2016): 157–73, 168, https://doi.org/10.1177/1464700116652835.

75. 'Incarceration Nation', *Monitor on Psychology* 45, no. 9 (October 2014), https://www.apa.org/monitor/2014/10/incarceration (last accessed 4 May 2020).

76. G. John Ikenberry, 'The Future of the Liberal World Order', *Foreign Affairs* 90, no. 3 (May/June 2011): 56–62, 63–7, https://www.foreignaffairs.com/articles/2011-05-01/future-liberal-world-order.

77. Immanuel Kant, *To Perpetual Peace: A Philosophical Sketch* (Indianapolis, IN: Hackett, 1983), https://www.hackettpublishing.com/philosophy/to-perpetual-peace.

78. Ikenberry, 'The Future of the Liberal World Order', 61.

79. See Khader, *Decolonizing Universalism*, for an argument for why women's empowerment does not conceptually require commitment to all of liberalism's core principles. But even if women's empowerment does not require liberalism, per se it does conceptually require greater respect for human rights and democracy than empowerment 3.0 allows.

80. 'Gates Foundation Criticised over Award to Indian PM Modi', Al Jazeera, 13 September 2019, https://www.aljazeera.com/news/2019/09/gates-foundation-criticised-award-indian-pm-modi-190913093713879.html.

81. Iain Marlow and Archana Chaudhary, 'Trump Stuck between Khan and Modi on India's Kashmir Crackdown', Bloomberg Quint, 24 September 2019, https://www.bloombergquint.com/global-economics/india-s-rising-power-mutes-criticism-of-modi-s-kashmir-crackdown.

82. 'India has Potential for Very Rapid Economic Growth, says Bill Gates', *The Economic Times*, 18 November 2019, https://economictimes.indiatimes.com/news/economy/policy/india-has-potential-for-very-rapid-economic-growth-says-bill-gates/articleshow/72094025.cms?from=mdr.

83. Raymond Zhong, 'Indian Hard-Liner Narendra Modi Leads in Prime Minister Race', *Wall Street Journal*, 4 April 2014, https://www.wsj.com/articles/indian-hard-liner-narendra-modi-leads-in-prime-minister-race-1396663753.

84. Shikha Dalmia, 'The West Was Profoundly Wrong About Modi', *The Week*, 20 December 2019, https://theweek.com/articles/884478/west-profoundly-wrong-about-modi.

85. Cited in Vidhi Doshi, 'Bill and Melinda Gates Foundation under Fire over Award for Narendra Modi', *The Guardian*, 12 September 2019, https://www.theguardian.com/world/2019/sep/12/bill-and-melinda-gates-foundation-under-fire-over-award-for-narendra-modi.

18. HUMANITARIANISM AND LIBERAL INTERNATIONAL ORDER: A NECESSARY RELATIONSHIP?

1. Bennett defines the formal international humanitarian system as an architecture of international agencies, UN agencies, major international NGOs, and the Red Cross

and Red Crescent movement, functioning alongside, and in association with, a range of international conventions and funding and coordination structures. See Christina Bennett, Matthew Foley, and Sara Pantuliano, *Time to Let Go: Remaking Humanitarian Action for the Modern Era* (London: Overseas Development Institute, 2016), 12.

2. Michael Barnett, *Empire of Humanity: A History of Humanitarianism* (New York, NY: Cornell University Press, 2011), 9.

3. Bennett et al., *Time to Let Go*, 19.

4. Christian Reus-Smit, 'The Liberal International Order Reconsidered', in *After Liberalism?*, ed. R. Friedman et al. (London: Palgrave Macmillan, 2013), 167–86.

5. Duncan Bell, 'What is Liberalism?', *Political Theory* 42, no. 6 (2014): 682–715; Barry Buzan and George Lawson, *The Global Transformation: History, Modernity and the Making of International Relations* (Cambridge: Cambridge University Press, 2015), 102.

6. See, for instance, Beate Jahn, 'Critique in a Time of Liberal World Order', *Journal of International Relations and Development* 15, no. 2 (2012): 145–57.

7. Reus-Smit, 'The Liberal International Order Reconsidered'.

8. G. John Ikenberry, 'The End of Liberal International Order?', *International Affairs* 94, no. 1 (January 2018): 7–23, 11.

9. Ibid., 11.

10. G. John Ikenberry, *Liberal Leviathan: The Origins, Crisis, and Transformation of the American World Order* (Princeton, NJ: Princeton University Press, 2011).

11. See Ikenberry, 'The End of Liberal International Order?'.

12. John J. Mearsheimer, 'Bound to Fail: The Rise and Fall of the Liberal International Order', *International Security* 43, no. 4 (2019): 7–50.

13. Francis Fukuyama, *The End of History and the Last Man* (New York, NY: Free Press, 1992).

14. Secretary of State Madeleine K. Albright, Interview on NBC-TV 'The Today Show' with Matt Lauer, 19 February 1998, https://1997–2001.state.gov/statements/1998/980219a.html. Unless otherwise stated, URLs cited were last accessed 15 October 2020.

15. Mearsheimer, 'Bound to Fail'.

16. National Intelligence Council, *Global Trends: Parodox of Progress* (Washington: ODNI, 2017), ix.

17. See House of Lords Select Committee on International Relations, *UK Foreign Policy in a Shifting World Order*, HL Paper 250 (December 2018).

18. UN Secretary-General, António Guterres, 'Remarks to the General Assembly on the Secretary-General's Priorities for 2020' (New York: United Nations, 22 January 2020), https://www.un.org/sg/en/content/sg/speeches/2020–01–22/remarks-general-assembly-priorities-for-2020.

19. Sarah Collinson, *Constructive Deconstruction: Making Sense of the International Humanitarian System*, HPG Working Paper (London: Overseas Development Institute, July 2016). *The State of the Humanitarian System* defines the IHS as, '[t]he

network of inter-connected institutional and operational entities that receive funds—directly or indirectly, from public donors and private sources, to enhance, support or substitute for within-country responses in the provision of humanitarian assistance and protection to a population in crisis'. See ALNAP, *State of the Humanitarian System 2018*, Inception Report (April 2017), 5, https://www.alnap.org/system/files/content/resource/files/main/alnap-sohs-2018-inception-report.pdf.

20. Where the state does not control particular areas, the same role is often taken up by the political groups that do.

21. Stuart Gordon and Sherine El Taraboulsi-McCarthy, *Counter-Terrorism, Bank De-Risking and Humanitarian Response: A Path Forward*, HPG Policy Brief 72 (London: Overseas Development Institute, August 2018). Kate Mackintosh and Patrick Duplat, *Study of the Impact of Donor Counter-Terrorism Measures on Principled Humanitarian Action* (New York: United Nations, 2013).

22. Michael Barnett, 'Humanitarianism Transformed', *Perspectives on Politics* 3, no. 4 (December 2005): 723–40.

23. In 2019, international humanitarian assistance sent directly to local and national actors as a proportion of all international humanitarian assistance was only 2.1 percent (US$444 million). Angus Urquhart, *Global Humanitarian Assistance Report 2019* (Bristol: Development Initiatives, 2020).

24. R. Kent, C. Bennett, A. Donini, and D. Maxwell, *Planning from the Future: Is the Humanitarian System Fit for Purpose?* (Boston, MA: Feinstein International Center, Tufts University, 2016), 1.

25. UN Secretary-General, António Guterres, 'Remarks to the Security Council on the Protection of Civilians in Armed Conflict' (New York, NY: United Nations, 23 May 2019), https://www.un.org/sg/en/content/sg/speeches/2019–05–23/remarks-security-council-protection-of-civilians-armed-conflict (last accessed 4 September 2020).

26. According to the UN Secretary-General's 2019 *Protection of Civilians in Armed Conflict* report, 90 percent of casualties from explosive weapons used in populated areas were civilians, https://reliefweb.int/sites/reliefweb.int/files/resources/S_2019_373_E.pdf.

27. Alex de Waal, cited in Christina Bennett, '2019's Biggest Challenge', Overseas Development Institute (blog), 10 January 2019, https://www.odi.org/blogs/10721–2019s-biggest-challenge-humanitarian-sell-out (last accessed 25 October 2020).

28. Bennett, '2019's Biggest Challenge'.

29. United Nations High Commission for Refugees, *Figures at a Glance* (Geneva, 18 June 2020), https://www.unhcr.org/figures-at-a-glance.html (last accessed 17 November 2020).

30. Urquhart, *Global Humanitarian Assistance Report 2019*.

31. Hannah B. Krebs, 'What You Need to Understand about Chinese Humanitarian Aid', Overseas Development Institute (blog), 6 November 2015, https://www.

odi.org/blogs/10066-what-you-need-understand-about-chinese-humanitarian-aid; Ankit Panda, 'China's Evolving Role in the Fight against Ebola: Beijing's Reaction to Africa's Most Serious Public Health Crisis in Years Represents a Shift in its Humanitarian Policy', *The Diplomat*, 16 September 2014, https://www.thediplomat.com/2014/09/chinas-evolving-role-in-the-fight-against-ebola/.

32. Eleanor Davey, *New Players Through Old Lenses*, HPG Policy Brief 48 (London: Overseas Development Institute, July 2012); Jin Sato, Hiroaki Shiga, Takaaki Kobayashi, and Hisahiro Kondoh, *How Do 'Emerging' Donors Differ from 'Traditional' Donors?*, JICA-RI Working Paper 2 (Tokyo: JICA-RI, March 2010).

33. In 2018, China established the China International Development Cooperation Agency as a coordinating body, but its impact is not yet clear. See Humanitarians Advocacy Group (HAG) and Denghua Zhang, *Positive Disruption? China's Humanitarian Aid*, Humanitarian Horizons Practice Paper Series (December 2019), https://humanitarianadvisorygroup.org/wp-content/uploads/2019/12/HH_China-Practice-Paper_Final-December–2019.pdf.

34. Miwa Hirono, *Exploring the Links between Chinese Foreign Policy and Humanitarian Action: Multiple Interests, Processes and Actors*, HPG Working Paper (London: Overseas Development Institute, 2018); HAG and Zhang, *Positive Disruption?*; Amy Lieberman, 'China Emerges as a Serious Player in Humanitarian Aid', Devex, 7 February 2018, https://www.devex.com/news/china-emerges-as-a-serious-player-in-humanitarian-aid-90974; Hannah B. Krebs, *The Chinese Way: The Evolution of Chinese Humanitarianism*, HPG Policy Brief 62 (London: Overseas Development Institute, 2014).

35. Deborah Bräutigam, 'Aid "with Chinese Characteristics": Chinese Foreign Aid and Development Finance Meet the OECD–DAC Aid Regime', *Journal of International Development* 23, no. 5 (2011): 752–64; Lieberman, 'China Emerges as a Serious Player'; Agnieszka Paczynska, *Emerging and Traditional Donors and Conflict-Affected States: The New Politics of Reconstruction* (Washington, DC: Stimson Center, 2016); Hirono, *Exploring the Links*.

36. One example is the initial paucity of aid China offered to the Philippines in the wake of Typhoon Haiyan in 2013.

37. Hirono, *Exploring the Links*, iii.

38. Urvashi Aneja, *South–South Humanitarianism*, Conference Report, 26–27 November 2014 (Center for Global Governance and Policy at the Jindal School of International Affairs).

39. Bennett et al., *Time to Let Go*.

40. Barnett, *Empire of Humanity*, 16; Antonio Donini, 'Decoding the Software of Humanitarian Action: Universal or Pluriversal?', in *Humanitarianism and Challenges of Cooperation*, ed. Volker M. Heins, Kai Koddenbrock, et al. (Abingdon: Routledge, 2016), 72–83.

41. See, for instance, Mika Aaltola, *Western Spectacle of Governance and the Emergence of Humanitarian World Politics* (New York, NY: Palgrave Macmillan, 2009); Antonio Donini, 'The Far Side: The Meta Functions of Humanitarianism in a Globalised

World', *Disasters* 34, S2 (2010): S220–S237; Michael Barnett and Peter Walker, 'Regime Change for Humanitarian Aid: How to Make Relief More Accountable', *Foreign Affairs* 94, no. 4 (July/August 2015): 130–41.

42. Michel Agier, 'Humanity as an Identity and its Political Effects (A Note on Camps and Humanitarian Government)', *Humanity: An International Journal of Human Rights, Humanitarianism, and Development* 1, no. 1 (2010): 29–45.

43. Ibid.; Davey, *New Players Through Old Lenses*.

44. Elena Fiddian–Qasmiyeh, 'Looking Forward: *Disasters* at 40', *Disasters* 43, S1 (April 2019): S36–S60.

45. Julia Pacitto and Elena Fiddian-Qasmiyeh, *Writing the 'Other' into Humanitarian Discourse: Framing Theory and Practice in South–South Humanitarian Responses to Forced Displacement*, Working Paper Series 93 (Refugee Studies Centre, University of Oxford, 2013).

19. TOWARDS AN ANTI-RACIST HUMANITARIANISM IN THE POST-LIBERAL WORLD

1. Office of the High Commissioner for Human Rights, 'Human Rights Council Adopts 14 Resolutions, Including on Excessive Use of Force by Law Enforcement Officers against Africans and People of African Descent' (Geneva, 19 June 2020), https://www.ohchr.org/EN/HRBodies/HRC/Pages/NewsDetail.aspx?NewsID=25981&LangID=E (last accessed 24 August 2020).

2. The previous time was in 2016 in the UN Human Rights Council, *Report of the Working Group of Experts on People of African Descent on its Mission to United States of America, 19–29 January 2016*, UN Doc. A/HRC/33/61/Add.2 (Geneva, 18 August 2016), https://documents-dds-ny.un.org/doc/UNDOC/GEN/G16/183/33/PDF/G1618333.pdf?OpenElement.

3. Nicholas De Genova, 'The "Migrant Crisis" as Racial Crisis: Do *Black Lives Matter* in Europe?', *Ethnic and Racial Studies* 41, no. 10 (2018): 1765–82; Patricia Ehrkamp, 'Geographies of Migration II: The Racial-Spatial Politics of Immigration', *Progress in Human Geography* 43, no. 2 (2019): 363–75.

4. On the necropolitical production of disposable lives, see Achille Mbembe, *Necropolitics* (Durham, NC: Duke University Press, 2019).

5. The terms 'global North' and 'global South' refer to areas classified in relation to their historical experience of European colonialism (former colonial powers and the areas inhabited by former and current colonised peoples respectively). 'The West' and 'Western' refer to the political–ideological bloc of countries that constituted the core of Euro-American capitalism during the Cold War.

6. Mbembe, *Necropolitics*, 162.

7. Alexander Weheliye, *Habeas Viscus: Racializing Assemblages, Biopolitics, and Black Feminist Theories of the Human* (Durham, NC: Duke University Press, 2014), 32.

8. Patricia Daley, 'From Livingstone to Geldof: Africa Not Yet Saved', *Pambazuka News*, 7 July 2005, http:www.pambazuka.org (last accessed 3 October 2020); Murali

Balaji, 'Racializing Pity: The Haiti Earthquake and the Plight of "Others"', *Critical Studies in Media and Communication* 28, no. 1 (2011): 50–67.

9. Michael Barnett, *Empire of Humanity: A History of Humanitarianism* (Ithaca, NY: Cornell University Press, 2011), 49.

10. B. S. Chimni, *Globalisation, Humanitarianism and the Erosion of Refugee Protection*, Working Paper 3 (Refugee Studies Centre, University of Oxford, 2000), 3.

11. Ibid, 4.

12. There is now a large and wide-ranging historiography on humanitarianism's roots in colonial empire. See, among many others, Alan Lester and Fae Dussart, *Colonization and the Origins of Humanitarian Governance: Protecting Aborigines Across the Nineteenth-Century British Empire* (Cambridge: Cambridge University Press, 2014); and Peter Stamatov, *The Origins of Global Humanitarianism: Religion, Empires, and Advocacy* (Cambridge: Cambridge University Press, 2015).

13. See Makau Mutua, 'Savages, Victims and Saviors: The Metaphor of Human Rights', *Harvard International Law Journal* 42, no. 1 (2001): 201–45; Patricia Daley, 'Rescuing African Bodies: Celebrities, Humanitarianism and Neoliberal Consumerism', *Review of African Political Economy* 40, no. 137 (2013): 375–93; Beverley Mullings, Marion Werner, and Linda Peake, 'Fear and Loathing in Haiti: Race and Politics of Humanitarian Dispossession', *ACME: An International Journal for Critical Geographies* 9, no. 3 (2010): 282–300; Tajudeen Abdul-Raheem, 'Western NGOs in Africa: Bodyguards of the Advancing Recolonization', *NGO Monitor* 1, no. 1 (Kampala: Pan African Movement Secretariat, October/December 1996); Yasmin Alibhai-Brown, 'Bob Geldof and the White Man's Burden', *The Independent*, 6 June 2005, http://www.independent.co.uk/voices/commentators/yasmin-alibhai-brown/yasmin-alibhai-brown-bob-geldof-and-the-white-mans-burden-493245.html (last accessed 3 October 2020); Abdul Rahman Mohamed Babu, 'Aid Dealers, Aid Pushers and Aid Addicts', *NGO Monitor* 1, no. 1 (Kampala: Pan African Movement Secretariat, October/December 1996): 21–2.

14. Aníbal Quijano, 'Coloniality and Modernity/Rationality', *Cultural Studies* 21, nos. 2–3 (2007): 168–78; Nelson Maldonado-Torres, 'On the Coloniality of Being: Contributions to the Development of a Concept', *Cultural Studies* 21, nos. 2–3 (2007): 240–70.

15. Maldonado-Torres, 'On the Coloniality of Being', 243.

16. African Rights, *Humanitarianism Unbound? Current Dilemmas Facing Multi-Mandate Relief Operations in Political Emergencies*, Discussion Paper 5 (London, 1994); David Rieff, 'Humanitarian Politics and the Spectre of Illegitimacy', *Journal of Humanitarian Affairs* 1, no. 1 (2019): 46–8.

17. See, among many others, David Rieff, *A Bed for the Night: Humanitarianism in Crisis* (New York, NY: Vintage, 2002); and Mark Duffield, *Development, Security and Unending War: Governing the World of Peoples* (Cambridge: Polity Press, 2007).

18. Aimé Césaire, *Discourse on Colonialism*, trans. Joan Pinkham (New York, NY: Monthly Review Press, 1972, 2000), 42.

19. Ibid., 39.

20. Ann Laura Stoler, 'Colonial Aphasia: Race and Disabled Histories in France', *Public Culture* 23, no. 1 (2011): 121–56.

21. Ibid., 125.

22. Ibid., 122.

23. See Brian Kwoba, Roseanne Chantiluke, and Athinangamso Nkopo, eds., *Rhodes Must Fall: The Struggle to Decolonise the Racist Heart of Empire* (London: Zed Books, 2019).

24. Orisanmi Burton, 'Black Lives Matter: A Critique of Anthropology', Hot Spots, *Fieldsights*, 29 June 2015. https://culanth.org/fieldsights/black-lives-matter-a-critique-of-anthropology.

25. Michel Foucault, *The History of Sexuality*, Vol. 1: *The Will to Knowledge* (London: Penguin Books, 1976), 139.

26. Weheliye, *Habeas Viscus*.

27. Frantz Fanon, *The Wretched of the Earth*, trans. Constance Farrington (London: Penguin Books, 2001).

28. Ibid., 32.

29. See Lucy Mayblin, *Asylum after Empire: Colonial Legacies in the Politics of Asylum Seeking* (London and New York: Rowman & Littlefield, 2017).

30. Mutua, 'Savages, Victims and Saviors'; Mayblin, *Asylum after Empire*.

31. Mutua, 'Savages, Victims and Saviors', 207.

32. Mayblin, *Asylum after Empire*.

33. Carol Anderson, *Eyes Off the Prize: The United Nations and the African American Struggle for Human Rights, 1944–1955* (Cambridge: Cambridge University Press, 2003); W. T. Whitney, Jr., '"We Charge Genocide"—Forerunner at UN of Black Lives Matter', *MRonline*, 30 July 2020, https://mronline.org/2020/07/30/we-charge-genocide-forerunner-at-un-of-black-lives-matter/ (last accessed 3 October 2020).

34. Steven L. B. Jensen, *The Making of International Human Rights: The 1960s, Decolonization, and the Reconstruction of Global Values* (Cambridge: Cambridge University Press, 2016).

35. Lawrence Summer, World Bank memo, 12 December 1991, http://www.whirledbank.org/ourwords/summers.html (last accessed 15 October 2020).

36. See, for example, Kaveri Qureshi, Ben Kasstan, Nasar Meer, and Sarah Hill, *Submission of Evidence on the Disproportionate Impact of COVID-19, and the UK Government Response, on Ethnic Minorities in the UK*, Working Paper (University of Edinburgh, 24 April 2020).

37. Mayblin, *Asylum after Empire*.

38. Roanne van Voorst, 'Praxis and Paradigms of Local and Expatriate Workers in "Aidland"', *Third World Quarterly* 40, no. 12 (2019): 2111–28.

39. Bram J. Jansen, 'The Humanitarian Protectorate of South Sudan? Understanding Insecurity for Humanitarians in a Political Economy of Aid', *Journal of Modern African Studies* 55, no. 3 (2017): 349–70.

40. Arnab Majumdar, 'Bearing Witness Inside MSF', *The New Humanitarian*, 18 August 2020, https://www.thenewhumanitarian.org/opinion/first-person/2020/08/18/MSF-Amsterdam-aid-institutional-racism (last accessed 3 October 2020).

41. Ibid.; Van Voorst, 'Praxis and Paradigms'.

42. Abdul-Raheem, 'Western NGOs in Africa'.

43. Amber Murrey and Nicholas Jackson, 'A Decolonial Critique of the Racialized "Localwashing" of Extraction in Central Africa', *Annals of the American Association of Geographers* 110, no. 3 (2020): 917–40.

44. A study conducted in 2018 shows that about 90 percent of humanitarian field staff were national (local) staff. See ALNAP, 'Data Story: What's the Shape and Size of the Humanitarian System?' (5 November 2018), https://sohs.alnap.org/blogs/data-story-whats-the-shape-and-size-of-the-humanitarian-system (last accessed 30 September 2020).

45. Alibhai-Brown, 'Bob Geldof'.

46. Balaji, 'Racializing Pity', 52.

47. Ibid., 51.

48. Ibid.

49. Lilie Chouliaraki, *The Ironic Spectator: Solidarity in the Age of Post-Humanitarianism* (Cambridge: Polity Press, 2013).

50. Mutua, 'Savages, Victims and Saviors'.

51. Mahmood Mamdani, *Saviors and Survivors: Darfur, Politics, and the War on Terror* (London: Verso, 2009).

52. Mullings et al., 'Fear and Loathing in Haiti', 293.

53. For more about the Uganda-based organisation, No White Saviors, see No White Saviors, 'If You're Not Uncomfortable, You're Not Listening' (n.d.), https://nowhitesaviors.org/ (last accessed 28 August 2020).

54. Mary Mostafanezhad, 'Volunteer Tourism and the Popular Humanitarian Gaze', *Geoforum* 54 (2014): 111–18.

55. Ibid., 117.

56. Babu, 'Aid Dealers, Aid Pushers'.

57. Gabrielle Daoust and Synne L. Dyvik, 'Knowing Safeguarding: The Geopolitics of Knowledge Production in the Humanitarian and Development Sector', *Geoforum* 112 (February 2020): 96–9.

58. Mayblin, *Asylum after Empire*; Hanno Brankamp and Patricia Daley, 'Laborers, Migrants, Refugees: Managing Belonging, Bodies, and Mobility in (Post)Colonial Kenya and Tanzania', *Migration & Society* 3, no. 1 (June 2020): 113–29; Olivia Rutazibwa, 'What's there to Mourn? Decolonial Reflections on (the End of) Liberal Humanitarianism', *Journal of Humanitarian Affairs* 1, no. 1 (2019): 65–7.

59. Balaji, 'Racializing Pity'; De Genova, 'The "Migrant Crisis" as Racial Crisis'; Lewis Turner, '"#Refugees Can be Entrepreneurs Too!" Humanitarianism, Race, and the Marketing of Syrian Refugees', *Review of International Studies* 46, no. 1 (January 2020): 137–55.

60. Mutua, 'Savages, Victims and Saviors', 205.

61. Daoust and Dyvik, 'Knowing Safeguarding', 97.

62. Ibid., 98.

63. That is, states with boundaries defined at the 1884–5 Berlin colonial conference to partition Africa.

64. Lisa Ann Richey, 'Conceptualizing "Everyday Humanitarianism": Ethics, Affects, and Practices of Contemporary Global Helping', *New Political Science* 40, no. 4 (2018): 625–39.

65. Robin Vandevoordt, 'Subversive Humanitarianism: Rethinking Refugee Solidarity through Grass-Roots Initiatives', *Refugee Survey Quarterly* 38, no. 3 (September 2019): 245–65.

66. Anne-Meike Fechter and Anke Schwittay, 'Citizen Aid: Grassroots Interventions in Development and Humanitarianism', *Third World Quarterly* 40, no. 10 (2019): 1769–80.

67. Francis B. Nyamnjoh, 'Incompleteness: Frontier Africa and the Currency of Conviviality, *Journal of Asian and African Studies* 52, no. 3 (2017): 253–70, 264.

68. Patricia Daley, 'Refugees, IDPs and Citizenship Rights: The Perils of Humanitarianism in the African Great Lakes Region', *Third World Quarterly* 34, no. 5 (2013): 893–912.

69. Mahmood Mamdani, 'The Invention of the *Indigène*', *Pambazuka News*, 13 January 2011, http://pambazuka.org/en/category/features/70061 (last accessed 3 October 2020).

70. Chouliaraki, *The Ironic Spectator*.

71. Mutua, 'Savages, Victims and Saviors', 208.

72. Robtel N. Pailey, 'De-centring the "White Gaze" of Development', *Development and Change* 51, no. 3 (2020): 729–45.

20. WHAT'S THERE TO MOURN? WHAT'S THERE TO CELEBRATE? DECOLONIAL RETRIEVALS OF HUMANITARIANISM

1. This chapter expands on an article originally published in the *Journal of Humanitarian Affairs*: Olivia U. Rutazibwa, 'What's there to Mourn? Decolonial Reflections on (the End of) Liberal Humanitarianism', *Journal of Humanitarian Affairs* 1, no. 1 (2019): 65–7.

2. 'Joe Biden Speech Condemning Capitol Protest: Transcript', 6 January 2021, https://www.rev.com/blog/transcripts/joe-biden-remarks-condemning-capitol-protest-transcript (last accessed 19 February 2021).

3. And Trump's predecessors! It is striking how they appear all of a sudden on the right side of history. The televised images of Barack Obama, Bill Clinton, and George W. Bush, Jr., at the military cemetery during Biden's inauguration, were evocative in that regard.

4. Julia Suárez-Krabbe, *Race, Rights and Rebels: Alternatives to Human Rights and Development from the Global South* (London: Rowman & Littlefield, 2015).

5. Eddie S. Glaude, Jr., *Begin Again: James Baldwin's America and its Urgent Lessons for Our Own* (New York, NY: Crown Publishing, 2020).

6. Ilan Kapoor, *Confronting Desire: Psychoanalysis and International Development* (Ithaca, NY: Cornell University Press, 2020).

7. Juliette Singh, *Unthinking Mastery: Dehumanism and Decolonial Entanglements* (Durham,

NC: Duke University Press, 2018); and Lewis Turner, 'The Politics of Labeling Refugee Men as "Vulnerable"', *Social Politics* (2019): 1–23.

8. MSNBC, 'Blaming Trump is Too Easy: This is Us', 5 August 2019, https://www.msnbc.com/deadline-white-house/watch/blaming-trump-is-too-easy-this-is-us-65354309615 (last accessed 19 February 2019).

9. Glaude, Jr., *Begin Again*, 7.

10. See, also, Gloria Wekker, *White Innocence: Paradoxes of Colonialism and Race* (Durham, NC: Duke University Press, 2016).

11. Olivia U. Rutazibwa, 'Hidden in Plain Sight: Coloniality, Capitalism and Race/ism as Far as the Eye Can See', *Millennium: Journal of International Studies* 48, no. 2 (2020): 221–41.

12. See, for example, Enrique Dussel, 'Eurocentrism and Modernity (Introduction to the Frankfurt Lectures)', *Boundary (2)* 20, no. 3 (1993): 65–76; Enrique Dussel, *Twenty Theses on Politics* (Durham, NC: Duke University Press, 2008); Ramón Grosfoguel and Ana Margarita Cervantes-Rodríguez, 'Introduction: Unthinking Twentieth-Century Eurocentric Mythologies: Universal Knowledge, Decolonization, and Developmentalism', in *The Modern/Colonial/Capitalist World-System in the Twentieth Century: Global Processes, Antisystemic Movements, and the Geopolitics of Knowledge*, ed. Ramón Grosfoguel and Ana Margarita Cervantes-Rodríguez (Westport, CT: Praeger Publishers, 2002), xi–xxix; Sabelo J. Ndlovu-Gatsheni, 'Coloniality of Power in Development Studies and the Impact of Global Imperial Designs on Africa', *Australasian Review of African Studies* 33, no. 2 (2012): 48–73; Sabelo J. Ndlovu-Gatsheni, 'Racism and "Blackism" on a World Scale', in *Routledge Handbook of Postcolonial Politics*, ed. Olivia U. Rutazibwa and Robbie Shilliam (Abingdon: Routledge, 2018), 72–86; Aníbal Quijano, 'Coloniality of Power and Eurocentrism in Latin America', *International Sociology* 15, no. 2 (2000): 215–32; and Aníbal Quijano, 'Coloniality and Modernity/Rationality', *Cultural Studies* 21, nos. 2–3 (2007): 168–78.

13. Wekker, *White Innocence*.

14. Cedric J. Robinson, *Black Marxism: The Making of the Black Radical Tradition* (Chapel Hill, NC: University of North Carolina Press, 2000).

15. W. E. B. Du Bois, 'Of Our Spiritual Strivings', in *The Souls of Black Folks* (Chicago, IL: A. C. McClurg and Co., 1903).

16. Sabelo Ndlovu-Gatsheni, 'The Cognitive Empire, Politics of Knowledge and African Intellectual Productions: Reflections on Struggles for Epistemic Freedom and Resurgence of Decolonisation in the Twenty-First Century', *Third World Quarterly* (2020): 1–20, https://doi.org/10.1080/01436597.2020.1775487; Ngugi wa Thiong'o, *Decolonising the Mind: The Politics of Language in African Literature* (Rochester, NY: James Currey, 1986).

17. Siba N. Grovogui, 'Sovereignty in Africa: Quasi-Statehood and Other Myths in International Theory', in *Africa's Challenge to International Relations Theory*, ed. Kevin Dunn and Timothy Shaw (London: Palgrave Macmillan, 2001), 29–45.

18. Amy Niang, 'The Colonial Origins of Extractivism in Africa', Al Jazeera Opinion,

17 August 2019, https://www.aljazeera.com/opinions/2019/8/17/the-colonial-origins-of-extractivism-in-africa (last accessed 19 February 2019).

19. Zubairui Wai, 'International Relations and the Discourse of State Failure in Africa', in *Recentering Africa in International Relations*, ed. Marta Iñiguez de Heredia and Zubairu Wai (London: Palgrave Macmillan, 2018), 31–58.

20. Meera Sabaratnam, *Decolonising Intervention: International Statebuilding in Mozambique* (London: Rowman & Littlefield, 2017).

21. Including my own: Olivia U. Rutazibwa, 'On Babies and Bathwater: Decolonizing International Development Studies', in *Decolonization and Feminisms in Global Teaching and Learning*, ed. Sara de Jong, Rosalba Icaza, and Olivia U. Rutazibwa (Abingdon: Routledge, 2018), 192–214.

22. Boaventura de Sousa Santos, *Epistemologies of the South: Justice Against Epistemicide* (Abingdon: Routledge, 2015).

23. The discussions about the distribution of the COVID-19 vaccine offer a poignant illustration of the point I am trying to make here. After they have secured double the number of necessary doses for their populations, Western countries like France are now offering to donate a percentage of those vaccines to countries in the South.

24. See Singh, *Unthinking Mastery*; Ariella Azoulay, *Potential History* (New York, NY: Verso, 2019); Kapoor, *Confronting Desire*; Turner, 'The Politics of Labeling Refugee Men as "Vulnerable"'.

25. Glaude, Jr., *Begin Again*, 184.

26. Eve Tuck and K. Wayne Yang, 'Decolonization is Not a Metaphor', *Decolonization: Indigeneity, Education & Society* 1, no. 1 (2012): 1–40.

INDEX

Page numbers followed by "n" refer to notes.

Aung San Suu Kyi, 59
Aaronson, Mike, 39, 42–3
Abbott, Tony, 99–100
Abdul-Raheem, Tajudeen, 360
Abraham Lincoln, USS, 43
Active Learning Network for
  Accountability and
  Performance, 40, 46
Adivasi (indigenous) women, 316,
  317
Adorno, Theodor W., 171, 180
Aegean Sea, 109, 110
Afghanistan, 91, 105, 117, 147,
  158, 187, 285, 344, 437n5
  invasion of (2001), 42, 252,
    255, 281, 337
  SCA funding and Australian
    troops in, 91, 105
Africa, slave trade in, 340
African Americans, 246, 358
  and decolonial thought, 12, 371
  fight for human rights, 358
  illegal migration, 111
  income inequality, 213, 232
'African Child' Conference
  (Geneva, 1931), 12, 31, 32

Agamben, Georgio, 178, 189
Agier, Michel, 348
AHRC (Australian Human Rights
  Commission), 89, 97, 99
Ahuja, Neel, 65
aid agencies, humanitarian. *See*
  humanitarian aid agencies
aid workers
  attacks on, global South, 290
  contribution to Western
    security strategies, 161
  as 'humanitarian system', 7–8
  no-go areas, 289, 290, 291
Albright, Madeleine K., 250, 337
Aldous, Richard, 138
Allison, Graham, 6
Al-Qaeda, 294, 337
America, poorhouse in, 201–2
American Civil War, 70
American exceptionalism, 229
American hegemony, 127, 128
American Indian reservation, 233,
  241
American liberalism, 228–9, 237
American power, 7, 177
'American universalism', 169, 257

Americans for Democratic Action (ADA), 409–10*n*30
Amesi Dimokratia Tora, 175
Amin, Samir, 12, 374
Amnesty International Australia, 93–4
Amnesty International, 89, 148
Anderson, Perry, 168
animal-adaptation, 65
anti-black racism, 351, 352
anti-Muslim pogrom (Delhi, 2020), 313
anti-Muslim riots (Gujarat, 2002), 316–17
anti-racist humanitarianism (in post-liberal world), 351–67
  colonial aphasia, 356
  coloniality and, 353–9
  decolonial approach and, 362–6
  humanitarian actors, racialist geopolitical categorisation of, 359–60
  policies on safeguarding, 363–4
  racialisation and, 353–9
  recent challenges to, 353
  violence against migrants (in African countries), 364–5
  Western humanitarianism, 353–9
  as a Western mode of governance, 353
anti-utopianism, 145–6, 151, 152
Appalachia region (United States), 229–30
Applebaum, Anne, 11
Arab Middle East (refugee humanitarianism). *See* refugee humanitarianism (in Arab Middle East)
Arab Spring (2011), 187, 205, 255, 265, 337

Arab states
  forced migration, governance of, 261–4
  UAE humanitarian role in, 306, 308, 309
Arantes, Paulo, 164, 172
Arendt, Hannah, 122–3, 131, 139, 172, 245
  on sacrificial model, 292
Aron, Raymond, 131, 162
'art of government' (concept), 163
ASEAN (Association of Southeast Asian Nations), 346
al-Assad, Bashar, 255–6
Association of Southeast Asian Nations (ASEAN), 346
Association pour l'Assistance aux Mutilés Pauvres (association for the relief of mutilated paupers), 73
asylum seeking
  asylum right, 117–19, 120
  Australia immigration and asylum policies, 87–90
  criminalisation of, 87, 111–14, 345, 352
  Jordan asylum system, 271–2
  political economy of, 260–1, 263
  securitisation of, 105
  see also Australia: NGO offshore detention management
AusAID (Australian development agency), 91
Australia: NGO offshore detention management, 16–17, 83–106
  anti-immigrant policy, 17
  asylum issues, lack of facilities, 94–5
  Border Force Act (mid-2015), 89, 97, 101

INDEX

children offshore imprisonment, 89–90, 92–4, 95–8, 101–6

'children overboard' scandal, 101–2

Christmas Island asylum boat tragedy (15 Dec2010), 93

DIBP transferred families, 95

Expert Panel asylum proposals (Aug 2012), 89–90

Gillard government offshore detention funding, 91

immigration and asylum policies, 87–90

immigration detention as business, 88

immigration detention review (2014), 89

immigration detention system, 84–5, 87–91

Liberal–National Party coalition, 98

'Nauru Files', 103–4

naval blockade (2013), 86

NGOs left offshore detention, 84, 90

NGOs marginalisation attempts, 99

NGOs' early commitments, 93

offshore detention as racialised politics, 88

offshore detention centres, 16–17

offshore detention, return of, 93

parliamentary debates on children immigration, 93

racialised politics, 87–8

SCA and TSA management, 84–91

territorial asylum approach, 106

violence against First Peoples, 87

Australian Border Force, 103

Australian Department of Immigration and Citizenship (DIAC), 86, 87

Australian Federal Police, 97

Australian Human Rights Commission (AHRC), 89, 97, 99

Australian Red Cross, 88

authoritarianism, 3, 9, 11, 177, 201

democratic authoritarianism, 295

automation, 165

Babu, A.M., 362

Bacevich, Andrew, 250–1

Balaji, Murali, 361

Baldwin, James, 371

Ballard, J.G., 163

Bamako (Mali), 208, 216, 218, 223

Bamako protests (Jun 2020), 219

Banerjee, Abhijit, 323

Bangladesh, 23, 56, 400n16

barbarism, 204, 356

Barcelona Process (1995), 265

Barnett, Michael, 6, 61, 64, 333, 343, 348

Barry, Brian, 142

al-Bashir, Omar, 102

Baudrillard, Jean, 169

Bauer, Peter, 159

Bauman, Zygmunt, 198, 222, 294

Bay, Guantanamo, 285

Bedau, Hugo, 120

Benjamin, Walter, 182, 295, 422n141, 422n142

Bennett, Christina, 333, 348, 452–3n1

Bennett, Tony, 71
Bennett-Jones, Peter, 52
Bentham, Jeremy, 155
Bergamaschi, Isaline, 214
Berlin General Act (1884), 340
Berlin Wall, 247
    fall of, 4, 248, 282
Berlin, 211
Bharatiya Janata Party (BJP), 314,
    315, 316. *See* Modi government
Biafra, 23, 25, 29, 39
Biafran War (1970), 14, 29
Biden, Joe, 2, 3, 177, 178, 210,
    246, 370
    on Capitol Hill insurrection,
        370
    crime bill (1994), 3
    as Democratic nominee, 246
    elected as president, 2, 3, 257
    electoral victory, 210
    His presidency, 370
'Big Pharma', 68, 80
biometric registration, 203–4
'biopower', 356–7
Birther movement, 227
BJP (Bharatiya Janata Party), 314,
    315, 316
black ghetto, 233, 234, 241
Black Lives Matter movement
    (BLM), 2, 210, 227–8, 245,
    351, 356, 359, 370
black poverty, 233, 239, 241
Black Radical Tradition, 240–1
Blair, Tony, 4, 24
    SCUS's Global Legacy Award,
        52
BLM *see* Black Lives Matter
    movement (BLM)
Boko Haram, 345
Bonaparte (Napoleon) Jena
    victory, 168
border crossing, irregular, 89,

110–12. *See* humanitarian
    interventions (at European
    borders)
Borrell, Josep, 217, 218, 231
Bosnia genocide, 23
Bosnia-Herzegovina, 254–5
bourgeois liberals, 178
Boutros-Ghali, Boutros, 166
Bowen, Chris, 91–2, 99
Brauman, Rony, 104, 159, 160,
    161
Brazil, 171, 172, 329, 346,
    418n90
'Brazilianisation', 172
Bretton Woods institutions, 130
Briskman, Linda, 96
Britain, 30, 175
    Brexit, 3, 4, 31, 299, 306
    Conservative government,
        30–1
    COVID-19 and state-society
        relationship, 177
    'digital-by-design' universal
        credit reforms, 203
    global leadership claims, 4
    international aid, 30–3
    liberal declinism in, 156–7
    liberalism in, 155–7
    miners' strikes in, 171
    state and aid agencies relations,
        4–5
British
    Colonial Office, 26
    Foreign Office, 32
    Hard Rock exercise (1982),
        193
    imperialism, 25, 26, 31, 32
    postcolonial foreign policy, 26
    slavery abolition, 31, 340
    war preparations, 192
British Anti-Slave Trade move-
    ment, 339

British warfare state, 192
    nuclear attack survival, 192–3
    war-fighting infrastructure,
        192–4
Brown, Mike, 235
Brown, Wendy, 182
Browne, Poppy, 102
Broyelle, Jacques, 159
Brussels conference (2020), 268,
    272, 274
Brussels Final Act (1890), 340
Brussels, 72, 211, 214, 217,
    220–1
Bucharest, 253
Buddhist nationalism, 59
Bundeswehr, 214
Burkina Faso, 217, 218
Bury, J.B., 178
Bush, George H.W., 250
Bush, George W., 43, 147, 148,
    176
    war on terror, 252
Buxton, Dorothy, 21–3, 24, 35

Cabrera, Luis, 122
California Consensus, 321–2, 324
Call to Action Summit (2015),
    314
Cambodia, 81, 282
Cameron, David, 4, 47, 50
    'One World Conservatism'
        strategy, 48–9
Campbell-Bannerman, Henry, 156
Cap Anamur (ship), 123
capitalism, 82, 149, 157, 158,
    163, 168, 178, 181, 186, 200,
    201, 292
    approximation, 165
    colonial capitalism, 25
    in Dubai, 304, 310, 311
    global capitalism, 187, 297
    global expansion, 164

industrial capitalism, 171–2
    'late capitalism', 165, 170, 171
    liberal capitalism, 168, 172,
        338
    logics of, 282
    neoliberal capitalism, 9
    poverty paradox, 202
    re-conceal attempts, 190
    visibility-invisibility relation-
        ship, 201
    Western capitalism, 4, 11
capitalist democracy, 29, 168, 175
CARAD (Coalition for Asylum
    Seekers, Refugees and
    Detainees), 88
CARE (charitable organization),
    161
Carnegie Endowment for
    International Peace, 304–5
Carter, Jimmy, 12, 238
Catherine II, 254
Catrambone, Christopher, 109
Catrambone, Regina, 109
Central Sahel, 207, 208, 209,
    214, 220, 222, 223
    European Global Strategy, 217
    European involvement in, 214
    Human rights violations,
        215–16
Centre International d'Études
    pour la Rénovation du
    Libéralisme (CIRL), 137
Césaire, Aimé, 55–6, 65, 66, 355
Chant, Sylvia, 320
Charbonneau, Bruno, 215, 218,
    222
Cheney, Dick, 250, 252
child rights, 28–9
children
    as focus of immigration debates,
        93
    liberal violence against, 292–3

offshore imprisonment of, 89–90, 92–4, 95–8, 101–6
Chimni, B.S., 274, 354
China, 175, 229, 248, 253, 338
  humanitarian responses, 346–7
  state capitalism, 11
Chloroquine (drug), 68
Chouliaraki, Lilie, 361
Christian Aid (aid organisation), 25
Christianity, 292, 356
Christmas Island, 88, 93
Cissé, Soumaïla, 219
Citoyenne, Roya, 112
civil society, 48, 59, 140, 157, 277, 342–3, 346–7
  Indian civil society, 330–1
  on labour permit, 273
  liberal democracies, 73, 99
  rely on private donations, 109–10
civil war (Libya), 116, 187
civil war (Yemen), 400n16
civil war theory, 189
Clinton, Bill, 147, 250
Clinton, Hillary, 241–2, 299
CNN (television channel), 2
Coalition for Asylum Seekers, Refugees and Detainees (CARAD), 88
Cobden, Richard, 155
Cold War, 7, 11, 12, 13, 127, 136, 139, 143, 144, 150, 161, 282, 337
  end of, 166, 195, 248, 249, 251, 283, 337, 354
  great tragedy, 408n13
  Liberalism, 129, 130–3
  post-Cold War period, 4, 14, 128, 147, 152, 236, 242
Coleman, Sophie, 97–8, 100
Colgan, Jeff, 9

'collateral damage', 200
Colombo, 57
  anti-Tamil pogrom (1983), 57
colonialism, 23, 28, 55
  anti-colonialism, 364
  and coloniality contrasts, 354–5, 356
  decolonisation, 23, 25–6, 72, 354
  European colonialism, 12, 235, 456n5
  formal colonialism, 372
coloniality, 353–9, 372
  decoloniality, 372, 374, 375–6
  destructive force of, 373–4
Communism, 129, 134, 139, 147, 336
  anti-communism, 161
'compassion fatigue', 362
Conditional cash transfer (CCT) programmes, 320
Congo, Democratic Republic of, 39
Conservative Party (UK), 4, 30–1, 47, 48–9, 50, 51, 156
Cooper, Frederick, 76
counter-revolution (1970), 161–2, 165, 171
Coup of 18 Brumaire, 157
Covenant of the League of Nations, 336, 340–1, 358
COVID-19 pandemic, 1, 15, 31, 53, 177, 338, 351, 369
  globalisation of, 67–9
  humanitarian aid realignment, 67–9
  impact on non-white peoples, 359
  vaccine research, 68
Cox's Bazar, 63
Craven-Matthews, Catriona, 222
Crimean War, 67

cybernetic 'science of warfare', 192, 202–3
Czech Republic, 254

DAC (Development Assistance Committee), 346
Daily Telegraph, 101, 102
Dalits, 313, 316, 317, 330
Danby, John Francis, 37–8
Daoust, Gabrielle, 363–4
data-knowledge contrasts, 201
Davos, 306
DAWN (women's organisations), 318
de Waal, Alex, 345
Debord, Guy, 165
DEC (Disasters Emergency Committee) [UK], 45, 48
decoloniality, 372, 374, 375–6
decolonisation, 23, 25–6, 72, 354
de-industrialisation, 171
Delhi, 313
Democratic Party (United States), 228, 238, 240, 241
Deneen, Patrick J., 9, 157
Department for International Development (DfID), 1, 30, 42, 49, 50, 52
  abolition of, 30, 53
  decolonisation process, 32
  'global leadership', 31
  into the Foreign and Commonwealth Office, 53
  right-wing nationalism, 31
Department of Immigration and Border Protection (DIBP), 95, 99–100, 101, 102, 103, 104
Department of Immigration and Citizenship (Australia), 86, 91
'dependency syndrome', 362
Depo-Provera, 317–18
Derg, 102, 102, 158

Derrida, Jacques, 168
Dewachi, Omar, 198
DfID (Department for International Development). *See* Department for International Development (DfID)
DIAC (Australian Department of Immigration and Citizenship), 86, 87
DIBP (Department of Immigration and Border Protection), 95, 99–100, 101, 102, 103, 104
Dicko, Mahmoud, 216, 220
digital workhouse, 187, 192, 201–4
Disasters Emergency Committee (DEC) [UK], 45, 48
dollar devaluation, 176
Donini, Antonio, 348
Dowd, Catriona, 221
drone warfare, 199, 287
Drugs for Neglected Diseases initiative (DNDi), 68
Du Bois, W.E.B., 240
Dubai: performance of modernity, 72, 303–11
  amnesty for workers declaration, 307
  capitalism, 304, 310, 311
  Carnegie report, 304–5
  domestic workers conditions in camps, 306–8, 309
  enabling global corruption, 304–5
  female domestic workers, violence against, 307–8
  as fifth largest aid donor, 308
  human rights abuses, 306–8, 309
  IGO's policy report, 309–10
  kafala system, 304–5, 307
  liberal order and threats, 305–6

markets of, 304
migrant labourers' abuses, 304–5
neoliberalism, 310
Dublin Regulations, 121–2
Duflo, Esther, 323
Dunant, Henri, 339
Dvorak, Suzanne, 90–1
Dyvik, Synne, 363–4

Eastern European secessionism, 195–8
Ebola crisis, 49–52, 346
Economic Times, The, 330
Economist, The, 9, 11
ECOWAS (Economic Community of West African States), 220–1
Edkins, Jenny, 124
Egypt, 262, 271, 298, 337
Ehrenberg, Alain, 180
Eichengreen, Barry, 145
El Salvador, 225, 226
11 September 2001 attacks. *See* 9/11 attacks
Emancipation, 144–5, 204
emergência, 164
Emmott, Bill, 11
empathy, 363
empire, 186, 374
collapse of, 179, 297
and humanitarian aid, 77, 105
in relation to neoliberalism, 185–6
Englebert, Pierre, 222
entitlement, 298–9
Ethiopia, 102, 158
Ethiopian famine (1980s), 23
EU Neighbourhood Policy (ENP) [2004], 265
Eubanks, Virginia, 202
EUCAP (European Union Capacity Building Mission in Mali), 214

Eurocentricity, 169
Eurocentrism, 12, 370, 374, 375–6
Europe
anti-immigrant groups, 175
'civilising mission', 357
exceptionalism, 219
external frontier security policy, 187–9, 198, 199
human rights diplomacy, 188
income inequality, 212–3
irregular migration to, 187–8
Mali integrated approach, 218, 219, 222–3
Mali intervention, 207–23
political action, 289–91
racial politics of immigration, 352
see also humanitarian interventions (at European borders)
European Central Bank, 186
European colonialism, 12, 235, 456n5
European Commission, 115, 116
European Economic Community (EEC), 130
European Enlightenment, 296, 325, 326, 328, 335, 339
European Union (EU) and Arab refugee diplomacy, 260, 262, 265–7, 275
EU–Jordan Case, 270–4
EU–Lebanon Case, 267–70
and refugee-hosting states cooperation, 259–60, 262, 265–77
European Union (EU), 110, 111, 112, 119, 186, 220, 248, 281, 306, 400n19
Action Plan Against Migrant Smuggling (2015), 116
Britain withdrawal, 3, 4, 31, 299, 306

INDEX

Charter of Fundamental Rights, 116

Common Defence and Security Policy, 216–7

controversial Facilitation Directive (2002), 113, 116

crisis governance imaginary (MAGYC 2020), 275

'European Neighbourhood Policy' (ENP), 187

external migration policy, 266

Global Strategy, 217

intersectoral policy approach adaptation, 266

Jordan Compacts (2016), 266, 271, 272, 273, 277

Khartoum Process, 187–8

Lebanon Compacts (2016), 266, 268

maximalism of, 219

Mediterranean migration cooperation, 264

Mediterranean SAR mission, 110, 111

Operation Irini, 115–16

Operation Sophia, 115

Sahel funding package, 214

SAR activities, resultant policy, 116

Supporting Syria and the Region conference (London, 2016), 268

unwillingness to rescued migrant's accommodation, 110, 111, 112, 114

European Union's Training Mission in Mali, 214

Evangelische Kirche Deutschlands (EKD), 400*n*15

Expert Panel, 89–90, 91, 93

'false consciousness', 296–7

Family Planning 2020 Summit (FP2020), 318

family-planning policy, 317–18

Fanon, Frantz, 179, 357

fascism, 28, 175, 282, 286, 294, 300–1

Fassin, Didier, 71

FASSTT (Forum of Australian Services for Survivors of Torture and Trauma), 88

Fechter, Anne-Meike, 364

Fejerskov, Adam, 322

female genital mutilation (FGM), 358

Ferguson, Niall, 6

Fiddian-Qasmiyeh, Elena, 349–50

FIHS. *See* 'formal international humanitarian system'(FIHS)

financial crisis (2008), 148, 175, 179, 205, 212, 337

Financial Times (newspaper), 237

Fisher, Mark, 204, 223

FitzGerald, David Scott, 86–7

Floyd (George), murder of, 2, 3, 245, 351, 370

Fondation Liberté Sans Frontières (LSF), 158, 159, 160, 161, 162

forced displacement, 259–60, 261–2

EU displacement approach, 276

geopolitical factors shaped, 260–1, 262, 270, 271, 274

human agency displacement, 287–8

Palestinian displacement, 261

Syrian displacement, 259, 262, 265–6, 267–70, 271–3, 276

forced migration. *See* forced displacement

Ford Foundation, 318

Ford, Glen, 243

Ford, James, 12

INDEX

Foreign Affairs (magazine), 6, 9, 232

Foreign and Commonwealth Office (UK), 1, 53

'formal international humanitarian system' (FIHS), 333–4, 339
and authority structures, 342–4
challenges to, 344–9
and institutions of, 340–2
and liberal order relationship, 333–4

Forsyth, Justin, 23–4, 48, 51, 52

Forum of Australian Services for Survivors of Torture and Trauma (FASSTT), 88

Fotaki, Marianne, 276

Foucault, Michel, 162–3, 296, 356–7

France, 111, 120
African policy, 208
'human rights and development' debates, 158
irregularised migration responses, 111, 112
as 'lost territory of the Republic', 209
Marseille, 209, 223
social division in, 174
see also Mali (France intervention of)

Franklin, H. Bruce, 163

Fraser, Malcolm, 102

fraternité principle, 112, 120

French army, 207

Freud, Sigmund, 178
on melancholia, 178–9, 180–1

Friedman, Milton, 142

Friedman, Thomas, 11

Friedrich, Carl, 137

Frontex (EU's border control agency), 109, 111, 115

FTE sector (finance, technology, and electronics), 212–13

Fukuyama, Francis, 5, 10, 11, 166, 167–8, 170, 228, 232, 233, 234, 236–8, 239, 240, 241, 281
'assimilation agenda', 237
blames Democrats, 241
Judeo-Christian eschatology, 168–9
liberal democracy crisis solution, 246
on Trump's victory, 231, 232, 237–8

Fundamental Principles of the Red Cross, 339

G5 Sahel Joint Force, 214

G5 Sahel summit (Nouakchott, Jun 2020), 215

G5 Sahel, 214, 218

Gandhi, Indira, 318

Gates Foundation, 313, 314–15, 316, 330, 331
Enlightenment teleological narrative, 325, 326–7
family-planning policy, 317–18
Global Goalkeeper Award to Modi, 313–14, 330–1
technocratic approaches to women's empowerment, 320, 321–4, 326
theory of change, 318–19

Gates, Bill, 167, 313–14, 321, 322

Gates, Melinda, 313, 321, 322, 324

GCC (Gulf Cooperation Council), 309

gender politics, 293

Geneva Convention, 70–1, 341, 345

Geneva School, 185, 186
two-world imaginary of world order, 189, 190, 195

geopolitical consensus, 352
geopolitics, 248, 249, 256, 287, 354
Georgian Armed Forces, 253
Germany, 21, 114, 119, 218, 248, 251
GI Bill, 240
Giddens, Anthony, 170
Gilbert, Jeremy, 11
Gilead (biopharmaceutical company), 81
Gillard government, 89, 91, 96
Gillard, Julia, 89
Gilman, Nils, 8
Giraldo, Isis, 327
Girard, René, 295
Gladstone, William Ewart, 155, 156
Gladwell, Malcolm, 243
Glaude, Eddie, Jr., 371
Gleeson, Madeline, 99–100
global economy, 251, 347, 356
global humanitarian sector, 26–7
global North, 104, 117, 264, 274, 285, 317, 352, 354, 359, 365, 456n5
    borders securitisation of, 123
    and global South gap, 194, 344, 345
    motive of, 50
    'popular humanitarianism', 362, 363
global South, 30, 33, 60, 79, 80, 117, 291, 297, 324, 326, 347, 349, 354, 355, 359–64, 374, 456n5
    attacks on aid workers, 290
    global North gap, 194, 344, 345
    humanitarian crises in, 352
    military intervention in, 283–4
    refugee aid, 274

white supremacy in, 357
Women's empowerment in, 315, 317, 318, 325
Global War on Terror, 209, 211, 235, 244, 251–3, 255, 285, 288, 365
    ethical failures of, 289
    narcissistic violence of, 284
globalisation, 188, 194, 198, 205, 337–8
    anglophile visions of, 291
Good Humanitarian Donorship Principles, 346
Gray, John, 211, 222
great food supplement (1867), 75
'great humanising movement', 155
Great War (1914–18). See World War I
Greece, 113, 119, 120, 175
Green Party (Australia), 101
Greening, Justine, 51
Greif, Mark, 169
Group of 77, 8
Group of Seven (G7), 249
Guardian, The (newspaper), 49, 94, 103, 228, 307
Guilhot, Nicolas, 137–8
Guilluy, Christophe, 3, 174, 213, 222
Guinea, 49
Gulf War I (1991), 198, 199, 248, 254
    and forced migration, 261
Guterres, António, 338

Haass, Richard, 5
Habermas, Jürgen, 149
Hague Convention, 341, 345
Haiti, 225, 226–7
Haitian earthquake (2010), 29, 79, 232, 235, 346, 361
Hammond, Philip, 51

Hargeisa, 373
Harrell-Bond, Barbara, 61, 62
Hashemite Kingdom, 271, 273–4
Havana Charter (1948), 130
Hayek, F.A., 136–7, 142, 177
hegemonic identities, mimicry of, 179–80
Henley Passport Index, 117
hepatitis C, 81
Herald Sun, The (newspaper), 83, 84, 98
Herrou, Cédric, 112, 114, 123
Hindus, 315
    Modi government women empowerment policies, 315–16, 317
    moral panic on women's honour, 315–16, 319
Hirono, Miwa, 347
historical closure, 10, 164, 165, 167–9
HIV, 80, 317
Hobbes, Thomas, 295
Hobhouse, L.T., 155, 156
Hobson, J.A., 155
Hochschild, Arlie Russell, 239
Hockey, Joe, 93
Hofstadter, Richard, 128, 139
Hollande, François, 207–9, 210
    Bamako visit (2013), 218
Hopgood, Stephen, 231
Hoppe, Hans-Hermann, 194
Höppner, Harald, 111
Horn of Africa, 77
HoSang, Daniel Martinez, 232, 240
Houthis, 308
human rights, 4, 14, 85, 89, 93, 108, 115, 117–18, 127, 128–30, 159, 228, 248, 265, 309, 325, 327, 328, 335, 351, 357, 363, 366, 370, 372, 373
    abuses in Dubai, 306–8, 309
    African Americans fight for, 358
    anti-political interpretation of, 162–3
    disobedience for, 119–23
    Europe human rights diplomacy, 188
    France 'human rights and development' debates, 158
    human rights agenda, 117–18
    international human rights regimes, 150, 305
    maximalist conception' of, 160
    minimalist conception of, 9
    Modi government's violations of, 314, 316–19, 330–1
    Moyn on, 10, 12–13, 14, 161–2, 378n16, 414n38
    NGOs on human rights law, 115, 124
    Universal Declaration of Human Rights (UDHR), 118, 336
    violations in Central Sahel, 215–16
    Western rhetoric of, 361
Human Rights Watch, 216, 308, 318
human smuggling, 115
human trafficking, 304, 305
humanitarian aid
    actants of aid, 76–9
    'command supply discipline', 77–80, 81, 82
    commercial use of trademarks and copyrighted emblems, 75
    critique of humanitarian goods, 81–2
    4x4 fleets development, 78
    humanitarian deployments, 74–80, 82
    humanitarian liberal market-

places and their objectors,
78–81
humanitarian objects of, 71–5
mass deployment of medicine,
76–7
procurement market, 74
treatment cost reduction, 81
humanitarian aid agencies, 8, 13,
26, 33, 262, 290–1
and commercial industries
relations, 166
during COVID-19 pandemic,
15
Ebola crisis responses, 49–52
fundraising activity, 166–7
'humanitarian wars' (1990s), 26
as hybrid radicalism, 13–14
local staff in, 360
racialised imagery usage, 361
and state relationship, 4, 26–7,
41, 43
see also Australia: NGO offshore
detention management; SAR
(search and rescue) missions
'humanitarian effectiveness',
166–7
humanitarian exhibitions. See
universal exhibitions
humanitarian idealism, 252
humanitarian operations (at
European borders), 107–24
agency of migrants, 122
asylum right, 117–19, 120
free movement right, 117–19
human rights agenda, 117–18
human rights, disobedience for,
119–23
humanitarian engagement
model, 124
international law of sea,
114–19
irregularised migrants, criminalisation of, 111–14

maritime civil disobedience,
119–23
migrants' legal transgressions,
122
non-governmental rescuers Vs.
European governments,
111–14
private rescuers and migrants'
relations, 111, 117, 121–2,
123–4
private SAR missions, 110–12,
113
'humanitarian interventions', 4–5,
40–1
humanitarian minimalism, 158
humanitarian minimum, 15, 158,
161, 167, 177, 178
humanitarian morality, 11–18
'humanitarian principles', 68–9
humanitarian protection, 260
humanitarian realism, 36, 37–8
'humanitarian space', 15–16, 166,
231–2, 359
'humanitarian system', 7–8
humanitarian trade fairs. See
universal exhibitions
'humanitarian wars' (1990s), 26
humanitarianism
challenges for, 5
conception of, 11–18
contemporary conceptions of,
334
decolonial histories of, 352–3
as a decolonial project of life,
370–2, 374–5
discourse and practices, 349,
352–9
'drift and shift' in nature of, 39,
54
institutions, establishment of,
7–8
international sacrificial order
role, 64

moral obligation, 104
moralisation of politics and, 166
objectives of 1990s, 248–57
as profession, 60–2
and third-worldist ideology, 159
'humanity law', 129, 142–3, 144
humanity, 11–13, 44, 61, 64, 105, 161, 181, 229, 294, 301, 309, 335, 339, 341, 352–3, 363, 366
search for meaning, 37
Hungary, 177, 254
Hurricane Katrina (2005), 235, 243–5, 290, 297
Hurricane Maria, 234, 242
Husain, Atiya, 64
Hussein, Saddam, 42
hydroxychloroquine (drug), 68

ICCPR (International Covenant on Civil and Political Rights) [1966], 115, 118
'identity politics', 153, 175, 238, 240–1, 246
in Arab Middle East, 261
IDP (Internally displaced person), 60, 217–18, 365, 425n34
IGO ('International Gulf Organization'), 309
IHL (International Humanitarian Law), 341–2, 344, 345, 349
IHRL (International human rights law), 150
Ikenberry, G. John, 5, 329, 335, 337
ILO (International Labour Organization), 150, 272, 309
IMF (International Monetary Fund), 145, 186
India, 343, 346
coercive sterilisation, 318

'family-planning' policies, 316–18
Indian civil society, 330–1
international organisations role in, 316–18
see also Modi government
Indian Ocean tsunami (2004), 44–5, 46, 343
Indonesia, 88, 343, 346
industrial capitalism, 171–2
'information age', 289
INGOs (international non-governmental organisations), 43, 262
insulation, legal, 186
Internally Displaced Persons (IDPs), 60, 217–18, 365, 425n34
International Committee of Military Medicine and Pharmacy, 72
international congresses (1960s), 72
International Convention for the Safety of Life at Sea (SOLAS Convention) [1974], 114
International Convention on Maritime Search and Rescue (SAR Convention) [1979], 114
International Courts and Tribunals, 144
International Covenant on Civil and Political Rights (ICCPR) [1966], 115, 118
International Criminal Court, 102
'international ethical order', 248
International Exposition (Paris, 1867), 69, 71, 82
'International Gulf Organization' (IGO), 309
International Labour Organization (ILO), 150, 272, 309
International Monetary Fund (IMF), 145, 186

International Organization for Migration (IOM), 108–9
International Red Cross movement (ICRC), 13, 15, 32, 46, 69, 70–1, 74, 340, 452–3n1
Code of Conduct, 346
emblem of, 75
Red Cross XXth Conference (Vienna, 1965), 72
world wars and, 71
intrauterine device (IUD), 318, 324
'inverted millenarianism', 170
IOM (International Organization for Migration), 108–9
Iphigenia, sacrifice of, 292, 293
Iran–Iraq war (1980s), 199
Iraq invasion (2003), 26, 170, 199, 337
as first 'humanitarian war' of 1990s, 248–9
forced migration and, 261, 262
Iraq War (2003), 23, 41, 147, 175
SCUK anti-war sentiment, 41–2
Iraq, 105, 194, 285, 344
aerial bombardment, 249
Canal Hotel bomb attack (Baghdad, 19 Aug 2003), 43
ISIS in, 294
modern public health system, 198–9
Iraq/Syria–Mali connection, 220
Isaacs, Mark, 94–5
ISIS, 290, 294, 337, 345
Islah party (Yemen), 308–9
Islamic State, 256, 305–6
Islamic world, 252, 252
Istanbul Cooperation Initiative, 255
Italy

criminalisation of SAR missions, 113, 114
irregularborder crossing, 111
maritime civil disobedience, 109
Operation Mare Nostrum, 109, 115
Operation Triton, 109

Jabali, Malaika, 241–2
Jackson, Nicholas, 360
Jadaliyya (website), 309
Jameson, Fredric, 163, 169
Jammu and Kashmir, 313
Japanese, 71
Jay, Michael, 49
Jebb, Eglantyne, 24–5, 27–8, 35, 44, 339
JEEAR (Joint Evaluation for Emergency Assistance to Rwanda), 39–40
Jensen, Steven, 358
Johnson Sirleaf, Ellen, 51
Johnson, Boris, 3–4
Johnson, Chalmers, 251
Joint Evaluation for Emergency Assistance to Rwanda (JEEAR), 39–40
Jones, Van, 2
Jordan, 43, 259, 260, 266, 276
asylum system, 271–2
civil society on labour permit, 273
granting employment right to Syrian refugees, 271–3, 276
labour market, 272, 273
mass protests (2018), 274, 277
refugee-hosting, 270–1
Syrian refugees in, 271–2, 274
Jugend Rettet, 109
Jung, Carl: theory of individuation, 181

Just War theory, 283, 292

Kachin Independence Army, 59
kafala system, 304–5, 307
Kant, Immanuel, 142, 281, 283, 328
Keïta, Ibrahim Boubacar, 216, 219, 220
Kenyan Emergency, 32, 106
Keohane, Robert, 9
Kerry Town (Sierra Leone), 50–1
Kerry Town Ebola Treatment Centre, 51
Keynes, John Maynard, 186
Keystone XL pipeline, 242
Khmer Rouge, 158
Kigali (Rwanda), 39
Kim Jong-un, 148
King, Martin Luther, Jr., 210. 375
Kojève, Alexandre, 168
Koselleck, Reinhart, 164, 172
Kosovo War (1999), 40, 255
Kosovo, 147
Kuwait, 43, 248

labour markets, 9, 171, 172, 266, 268, 272, 273
Labour Party (UK), 4
Lampedusa migrant shipwreck (2013), 109
Lasch, Christopher, 164, 173
'late capitalism', 165, 170, 171
Le Monde, 159
Le Pen, Marine, 3–4
le Play, Frédéric, 69
League of Nations Child Welfare Committee, 25, 28
League of Nations Health Organization, 31
League of Nations, 31, 185, 336

Lebanon, 259, 260, 266
    displaced people's rates, 267
    EU and Lebanese state cooperation, 277
    financial collapse of, 269
    October uprising (2019), 267, 277
    open-border policy adaptation, 267
    politicians on Syrian refugees, 270
    sectarian power-sharing, 270
    Syrian displacement in, 267–70
    Syrian refugees sit-in (Tripoli), 277
    use of EU's diplomacy, 276
Lewis, W. Arthur, 212, 213
liberal constitutionalism, 168
liberal declinism, 10, 17, 156
liberal democracies, 161, 232
    anti-utopian teleology threat to, 151
    civil society on, 73, 99
    military interventions as toolbox of, 209–10, 211
    Western liberal democracies, 213, 305, 327–8, 336
liberal despondency, 158
liberal hegemony, 157, 196–7, 283
liberal humanism, 291
liberal humanitarianism. *See* liberal international order
liberal innocence, 371–2
liberal interventionism, 290
liberal melancholy, 178–9
liberal multiculturalism, 299
liberal order
    challenges to, 338
    characterisations of, 335–6
    conception of, 6–7
    current crisis of, 145–51, 153

decolonial approach, 362–6
defenders, 5–6
defensive liberalism, 132–3, 135
emerging humanitarian actors as
    disruptors, 344, 346
end of, 9–11
'the Golden Age' of (1990 and
    2004), 337–8
in post-1945 era, 128, 129, 131
institutionalisation of, 129, 130
international refugee regime,
    challenges to, 344–50
laws of war, 344–5
liberal democracy, 133–4, 136,
    142, 143, 144, 168, 170,
    305–6
liberal international order, 127–
    53, 334
liberal international order and
    humanitarianism, 339–49
liberal international order
    mobilisation of, 257
post-World War II order-build-
    ing project, 335–6
proximity strategy, 36
re-historicising, 353
societies and democracy
    relations, 298
Soviet Union and, 337
term usage, 8
triumphalism of the early
    1990s, 337–8
Truman 'four freedoms' speech
    (1945), 132
see also formal international
    humanitarian system' (FIHS);
    liberal international order
    and humanitarianism;
    political minimalism;
    post-liberal world, violence
    emergence in

liberal revivalism, 282
liberal sensibility, 200
'liberal space', 231–2, 246, 291
    'ideal-framework', 233–4
    racial ordering within, 232
liberal technology, 284
liberal tolerance, 297
liberal utopianism, 140, 178
liberal warfare
    digitalised, 286–7
    drone technologies in, 287
    as faith-based, 293
    nature of, 285–6
    victim's sacralisation, 292–3
'liberal', 328
liberalism
    as biopolitical regime, 282
    death of, 297–8, 300
    founding fathers, 196
    historical mutations, 282
    left–right dialectic, 194–8, 204
    ruins of, 281, 284–5
    threat to, 9
    tolerance idea, 299
Liberia, 49, 51
Libya, 108, 119, 285
    violent assault (2011), 282
Libyan coast, 109
Libyan coastguard, 111, 116
Libyan War, 254–5
Liebig stock cubes, 75
Lilla, Mark, 153
Live Aid, 166
long-acting contraception,
    317–18, 323
Losurdo, Domenico, 196
Louisiana Gulf, 245
Lowndes, Joseph E., 232, 240
LSF. See Fondation Liberté Sans
    Frontières (LSF)
Luce, Edward, 11

Lyons national exhibition (1885), 73

Mac Ginty, Roger, 78
MacAndrew, Nick, 41
Macron, Emmanuel, 215, 217, 218
malaria, 76, 86
Malhuret, Claude, 159, 160, 161
Mali (France intervention of), 207–23
  Bauman's retrotopia, 222
  Europe's policies in Mali, 210–12
  French soldiers deployment, 214, 215
  Opération Barkhane, 209, 214, 215
  Opération Serval, 207–9, 214, 215
Mali
  Anti-terrorism forces, 219
  Bamako protests (Jun 2020), 219
  collapse of state authorities in, 215
  humanitarian aid support to, 214–15
  internally displaced people, rise of, 218
  military coup (18 Aug 2020), 216, 220
  military junta, 220–1
  North Mali conflict (2012), 218
  political and economic blockade on, 220
  return of the state, 215–16, 221
  violence in, 215–18, 221
  see also Mali (France intervention of)
Malian Armed Forces, 221

Malian diaspora, 208
Mali–Marseille connection, 209–10, 222
Malkki, Liisa, 119
Malta, 108, 109, 113, 114
Mamdani, Mahmood, 57–8
Mandel, Ernest, 165, 170–1
Mann, Geoff, 412n12
Mann, Gregory, 219–20
Mann, Itamar, 117
Manus Island (Papua New Guinea), 83–5, 86, 106
  detention centre conditions, 86
  provisions for families, 91–2
Marchal, Roland, 208
Marcuse, Herbert, 412n39
Mariam, Mengistu Haile, 102
Marxists, 296
Mauritania, 218
Mbembe, Achille, 352
McAllister, David, 305, 306
McCarthyism era, 133
McNevin, Anne, 88
'me too' movement (2016), 24
Mearsheimer, John, 7
Médecins Sans Frontières (MSF), 12–13, 49, 77, 102, 158, 160, 161, 342, 398–9n5, 400n19
  protest against Soviet attacks, 158
  SAR missions, 109, 110
  as Toyota dealership, 78
medical economy, 76
Medical Emergency Relief International (Merlin), 49, 50
Mediterranean Dialogue, 255
Mediterranean Sea
  as deadliest migrant route, 108–9
  mass drownings in, 200
  migrant deaths, 109

search and rescue (SAR)
mission in, 107, 108–10
see also humanitarian interventions (at European borders)
melancholia, 178–81
Mexico, 171, 235
Middle East and North Africa
Region (MENA), 265
Middle Eastern states internal
antagonisms, 199–200
Mignolo, Walter, 327
Migrant Offshore Aid Station
(MOAS), 109, 110, 114,
400*n*16
migration, irregular/migrants,
111, 425*n*34, 398*n*4
Arab states governance of,
261–4
civil networks support for, 111
'conviviality' concept, 364–5
criminalisation of humanitarian
assistance, 87, 111–14, 345,
352
detention services contracts,
84–5, 88–9, 90–4, 95
EU external migration policy,
266
towards Europe, 187–8
self-settled refugees, 365
violence against, in African
countries, 364–5
Western conceptions of, 235–6
see also Australia: NGO offshore
detention management;
forced displacement;
humanitarian interventions
(at European borders); SAR
(search and rescue) missions
militarism and welfare relationship, 190
Mill, John Stuart, 155
Millennium Development Goals,
211

Miller, Simon, 97–8, 100
Mills, Charles W., 227, 233
MINUSMA (United Nations
Multidimensional Integrated
Stabilization Mission), 214
Mishra, Pankaj, 10, 174, 179, 223
Mission Lifeline, 109
MOAS (Migrant Offshore Aid
Station), 109, 110, 114, 400*n*16
modern inter-state warfare, 190–1
Modi government, 313
action against rape, 315–16
anti-Muslim pogrom, 313
criminalising Muslim men, 316
and Gates Foundation, 313–15,
316, 330
promoting coercive sterilisation, 316–18
public relations war, 331
sterilisation abuse, 317–18
toilet-building project, 314,
315, 319
triple *talaq* illegalisation, 316
vote of no confidence (Jul
2018), 314
winning Western actors
support, 329
and women's empowerment,
314–19, 323, 325
Modi, Narendra, 313–15, 330–1
'Beti Bachao Beti Padhao'
('Save the daughter, educate
the daughter') programme,
315
Global Goalkeeper Award,
313–14, 330–1
hosting FP2020 Summit, 318
and women's empowerment
programmes, 314–19
see also Modi government
money laundering, 304
Morefield, Heidi, 321, 324
Morgenthau, Hans, 136, 253

Morrison, Scott, 83, 84, 94, 98, 101

Morrison, Toni, 59

Moss, Philip, 102

Most Excellent Order of the British Empire, 64

Mostafanezhad, Mary, 362

Moulds, Paul, 92, 94

Moulds, Robbin, 92, 94

Mouvement du 5 juin— Rassemblement des Forces Patriotiques (M5-RFP), 216, 219, 220, 221

Movimiento 15-M, 175

Moyn, Samuel, 10, 12, 14, 131, 161–2, 412*n*38

Moynier, Gustave, 70–1

Moynihan, Daniel Patrick, 233

Muhammadiyah (Indonesian Muslim social movement), 346

Mullings, Beverley, 361

multiculturalism, 174, 195, 227, 240

Munich Security Conference (Feb 2019), 305, 306

Murrey, Amber, 360

Mutua, Makau, 358, 361, 363, 366

Myanmar, 58–60, 105

mythical violence, 294–7

NAFTA (North American Free Trade Agreement), 186

narcissism, 173, 286

National Review articles, 229–30, 237

National Security Act (1947), 132–3

National warfare states, 194–5

NATO (North Atlantic Treaty Organization), 130, 149, 251, 253, 255

Libyan intervention (2011), 254–5, 337

Nauru, 84, 91–2, 101, 106

detention camps conditions and procedures, 96

SCA in, 84, 85, 94

Topside camp (detention site), 86

Ndlovu-Gatsheni, Sabelo, 374

necropolitics, 200, 357

Neilson, Brett, 89

neoliberal bourgeoisie, 173

neoliberal fundamentalism, 176

neoliberal humanitarianism, 358

neoliberal modernity, 304

neoliberalism, 136–7, 138, 145, 146, 161, 176, 185–6

for social democrats, 186

minimalist politics, 354

new wars redux, 194–6

opposition to imperialism, 196

privatisation and destruction, 192–4, 205

rise of, 8–9

and social reproduction, 191–2, 193, 205

'two world' imaginary of, 186, 189–90

warfare nexus and secessionism, 187

world economy, politicisation of, 189–90

Nepal earthquake (2015), 346

'network-centric warfare', 445*n*11

Neumann, Klaus, 87

New Deal, 238, 240

liberalism, 129, 132

'new imperialism', 379*n*26

New International Economic Order (NIEO), 8, 145, 150, 152

New Orleans, 243–4, 297
    Hurricane Katrina (2005), 235,
    243–5, 290, 297
'new wars', 188, 189, 194–6,
    205, 285
New York Magazine (magazine), 228
New York Times (newspaper), 231
New Yorker, The (newspaper), 243
News Corp daily, 93
newspaper subscriptions (1870
    and 1914), 74
NGOs (Non-governmental
    organisations), 342–3, 353
    domestic poverty reduction
        role, 15–16
    and international law of sea,
        114–19
    irregular migration assistance,
        111
    Mediterranean SAR missions,
        109–19
    role non-Western NGOs,
        346–7
    see also Australia: NGO offshore
        detention management;
        humanitarian aid (NGO);
        humanitarian aid agencies
Ngugi wa Thiong'o, 374
Niebuhr, Reinhold, 133–5, 137,
    138, 141, 152, 409–10n30
    on political minimalism, 133–4
NIEO (New International
    Economic Order), 8, 145, 150,
    152
Niethammer, Lutz, 167–8
Nietzsche, Friedrich, 174, 179
Niger, 217
9/11 attacks, 170, 172, 175, 197,
    252, 297
    theological rage of, 293–4
Nitze, Paul, 135
Nixon, Richard, 227, 238, 239

Nobel Prize for Economic
    Sciences (2019), 323
North Atlantic Treaty
    Organization (NATO). *See*
    NATO (North Atlantic Treaty
    Organization)
Not-for-profit Sector Freedom to
    Advocate Act (2013), 96
Nunes, Rodrigo, 177
Nyamnjoh, Francis, 364
Nye, Joseph, 5, 6

O'Reilly, Bill, 243–4
Obama, Barack, 135, 176, 227,
    229, 236, 241, 242
Occupy Wall Street, 175
OECD (Organisation for
    Economic Co-operation and
    Development), 105
Oedipus, 295
Oliveira, Francisco de, 419n97
'open society', 9, 283
Opération Barkhane, 209, 214, 215
Operation Desert Shield (Aug
    1990), 249
Operation Irini, 115–16
Operation Mare Nostrum, 109, 115
Opération Serval, 207–9, 214, 215
Operation Sophia, 115
Operation Triton, 109
Organisation of African Unity
    (OAU), 364
Organisation of Islamic
    Cooperation (OIC), 346
Osborne, George: Autumn
    Statement, 51
Ottoman empire, 71, 198
Owen, Gareth, 90
Oxfam (aid organisation), 25,
    161, 342

Packer, George, 11

Padilla affair in Cuba, 159
Pailey, Robtel, 366
Palais de l'Élysée (France), 209
Palestinian–Israeli conflict, 262
Papua New Guinea (PNG), 83–5,
    86, 95
    detainee crisis, 83–5, 86
    families removal from, 98
    provisions for families, 91–2
Paradise Lost vision, 294–7, 301
Paris, 211
    International Exposition
        (1867), 69, 71, 82
    medical conferences (1931–3),
        76
    siege of 1871, 75
    Walter Lippmann Colloquium
        (1938), 137
Parker, Alan, 47, 48, 49, 52
PATH (reproductive health
    technology organisation), 324
Pax Americana, 248
Penrose, Mike, 90, 91
Perera, Suvendrini, 84, 88
Perrin, Andrew, 240
Peter the Great, 254
Pfizer (American pharmaceutical
    company), 317, 322
pharmaceutical industries, 76, 77,
    80, 81
philanthropy, 314–31
    see also Gates Foundation
Piketty, Thomas, 212
Pinel, Jacques, 78
Pinker, Steven, 178, 282
Pirson, Michael, 44
Poland, 177, 254
political economy, 195
    of asylum, 260–1, 263
political integration, 195
political minimalism, 128, 144
    anti-democratic instincts,
        137–8

between national and interna-
    tional stage, 140–5
emerge in US, 133, 140, 145
essence of, 139
ethos of, 128–9, 133–4, 136,
    139, 141, 145, 149, 151–2
in (post-1945), 129, 130–40
and new social movements, 140
political orders
    key elements of, 334
    power and authority contrasts,
        334–5, 342–4
political realism, 134–5, 138,
    145, 146, 253–4
pop culture, 167
populism, 195, 230, 237, 338
populist nationalism, 283
Port-au-Prince earthquake (Haiti,
    2010), 79
post-liberal world, violence
    emergence in, 281–301
    Anthropocene notion, 289
    human agency displacement
        and, 287–8, 289, 290
    individualisation of sacrificial
        actions, 294
    liberal regimes military
        intervention (in global
        South), 283–4
    liberal regimes relied upon
        digital recoupment, 285–7
    onto-theological tensions,
        292–4
    political theology, 288–9
    post-9/11 setting, 300
    resilience doctrine deployment,
        288, 300
    sacred object for power and
        violence, 292–4
Postmodernism, 163–4, 169–70,
    173

Post-traumatic stress disorder (PTSD), 287–8
Powell, Colin, 42
PPE equipment, 68
presentism, 164, 182
Proactiva Open Arms, 109, 110
Prose, Francine, 2
Puerto Rico, 235
Putin, Vladimir, 256

QAnon conspiratorialism, 170
Qatar, 347

racial imbalance, 357–60
racial liberalism, 3, 227
'racial transposition', 232–3, 240
racism, 57–9, 240
    anti-black racism, 351, 352
    institutional racism, 366–7
Rackete, Carola, 114, 119, 120, 121, 123
'radical humanism', 123
radical liberalism, 156
Raleigh, Clionadh, 221
RAND corporation, 202
Rawls, John, 120–1, 140, 141, 144, 149, 151, 152, 410n31
    theory of justice, 141–4
Reagan, Ronald, 87, 234, 236, 437n5
recalcitrant states, 200–1
Red Cross and Red Crescent movement. See International Red Cross movement (ICRC)
Reddy, Sanjay, 320–1
Refugee Action Coalition (RAC), 92
Refugee Convention (1951), 117, 261, 341, 345, 346
    1967 Protocol, 261, 341
refugee crisis (2015), 122
refugee crisis (mid-1990s), 29

refugee humanitarianism (in Arab Middle East), 259–77
    as arena for frictional encounters, 274–7
    external aid strategies, 264
    forced migration politics, 260
    global North fund allocation, 264
    'guesthood' notion, 261–2
    politics of refugee hospitality, 275–6
    politics of refugee reception, 262
    refugee (dis)ordering processes, 260, 261–4
    refugees and host communities, 276–7
    see also European Union (EU) and Arab refugee diplomacy
refugee humanitarianism
    'grand compromise', 259–60, 263
    refugee camps, growth of, 77
    see also asylum seeking; migration, irregular/migrants; refugee humanitarianism (in Arab Middle East)
'regional processing centres' (RPCs), 83–4, 85
Regional Refugee and Resilience Plans (3RP), 263
Reid-Henry, Simon, 214
reindividualisation, 192–3, 202
Republican Party, 149, 237, 238, 240
'resilience' of refugees, 200
'resiliency humanitarianism', 260, 266–9, 275, 277
    'resilience-building' efforts, 266, 268–70, 271
Responsibility to Protect doctrines, 143, 150

INDEX

ressentiment, 174, 179

'retrotopia', 294

Reuther, Walter, 409–10n30

'rewesternisation', 327

Rhodes Must Fall student protests, 356

Rice, Condoleezza, 253

RISE (Refugees, Survivors and eX-detainees), 85, 87, 104

Rockefeller Foundation, 61, 77

Rodney, Walter, 12

Rohingya exodus, 59–60

Rohingya peoples (ethnic group), 65

Rohingya refugee, 62–3

Rome, Treaty of (1957), 130

Ronalds, Paul, 96, 99, 102, 103, 105

Roosevelt New Deal programme, 136, 240

Roosevelt, Eleanor, 409–10n30

Röpke, Wilhelm, 8

Rothbard, Murray, 190–1

Roy, Olivier, 160

Roya Valley (France), 111, 112, 122

Rubenstein, Jennifer, 104

Rules of Origin (RoO), 272

Rumsfeld, Donald, 252

Russia, 209–10, 248, 251, 253, 338

military action in Syria, 256–7

Russian Air Force, 253

Russian Armed Forces, 254

Russian Army, 253

Russian famine, 13, 26

Russian Revolution, 185

Russo-Georgian War (2008), 253–4

Russo-Turkish wars (1877–8), 74

Rutazibwa, Olivia, 12

Rwanda, 372

génocidaires, 104–5

genocide against Tutsi, 373

SCUK in, 39

Rwandan genocide, 23, 29, 39–40, 104, 166

Rwandan Patriotic Front, 39

Sabaratnam, Meera, 218, 374–5

Sahel Alliance, 215, 217, 221

Salem, Sara, 369

Salvation Army (TSA), 16, 84, 85, 91, 94

immigration detention services contracts, 84, 94

offshore operations, 84, 92, 94–5, 99

San Francisco insurance summit, 71

Sanders, Bernie, 242

sans-frontiériste principle of *témoignage*, 158–9, 160, 161, 162

SAR (search and rescue) missions, 400n15

criminalisation of, 113, 114

EU Mediterranean SAR mission, 110, 111, 116

Germany activists fundraising for, 114

maritime civil disobedience, 109, 119–23

in Mediterranean, 109–19

private SAR missions, 111–12, 113, 123, 124

United4Rescue, 400n15

see also humanitarian interventions (at European borders); SOS MEDITERRANEE

Sartre, Jean-Paul, 162

Saturday Paper, The (newspaper), 95

Saudi Arabia, 346, 347

INDEX

Save the Children Australia (SCA), 84, 85, 91, 92–3, 94, 98
  Afghanistan contracts, 91
  criticism on, 92
  disconnection within, 100–1
  'Holistic Support Approach' to Nauru, 100
  humanitarian operation expansion, 90
  immigration detention services contracts, 84–5, 88, 90–4, 95
  leadership, 97–8, 100–1
  Manus Island detention centres operations, 83–5, 86, 94, 95, 106
  Manus Island, departure from, 84, 95
  members' fabrication of abuse, 100–4
  Morrison on, 98–9
  Moss report (2015), 102–3
  Nauru welfare services, 95–6, 98
  offshore detention funds, 91
  opposition to detention of children, 96
  public inquiries submission into offshore detention, 96–7
  public statements, 100
  roots of, 105–6
  tensions between DIBP and, 99–100, 102
Save the Children International (SCI), 36, 47–8, 90
  Ebola crisis, 49–51
  Indian Ocean tsunami (2004), 44–5, 46
  Iraq invasion (2003), 42–3
  Kashmir earthquake (2005), 46
  Kosovo War, 40
  Niger famine (2005), 46

Rwandan genocide, 39, 40
Save the Children UK (SCUK), 35, 36–54, 90
  annual income, 36
  economic and political power relationship, 53
  economistic drives, 44
  'Emergency Strategy', 41–3
  entered Kigali, 39
  expansion of, 46–7, 48
  'Global Programme Strategy', 40, 46
  as health humanitarian front-line, 49, 50
  humanitarian agenda, 36–8
  humanitarian ambition, re-politicisation of, 48–54
  humanitarian corporatism, rise of, 46–8
  Iraq anti-war sentiment, 41–3
  in Kosovo War, 40
  leadership, 36–7, 46–8
  leadership's political strategy, 49–53
  new fundraising techniques, 41
  and the 'new humanitarian' era, 39–41
  Rwandan genocide responses, 39
  sexual harassment scandal (2018), 52
  two-tier governance system, 38
  and UK government engagement, 41
Save the Children US (SCUS), 42
Save the Children/Save the Children Fund, 4, 15, 16, 17, 21–30, 31, 35–54, 148, 161
  'African Child' Conference (Geneva, 1931), 12, 31, 32
  annual income, 36
  and British state relations, 4, 23–4

centenary conference (Apr 2019), 22–4, 27, 31, 32, 52
child rights as a framing device for its work, 28
children protection in war report (1938), 30
Declaration of the Rights of the Child, introduction of (1924), 27–8
establishment of, 4, 21
expansion into British empire, 23
first family reunification programme, 29–30
history of, 21–4
humanitarianism function shifts, 25–6
humanitarianism training course launch (2019), 32
and imperial British empire relations, 25–7, 31–2
leadership shifts, 25–6, 28–9
liberal internationalism, 22, 25
logo of, 29
rise of, 23
SAR mission in Mediterranean, 109, 110, 114
success in altering restrictive immigration policies, 30
theme of, 36
UK branch annual income, 23
under Jebb leadership, 25–6
vision of, 36
Sayana Press injection, 317, 322, 323, 324
SCA. *See* Save the Children Australia (SCA)
Scheuerman, William, 121
Schlesinger, Arthur, Jr., 138–9
Schmitt, Carl, 186, 295
Schumpeter, Joseph, 409–10n30
Schwittay, Anke, 364

SCI. See Save the Children International (SCI)
Science (magazine), 324
Scott-Smith, Tom, 75
SCUK. *See* Save the Children UK (SCUK)
SCUS (Save the Children US), 42
Sea-Eye, 109
Sears, Jonathan M., 215, 218, 222
Seattle WTO protests (1999), 152–3, 205
Sea-Watch 3 (vessel), 114, 119–20, 123
Sea-Watch 4 (vessel), 401n25
Sea-Watch, 109, 110–12, 114, 122, 401n25
aims of, 110, 112
private SAR missions, 111–12, 113, 123, 124
Seebrücke (German network), 114, 119
'self-expression', 170
Sen, Amartya, 8–9, 298
Shakespeare, William, 37
shifting nature of humanitarianism, 275
Shklar, Judith, 129, 130–1, 135, 138, 140–2, 144, 152, 153, 177, 408n12, 408–9n14, 410n31
liberalism of, 131–2, 133, 151
Sida, Lewis, 24, 27
Sierra Leone: Ebola crisis and measures, 49, 50–1
Silverstein, Jordana, 93
slave trade abolition, 340–1
Slim, Hugo, 43
Slobodian, Quinn, 8, 185, 419n105
Smirl, Lisa, 78
Smith, Stephen, 208
'social commons', 191–2

INDEX

social democracy, 188–9
social liberalism, 136, 137, 140
Social Security Act (1935), 133
Socialism, 35, 298
Society for the Abolition of Slave Trade, 340
Solnit, Rebecca, 244
Solzhenitsyn, Aleksandr, 159
Somalia, 196, 337
    Mogadishu line in, 282
Somaliland, 373
Somers, Margaret, 243, 244, 245
SOS MEDITERRANEE, 107, 108, 122, 123, 124, 398–9n5
    aim of, 108
    SAR missions, 107, 108
South Africa, 171
South China Sea, 123
South Ossetia, 253
South Sudan, 337
'southern humanitarianisms', 32
Soviet Union (USSR), 130, 132, 134, 135, 167, 252, 254, 336–7
    communism, collapse of, 168
    dissolution of, 248, 249, 254
    'Westernisation' of post-Soviet states, 254
Spain, 175, 214, 218
Special Economic Zones (SEZ), 272, 273
Sri Lanka, 55, 57–8, 61–2, 64
Sriskandarajah, Danny, 4
Stafford House Committee, 74
Stansted 15 (human rights activists' group), 113
Steel, Charles, 52
Stierl, Maurice, 120
Stiglitz, Joseph, 8–9
Stoler, Ann, 355
Structural Adjustment Programs (SAPs), 319

Sudan, 15
    civil war (1980s), 23
Sudanese Revolution, 205
Summers, Lawrence, 358
Sun, The (newspaper), 41
Sunak, Rishi, 1, 53
Swach Bharat programme, 316
Sweetman, Caroline, 320
Syria/Syrian, 285, 337, 344, 345
    conflict forced migration, 259, 262, 267–70
    displacement in Lebanon, 267–70
    people displacement, 265–6
    refugee governance in, 263
    refugees as Sunni, 270
    refugees in Jordan, 271–3, 274, 276
    refugees, return of, 267
    on 'resiliency humanitarianism', 275
    Russia military action in, 256–7
    state attitude to hosting refugees, 262
    Turkey's hosting of refugees, 346
Syrian War (2011), 187, 255–7, 267

Tamil Rehabilitation Organisation (TRO), 57–8, 63, 65, 66
Tamils peoples, 57–8, 65
Tea Party, 175, 242
Teitel, Ruti, 144
Temin, Peter, 212–13
temporal horizon, 164–5
Temporary Protected Status (TPS), 225, 226, 235
terrestrial cartography, 291–2
Thailand, 45
Third World, 162–6
    ideology, 158–62

Thompson, Kenneth, 135
tiers-mondisme, 159, 160
Tigers (Tamil militant organization), 58, 64, 65
Times, The, 47
Tinkler, Mat, 99, 100
Tocqueville, Alexis de, 16
Tories (British political party), 47
Torres, Maldonado, 354
totalitarian violence, 182
Totalitarianism, 137
trade tariffs, 156
trade union, 191
transnational humanitarianism, 365–6
Traverso, Enzo, 172–3
TRO (Tamil Rehabilitation Organisation), 57–8, 63, 65, 66
Truman, Harry S., 132
  'four freedoms' speech (1945), 132
Trump administration, 225
  COVID-19 pandemic, mishandling of, 228
  Hurricane Maria responses, 234–5, 242
  on immigration, 225–6
'Trump Doctrine', 229
Trump, Donald, 2, 3, 148–9, 176, 227, 256, 306
  'America First' policy (2016), 249, 257
  'American carnage', 228–9, 242–3
  anti-immigrant rhetoric, 225–6
  assault on 'globalism', 257
  His candidacy announcement, 226
  controversial policies, 227
  discriminatory policies, 236
  election defeat, 177
  Hydroxychloroquine promoted by, 68

illiberalism, 228
India visit (2020), 330
MAGA campaign, 245
'Make America Great Again' campaign, 227
Moyn on, 177
new trade tariffs introduction, 176
as Nixon's Silent Majority, 227
His populism, 230
racist revanchism, 246
'shithole countries' remarks, 225, 226, 233
supporters stormed Capitol (6 Jan 2021), 3, 370
victory as encroachment of the Big White Ghetto, 237–8, 241
White House departure, 2
see also Trump administration
Trumpism and liberalism, 3, 174, 176–7, 225–46
TSA (Salvation Army). *See* Salvation Army (TSA)
Tsunami Evaluation Coalition (TEC), 46
Tsunami, 44–6
  Indian Ocean tsunami (2004), 44–5, 46, 343
Tuareg uprising (2012), 218, 221
Turkey, 209–10, 346
Turner, Lewis, 275
'Twenty-Year War', 282
Tyrrell, R. Emmett, Jr., 157

UAE. *See* United Arab Emirates (UAE)
UDHR (Universal Declaration of Human Rights), 118, 336
U-Haul (firm), 243
Ukraine, 256
UN Charter, 207, 336
  Article 1(3), 340

UN Church Center, 61

UN Convention Against Transnational Organised Crime (2000), 116

UN Convention on the Law of the Sea (UNCLOS) [1982], 114, 120

UN Convention on the Rights of the Child, 29

UN Convention Relating to the Status of Refugees, 87

UN funding for Indian sterilisation programmes, 318

UN High Commissioner for Refugees, 341

UN Human Rights Council, 176

UN Industrial Development Organization (UNIDO), 150

UN Protocol Against the Smuggling of Migrants (2000), 116

UN Relief and Works Agency for Palestinian Refugees, 341

UNCTAD (United Nations Conference on Trade and Development), 145, 150

UNHCR (UN Refugee Agency), 263, 267, 268, 269, 277, 400n16

UNHRC (United Nations Human Rights Council), 351–2

UNICEF (United Nations International Children's Emergency Fund), 28, 78, 341

United Arab Emirates (UAE), 10, 303–11

  duplicity in Yemen, 308–9

  Emirati justice system, 309

  financial crimes, 304–5

  humanitarian donorship, 306, 308, 309

  humanitarian role, 306, 308, 309

  liberal modernity, 303–5, 306, 310–11

  support for Saudi Arabia, 308

  veneer of humanity, 309

United Kingdom (UK), 1, 298

  aid budget, 47, 48–9, 50

  Brexit referendum (Jun 2016), 3

  COVID-19 and lockdown, 1, 53, 67–8

  decisions to cut foreign aid, 1, 4, 16, 53

  Ebola crisis responses, 49–51

  general election (7 May 2015), 49, 50, 51

  Iraq Dossier, 41–2

  Ministry of Defence (MoD), 50

  and Sierra Leone relations, 50

  see also Department for International Development (DfID)

United Nations (UN), 46, 61, 62, 130, 199, 255, 305, 337, 353, 357

  coordination meeting, 8

  Declaration of the Rights of the Child relaunch, 28

  General Assembly, 118, 150, 158, 166, 250, 336

  Millennium Development Goals (MDG), 322

  refugee's governance, 262

  'responsibility to protect', 255

  Security Council, 115–16, 207, 254, 255, 256, 336, 341

  specialised agencies establishment, 341

  Sustainable Development Goals, 217, 322

United Nations Human Rights Council (UNHRC), 351–2

United Nations Multidimensional

Integrated Stabilization Mission (MINUSMA), 214

United Nations Relief and Rehabilitation Administration, 77

United Nations World Summit (2005), 248

United States (US), 2, 7, 12, 30, 87, 127, 142, 220, 289, 298–9, 304, 305, 337, 345, 371–2
Afghanistan invasion (2001), 42, 252, 255, 281, 337
anti-ballistic missile defence system installation announcement, 252–3
Anti-Ballistic Missile Treaty withdrawal, 252
anti-racist protests (2020), 228
Capitol Hill insurrection (6 Jan 2021), 370
Cold War Liberalism, 129, 130–3
COVID-19 and Trump administration, 177, 242, 245
Danziger Bridge shootings (2005), 244
domestic liberalism, 139
economic dominance (in the wake of Cold War), 251
financial sector expansion, 171
Floyd (George) public lynching (May 2020), 2, 3, 245, 351, 370
foreign policy, 132–6, 138, 248–57, 437n5
global power, expansion of, 248–57
Global War on Terror, 209, 211, 235, 244, 251–3, 255, 284, 285, 288, 289, 365
'globalism', 145

humanitarian responses and Iraq invasion (2003), 42–3, 249
'humanitarian' logic of engagement, 147–8
'Immediate Response' joint military exercise (2008), 253
income inequality, 212–3
as 'the indispensable nation', 337
liberal order as global hegemony, 7, 129–36, 138, 140–2, 147–8
'liberal' term usage, 328
migrants illegal border crossing, 111
military doctrine, 252–3
military interventions list, 250–1
National Intelligence Council report (2017), 338
NATO role in US geostrategy, 255
neoconservatives, political decline of, 175
9/11 attacks, 170, 172, 175, 197, 252, 293–4, 297
Operation Desert Shield (Aug 1990), 249
political minimalism, 130, 133–5, 138, 146
political realism, 135–6
post-Cold War American political class, 242
power in twentieth century, 257
Promise for democracy, 140, 142
pursued imperial power, 251–7
racial liberal ordering, 229–37
racial liberalism, 229–37, 238, 241
Shock & Awe doctrine, 199

sovereign power limits in
Georgia, 253–4
state pressure on NGOs, 42–3
state's relationship to right to
life, 177
Syrian War intervention, 256
threat of black gangs, 244
Truman 'four freedoms' speech
(1945), 132
Trump new national security
doctrine (2017), 256
Trump presidency, 371
US troops withdrawal from
Syria, 256
War on Drugs, 235
'the Western idea', 169
white ghetto's dysfunction,
229–34, 236
white poverty, 229–33, 241
United States State Department,
169
Universal Declaration of Human
Rights (UDHR), 118, 336
universal exhibitions, 69–71
humanitarian medicine summits,
69–75
humanitarian objects, liberal
origins of, 69–71
Lyons national exhibition
(1885), 73
objectives of, 71–5
universalism, 12, 32–3, 169, 173,
229, 257
moral universalism, 9, 12
Western universalism, 12, 32–
3, 352
urbicide, 200
urgence, 160, 162, 164, 177
Uruzgan province (Afghanistan),
91, 105
utopianism, 10, 140, 149, 158–62,
178

anti-utopianism, 145–6, 151,
152

Vidal, Claudine, 78
Vieira de Mello, Sérgio, 43
Vietnam war, 134, 143
Vietnam, 282
Vietnamese boat people rescue
campaigns (1979), 162
Vijayan, Suchitra, 331
voluntarism, 362

Wall Street Journal (newspaper),
The, 331
Walter Lippmann Colloquium
(Paris, 1938), 137
'war on poverty', 202
war on welfare, 202
Warsaw Pact, 248, 254
Washington Consensus, 145
Washington Post (newspaper), 231
WatchTheMed's Alarm Phone
initiative, 120
Watkins, Kevin, 4, 52
Weber (firm), 73
Weheliye, Alexander, 352, 356
West Africa: Ebola crisis, 49–52,
346
Westad, Odd Arne, 133
Western bourgeoisie, 171–2, 173
Western corporations, 175–6
Western countries
income inequality affects middle
classes, 212–13
migration, conceptions of,
235–6
NGOs role in domestic poverty
reduction, 15–16
political culture, 189
societies, humanitarianisation
of, 15–16
Western democracy, 231

Western hegemony, 329
Western humanitarianism, 105, 353–9
    commercialisation of, 166–7
Western imperialism, 22
Western states
    humanitarian organisations funding, 26–7
    securitisation of asylum, 105
    self-conception as liberal, 328–9
Whitbread, Jasmine, 46, 47, 48, 90
White House, 225
white nationalism, 227, 233, 237, 245
white supremacy, 233, 246, 351–2, 355, 356–62, 365–7
'white working class'
    social mobility of, 238–40
    and support for Republicans, 238
    and financial crash (2007–8), 238–9, 241
    liberal identification of, 240
Wilhelm, Lola, 75
Williamson, Kevin D., 229–30, 233–6, 238, 241
Wilson Security, 101, 104
Wilson, Kalpana, 316, 317
Wilson, Woodrow, 250
women's empowerment, 314–31
    as part of a 'security paradigm', 315
    Enlightenment teleological narrative, 325, 326–8
    feminist organisations and, 319–20
    moral progress notion, 325–6, 327
    neoliberal conception, 319–20
    redefining women's empowerment, 324–31

technocratic reconceptualisation of, 314–24
theory of change, 319–24
understanding, 319–20
women's participation in parliament, 315
Women's International League for Peace and Freedom, 21
World Bank, 145, 186, 319, 358
    Community-Driven Development (CDD) programmes, 191
World Economic Forum, 306
'world economy', 185–7
World Food Programme, 341
World Health Organization (WHO), 50, 51, 77, 78, 149, 176, 314, 317, 326, 338, 341
World Humanitarian Summit (Istanbul, 2016), 72–3, 81
World Medical Association, 72
World Politics Review, 228
World War I, 4, 7, 21, 24, 35, 71, 73, 77, 164, 185, 335, 353, 379n26
World War II, 4, 7, 13–14, 25, 28, 68, 71, 77, 127, 130, 135, 165, 171, 212, 226, 282, 335, 341, 345, 353
    humanitarian medicine summits, 71–2
WTO (World Trade Organization), 150, 186 Seattle protests (1999), 152–3, 205

xenophobic nationalism, 365, 366

Yangon (Myanmar), 59
Yaoundé Convention (1963), 130
Yemen, 308, 337, 344
    port of Aden, 309

UAE duplicity in, 308–9
Youth with a Mission (YWAM),
 88
Yugoslav wars, 249

Yugoslavia, 199
 breakup of, 187, 194, 198, 200
YWAM (Youth with a Mission),
 88